Urban Underground Space Design: Structural Stability and Mechanics Analysis

Urban Underground Space Design: Structural Stability and Mechanics Analysis

Guest Editors

Jun Wu
Hao Zhang
Zhehao Zhu
Yi Rui

Basel • Beijing • Wuhan • Barcelona • Belgrade • Novi Sad • Cluj • Manchester

Guest Editors

Jun Wu
School of Civil Engineering
Shanghai Normal University
Shanghai
China

Hao Zhang
College of Environmental
Science and Engineering
Donghua University
Shanghai
China

Zhehao Zhu
School of Civil Engineering
Shanghai Normal University
Shanghai
China

Yi Rui
Department of Geotechnical
Engineering
Tongji University
Shanghai
China

Editorial Office
MDPI AG
Grosspeteranlage 5
4052 Basel, Switzerland

This is a reprint of the Special Issue, published open access by the journal *Buildings* (ISSN 2075-5309), freely accessible at: www.mdpi.com/journal/buildings/special_issues/6U5F547YLT.

For citation purposes, cite each article independently as indicated on the article page online and as indicated below:

Lastname, A.A.; Lastname, B.B. Article Title. *Journal Name* **Year**, *Volume Number*, Page Range.

ISBN 978-3-7258-4032-8 (Hbk)
ISBN 978-3-7258-4031-1 (PDF)
https://doi.org/10.3390/books978-3-7258-4031-1

© 2025 by the authors. Articles in this book are Open Access and distributed under the Creative Commons Attribution (CC BY) license. The book as a whole is distributed by MDPI under the terms and conditions of the Creative Commons Attribution-NonCommercial-NoDerivs (CC BY-NC-ND) license (https://creativecommons.org/licenses/by-nc-nd/4.0/).

Contents

Preface vii

Linhai Lu, Xin Zhang, Xiaojun Li and Yanyun Lu
Application of Advanced Multi-Parameter Monitoring in Concrete Structure Defect Detection: Integrating Thermal Integrity Profiling and Strain Analysis
Reprinted from: *Buildings* 2025, *15*, 1350, https://doi.org/10.3390/buildings15081350 1

Xijun Liu, Bokai Song, Zhuanqin Sun and Wenxiu Jiao
Critical Filling Height of Embankment over Soft Soil: A Three-Dimensional Upper-Bound Limit Analysis
Reprinted from: *Buildings* 2025, *15*, 395, https://doi.org/10.3390/buildings15030395 28

Tianwen Li and Jieyun Xing
Research on the 3D Visualization Method of Web-Based Seismic Wave CT Results and the Application in Underground Caverns
Reprinted from: *Buildings* 2024, *14*, 3622, https://doi.org/10.3390/buildings14113622 46

Bingxiong Tu, Meng Han, Jinqing Jia, Zhaoyun Xiao and Lulu Liu
Improved Mobilized Strength Design Method for Multi-Support Excavation Deformation Analysis
Reprinted from: *Buildings* 2024, *14*, 3630, https://doi.org/10.3390/buildings14113630 60

Lichao Chen, Chengchao Guo, Yanhui Pan, Huqing Liang, Mengxiong Tang and Kejie Zhai
Influence of Excavation Radius on Behavior of Circular Foundation Pits Supported by Prefabricated Recyclable Structures: Full-Scale Experimental and Numerical Analysis
Reprinted from: *Buildings* 2024, *14*, 3110, https://doi.org/10.3390/buildings14103110 82

Qinyi Chen, Guo Hu and Jun Wu
Prediction of the Unconfined Compressive Strength of a One-Part Geopolymer-Stabilized Soil Using Deep Learning Methods with Combined Real and Synthetic Data
Reprinted from: *Buildings* 2024, *14*, 2894, https://doi.org/10.3390/buildings14092894 102

Huaqiao Zhong, Zhehao Zhu, Jiajin Zhao, Lanyi Wei, Yanyan Zhang, Jiayu Li, et al.
Influence of Fine Content and Mean Diameter Ratio on the Minimum and Maximum Void Ratios of Sand–Fine Mixtures: A Discrete Element Method Study
Reprinted from: *Buildings* 2024, *14*, 2877, https://doi.org/10.3390/buildings14092877 133

Lili Jin and Youfang Liao
Upper Bound Analysis of Two-Layered Slopes Subjected to Seismic Excitations Using the Layer-Wise Summation Method
Reprinted from: *Buildings* 2024, *14*, 1990, https://doi.org/10.3390/buildings14071990 149

Rudong Wu, Kaixin Liu, Peng Zhang, Cong Zeng, Yong Xu and Jiahao Mei
Structural Stability and Mechanical Analysis of PVC Pipe Jacking under Axial Force
Reprinted from: *Buildings* 2024, *14*, 1884, https://doi.org/10.3390/buildings14061884 166

Xiannian Zhou, Yurui He, Wanmao Zhang and Dunwen Liu
Multifractal Characteristics and Displacement Prediction of Deformation on Tunnel Portal Slope of Shallow Buried Tunnel Adjacent to Important Structures
Reprinted from: *Buildings* 2024, *14*, 1662, https://doi.org/10.3390/buildings14061662 187

Haochuan Zhao, Fan Zeng, Xiaowei Feng, Shouqian Wang, Chao Huang, Na Liu and Jian Zhang
Dynamic Response Analysis Method of a High-Strength RC Beam Subjected to Long-Duration Blast Loading
Reprinted from: *Buildings* **2024**, *14*, 1612, https://doi.org/10.3390/buildings14061612 . . . . . . **211**

Jiani Zhang, Zhenkun Yang and Rafig Azzam
Parametric Study of the Deep Excavation Performance of Underground Pumping Station Based on Numerical Method
Reprinted from: *Buildings* **2024**, *14*, 1569, https://doi.org/10.3390/buildings14061569 . . . . . . **229**

Binhui Xiang, Ying Liu, Jifei Cui and Zhenkun Yang
Analytical Solution for the Deformation of Pipe Galleries Adjacent to Deep Excavation
Reprinted from: *Buildings* **2024**, *14*, 1103, https://doi.org/10.3390/buildings14041103 . . . . . . **246**

Preface

The rapid pace of urbanization has led to increasing demands on surface space, prompting cities to explore the potential of underground environments for sustainable development. This reprint addresses the multifaceted challenges and innovative solutions associated with designing and constructing urban underground spaces, with a particular focus on structural stability and mechanical analysis.

The impetus for this work arises from the need to consolidate contemporary research and practical insights that tackle the complexities inherent in subterranean construction within urban settings. Our objective is to provide a comprehensive resource that bridges theoretical frameworks with real-world applications, thereby enhancing understanding and informing practice in this specialized field.

This volume is intended for a diverse audience, including civil and geotechnical engineers, urban planners, architects, researchers, and graduate students. By presenting a curated collection of peer-reviewed studies and case analyses, we aim to support professionals engaged in the planning, design, and implementation of underground urban projects.

The contributing authors, drawn from esteemed academic and industry backgrounds, contributed a wealth of knowledge and experience. Their collective efforts were instrumental in shaping the content and direction of this book. We extend our sincere gratitude to each contributor for their invaluable input.

The editors acknowledge the financial support provided by the National Natural Science Foundation of China (Grant No. 42307190). It is our hope that this book serves as both a foundational text and catalyst for future innovations in urban underground development.

Jun Wu, Hao Zhang, Zhehao Zhu, and Yi Rui
Guest Editors

Article

Application of Advanced Multi-Parameter Monitoring in Concrete Structure Defect Detection: Integrating Thermal Integrity Profiling and Strain Analysis

Linhai Lu [1], Xin Zhang [2,*], Xiaojun Li [2] and Yanyun Lu [2]

[1] Jinan Transportation Development Investment Co., Ltd., Jinan 250014, China; sucllh@126.com
[2] Department of Geotechnical Engineering, Tongji University, 1239 Siping Road, Shanghai 200092, China; lixiaojun@tongji.edu.cn (X.L.); yanyunlu@tongji.edu.cn (Y.L.)
* Correspondence: 2210342@tongji.edu.cn

Abstract: Thermal Integrity Profiling (TIP) effectively monitors concrete integrity. TIP detects structural defects and locates them through anomalies in hydration–temperature curves. However, TIP alone cannot accurately identify the defect types. To resolve this limitation, strain monitoring is integrated with TIP. A dual-parameter temperature–strain monitoring system using fiber-optic sensing was implemented in a diaphragm wall of Weizishan Station, Jinan. This study investigated the spatial distribution and variation patterns of concrete temperature–strain during the different stages of hydration. A thermal–mechanical–chemical multi-field coupling model was established based on the concrete mix ratio and the theoretical thermal parameters, and its feasibility was verified. This study also analyzed the impact mechanisms of four defect types—voids, mud inclusions, necking, and widening—on the surrounding concrete's heat release and deformation during hydration. It presents specific hydration–temperature–strain characteristic curves that can accurately differentiate the defect types and established the correspondence between the defect types and these characteristic patterns. Finally, a rapid and accurate defect identification process is proposed for practical application, improving efficiency and precision in detecting anomalies. The findings provide a reference for implementing appropriate defect prevention and remediation measures on-site and hold promise for enhancing the prediction and control of defects during the hydration period of concrete structures.

Keywords: concrete structure defects; multi-parameter monitoring; fiber-optic sensing technology; multi-field coupling model; concrete hydration process

1. Introduction

Underground continuous wall (UCW) systems have become the preferred form of retaining structure in deep foundation pits due to their reliable performance and dual role in support and structural load-bearing [1,2]. However, various factors such as the construction conditions, geology, and workmanship can introduce defects (e.g., voids, mud inclusions, necking, and misalignment) that jeopardize UCW integrity [3,4]. Undetected defects severely threaten the stability of foundation pits, making it difficult to assess the wall capacity or take timely corrective measures. Thus, the rapid and effective quality monitoring of UCWs is crucial for ensuring safety [5].

Ensuring UCW construction quality is challenging because the wall is deeply embedded and largely concealed in soil [3,6]. The traditional integrity detection methods (core sampling, acoustic transmission, impact echoes, resistivity, etc.) each have limitations [7].

For example, core sampling provides direct evidence, but is destructive and may miss the defects between cores [8]. Acoustic methods (e.g., cross-hole sonic logging) rely on pre-installed pipes and suffer from signal attenuation in concrete, making them less effective for large-scale walls [9,10]. Impact echoes can only roughly locate defects and cannot determine their nature or size [11,12]. Electrical resistivity requires a high data density for accuracy, resulting in low efficiency, and serves only as an auxiliary tool. To meet the demands of large, deep excavations and overcome these limitations, other researchers have developed new non-destructive monitoring technologies for concrete quality [13,14].

Temperature-based methods have shown particular promise. The Temperature Tracer Method (TTM) [15,16], as introduced by Fengfei He et al., has been widely employed in the structural health monitoring of underground structures, pipelines, and concrete structures due to its distinct advantages of distributed monitoring capabilities, good stability, low cost, and environmental friendliness. In addition to the temperature-based methods, ultrasonic coda wave (UCW) monitoring offers a complementary high-resolution approach. UCW is highly sensitive to subtle internal changes, enabling the detection of minute defects, such as micro-cracks and stress changes that may not manifest in global temperature trends. Despite the challenges in data interpretation due to environmental influences, UCW can directly sense internal structural defects, enhancing structural integrity assessments. Moreover, environmental temperature effects, such as daily and seasonal fluctuations, can induce structural deformations, further complicating monitoring efforts. Recent studies have integrated environmental temperature data with advanced remote sensing technologies, like the Multi-Temporal Interferometry Synthetic Aperture Radar (MTInSAR)-based early warning system developed by Mirko Calò et al. [17]. This system integrates environmental temperature data and satellite radar information to monitor deformation in simply supported concrete bridges, highlighting the crucial role of temperature in assessing structural health. Fiber-optic sensing technology, with its capabilities for rapid, continuous data acquisition and strong anti-interference, has also attracted significant attention. This technology has been applied to the Thermal Integrity Profiling (TIP) of concrete and achieved promising defect detection results. TIP, which leverages embedded fiber-optic temperature sensors, has been successfully used to assess the integrity of cast-in-place deep foundations for the last decade. Compared to the conventional sonic or coring tests, TIP provides real-time, full-length temperature profiles of curing concrete, enabling earlier and more comprehensive anomaly detection [18].

The principle behind TIP is to exploit the heat released during hydration during concrete curing. As cement hydrates, it releases heat; defects (e.g., inclusions or cross-sectional changes) locally alter the thermal profile [19,20]. By embedding distributed temperature sensors (e.g., fiber-optic cables or Bragg grating arrays) along the reinforcement prior to casting, one can continuously monitor the internal temperature rise [21,22]. Any abnormal temperature drop or deviation indicates a potential defect region. Some studies have shown that this method yields continuous, high-precision data for quantitative internal quality assessment, offering substantial advantages over the older techniques. For instance, TIP outperforms conventional cross-hole sonic logging in anomaly detectability and coverage, while also reducing the testing costs. Furthermore, Sun et al. [8] enhanced TIP interpretation by integrating finite element simulations of pile curing, which significantly increased the anomaly detection accuracy relative to that of the standard empirical methods. However, hydration–temperature as a single diagnostic parameter has its limitations. Different defect types can sometimes produce similar temperature anomalies, impeding confident identification. For example, Sun et al. [20] demonstrated that distributed temperature profiles can distinguish various pile defect types based on characteristic heat loss signatures. Nonetheless, certain defect scenarios yield overlapping thermal responses, making it difficult to uniquely identify the defect nature from the temperature data alone [23,24].

Increasing evidence suggests that incorporating mechanical strain monitoring can resolve some of these ambiguities [25,26]. The abnormal deformation behavior of new concrete (e.g., unusual strain spikes or distortions during curing) often correlates with internal flaws [27,28]. Thus, tracking the strain evolution alongside temperature is essential for a more complete integrity assessment [29]. Recently made concrete undergoes thermal expansion, autogenous and drying shrinkage, and creep; excessive or non-uniform strain may indicate cracking or weak zones, making strain a critical indicator of structural health [30,31]. Measuring the strain in curing concrete is challenging due to concrete's early-stage properties and the multitude of influencing factors, and until recently there has been limited research linking distributed strain profiles to specific defect types in situ [32,33]. Some initial studies have applied distributed fiber-optic strain sensing in cast-in-place piles, obtaining that high-resolution strain data can be collected during curing. However, those works focused on the overall structural behavior and did not develop robust criteria to identify the defect signatures from the strain data. In other words, a comprehensive monitoring framework combining temperature and strain metrics had yet to be fully established. This gap pointed to the urgent need for a rapid, accurate, and easily interpretable multi-parameter monitoring method for UCWs, one capable of determining the defect type, location, and characteristics, thereby guiding timely remediation.

Against this background, this study innovatively builds upon conventional TIP by introducing simultaneous strain measurement as part of the monitoring system [34–36], offering a new multi-parameter approach. Notably, unlike most previous TIP research that focused on concrete piles, our work applies combined temperature–strain monitoring to an underground continuous wall, extending integrity monitoring to this different structural context [37]. Fiber-optic sensors were used to capture both the hydration–temperature and the strain of the wall, providing a more thorough, dual-modal dataset for analysis [38]. During hydration, different defect types induce distinctive patterns in temperature and strain. Temperature anomalies primarily reflect the changes in heat release, while strain anomalies can reveal localized deformation and stress concentrations [39]. By analyzing the two signals together, one can more accurately pinpoint the abnormal zones in the UCW and infer the likely defect types, significantly improving the accuracy and reliability of defect identification. In summary, the synergy of temperature and strain monitoring yields a multidimensional defect signature, greatly improving identification confidence compared to that of temperature-only diagnostics [40]. Nevertheless, prior to our work, research on such integrated temperature–strain evaluation remained nascent, with many fundamental issues (e.g., quantitative defect characterization and automated interpretation) yet to be fully addressed.

This study focuses on the underground continuous wall of Weizishan Station in Jinan as an engineering case study. Bragg fiber grating temperature–strain sensors were employed to perform the real-time monitoring of the hydration process, capturing the spatial and temporal evolution of temperature and strain in the concrete. Based on the physical and thermal properties of the concrete obtained from the field measurements, a high-fidelity thermal–mechanical–chemical multi-field finite element model was developed and validated. Utilizing this model, a series of numerical simulations were carried out to investigate the thermal integrity and strain responses in concrete structures containing different types of defect. This paper is structured as follows: Section 2 outlines the field implementation of the multi-parameter monitoring system, including the deployment of Thermal Integrity Profiling (TIP) and the strain sensors and the recording of temperature and strain behaviors during hydration. Section 3 describes the development and validation of the coupled finite element model. Section 4 presents the analysis of the four representative defect types—voids, mud inclusions, necking, and widening—highlighting their respective effects on the hydration-induced responses. Section 5 proposes a practical defect identification framework based on the combined temperature–strain data. This integrated approach not only enables the rapid and accurate identification of defect types during construction, but also supports long-term structural health monitoring, contributing to the safety and durability of underground concrete structures.

2. Field Monitoring of Temperature and Strain in Underground Continuous Walls During Hydration

To investigate the spatial distribution and evolution of hydration–temperature and strain in underground continuous walls, field monitoring experiments were conducted at a subway station's underground continuous wall project. This study examined the heat release and temperature rise during concrete hydration at different stages, along with the temporal changes in concrete strain. These findings provide crucial data support for the development of the subsequent thermal–mechanical–chemical multi-field coupling model.

2.1. Project Overview

Weizishan Station is located in Jinan, Shandong Province, China. It is an underground station with two levels and a single-island platform. The station uses a combined "two-wall integrated" structure, where the retaining and main structures are integrated. The underground continuous wall has a thickness of 1.2 m and is connected using the "roughening + rebar anchoring" method. Concrete strength is rated C45, with double-layer, bidirectional reinforcement (Φ25@100mm), grade II steel. The protective layer thickness of upper steel reinforcement is 25 mm. After the model was poured, the side walls were insulated with wooden formwork, while the top surface was insulated using a thin film and burlap. The continuous wall was poured over a length of 12 m and a height of 4.8 m. The formwork was removed 48 h after concrete pouring, and further curing was carried out.

2.2. Sensors and Monitoring Plan

This project uses a real-time, dynamic Bragg fiber-optic grating monitoring system. Fiber Bragg grating (FBG) sensors detect the changes in external parameters, such as temperature and strain, by modulating the Bragg center wavelength. This type of fiber-optic sensor operates by using a broadband light source, which travels along the fiber core. After passing through the grating period, part of the light is reflected back along the core, forming reflected light, while the remaining light forms transmitted light. Changes in physical parameters like strain and temperature alter the Bragg grating's center wavelength, causing it to shift (Figure 1). The basic expression for the reflected wavelength of the fiber grating is [41]:

$$\lambda_B = 2n_{eff} \cdot \Lambda \tag{1}$$

In this equation, λ_B represents the center wavelength of the FBG; n_{eff} is the effective refractive index of the fiber core; and Λ is the modulation period of the fiber grating's refractive index. Equation (1) represents the fundamental Bragg condition for FBG sensors. It indicates that a specific wavelength λ_B will be strongly reflected when the grating period (Λ) and the fiber's effective refractive index (n_{eff}) satisfy this relationship. Physically, if either Λ or n_{eff} changes (for example due to strain or temperature), the Bragg wavelength shifts accordingly. This principle underpins the operation of FBG sensors, as external stimuli can be detected by monitoring the resulting shifts in the reflected wavelength.

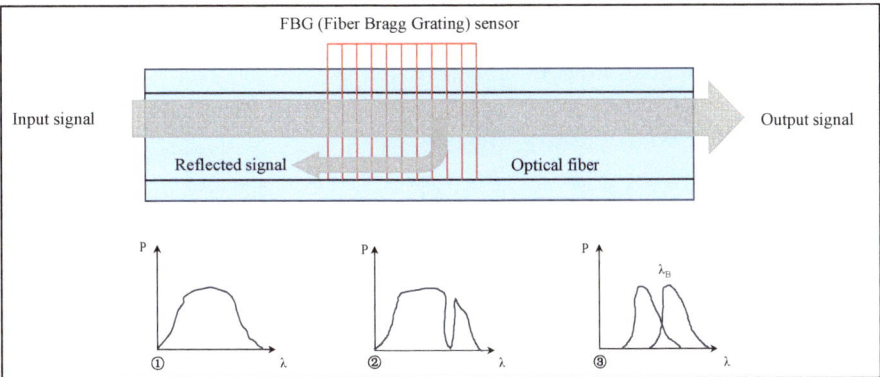

Figure 1. Principle of fiber Bragg grating (FBG) monitoring system.

The refractive index of the FBG varies periodically along the fiber axis, offering excellent wavelength selectivity. Incident light that satisfies the Bragg diffraction condition (with a wavelength of λ_B) is coupled and reflected at the FBG, while light of other wavelengths passes through unaffected. As shown in Figure 1, the reflection spectrum exhibits a peak at the center wavelength λ_B of the FBG. Both temperature and strain changes can cause shifts in λ_B, following the linear relationship described by Equation (2):

$$\frac{\Delta\lambda}{\lambda_B} = (1 - P_e)\varepsilon + (\alpha + \zeta)\Delta T \qquad (2)$$

In this equation, $\Delta\lambda$ represents the change in the FBG wavelength, ε is the axial strain in the fiber, ΔT is temperature change, P_e is the fiber's photoelastic coefficient, α is the fiber's thermal expansion coefficient, and ζ is the fiber's thermo-optic coefficient [42]. Equation (2) quantitatively relates the fractional change in Bragg wavelength ($\frac{\Delta\lambda}{\lambda_B}$) to the applied strain and temperature change. The first term, $(1 - P_e)\varepsilon$, represents the effect of mechanical strain; stretching the fiber (ε) increases the grating period and alters the refractive index via the photoelastic effect, producing a proportional shift in λ_B. The second term, $(\alpha + \zeta)\Delta T$, represents thermal effects; a temperature rise causes the fiber to expand (α) and its refractive index to change (ζ), together shifting. This linear model underpins the FBG sensor's ability to simultaneously measure strain and temperature by distinguishing their respective contributions to the wavelength shift.

Based on the above principles, this system enables the dynamic and precise measurement of both temperature and strain in structures. It features corrosion resistance, immunity to electromagnetic interference, and lightning protection. Additionally, due to the lightweight and flexible nature of optical fibers, the sensors are compact and lightweight, making installation easier. Moreover, the sensors have minimal impact on the material properties and mechanical parameters of the installation site, allowing for non-destructive embedding. Fiber Bragg grating (FBG) strain and temperature sensors are embedded at different locations within the wall, allowing for multi-channel remote monitoring via a bus system. These sensors are connected to an FBG wireless demodulator for the real-time, automatic collection and storage of strain and hydration–temperature data.

To investigate the evolution of temperature and strain during the hydration period of the continuous wall, two monitoring sections were set up along the wall's thickness direction: one at the center layer and one at the outer layer. The temperature and strain measurement points were arranged at both the sections, with the temperature sensors for the center and outer layers labeled T_1 and T_2, respectively, and the strain sensors labeled S_1

and S_2. The outer layer monitoring points are located approximately 300 mm from the wall surface, while the center layer points are about 600 mm away. Both the points are located at an absolute height of 2400 mm. The FBG temperature and strain sensors were installed using the main reinforcement binding method. A diagram of the sensor layout is shown in Figure 2.

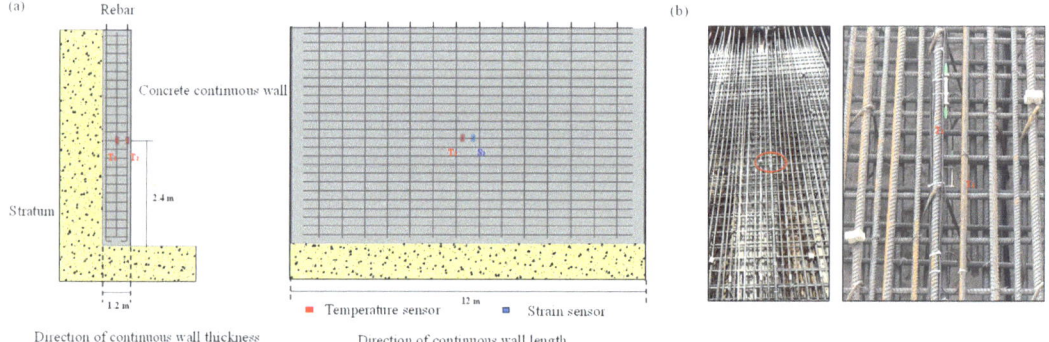

Figure 2. On-site monitoring plan: (**a**) schematic diagram of sensor layout for monitoring hydration–temperature and strain in continuous wall; (**b**) on-site installation of sensors for monitoring hydration–temperature and strain in continuous wall.

Given the thin wall thickness, efforts were made to minimize the impact of sensor embedding on the quality of concrete pouring. To avoid sensor damage during concrete vibration, the sensors were securely fixed, and their lead wires were organized, marked, and protected. During the concrete pouring process, the sensors and their lead wires were not to be directly impacted by the material, and the vibrator should not come into contact with the sensors or lead wires. A full-process monitoring approach was implemented to ensure the safety of the sensors, lead wires, and measuring instruments. All the fiber Bragg grating (FBG) temperature and strain sensors were factory-calibrated by the manufacturer, and their accuracy was verified under controlled laboratory conditions prior to deployment. Although no independent reference sensors (such as thermocouples or resistive strain gauges) were used for side-by-side calibration, manufacturer-provided calibration curves were used to convert the raw sensor measurements to engineering units. The consistency of sensor readings was also checked before and after the monitoring period to ensure a stable performance and measurement accuracy. The monitoring began immediately after the completion of concrete pouring, with a monitoring period of 28 days and a frequency of every 0.2 h.

2.3. Analysis of Monitoring Results

The temperature evolution curves at the different monitoring points of the continuous wall during hydration are shown in Figure 3a. The temperature trends at all the points are generally consistent, with each point experiencing an initial increase followed by a decrease. Based on the temperature curve, the hydration–temperature change can be divided into three stages:

1. Rapid Hydration and Accelerated Temperature Rise: After concrete pouring is completed, the hydration effect becomes significant. During this stage, the hydration degree of the concrete increases rapidly, and the heat released from the hydration reaction exceeds heat loss from the surrounding environment due to convection and heat conduction, causing a rapid increase in concrete temperature. At 21 h after pouring (Point A), the rate of heat release reaches its maximum.

2. Slower Hydration and Continuous Temperature Rise: After 21 h, the hydration heat effect slows down, and the internal temperature of the concrete continues to rise steadily until 44 h after pouring (Point B), at which point the internal and external temperatures of the wall reach their peak. This characteristic time point (44 h) was identified by analyzing the measured temperature evolution curves obtained from the fiber-optic sensing system during the transition from temperature rise to decline.
3. Hydration Cooling Stage: In this phase, the hydration rate decreases, and the heat released is less than heat loss caused by convection and heat conduction. As a result, the concrete temperature decreases. The temperature continues to decrease until 153 h after pouring (Point D), when the hydration effect is essentially complete. This point (153 h) was selected based on the observation that the concrete temperature stabilized, indicating the hydration process was essentially complete. The hydration heat effect shows a phased pattern, initially slowing, and then accelerating, followed by stabilization and gradual dissipation. The temperature changes throughout the hydration stage are influenced by both the heat generated from hydration and heat dissipation from the concrete surface.

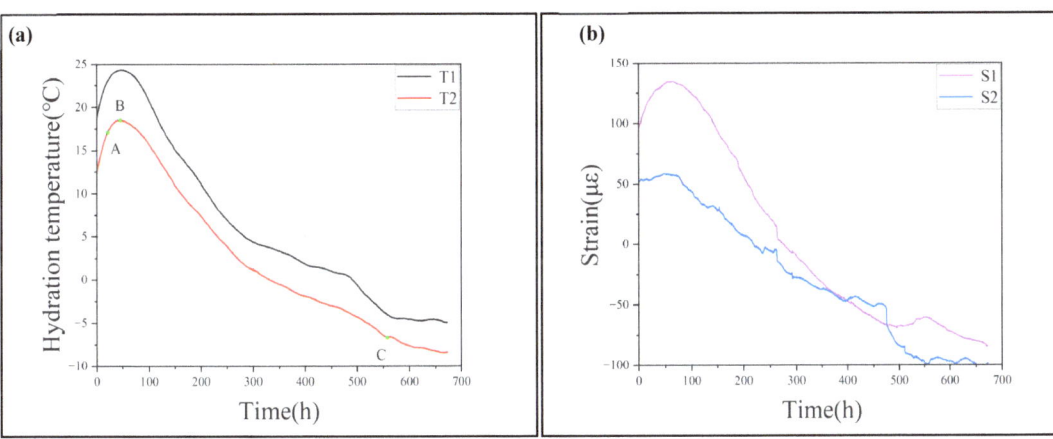

Figure 3. Evolution of temperature and strain in continuous wall during hydration: (**a**) evolution of hydration–temperature at different monitoring points of continuous wall; (**b**) evolution of internal strain in continuous wall during hydration.

Despite the overall consistency in the temperature trends across the different points, the peak temperatures at each monitoring point vary significantly. At 44 h, the center and outer layer points reach their peak temperatures. The peak temperature at the center point (T_1) is 24.3 °C, while the peak temperature at the outer point (T_2) is 18.5 °C, 23.8% lower than that at T1. This difference occurs because the surface of the continuous wall can exchange heat more easily with the surrounding environment, while the center of the wall cannot, resulting in poorer heat dissipation conditions. Therefore, the maximum temperature increases with the thickness of the concrete protective layer.

Based on these findings, it can be further inferred that assuming the concrete is homogeneous and defect-free, the temperature differences generated at the different locations in the concrete during hydration can be used to precisely identify the thickness of the concrete protective layer. The heat produced during the hydration process spreads through the surrounding soil and atmosphere. The rates of heat generation and diffusion depend on the internal conditions of the concrete, such as the cement content, the type of cement material, and the presence of defects. If a distinct temperature anomaly is observed in the temperature distribution along the wall in the early hydration stage, it can be compared with the ideal temperature distribution for the wall to identify potential defects. However, different defect types can result in similar temperature profiles during hydration, making it difficult to accurately distinguish between them based on temperature data alone. This similarity increases the risk of misidentifying the defect type if temperature is used as the sole diagnostic parameter. Additional parameters are needed for precise defect identification.

Strain evolution curves inside the wall during the hydration period are shown in Figure 3b. Two measurement points, constrained by the bottom and lateral sides, initially experience compressive strain in the early hydration stage after pouring is complete. As the concrete's hydration heat causes temperature rise, the compressive strain gradually increases, reaching its maximum value at 62 h. The compressive strain then gradually decreases, and during the cooling phase, it decreases to zero and transitions into tensile strain. Subsequently, the tensile strain increases until hydration is complete, and strain eventually stabilizes.

Analyzing the hydration–temperature curve, in the early hydration stage, the rapid temperature rise causes concrete to expand, and this expansion, under external constraints, leads to significant compressive strain. As hydration progresses, the temperature rise slows down, and the autogenous shrinkage effect gradually becomes more evident, counteracting deformation caused by thermal expansion. The compressive strain begins to decrease. As hydration continues, the concrete temperature starts to decrease, and the material transitions from thermal expansion deformation to shrinkage deformation, with shrinkage gradually dominating. This process reduces compressive strain until tensile strain is generated, which increases as the age of the concrete progresses until hydration is complete.

3. Finite Element Modeling

3.1. Basic Principles

This paper introduces a new multi-physics computational framework based on the COMSOL multiphysics® 6.2 finite element software, enabling the capture and analysis of the complex thermo-mechanical–chemical (TMC) properties of concrete during its hydration period. The model couples the essential thermo-mechanical–chemical processes to describe temperature evolution, the changes in hydration degree, and mechanical behavior, incorporating age-related effects to represent the changes in material properties. The model also accounts for heat conduction/convection between the solid material and the environment at temperature T0. The specific principles are detailed below.

3.1.1. Heat Generation and Thermal Diffusion

During the early-stage curing of concrete, hydration reactions release heat, causing the material to heat up and expand. Subsequently, heat transfer processes such as conduction and convection lead to a gradual reduction in temperature after reaching their peak, inducing shrinkage deformation. Therefore, heat generation and diffusion are two critical concepts in the TIP testing process. The thermodynamic equilibrium of concrete during hydration follows Fourier's law. The heat generation equation and the heat conduction equation can be expressed as follows [43]:

$$\rho c_t \frac{\partial T}{\partial t} = -\nabla \cdot q + \dot{Q}_c \tag{3}$$

$$q = -\lambda \nabla T \tag{4}$$

where ρ is the density of concrete, c_t is the specific heat capacity, T is temperature, q is heat flux, and $\dot{Q}_c$ is the heat generation rate per unit volume due to cement hydration. λ is the material's thermal conductivity coefficient.

3.1.2. Stress–Strain Constitutive Relationship

The strain equation for concrete under hydration can be expressed as follows [44]:

$$\varepsilon = \varepsilon_m + \varepsilon_t + \varepsilon_a \tag{5}$$

$$\varepsilon_t = \eta_t(\theta - \theta_0) \tag{6}$$

$$\varepsilon_a = -\eta_a \xi(\chi) \tag{7}$$

In this equation, ε_m represents mechanical strain, ε_t represents thermal expansion strain, and ε_a represents autogenous shrinkage strain. η_t is the thermal expansion coefficient, which characterizes the thermal expansion strain related to the difference between the current temperature θ and the initial temperature. χ is the degree of hydration. When the degree of hydration χ exceeds the threshold χ_0 ($\chi_0 = 0.03$), concrete undergoes autogenous shrinkage, and its magnitude is related to the coefficient η_a. $\xi(\chi)$ is a truncated linear function expressed as follows:

$$\xi(\chi) = \left\langle \frac{\chi - \chi_0}{\chi_\infty - \chi_0} \right\rangle \tag{8}$$

$$\chi_\infty = 1 - exp(-3.3\frac{w}{c}) \tag{9}$$

The final degree of hydration of concrete, χ_∞, follows the above exponential relationship with the water-to-cement ratio.

3.1.3. Hydration Equation

$$\dot{\chi} = \phi(\chi) exp\left(-\frac{E_a}{R \cdot \theta}\right) \tag{10}$$

In this equation, θ represents the current temperature, E_a is activation energy, which characterizes the rate of heat generation, and $R = 8.314$ J/(K·mol) is the ideal gas constant [45].

3.1.4. Concrete Ageing Effects

As the age of concrete increases, it exhibits noticeable ageing effects. Specifically, the elastic modulus (E_0), compressive strength (f_t), and fracture energy (G_f) gradually increase, while Poisson's ratio (v_0) remains relatively constant. To simplify, we assume that the hydration degree threshold for the development of the elastic modulus, compressive strength, and fracture energy in the recently made concrete is the same as that for the autogenous shrinkage strain, denoted as χ_0. The concrete ageing effect is considered as follows [46,47]:

$$E_0(\chi) = E_\infty \xi(\chi) \tag{11}$$

$$G_f(\chi) = G_{f\infty} \xi(\chi) \tag{12}$$

$$f_t(\chi) = f_{t\infty} \xi(\chi) \tag{13}$$

In this equation, the function $\xi(\chi)$ is given by Equation (8), and E_∞, $G_{f\infty}$, and $f_{t\infty}$ represent the elastic modulus, fracture energy, and tensile strength when the degree of hydration reaches saturation at χ_∞, respectively [48,49].

3.2. Model Parameters

For simulating the underground continuous wall, the relevant material parameters were obtained through on-site measurements, as shown in Table 1. The critical hydration degree at which the cement material begins to gain strength is defined as follows: when the degree of hydration exceeds $\chi_0 = 0.03$, autogenous shrinkage strain is activated. Throughout the simulation, the environmental temperature is assumed to be constant, with an initial temperature of $T_0 = 0\ °C$ for the entire system. The structure is influenced by the convective boundary conditions, where the radiation/convection coefficient is assumed to be independent of wind speed, with a value of $h = 6\ [W/(m^2 \cdot K)]$.

Table 1. Material property parameters.

Material Property Name, Symbol (Unit)	Value
Concrete density, ρ (kg/m^3)	2450
Convective heat-transfer coefficient of sidewall template (W/(m^2 K))	2.75
Concrete heat capacity, c_t (J/(kg K))	940
Heat conductivity, λ (W/(m K))	2.4
Convective heat-transfer coefficient of side-wall concrete surface (W/(m^2 K))	6.0
Specific heat capacity of the foundation, (J/(kg K))	1005
Initial temperature of concrete and environment, T_0 (K)	293
Solid bulk modulus, K_r (GPa)	44

Additionally, to match the on-site conditions, constraints are applied to the x displacement at the left end of the wall and to the y displacement at the lower end. The y displacement at the upper end is free. The structure is meshed using triangular elements with a maximum element size of $h_{max}\ e = 0.0022$ m and a minimum element size of $h_{min}\ e = 0.0013$ m. For the first 200 time steps, the time increment is set at $\Delta t = 300$ s, and for the remaining 2500 time steps, the increment is set at $\Delta t = 600$ s. The goal is to ensure appropriate soil medium dimensions, boundary condition definitions, and element meshing, so that the model size is manageable and provides convergence. The final configuration includes 22,434 nodes and 19,146 elements (Figure 4a).

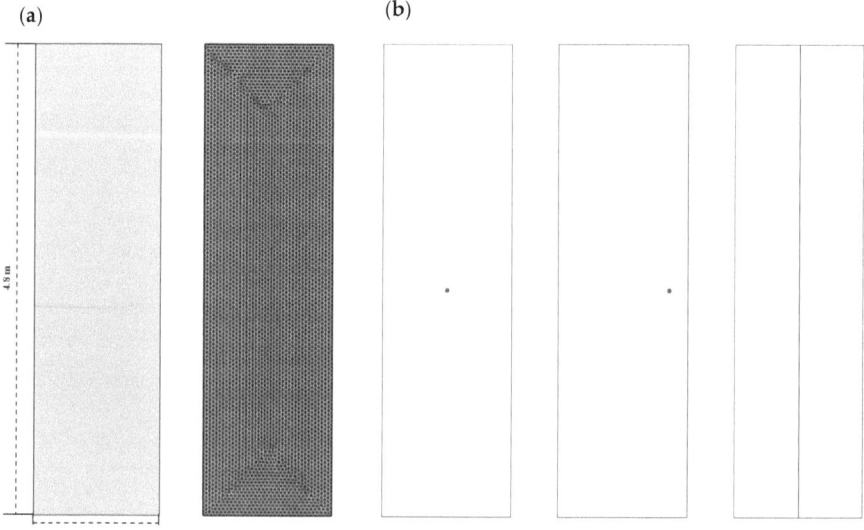

Figure 4. Numerical model construction. (**a**) Numerical model mesh division; (**b**) set monitoring points and monitoring lines.

3.3. Validation with Experimental Data

To validate the effectiveness of the developed finite element model, two monitoring points were set in the numerical model (as shown in Figure 4b). Temperature–time and strain–time curves were extracted from the finite element model at both the points, as shown in Figure 5. The results indicate that the numerical coupled model aligns with the observed temperature–strain variations over time from the field measurements. The data from the coupled model closely match the field measurements in terms of the temporal domain. To further quantify the model's accuracy, statistical validation metrics were calculated. In particular, the Root Mean Square Error (RMSE) and the Pearson correlation coefficient (R) were employed to evaluate the differences between the simulated and experimental time-series data. The RMSE is defined as follows:

$$RMSE = \sqrt{\frac{1}{N}\sum_{i=1}^{N}(Y_i^{sim} - Y_i^{exp^2})} \tag{14}$$

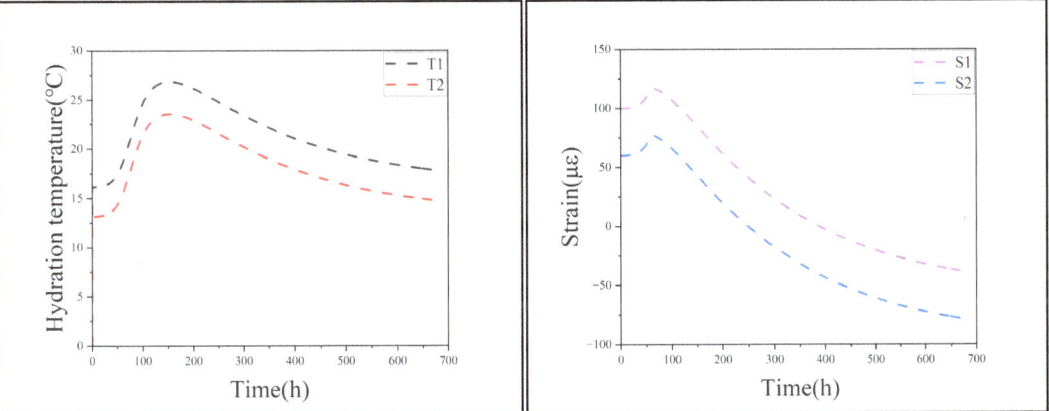

Figure 5. Temperature and strain evolution curves at two points of continuous wall during hydration based on numerical coupled model.

This metric represents the average magnitude of the error between the simulation (Y_i^{sim}) and experiment (Y_i^{exp}) over N data points. Similarly, the Pearson correlation coefficient is given as follows:

$$R = \frac{\sum_{i=1}^{N}\left[\left(Y_i^{sim} - \overline{Y}_i^{sim}\right)\left(Y_i^{exp} - \overline{Y}_i^{exp}\right)\right]}{\sqrt{\sum_{i=1}^{N}\left(Y_i^{sim} - \overline{Y}_i^{sim}\right)^2 \sum_{i=1}^{N}\left(Y_i^{exp} - \overline{Y}_i^{exp}\right)^2}} \tag{15}$$

It measures the strength of linear correlation (with $R = 1$ indicating a perfect positive correlation and $R = 0$ indicating no correlation). Using these metrics, the model predictions show excellent agreement with the experimental data. For the temperature–time curves at Point 1 and Point 2, the RMSEs between the simulated and measured temperatures are approximately 1.1 °C and 1.3 °C, with Pearson correlation coefficients of 0.98 and 0.97, respectively. For the strain–time curves, the RMSE is on the order of 5–6 με for the two monitoring points, with R values of 0.96 and 0.95, respectively. All the correlation coefficients exceed 0.95, indicating a very strong linear relationship between the model and the experimental results. These low RMSE values and high correlations quantitatively confirm that the finite element model can accurately reproduce the thermal and mechanical responses observed in the field. Table 2 summarizes the validation metrics for each monitoring point.

Table 2. Statistical validation of the finite element model against experimental measurements at two monitoring points (temperature in °C; strain in με).

Monitoring Point	RMSE (Temperature)	R (Temperature)	RMSE (Strain)	R (Strain)
Point 1	1.1 °C	0.98	5 με	0.96
Point 2	1.3 °C	0.97	6 με	0.95

Overall, the finite element modeling approach used in this study is deemed sufficient and capable of accurately simulating the TIP process, including the maximum temperature, the temperature differences caused by defects, and the temperature–time history. Consequently, the finite element model was used for further defect analysis.

Additionally, a monitoring line was placed vertically from the bottom to the top of the model (as shown in Figure 4b) to extract the spatial distribution of hydration–temperature and strain at a specific moment, as presented in Figure 6. In the absence of defects, the temperature and strain curves of the wall are smooth and continuous. Across the wall's depth, the temperature and strain values gradually change and remain relatively stable, without significant jumps or discontinuities. The convective heat transfer coefficient at the top of the wall is significantly higher than those at the middle and bottom of the wall. As a result, during hydration, the temperature at the top of the wall at the same time is approximately 3 °C lower than at the middle, and the temperature of the concrete gradually decreases from the top to the middle. This phenomenon is consistent with the experimental results observed by Rui et al. [50].

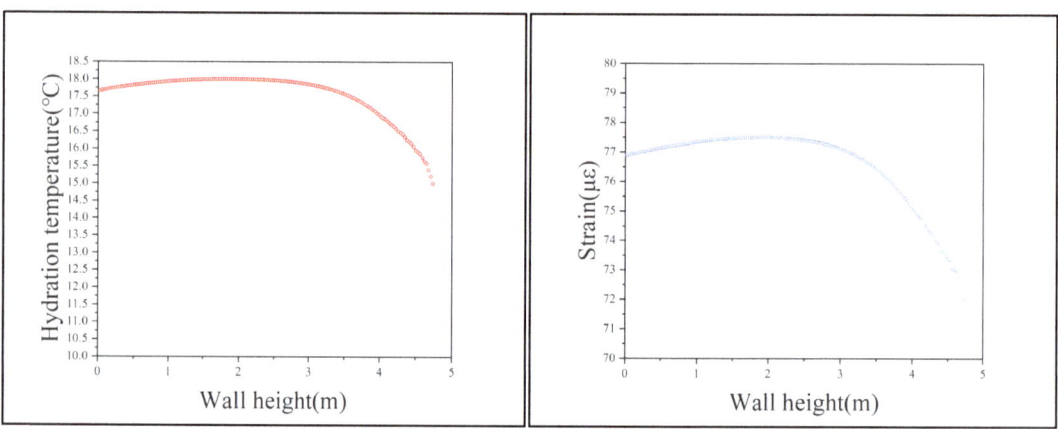

Figure 6. Evolution curves of temperature and strain with wall height at specific moment during hydration based on numerical coupled model.

In the early stages of hydration, if the temperature and strain profiles along the wall show smooth, uniform trends without significant anomalies, this indicates a uniform heat distribution and a defect-free condition within the wall. However, if the temperature and strain curves exhibit distinct anomalies—such as sharp changes at certain depths—this suggests the presence of defects (e.g., voids, mud inclusions, or cross-sectional narrowing/widening). The further analysis of the coupled temperature–strain behavior can help determine the specific nature of the defect. This integrated analysis approach is crucial for comprehensively assessing the wall's integrity and providing reliable defect diagnosis.

4. Analysis of the Influence of Different Defect Types on the Temperature and Strain Evolution of the Wall During Hydration

This section builds upon the concrete hydration model established in the previous section, introducing the different defect types (Table 3). By analyzing the impact of these defects on temperature and strain during the hydration process, we study the relationship between the defect types and the temperature–strain characteristic curves, enabling the accurate identification of defect types. Underground continuous walls are prone to a range of structural quality issues after pouring, influenced by factors such as the geological conditions, construction equipment, and technician skill levels. The main types of defects include necking, widening, mud inclusion, and voids. This section builds upon the concrete hydration model established in the previous section, introducing the different defect types (Figure 7). These defects not only reduce the wall's load-bearing capacity, but also pose serious risks related to the stability of the structure. In the experiments, in addition to the defect-free model, four sets of intentionally created defects were included. To improve computational efficiency and convergence, the mud inclusion and void defect zones were modeled as circular areas with a radius of 0.3 m. The distance from the defect boundary to the left wall boundary is 0.1 m, and the height is 1.8 m. In the case of the void defects, the area is filled with air, while the mud inclusion defect area is filled with soil. The widening and necking defects are represented as protrusions and recesses along the left and right boundaries of the wall, with a 0.1 m distance from the defect boundary to the wall. For the necking defect, the recessed area is filled with the surrounding soil. The grid size for the four defect groups is similar to that of the baseline model.

Table 3. Continuous wall types and their definitions.

Type	Concept
Intact Wall	A continuous wall with a uniform structure and no internal defects.
Void	An internal cavity in the continuous wall where concrete is absent.
Mud Inclusion	A layer of mud or weak material embedded within the continuous wall.
Necking	A local reduction in the thickness of the continuous wall.
Widening	A local increase in the thickness of the continuous wall.

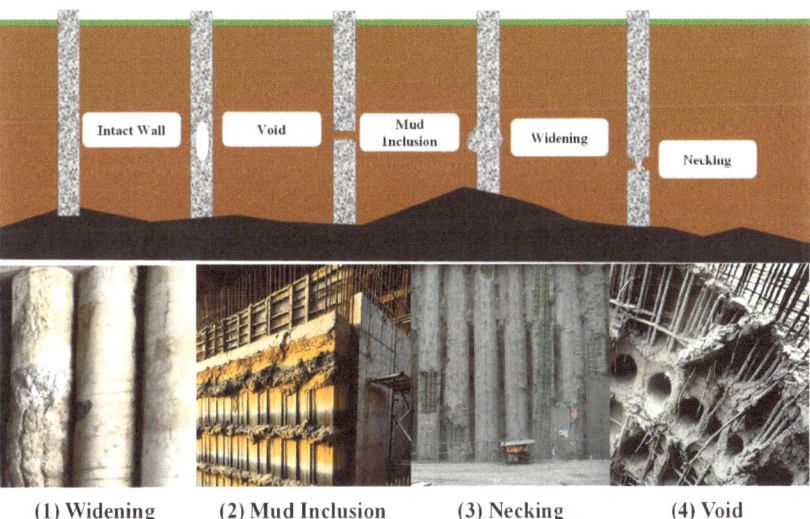

Figure 7. Typical defect types in underground continuous walls: schematics and on-site examples.

A distributed fiber-optic monitoring line is used in the model to monitor the changes in temperature and strain along the wall's height during hydration. It is important to note that depending on the relative distance between the monitoring line and the defect location, two scenarios arise: the monitoring line either passes through the defect zone, or does not (Figure 8). The position of the monitoring line significantly affects the results, so this section analyzes both the scenarios separately.

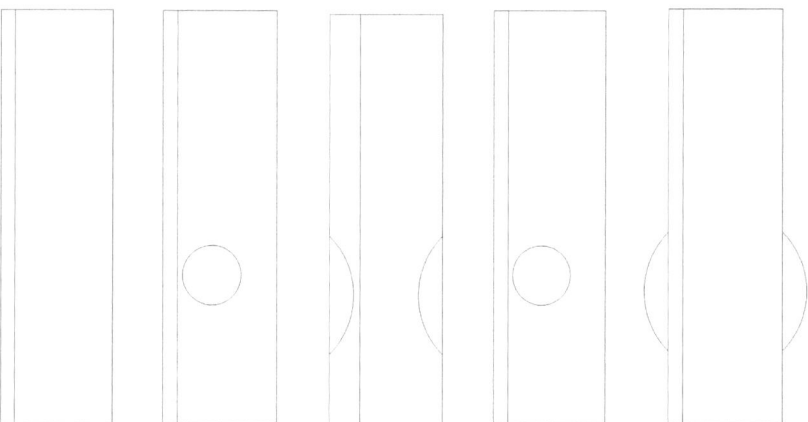

Monitoring line not passing through the defect zone.

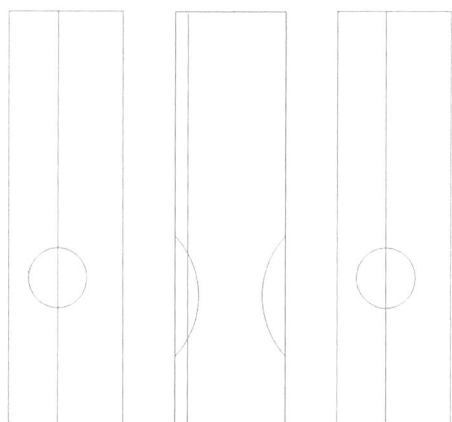

Monitoring line passing through the defect zone.

Figure 8. Schematic diagram of the relationship between the monitoring line layout and the defect zone location.

4.1. Temperature and Strain Distribution of the Wall During Hydration When the Monitoring Line Does Not Pass Through the Defect Zone

Figure 9 presents distribution maps of hydration–temperature and strain in the continuous wall for the different defect types (void, mud inclusion, widening, and necking) at three stages: early, middle, and late hydration. Comparing with the control group (no defects), it is clear that the different defect zones have a significant impact on the hydration–temperature and deformation of the surrounding concrete, with varying degrees of influence depending on the defect type. To further distinguish the defect types, the data from the monitoring line were extracted, and the spatial distribution curves of the wall's hydration–temperature at the same time under different the defect conditions were compared (Figure 10). It is observed that except for the widening defect zone—where the concrete temperature is significantly higher than that in the non-defect area during hydration—the concrete temperatures around the void, mud inclusion, and necking defect zones are all noticeably lower than those in the non-defect area.

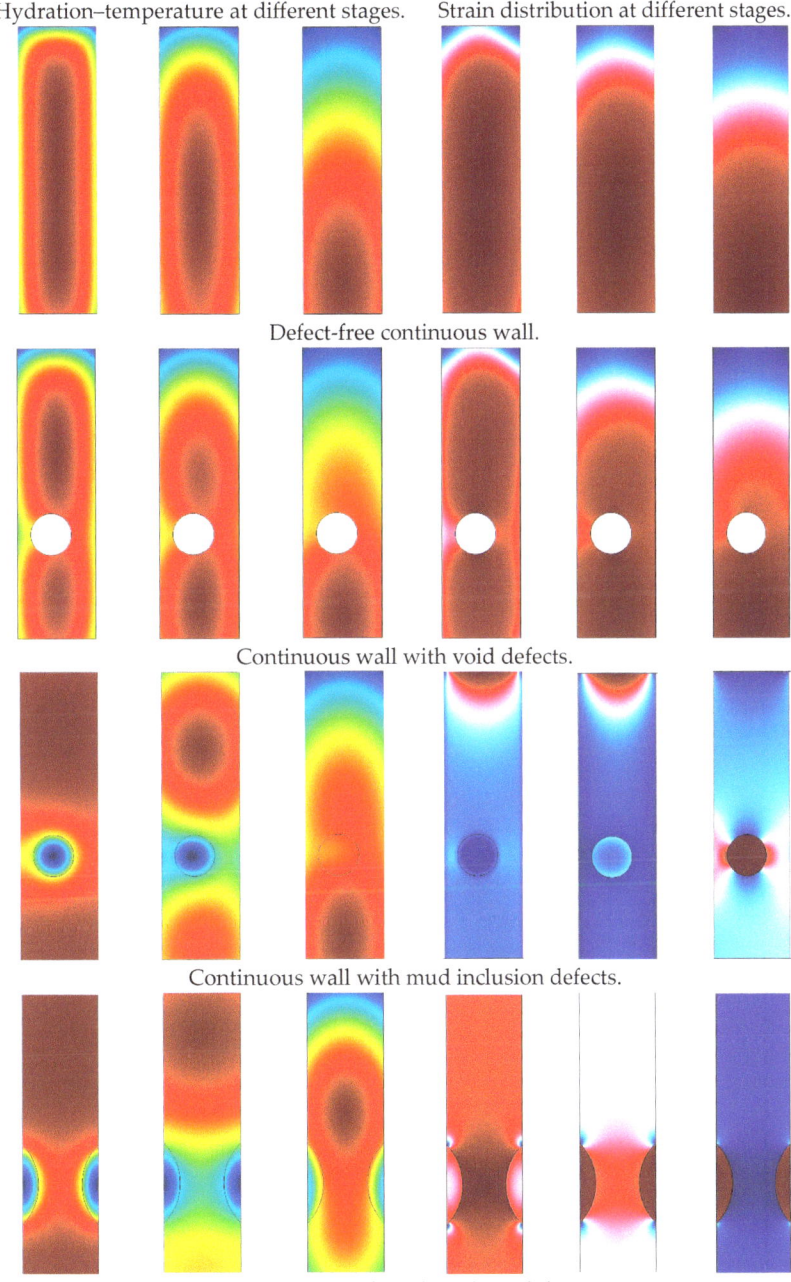

Hydration–temperature at different stages.   Strain distribution at different stages.

Defect-free continuous wall.

Continuous wall with void defects.

Continuous wall with mud inclusion defects.

Continuous wall with necking defects.

Figure 9. *Cont.*

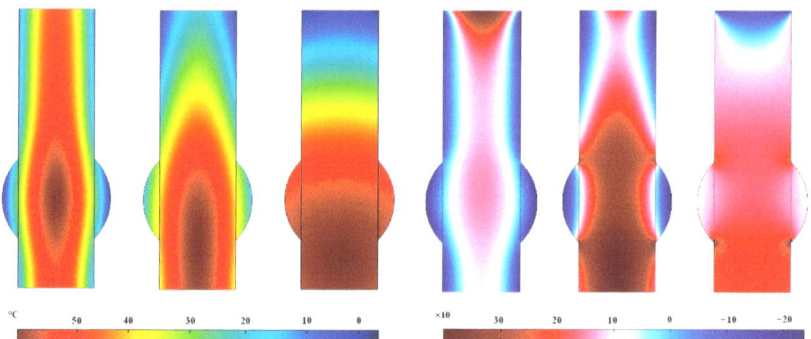

Continuous wall with widening defects.

Figure 9. Distribution maps of hydration–temperature and strain in continuous wall for different defect types.

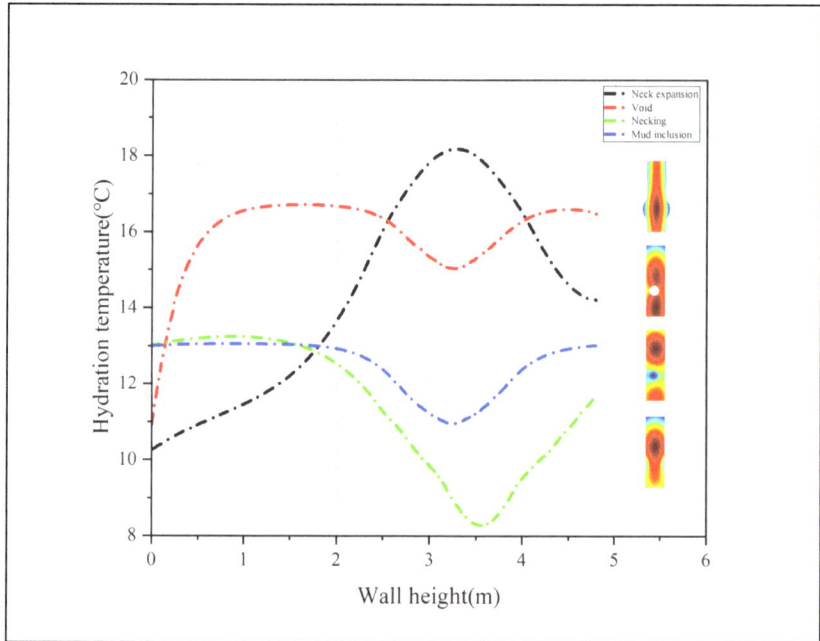

Figure 10. Hydration–temperature curves of wall at same moment for different defect types.

For the widening defect, the elevated temperature is attributable to the greater volume of cementitious material in that region, which releases more heat during hydration. In a larger cross-section, the heat generated by cement hydration is not able to dissipate, leading to the accumulation of heat in the widening zone. This well-known "mass effect" in concrete implies that thicker or bulging sections attain higher internal temperatures than those in the normal sections. As a result, the temperature in the widening region is significantly higher than that in the normal zones, and this distinct thermal signature enables the accurate identification of widening (bulging) defects.

By contrast, void defects, mud inclusions, and necking (under-sized cross-section) defects lack cement, so little to no hydration heat is generated in those areas [51]. The void defect (air pocket) not only fails to produce heat, but also acts as a thermal insulator that blocks heat flow, causing the area around the void to remain cooler than the surrounding concrete. A mud inclusion (soil-filled void) similarly does not contribute to hydration heat, and the presence of soil (an inert material) in that zone leads to a "cold spot" during curing; although soil has higher thermal conductivity than air, it still cannot compensate for the absence of exothermic cement hydration [52]. Likewise, a necking defect (reduced cross-sectional area) contains a smaller concrete volume; accordingly, it generates less heat and has a higher surface-to-volume ratio, allowing for faster heat loss. This means the necked region will exhibit a lower temperature rise compared to that of the intact sections.

The temperature differences manifest as abrupt changes in the temperature–depth curve along the monitoring line, providing a reliable basis for identifying internal defects. Notably, cooler-than-average temperature readings along the wall indicate the presence of voids, mud inclusions, or necking (insufficient concrete), whereas warmer-than-average readings indicate the likely widening or bulging of the cross-section. These trends are consistent with the findings in the recent literature and practical thermal profiling methods, which report that internal concrete defects or inclusions lead to locally depressed temperatures, while enlarged sections yield higher temperatures (The strain distribution results at different stages show analogous trends and are discussed in Section 4.2.)

Note that the temperature distributions in the wall caused by these three types of defect shows distinct differences. At the same time, the temperature difference around the void defect is the small compared to that of the non-defect area, followed by the mud inclusion defect, with the necking defect showing the largest temperature difference. This is due to the different materials filling the defect zones, with the differences in thermal conductivity leading to variations in temperature. The void defect is filled with air, while the mud inclusion and necking defects are filled with soil. Air is a poor thermal conductor with an extremely low level of thermal conductivity, which results in low efficiency in heat transfer and dissipation. This leads to a smaller temperature difference between the concrete in the defect zone and the non-defect area. In contrast, soil has a relatively higher thermal conductivity. The particles and water molecules in the soil effectively transfer heat, causing heat to diffuse rapidly. As a result, the temperature difference around the defect zones of mud inclusion and necking defects is more pronounced.

However, there is a further distinction between the two. The heat transfer mode for these two defects differs. The mud inclusion defect is surrounded by concrete, allowing for heat exchange only between the defect zone and the surrounding concrete, causing heat to accumulate and the temperature to rise quickly. On the other hand, the soil side of the necking defect not only absorbs heat from the surrounding concrete, but also connects to the deeper soil layers, allowing for heat to dissipate into the soil. Consequently, the necking defect has a higher heat dissipation rate, and its temperature is significantly lower than that of the mud inclusion defect. This difference in heat transfer directly impacts temperature distribution during the hydration process of the two defect types.

It should be noted that for these three defect types, which all exhibit cooling characteristics, relying solely on the temperature difference from the non-defect concrete is insufficient for accurate identification. The temperature differences among the three defect types are relatively small, so the additional analysis of the strain curve characteristics is necessary. The field experiments by Rui et al. [50] demonstrated that the deployment of distributed fiber-optic sensors within piles effectively captured abnormal temperature variations along the pile depth during early hydration, thereby identifying defects, such as cross-sectional widening and narrowing. These observations align closely with the temperature distribution patterns obtained from the numerical simulations in this study for the various defect types. Furthermore, Sun et al. [20] conducted the field monitoring of temperature distributions in cast-in-place piles and found distinct inflection points in temperature curves at the defect locations, thus validating the reliability of Thermal Integrity Profiling methods for practical applications. Similarly, model experiments by Wang et al. [37] highlighted significant differences in the temperature responses between intact piles and piles with defects, consistent with the monitoring results presented in this study. These comparative analyses with existing real-world case studies from the literature provide substantial evidence of the practical applicability and validity of the proposed temperature–strain combined monitoring method. This integrated analysis will improve the accuracy of identifying and distinguishing internal concrete defects.

Figure 11 shows strain distribution curves along the wall height for both the early and late hydration stages for the walls with the four different defect types. The strain values in the widening defect zone are significantly higher than those in the non-defect region during both the early hydration compressive strain phase and the late hydration tensile strain phase. This is because the widening defect contains more cement material, which releases more heat during hydration. This results in greater volume expansion during the temperature rise, causing significant compressive strain. During the cooling phase, the higher cement content causes a larger volume shrinkage, leading to pronounced tensile strain. As a result, the strain values in the defect zone are significantly higher than those in the normal area during both the stages of hydration.

For the void defect type, during the hydration expansion and contraction of concrete, the strain around the void is smaller than that in the normal area, both for compressive and tensile strain. This is because the void region lacks cement material and does not participate in the hydration reaction. Therefore, during the expansion phase, there is no volumetric expansion or compressive effect on the surrounding concrete, leading to smaller compressive strain around the void. Similarly, during the contraction phase, the void region lacks internal constraints, meaning it does not induce tensile stress on the surrounding concrete, resulting in significantly lower tensile strain compared to that in the normal area. This distinctive strain curve characteristic is the most typical feature used for identifying void defects.

For the mud inclusion defect type, the strain curve during the early hydration phase differs from that of the void defect. In the defect zone, a peak forms, indicating larger compressive strain around the mud inclusion defect. This is because during the early hydration phase, the concrete is still in a plastic state, with an elasticity modulus lower than that in the surrounding compacted soil in the mud inclusion zone. As the temperature rises, the soil in the mud inclusion area compresses the surrounding concrete, resulting in significant compressive strain. However, as the concrete hardens, its elasticity modulus increases rapidly and soon exceeds that of the surrounding soil, causing the strain curve in the mud inclusion zone to resemble that of the void defect. At this point, the compressive strain becomes noticeably smaller than that in the non-defective region. Therefore, the occurrence of high strain in the defect zone during the early hydration phase is the most typical characteristic for distinguishing mud inclusions from void defects.

For the necking defect type, whether during the compressive strain phase in early hydration or the tensile strain phase in later hydration, the strain in the necking defect zone is significantly greater than that in the normal area. This is due to the sudden reduction in wall thickness at the necking region, causing localized stress concentration. Additionally, the compression and constraint exerted by the surrounding soil on both sides of the necking defect further amplifies the stress concentration. This results in significant strain in both the expansion and contraction phases. Therefore, the strain curve in the defect zone exhibits prominent peaks and valleys. This characteristic is the most typical feature used for distinguishing necking from void and mud inclusion defects.

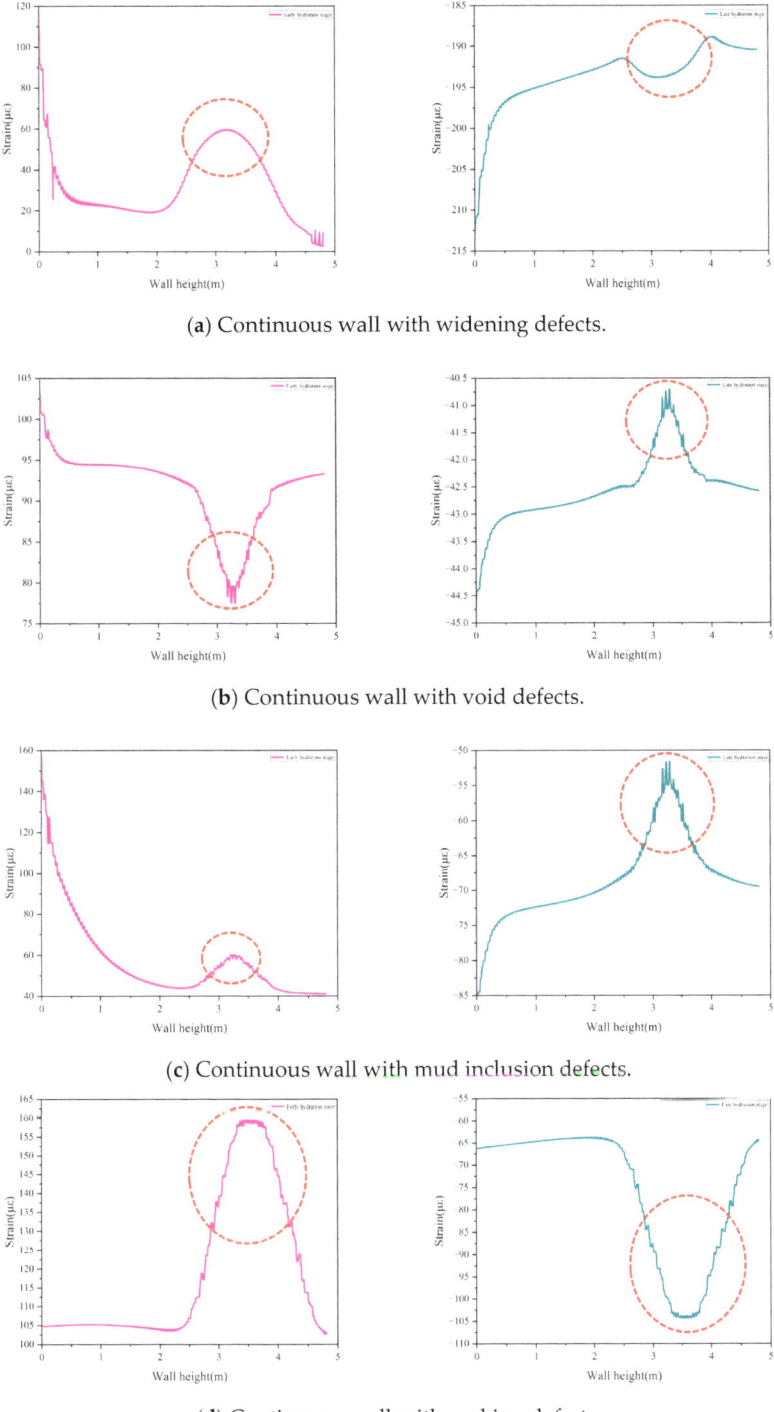

(a) Continuous wall with widening defects.

(b) Continuous wall with void defects.

(c) Continuous wall with mud inclusion defects.

(d) Continuous wall with necking defects.

Figure 11. Strain distribution curves along wall height for early and late hydration stages: (**a**) continuous wall with widening defects; (**b**) continuous wall with void defects; (**c**) continuous wall with mud-inclusion defects; (**d**) continuous wall with necking defects.

In conclusion, the four defect types—necking, widening, mud inclusion, and voids—each exhibits unique temperature–strain distribution characteristics during the hydration process. These characteristics can be leveraged for the accurate identification of specific defect types. This method provides a new and effective approach for assessing the health status of engineering structures. It enables the timely detection and correction of defects during construction and allows for the long-term health monitoring of the underground continuous wall after installation, helping prevent potential issues.

4.2. Distribution Patterns of Hydration–Temperature and Strain in the Wall When the Monitoring Line Passes Through the Defect Zone

In the previous section, we examined the case where the monitoring line does not pass through the defect zone. This section focuses on the results when the monitoring line passes through the defect zone. It is important to note that since the monitoring line is embedded within the internal framework of the wall, the monitoring line cannot pass through the protruding area of the widening defect. Therefore, only the cases where the monitoring line passes through the necking, mud inclusion, and void defects are considered in this section.

As seen in the temperature distribution patterns for the different defect types, the conclusion remains consistent with the previous section; the temperature in the different defect zones decreases variably, so no further discussion is needed. However, the strain distribution patterns differ across the defect types. When the monitoring line passes through the defect zone, the strain curve shows distinct breakpoints and layering (Figure 12), which is notably different from the strain curve when the monitoring line does not pass through the defect zone. This phenomenon occurs because the areas representing the materials intersected by the monitoring line have different thermal expansion coefficients. During both the heating and cooling phases, the responses of each material to temperature changes differ significantly, causing the strain curve to display clear layers and jumps between the different materials. This strain variation reflects the differences in the stress transfer properties of the optical fibers in different materials, serving as a crucial basis for identifying whether the monitoring line passes through the defect zone. This information can then be used to further identify the defect type.

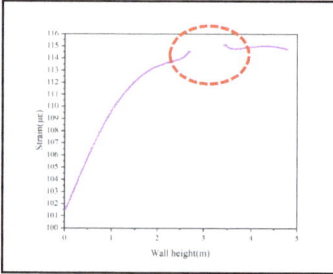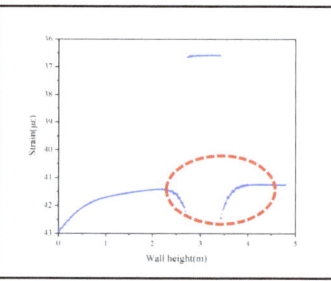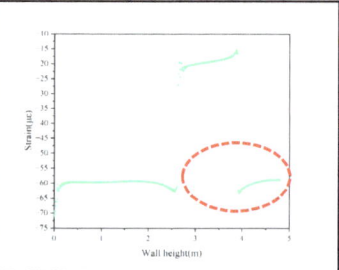

Figure 12. Strain distribution curves along wall height when monitoring line passes through different defect zones.

For the void defect type, during the concrete hydration process, the strain curve of the defect-free concrete remains smooth and continuous, without noticeable jumps. When the monitoring line passes through the void defect zone, the strain drops abruptly to zero, and a clear break appears in the strain curve for the defect. This is because the internal medium of the defect is air, and the optical fiber cannot detect strain, resulting in a strain value close to zero. For the mud inclusion and necking defect types, when the monitoring line passes through the defect area, the strain curve also shows a noticeable jump, but the strain value does not drop to zero. Instead, a certain strain value remains in these defect zones, leading to a layered phenomenon in the curve. The presence of layers in the strain curve indicates the presence of soil inclusion at these positions. This is in contrast to the void defect type, where the strain curve shows a clear break. Thus, the presence of a noticeable break in the strain curve is an important indicator for identifying when the optical fiber passes through a void defect.

To further distinguish between the mud inclusion and necking defect types, it can be observed that since both the defect zones are filled with soil, their strain curves are relatively similar during the early hydration phase. However, significant differences emerge during the late hydration phase when the wall undergoes contraction. When the monitoring line passes through the edge of the mud inclusion defect zone, the strain curve forms a distinct "funnel" shape. These funnel shapes indicate a rapid increase in tensile strain at these positions, followed by a quick rebound. In contrast, for the necking defect type, the strain curve near the defect edge changes more gradually, without forming a noticeable funnel shape.

This difference can be attributed to the fact that the mud inclusion defect zone is completely surrounded by concrete and is not connected to the surrounding soil. During the late hydration phase, concrete shrinkage around the defect zone creates concentrated tensile stress, causing the strain to change abruptly at the defect's edge. On the other hand, the edge of the necking defect zone is connected to the surrounding soil, which does not participate in the hydration reaction. Therefore, the tensile stress at the necking defect edge is lower, and the strain curve does not exhibit the sharp stress concentration seen in the mud inclusion defect. As a result, the strain curve near the necking defect edge does not form a funnel shape.

In the late hydration phase, the strain distribution at the defect edge serves as the key characteristic used to differentiate between the mud inclusion and necking defects. Based on the combined analysis of hydration–temperature and strain, the identification of jumps and layering in the strain curve can accurately distinguish whether the monitoring line passes through the defect zone, further enabling the determination of the different defect types within the concrete.

From an engineering perspective, each defect type introduces distinct geometric and material conditions that alter the hydration heat development and structural response of the concrete wall, thereby explaining the unique temperature and strain evolution observed for each case. Specifically, a widening defect increases the cross-sectional area of the wall, providing more cement material to react and release heat; a larger volume and reduced surface-to-volume ratio lead to heat accumulation and a significantly higher local temperature. This elevated thermal energy causes more pronounced expansion during early hydration (greater compressive strain) and greater contraction upon cooling (greater tensile strain), so the strains in the widening zone are much higher than those in the intact section during both the phases. In contrast, a necking defect creates an abrupt reduction in wall thickness, which causes a local stress concentration. The narrowed region is strongly confined by the adjacent soil, amplifying the strain response in that area. Therefore, even though the necking zone contains little or no cement (and thus generates a local temperature deficit similar to a void), it experiences considerably higher strain than the normal wall, with pronounced peaks in the strain curve during both the expansion and contraction stages. For a void defect, the absence of concrete means no hydration occurs in that zone, yielding a local temperature dip and eliminating any internal expansion or contraction. Consequently, the surrounding concrete experiences much less thermal strain (both compressive and tensile) near the void compared to the defect-free region, resulting in a relatively flat strain profile through the void area. The mud inclusion defect exhibits an intermediate behavior; like a void, it produces no hydration heat (causing a lower temperature in the defect region), but in the early hydration stage, the soil inclusion is stiffer than fresh concrete. This stiffness mismatch causes the expanding concrete to be constrained by the mud inclusion, leading to a pronounced compressive strain peak around the defect. As the concrete cures and its stiffness surpasses that of the surrounding soil, the inclusion's influence diminishes, and the strain pattern around the mud inclusion begins to resemble that of a void (with much lower strain than in sound concrete). Thus, each defect type (widening, necking, void, and mud inclusion) produces a characteristic temperature and strain response that is logically consistent with its structural characteristics and the associated physical mechanisms, confirming that the observed differences in the curves are physically reasonable.

5. Concrete Defect Type Identification Process Based on Temperature–Strain Combined Monitoring and Application Study

Based on the research findings, a specific process for identifying defect types is proposed to more accurately interpret the monitoring results in practical applications (Figure 13). The process is as follows: First, construct the hydration–temperature–strain curve of the wall. Determine if the monitoring line passes through the defect zone. If the strain curve exhibits a breakpoint or layering, it indicates that the monitoring line passes through the defect zone. Conversely, if the strain curve is continuous, the monitoring line does not pass through the defect zone. The following sections explain both these scenarios, when the monitoring line passes through and when it does not pass through the defect zone.

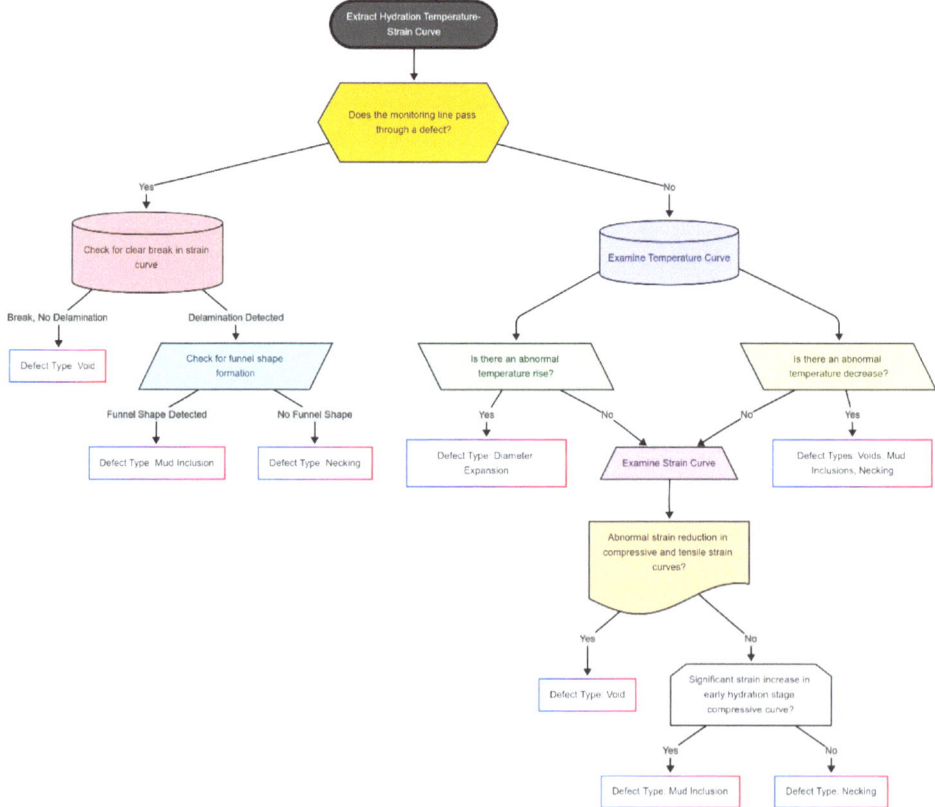

Figure 13. Concrete defect type identification process based on temperature–strain combined monitoring.

If the monitoring line does not pass through the defect zone, the next step is to observe if the temperature curve shows an abnormal increase. If so, the defect type is identified as widening. If the temperature curve shows a significant decrease, the defect type is identified as a void, mud inclusion, or necking. The further examination of the strain curve is then performed. If both the compressive strain curve during early hydration and the tensile strain curve during later hydration show a significant reduction, the defect type is identified as a void. If the compressive strain curve during early hydration shows a significant increase and the tensile strain curve during later hydration shows a reduction, the defect type is identified as a mud inclusion. If both the compressive strain curve during early hydration and the tensile strain curve during later hydration show significant increases, the defect type is identified as necking.

If the monitoring line passes through the defect zone and the strain curve shows a clear break without layering, the defect type is identified as a void. If the strain curve exhibits layering and a distinct funnel shape appears in the strain curve during late hydration, the defect type is identified as a mud inclusion. If the funnel shape is not observed, the defect type is identified as necking.

The proposed identification process effectively categorizes and localizes the defects based on temperature–strain monitoring, providing critical information for prompt intervention during construction. Moreover, from a structural engineering perspective, identifying these defects at an early stage is essential due to their potential impact on long-term structural reliability. Voids and mud inclusions, for instance, introduce internal discontinuities that reduce the effective load-bearing cross-section, leading to stress concentrations that accelerate crack initiation and propagation around defect zones. These discontinuities also compromise durability by creating pathways for water ingress and aggressive agents, adversely affecting the wall's watertightness and potentially accelerating steel corrosion or concrete deterioration over time. Necking defects, characterized by a localized reduction in cross-sectional area, represent structural weaknesses where elevated stresses can trigger progressive cracking and deformation, significantly diminishing he overall load-bearing capacity and stability throughout a wall's service life. Even widening defects, despite their locally enlarged cross-section, create geometric irregularities that can induce differential shrinkage or thermal strains, initiating micro-cracks in adjacent concrete. If left unmitigated, the presence of these defects and their associated cracking can lead not only to the immediate weakening of its structural performance, but also secondary damage, such as reinforcement corrosion or increased leakage, ultimately compromising the structure's long-term serviceability and safety.

The goal of this process is to help engineers more effectively utilize the temperature–strain combined monitoring method, enabling the more accurate and efficient detection of abnormalities in practical applications. While the proposed defect identification approach demonstrates strong capabilities in capturing and classifying various defects and their potential impacts on structural integrity, it is also important to recognize certain practical limitations inherent to this monitoring method. For instance, extremely minor or composite defects may only produce subtle thermal or strain anomalies that are challenging to reliably detect and differentiate based on current monitoring resolution. Additionally, the accuracy of defect detection is highly dependent on sensor deployment density and installation quality. Insufficient sensor coverage or improperly installed sensors could result in incomplete or inaccurate data, thereby reducing the reliability of defect classification. Moreover, the monitoring system can be sensitive to environmental disturbances, such as ambient temperature fluctuations, which may mask or mimic defect-induced anomalies in the measured temperature–strain response. Clearly acknowledging these limitations allows for a more comprehensive understanding of the method's applicability under various field conditions, thereby guiding appropriate engineering practices and the interpretation of monitoring outcomes. These findings provide valuable insights for implementing defect prevention and control measures on-site and are expected to play a significant role in predicting and controlling defects during the concrete hydration phase.

6. Conclusions

Based on the above findings, the main conclusions of this study are summarized as follows:

1. The combination of Thermal Integrity Profiling and fiber Bragg grating strain monitoring effectively provided the detailed, real-time tracking of the concrete hydration process within underground walls. The data verified the typical three-stage hydration process (rapid temperature rise, peak temperature, and gradual cooling) and highlighted a clear linear relationship between peak temperature and protective layer thickness. Notably, the multi-parameter approach successfully detected anomalous temperature and strain patterns, proving valuable for the early detection of hidden structural defects.
2. An advanced thermal–mechanical–chemical multi-field coupled finite element model was created to simulate temperature and strain behaviors throughout the concrete hydration period, accounting for the presence of defects. This innovative model integrates chemical hydration heat generation, thermal conduction, and mechanical deformation comprehensively. The model was validated rigorously against field measurements, achieving excellent consistency between the simulation and experimental data, underscoring its potential as an effective analytical tool for studying early-stage defects in concrete structures.
3. Defect Identification Mechanisms and Accuracy: By analyzing the combined temperature and strain data, the distinct impact mechanisms of different defect types were elucidated, enabling the accurate identification of defect nature and location. Four major defect types in the continuous wall—voids, mud inclusions, necking, and widening—were successfully distinguished by their unique temperature–strain signature patterns (e.g., variations in peak temperature drop, the heat dissipation rate, and strain anomalies during hydration). This dual-parameter approach overcomes the limitation of TIP alone by linking each observed anomaly to a specific defect mechanism.
4. This study proposes a rapid and systematic defect identification procedure based on the integrated monitoring and modeling results, which offers a new technological approach for concrete structural health assessment. This procedure was successfully demonstrated on the Weizishan Station underground wall and is readily transferable to similar underground concrete structures (e.g., diaphragm walls, deep foundation elements, and tunnel linings). The proposed multi-parameter monitoring and analysis framework significantly enhances the efficiency and precision of defect detection in recently made concrete, enabling timely intervention and long-term health monitoring.

To further enhance the practical applicability and broaden the scope of this research, future studies should focus on optimizing the monitoring process, including refining analytical algorithms and developing more effective sensor placement strategies. Additionally, exploring alternative sensing technologies, such as distributed fiber-optic sensing systems or low-cost wireless sensor networks, may provide additional capabilities and reduce deployment complexity. Finally, evaluating the adaptability and scalability of the proposed method to other structural forms, such as tunnel linings and raft foundations, and assessing its feasibility in large-scale engineering projects will be crucial for verifying and maximizing its potential impact on engineering practice.

Author Contributions: Conceptualization, X.Z.; methodology, L.L.; software, X.Z.; validation, X.L. and Y.L.; formal analysis, X.Z.; investigation, X.Z.; resources, L.L.; data curation, X.L.; writing—original draft preparation, X.Z.; writing—review and editing, X.Z.; visualization, X.Z.; supervision, X.Z.; project administration, L.L.; funding acquisition, X.L. All authors have read and agreed to the published version of the manuscript.

Funding: The authors greatly appreciate the Key R&D Plan of Shandong Province (2021CXGC011203) and the Shandong Province Housing and Urban Rural Construction Science and Technology Plan (2019-K7-12).

Data Availability Statement: Data will be made available upon request.

Conflicts of Interest: Author Linhai Lu was employed by the company Jinan Transportation Development Investment Co., Ltd. The remaining authors declare that the research was conducted in the absence of any commercial or financial relationships that could be construed as a potential conflict of interest.

References

1. Liu, Y.X.; Zhao, J.; Zhang, Q.B. A modular automated modelling framework for cut-and-cover excavations in mixed ground conditions. *Tunn. Undergr. Space Technol.* **2025**, *158*, 106384. [CrossRef]
2. Bai, B.W.; Liang, J.R.; Xu, H.Q.; Jiang, P.M.; Zhou, A.Z.; Lv, Y.Y. Study on hydraulic conductivity of dredged sediment-attapulgite vertical cutoff walls under confining pressure. *Environ. Res.* **2024**, *255*, 119110. [CrossRef]
3. Choi, J.Y.; Ahn, D.H. Displacement Monitoring of Subway Tracks and Tunnels According to Adjacent Construction. *Appl. Sci.* **2024**, *14*, 1887. [CrossRef]
4. Wu, J.R.; Chen, J. Experimental Research on the Floating Amount of Shield Tunnel Based on the Innovative Cumulative Floating Amount Calculation Method. *Buildings* **2024**, *14*, 1228. [CrossRef]
5. Miao, R.C.; Gu, Z.H.; Wang, C.; Cui, W. Study on rock-breaking mechanism of impact trenching in underground diaphragm wall with consideration of slurry effects. *Comput. Geotech.* **2025**, *179*, 106998. [CrossRef]
6. Peng, H.; Li, Y.J.; Niu, X.K.; Tang, H.D.; Meng, X.; Li, Z.C.; Wan, K.D.; Li, W.; Song, W. Characteristics analysis of leakage diseases of Beijing underground subway stations based on the field investigation and data statistics. *Transp. Geotech.* **2024**, *48*, 101317. [CrossRef]
7. Liang, R.Z.; Zhang, Z.W.; Li, Z.C.; Cao, S.; El Naggar, M.H.; Xiao, M.Z.; Wu, W.B. Simplified Method for Predicting the Shield Tunnel Longitudinal Responses to Over-Crossing Tunneling Considering Circumferential Joint Effect. *Int. J. Geomech.* **2024**, *24*, 04024140. [CrossRef]
8. Sun, Q.; Elshafie, M.Z.; Xu, X.; Schooling, J. Pile defect assessment using distributed temperature sensing: Fundamental questions examined. *Struct. Health Monit.-Int. J.* **2024**, *23*, 1701–1724. [CrossRef]
9. Torigoe, I.; Mori, K.; Spagnoli, A. Signal processing procedure for non-destructive test of concrete structure integrity. *NDT E Int.* **2005**, *38*, 575–581. [CrossRef]
10. Ni, S.-H.; Lo, K.-F.; Lehmann, L.; Huang, Y.-H. Time-frequency analyses of pile-integrity testing using wavelet transform. *Comput. Geotech.* **2008**, *35*, 600–607. [CrossRef]
11. Tennyson, R.C.; Coroy, T.; Duck, G.; Manuelpillai, G.; Mulvihill, P.; Cooper, D.J.F.; Smith, P.W.E.; Mufti, A.A.; Jalali, S.J. Fibre optic sensors in civil engineering structures. *Can. J. Civ. Eng.* **2000**, *27*, 880–889. [CrossRef]
12. Pelecanos, L.; Soga, K.; Elshafie, M.Z.E.B.; de Battista, N.; Kechavarzi, C.; Gue, C.Y.; Ouyang, Y.; Seo, H.-J. Distributed Fiber Optic Sensing of Axially Loaded Bored Piles. *J. Geotech. Geoenviron. Eng.* **2018**, *144*, 04017122. [CrossRef]
13. Sun, Q.; Elshafie, M.; Barker, C.; Fisher, A.; Schooling, J.; Rui, Y. Thermal integrity testing of cast in situ piles: An alternative interpretation approach. *Struct. Health Monit.-Int. J.* **2021**, *20*, 2493–2512. [CrossRef]
14. Chen, J.W.; Liao, Y.S.; Ma, F.; Tang, S.W. Effect of ground granulated blast furnace slag on hydration characteristics of ferrite-rich calcium sulfoaluminate cement in seawater. *J. Cent. South Univ.* **2025**, *32*, 189–204. [CrossRef]
15. He, F.F.; Chen, J.; Li, C.Z.; Xiong, F. Temperature tracer method in structural health monitoring: A review. *Measurement* **2022**, *200*, 111608. [CrossRef]
16. Zhu, J.S.; Wang, Z.Y. Experimental modeling and quantitative evaluation of mitigating cracks in early-age mass concrete by regulating heat transfer. *J. Build. Eng.* **2024**, *96*, 110641. [CrossRef]
17. Calo, M.; Ruggieri, S.; Nettis, A.; Uva, G. A MTInSAR-Based Early Warning System to Appraise Deformations in Simply Supported Concrete Girder Bridges. *Struct. Control Health Monit.* **2024**, *2024*, 8978782. [CrossRef]
18. Chu, I.; Kwon, S.H.; Amin, M.N.; Kim, J.-K. Estimation of temperature effects on autogenous shrinkage of concrete by a new prediction model. *Constr. Build. Mater.* **2012**, *35*, 171–182. [CrossRef]

19. Xiao, Z.P.; Di Murro, V.; Osborne, J.A.; Zhu, H.H.; Li, Z.L. Distributed fibre optic sensing and novel data processing method for tunnel circumferential deformation—A case study of an ageing tunnel at CERN. *Tunn. Undergr. Space Technol.* **2024**, *153*, 106014. [CrossRef]
20. Sun, Q.; Elshafie, M.Z.E.B.; Barker, C.; Fisher, A.; Schooling, J.; Rui, Y. Integrity monitoring of cast in-situ piles using thermal approach: A field case study. *Eng. Struct.* **2022**, *272*, 114586. [CrossRef]
21. Phan, L.T.; Lawson, J.R.; Davis, F.L. Effects of elevated temperature exposure on heating characteristics, spalling, and residual properties of high performance concrete. *Mater. Struct.* **2001**, *34*, 83–91. [CrossRef]
22. Khan, I.; Yong, G.T. Role of supplementary cementiteous materials in mitigating heat of hydration in mass concrete elements. *Constr. Build. Mater.* **2024**, *431*, 136482. [CrossRef]
23. Hernandez-Bautista, E.; Bentz, D.P.; Sandoval-Torres, S.; Cano-Barrita, P.F.d.J. Numerical simulation of heat and mass transport during hydration of Portland cement mortar in semi-adiabatic and steam curing conditions. *Cem. Concr. Compos.* **2016**, *69*, 38–48. [CrossRef] [PubMed]
24. Hu, J.; Ge, Z.; Wang, K. Influence of cement fineness and water-to-cement ratio on mortar early-age heat of hydration and set times. *Constr. Build. Mater.* **2014**, *50*, 657–663. [CrossRef]
25. Zhao, D.P.; Zhu, L.; Shen, Z.D.; Miu, Z.C.; Liu, X.H. Effect of hydration heat of super-large-section tunnel-lining concrete on structural stress and its mitigation measures. *Tunn. Undergr. Space Technol.* **2025**, *157*, 106324. [CrossRef]
26. Wang, L.G.; Wang, Y.C.; Miao, Y.C.; Ju, S.Y.; Sui, S.Y.; Wang, F.J.; Liu, Z.Y.; Jiang, J.Y. Temperature damage assessment of mass concrete based on the coupling mechanism of hydration-temperature-humidity-constraint factors. *J. Build. Eng.* **2024**, *90*, 109211. [CrossRef]
27. Gottsäter, E.; Johansson, M.; Plos, M.; Ivanov, O.L. Crack widths in base restrained walls subjected to restraint loading. *Eng. Struct.* **2019**, *189*, 272–285. [CrossRef]
28. Li, H.; Liu, J.; Wang, Y.; Yao, T.; Tian, Q.; Li, S. Deformation and cracking modeling for early-age sidewall concrete based on the multi-field coupling mechanism. *Constr. Build. Mater.* **2015**, *88*, 84–93. [CrossRef]
29. Saeed, M.K.; Rahman, M.K.; Alfawzan, M.; Basha, S.; Dahish, H.A. Recycling of date kernel powder (DKP) in mass concrete for mitigating heat generation and risk of cracking at an early age. *Constr. Build. Mater.* **2023**, *376*, 131033. [CrossRef]
30. Chu, I.; Lee, Y.; Amin, M.N.; Jang, B.-S.; Kim, J.-K. Application of a thermal stress device for the prediction of stresses due to hydration heat in mass concrete structure. *Constr. Build. Mater.* **2013**, *45*, 192–198. [CrossRef]
31. Schackow, A.; Effting, C.; Gomes, I.R.; Patruni, I.Z.; Vicenzi, F.; Kramel, C. Temperature variation in concrete samples due to cement hydration. *Appl. Therm. Eng.* **2016**, *103*, 1362–1369. [CrossRef]
32. Chen, B.F.; Tang, G.Q.; Lu, X.C.; Xiong, B.B.; Guan, B.; Tian, B. Thermal property evolution and prediction model of early-age low-heat cement concrete under different curing temperatures. *J. Build. Eng.* **2024**, *82*, 108020. [CrossRef]
33. Mardmomen, S.; Chen, H.L. Prediction of the early age thermal behavior of mass concrete containing SCMs using ANSYS. *J. Therm. Anal. Calorim.* **2023**, *148*, 7899–7917. [CrossRef]
34. Bazant, Z.P.; Baweja, S. Justification and refinements of model b3 for concrete creep and shrinkage 1. statistics and sensitivity. *Mater. Struct.* **1995**, *28*, 415–430. [CrossRef]
35. Madsen, H.O.; Bazant, Z.P. Uncertainty analysis of creep and shrinkage effects in concrete structures. *J. Am. Concr. Inst.* **1983**, *80*, 116–127.
36. Dwairi, H.M.; Wagner, M.C.; Kowalsky, M.J.; Zia, P. Behavior of instrumented prestressed high performance concrete bridge girders. *Constr. Build. Mater.* **2010**, *24*, 2294–2311. [CrossRef]
37. Wang, C.; Chen, Y.; Zhou, M.; Chen, F. Control of Early-Age Cracking in Super-Long Mass Concrete Structures. *Sustainability* **2022**, *14*, 3809. [CrossRef]
38. Dias, I.F.; Oliver, J.; Lemos, J.V.; Lloberas-Valls, O. Modeling tensile crack propagation in concrete gravity dams via crack-path-field and strain injection techniques. *Eng. Fract. Mech.* **2016**, *154*, 288–310. [CrossRef]
39. Klemczak, B.; Knoppik-Wrobel, A. Reinforced concrete tank walls and bridge abutments: Early-age behaviour, analytic approaches and numerical models. *Eng. Struct.* **2015**, *84*, 233–251. [CrossRef]
40. Boeckmann, A.Z.; Loehr, J.E. Evaluation of Thermal Integrity Profiling and Crosshole Sonic Logging for Drilled Shafts with Concrete Defects. *Transp. Res. Rec.* **2019**, *2673*, 86–98. [CrossRef]
41. Farahani, M.A.; Gogolla, T. Spontaneous raman scattering in optical fibers with modulated probe light for distributed temperature Raman remote sensing. *J. Light. Technol.* **1999**, *17*, 1379–1391. [CrossRef]
42. Zhu, H.H.; Ho, A.N.L.; Yin, J.H.; Sun, H.W.; Pei, H.F.; Hong, C.Y. An optical fibre monitoring system for evaluating the performance of a soil nailed slope. *Smart Struct. Syst.* **2012**, *9*, 393–410. [CrossRef]
43. Schindler, A.K.; Folliard, K.J. Heat of hydration models for cementitious materials. *ACI Mater. J.* **2005**, *102*, 24–33.
44. Ulm, F.J.; Coussy, O. Couplings in early-age concrete: From material modeling to structural design. *Int. J. Solids Struct.* **1998**, *35*, 4295–4311. [CrossRef]
45. Briffaut, M.; Benboudjema, F.; Torrenti, J.M.; Nahas, G. Numerical analysis of the thermal active restrained shrinkage ring test to study the early age behavior of massive concrete structures. *Eng. Struct.* **2011**, *33*, 1390–1401. [CrossRef]

46. De Schutter, G. Finite element simulation of thermal cracking in massive hardening concrete elements using degree of hydration based material laws. *Comput. Struct.* **2002**, *80*, 2035–2042. [CrossRef]
47. Thanh-Tung, N.; Weiler, M.; Waldmann, D. Experimental and numerical analysis of early age behavior in non-reinforced concrete. *Constr. Build. Mater.* **2019**, *210*, 499–513. [CrossRef]
48. De Schutter, G.; Taerwe, L. Degree of hydration-based description of mechanical properties of early age concrete. *Mater. Struct.* **1996**, *29*, 335–344. [CrossRef]
49. De Schutter, G.; Taerwe, L. Fracture energy of concrete at early ages. *Mater. Struct.* **1997**, *30*, 67–71. [CrossRef]
50. Rui, Y.; Kechavarzi, C.; O'Leary, F.; Barker, C.; Nicholson, D.; Soga, K. Integrity Testing of Pile Cover Using Distributed Fibre Optic Sensing. *Sensors* **2017**, *17*, 2949. [CrossRef]
51. Li, Z.; Li, M.; Guo, H.; Wu, Y.; Sheng, L.; Jiao, J.; Li, Z.; Sui, W. Experimental Investigation of the Evaluation of the Cement Hydration Process in the Annular Space Using Distributed Fiber Optic Temperature Sensing. *Sensors* **2025**, *25*, 958. [CrossRef] [PubMed]
52. Rui, Y.; Sun, Q.C. Measurement of Pile Cover Thickness Using Distributed Fibre Optic Sensors. In Proceedings of the 3rd International Conference on Information Technology in Geo-Engineering (ICITG), Guimaraes, Portugal, 29 September–2 October 2019.

Disclaimer/Publisher's Note: The statements, opinions and data contained in all publications are solely those of the individual author(s) and contributor(s) and not of MDPI and/or the editor(s). MDPI and/or the editor(s) disclaim responsibility for any injury to people or property resulting from any ideas, methods, instructions or products referred to in the content.

Article

Critical Filling Height of Embankment over Soft Soil: A Three-Dimensional Upper-Bound Limit Analysis

Xijun Liu [1,2], Bokai Song [1,*], Zhuanqin Sun [1] and Wenxiu Jiao [1]

[1] School of Highway, Chang'an University, Xi'an 710064, China; 2022021503@chd.edu.cn (X.L.); 2021221105@chd.edu.cn (Z.S.); jiaowenxiu@chd.edu.cn (W.J.)
[2] Guangzhou Expressway Co., Ltd., Guangzhou 510100, China
* Correspondence: 2024221211@chd.edu.cn

Abstract: This paper investigates the critical filling height of embankments over soft soil using three-dimensional (3D) upper-bound limit analysis based on a rotational log-spiral failure mechanism. Soft soils are characterized by low shear strength and high compressibility, making the accurate determination of critical filling height essential for evaluating embankment stability. Unlike conventional two-dimensional (2D) analyses, the proposed 3D method captures the true failure mechanism of embankments, providing more realistic and reliable results. The upper-bound analysis equations are derived using the principle of virtual work and solved efficiently through the genetic algorithm (GA), which avoids the limitations of traditional loop and random searching algorithms. The proposed solution is validated by comparing it with existing studies on slope stability and demonstrates higher accuracy and computational efficiency. Parametric studies are conducted to evaluate the influence of the depth–height ratio (the ratio of soft soil depth to embankment height) on the failure width of the embankment, the critical failure surface, and the critical filling height. Results show that the critical failure surface is tangential to the bottom of the soft soil layer and the critical filling height increases as the depth–height ratio decreases. The findings provide a set of critical filling heights calculated under various soft soil depths, strength parameters, and embankment geometries, offering practical guidance for embankment design.

Keywords: critical filling height; embankment; soft soil; genetic algorithm; upper-bound limit analysis

Academic Editor: Eugeniusz Koda

Received: 26 November 2024
Revised: 23 December 2024
Accepted: 30 December 2024
Published: 26 January 2025

Citation: Liu, X.; Song, B.; Sun, Z.; Jiao, W. Critical Filling Height of Embankment over Soft Soil: A Three-Dimensional Upper-Bound Limit Analysis. *Buildings* **2025**, *15*, 395. https://doi.org/10.3390/buildings15030395

Copyright: © 2025 by the authors. Licensee MDPI, Basel, Switzerland. This article is an open access article distributed under the terms and conditions of the Creative Commons Attribution (CC BY) license (https://creativecommons.org/licenses/by/4.0/).

1. Introduction

Soft soils possess the characteristics of low shear strength and strong compressibility [1,2] and are always encountered in engineering constructions [3]. When embankments are built on soft soils and the filling height exceeds the critical filling height, i.e., the highest filling height that a natural foundation can bear, lateral displacement and collapse can be caused [4]. Therefore, the critical filling height is a valuable indicator to evaluate the stability of the embankment [5]. The limit equilibrium method and finite element method are popularly used to explore the critical filling height of embankments [6–11]. Although the limit equilibrium method has clear mechanical concepts and simple calculation methods, it only considers stress equilibrium and neglects the constitutive relationship of the soil. Therefore, the solution solved by the limit equilibrium method is neither a strict upper limit value nor a strict lower-bound value. The finite element limit analysis method can simulate the process of embankment failure and obtain the distribution of stress–strain fields during embankment instability [12]. However, the modeling process of the finite element analysis is not only very complicated but also, the constitutive model parameters utilized are difficult to determine. More importantly, the precision of the selected parameters greatly determines the accuracy of the calculation results [11,13].

Recently, the upper-bound limit analysis was used to determine the critical state of embankments. For example, Chen et al. [14] calculated the critical filling height of a pile-supported embankment by using two-dimensional (2D) limit analysis; Gong et al. [15] evaluated the seismic stability of embankments considering the anisotropy and nonhomogeneity of soils; and Li et al. [15] assumed a rigid block sliding along two logarithmic spiral surfaces and two-dimensional (2D) limit analysis to explore the critical filling height of the embankment. However, the embankment failures are 3D in nature. Recent studies have increasingly focused on incorporating three-dimensional features to improve the accuracy of stability predictions. These efforts include the exploration of complex soil behaviors, irregular geometries, and dynamic loading conditions. While promising, many of these approaches remain computationally intensive and are challenging to apply in large-scale engineering projects. Building on this foundation, this study integrates a 3D upper-bound limit analysis with a genetic algorithm (GA) to provide a practical and efficient solution for embankments over soft soils.

However, due to the difficulty of constructing admissible base failure mechanisms of embankments, the 3D analysis method for embankments is not as common as other methods, and a limited number of attempts have been conducted so far. Giger and Krizek [16] firstly utilized the 3D limit analysis method to explore the stability of a soil slope. Qu [17] conducted 3D finite element analyses on three full-scale embankments to assess their failure mechanisms over soft clay deposits. Zhuang and Wan analyzed four cases of embankments rapidly loaded to failure by using the 3D total stress circular arc stability analysis. Berrabah et al. [18] employed the 3D numerical method to analyze the stability of the embankment constructed over locally weak zones. Yang et al. [11] adopted a limit equilibrium-based 3D rotational failure mechanism to explore the stability of convex embankments. Another worthy point to note is that traditional loop algorithm and the random searching algorithm are the more commonly applied algorithms to search the most critical slip surface in current research [10,19]. However, the loop algorithm exhibits not only limited computational efficiency but also the potential to overlook the global minimum value if the incremental step is insufficiently small [19,20]. Moreover, although the random search technique proposed by Chen [14] could provide high computational efficiency, it would get trapped in local minimums. These limitations make it difficult to apply such methods to large-scale or highly complex embankment systems, necessitating the development of more efficient and versatile approaches. Compared to these traditional algorithms, the genetic algorithm (GA) utilized in this study significantly enhances computational efficiency and avoids local minima, leading to more reliable results. Therefore, the genetic algorithm (GA) is adopted to search for the critical safety factor of embankments over soft soil. Due to parameter limitations and the adjustment of the search direction during the search process, the genetic algorithm can effectively avoid missing the global minimum [21,22].

This study explores the critical filling height of embankments over soft soil using 3D upper-bound limit analysis. An admissible rotational log-spiral failure mechanism proposed by Michalowski and Drescher [23] is utilized to replicate the embankment failure. The log-spiral failure surface is composed of two sub-failure surfaces, one passing through the embankment and the other passing through the soft soil. Surcharge loads that may be caused during embankment construction are also considered. The critical filling height is determined by balancing the energy rates of external loads, including the equilibrium between soil weight and surcharge loads, and the frictional force acting along the failure surface. Compared to existing 2D methods, which often oversimplify the complex three-dimensional nature of embankment failure, the proposed approach provides a more accurate representation of the failure mechanisms by directly incorporating 3D effects. Additionally, traditional algorithms such as loop searching and random searching methods are limited in computational efficiency and often fail to locate the global minimum, highlighting the need for a more robust optimization approach. The GA with the advantage of computation efficiency and accuracy is used to solve the formulation and find the most critical filling height and critical failure surface. The solution is validated by degenerating the proposed embankment failure mechanism into the general slope mechanism and then comparing it with existing solutions. Parametric studies are conducted to investigate the influence of the ratio of the soft soil depth to the embankment height on the failure width of the embankment, the critical failure surfaces, and the critical filling heights.

2. Base Failure of Embankment over Soft Soil

2.1. Log-Spiral Failure Mechanism

The upper-bound limit analysis theorem relies on the conservation of energy principle and is designed to assess the maximum limit load or failure boundary of materials exhibiting elastic perfectly plastic behavior [24]. The energy rate equilibrium dictates that the strain rate of the failure mechanism must adhere to both the boundary condition and the corresponding flow rule of the yield criterion simultaneously (Appendix A). Hence, the 3D rotational mechanism proposed by Michalowski and Drescher [23] is the most reasonable failure model for a given frictional-cohesive soil embankment. In this paper, the 3D failure mechanism presented by Michalowski and Drescher [23] for a single-layer slope is further developed and extended for the base failure mechanism of embankments over soft soil. Moreover, according to the characteristics that the embankment is compacted while the foundation is not compacted, the failure mechanism is established by combining the layering characteristics of the embankment and the foundation. The failure mechanism of an embankment over soft soil is shown in Figure 1.

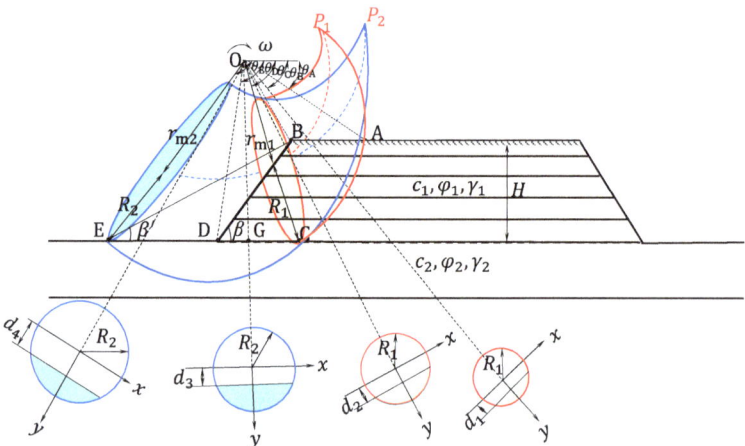

Figure 1. 3D failure mechanism of embankment over soft soil.

Figure 1 shows the log-spiral failure mechanism of the embankment over soft soil. Based on the layering characteristics of the embankment and the foundation, the failure mechanism is composed of two curvilinear cones with the same symmetry plane, and the surfaces must be tangential to a cone with apex angle 2φ shown as P_1, P_2. The schematic illustrations of the embankment failure and soft soil failure are shown as red and blue curves, respectively. The lower outline of two curvilinear cones forming the failure surface can be formulated as two log spirals (i.e., the lines AC and AE).

$$r_1 = r_0 e^{(\theta - \theta_A)\tan\varphi_1}$$
$$(\theta_A \leq \theta \leq \theta_C) \tag{1}$$

$$r_2 = r_C e^{(\theta - \theta_C)\tan\varphi_2}$$
$$(\theta_C < \theta \leq \theta_E) \tag{2}$$

where r_0, i.e., OA, is the initial radius of log spirals; θ_A and θ_E are the initial angle and the final angle describing the rotational mechanism, respectively; θ_C is the angle that the failure surface just passes through the interface between the embankment and soft soil foundation; r_C is the radius of the log spiral when the failure surface just crosses the interface between the embankment and the soft soil foundation; and φ_1 and φ_2, separately, represent the internal frictional angles of the embankment and the soft soil. The auxiliary angle, β', is introduced to ensure that the embankment failure penetrates the soft foundation, and this angle is smaller than the slope angle, β. The shaded area of the circle denotes the location where the failure mechanism just hit the soft soil surface. In the cross-sectional circles, d_i ($i = 1, 2, 3$) represents the separation between the center of the cross-sectional circle and the surface of the embankment; d_4 is the distance between the center of the cross-sectional circle and the surface of soft soil; R_i ($i = 1, 2$) are the radii of the rotating circle; and c_1 and c_2 are the cohesions of the embankment and the soft ground, respectively.

2.2. Energy Rate Balance

In upper-bound limit analysis, the energy rate balance is employed to establish formulations, ensuring that the work performed by external loads equals the energy dissipated along the failure surface [24]. Note that the rotational block is assumed to be rigid and without deformation and volume change [23]. Therefore, the internal energy is only dissipated along the sliding failure surfaces. The effect of surcharge loads is taken into account in this study. During embankment construction, surcharge loads are primarily caused by the weight of large rollers or construction debris, which can significantly affect the stability of the embankment by increasing the external work rates [25]. Hence, the forces contributing to the external work rates consist of the soil weight and surcharge loads, which are illustrated in Figure 2.

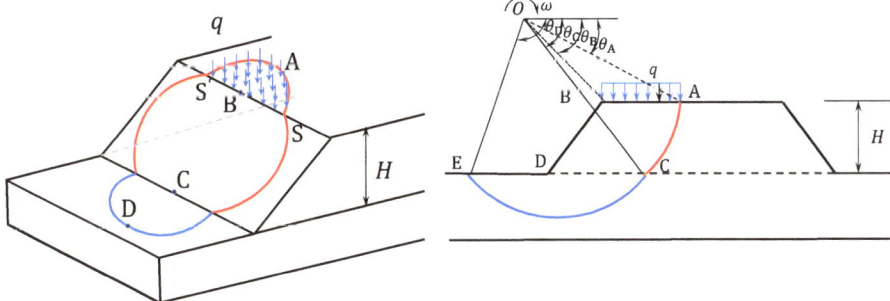

Figure 2. Surcharge loads on the embankment crest.

Then, the energy rate balance equation can be written as

$$W_\gamma^{3D} + W_q^{3D} = D_\gamma^{3D} \tag{3}$$

where D_γ^{3D} is the rate of internal energy dissipation of the failure mechanism; W_γ^{3D} is the work rate of the soil weight; and W_q^{3D} is the work rate due to the surcharge loads. The existing literature Zheng et al. [26] has given the details of deriving D_γ^{3D} and W_γ^{3D}.

2.3. Work Rate of Surcharge Loads

The uniform load, q, is introduced to represent the surcharge loads on the embankment. The magnitude of uniform load is computed based on the entire failure area involved. The rotating mechanism is created by progressively rotating a circle with an expanding diameter around the axis. Consequently, numerous potential failure regions emerge from the intersection of the embankment's crest with the rotating mechanism during the search for the failure surface [23,27,28]. The detailed expressions of failure area, S, can be written as

$$S = \frac{1}{2}\pi - 2\vartheta \left[\frac{(r_0\cos\theta_A - r_0\sin\theta_A\cot\theta_B)^2 + d_B^2}{2(r_0\cos\theta_A - r_0\sin\theta_A\cot\theta_B)} \right]^2 - \frac{d_B^2 - (r_0\cos\theta_A - r_0\sin\theta_A\cot\theta_B)^2}{2(r_0\cos\theta_A - r_0\sin\theta_A\cot\theta_B)}\sqrt{R_1^2 - d_1^2} \quad (4)$$

where d_B is the length of BS in Figure 2 and ϑ is the angle corresponding to the trajectory ASS'. The expressions of the two parameters can be calculated as

$$d_B = \sqrt{R_1^2 - \left(\frac{r_0 sin\theta_A}{sin\theta_B} - r_{m1}\right)^2} \quad (5)$$

$$\vartheta = \arctan\left[\frac{(R_1^2 - d_B^2) - r_0^2(\cos\theta_A - \sin\theta_A\cot\theta_B)^2}{2r_0\sqrt{R_1^2 - d_B^2}(\cos\theta_A - \sin\theta_A\cot\theta_B)}\right] \quad (6)$$

The surcharge loads are considered as a body force. The rate of work of the surcharge load is calculated by multiplying the sum of the forces on the failure surface ASS' by the distance from the centroid of the failure surface to the center of rotation, O. Moreover, the work rate of the surcharge load, W_q^{3D}, is dependent on the angular velocity, ω, and the equation can be written as

$$W_q^{3D} = \omega Sq \left\{ \begin{array}{c} r_0 sin\theta_A cot\theta_B + \\ \frac{4[(r_0\cos\theta_A - r_0\sin\theta_A\cot\theta_B)^2 + d_B^2]\cos\vartheta}{6(r_0\cos\theta_A - r_0\sin\theta_A\cot\theta_B)(\pi - 2\vartheta)} \end{array} \right\} \quad (7)$$

Furthermore, in addition to the special distribution form of surcharge load described above, the rectangular distribution form of surcharge load is also taken into account. Surcharge load is evenly distributed on the embankment crest, and the diagrammatic drawing is illustrated in Figure 3.

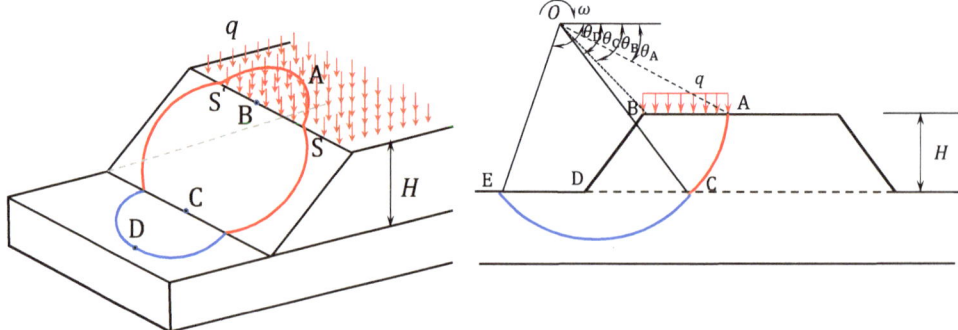

Figure 3. Surcharge loads of a rectangle on the embankment crest.

In the case of rectangular distribution, the work rate of the surcharge load can be defined as the scalar product of the uniform load and the velocity vector. The rate of external work due to the surcharge load can be written as follows:

$$W_q^{3D} = 2\omega r_0^2 \sin^2\theta_A \int_{\theta_A}^{\theta_B} q \frac{\cos\theta}{\sin^3\theta} \sqrt{R_1^2 - d_1^2}\, d\theta \tag{8}$$

2.4. Critical Filling Height of Embankment

The critical filling height of the embankment is the highest filling height that the natural foundation can bear and is an important metric to evaluate the stability of the embankment [25]. By utilizing the upper-bound theorem of limit analysis and balancing the work rate of external forces with the energy dissipation rate along the failure surface, the stability factor is determined as follows:

$$\frac{\gamma H}{c} = f\left(\theta_A, \theta_E, \beta', D_{cr}, \frac{r'_{01}}{r_{01}}, \frac{r'_{02}}{r_{02}}\right) \tag{9}$$

where γ is the unit weight of the soil. The embankment height, H, is not defined, so H needs to be determined from the geometrical and trigonometric relations as

$$H = r_0\left[e^{(\theta_A - \theta_C)\tan\varphi_1 + (\theta_E - \theta_C)\tan\varphi_2}\sin\theta_E - \sin\theta_A\right] \tag{10}$$

The function $f(\theta_A, \theta_E, \beta', D_{cr}, r'_{01}/r_{01}, r'_{02}/r_{02})$ can reach a minimum value, i.e., the least upper-bound value, when θ_A, θ_E, β', D_{cr}, r'_{01}/r_{01} and r'_{02}/r_{02} satisfy the following conditions:

$$\frac{\partial F_s}{\partial \theta_A} = 0 \tag{11}$$

$$\frac{\partial F_s}{\partial \theta_E} = 0 \tag{12}$$

$$\frac{\partial F_s}{\partial \beta'} = 0 \tag{13}$$

$$\frac{\partial F_s}{\partial D_{cr}} = 0 \tag{14}$$

$$\frac{\partial F_s}{\partial \frac{r'_{01}}{r_{01}}} = 0 \tag{15}$$

$$\frac{\partial F_s}{\partial \frac{r'_{02}}{r_{02}}} = 0 \tag{16}$$

where ∂F_s is the stability factor increment; $\partial \theta_A$ and $\partial \theta_E$ are the rotation angle increments; ∂D_{cr} is the increment of the ratio of the soft soil depth to embankment height; and $\partial \beta'$ is the auxiliary angle increment. When the derivatives of the reduction factor F_s with respect to θ_A, θ_E, β', D_{cr}, r'_{01}/r_{01} and r'_{02}/r_{02} are equal to zero, the function $f(\theta_A, \theta_E, \beta', D_{cr}, r'_{01}/r_{01}, r'_{02}/r_{02})$ reaches the minimum value. Consequently, the critical filling height can be expressed as

$$H_{cr} \leq \frac{c}{\gamma}\min\left[f\left(\theta_A, \theta_E, \beta', D_{cr}, \frac{r'_{01}}{r_{01}}, \frac{r'_{02}}{r_{02}}\right)\right] \tag{17}$$

3. Optimization Procedure

The genetic algorithm (GA), as a machine learning method, is utilized to search for the critical value of $\gamma H/c$ and identify all possible critical failure surfaces based on the energy rate balance equation derived for the failure mechanisms. Compared to conventional traversal search algorithms, the GA significantly improves computational efficiency by leveraging evolutionary strategies such as selection, crossover, and mutation [29]. These strategies allow the GA to effectively explore a larger solution space and converge more quickly to the optimal solution, making it more advantageous than loop searching and random searching methods. The calculation flowchart of the GA for the problem considered is illustrated in Figure 4.

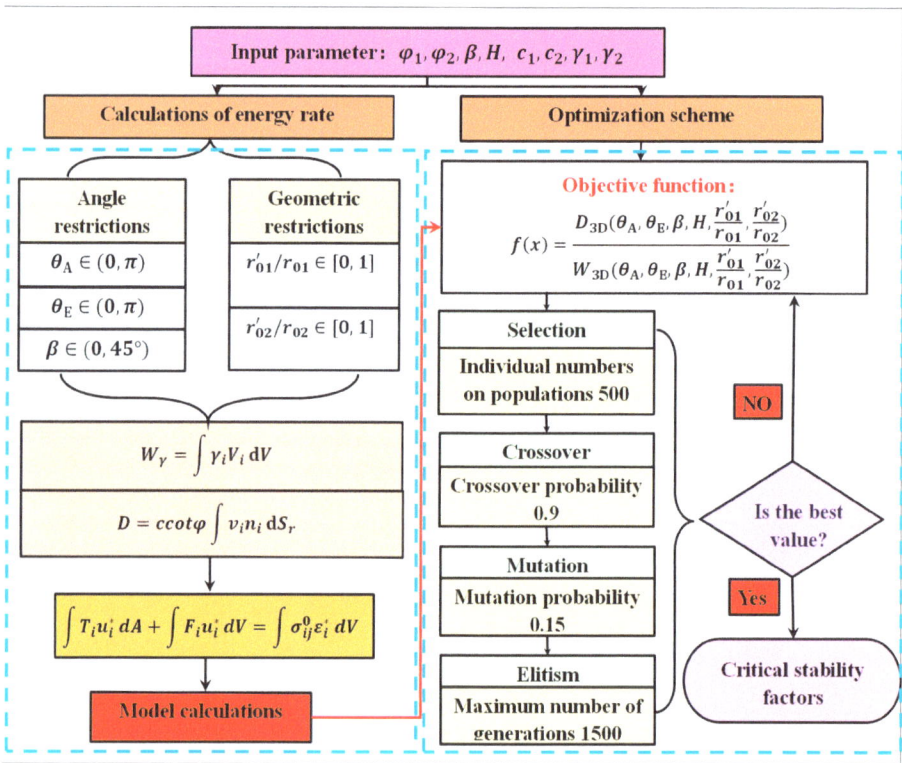

Figure 4. Workflow of the genetic algorithm (GA) optimization process for determining critical stability factors.

Figure 4 shows the flowchart employed to search the least upper bound to $\gamma H/c$. This scheme presents the search process of the genetic algorithm. For the given constraints of values of the embankment over soft soil c_1, c_2, φ_1, φ_2, γ_1, γ_2, and β, new individuals in a population are generated. Each generated individual corresponds to a value with independent variables ($\theta_A, \theta_E, \beta', D_{cr}, r'_{01}/r_{01}, r'_{02}/r_{02}$). The independent variables θ_A, θ_E, β', D_{cr}, r'_{01}/r_{01} and r'_{02}/r_{02} are introduced as the input variables because the geometric shape of the failure embankment can be uniquely defined by these variables. In order to explore the critical filling height of the embankment over different depths of soft soil, the depth restriction, D_{cr}, is introduced. D_{cr} is defined as the ratio of soft soil depth to embankment height, which constrains the depth of failure and requires that the failure surface is tangential to the bottom of the soft soil. The depth of failure mechanism satisfies the geometric restrictions, which are presented as follows:

$$m_1 = \left\{ r_0 e^{[(\theta_C - \theta_A)\tan\varphi_1 + (\theta - \theta_C)\tan\varphi_2]} - \frac{r_E \sin\theta_E}{\sin\theta} \right\} \sin\theta \tag{18}$$

$$m_2 = \left(R_2 - \frac{\sin\theta_E}{\sin\theta} r_E + r_{m2} \right) \sin\theta \tag{19}$$

$$d = \max(m_1, m_2) \tag{20}$$

$$D_{cr} = \frac{d}{H} \tag{21}$$

A set of sliding surfaces can be obtained when depth is limited. By utilizing genetic algorithms, the most dangerous slip surface can be searched. The objective function in the search procedure is developed as follows:

$$f(x) = \frac{\gamma H}{c} = \frac{W_{3D}\left(\theta_A, \theta_E, \beta', D_{cr}, \frac{r'_{01}}{r_{01}}, \frac{r'_{02}}{r_{02}}\right)}{D_{3D}\left(\theta_A, \theta_E, \beta', D_{cr}, \frac{r'_{01}}{r_{01}}, \frac{r'_{02}}{r_{02}}\right)} \tag{22}$$

The best individual is chosen through a set of selection, crossover, mutation, and elitism. Finally, the optimal results with the highest fitness are generated through constant updates.

4. Validation

To confirm the log-spiral failure mechanism of the embankment over soft soil, the embankment failure mechanism is simplified to the general slope failure, and the outcomes are juxtaposed with those from Michalowski and Drescher [23] and Gao et al. [30]. It is worth noting that Michalowski and Drescher [23] utilized the loop searching method, which systematically evaluates potential solutions within a predefined range, while Gao et al. [30] adopted the random searching technique, which explores potential solutions by generating random values within a specified domain. Both approaches aim to identify the critical height of $\gamma H/c$, but they differ in terms of their searching strategies and computational efficiency. The comparisons in Figure 5 show the variation in the critical height of $\gamma H/c$ with the ratio of width to the height of the slope for different slope angles, β. The values of $\gamma H/c$ computed by genetic algorithms (GAs) are comparable to or even lower than the outcomes determined by the loop searching method and the random searching technique. This suggests that the $\gamma H/c$ value obtained via the GA is closer to the actual value for the slope. The above validation demonstrates that the optimization method, the GA, is more efficient in searching the least upper-bound value of the critical filling height.

To further validate the feasibility of the present methodology for failure surface projections, the critical slip surface obtained from the limit analysis has been compared with that of the failure surface obtained from [28]. The associated parameters have been defined in Figure 6, which are listed as follows: $\varphi_1 = 30°$, $\varphi_2 = 40°$, $\beta = 20°$, $H = 10\,\text{m}$, $D_{cr} = 1$, and $B = 57\,\text{m}$, $B_0 = 90\,\text{m}$.

In Figure 6, it also has been noted that the critical slip surface of the present study and failure surface generated by Mohapatra [29] are well matched with each other. The validation of failure surface projections demonstrates that the GA and the three-dimensional rotational mechanism utilized by the present study are efficient in searching the critical failure surface.

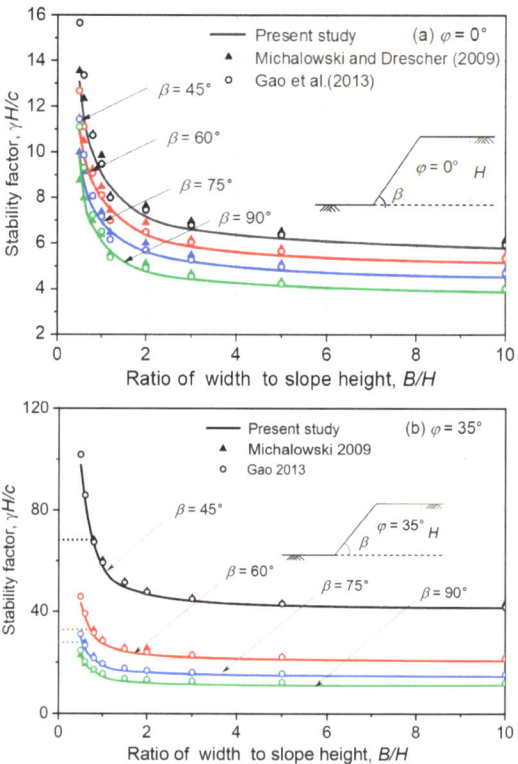

Figure 5. Comparison of critical value of $\gamma H/c$ from present study and Michalowski and Drescher and Gao et al. [30].

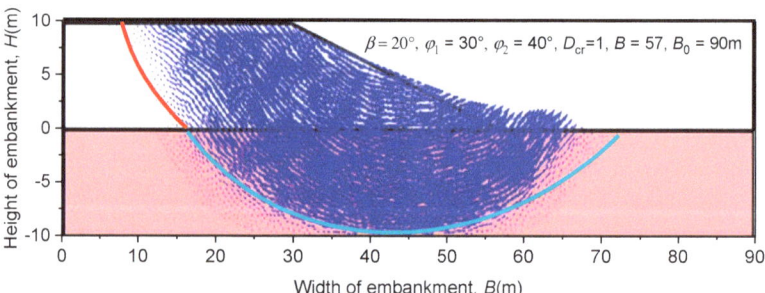

Figure 6. Comparison of failure surface projection from present study and Mohapatra [30].

5. Parametric Study

The effects of the cohesion of soft soil, the depth–height ratio, and the surcharge loads on the critical filling height of the embankment are first explored. Then, the effect of the depth–height ratio on the failure width of the embankment is investigated. Finally, the projections of the maximum critical failure surfaces for different conditions are plotted. These analyses are conducted by using nondimensional charts to efficiently cover a wide range of possible parameters.

5.1. Soft Soil Cohesion

Figure 7 shows the critical filling height for the base failure of embankments with different values of c_2/c_1 and β. The internal frictional angle and cohesion of embankment soil are taken as $\varphi_1 = 30°$ and $c_1 = 5$ kPa, respectively. The slope angles of the embankment are taken as $\beta = 45°, \beta = 60°$, and $\beta = 75°$ and the permitted embankment width is $L = 5H$. Note that because the cohesions of embankment soil and soft soil are different, the equivalent cohesion, $\bar{c} = (c_1 H + c_2 d)/(H + d)$, is employed to describe the soil cohesion.

The figure illustrates that the critical filling height initially shows a gradual increase, followed by a sharp rise as the cohesion of soft soil increases. When the soft soil has higher strength, the critical filling height becomes significantly larger. For instance, in the case of $\varphi_2 = 5°$, the critical filling height remains below 18 when the ratio of c_2/c_1 ranges between 1 and 5, but it increases sharply when c_2/c_1 exceeds six. In contrast, when φ_2 is relatively small, the critical slip surface tends to pass through the intersection of the embankment and soft soil interface. As shown in Figure 7a–c, for all the slope angles of the embankment considered, the critical filling height of the embankment over soft soil decreases as the slope angle increases, particularly for soft soils with smaller friction angles. Additionally, the use of nondimensional charts in this analysis allows for efficient representation and comparison of a wide range of parameters, providing a clearer understanding of the relationships among key factors affecting the embankment stability.

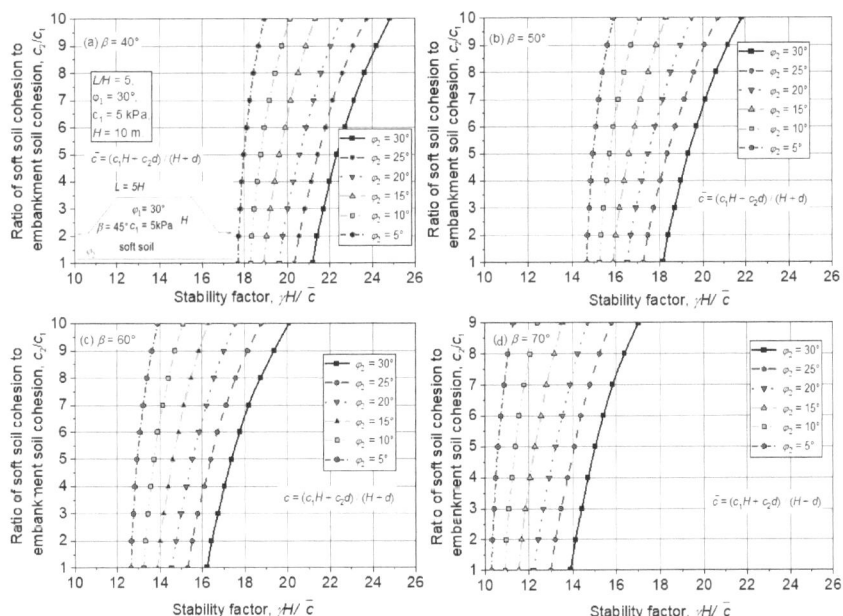

Figure 7. Critical stability factor with ratio of soil cohesion: (**a**) $\beta = 40°$, (**b**) $\beta = 50°$, (**c**) $\beta = 60°$, and (**d**) $\beta = 70°$.

5.2. Depth–Height Ratio

The variation in the critical height of $\gamma H/\bar{c}$ in terms of the depth–height ratio, D_{cr}, is plotted in Figure 8. The internal frictional angle and cohesion of embankment soil are also taken as $\varphi_1 = 30°$ and $c_1 = 5$ kPa, respectively. The normalized embankment width, $L = 5H$, is adopted to limit the embankment width.

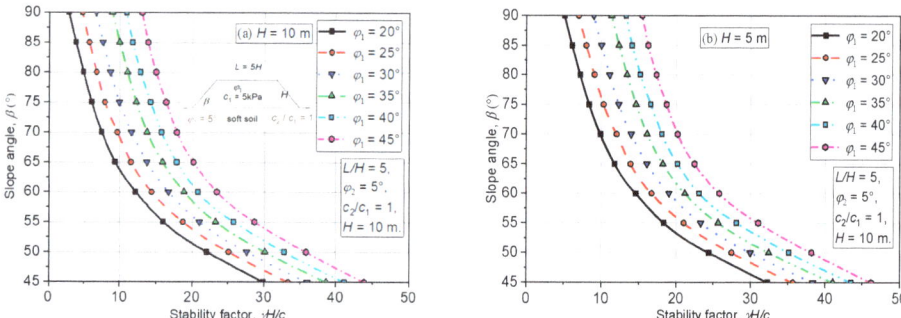

Figure 8. Critical stability factor with slope angles of (**a**) $H = 10$ m and (**b**) $H = 5$ m.

According to an overall observation of the evolution of the critical filling height of $\gamma H/c$, the process of change can be divided into three stages, namely a rapid change stage when $d/H \leq 1$, a moderate change stage when $1 < d/H \leq 1.5$, and a stable change stage when $d/H > 1.5$. This indicates that the internal energy should dissipate rapidly to expand failure to the depth of soft soil at the initial stage, resulting in dissipating much more rapidly in the early stage of failure occurrence than the later stage. For instance, for $\varphi_2 = 30°$ and $\beta = 45°$, the critical filling height of the embankment is reduced by 26.65% when d/H is at rapid change stage. However, the critical filling height of the embankment is reduced by 3.57% when d/H is at stable change stage. This indicates that the critical failure surface tends to develop in the weaker soil of the embankment.

5.3. Surcharge Loads

The geometric restriction and the surcharge load against the stability of the embankment over the soft foundation are depicted in Figures 9 and 10, respectively. The embankment width, $L = 5H$, is used. The depth–height ratio, D_{cr}, is equal to one. The slope angle β changes from $45°$ to $80°$, and the ratio c_2/c_1 varies from 1 to 10.

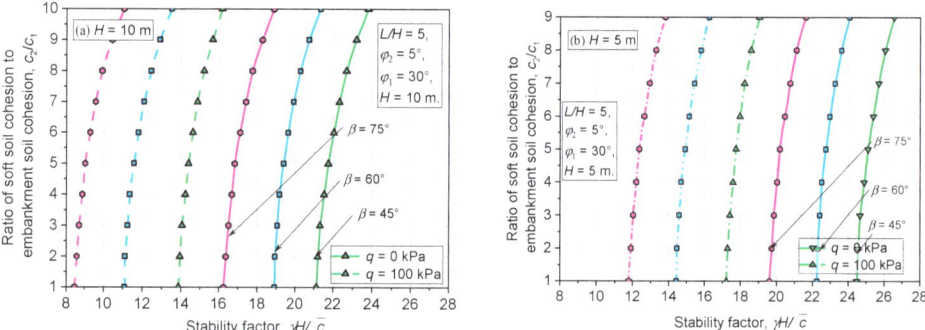

Figure 9. Critical stability factor with ratio of soil cohesion considering surcharge loads of (**a**) $H = 10$ m and (**b**) $H = 5$ m.

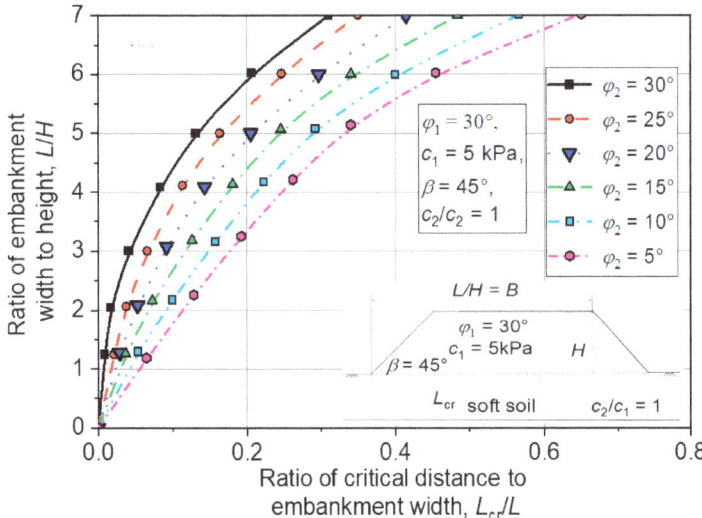

Figure 10. Limitation on width of failure mechanism for embankment over soft soil.

Figure 9 shows that the critical filling height decreases dramatically with the increase in the slope angle of the embankment, β. For $\varphi_1 = 45°$, $\gamma H/c$ decreases from 43.87 to 14.96 when the slope angle β increases from 45° to 80°. On the contrary, the value of $\gamma H/c$ increases with the increase in φ_1 and φ_2 of the embankment. For the embankment with low soil strength, base failure is more likely to occur as the friction angle of the foundation decreases. Thus, the parameters of slope geometry, β, show a significant impact on the stability of the embankment over soft soil, which can be interpreted by the fact that the flatter inclination of the embankment can provide higher resistance [31].

Figure 10 shows a comparison between surcharge loads $q = 100$kPa and $q = 0$kPa for three different slope angles, i.e., $\beta = 45°$, $\beta = 60°$, and $\beta = 75°$. When the embankment crest has surcharge loads, the external work rate, W_{3D}, is not only provided by the soil but also surcharge loads; hence, the filling height of the embankment under surcharge loads is more critical. Taking $\beta = 45°$ as an example, the value of $\gamma H/c$ decreases by 37% for the cases of $q = 100$ kPa and $q = 0$ kPa as compared with the case $c_2/c_1 = 1$. This indicates that the surcharge loads have a negative effect on improving the critical filling height of the embankment over soft soil.

5.4. Failure Width

Figure 11 shows the variations in failure width of the embankment with the depth–height ratio, where $c_2/c_1 = 1$, $\beta = 45°$, $\varphi_1 = 30°$, and $\varphi_2 = 5°$. Since the projection width of the failure mechanism has a finite width, L, the critical base failure of the embankment needs to be checked if the embankment has inadequate stability. Therefore, the distribution of the projection width should be evaluated so that the critical filling height is determined.

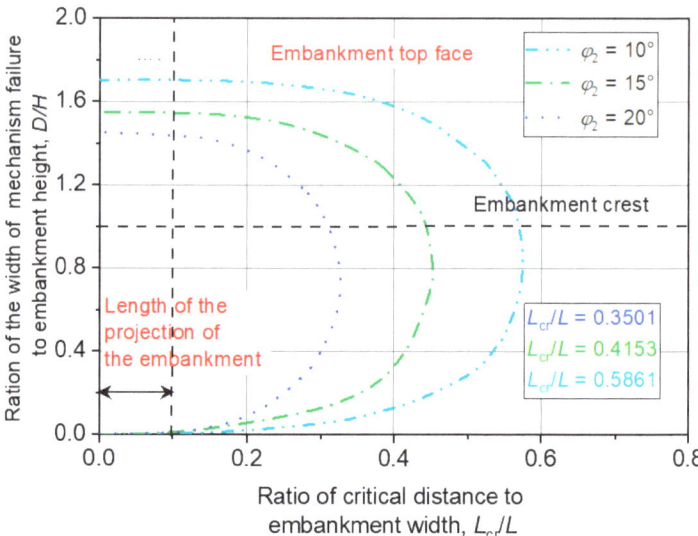

Figure 11. Critical slip surfaces on embankment top face.

In Figure 11, it is shown that the ratio of L_{cr}/L increases from 0 to 0.68 when D_{cr} increases from 0 to 2 and L/H is equal to five. When L_{cr}/L is smaller than one, the failure width of the embankment is included within the embankment width. To study the impact of the depth–height ratio on the failure width of the embankment over soft soil, $L/H = 15$, $L/H = 10$, $L/H = 15$, and $L/H = 20$ are employed to describe the permitted width of the embankment. For $L/H = 5$, L_{cr}/L increases by 254% when the depth–height ratio increases from 0.5 to 1.5. This is not surprising, since the increase in the failure width is associated with the change in the curvature of the failure surface. Thus, the critical filling height indicates that the constraint on the depth–height ratio has a significant impact on the critical failure width of the mechanism.

5.5. Projection of Critical Failure Surface

Figure 12a plots the 3D failure mechanism of the embankment over the soft ground, and the projections of the maximum cross-section of the critical failure surface are shown in Figure 12b,c. The slope angle of embankment, β, is taken as 45°. In Figure 12a, $D_{cr} = 1$, $\varphi_1 = 30°$, $c_2/c_1 = 5$, and $c_2/c_1 = 1$. In Figure 11, $D_{cr} = 0.5$, $\varphi_1 = 40°$, $c_1 = 10$ kPa, $\varphi_2 = 5°$, and $\varphi_2 = 20°$. Figure 12c is the corresponding 3D failure mechanism.

Figure 12a shows that the critical failure surface is flat when the soft soil has stronger strength, i.e., $c_2/c_1 = 5$. Moreover, the slip surface expands with a decreasing ratio of c_2/c_1, and the critical failure mechanism changes gradually from embankment failure to soft soil failure as the ratio of c_2/c_1 decreases. Apart from the cohesion of soil, the internal friction angle of soft soil is also an important factor for the critical slip failure, as shown in Figure 12b. It can be found that critical failure surface tends to develop in weaker soil. By comparing a family of the projections of failure surface curves in Figure 12a,b, the failure width of the embankment is affected by the depths of soft soil and the soil strength. The deeper the depths of soft soil, the greater the failure width. However, when the soil strength of the embankment is large, it will weaken the increase in failure width to a certain extent.

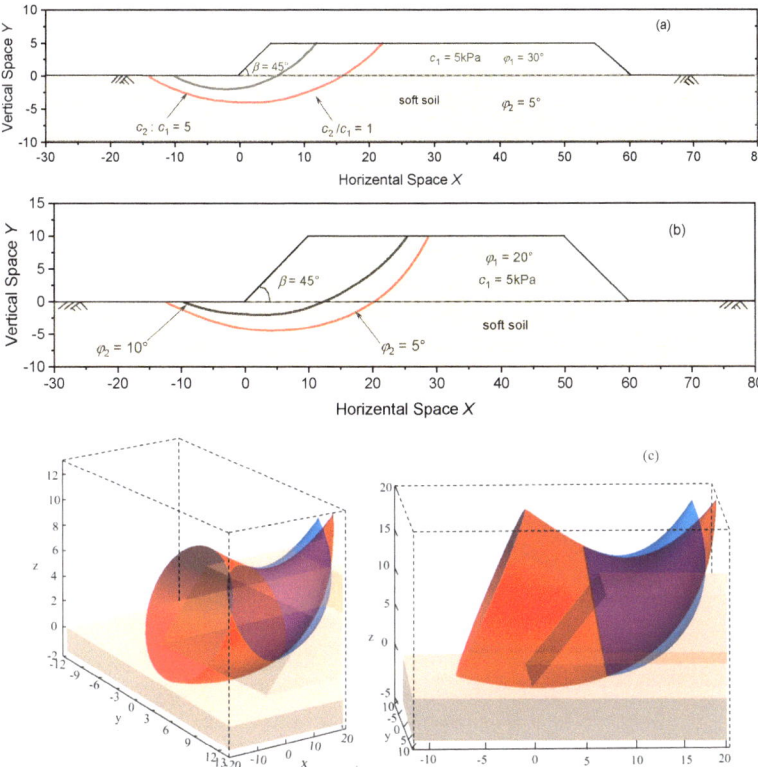

Figure 12. Critical failure surfaces for different ratios of cohesion and friction angles of embankment, (a) $Y/H = 5$, (b) $Y/H = 10$, and (c) 3D failure mechanism.

6. Conclusions

This study investigated the critical filling height of embankments over soft soil using a 3D upper-bound limit analysis with a kinematically rotational log-spiral failure mechanism. The critical filling height was determined by balancing energy rates, and the highly efficient genetic algorithm (GA) was employed to optimize the failure mechanism. The main findings are summarized as follows:

(a) The proposed failure mechanism effectively extends to scenarios involving soft soil. Solutions obtained using the GA are more stringent compared to loop searching and random searching techniques, with critical slip surfaces aligning well with finite element limit analysis results.

(b) The most critical failure surfaces are tangential to the base of the soft soil layer. The study also revealed a negative correlation between the critical filling height and the ratio of soft soil depth to embankment height, with the critical filling height increasing as this ratio decreases.

(c) Constraining the failure mechanism to embankment dimensions prevents an indefinite expansion of the mechanism and ensures achievable minimum upper-bound values.

(d) Soil strength parameters (cohesion and internal friction), the depth–height ratio, and surcharge loads significantly influence the critical failure surfaces, with embankment failure dimensions increasing as both the depth–height ratio and surcharge loads increase.

(e) Compared to conventional 2D approaches, the proposed 3D upper-bound limit analysis provides more realistic predictions of critical filling heights, better capturing the three-dimensional nature of failure mechanisms. Additionally, the genetic algorithm (GA) enhances computational efficiency, outperforming traditional optimization techniques in terms of both speed and accuracy.

However, the method relies on idealized soil models and predefined failure mechanisms, which may not fully capture the complexities of real-world embankments. Experimental validation and field applications are needed to further verify the robustness of the proposed approach.

To ensure practical applicability, the proposed GA-based method can be adapted to different soil conditions by calibrating soil parameters such as cohesion, friction angle, and unit weight, providing engineers with a flexible and efficient tool for embankment design in diverse geotechnical settings.

Author Contributions: Conceptualization, X.L. and B.S.; methodology, X.L.; software, X.L.; validation, X.L., B.S., and Z.S.; formal analysis, X.L.; investigation, X.L.; resources, W.J.; data curation, X.L.; writing—original draft preparation, X.L.; writing—review and editing, B.S.; visualization, X.L.; supervision, B.S.; project administration, W.J.; funding acquisition, X.L. All authors have read and agreed to the published version of the manuscript.

Funding: This research was funded by Research and Development Project of China Railway 17th Bureau Group (Guangzhou), grant number [220221230169], and National Natural Science Foundation of China, grant number [52208418]. The APC was funded by [220221230169].

Data Availability Statement: Some or all data, models, or code generated or used during the study are available from the corresponding author upon request.

Acknowledgments: The authors acknowledge the financial support provided by the National Natural Science Foundation of China (grant no. 52108297); the Special Support Project of China Postdoctoral Foundation (2023T160560); the Postdoctoral Research Foundation of China (grant no. 2021M692742); the Qing Chuangyuan Innovation and Entrepreneurship Project (grant no. QCYRCXM-2022-29); and supported by the Fundamental Research Funds for the Central Universities, CHD (grant no. 300102212301, 300102214303).

Conflicts of Interest: Author Xijun Liu was employed by the company Guangzhou Expressway Co., Ltd. The remaining authors declare that the research was conducted in the absence of any commercial or financial relationships that could be construed as a potential conflict of interest.

Appendix A

The failure mechanism involves two log-spiral curves and the details of r_1, r'_1, r_2 and r'_2 are written as

$$r_1 = r_0 e^{(\theta - \theta_A)\tan\varphi_1}$$
$$(\theta_A \leq \theta \leq \theta_C) \tag{A1}$$

$$r'_1 = r'_0 e^{-(\theta - \theta_A)\tan\varphi_1}$$
$$(\theta_A \leq \theta \leq \theta_C) \tag{A2}$$

$$r_2 = r_0 e^{[(\theta_C - \theta_A)\tan\varphi_1 + (\theta - \theta_C)\tan\varphi_2]}$$
$$(\theta_C \leq \theta \leq \theta_E) \tag{A3}$$

$$r'_2 = r'_0 e^{[-(\theta_C - \theta_A)\tan\varphi_1 - (\theta - \theta_C)\tan\varphi_2]}$$
$$(\theta_C \leq \theta \leq \theta_E) \tag{A4}$$

$$R_1 = \frac{r_0 e^{(\theta - \theta_A)\tan\varphi_1} - r'_0 e^{-(\theta - \theta_A)\tan\varphi_1}}{2}$$
$$(\theta_A \leq \theta \leq \theta_C) \tag{A5}$$

$$R_2 = \frac{r_0 e^{[(\theta_C - \theta_A) \tan \varphi_1 + (\theta - \theta_C) \tan \varphi_2]} - r_0' e^{[-(\theta_C - \theta_A) \tan \varphi_1 - (\theta - \theta_C) \tan \varphi_2]}}{2} \quad (\theta_C \leq \theta \leq \theta_E) \tag{A6}$$

$$r_{m1} = \frac{r_0 e^{(\theta - \theta_A) \tan \varphi_1} + r_0' e^{-(\theta - \theta_A) \tan \varphi_1}}{2} \quad (\theta_A \leq \theta \leq \theta_C) \tag{A7}$$

where r_m is the centerline of the log-spiral mechanism; R is the radius of the circular cross-section; r_{mi} ($i = 1, 2$) and R_i ($i = 1, 2$) are the centerline of the log-spiral mechanism and the radius of the circular cross-section for two log-spiral failure mechanisms; d_i ($i = 1, 2, 3, 4$) are the distances from the midline of the curvilinear cone to the surface of the embankment; and d^* is the distance from the midline of the curvilinear cone to the interface of the embankment and soft ground. The detail of d_i ($i = 1, 2, 3, 4$) is expressed as follows:

$$d_1 = \frac{\sin \theta_A r_0}{\sin \theta} - r_{m1} \tag{A8}$$

$$d_2 = \frac{r_E \sin \theta_E \sin(\beta + \theta_D)}{\sin \theta_D \sin(\beta + \theta)} - r_{m1} \quad (\theta_B \leq \theta \leq \theta_C) \tag{A9}$$

$$d_3 = \frac{r_E \sin \theta_E \sin(\beta + \theta_D)}{\sin \theta_D \sin(\beta + \theta)} - r_{m2} \quad (\theta_C \leq \theta \leq \theta_D) \tag{A10}$$

$$d_4 = \frac{\sin \theta_E}{\sin \theta} r_0 e^{[(\theta_C - \theta_A) \tan \varphi_1 + (\theta_E - \theta_C) \tan \varphi_2]} - r_{m2} \quad (\theta_D \leq \theta \leq \theta_E) \tag{A11}$$

$$d^* = \frac{r_0 e^{[(\theta_C - \theta_A) \tan \varphi_1 + (\theta_E - \theta_C) \tan \varphi_2]} \sin \theta_E}{\sin \theta} - r_{m2} \quad (\theta_C \leq \theta \leq \theta_E) \tag{A12}$$

where θ_B and θ_D are the angles from the horizontal line passes point O to lines OB and OD; the details of θ_B and θ_D can be written as

$$\theta_B = \arctan \left\{ \frac{r_0 e^{[(\theta_C - \theta_A) \tan \varphi_1 + (\theta_E - \theta_C) \tan \varphi_2]} \sin \theta_E - H}{H \cot \beta' + r_0 e^{[(\theta_C - \theta_A) \tan \varphi_1 + (\theta_E - \theta_C) \tan \varphi_2]} \cos \theta_E} \right\} \tag{A13}$$

$$\theta_D = \arctan \left[\frac{r_0 e^{[(\theta_C - \theta_A) \tan \varphi_1 + (\theta_E - \theta_C) \tan \varphi_2]} \sin \theta_E}{H(\cot \beta' - \cot \beta) + OE \cos \theta_E} \right] \tag{A14}$$

To calculate the work of the soil weight, the equation of the work of the soil weight now can be written as follows:

$$W_\gamma^{3D} = 2\omega \gamma_1 \left[\int_{\theta_A}^{\theta_B} \int_{d_1}^{R_1} \int_0^{\sqrt{R_1^2 - y^2}} (r_m + y)^2 \cos \theta \, dx \, dy \, d\theta \right.$$
$$+ \int_{\theta_B}^{\theta_C} \int_{d_2}^{R_1} \int_0^{\sqrt{R_1^2 - y^2}} (r_m + y)^2 \cos \theta \, dx \, dy \, d\theta$$
$$\left. + \int_{\theta_C}^{\theta_D} \int_{d_3}^{d^*} \int_0^{\sqrt{R_2^2 - y^2}} (r_m + y)^2 \cos \theta \, dx \, dy \, d\theta \right]$$
$$+ 2\omega \gamma_2 \left[\int_{\theta_C}^{\theta_D} \int_{d^*}^{R_2} \int_0^{\sqrt{R_2^2 - y^2}} (r_m + y)^2 \cos \theta \, dx \, dy \, d\theta \right] \tag{A15}$$

Moreover, the rate of internal energy dissipation of the failure mechanism can be written as

$$\begin{aligned} D_c^{3D} = & -2\omega c_1 \cot\varphi_1 \Big[(r_0 \sin\theta_A)^2 \int_{\theta_A}^{\theta_B} \frac{\cos\theta}{\sin^3\theta} \sqrt{R_1^2 - d_1^2} d\theta \\ & + r_1^2 \frac{\sin^2(\theta_D + \beta)\sin\theta_E}{\sin^2\theta_D} \int_{\theta_B}^{\theta_C} \frac{\cos(\theta+\beta)}{\sin^3(\theta+\beta)} \sqrt{R_1^2 - d_2^2} d\theta \\ & + r_2^2 \frac{\sin^2(\theta_D + \beta)\sin\theta_E}{\sin^2\theta_D} \int_{\theta_C}^{\theta_D} \frac{\cos(\theta+\beta)}{\sin^3(\theta+\beta)} \sqrt{R_2^2 - d_3^2} d\theta \Big] \\ & + 2\omega c_2 \cot\varphi_2 r_2^2 \sin^2\theta_E \int_{\theta_D}^{\theta_E} \frac{\cos\theta}{\sin^3\theta} \sqrt{R_2^2 - d_4^2} d\theta \\ & - 2\omega r_1^2 \sin^2\theta_C \Big(c_1 \cot\varphi_1 \int_{\theta_C}^{\theta_D} \frac{\cos(\theta+\beta)}{\sin^3(\theta+\beta)} \sqrt{R_2^2 - d_3^2} d\theta \\ & - c_2 \cot\varphi_2 \int_{\theta_C}^{\theta_D} \frac{\cos(\theta+\beta)}{\sin^3(\theta+\beta)} \sqrt{R_2^2 - d_3^2} d\theta \Big) \end{aligned} \quad (A16)$$

References

1. Kaniraj, S.R. Rotational stability of unreinforced and reinforced embankments on soft soils. *Geotext. Geomembr.* **1994**, *13*, 707–726. [CrossRef]
2. Balasubramaniam, A.S.; Cai, H.; Zhu, D.; Surarak, C.; Oh, E.Y.N. Settlement of embankments in soft soils. *Geomechnics Eng.* **2010**, *41*, 61–80.
3. Indraratna, B.; Balasubramaniam, A.S.; Balachandran, S. Performance of test embankment constructed to failure on soft marine clay. *J. Geotech. Geoenvironmental Eng.* **1992**, *118*, 12–33. [CrossRef]
4. Zhao, J.; Zhu, Z.; Zhang, D.; Wang, H.; Li, X. Assessment of fabric characteristics with the development of sand liquefaction in cyclic triaxial tests: A DEM study. *Soil. Dyn. Earthq. Eng.* **2024**, *176*, 108343. [CrossRef]
5. Naughton, P.J. The significance of critical height in the design of piled embankments. *Soil. Improv.* **2007**, *172*, 1–10. [CrossRef]
6. Jewell, R.A. The mechanics of reinforced embankments on soft soils. *Geotext. Geomembr.* **1988**, *7*, 237–273. [CrossRef]
7. Borges, J.L.; Cardoso, A.S. Overall stability of geosynthetic-reinforced embankments on soft soils. *Geotext. Geomembr.* **2002**, *20*, 395–421. [CrossRef]
8. Karim, M.R.; Manivannan, G.; Gnanendran, C.T.; Lo, S.R. Predicting the long-term performance of a geogrid-reinforced embankment on soft soil using two-dimensional finite element analysis. *Can. Geotech. J.* **2011**, *48*, 741–753. [CrossRef]
9. Abusharar, S.W.; Han, J. Two-dimensional deep-seated slope stability analysis of embankments over stone column-improved soft clay. *Eng. Geol.* **2011**, *120*, 103–110. [CrossRef]
10. Carreira, M.; Almeida, M.; Pinto, A. A numerical study on the critical height of embankments supported by geotextile encased granular columns. *Geomechnics Eng.* **2016**, *143*, 1341–1349. [CrossRef]
11. Li, Z.; Yang, X. Three-dimensional active earth pressure for retaining structures in soils subjected to steady unsaturated seepage effects. *Can. Geotech. J.* **2020**, *15*, 2017–2029. [CrossRef]
12. Yao, C.; Zhong, H.; Zhu, Z. Development of a Large Shaking Table Test for Sand Liquefaction Analysis. *Lithosphere* **2024**, *2024*, 44. [CrossRef]
13. Gong, W.; Zekkos, D.; Clark, D.; Manousakis, J.; Kirschbaum, D. Regional 3D stability analyses of the Egkremnoi coastline and comparison with landsliding caused by the 2015 Lefkada earthquake. In Proceedings of the International Foundations Congress and Equipment Exposition (IFCEE), Dallas, TX, USA, 10–14 May 2021; pp. 130–138. [CrossRef]
14. Chen, R.P.; Chen, Y.M.; Han, J.; Xu, Z.Z. A theoretical solution for pile-supported embankments on soft soils under one-dimensional compression. *Can. Geotech. J.* **2008**, *45*, 611–623. [CrossRef]
15. Gong, W.; Li, J.; Li, L. Limit analysis on seismic stability of anisotropic and nonhomogeneous slopes with anti-slide piles. *Sci. China Technol. Sci.* **2018**, *61*, 140–146. [CrossRef]
16. Giger, M.W.; Krizek, R.J. Stability analysis of vertical cut with variable corner angle. *Soils Found.* **1975**, *15*, 63–71. [CrossRef]
17. Qu, G.; Hinchberger, S.D.; Lo, K.Y. Case studies of three-dimensional effects on the behavior of test embankments. *Can. Geotech. J.* **2009**, *46*, 1356–1370. [CrossRef]
18. Berrabah, F.; Benmebarek, S.; Benmebarek, N. Three-dimensional numerical analysis of geosynthetic-reinforced embankment over locally weak zone. *J. Geotech. Geoenviron. Eng.* **2020**, *7*, 269–296. [CrossRef]
19. Jamsawang, P.; Phongphinittana, E.; Voottipruex, P.; Bergado, D.T.; Jongpradist, P. Comparative performances of two-and three-dimensional analyses of soil-cement mixing columns under an embankment load. *Mar. Georesources Geotechnol.* **2019**, *37*, 852–869. [CrossRef]
20. Azzouz, A.S.; Baligh, M.M.; Ladd, C.C. Three-dimensional stability analyses of four embankment failures. In Proceedings of the 10th International Conference on Soil Mechanics and Foundation Engineering, Stockholm, Sweden, 15–19 June 1981; Volume 3. [CrossRef]
21. McCombie, P.; Wilkinson, P. The use of the simple genetic algorithm in finding the critical factor of safety in slope stability analysis. *Comput. Geotech.* **2002**, *29*, 699–714. [CrossRef]

22. Mitchell, M. *An Introduction to Genetic Algorithms*; MIT Press: Cambridge, MA, USA, 1998. [CrossRef]
23. Michalowski, R.L.; Drescher, A. Three-dimensional stability of slopes and excavations. *Géotechnique* **2009**, *59*, 839–850. [CrossRef]
24. Chen, W.F. *Limit Analysis and Soil Plasticity*; Elsevier: Amsterdam, The Netherlands, 2013. [CrossRef]
25. Hatami, K.; Bathurst, R.J. Numerical model for reinforced soil segmental walls under surcharge loading. *J. Geotech. Geoenviron. Eng.* **2006**, *132*, 673–684. [CrossRef]
26. Zheng, L.; Li, L.; Li, J. Development of three-dimensional failure mechanisms and genetic algorithm for limit analysis of two-layer slopes. *Natural Hazards* **2020**, *103*, 3181–3212. [CrossRef]
27. Drescher, A. Limit plasticity approach to piping in bins. *J. Appl. Mech.* **1983**, *50*, 549–553. [CrossRef]
28. Jenck, O.; Dias, D.; Kastner, R. Three-dimensional numerical modeling of a piled embankment. *Int. J. Geomech.* **2009**, *9*, 102–112. [CrossRef]
29. Mohapatra, D.; Kumar, J. Homogenization based kinematic limit analysis for finding the stability of an embankment over soft clay reinforced with granular columns. *Comput. Geotech.* **2022**, *142*, 104562. [CrossRef]
30. Yang, S.; Gao, Y.; Leshchinsky, B.; Cui, K.; Zhang, F. Internal stability analysis of reinforced convex highway embankments considering seismic loading. *Geotext. Geomembr.* **2020**, *48*, 221–229. [CrossRef]
31. Chen, W.; Song, Y.; Wu, Z.; Zeng, J.; Li, C. Stability of double-step muck slope under different overload conditions. *Geotech. Geol. Eng.* **2021**, *25*, 245–263. [CrossRef]

Disclaimer/Publisher's Note: The statements, opinions and data contained in all publications are solely those of the individual author(s) and contributor(s) and not of MDPI and/or the editor(s). MDPI and/or the editor(s) disclaim responsibility for any injury to people or property resulting from any ideas, methods, instructions or products referred to in the content.

Article

Research on the 3D Visualization Method of Web-Based Seismic Wave CT Results and the Application in Underground Caverns

Tianwen Li [1] and Jieyun Xing [2,*]

1. School of Mathematical Science, Tongji University, Shanghai 200092, China; aster@tongji.edu.cn
2. PowerChina Northwest Engineering Corporation Limited, Xi'an 710016, China
* Correspondence: xingjieyun@nwh.cn; Tel.: +86-17791857668

Abstract: This paper introduces a novel 3D visualization technique for seismic tomography results utilizing WebGL technology, which operates independently of specific software platforms and offers highly efficient visualization. The method constructs the mesh using wave velocity as a reference point, applies vertex and surface coloring techniques to the model, and integrates CT detection data, resulting in a detailed color rendering and a clear visual representation of the model. The visualization outcomes are presented on an intelligent construction platform with a response time maintained within 2 s. To validate the efficacy of the proposed method, it was applied to the underground cavern project of a hydropower station and compared with the geological 3D design software developed independently by the Northwest China Institute of Architectural Engineering. The comparative results demonstrate that the proposed visualization technique effectively identifies weak geological layers and displays the distribution of surrounding rock types in underground structures. This provides intuitive references for devising support schemes for underground structures and facilitates digital management during project construction.

Keywords: 3D visualization; seismic tomography; WebGL technology; intelligent construction platform

Citation: Li, T.; Xing, J. Research on the 3D Visualization Method of Web-Based Seismic Wave CT Results and the Application in Underground Caverns. *Buildings* **2024**, *14*, 3622. https://doi.org/10.3390/buildings14113622

Academic Editor: Humberto Varum

Received: 7 August 2024
Revised: 7 November 2024
Accepted: 11 November 2024
Published: 14 November 2024

Copyright: © 2024 by the authors. Licensee MDPI, Basel, Switzerland. This article is an open access article distributed under the terms and conditions of the Creative Commons Attribution (CC BY) license (https://creativecommons.org/licenses/by/4.0/).

1. Introduction

In geological exploration, seismic tomography imaging is extensively employed due to its high accuracy and resolution capabilities [1,2]. The propagation velocity of seismic waves is influenced by the physical properties of rock, such as density and elastic modulus, as well as the structural features of rock masses. This technique leverages the propagation characteristics of seismic waves through geological strata to analyze and infer the physical properties and structural attributes of formations, including karst terrains, faults, and fractured rock masses [3–6].

However, the results of seismic wave CT are typically scattered and consist of independent two-dimensional profile data, making it challenging to analyze data correlation and connectivity across profiles. Consequently, it fails to intuitively convey the distribution, direction, spatial location, and morphology of underground anomalies, thus lacking in intuitive comprehension, particularly for non-geologists. This limitation complicates the establishment of three-dimensional spatial spreading scenarios, adversely affecting the visualization of detection results [7]. Understanding the anomalous distribution, spatial positioning, and morphological features of three-dimensional strata structures based solely on 2D profiles is a complex process.

To address these limitations, researchers have explored three-dimensional visualization techniques for seismic tomography CT. Li Zuneng [8] employed Voxler 3D visualization software to establish a three-dimensional numerical model of seismic wave velocities. This model was processed through slicing, volume rendering, and surface rendering to analyze and delineate seismic wave velocity ranges of various lithological bodies, stratigraphic layers, and boundaries of karst development zones. Hu Junjie et al. [9] utilized cross-hole electromagnetic CT methods to detect karst development in bridge foundation areas, demonstrating the regional distribution of karst development zones through three-dimensional modeling. Yu Bo [10] applied quasi-three-dimensional cross-hole seismic CT detection technology and Voxler software for three-dimensional data gridding, achieving visualization of geological structures, bedrock surfaces, and the three-dimensional spatial morphology of karst in the survey area. Liang Juan [11], using Blender software and Python programming language, rapidly constructed dynamic three-dimensional visualization models of seismic wave propagation, dynamically simulating and analyzing wave effects using the aforementioned methods.

There have been significant international efforts in the development of three-dimensional geological visualization software. For instance, the Vulcan software developed by MAPTEK in Australia [12] visualizes three-dimensional geological models with exploration data and provides modules for road design and quarry modeling, which are crucial for open-pit mining planning. Similarly, the Mining Visualization System (MvS) series developed by CTECH in the United States [12] enables visualization of geological models and related spatial analyses. This software supports true three-dimensional geological modeling, statistical analysis, structural analysis, and geological engineering calculations.

With advancements in computer hardware and software, three-dimensional visualization techniques for seismic tomography CT have matured, offering richer display effects [13]. However, the current predominant approach involves presenting and analyzing geological data within specialized visualization software, which requires complex operational steps and professional technical support. These software packages often necessitate high-performance computers and dedicated graphics processors, limiting their accessibility and widespread adoption [14]. In contrast, significant advancements have been made in WebGL-based visualization for medical CT, demonstrating that user-friendly web interfaces can provide precise and efficient algorithmic services [15–17]. WebGL-based visualization addresses the limitations of poor mobility performance on PCs and offers significant advantages in data transmission speed and display smoothness. In the field of underground engineering, researchers have also explored WebGL-based visualization of stratigraphic models. For example, Xinshan Xu [18] developed a convex hull fit for the body side of stratigraphy and TINs for top and bottom surfaces, achieving visualization of geological body models. Despite these advances, the application of WebGL technology for the visualization of exploration results on the web remains underdeveloped.

This paper proposes a three-dimensional visualization method for seismic tomography CT results based on WebGL technology, which is independent of specific software and offers high visualization efficiency. This method utilizes wave velocity reference points to create grids and applies vertex and surface coloring to the model. By processing model profiles with color adjustments based on CT detection data, it achieves model coloration and visualization display. The visualization results are showcased on an intelligent construction platform with response times controlled within 2 s. The proposed visualization method was validated and applied to underground chamber projects at a hydropower station. Comparative validation with geological three-dimensional design software, independently developed by the China Northwest Institute of Civil Engineering and Architecture, demonstrated the effectiveness and practicality of the method. The WebGL-based visualization results can reveal weak geological layers, display the distribution of surrounding rock types in underground structures, and provide intuitive references for support schemes of underground structures, thus promoting the digital management process during engineering construction periods.

2. Research Method

There are many methods for processing discrete data by difference, and the most widely used methods at present include Kriging interpolation, inverse square distance interpolation, and DSI interpolation.

The Kriging method is a geostatistical approach used for spatial data interpolation. It is widely employed in geological exploration, environmental science, and geographic information systems [19]. This method estimates the values at unknown locations based on known discrete point data to achieve numerical predictions for the entire region. The advantage of the Kriging interpolation method is that it considers the correlation between spatial data, providing accurate estimates for unknown points and assessing the confidence of the interpolation results. However, its drawbacks include the need for extensive computations on large-scale data and the complexity of parameter tuning and model selection [20,21].

The IDW method is a commonly used interpolation technique that calculates the value of an unknown point based on the weight of the value of known points, with the weight being inversely proportional to the distance from the unknown point [22,23]. The advantage of this method is its simplicity and ease of use, allowing it to reasonably weight neighboring points according to their distance, so that points closer to the unknown point contribute more to the estimated value. However, it also has disadvantages, such as the potential for uneven distribution of dense and sparse points, which may lead to discontinuous interpolation results. Therefore, in practical application, it needs to be balanced and adjusted according to the specific situation [24].

The DSI interpolation method was first proposed by Professor Mallet of the University of Nancy in France [25]. The basic idea of DSI interpolation is to establish an interconnected network among discrete data points. If the known node values on the network satisfy certain constraint conditions, the unknown node values can be obtained by solving linear equations. The DSI difference method only relies on the topological relationships between nodes and is an interpolation algorithm that is not limited by dimension. The interpolation calculation of unknown points only depends on the topological grid, not on the plane or spatial coordinates, and the calculation process is generally iterative, which is conducive to dynamically approaching sampling points and is suitable for interpolation problems of multi-valued surfaces. The DSI interpolation method can consistently maintain the geometric detail features of the optimized grid and the original grid, impose discrete control point constraints, ensure consistency with the original grid during optimization, and can greatly improve the grid quality, thereby significantly improving the data visualization effect. Since the DSI interpolation method has high interpolation accuracy and calculation efficiency, it is widely used in geological modeling and earth physical data processing.

WebGL (Web Graphics Library) is a JavaScript API that presents interactive 3D and 2D graphics in web browsers. WebGL can achieve efficient real-time graphic rendering and is more suitable for large-scale data visualization than traditional 2D graphic technology. It can provide smoother rendering effects and faster response speeds and can enable graphic viewing at any time on the web end.

In this paper, the DSI interpolation method is used to perform differential processing on the discrete seismic wave CT result data. At the same time, in order to improve the visualization degree and convenience of browsing, the seismic wave CT three-dimensional results are realized in the web-based platform through WebGL technology, and the three-dimensional visualization display is achieved.

It is important to note that although the DSI interpolation method performs well in handling noisy or incomplete seismic data, its effectiveness is also influenced by factors such as data quality, the extent of missing data, and interpolation parameters. Therefore, when processing noisy seismic data with the DSI interpolation method, it is often combined with other denoising techniques, such as filtering methods, to identify and filter out noise in the seismic data. This approach utilizes the selectivity of effective signals and noise in specific domains to eliminate the noise. When dealing with incomplete seismic data, the DSI interpolation method takes into account the spatial correlation of the seismic data, using the spatial distribution and correlation of known data points to predict the values of unknown data points, thereby filling in the missing data.

3. Visualization Process

3.1. Creation of Wave Velocity Reference Point Grid

The color grid defined in this paper consists of multiple vertices and the corresponding wave velocity values. By setting the bounds, the wave velocity at each point in the model can be quickly calculated. Finally, an appropriate interpolation method is chosen to determine the wave velocity at each point within the mesh.

3.1.1. Determine the Bounds

The bounds should encompass the entire model that needs to be rendered. The bounds form the smallest hexahedron with edges parallel to the coordinate axes and vertices with three-dimensional integer coordinate values. The minimum values of the BIM model coordinate points in the X, Y, and Z directions are x_{min}, y_{min}, and z_{min}. The maximum values are x_{min}, y_{min}, and z_{min}, respectively. The bounds can be represented as follows.

$$\text{bb} = [\lfloor x_{min} \rfloor, \lfloor y_{min} \rfloor, \lfloor z_{min} \rfloor, \lceil x_{max} \rceil, \lceil y_{max} \rceil, \lceil z_{max} \rceil] \tag{1}$$

The coordinates x, y, and z of all points at the boundary and interior of the bounding box satisfy the following equation.

$$\begin{cases} \lfloor x_{min} \rfloor \leq x \leq \lceil x_{max} \rceil \\ \lfloor y_{min} \rfloor \leq y \leq \lceil y_{max} \rceil \\ \lfloor z_{min} \rfloor \leq z \leq \lceil z_{max} \rceil \end{cases} \tag{2}$$

3.1.2. Grid Distribution Density

In geological 3D modeling systems, grid technology requires that each unit can store information and perform data interpolation operations. Compared to finite element models, the number of grids used for geological analysis services is 2–3 orders of magnitude higher. Generally, the number of mesh elements in a three-dimensional finite element model is within one million, with some models reaching several million elements. However, the quality grading and parameter values of geological rock masses often involve grids numbering in the millions, typically tens of millions, and in some cases, even billions.

Generate a point set Ω based on the set step size λ and store it in an array. The size of Ω is given by $\|\Omega\| = (i+1) \times (j+1) \times (k+1)$. Any point in the point set can be represented by T and can be expressed as the following equation.

$$T[i][j][k] = (\lfloor x_{min} \rfloor + \lambda * i, \lfloor y_{min} \rfloor + \lambda * j, \lfloor z_{min} \rfloor + \lambda * k) \tag{3}$$

where

$$0 \leq i \leq \left\lceil \frac{\lceil x_{max} \rceil - \lfloor x_{min} \rfloor}{\lambda} \right\rceil, 0 \leq j \leq \left\lceil \frac{\lceil y_{max} \rceil - \lfloor y_{min} \rfloor}{\lambda} \right\rceil, 0 \leq k \leq \left\lceil \frac{\lceil z_{max} \rceil - \lfloor z_{min} \rfloor}{\lambda} \right\rceil \tag{4}$$

Considering computational efficiency, the step size λ is primarily determined by the complexity of the actual scene and model. In practical applications, it is recommended to generate fewer than 500,000 grid reference points to ensure real-time computational efficiency.

3.1.3. Interpolation and Processing of Wave Velocity of Mesh

Table 1 shows a sample of the detection data. The set of all points from the probe data is denoted by Ψ. The wave speeds of all points in Ω need to be obtained through interpolation based on the wave speed values of all points in Ψ.

Table 1. Examples of CT detection data.

X/m	Y/m	Z/m	Wave Velocity/m/s
3,495,795.276	507,375.641	2152	4287
3,495,795.023	507,375.641	2152	4294
3,495,794.771	507,375.641	2152	4300
3,495,794.518	507,375.641	2152	4306
3,495,794.266	507,375.641	2152	4312
3,495,794.013	507,375.641	2152	4318
3,495,793.761	507,375.641	2152	4325
3,495,793.508	507,375.641	2152	4331
3,495,793.256	507,375.641	2152	4341
3,495,793.003	507,375.641	2152	4352
3,495,792.751	507,375.641	2152	4363
3,495,792.498	507,375.641	2152	4374
3,495,792.246	507,375.641	2152	4385
3,495,791.993	507,375.641	2152	4396
3,495,791.741	507,375.641	2152	4407

DSI uses discrete sampling points to estimate values between these points through a smooth interpolation method, generating smooth surfaces or curves. This feature makes DSI suitable for applications in image processing, computer vision, and 3D reconstruction. The primary goal of the DSI algorithm is to estimate values between a set of discrete samples by employing a smooth interpolation method to produce smooth surfaces or curves. DSI establishes an objective function $R^*(\phi) = R(\phi) + \rho(\phi)$ for calculating the optimal solution on mesh nodes, where $R(\phi)$ is the global roughness function and $\rho(\phi)$ is the linear constraint violation function. By minimizing this objective function, two main objectives are achieved. First, minimizing $R^*(\phi)$ ensures that the value of the function at any given node approximates the average of the values at the surrounding nodes. Second, minimizing $\rho(\phi)$ ensures that the raw sampled data are converted into linear constraints on the nodes, making the node values as close as possible to the sampled data by maximizing compliance with the linear constraints [26,27].

Table 1 provides an example of the detection data. The DSI method is represented by G. For any point $p \in \Omega$, the computation of its velocity v can be expressed by the following equation.

$$v = G(p) \tag{5}$$

3.2. Color Rendering of Model Surface Based on WebGL Technology

Model surface coloring requires determining the corresponding color for each point in the model based on the calculated wave speed values, followed by the rendering process. The rendering described in this paper is based on WebGL technology. WebGL allows developers to directly use the GPU to render 3D graphics within a browser, incorporating rich visual effects into web design. Color rendering through WebGL relies on shaders [28–30]. Shaders enable customization of the graphics card rendering algorithm, allowing the image to achieve the desired visual effect. There are two types of shaders: vertex shaders and fragment shaders, which handle data at the vertex and pixel levels, respectively.

3.2.1. Preprocessing of Vertex Colors

Colors are uniformly encoded using the RGB color mode, which employs three variables to represent the intensity of red, green, and blue [31,32]. This mode provides a unique numerical code for each color. Subsequently, color bands are customized to preprocess the colors of points with different wave speeds. The color band consists of the following components.

① minNum (minimum value).
② maxNum (maximum value).
③ count ($5 \leq$ count ≤ 30, Color quantity).

④ minColor (starting color RGB, minimum value).
⑤ maxColor (termination color RGB, maximum value).
The set of color bands is denoted by color ($Color_i \in Color, 0 \leq i \leq count - 1, i \in N$). Arranging the colors in RGB from small to large, each color band $Color_i$ and the corresponding wave velocity value $F(Color_i)$ can be expressed, respectively.

$$Color_i[j] = \left(minColor[j] + \left[i \frac{|maxColor[j] - minColor[j]|}{count - 1} \right] \right) \quad (6)$$

$$(0 \leq j \leq 2, j \in N)$$

$$F(Color_i) = \begin{cases} \left[minNum + i\frac{Num}{count}, maxNum \right], i = count - 1 \\ \left[minNum + i\frac{Num}{count}, minNum + (i+1)\frac{Num}{count} \right], else \end{cases} \quad (7)$$

$$Num = maxColor - minColor$$

3.2.2. Drawing of Model Surface Colors

In this paper, the surface of the model is colored using shaders. During the graphics rendering process, the graphics rendering pipeline visualizes the vertex data of the model. When the graphics card processes the triangle drawing task, it generates additional pixel fragments during the rasterization stage to ensure accurate rendering of the triangle [33–35].

The positions of the fragments are determined based on their relative positions within the triangle. The graphics card interpolates the input variables of the fragment shader using this location information. Subsequently, the fragment shader automatically interpolates the color of each pixel within the triangle. To achieve the effect of seismic wave CT contour cloud image rendering, the color of each pixel must be accurately calculated in the fragment shader. This allows the graphics card to present a colored contour cloud map on the surface or section of the model after rendering is complete, providing an intuitive visual presentation for scientific research and data analysis.

The specific operation steps are as follows.

(1) Coordinate information input: input model vertices, projection matrix, observation matrix, model matrix M_{model}, and the texture buffer containing reference point set data into the shader.

(2) Information transmission: transfer the vertex coordinates of the model to the tile shader in the vertex shader.

(3) Coordinate calculation: calculate the world coordinates of the current point in the tile shader.

$$V_{world} = M_{model} \cdot V_{local} \quad (8)$$

(4) Reference point query: obtain the coordinates of the 8 closest reference points to the current point based on the world coordinate V_{world}, and calculate the wave velocity values of these 8 reference points in the texture buffer. The position relationships of these points are illustrated in Figure 1. Assuming that the world coordinates of the current point are $p_0(x_0, y_0, z_0)$, the relevant points can be calculated using the step size λ. The eight reference points are as follows.

$$\begin{array}{c} T[i][j][k] \\ T[i][j+1][k] \\ T[i][j][k+1] \\ T[i][j+1][k+1] \\ T[i+1][j][k] \\ T[i+1][j+1][k] \end{array} \quad (9)$$

$$T[i][j][k+1]$$
$$T[i+1][j][k+1]$$

where, $i = \left\lfloor \frac{x_0 - bb[0]}{\lambda} \right\rfloor, j = \left\lfloor \frac{y_0 - bb[1]}{\lambda} \right\rfloor, k = \left\lfloor \frac{z_0 - bb[2]}{\lambda} \right\rfloor$.

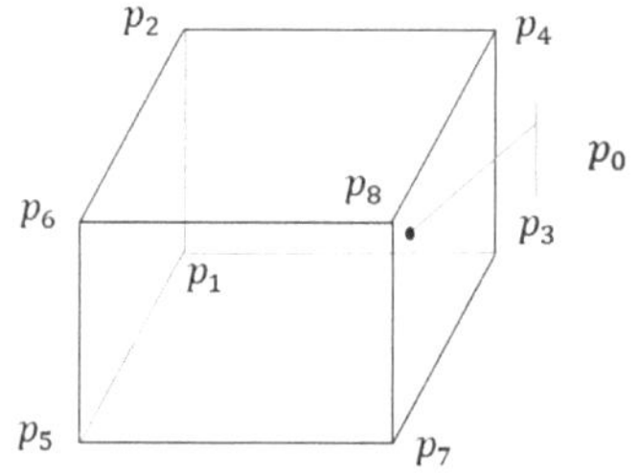

Figure 1. Schematic diagram of reference points.

(5) Calculation of wave velocity values: perform trilinear interpolation on the wave velocity values of the 8 reference points to obtain the wave velocity v of vertex p_0.

(6) Visualization result: obtain the final color of the pixel based on the wave velocity value and color band division. This 3D model can display wave velocity information through surface color.

By following these steps, the graphics card can accurately render the model surface with colors that represent the seismic wave velocities, providing a clear visual representation for analysis.

3.3. Color Determination of Model Profiles

To improve the update speed of real-time display results in this study, the pixel color of points outside the reference point set is set to semi-transparent white, and the calculation and processing of profile contours are omitted. The steps for drawing a profile are as follows:

(1) Generate the four vertices of the profile based on the location information that the user intends to view.

(2) Pass the profile vertices, projection matrix, observation matrix, model matrix M_{model}, and texture buffer containing reference point set data into the shader.

(3) Transfer the vertex coordinates of the profile to the tile shader in the vertex shader.

(4) Calculate the world coordinates of the current point in the tile shader using the formula.

(5) If the coordinate point lies within the range of the reference point set, retrieve the coordinates of the eight closest reference points based on the world coordinate V_{world}, and obtain the wave velocity values of these eight reference points from the texture buffer. If it is outside the range of the reference point set, set the pixel color of the point to semi-transparent white.

(6) Calculate the wave velocity value of pixels within the reference point set range.

(7) Using the wave velocity values and color band division results, generate a profile that represents the wave velocity information using surface colors.

4. Visualization Results

The visualization method presented in this paper is applied within the intelligent construction platform (management platform of the design institute of the China Electric Construction Group). The basic environment configuration of the platform is detailed in Table 2, and the geological model along with the seismic wave visualization results are illustrated in Figure 2. During the seismic wave assignment process, if the profile is colored after performing detailed calculations, the average response time ranges from 5 to 15 s.

However, the approach outlined in this paper reduces the final response time to less than 2 s, significantly enhancing visualization efficiency.

Table 2. Basic environment configuration of the experimental platform.

Browser	Microsoft Edge Version: 113.0.1774.57 (official version) (64 bit)
Operating System	Windows 11 Professional Edition
Processor	Intel(R) Core (TM) i7-9750H CPU @ 2.60 GHz 2.59 GHz
Graphics card	Intel(R) UHD Graphics 630
Rack RAM	16.0 GB (15.8 GB available)
System type	64-bit operating system, based on x64 processors

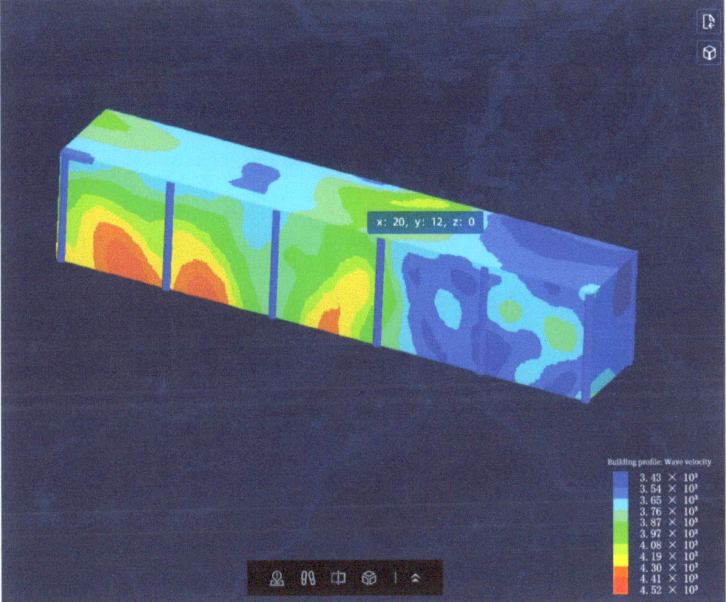

Figure 2. Visualized results of web-based CT seismic wave.

5. Applications in Engineering

5.1. Project Introduction

The hydropower station features a concrete face rockfill dam, an underground water diversion and power generation system on the left bank, and a spillway and flood discharge tunnel on the right bank. The project includes multiple underground caverns, with diversion and flood discharge tunnels situated on the right bank and water diversion and power generation systems located on the left bank. Key structures include the underground powerhouse, main transformer cavern, and tailrace gate operation room, which are arranged in parallel with their axes oriented directly north–south, forming an angle of approximately 30° to 40° with the rock strata. The underground powerhouse has dimensions of 183.5 m × 25.3 m × 64.25 m, the main transformer cavern measures 117.2 m × 16.5 m × 30.8 m, and the tailrace gate operation room is 115.6 m × 10.2 m × 59.1 m. The cavern spans are 25.3 m, 16.5 m, and 10.2 m, respectively, with distances of 39.7 m, 19.8 m, and 19.8 m between these structures.

The scale of the underground cavern group is substantial, with the largest span being 25.3 m for the powerhouse. The caverns are interspersed with thin rock layers between some, and the geological conditions are complex. Preliminary surveys indicate that the rock formations primarily consist of T3Z2 (3) to T3Z2 (5). The main powerhouse, main transformer cavern, and tailrace gate operation room are surrounded by type IV2 rock. Several unfavorable geological features, such as the steeply dipping f31 fault and PH strips, pose challenges to the stability of the surrounding rock.

By combining seismic wave CT visualization methods with investigation data and underground engineering excavation, we achieve a visual display of geological properties and surrounding rock classifications.

5.2. Comparison and Validation

Utilizing Web-GL technology, the physical exploration results of this underground cavern are visualized and compared with the visualization results obtained from geological 3D design software (V1.0). This geological 3D design software, developed independently by the Northwest Institute of China Electric Construction, employs the DSI interpolation algorithm as its core modeling substrate. It integrates a geological database and uses survey data or manual judgment as modeling constraints, achieving step-by-step approximation and fitting to ensure geological analysis and rationality. This software has been widely promoted and applied in the survey and design of many hydropower station projects, such as Jinchuan and Mar block. It boasts extensive practical experience in the professional application of rock mass grading, geotechnical engineering analysis, and design within the 3D geological model.

Figure 3 presents the visualization results generated by the geological 3D design software, while Figure 4 displays the visualization results based on Web-GL technology (Version: 1.0.1). The two visualizations are consistent with each other, and the CT wave velocity calculations yield identical results. The 3D visualization method of seismic wave CT results, as implemented on the Web terminal in this paper, can accurately represent the physical exploration findings. This method offers a convenient display technique for the digital management of construction projects.

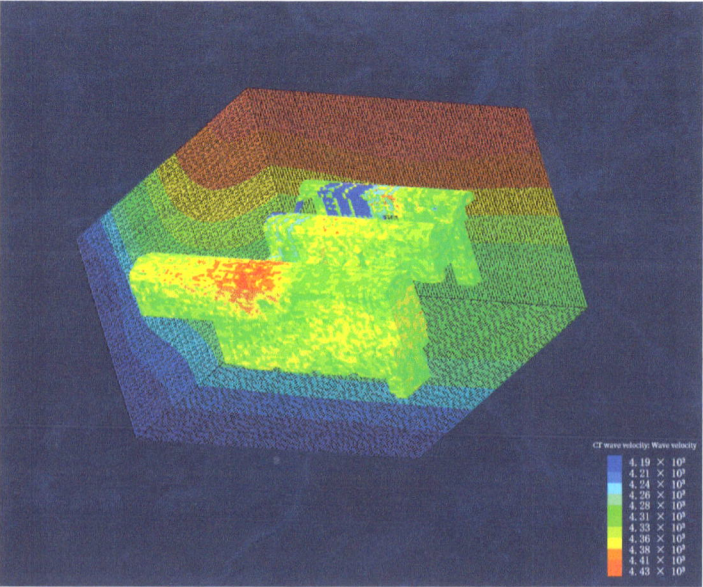

Figure 3. Three-dimensional wave velocity visualization results of underground cavern based on WebGL technology.

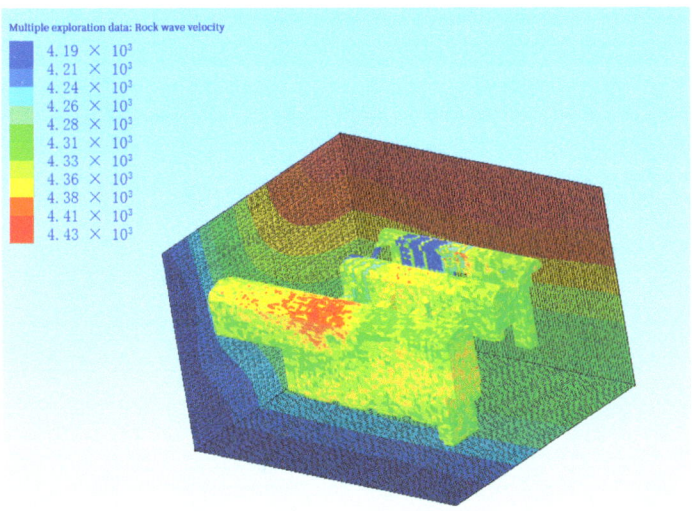

Figure 4. Three-dimensional wave velocity visualization results of underground cavern based on software.

5.3. Results and Analyses

Based on the intelligent construction platform described in Section 3, the geophysical visualization results of the underground cavity group can be obtained. Figure 5 illustrates the enclosing mesh body that completely contains the underground caverns. Figure 6 presents the attribute data and rock mass quality classification data within the enclosure mesh. The blue area denotes the weak zone, which requires special attention during the excavation and support process of the underground powerhouse cavern group, while the red area represents areas with good rock mass quality.

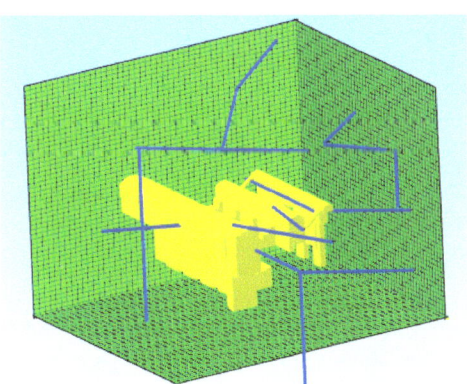

Figure 5. Cubic mesh surrounding the underground chamber. (The blue lines in Figures 5 and 6 represent boreholes and flat holes).

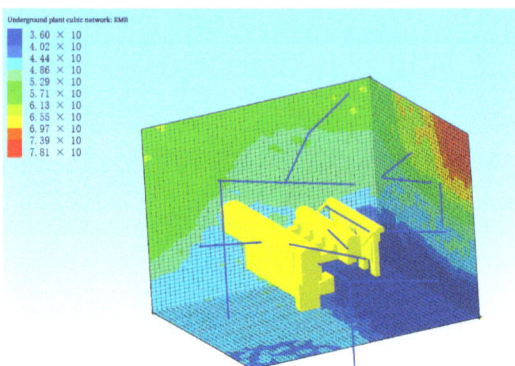

Figure 6. Spatial data of cubic network created and interpolated based on assigned data.

By assigning the geophysical wave velocity data on the cubic network to the surface of the underground engineering structure model, the seismic wave velocity distribution of the underground powerhouse cavern group is depicted in Figure 7. The non-uniformity of wave velocity distribution reflects the differences in the physical properties of underground rocks, providing an important basis for evaluating the quality of surrounding rocks.

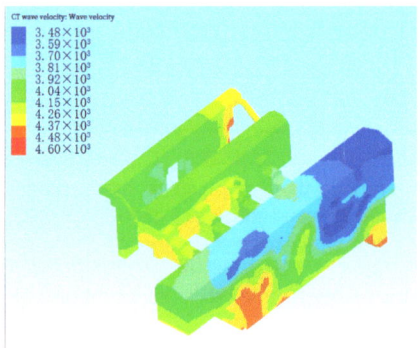

Figure 7. The geophysical wave velocity data of the cubic network is assigned to the underground engineering surface model.

Figure 8 shows the result of assigning the surrounding rock classification data from Figure 6 to the underground engineering model. The distribution of surrounding rock quality is uneven, with multiple weak zones and unstable areas. Corresponding reinforcement measures need to be implemented during the design and construction process in these areas to ensure the stability and safety of the underground cavity group.

The web-based 3D visualization technology of seismic waves intuitively displays the geological conditions and surrounding rock mass distribution, providing robust support for engineering design and construction. Additionally, web-based visualization offers high efficiency and significantly enhances digital management during the construction period of engineering projects. The 3D visualization technology of seismic waves on the web can intuitively display the geological conditions and rock mass distribution of underground powerhouse caverns, providing essential support for engineering design and construction. Additionally, web-based visualization updates are highly efficient, promoting effective digital management throughout the construction period of engineering projects.

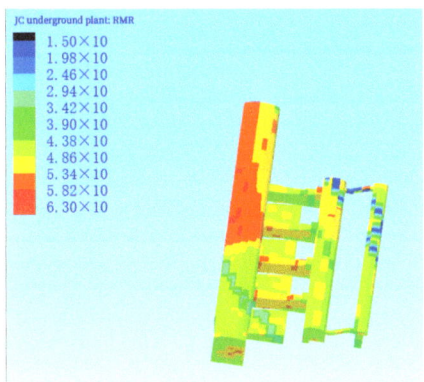

Figure 8. Surrounding rock quality classification model obtained by assigning cubic network data to the underground engineering model.

The three-dimensional visualization method of seismic wave CT results has broad scalability. This method relies on advanced algorithms, and as these algorithms are continuously optimized and upgraded, the visualization effects and computational efficiency can be improved. With the ongoing enhancement of computer hardware performance, such as the acceleration capabilities of GPUs and increased memory capacity, the seismic wave CT three-dimensional visualization method can better utilize these hardware resources to achieve higher resolutions and visualize more complex scenes. This method is not only applicable to the field of seismic exploration but can also be extended to other areas such as geological exploration, geotechnical engineering, and environmental engineering. For instance, when conducting engineering construction in karst-prone areas, it is often necessary to grout karst caves. The precise acquisition of the location and three-dimensional morphology of underground karst formations is crucial for assessing the degree of karst development and calculating the volume of grouting required. Through three-dimensional visualization technology of seismic wave CT results, the morphology of karst caves can be finely detected, enabling more accurate calculations of grouting volume and effectively reducing material waste in construction projects. Mineral reserves are an important basis for the evaluation of mineral resources, serving as a critical reference for assessing the industrial significance of ore deposits, determining the production scale of mining enterprises, investment scale, and service life. The three-dimensional visualization technology of seismic wave CT results enables accurate estimation of underground mineral reserves, which is significant for the exploration and production design of mines, production planning, reserve management, and production economic management. In addition, this technology can also be applied to the fine detection of adverse geological bodies underground and the delineation of groundwater bodies and lens profiles.

6. Conclusions

Aiming at the problems that the post-processing of CT detection results in geological specialties is restricted by specific software, low processing efficiency, cumbersome processing procedures, and is unable to be displayed conveniently, this paper proposes a three-dimensional visualization method of seismic wave CT results based on WebGL technology. The specific conclusion is as follows.

1. Firstly, generate an integer enclosing box based on the target 3D model, and calculate the wave velocity values of all reference points using the DSI interpolation calculation method. Secondly, calculate the wave velocity values of all the points to be rendered using the wave velocity values of the reference points. Finally, determine the color values of the points to be rendered and render the model and profile in real-time using shaders.

2. The visualization results of the research method in this paper were displayed on the intelligent building platform with a response time controlled within 2 s. The comparative validation of the visualization results between the proposed method and the geological 3D design software (independently developed by the Northwest China Institute of Civil Engineering and Architecture) proves the effectiveness, efficiency, and practicality of the proposed method.

3. The method was used to represent the geological information and classification of the enclosing rocks of an underground cavern, and the visualization results provide an intuitive demonstration of weak strata and unstable areas. The results present a visual reference for the support scheme of the underground structure and facilitate the digital management process during the construction of the project.

Author Contributions: Conceptualization, T.L. and J.X.; methodology, J.X.; software, T.L.; validation, T.L. and J.X.; formal analysis, T.L.; investigation, T.L.; resources, J.X.; data curation, T.L.; writing—original draft preparation, T.L.; writing—review and editing, J.X.; visualization, J.X.; supervision, T.L.; project administration, J.X.; funding acquisition, J.X. All authors have read and agreed to the published version of the manuscript.

Funding: This research was funded by National Key Research and Development Program fund, grant number 2023YFF0905500.

Data Availability Statement: Data are contained within the article.

Conflicts of Interest: Author Jieyun Xing was employed by the company PowerChina Northwest Engineering Corporation Limited. The remaining authors declare that the research was conducted in the absence of any commercial or financial relationships that could be construed as a potential conflict of interest.

References

1. Wang, H.; Chai, L.; Huang, Z.; Yang, X. Convergence analysis on seismic tomography for inverse problems of acoustic wave propagation. *Commun. Math. Sci.* **2022**, *20*, 1551–1565. [CrossRef]
2. Bergman, B.; Tryggvason, A.; Juhlin, C. Seismic tomography studies of cover thickness and near-surface bedrock velocities. *Geophysics* **2006**, *71*, U77. [CrossRef]
3. Lin, S.; Wang, W.; Jin, C.; Deng, X.; Liu, Z. Application and Discussion of Seismic CT in Detailed Karst Detection: A Case of Shenzhen Metro Line 14. *Sci. Technol. Eng.* **2019**, *19*, 18–23.
4. Cuny, J.E.; Dunn, R.A.; Hackstadt, S.T.; Harrop, C.W.; Hersey, H.H.; Malony, A.D.; Toomey, D.R. Building Domain-Specific Environments For Computational Science: A Case Study In Seismic Tomography. *Int. J. High Perform. Comput. Appl.* **1997**, *11*, 179–196. [CrossRef]
5. Xie, P.; Li, J.; Wang, B.; Wu, G.; Wang, Q.; Lin, S. Application of SPAC method and electromagnetic wave CT in karst detection of Wuhan Metro Line 8. *Geod. Geodyn.* **2023**, *14*, 513–520. [CrossRef]
6. Cifeng, C.; Pengfei, L. Application of Ground Penetrating Radar in the Survey of Hidden Karst for Subway Foundation Pit. *Geotech. Eng. Tech.* **2012**, *26*, 321–323.
7. Xu, J.; Zhu, L.; Zhai, P. 3D visualization of electrical data volume based on Voxler platform. *Chin. J. Eng. Geophys.* **2014**, *11*, 772–775.
8. Li, Z. Research on three-dimensional modeling of karst detection based on Voxler platform seismic wave CT. *Found. Earth Eng.* **2018**, *32*, 88–92.
9. Hu, J.J.; Xu, H.M.; Wang, P.; Duan, C.L. Application of Cross-hole Electromagnetic Wave Tomography Based on 3D Visualization in Karst Exploration. *Chin. J. Eng. Geophys.* **2022**, *19*, 443–449.
10. Yu, B. Application of Quasi-three-dimensional Cross-hole Seismic-wave Tomography in Karst investigation of Bridge Pile Foundation. *Chin. J. Eng. Geophys.* **2023**, *20*, 491–499.
11. Liang, J.; Zhu, Q.J.; Zhang, Z.; Zhang, E.H. Modelling and simulation of seismic wave propagation based on Blender. *J. North China Inst. Sci. Technol.* **2019**, *16*, 59–66.
12. Ma, C.Y.; Wang, Z.C.; Zhang, L.H.; Yao, Y.T.; Qiao, Y.K. A New3D Geological Modeling Method and its Application in Chengdu-Chengdu Region Modeling. *Northwestern Geol.* **2022**, *55*, 82–92.
13. Yu, M.C.; Wu, J.H.; Wang, Y.; Shi, W.H.; Wang, X. 3D Geological Modeling and Its Application in Underground Space Development. *J. Disaster Prev. Mitig. Eng.* **2023**, *43*, 588–595+636.
14. Brassel, K. A Model for Automatic Hill—Shading Cartography & Geographic Information Science. *Am. Cartogr.* **1974**, *1*, 15–27.
15. Zhou, Z.; Wellinghoff, J.; Fan, M.; Hsieh, S.S.; Holmes, D.; McCollough, C.H.; Yu, L. Automated Web-based Software for CT Quality Control Testing of Low-contrast Detectability using Model Observers. *Proc. SPIE Int. Soc. Opt. Eng.* **2024**, *12925*, 129252J.

16. Saltybaeva, N.; Platon, A.; Poletti, P.A.; Hinzpeter, R.; Merce, M.S.; Alkadhi, H. Radiation Dose to the Fetus from Computed Tomography of Pregnant Patients-Development and Validation of a Web-Based Tool. *Investig. Radiol.* **2020**, *55*, 762–768. [CrossRef]
17. Münch, H.; Engelmann, U.; Schroeter, A.; Meinzer, H. Web-based distribution of radiological images from PACS to EPR. *Int. Congr. Ser.* **2003**, *1256*, 873–879. [CrossRef]
18. Xu, X.S.; Zhang, Z.H. The 3D visualization of stratum information based on WebGL. *Geomat. Spat. Inf. Technol.* **2016**, *39*, 65–68. (In Chinese with English abstract)
19. Kerry, K.E.; Hawick, K.A. Kriging Interpolation on High-Performance Computers. In Proceedings of the High-Performance Computing and Networking, International Conference and Exhibition, HPCN Europe 1998, Amsterdam, The Netherlands, 21–23 April 1998. [CrossRef]
20. Zimmerman, D.; Pavlik, C.; Ruggles, A.; Armstrong, M.P. An Experimental Comparison of Ordinary and Universal Kriging and Inverse Distance Weighting. *Math. Geol.* **1999**, *31*, 375–390. [CrossRef]
21. Homayoon, S.R.; Keshavarzi, A.; Gazni, R. Application of Artificial Neural Network, Kriging, and Inverse Distance Weighting Models for Estimation of Scour Depth around Bridge Pier with Bed Sill. *J. Softw. Eng. Appl.* **2010**, *3*, 944–964.
22. Vu, T.D. Comparison of Ordinary Kriging and Inverse Distance Weighting Interpolation Methods: A Case Study at Ta Thiet Deposit of Cement Limestone Deposits, Binh Phuoc Province. 2018. Available online: https://www.researchgate.net/publication/341160924_Comparison_of_Ordinary_Kriging_and_Inverse_Distance_Weighting_Interpolation_methods_A_Case_Study_at_Ta_Thiet_deposit_of_Cement_Limestone_Deposits_Binh_Phuoc_province (accessed on 1 November 2024).
23. Diodato, N.; Ceccarelli, M. Interpolation processes using multivariate geostatistics for mapping of climatological precipitation mean in the Sannio Mountains (southern Italy). *Earth Surf. Process. Landf.* **2005**, *30*, 259–268. [CrossRef]
24. Chen, C.; Zhao, N.; Yue, T.; Guo, J. A generalization of inverse distance weighting method via kernel regression and its application to surface modeling. *Arab. J. Geosci.* **2015**, *8*, 6623–6633. [CrossRef]
25. Mallet, J.L. Discrete smooth interpolation. *ACM Trans. Graph.* **1989**, *8*, 121–144. [CrossRef]
26. Lee, C.; Lee, J.; Seo, G. Direct Encoding for Sampled Color Pictures with Location Consideration. In Proceedings of the Advances in Visual Computing: 9th International Symposium, ISVC 2013, Rethymnon, Crete, Greece, 29–31 July 2013; Volume 8034.
27. Rui, D.; Zitong, Z.; Lian, X.; Ren, T.; Zhou, X.; Thung, Y.T.; Ta, V.D.; Su, J.Y.H. Dome-shaped mode lasing from liquid crystals for full-color lasers and high-sensitivity detection. *Chem. Commun.* **2023**, *59*, 1641–1644.
28. Ruta, D.; Jordan, L.; Fox, T.J.; Boakes, R. WebSight: Using AR and WebGL shaders to assist the visually impaired. In Proceedings of the 15th International Web for All Conference, Lyon, France, 23–25 April 2018. [CrossRef]
29. Calabuig-Barbero, E.; Davia-Aracil, M.; Mora-Mora, H.; Herrero-Pérez, F. Computational model for hyper-realistic image generation using uniform shaders in 3D environments. *Comput. Ind.* **2020**, *123*, 103337. [CrossRef]
30. Chang, X.; Yuksel, K.; Skarbek, W. WebGL and web audio software lightweight components for multimedia education. In Proceedings of the Photonics Applications in Astronomy, Communications, Industry, and High Energy Physics Experiments, Wilga, Poland, 28 May–6 June 2017.
31. Mallet, J.L. Discrete smooth interpolation in geometric modelling. *Comput. Aided Des.* **1992**, *24*, 178–191. [CrossRef]
32. Guo, J.; Wang, X.; Wang, J.; Dai, X.; Wu, L.; Li, C.; Li, F.; Liu, S.; Jessell, M.W. Three-dimensional geological modeling and spatial analysis from geotechnical borehole data using an implicit surface and marching tetrahedra algorithm. *Eng. Geol.* **2021**, *284*, 106047. [CrossRef]
33. Ai, X.; Wang, Y.; Wu, Y.; Kou, S. WebLFR: An interactive light field renderer in web browsers. *Multimed. Tools Appl.* **2024**, *83*, 77377–77392. [CrossRef]
34. Mlakar, D.; Steinberger, M.; Schmalstieg, D. End-to-End Compressed Meshlet Rendering. *Comput. Graph. Forum* **2024**, *43*, e15002. [CrossRef]
35. Kim, M.; Baek, N. A 3D graphics rendering pipeline implementation based on the openCL massively parallel processing. *J. Supercomput.* **2021**, *77*, 7351–7367. [CrossRef]

Disclaimer/Publisher's Note: The statements, opinions and data contained in all publications are solely those of the individual author(s) and contributor(s) and not of MDPI and/or the editor(s). MDPI and/or the editor(s) disclaim responsibility for any injury to people or property resulting from any ideas, methods, instructions or products referred to in the content.

Article

Improved Mobilized Strength Design Method for Multi-Support Excavation Deformation Analysis

Bingxiong Tu [1], Meng Han [2,*], Jinqing Jia [2], Zhaoyun Xiao [1] and Lulu Liu [3,*]

[1] Fujian Engineering Technology Research Center for Tunnel and Underground Space, Huaqiao University, Xiamen 361021, China; tubingxiong@hqu.edu.cn (B.T.); zyxiao@hqu.edu.cn (Z.X.)
[2] State Key Laboratory of Coastal and Offshore Engineering, Dalian University of Technology, Dalian 116024, China; jiajq@dlut.edu.cn
[3] State Key Laboratory for Geomechanics and Deep Underground Engineering, China University of Mining and Technology, Xuzhou 210096, China
* Correspondence: hanmeng320@mail.dlut.edu.cn (M.H.); believeliululu@163.com (L.L.)

Abstract: The safe and reliable design of underground spaces ensures the safety of a structure itself and its surroundings. The traditional Mobilized Strength Design (MSD) method for a multi-support excavation deformation analysis ignores the effects of soil parameters and excavation boundary conditions. Therefore, to compensate for the shortcomings of the existing MSD method, this paper proposes an improved mobilized strength design (IMSD) method for a multi-support excavation deformation analysis. The improved incremental deformation mechanism further considers the effect of the soil friction angle, and the effect of excavation depth and the first support on deformation energy are also considered. Further, the excavation calculation process based on the IMSD method is given, and the effects of different calculation parameters on the IMSD solution of excavation deformation are discussed. The results show that the IMSD method can effectively consider the effect of boundary conditions and the excavated process on the excavation deformation. The traditional MSD method underestimates the excavation deformation and surface settlement by an average of 15–23%, while the IMSD solution is more consistent with the measured values. The study results can provide a theoretical reference for the design of multi-support excavation.

Keywords: IMSD method; excavation deformation; surface settlement; incremental method; deformation energy

1. Introduction

With the implementation of the strategy of a country with a strong transportation network, urban infrastructure construction and rail transportation have been rapidly developed [1–4]. The construction of underground projects has been required due to the massive construction of high-rise buildings, commercial centers, and subway projects [5–7]. Underground projects have been mostly located in urban centers, where the environment was very complex, especially around subway excavation with dense buildings, roads, and lifelines [8–10]. Once an excavation failed, it would be a fatal disaster for the surrounding buildings and lifelines [11–13]. Therefore, to ensure the safety of an excavation, surrounding buildings, and lifelines, it is very significant to study a reliable theoretical system to accurately predict excavation deformation and force.

With the continuous development of urban construction, the building environment around urban excavation has been becoming increasingly complex, making the deformation control design of excavation engineering increasingly significant [14,15]. Therefore, the prediction method of excavation deformation has received extensive attention. The current methods for analyzing excavation deformation and forces have been divided into three main categories: (1) the classical method; (2) the elastic foundation beam method; and (3) the finite element method [16]. The classical method simplifies the excavation boundary conditions and differs from the actual force pattern [17]. The elastic foundation beam method treats the soil as a homogeneous elastic semi-infinite body, ignoring the plastic deformation of the soil [18]. The finite element method has a complex selection of constitutive models with uncertainties in the input parameters [7,9,19]. Therefore, it is of great significance to investigate new reliable methods for excavation design.

With the development of the excavation theory, a new method from the energy point of view has emerged: the Mobilized Strength Design (MSD) method [20–22]. The MSD method adopted the plastic deformation mechanism to predict the excavation deformation and surface settlement through the energy conservation relationship between the soil and the supporting system [23–25]. Overall, compared with traditional design methods, the MSD method has three major advantages: (1) tightly formulated derivations using energy conservation and clear physical concepts [26,27]; (2) the nonlinear relationship of soil stress–strain and the dynamic development of excavation deformation can be considered; and (3) the non-homogeneous soil condition, burial depth of soil, and the soil principal stress rotation caused by the excavation can be considered [28].

Currently, the MSD method has been successfully applied to cantilever retaining walls [29–31], ground surface settlement caused by tunnel excavation [32–34], excavation-induced deformation and ground surface settlement [35–37], and nonlinear pile group response [38,39]. Bolton et al. [20,23] first proposed the mobilizable strength design (MSD) method and successfully applied it to wall displacement and stability studies in over-consolidated clays. Osman and Bolton [40] proposed a design method for cantilevered excavation considering the nonlinear soil stress–strain relationship based on the MSD method and elastoplasticity theory. Then, the effect of anisotropic soil was considered, and the application of the MSD method in excavation was further extended and improved [37]. Lam and Bolton [21] proposed different deformation mechanisms for wide and narrow excavation, considering the effect of excavation width on the surrounding soil deformation pattern. Moreover, the accuracy of the excavation MSD method, considering the mobilized shear strength of soils with different burial depths, has been verified and improved by model experiments and engineering cases [28,35]. Further, Liu et al. [41] and Wang et al. [22,42] considered the effect of soil non-homogeneity and anisotropy and introduced the compression deformation energy and bending deformation energy of supporting structures in the energy conservation equation.

However, the traditional incremental deformation mechanism adopted for excavation is inconsistent with the actual situation. The current MSD method to calculate the excavation deformation does not consider the effect of the soil friction angle. The range of plastic deformation caused by excavation only considers the length effect of the supporting piles, ignoring the effect of the excavation depth on the deformation energy. In addition, the traditional energy conservation formula does not give enough consideration to the deformation energy of the excavation supporting structure, especially the deformation energy generated by the first support.

Therefore, to address the above research deficiencies, this paper proposes an improved mobilized strength design (IMSD) method for multi-support excavation deformation analysis. The improved incremental deformation mechanism further considers the effect of soil friction angle, and the effect of excavation depth and first support on deformation energy is also considered. The reasonableness and accuracy of the newly proposed IMSD method were verified using engineering examples. Finally, the effects of different parameters on the IMSD solution of excavation deformation were discussed. These study results improve the prediction accuracy of excavation deformation and provide a theoretical basis for the excavation design.

2. Application of the IMSD Method in Excavation

2.1. Traditional MSD Method

The selection of the incremental deformation mechanism is the key to the MSD method. The MSD method proposed by Lam and Bolton [21] assumed that the incremental deformation function should be a cosine function, as in Equation (1). However, this method only considered the soil deformation between the lowest support and the hard soil layer, which was not consistent with the actual excavation deformation. Liu et al. [41] further improved the incremental deformation function by considering the soil deformation between the pile top and the hard soil layer. The incremental deformation curve was assumed to be a segmented cosine function based on the excavation deformation in the layered strata, as in Equation (2).

$$\delta_x = \frac{\delta_{\max}}{2}\left[1 - \cos\left(\frac{2\pi y}{\lambda}\right)\right] \qquad (1)$$

$$\begin{cases} \delta_x = \frac{\delta_{\max}}{2}\left[1 - \cos\left(\frac{\pi y}{k\lambda}\right)\right], -k\lambda \le y \le 0 \\ \delta_x = \frac{\delta_{\max}}{2}\left[1 - \cos\left(\frac{\pi(y-(1-2k)\lambda)}{(1-k)\lambda}\right)\right], -\lambda \le y \le -k\lambda \\ \lambda = \alpha s \end{cases} \qquad (2)$$

where y is the distance from the lowest support of any point below the lowest support, δ_x is the incremental displacement of the wall at y, $\delta_{\max}$ is the maximum incremental displacement of the soil, s is the length of the supporting structure below the lowest support, λ is the deformation wavelength, k is the ratio of the distance from the peak to the origin to the wavelength, defined as the crest coefficient of variation, and α is the deformation influence coefficient, which takes the value of 0.5–2.

2.2. Improved MSD Method

2.2.1. Plastic Deformation Mechanism of Excavation

To compensate for the shortcomings of the traditional MSD method, the incremental deformation mechanism of the excavation was improved (see Figure 1). In this paper, the range of incremental deformation outside the excavation lay between O'rourke [43] and Liu et al. [41], while the influence range inside the excavation was reduced. From Figure 1, the plastic deformation flow is shown as the dashed line with arrows, including active zone ABCF, sectors CEF and EHF, and passive zone FHI. The ABCF zone considers the horizontal displacement of the area above the excavation surface and forms a quadrilateral zone where the angle between the flow line and the horizontal is the angle of internal friction. The CFE zone is a sector centered at point F. The angle between the sideline CF and the vertical is the angle of internal friction. The FH line is perpendicular to the CF line, dividing the sector FEH zone and the triangle FHI zone. The influence range of the improved incremental deformation mechanism varies with the excavation depth. In addition, a plastic deformation field, considering the displacement coordination and soil friction angle, is proposed.

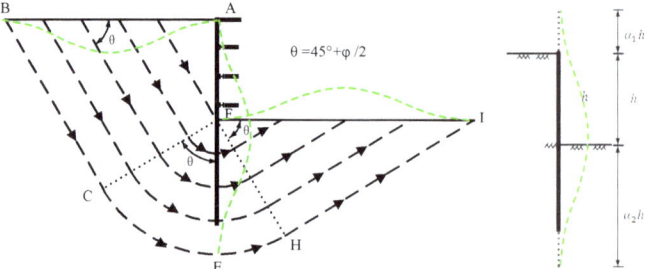

Figure 1. Improved incremental deformation mechanism of MSD method.

It is assumed that the excavation width is greater than $2(1+\alpha_2)h\sec\theta$, and the deformation is not affected by the interaction of the two sides of the supporting structures. According to the excavation deformation in the actual layered stratigraphy, the virtual top deformation zero point of the deformation curve is assumed to be located above the excavation top. The improved plastic deformation field further considers the effect of the soil friction angle. Meanwhile, two parameters, the virtual fixed point location coefficient, α_1, and the influence range coefficient of excavation depth, α_2, are introduced into the incremental deformation function so as to reflect the influence of excavation depth and the first support on the deformation energy. If the incremental deformation function ignores the compression deformation energy of the first support, the calculated excavation top displacement is always zero. In addition, if the deformation increment function assumes that the deformation wavelength is a fixed value and fails to correlate with the excavation depth, the influence range of soil deformation is quite different from the actual situation when the excavation depth is small.

The improved incremental deformation cosine function is expressed as follows:

$$\delta_x = \frac{\delta_{\max}}{2}\left[1 - \cos\left(\frac{2\pi(y + \alpha_1 h)}{\lambda}\right)\right] \tag{3}$$

$$\lambda = (1 + \alpha_1 + \alpha_2)h \tag{4}$$

$$k = \frac{h}{\lambda} \tag{5}$$

where α_1 is the coefficient of the virtual fixed point position, α_2 is the influence range coefficient of excavation depth, h is the excavation depth, λ is the deformation wavelength, and k is the crest coefficient of variation.

2.2.2. Total Loss of Potential Energy of the Soil

Excavation unloading disrupts the initial stress balance. Horizontal additional stresses caused by excavation act to deform the supporting structure, and the soil behind the supporting structure is also displaced horizontally and vertically. The tendency of soil bodies to move relative to each other results in shear stresses and, hence, shear displacements. This result is accompanied by the bending deformation of the supporting structure and the compression deformation of the inner support, which generates the corresponding deformation energy, respectively. Based on Lam and Bolton [21], the effect of the incremental compression deformation energy of internal supports was further considered in the energy conservation equation:

$$\Delta P = \Delta W + \Delta U + \Delta V \tag{6}$$

where ΔP is the total loss of potential energy of the soil, ΔW is the total work carried out in shearing the soil, ΔU is elastic strain energy, and ΔV is the incremental compression deformation energy of the internal support.

The increment of the total potential energy of the excavation system in the mth stage of construction can be expressed as follows:

$$\Delta P = \sum_{i=1}^{n}\left[\int \gamma_{sat}(m,i)\delta_y(m,i)dA\right] \tag{7}$$

where $\gamma_{sat}(m,i)$ is the saturated unit weight of soil in the ith layer for the mth construction, $\delta_y(m,i)$ is the vertical component of displacement of soil in the ith layer for the mth construction, and A is the site soil area within the influence range.

According to the deformation mechanism shown in Figure 1, the excavation soil body can be divided into four deformation zones: ABCF, CEF, EHF, and FHI. The incremental displacement at the mth excavation condition can be expressed as follows:

$$\delta_y = y(\delta_{\max}) \tag{8}$$

$$\delta_x = x(\delta_{\max}) \tag{9}$$

The details are shown in the following Equations (10)–(17), where $r^2 = x^2 + y^2$, r and x with the same positive and negative sign.

(1) In the zone ABCF, with point A as the origin of the coordinates, then:

$$\delta_x = -\frac{\delta_{max}}{2}\left[1 - \cos\left(\frac{2\pi\left(\sqrt{x^2+y^2}+(1+\alpha_1)h\right)\tan\theta}{(1+\alpha_1+\alpha_2)h}\right)\right]\sin\theta \quad (10)$$

$$\delta_y = \frac{\delta_{max}}{2}\left[1 - \cos\left(\frac{2\pi\left(\sqrt{x^2+y^2}+(1+\alpha_1)h\right)\tan\theta}{(1+\alpha_1+\alpha_2)h}\right)\right]\cos\theta \quad (11)$$

(2) In the zone CEF, with point F as the origin of the coordinates, then:

$$\delta_x = -\frac{\delta_{max}}{2}\left[1 - \cos\left(\frac{2\pi\left(\sqrt{x^2+y^2}+(1+\alpha_1)h\right)}{(1+\alpha_1+\alpha_2)h}\right)\right]\frac{y}{\sqrt{x^2+y^2}} \quad (12)$$

$$\delta_y = \frac{\delta_{max}}{2}\left[1 - \cos\left(\frac{2\pi\left(\sqrt{x^2+y^2}+(1+\alpha_1)h\right)}{(1+\alpha_1+\alpha_2)h}\right)\right]\frac{x}{\sqrt{x^2+y^2}} \quad (13)$$

(3) In the zone FEH, with point F as the origin of the coordinates, then:

$$\delta_x = \frac{\delta_{max}}{2}\left[1 - \cos\left(\frac{2\pi\left(\sqrt{x^2+y^2}+(1+\alpha_1)h\right)}{(1+\alpha_1+\alpha_2)h}\right)\right]\frac{y}{\sqrt{x^2+y^2}} \quad (14)$$

$$\delta_y = -\frac{\delta_{max}}{2}\left[1 - \cos\left(\frac{2\pi\left(\sqrt{x^2+y^2}+(1+\alpha_1)h\right)}{(1+\alpha_1+\alpha_2)h}\right)\right]\frac{x}{\sqrt{x^2+y^2}} \quad (15)$$

(4) In the zone FHI, with point F as the origin of the coordinates, then:

$$\delta_x = \frac{\delta_{max}}{2}\left[1 - \cos\left(\frac{2\pi\left(\frac{x}{\tan\theta}+y+(1+\alpha_1)h\right)}{(1+\alpha_1+\alpha_2)h}\right)\right]\sin\theta \quad (16)$$

$$\delta_y = -\frac{\delta_{max}}{2}\left[1 - \cos\left(\frac{2\pi\left(\frac{x}{\tan\theta}+y+(1+\alpha_1)h\right)}{(1+\alpha_1+\alpha_2)h}\right)\right]\cos\theta \quad (17)$$

2.2.3. The Total Work Performed in Shearing the Soil

The calculation of the internal energy increment of the soil can be referred to Liu et al. [41]:

$$\Delta W = \sum_{i=1}^{n}\left[\int C_{u,mob}(m,i)|\delta_\gamma(m,i)|dA\right] \quad (18)$$

where $C_{u,mob}(m,i)$ is the undrained shear strength of soil in the ith layer for the mth stage of construction, and $\delta_\gamma(m,i)$ is the shear strain increment of soil in the ith layer for the mth stage of construction.

$\delta_\gamma(m,i)$ can be expressed as a partial differential function of the displacement:

$$\delta_\gamma(m,i) = \sqrt{\left(\frac{\partial \delta_x}{\partial y}+\frac{\partial \delta_y}{\partial x}\right)^2 - 4\frac{\partial \delta_x}{\partial x}\cdot\frac{\partial \delta_y}{\partial y}} \quad (19)$$

In the zone ABCF:

$$\delta_\gamma = \frac{2\pi\delta_{max}}{(1+\alpha_1+\alpha_2)h}\left|\sin\theta\times\sin\left(\frac{2\pi(x+y\cot\theta)\tan\theta}{(1+\alpha_1+\alpha_2)h}\right)\right| \quad (20)$$

In the zones CEF and EHF:

$$\delta_\gamma = \frac{\delta_{\max}}{\sqrt{2}(1+\alpha_1+\alpha_2)hr}\left|\sin\left(\frac{\pi(h+r)}{(1+\alpha_1+\alpha_2)h}\right) \times \left[4\pi^2 r^2\left(1+\cos\left(\frac{2\pi(h+r)}{(1+\alpha_1+\alpha_2)h}\right)\right)+\right.\right.$$
$$\left.\left.(1+\alpha_1+\alpha_2)^2 h^2\left(1-\cos\left(\frac{2\pi(h+r)}{(1+\alpha_1+\alpha_2)h}\right)\right) - 4\pi r(1+\alpha_1+\alpha_2)h \times \sin\left(\frac{2\pi(h+r)}{(1+\alpha_1+\alpha_2)h}\right)\right]\right| \tag{21}$$

In the zone EFI:

$$\delta_\gamma = \frac{\pi\delta_{\max}}{(1+\alpha_1+\alpha_2)h}\left|\csc\theta \times \sin\left(\frac{2\pi(h+y+x\cot\theta)}{(1+\alpha_1+\alpha_2)h}\right)\right| \tag{22}$$

2.2.4. Elastic Strain Energy

Elastic strain energy can be obtained by integrating the bending stiffness with the incremental horizontal displacement within the burial wall depth:

$$\Delta U = \frac{EI}{2}\int_0^h \left[\frac{d^2\delta_x}{dy^2}\right]^2 dy \tag{23}$$

The excavation deformation curve conforms to the cosine function:

$$\Delta U = \frac{\pi EI\delta_{\max}}{2(1+\alpha_1+\alpha_2)^2 h^2}\left[\sin\frac{2\pi(1+\alpha_1)}{(1+\alpha_1+\alpha_2)} - \sin\frac{2\pi\alpha_1}{(1+\alpha_1+\alpha_2)}\right] \tag{24}$$

where EI is the bending stiffness of the supporting structure.

2.2.5. Compression Deformation Energy of the Internal Support

The calculation of compression deformation energy of the internal support can be referred to Liu et al. [41]:

$$\Delta V = \sum\left[\frac{E_P A_P}{2l_P}(\delta_{x,p})^2 \sin\theta\right] \tag{25}$$

where $E_P A_P$ is the bending stiffness of internal support.

2.3. Determination of Calculation Parameters

Three significant calculation parameters affect the IMSD solution, including the following: (1) the deformation-influenced wavelength, (2) the soil shear strength, and (3) the soil stress–strain curve. To match the actual engineering, these significant calculation parameters in the IMSD method were improved.

2.3.1. Improved Deformation-Influenced Wavelength

The current incremental deformation function assumes the deformation-influenced wavelength as a fixed value and fails to account for the effect of excavation depth. When the excavation depth is small, the influence scope of soil deformation differs greatly from the actual deformation. Compared with the fixed deformation-influenced wavelength in the traditional MSD method, the deformation-influenced wavelength determined by the support load-sharing method introduced in this paper can more realistically reflect the influence range of the soil body [27,41]. Therefore, the support load-sharing method was used to determine the deformation-influenced wavelength in the MSD method.

It is assumed that the maximum soil deformation influence range of the excavation is two times the actual insertion depth of the soil. Therefore, the deformation-influenced wavelength can be expressed as a relation between the insertion depth below and above the reverse bend points of the supporting structure and the excavation depth (see Figure 2). The improved deformation-influenced wavelength is calculated as follows:

$$\lambda = 2(x+y) + h \tag{26}$$

where λ is the deformation wavelength, x and y are the insertion depth below and above the reverse bend points of the supporting structure, respectively, and h is the excavation depth.

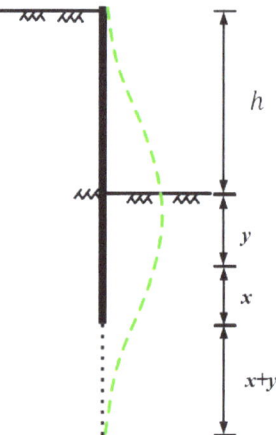

Figure 2. Calculation of improved deformation-influenced wavelength.

2.3.2. Soil Shear Strength

Stress changes in the soil caused by excavation in soft clay can be regarded as undrained behavior, and the soil strength eigenvalues for this process can be adopted as undrained shear strength. The undrained shear strength of soft clays is characterized by anisotropy due to the depositional history and initial consolidation state and is related to the overlying effective stress. Due to the soil stress spindle rotation caused by the excavation unloading, the soil stress state is different at different excavation locations, so the soil shear strength at different locations is different. Based on the model proposed by Casagrande and Carillo [44], formulas for the shear strength of soils considering different stress states and depth conditions are obtained:

$$s_{u\alpha} = \eta\xi + \xi(1-\eta)\cos^2(\theta - \frac{\pi}{4} + \frac{\varphi'}{2})\sigma'_v \qquad (27)$$

$$\sigma'_v = \sum_i \gamma_{sat,i} z_i \qquad (28)$$

where $s_{u\alpha}$ is the soil shear strength, η is the anisotropy ratio, ξ is the ratio of the vertical undrained shear strength to the overlying effective stress, θ is the deflection angle of the main axis, σ'_v is the overlying effective stress, φ' is the effective angle of internal friction, γ_{sat} is the saturated unit weight of the soil, and z is the depth.

2.3.3. Stress–Strain Curve of Soil

The theoretical core of the MSD method is the shear strength mobilization coefficient of the soil and the function of soil shear strain. Vardanega and Bolton [33] obtained undrained shear stress–strain curves for cohesive soils conforming to an exponential function considering the effects of soil nonlinearity:

$$\beta = \frac{S_{u,mob}}{S_u} = a\left(\frac{\gamma}{\gamma_{0.5}}\right)^b \qquad (29)$$

where $S_u(i)$ is the peak strength of the stress–strain curve in the ith layer, $\gamma_{0.5}(i)$ is the shear strain at corresponding to $0.5S_u(i)$ on the stress–strain curve, a and b are the fitting parameters, and β is the undrained shear strength exertion coefficient.

3. Suggested Calculation Process

This paper proposes a multi-support excavation deformation analysis method based on the improved MSD method. The main calculation process is divided into eight steps (see Figure 3):

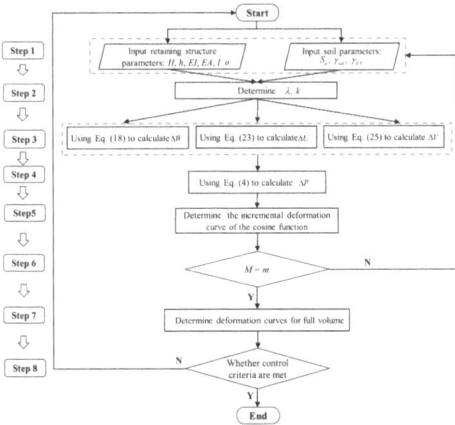

Figure 3. Calculation flow chart.

(1) **Input the basic parameters**: Input soil parameters, such as saturated unit weight, γ_{sat}, shear stress, S_u, and shear strain, $\gamma_{0.5}$. Input the supporting structure parameters, such as bending stiffness (EI), length (l), and compressive stiffness (EA) of the inner support, the angle between the support and the horizontal direction of the supporting structure (θ), excavation depth (h), and the layered excavation depth.

(2) **Calculate wavelength and crest variation coefficient**: Calculate the wavelength, λ, and crest variation coefficient, k, using Equation (3).

(3) **Calculate the increment of different systems**: Equations (18), (23) and (25) are used to calculate the total work performed in shearing the soil, ΔW, the elastic deformation energy, ΔU, and the incremental compression deformation energy of the internal support, ΔV, respectively.

(4) **Calculate the total loss of potential energy of the soil**: According to the energy conservation in the excavation system, the total loss of potential energy of the soil, ΔP, is calculated by Equation (6).

(5) **Determine the cosine function of the incremental deformation curve**: The maximum horizontal displacement increment of the supporting structure is determined, and the cosine function of the incremental deformation curve is then determined

(6) **Determine whether the excavation step m is equal to the final excavation step M**: If $m = M$, output the full deformation curve. If $m \neq M$, continue to input parameters for the superposition of incremental deformation.

(7) **Judge whether to meet the control standard**: When the obtained deformation does not meet the requirements of the control standards, the excavation construction program can be adjusted appropriately and repeatedly accounted for until the requirements are met.

(8) **Output the results of excavation calculation**: Output the results of the excavation displacement and the ground surface settlement.

4. Engineering Verification

4.1. Case 1

Liu et al. [41] analyzed the excavation deformation characteristics using the MSD method. The Jinzhongjie Station excavation of Tianjin Metro Line 6 was 499.9 m long × 16.6 m deep × 20.7 m wide. The support system adopted a combination of a diaphragm wall

(0.8 m wide × 34.1 m deep) and mixed internal support with the 1st concrete strut (0.8 × 0.8 m in section size, $EI = 1.28 \times 10^6$ kN·m^2) and 2nd, 3rd, and 4th steel pile struts (0.609 m or 0.8 m in diameter and 0.016 m in thickness, $E = 210$ GPa). The soil around the excavation was mainly silty clay and fine sand. Excavation resulted in a weakened resistance of the supporting structure to the soil. The horizontal resistance coefficients for the soils below and above the excavation surface were 2.4×10^6 N·m^{-3} and 1.2×10^6 N·m^{-3}, respectively. The corresponding deformation coefficients for different soil resistance coefficients were 0.1195 and 0.1005, respectively. Refer to Liu et al. [41] for specific project overview details.

Figure 4 compares the pile deformation and surface settlement calculated by different methods. By comparing the measured values and the MSD solution proposed by Liu et al. [41], the IMSD solution proposed in this paper was more consistent with the measured pile deformation and ground surface settlement. This finding was because the proposed IMSD solution adopted a plastic incremental deformation mechanism considering the internal friction angle, which could more accurately reflect the soil deformation and significantly improve the accuracy of the maximum excavation displacement. In addition, the MSD solution proposed by Liu et al. [41] underestimated the measured pile deformation, which differs from the measured value. This result was because the same incremental deformation function was used for the surface settlement and pile deformation in the plastic incremental deformation mechanism. The incremental deformation mechanism adopted by Liu et al. [41] ignored the effect of excavation depth and first support on deformation energy. In addition, the proposed model solution had an error of 5% with the measured data, but the accuracy was improved by 20–30% compared with the traditional model solution, so the error was within the controllable range. The reason for the error was that there was some error in the selection of the soil pressure model in the deformation influence wavelength of the method in this paper. The determination of earth pressure parameters requires the improvement of existing earth pressure models. This is an important research component that will be further investigated in the future.

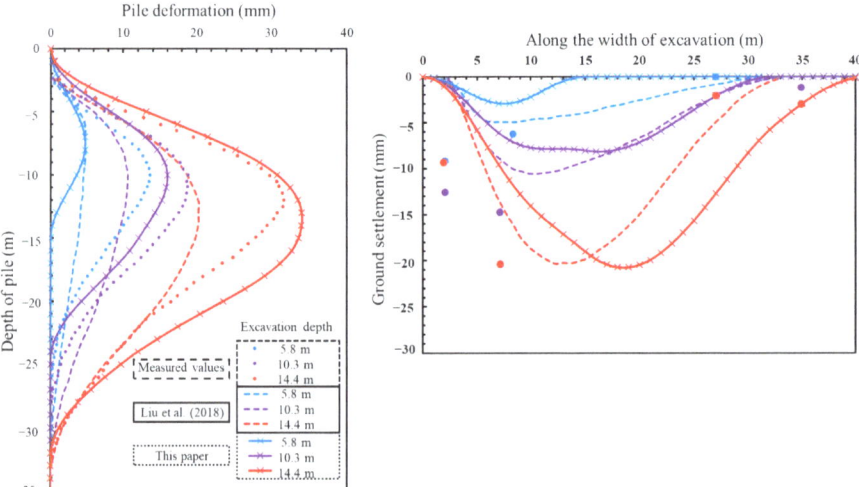

Figure 4. Comparison of calculation results of pile deformation and ground surface settlement of different methods [41].

Figure 5 shows the relationship between the calculated parameters and excavation depth under different zones. From Figure 5, the potential energy increment and internal energy increment of the soil were positively correlated with the excavation depth. This positive correlation was due to the increase in the deformation influence range caused by the increase in excavation depth. The most sensitive of each energy increment to excavation depth was the potential energy increment in the ABCF zone, with the least significant change in the FEH zone. This finding was because excavation depth affected the area of each plastic deformation zone differently. The incremental change in internal energy for each zone was more similarly affected by the increase in excavation depth, and the shear strain in zone ABCF was the largest in all zones. However, considering that the soil shear strength was positively correlated with the burial depth, the internal energy increment in the ABCF zone was slightly smaller than that in the CEF zone.

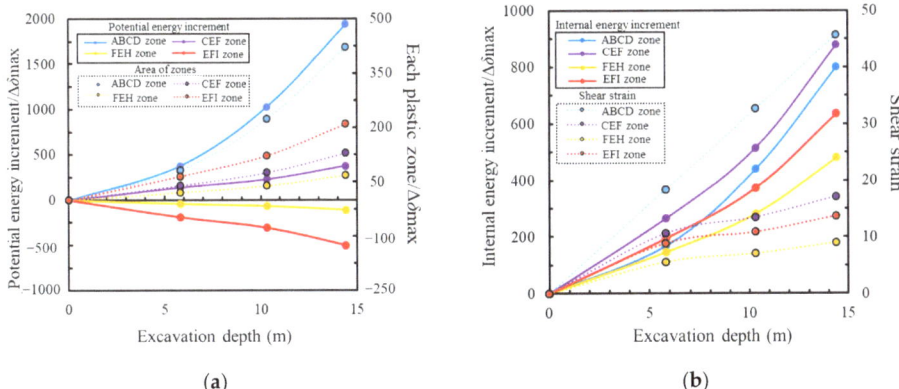

Figure 5. Relationship between calculated parameters and excavation depth: (**a**) potential energy increment; (**b**) internal energy increment.

4.2. Case 2

Tan et al. [45] studied the characterization of semi-top-down excavation for a subway station in Shanghai soft ground based on measured data. The excavation with a dimension of 139.6 × 21.8 × 24.8 m (length × width × depth) and the supporting structures consisting of the diaphragm wall (1 m wide) and mixed strut systems were adopted. The six internal support systems with the 1st concrete strut (0.8 × 1 m in section size and 6 m in horizontal spacing) and 2nd–6th steel pile struts (0.609 m in diameter, 2–3 m in horizontal spacing) were adopted. The soils around the excavation were mostly silty clay, muddy clay, clay and silty clay, and silty sand. For details of the excavation, refer to Tan et al. [45].

Figure 6 shows the comparison of measured and calculated wall displacement under different working conditions. From Figure 6, the wall displacement calculated by the proposed method was consistent with the measured values in the overall trend. The depth where the maximum wall deformation was basically the same as the measured values. When excavating to 12.3 m, 19.3 m, and 24.8 m, respectively, the average error between the measured and calculated wall displacement was 6.07%. This value verified the accuracy of the proposed calculation model in this paper. The main reasons for this error were (1) the influence of cyclic traffic loads on the excavation and (2) the temperature effect on excavation deformation. It is worth noting that there is some error between the measured and calculated wall bottom displacement. This outcome is due to the fact that the proposed model in this paper is mainly applied to special cases in which the basal strata is too soft, or the length of embedded retaining wall is insufficient.

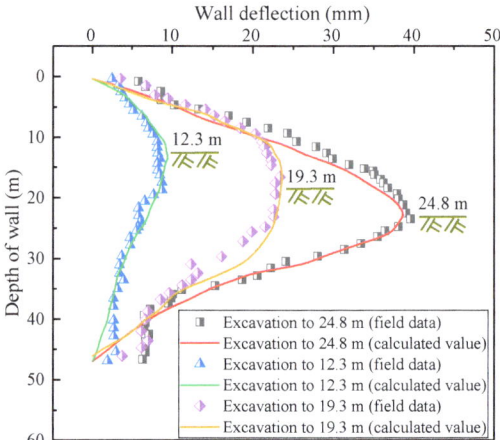

Figure 6. Comparison of measured and calculated wall displacement under different working conditions.

4.3. Case 3

This paper relied on the subway excavation project in soft soil at Daliang Station (266 m long × 25.3 m deep × 19.9 m wide) reported by Han et al. [15]. The excavation support structure consisted of a diaphragm wall (0.8 m wide × 30 m deep) and four layers of hybrid internal support. The first layer was concrete support (0.7 × 0.9 m in cross-section size) and the second to fourth layers were steel supports (0.609 m in diameter, 0.016 m in thickness). The concrete and steel supports were spaced horizontally at 9 m and 4.5 m, respectively. The soils around the excavation were mainly silty clay, muddy soil, fully weathered muddy siltstone, and strongly weathered muddy siltstone. See Han et al. [15] for an overview of specific projects. The length of the diaphragm wall for subway excavation at Daliang Station was 30 m, and the embedment depth was 5 m. According to the geological condition and design data, the embedded depth of the excavation wall of Daliang station was insufficient, and the soil condition was soft soil, which belongs to the special excavation case to which the model of this paper applies.

Figure 7 shows a comparison of wall deformation when excavating to the third and fourth support positions. From Figure 7, the measured wall displacements were consistent with the overall trend of this paper's solution, which demonstrates the reasonableness and accuracy of the proposed calculation model. As the excavation top support in the Foshan area was affected by the temperature, it led to the wall top deformation towards the outside of the excavation. And the proposed method in this paper does not consider the influence of temperature effect, so there is some error in the displacement value at the top of the wall. Therefore, the model proposed in this paper applies to the special case where the embedment depth of the wall of Daliang Station is insufficient and the soil condition situation is soft soil. In addition, the method proposed by Liu et al. [41] underestimated the wall displacement, while the method proposed by Lam and Bolton [21] overestimated the wall displacement, especially the large difference in displacement at the top and bottom of the wall. This finding was because these two methods proposed by Liu et al. [41] and Lam and Bolton [21] did not consider the actual boundary conditions of the excavation.

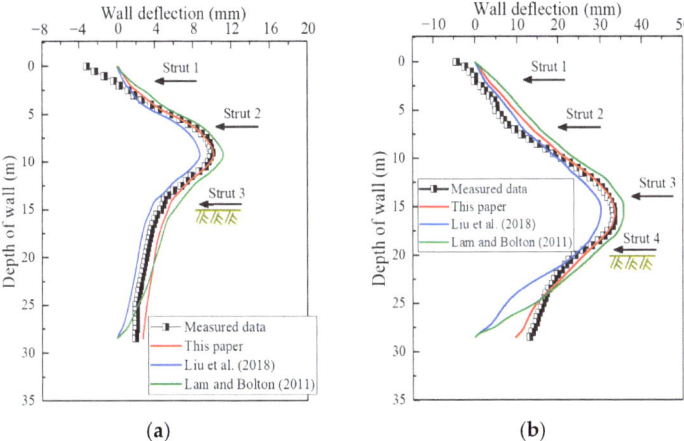

Figure 7. Comparison of wall deformation under different excavation conditions: (**a**) excavation to 14.55 m; (**b**) excavation to 19.75 m [21,41].

Figure 8 and Table 1 show the comparison of measured and predicted wall displacements. From Figure 8 and Table 1, the IMSD solution proposed in this paper can predict the wall displacements better and can improve the prediction accuracy of the MSD method, with the error basically in the range of 10–15%. Compared with the measured wall displacements, the method proposed by Liu et al. [41] underestimated the wall displacements, while the method proposed by Lam and Bolton [21] overestimated the wall displacements, with the error basically within 25%. When the wall displacement was small, the error between the predicted and measured values was relatively large. This result was because the methods proposed by Liu et al. [41] and Lam and Bolton [21] both ignored the effect of the actual boundary conditions of the excavation.

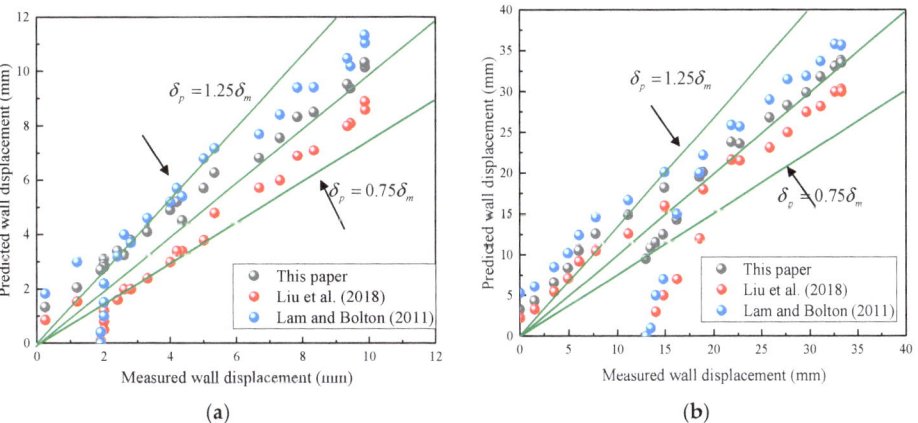

Figure 8. Comparison of measured and predicted wall displacement: (**a**) excavation to 14.55 m; (**b**) excavation to 19.75 m [21,41].

Table 1. Comparison of wall displacement.

Depth (m)	Wall Displacement When Excavating to 14.55 m (mm)				Depth (m)	Wall Displacement When Excavating to 19.7 m (mm)			
	Measured Values	This Paper	Liu et al. [41]	Lam and Bolton [21]		Measured Values	This Paper	Liu et al. [41]	Lam and Bolton [21]
0	−3.21	0.15	0	0	0	−4.31	0	0.12	0
2	0.25	1.32	0.86	1.83	2	0	2	3.26	2
2.5	1.2	2.05	1.54	3	2.5	1.5	2.5	4.32	2.5
3.5	2.6	3.25	2	4	3.5	3.5	3.5	6.57	3.5
4.5	4.36	4.52	3.4	5.4	4.5	4.9	4.5	8.38	4.5
5.5	6.68	6.82	5.72	7.7	5.5	6	5.5	10.51	5.5
6.5	8.34	8.51	7.1	9.42	6.5	7.72	6.5	12.58	6.5
7.5	9.44	9.38	8.1	10.2	7.5	11.12	7.5	14.88	7.5
8.5	9.88	10.15	8.6	11.05	8.5	14.94	8.5	18.2	8.5
9.5	9.87	10.33	8.9	11.34	9.5	18.89	9.5	20.08	9.5
10.5	9.34	9.53	8	10.48	10.5	22.69	10.5	23.6	10.5
11.5	7.85	8.33	6.9	9.41	11.5	25.85	11.5	26.8	11.5
12	7.32	7.56	6	8.42	12	27.69	12	28.3	12
13.5	5.34	6.27	4.8	7.18	13.5	31.13	13.5	31.8	13.5
14	5.01	5.7	3.8	6.8	14.5	32.61	14.5	33.07	14.5
15.5	4.2	5.2	3.4	5.7	15.5	33.27	15.5	33.8	15.5
16	4	4.9	3	5.2	16	33.31	16	33.5	16
18.5	3.3	4.1	2.4	4.6	18.5	29.64	18.5	29.87	18.5
21	2.8	3.8	2	3.7	21	21.8	21	23.8	21
23	2.4	3.4	1.6	3.2	23	18.5	23	19.5	23
25	2	3.1	1.2	2.2	25	16.2	25	14.3	25
26.5	2	2.9	0.8	1.5	26.5	14.8	26.5	12.5	26.5
27.5	2	2.8	0.5	1	27.5	14	27.5	11.5	27.5
28	1.9	2.7	0.1	0.4	28	13.5	28	10.8	28
28.5	1.9	2.7	0	0	28.5	13	28.5	9.5	28.5

5. Parametric Analysis

The accuracy of the IMSD solution relies on the selection of parameters. Parameters affecting the IMSD solution can be divided into two categories: internal and external parameters. Various parameter combinations affect the deformation energy to different degrees. Therefore, the selection of parameter combinations, such as the size of α_1 and α_2, and the determination of the deformation wavelength may present some challenges and uncertainties. The internal parameters include two parameters used in the deformation mechanism: the coefficient of the virtual fixed point location, α_1, and the influence range coefficient of excavation depth, α_2. The external parameters include parameters such as the soil internal friction angle, φ, the soil shear strength factor, ξ, the flexural stiffness of pile or wall, EI, and the compressive stiffness of support, EA. The internal parameters mainly change the deformation function form, and the external factors affect the maximum displacement increment of the MSD solution.

5.1. Effect of Virtual Fixed-Point Position Coefficients

Figure 9 shows the excavation displacements under different α_1. When $\alpha_1 = 0$, the excavation top displacement was zero, and the maximum displacement was near the excavation surface. As α_1 increased, the maximum excavation displacement and pile top displacement grew gradually, and the depth of the maximum excavation displacement shifted upward. When α_1 was small, the depth of the maximum pile displacement was positively correlated with the excavation depth. When α_1 increased to a certain extent, the depth of the maximum pile displacement gradually shifted upward with the excavation depth. When the maximum pile displacement occurred at the excavation top, it corresponded to the deformation pattern of the cantilevered excavation. Therefore, different values of α_1

can reflect the excavation deformation under different support conditions. A reasonable value of α_1 can be selected to calculate the MSD solution for different excavation types.

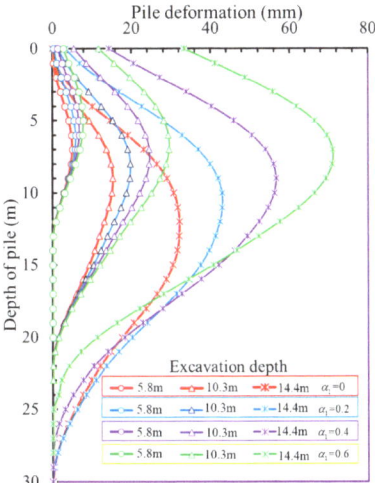

Figure 9. Pile deformation under different α_1.

Figure 10 shows the relationship between excavation depth and different increments under different α_1. From Figure 10, α_1 was positively correlated with the strength mobilization coefficient and maximum displacement increment. At the same excavation depth, the potential energy increment of the ABCF zone decreased and the maximum displacement increment gradually increased with increasing α_1. This result was because α_1 stretched the wavelength of the deformation function by $\alpha_1 h$ such that the actual integral area of the deformation function decreased. As α_1 increased, the more integral area was lost, and the internal energy incremental decreased more than the potential energy incremental. When the excavation depth was certain, compared to $\alpha_1 = 0$, the potential energy increment was reduced by 3%, 6.3%, and 10.6% when $\alpha_1 = 0.2, 0.4, 0.6$, while the internal energy increment was reduced by 8.9%, 16.7%, and 19.2%, respectively.

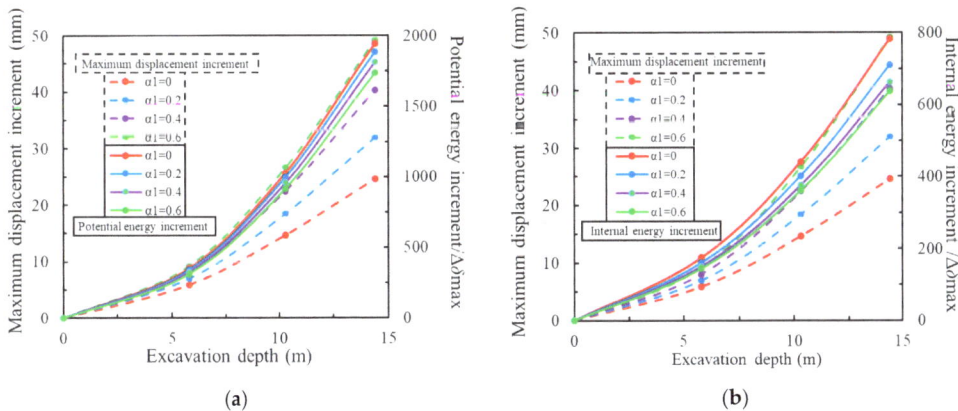

Figure 10. Relationship between excavation depth and different increments at different α_1: (**a**) potential energy increment; (**b**) internal energy increment.

5.2. Effect of the Influence Range Coefficient of Excavation Depth

Four sets of calculations with α_2 equal to 1, k (=1–1.5), 1.5, and 2, respectively, were taken to solve for the pile deformation by the IMSD method, where $\alpha_2 = k$ referred to the influence range determined by the method of calculating embedment depth. Similarly, the effect of the retaining structure and internal support on the deformation was not considered during the calculation of the MSD solution.

Figure 11 shows pile deformation under different α_2. From Figure 11, the increase of α_2 not only made the pile deformation pattern change but also significantly affected the maximum pile deformation. Contrary to the effect of α_1, α_2 caused a reduction in the depth of the maximum pile deformation. The pile bottom deformation, which was positively correlated with α_2, was zero for the pile with good embedment depth ($\alpha_2 < k$). When the excavation influence area exceeds the pile depth, the pile bottom may undergo a "kicking" deformation pattern with $\alpha_2 = 2$. When α_2 doubled, the maximum pile deformation was about a quarter of the original pile deformation. The depth of maximum pile deformation decreased by about $0.5h$, and the deformation influence range increased dramatically. In addition, α_2 can reflect the excavation deformation under different soil conditions. When α_2 was small, the deformation pattern was consistent with the excavation under better soil conditions. As α_2 increased, the deformation pattern was more similar to the excavation deformation characteristics in soft soil areas [5,19].

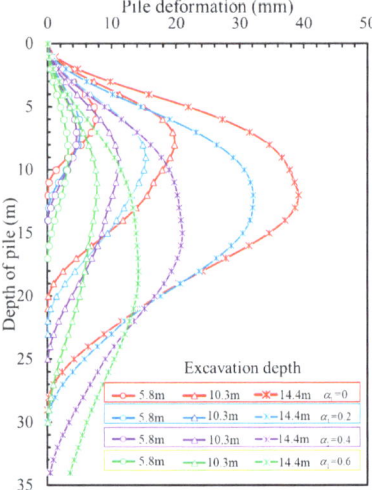

Figure 11. Pile deformation under different α_2.

Figure 12 shows the variation in energy increments with α_2 in different regions. From Figure 12, as α_2 kept increasing, the potential energy increment and internal energy increment in each zone increased, while the maximum displacement increment gradually became smaller. This change was because α_2 significantly increased the negative potential energy increment in the EFI zone. The increase in the sum of the potential energy increments in each zone was less than that of the internal energy increments. According to the formula $\int_A \gamma_{sat} \triangle \delta_v dA = \int_A \beta s_u \delta \gamma dA$, the mobilized soil strength coefficient, β, decreased with the increase of α_2, which resulted in the consequent decrease in the maximum pile displacement. The internal energy increment in the ABCD, CEF, FEH, and EFI regions when $\alpha_2 = 2$ was 1.3, 3, 3.1, and 3.3 times that of the $\alpha_2 = 1$, respectively.

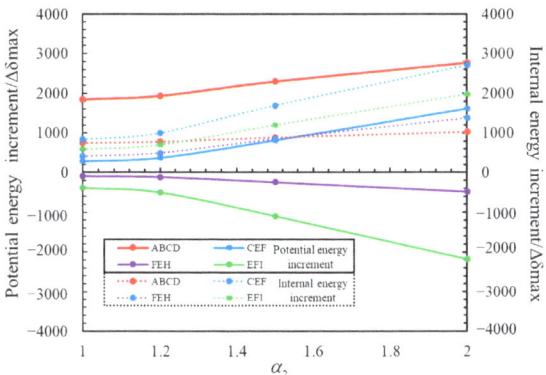

Figure 12. Variation rules of energy increment with α_2 in different zones.

5.3. Effect of Pile Bending Stiffness and Internal Support Stiffness

To analyze the role of α_1 and α_2 in the deformation mechanism, the effect of the retaining structure and internal support on the deformation energy was neglected. However, the deformation energy stored by retaining structure and internal support cannot be ignored in actual excavation engineering. The improved MSD method using an iterative method to calculate the maximum incremental deformation is a necessary improvement.

Figure 13 shows the relationship between the maximum displacement increment and excavation depth under different α_1 and α_2. From Figure 13a, the maximum displacement increment was inversely proportional to α_1. This result was because α_1 increased the pile top deformation and decreased the deformation influence wavelength. This action increased the incremental deformation energy of both the supporting structure and internal support, resulting in a decrease in the soil strength mobilization factor, which in turn suppressed the maximum incremental deformation in the MSD solution. From Figure 13b, the maximum displacement increment decreased only when α_2 was small. This change was because α_2 caused the deformation function value at the internal support position to decrease substantially, and the decrease degree was greater as α_2 increased. Therefore, the bending deformation energy incremental of the retaining structure and the compression deformation energy incremental of the internal support were positively and negatively correlated with α_1 and α_2, respectively.

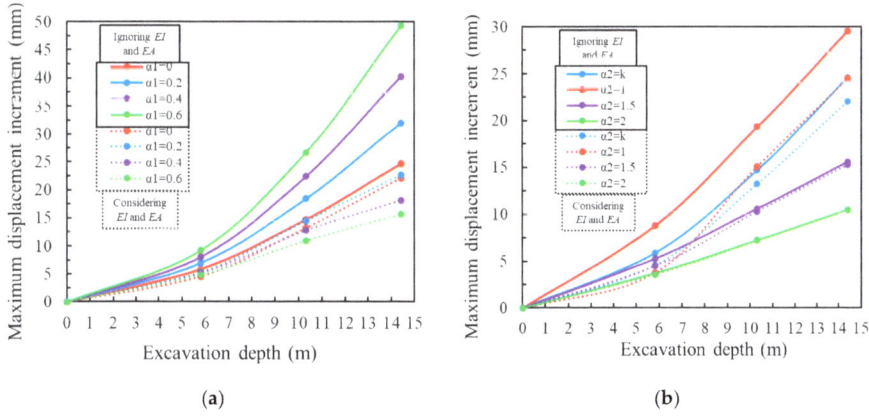

Figure 13. Relationship between maximum displacement increment and excavation depth: (**a**) different α_1; (**b**) different α_2.

Figure 14 shows the effect of different stiffness of the retaining structure and internal support on excavation deformation, where k_u and k_v refer to the bending stiffness discount factor of the pile and support, respectively. From Figure 14, the compressive stiffness of the internal support inhibited the excavation deformation more than the pile stiffness. When the excavation depth was small, the pile bending stiffness could play a better inhibiting deformation effect more than the compressive stiffness of internal support, and the pattern was reversed for larger excavation depths. This action was because the bending deformation energy incremental depended on the pile deformation curvature, and the compression deformation energy incremental of the internal support depended on the displacement at the support.

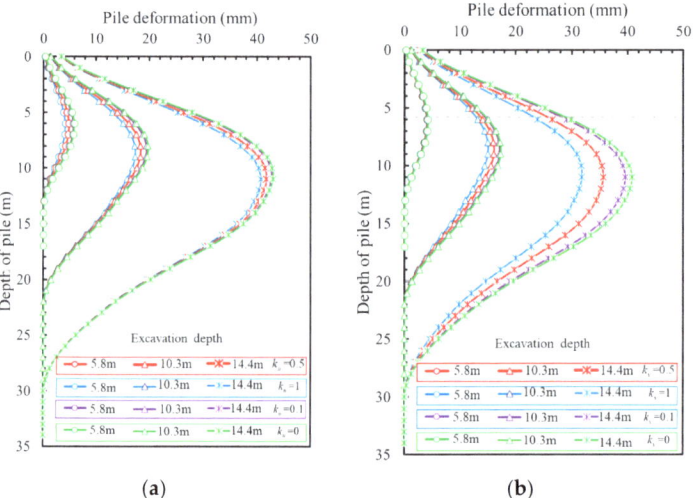

Figure 14. Effect of different retaining structure stiffness on excavation deformation: (**a**) piles; (**b**) internal support.

5.4. Effect of Soil Friction Angle

In the modified MSD method, the angle of internal friction not only affects the plastic deformation mechanism and soil shear strength but also affects the deformation-influenced wavelength. Three sets of calculations with $\varphi = 20°$, $24°$, $28°$ were taken to solve for pile deformation by the IMSD method.

Figure 15 shows the pile deformation under different internal friction angles. From Figure 15, pile deformation was inversely correlated with the soil friction angle. Pile deformation increased nonlinearly with decreasing internal friction angle, which was consistent with Liu et al. [41]. Relevant measured results [46] show that the maximum pile displacement was about $0.25H$ above the excavation surface when the soil conditions were good. While the soil condition was poor, the maximum pile displacement was near the excavation surface. When $\varphi = 20°$, the deformation influence range was more than the embedment depth of the pile. Horizontal displacements were observed at the pile bottom, which was a typical deformation pattern when the embedment depth was insufficient.

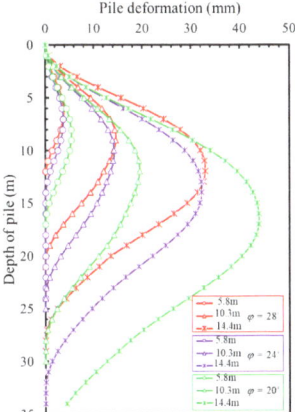

Figure 15. Pile deformation for different internal friction angles.

5.5. Effect of Soil Shear Strength Coefficients

The soil shear strength coefficients play an important role in calculating the internal energy increment in each plastic deformation zone. In this paper, an undrained shear strength formula considering the soil anisotropy was used. Taking $K_0 = 0.5$, $\varphi' = 33°$, $C_c = 0.33$, and $C_s = 0.027$, the ratio of the undrained shear strength to the overlying effective stress for different angles, ξ, can be obtained (see Table 2). The effect of four sets of calculations with soil shear strength coefficients taken as k, 0.2, 0.25, and 0.3 on the excavation MSD solution was investigated.

Table 2. The ratio of undrained shear strength to overlying effective stress for different angles.

θ	0°	30°	45°	60°	90°	Average Value
$S_{u\alpha}/\sigma_v$	0.255	0.313	0.300	0.262	0.153	0.257

Figure 16 shows the pile deformation under different soil shear strength coefficients. From Figure 16, the pile deformation was inversely proportional to ξ. The undrained soil shear strength formula used in this paper yielded pile deformation very close to $\xi = 0.25$. This result was because the ξ of this example was closer to the average value of ξ. The change in the soil shear strength coefficients directly affected the internal energy increment in the MSD method. A smaller ξ meant that the soil shear strength was lower; the greater the mobilization coefficient produced by exerting the same shear strength. The soil body needed to produce large deformations for the deformation mechanism to reach equilibrium.

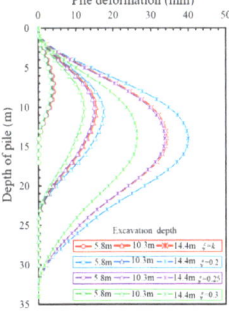

Figure 16. Pile deformation under different ξ.

6. Discussion

The deformation mechanisms proposed by Lam and Bolton [21] and Liu et al. [41] suffered from the problems of uncoordinated displacements and the inability to consider the effects of soil parameters. And the incremental deformation function ignored the compressive deformation energy of the first support. Therefore, based on the studies of Lam and Bolton [21] and Liu et al. [41], this paper proposes an improved plastic deformation field that can consider the effect of soil friction angle. Meanwhile, two parameters, the virtual fixed point location coefficient and the influence range coefficient of excavation depth, were introduced into the incremental deformation function, so as to reflect the influence of excavation depth and the first support on the deformation energy. Compared with the models proposed by Lam and Bolton [21] and Liu et al. [41], the accuracy of the proposed model in this paper was improved by 20–30%. This result indicated that the improved plastic deformation mechanism and incremental deformation function in this paper better reflected the actual incremental deformation of the excavation.

The model proposed in this paper is suitable for use in excavation projects with multiple internal supports combined with flexible retaining walls under stratified soil conditions. However, the proposed model does not consider the influence of complex factors such as overloading. And the selection of the soil pressure model in the deformation influence wavelength leads to a certain error in the calculated value, which needs further research.

7. Limitation

Massive field instrumentation data have already demonstrated that basal heave within an excavation enclosure results largely from the rebound of basal strata below excavation levels rather than the flow of ground behind the retaining wall into the excavation, the ground settlement behind the retaining wall derived from lateral wall movement rather than contributing to the basal heave [47,48]. For most cases in practice, the soft basal strata would be improved by ground treatment prior to soil removal, and the retaining wall would be designed with an adequate embedment length [49–51]. The ground movement pattern assumed in the MSD model (Figure 1) only works for a special condition, i.e., the basal strata is too soft or the length of embedded retaining wall is insufficient to constrain a kicking-out failure of the retaining wall, and then the ground behind the wall would slide into the excavation pushing the basal strata upwards. Therefore, further research and improvement of the ground movement pattern assumed in the MSD model (Figure 1) is needed in the future.

8. Conclusions

This paper mainly proposes a multi-support excavation deformation analysis method based on the improved MSD method. The main conclusions follow:

(1) Based on the traditional MSD method, an improved mobilized strength design (IMSD) method for multi-support excavation deformation analysis is proposed. The proposed model compensates for the shortcomings of the traditional MSD method; the improved incremental deformation mechanism further considers the effect of the soil friction angle, and the effect of excavation depth and the first support on deformation energy is also considered. The proposed IMSD method effectively improves the accuracy and reliability of soil deformation predictions by establishing virtual fixed points and excavation depth influence coefficients.

(2) Through an engineering case study, we found that the traditional MSD method underestimates the excavation deformation by 25% and the surface settlement by 13% compared to the measured results. The accuracy of the improved MSD solution has increased by 20–30%, which is more consistent with the measured data. This finding indicates that the IMSD method, considering the effect of soil parameters and boundary conditions, is more reasonable.

(3) The effect of internal and external parameters on the excavation deformation is discussed. The influence degree of internal and external parameters on excavation defor-

mation is 30–40% and 10–20%, respectively. The virtual fixation point location coefficient and the soil friction angle have the greatest influence degree on the excavation deformation. The $α_1$ mainly affects the deformation pattern, while $α_2$ and the stiffness of the retaining structure mainly affects the maximum displacement increment.

(4) Potential applications of this method in different types of underground projects (such as subway construction and high-rise building foundations) can be explored, along with how to address challenges posed by complex environments. Furthermore, optimizing parameter selection, integrating new technologies (like artificial intelligence or machine learning) to enhance the intelligence level of the model, or developing adaptive models to respond to changes in different geological conditions will be studied in the future.

Author Contributions: Conceptualization, B.T. and M.H.; methodology, L.L.; validation, L.L. and Z.X.; formal analysis, J.J.; investigation, L.L., Z.X. and J.J.; resources, L.L.; data curation, B.T.; writing—original draft preparation, M.H.; writing—review and editing, M.H.; visualization, J.J. and Z.X.; supervision, L.L. funding acquisition, B.T., Z.X., J.J. and L.L. All authors have read and agreed to the published version of the manuscript.

Funding: This research was funded by the Collaborative Innovation Platform Project of Fuzhou-Xiamen-Quanzhou National Self-Innovation Zone, grant number 3502ZCQXT2022002; Science and technology plan of Fujian Province, grant number 2022I0014, 2023Y4007; Fundamental Research Funds for the Central Universities, grant number ZQN-1012; National Nature Science Foundation of China, grant number 52278332; and the Youth Program of Natural Science Foundation of Jiangsu Province, grant number BK20221136.

Data Availability Statement: Data will be made available upon request.

Conflicts of Interest: The authors declare no conflicts of interest.

References

1. Du, C.; Xu, Z.; Yi, F.; Gao, J.; Shi, K. Bearing capacity mechanism of soilbagged graphite tailings. *Bull. Eng. Geol. Environ.* **2024**, *83*, 24. [CrossRef]
2. Li, Q.; Zhu, Z. Calibration of an elastoplastic model of sand liquefaction using the swarm intelligence with a multi-objective function. *J. Rock. Mech. Geotech.* **2023**, *15*, 789–802. [CrossRef]
3. Yang, M.; Wu, R.; Tong, C.; Chen, J.; Tang, B. Displacement Analyses of Diaphragm Wall in Small-Scale Deep Excavation Considering Joints between Panels. *Buildings* **2024**, *14*, 1449. [CrossRef]
4. Zhang, D. Influences of Deep Foundation Pit Excavation on the Stability of Adjacent Ancient Buildings. *Buildings* **2023**, *13*, 2004. [CrossRef]
5. Han, M.; Chen, X.; Jia, J.; Tu, B. Coupled analytical method for braced excavation based on the Pasternak foundation model and nonlinear p–y curve model. *Int. J. Geomech.* **2024**, *24*, 04024180. [CrossRef]
6. Lu, D.; Liang, J.; Du, X.; Ma, C.; Gao, Z. Fractional elastoplastic constitutive model for soils based on a novel 3D fractional plastic flow rule. *Comput. Geotech.* **2019**, *105*, 277–290. [CrossRef]
7. Lu, D.; Ma, C.; Du, X.; Jin, L.; Gong, Q. Development of a new nonlinear unified strength theory for geomaterials based on the characteristic stress concept. *Int. J. Geomech.* **2017**, *17*, 04016058. [CrossRef]
8. Yao, C.; Zhong, H.; Zhu, Z. Development of a Large Shaking Table Test for Sand Liquefaction Analysis. *Lithosphere* **2024**, *2024*, 137. [CrossRef]
9. Zhao, J.; Zhu, Z.; Zhang, D.; Wang, H.; Li, X. Assessment of fabric characteristics with the development of sand liquefaction in cyclic triaxial tests: A DEM study. *Soil. Dyn. Earthq. Eng.* **2024**, *176*, 108343. [CrossRef]
10. He, B.G.; Lin, B.; Li, H.P.; Zhu, S.Q. Suggested method of utilizing soil arching for optimizing the design of strutted excavations. *Tunn. Undergr. Sp. Tech.* **2024**, *143*, 105450. [CrossRef]
11. Zheng, G.; Guo, Z.; Zhou, H.; He, X. Design method for wall deformation and soil movement of excavations with inclined retaining walls in sand. *Int. J. Geomech.* **2024**, *24*, 04024042. [CrossRef]
12. Wu, S.; Han, L.; Cheng, Z.; Zhang, X.; Cheng, H. Study on the limit equilibrium slice method considering characteristics of inter-slice normal forces distribution: The improved Spencer method. *Environ. Earth. Sci.* **2019**, *78*, 611. [CrossRef]
13. Zhang, Z.; Huang, M.; Xu, C.; Jiang, Y.; Wang, W. Simplified solution for tunnel-soil-pile interaction in Pasternak's foundation model. *Tunn. Undergr. Sp. Tech.* **2018**, *78*, 146–158. [CrossRef]
14. Han, M.; Chen, X.; Li, Z.; Jia, J. Improved inverse analysis methods and modified apparent earth pressure for braced excavations in soft clay. *Comput. Geotech.* **2023**, *159*, 105456. [CrossRef]
15. Han, M.; Li, Z.; Jia, J.; Bao, X.; Mei, G.; Liu, L. Force system conversion mechanisms of retaining structures for subway excavation in soft soil. *Bull. Eng. Geol. Environ.* **2023**, *82*, 262. [CrossRef]

16. Mu, L.; Huang, M. Small strain based method for predicting three-dimensional soil displacements induced by braced excavation. *Tunn. Undergr. Sp. Tech.* **2016**, *52*, 12–22. [CrossRef]
17. Kung, G.T.; Juang, C.H.; Hsiao, E.C.; Hashash, Y.M. Simplified model for wall deflection and ground-surface settlement caused by braced excavation in clays. *J. Geotech. Geoenviron.* **2007**, *133*, 731–747. [CrossRef]
18. Mu, L.; Chen, W.; Huang, M.; Lu, Q. Hybrid method for predicting the response of a pile-raft foundation to adjacent braced excavation. *Int. J. Geomech.* **2020**, *20*, 04020026. [CrossRef]
19. Han, M.; Chen, X.; Jia, J. Analytical solution for displacement-dependent 3D earth pressure on flexible walls of foundation pits in layered cohesive soil. *Acta Geotech.* **2024**, *19*, 5249–5275. [CrossRef]
20. Bolton, M.; Powrie, W.; Symons, I. The design of stiff in-situ walls retaining overconsolidated clay: Part II, long term behaviour. *Ground Eng.* **1990**, *23*, 24–28.
21. Lam, S.; Bolton, M. Energy conservation as a principle underlying mobilizable strength design for deep excavations. *J. Geotech. Geoenviron.* **2011**, *137*, 1062–1074. [CrossRef]
22. Wang, L.; Liu, Y.; Hong, Y.; Liu, S. Predicting deformation of multipropped excavations in soft clay with a modified mobilizable strength design (MMSD) method. *Comput. Geotech.* **2018**, *104*, 54–68. [CrossRef]
23. Bolton, M.; Powrie, W.; Symons, I. The design of stiff in situ walls retaining overconsolidated clay part 1: Short term behaviour. *Ground Eng.* **1990**, *23*, 10–21.
24. Bolton, M.D.; Lam, S.-Y.; Vardanega, P.J.; Ng, C.W.; Ma, X. Ground movements due to deep excavations in Shanghai: Design charts. *Front. Struct. Civ. Eng.* **2014**, *8*, 201–236. [CrossRef]
25. Li, S.; Huang, M.; Yu, J. Continuous field based upper-bound analysis for the undrained bearing capacity of strip footings resting near clay slopes with linearly increased strength. *Comput. Geotech.* **2019**, *105*, 168–182. [CrossRef]
26. Dan, K.; Sahu, R. A theoretical study on ground movement prediction for braced excavation in soft clay. *Int. J. Geotech. Eng.* **2012**, *6*, 53–64. [CrossRef]
27. Lei, G.; Gong, X. Analysis of lateral displacement law of deep foundation pit support in soft soil based on improved MSD method. *Adv. Civ. Eng.* **2021**, *2021*, 5550214. [CrossRef]
28. Lam, S.; Ma, X.; Bolton, M. Analysis of Case Histories on Deep Excavations in Marine Clay. In *Deep and Underground Excavations*; ASCE: Reston, VA, USA, 2010; pp. 37–42.
29. Bolton, M. Using centrifuge models to define deformation mechanisms and generate design methods. In *Deformation Characteristics of Geomaterials*; ISSMGE-TC29; IOS Press: Amsterdam, The Netherlands, 2011; pp. 181–197.
30. Zheng, G.; He, X.; Zhou, H. A Prediction Model for the Deformation of an Embedded Cantilever Retaining Wall in Sand. *Int. J. Geomech.* **2023**, *23*, 06023001. [CrossRef]
31. Zheng, G.; Wang, F.; Nie, D.; Diao, Y.; Yu, D.; Cheng, X. Mobilizable strength design for multibench retained excavation. *Math. Probl. Eng.* **2018**, *2018*, 8402601. [CrossRef]
32. Liu, X.; Fang, Q.; Zhang, D.; Liu, Y. Energy-based prediction of volume loss ratio and plastic zone dimension of shallow tunnelling. *Comput. Geotech.* **2020**, *118*, 103343. [CrossRef]
33. Vardanega, P.; Bolton, M. Strength mobilization in clays and silts. *Can. Geotech. J.* **2011**, *48*, 1485–1503. [CrossRef]
34. Vardanega, P.; Bolton, M. Design of geostructural systems. *ASCE-ASME J. Risk Uncertain. Eng. Syst. Part A Civ. Eng.* **2016**, *2*, 04015017. [CrossRef]
35. Lam, S.; Haigh, S.; Bolton, M. Understanding ground deformation mechanisms for multi-propped excavation in soft clay. *Soils Found.* **2014**, *54*, 296–312. [CrossRef]
36. McMahon, B.; Bolton, M. Centrifuge experiments on the settlement of circular foundations on clay. *Can. Geotech. J.* **2014**, *51*, 610–620. [CrossRef]
37. Osman, A.S.; Bolton, M.D. Ground movement predictions for braced excavations in undrained clay. *J. Geotech. Geoenviron.* **2006**, *132*, 465–477. [CrossRef]
38. Bhattacharya, S.; Lombardi, D.; Amani, S.; Aleem, M.; Prakhya, G.; Adhikari, S.; Aliyu, A.; Alexander, N.; Wang, Y.; Cui, L. Physical modelling of offshore wind turbine foundations for TRL (technology readiness level) studies. *J. Mar. Sci. Eng.* **2021**, *9*, 589. [CrossRef]
39. Klar, A.; Leung, Y.-F. Simple energy-based method for nonlinear analysis of incompressible pile groups in clays. *J. Geotech. Geoenviron.* **2009**, *135*, 960–965. [CrossRef]
40. Osman, A.S.; Bolton, M.D. A new design method for retaining walls in clay. *Can. Geotech. J.* **2004**, *41*, 451–466. [CrossRef]
41. Liu, M.; Qian, F.; Dingli, Z.; Yanjuan, H. Prediction of dynamic deformation of excavation based on improved msd method. *Chin. J. Rock Mech. Eng.* **2018**, *37*, 1700–1707.
42. Wang, H.; Wang, W.; Huang, M.; Xu, Z. Modified mobilizable strength design (MSD) method on deformation predictions of foundation pit. *Chin. J. Rock Mech. Eng.* **2011**, *30* (Suppl. S1), 3245–3251.
43. O'rourke, T.D. Base stability and ground movement prediction for excavations in soft clay. In *Retaining Structures*; Robinson Coll: Cambridge, UK, 1993; pp. 657–686.
44. Casagrande, A.; Carillo, N. Shear failure of anisotropic soil. *J. Boston Soc. Civ. Eng.* **1944**, *31*, 74–87.
45. Tan, Y.; Zhu, H.; Peng, F.; Karlsrud, K.; Wei, B. Characterization of semi-top-down excavation for subway station in Shanghai soft ground. *Tunn. Undergr. Sp. Tech.* **2017**, *68*, 244–261. [CrossRef]

46. Han, M.; Li, Z.; Mei, G.; Bao, X.; Jia, J.; Liu, L.; Li, Y. Characteristics of subway excavation in soft soil and protective effects of partition wall on the historical building and pile foundation building. *Bull. Eng. Geol. Environ.* **2022**, *81*, 307. [CrossRef]
47. Tan, Y. Discussion of "Numerical Study of the Effect of Ground Improvement on Basal Heave Stability for Deep Excavations in Normally Consolidated Clays". *J. Geotech. Geoenviron.* **2024**, *150*, 07024005. [CrossRef]
48. Tan, Y.; Lu, Y.; Wang, D. Synchronous-cross zoned excavation of the oversized basement of Shanghai International Financial Centre by combination of bottom-up and top-down methods: Structural and geotechnical behaviors. *Tunn. Undergr. Space Technol.* **2024**, *153*, 106023. [CrossRef]
49. Long, M. Database for retaining wall and ground movements due to deep excavations. *J. Geotech. Geoenviron.* **2001**, *127*, 203–224. [CrossRef]
50. Moormann, C. Analysis of wall and ground movements due to deep excavations in soft soil based on a new worldwide database. *Soils Found.* **2004**, *44*, 87–98. [CrossRef]
51. Tan, Y.; Fan, D.; Lu, Y. Statistical analyses on a database of deep excavations in Shanghai soft clays in China from 1995–2018. *Pract. Period. Struct.* **2022**, *27*, 04021067. [CrossRef]

Disclaimer/Publisher's Note: The statements, opinions and data contained in all publications are solely those of the individual author(s) and contributor(s) and not of MDPI and/or the editor(s). MDPI and/or the editor(s) disclaim responsibility for any injury to people or property resulting from any ideas, methods, instructions or products referred to in the content.

Article

Influence of Excavation Radius on Behavior of Circular Foundation Pits Supported by Prefabricated Recyclable Structures: Full-Scale Experimental and Numerical Analysis

Lichao Chen [1,2,3], Chengchao Guo [1,2,3,4,*], Yanhui Pan [4], Huqing Liang [5], Mengxiong Tang [5] and Kejie Zhai [6,*]

[1] School of Civil Engineering, Sun Yat-sen University, Zhuhai 519082, China; chenlch8@mail3.sysu.edu.cn
[2] Southern Marine Science and Engineering Guangdong Laboratory, Zhuhai 519000, China
[3] Guangdong Research Center for Underground Space Exploitation Technology, Guangzhou 510275, China
[4] Best Dr Infrastructure Hospital, Zhumadian 463000, China; pyh511@126.com
[5] Guangzhou Municipal Construction Group Co., Ltd., Guangzhou 510275, China
[6] School of Water Conservancy and Transportation, Zhengzhou University, Zhengzhou 450001, China
* Correspondence: guochch25@mail.sysu.edu.cn (C.G.); kejiezhai@zzu.edu.cn (K.Z.)

Abstract: A foundation pit's excavation area, which is determined by its radius in a circular foundation pit, exerts a considerable influence on the pit's behavior. Using a full-scale experiment on a circular foundation pit retained by a prefabricated recyclable supporting structure (PRSS), this study develops a series of axisymmetric numerical models to systematically investigate the influence of excavation radius on the pit's deformation, stress, and stability. Furthermore, simulation results from axisymmetric models are compared with those from plane strain models to illustrate the influence mechanism. The results show that at a given excavation depth, the deflection and bending moments of the supporting piles, the earth pressure on the non-excavation side, and ground surface settlement increase with the enlarged excavation radius, but the increase rate progressively decreases. However, the foundation pit's safety factor decreases with an increasing excavation radius and gradually stabilizes. When the excavation radius exceeds 50 m, its influence on the foundation pit's behavior significantly diminishes. The axisymmetric model results closely approximate those from the plane strain models, suggesting that the spatial arching effects of the circular foundation pit can be disregarded.

Keywords: circular foundation pit; recyclable structure; full-scale experiment; numerical simulation; deformation; earth pressure; stability

Citation: Chen, L.; Guo, C.; Pan, Y.; Liang, H.; Tang, M.; Zhai, K. Influence of Excavation Radius on Behavior of Circular Foundation Pits Supported by Prefabricated Recyclable Structures: Full-Scale Experimental and Numerical Analysis. *Buildings* **2024**, *14*, 3110. https://doi.org/10.3390/buildings14103110

Academic Editor: Eugeniusz Koda

Received: 23 August 2024
Revised: 19 September 2024
Accepted: 26 September 2024
Published: 27 September 2024

Copyright: © 2024 by the authors. Licensee MDPI, Basel, Switzerland. This article is an open access article distributed under the terms and conditions of the Creative Commons Attribution (CC BY) license (https://creativecommons.org/licenses/by/4.0/).

1. Introduction

The rapid urbanization of China has accelerated the expansion of underground infrastructure, resulting in a substantial rise in foundation pit projects. Consequently, foundation pits with varying excavation areas have become increasingly prevalent. The performance of a foundation pit is significantly influenced by the dimensions of its planar excavation area [1,2]. However, this influence is not considered in the current design methodologies for foundation pit supporting structures [3], resulting in a large deviation in observed forces and deformations compared with those calculated in designs [4]. Thus, analyzing the behavior of foundation pits with different excavation areas is essential for practical applications.

Field monitoring data indicate that, for similar excavation depths and geological conditions, the movements of retaining walls and the surrounding soil are more significant in foundation pits with larger excavation areas than in pits with smaller excavation areas [5–8]. In a rectangular foundation pit, the excavation width determines the excavation area, whereas for a circular foundation pit, the determining parameter is the excavation radius. Using 2D finite-element analysis, Mana and Clough [9] studied foundation pit deformation relative to excavation width. Based on a theoretical analysis, Wang [10] pointed out that a smaller excavation width results in a higher safety factor for the foundation pit. Based on several case studies of foundation pits with various excavation widths, Xiao et al. [11] and Park [12] claimed that increasing the excavation width initially increases both lateral wall deflection and ground settlement, though these values generally stabilize afterward. Furthermore, the impact of width on foundation pit performance appears to be largely independent of the retaining wall type. In a comparative analysis of monitoring data from several circular foundation pits, Tan and Wang [13] found that for foundation pits exceeding 30,000 m^2 in area, deformations are three to five times greater than those of typical small foundation pits with areas not exceeding 6,000 m^2. Additionally, the influence zone of large foundation pits extends much further than that of small foundation pits. Zeng et al. [14] indicated that the deformation in retaining walls and surrounding soil due to pre-excavation dewatering increases when the foundation pit widens. However, a critical foundation pit width exists, within which deformations escalate rapidly; beyond this critical width, the foundation pit's behavior slightly varies. Huang et al. [15] concluded that at a given excavation depth, the passive zone's capacity to reduce deformations caused by excavation decreases as the excavation width expands. This increases deformations in the retaining wall and the surrounding soil, though the increase rate gradually decreases.

Compared with the many studies on the influence of excavation width on the performance of rectangular foundation pits, there have been limited investigations of the impact of excavation radius on the performance of circular foundation pits. Nevertheless, some researchers have noted the behavior of circular foundation pits during construction and observed that deformations in these pits significantly differ from typical deformation patterns in retaining walls [16–18]. This is because the behavior of the soil surrounding circular foundation pits is influenced by the arching effect [19], wherein lateral earth pressures tangentially compress and radially extend. Earth pressure on retaining walls in circular foundation pits decreases with an increasing radius [20,21]. Moreover, for circular foundation pits, the diameter rather than the penetration ratio of the retaining wall plays a primary role in determining the pit's behavior [22]. Most numerical simulations of circular foundation pit issues use 2D axisymmetric models [23–27]. Keshavarz and Ebrahimi [28] demonstrated that passive lateral earth pressure in axial symmetry yields greater results than those under plane strain conditions. The above research on the influence of excavation radius on circular foundation pits has primarily involved experimental or theoretical studies of soil pressure distribution or case studies on the performance of foundation pits with specific radii. There is a lack of research using numerical modeling methods to study the performance of circular foundation pits with different radii.

PRSS is a novel retaining system that consists of supporting piles, walings, steel plates, and resilient waterproofing polymers [29–32]. Due to its high construction efficiency, reusability, and excellent structural performance, it is widely used in circular foundation pits with varying excavation radii, such as working shafts, underground grain silos, and automated underground parking garages [33,34]. Therefore, it is necessary to study the influence of excavation radius on the behavior of circular foundation pits to deepen our understanding of those supported by PRSSs or other retaining wall types [35,36]. This study includes a full-scale experiment on a circular foundation pit supported by PRSSs. Subsequently, a series of 2D axisymmetric numerical models were developed based on this experiment, and field monitoring data were used for validation. The influence of excavation radius on the behavior of the circular foundation pit, including the deflection and bending moments of the supporting piles, earth pressure, ground surface settlement, and the safety factor, was systematically analyzed. In addition, simulation results from axisymmetric models are compared with those from plane strain models to illustrate this influence mechanism. Through a thorough investigation of these factors, this study significantly enhances our understanding of how excavation radius impacts the behavior of circular foundation pits supported by PRSSs or similar retaining systems.

2. Full-Scale Experimental Scheme

2.1. Site and Structure Description

The full-scale experiment took place in Pingyu County, Zhumadian, China. Figure 1 shows that the foundation pit is cylindrical, with a 5 m radius and a maximum depth of 9 m. The supporting piles are 12 m long, spaced 1.57 m apart [37]. Additionally, a waling is set up at each 3 m interval beneath the ground surface. Steel plates support the soil between the support piles, with dimensions of 12 m in length, 1.45 m in width, and 8 mm in thickness. To prevent excessive deformation in these plates, 12 m long beams are embedded in front of them.

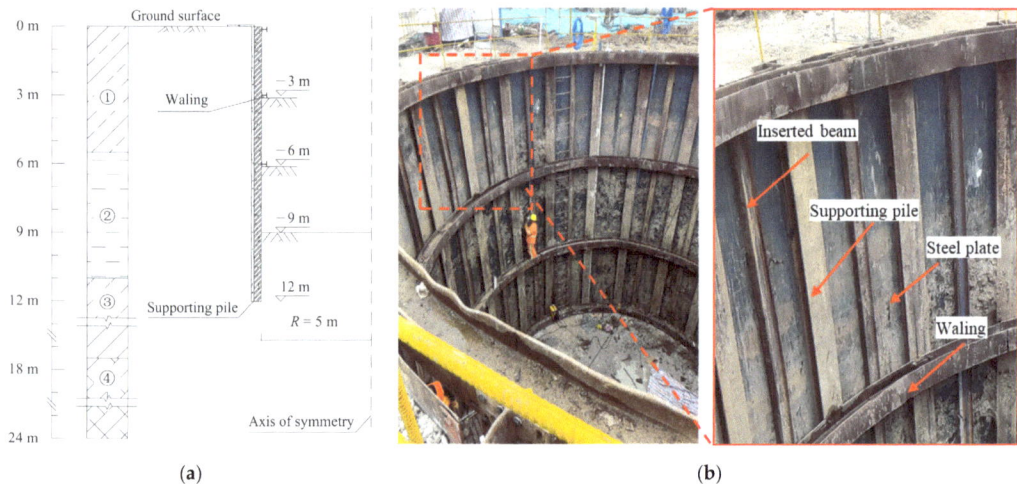

Figure 1. The circular foundation pit supported by PRSSs: (**a**) schematic diagram of profile view; (**b**) aerial top view.

A thorough geotechnical investigation revealed the presence of four soil layers within a depth range of 24 m, all classified as silty clay. These layers are designated as ①, ②, ③, and ④, and their fundamental properties are detailed in Table 1. In Table 1, the cone penetration resistance in the cone penetration test (CPT) and the blow counts of the standard penetration test (SPT) were obtained through field investigation, with other parameters obtained from laboratory testing of soil samples. Additionally, the groundwater table was 3.5 m beneath the surface.

Table 1. Basic parameters of soil layers at the site.

Soil Layers	Unit Weight, γ (kN/m³)	Water Content, w (%)	Void Ratio, e	Effective Cohesion, c' (kPa)	Effective Friction Angle, φ' (°)	Plasticity Index, I_P (%)	Liquidity Index, I_L	Compression Modulus, E_s (MPa)	Cone Resistance in CPT, q_c (MPa)	Blow Count of SPT, N	Permeability Coefficient, K (m/day)
①	19.18	23.6	0.719	28.5	13.3	12.7	0.38	7.76	1	4.5	0.08
②	19.43	23.8	0.704	31.6	14.2	13.9	0.33	8.09	1.3	10.3	0.08
③	19.18	24.7	0.738	30.8	13.4	13.9	0.33	8.37	2.2	8.9	0.12
④	19.38	23.3	0.702	31.5	14.6	13.8	0.29	9.01	1.8	16.4	0.09

2.2. Construction Process

Figure 2 illustrates the construction process for a foundation pit supported by a PRSS. The process begins with installing supporting piles in bored holes. Next, a first-level waling is assembled to connect these supporting piles. Steel plates are then embedded in the soil.

Subsequently, the groundwater level inside the foundation pit is lowered to −10 m below the ground surface through four dewatering wells. After excavating to the first design depth, a second-level waling is installed. To improve the PRSS's impermeability, expanded polyurethane is used as a grouting material behind the steel plates. This polyurethane expands upon application, filling gaps and voids to create a more effective barrier against water infiltration, significantly enhancing the PRSS's ability to prevent water from penetrating the structural components. The excavation, waling installation, and grouting cycle is repeated until the final depth is achieved. A more detailed PRSS construction procedure in practical engineering can be found in studies by Wang et al. [38] and Pan et al. [33].

Figure 2. Construction process: (**a**) installing supporting piles; (**b**) installing first-layer waling; (**c**) installing steel plates; (**d**) excavating soil and installing second-layer waling; (**e**) injecting polyurethane behind the steel plates; (**f**) repeating steps (**d**,**e**) until the final depth is reached.

2.3. Instrumentation

To monitor the foundation pit's behavior, various instruments were installed, as depicted in Figures 3 and 4. Inclinometer casings were placed on the supporting piles to measure lateral displacement caused by excavation and dewatering processes. The DM601 inclinometer is utilized, offering an accuracy of ±2 mm per 25 m. Horizontal displacements at the top of the supporting piles were measured using a total station, which served as a reference point for correcting the deflection of the supporting piles. Earth pressure cells were positioned on the non-excavation side of the supporting piles to assess pressure changes. The type of the soil pressure cell is DMTY, with an accuracy of ≤0.5% FS. Prior to installation, the earth pressure cells undergo a calibration process, after which their initial value is recorded upon completion of the installation. Additionally, strain-sensing optical fibers were attached to the supporting piles to measure bending moments. The NZS-DSS-C06 strain-sensing optical fiber is utilized, which exhibits excellent coupling with the measured object through the use of adhesives, ensuring high strain transfer performance. Furthermore, the DM-JL hydrostatic levels were positioned at the ground surface outside the foundation pit to monitor ground surface settlement, with an accuracy of 0.001 mm. To minimize external disturbances, the instrument's base is anchored in concrete at a depth of 0.5 m below the surface. Corrections for the measured settlement are performed using reference points located outside the excavation's area of influence. Additionally, four dewatering wells were uniformly installed 1.5 m around the foundation pit to keep the working face dry during construction. Moreover, groundwater observation wells were installed outside the excavation to monitor groundwater level variations.

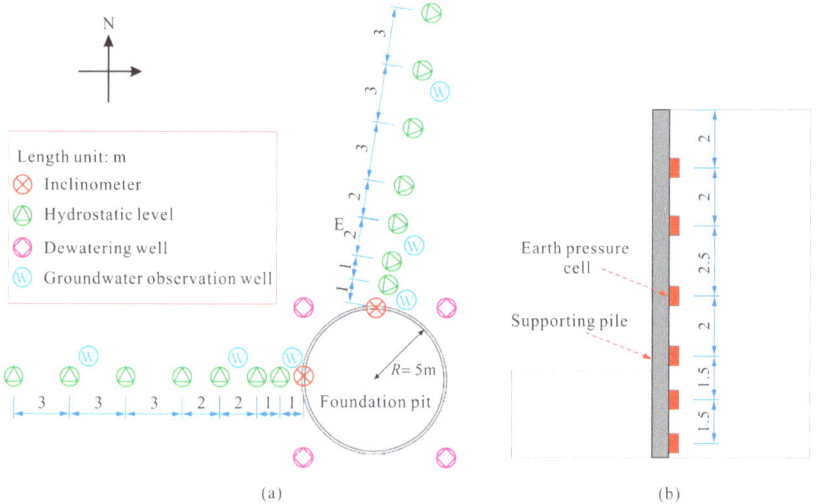

Figure 3. Instrumentation layout: (**a**) plane view; (**b**) cross-section view.

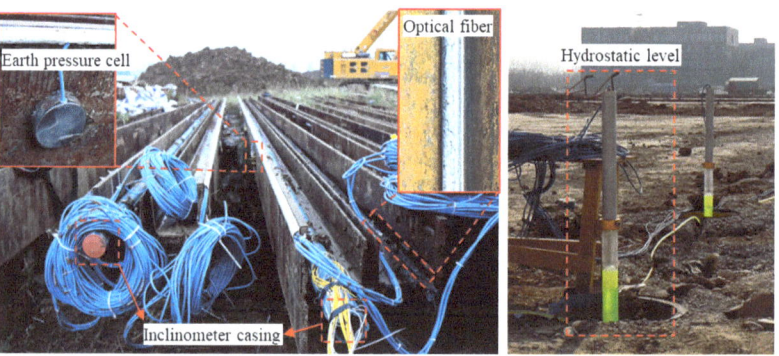

Figure 4. Instrumentation details.

3. Numerical Simulation

3.1. Finite-Element Model and Boundary Conditions

Extensive analyses of the foundation pit were performed using the finite-element software Plaxis 2D, version 2023.2. A series of 2D axisymmetric models were established, as was a plane strain model. The basic axisymmetric and plane strain models are presented in Figure 5; H_p is the length of the supporting pile, which is equal to the sum of the excavation depth (H_e) and the embedment depth (H_d). The model dimensions used in the analysis are $R + 5H_e$ in length and $2H_p$ in width, ensuring that the numerical results are not affected by the boundaries [39]. Horizontal movement constraints (roller support) are applied to the vertical boundaries of the models, while both horizontal and vertical movement constraints (pin support) are employed at the bottom of the models. The axis of symmetry in the symmetric model is along the left edge. The soil is represented by 15-noded triangular elements. The supporting structure consists of supporting piles, inserted beams, and steel plates, and it is equivalently modeled as a wall based on the principle of equal bending stiffness and simulated using plate elements. Interfaces are set up between the soil and supporting structure to simulate their interaction. The support effect from walings is simulated using a fixed-end anchor [40]. The soil mesh surrounding the PRSS is adjusted to enhance computational efficiency and accuracy. Near the foundation pit—where detailed analysis is crucial owing to the high complexity of interactions and potential stress concentrations—the mesh is refined to provide more precise modeling. Conversely, at greater distances from the pit, where the effects are less pronounced, the mesh is coarsened to reduce computational demands while maintaining sufficient model accuracy. An optimized mesh size is determined by comparing calculation results using different mesh densities, with further refinement showing negligible differences in the computations.

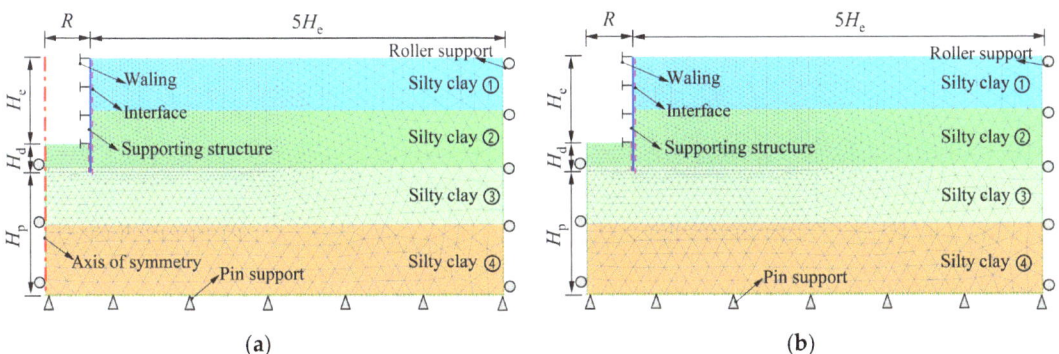

Figure 5. Typical FE models: (**a**) axisymmetric condition; (**b**) plane strain condition.

3.2. Material Constitutive Model and Parameters

The HSS model developed by Benz [41] has been extensively adopted in foundation pit analysis owing to its capacity to reflect the soil's small strain behavior [2,42,43]. In this model, the small strain behavior of the soil is determined by two parameters: the reference shear modulus (G_0^{ref}) at a given stress level and the shear strain ($\gamma_{0.7}$) at which the shear modulus decreases to about 70% of G_0^{ref}. The reference shear modulus is obtained from the relationship introduced by Hardin and Black [44]. The formula proposed by Benz [41] determines the threshold shear strain. Table 2 provides a detailed list of the soil parameters utilized for the HSS in this study. The relationship of the stiffness parameters ($E_s : E_{oed}^{ref} : E_{50}^{ref} : E_{ur}^{ref} = 1 : 1 : 1 : 3$) is used in this paper [45,46].

Table 2. Soil parameters for the HSS model used in the numerical analyses.

Soil Layers	Tangent Referential Stiffness, E_{oed}^{ref} (MPa)	Secant Referential Stiffness, E_{50}^{ref} (MPa)	Unloading–Reloading Referential Stiffness, E_{ur}^{ref} (MPa)	Poisson's Ratio for Unloading-Reloading, v_{ur}	Reference Shear Modulus at Very Small Strains, G_0^{ref} (kN/m²)	Shear Strain for 70% of G_0, $\gamma_{0.7}$ (10^{-4})	Power for Stress-Level Dependency of Stiffness, m	Failure Ratio, R_f	Interface Reduction Factor, R_{inter}
①	7.76	7.76	23.28	0.2	97.27	2.59	1.0	0.9	0.65
②	8.09	8.09	24.27	0.2	99.44	2.48	1.0	0.9	0.65
③	8.37	8.37	25.11	0.2	94.59	2.62	1.0	0.9	0.65
④	9.01	9.01	27.03	0.2	99.73	2.87	1.0	0.9	0.65

The interfaces adhere to the Mohr–Coulomb criterion, and their material properties are derived from the surrounding soil with a reduction factor (R_{inter}) [47]. In accordance with the friction coefficient between soil and steel recommended by Potyondy [48], the interaction parameter, R_{inter}, is uniformly assigned a value of 0.65 for each soil layer in the model.

The numerical analyses assume that the supporting structure and walings display linear elastic behavior. Table 3 offers comprehensive details on their properties and parameters, which were obtained from the specifications of "Hot-Rolled H Sections and Cut T Sections" [49]. Owing to the thin steel plates between the piles and their lack of fixed connection to the piles, the supporting structure composed of piles, inserted beams, and steel plates exhibits orthotropic elastic behavior, similar to a contiguous pile wall [50]. Therefore, the out-of-plane axis stiffness is neglected and set to zero.

Table 3. Structural parameters used for numerical analyses.

Structural Element	Element Type	Material Type	Axis Stiffness of the Anchor or the In-Plane Axis Stiffness of the Plate EA_1 (kN)	Out-of-Plane Axis Stiffness, EA_2 (kN)	Flexural Rigidity EI (kN·m^2)	Spacing of Supporting Piles $L_{spacing}$ (m)
Supporting structure	Plate	Elastic	2.31×10^6	0	5.22×10^4	--
Waling	Anchor	Elastic	1.43×10^5	--	--	1.57

3.3. Simulation Procedures

The foundation pit construction simulation was achieved in several steps, including activating and deactivating relevant element meshes and boundary conditions. In the initial stage, boundary conditions are activated to establish the initial stress field on-site. Subsequently, supporting structures and crown beams are installed, and soil and structure displacements are reset to zero, disregarding the installation effects. Following this, in the models used for validation, the groundwater level is lowered based on the observed groundwater level results. In the models used for parametric analysis, given that the influence of groundwater was not considered, the groundwater level in all simulation steps is uniformly set to -10 m beneath the ground surface to improve computational efficiency. Then, the soil is removed layer by layer according to the construction procedures, and the corresponding walings are activated. Finally, the excavation and waling installation are repeated alternately until the excavation reaches the designed depth. Furthermore, a stability analysis of the ultimate excavation conditions is conducted using the strength reduction method [40] to assess the relationship between the excavation radius and the foundation pit's stability. The analysis covers four key excavation stages: Stage 0 ($H_e = 0$ m), Stage 1 ($H_e = 3$ m), Stage 2 ($H_e = 6$ m), and Stage 3 ($H_e = 9$ m).

4. Results and Discussion

4.1. Comparison of Experimental and Numerical Results

To validate the numerical simulation, the observed and calculated results from various excavation stages are compared, as indicated in Figure 6. The deflections of the supporting piles exhibit a bulging profile. The maximum pile deflections measured during the three excavation stages were 1.9 mm, 4.6 mm, and 9.3 mm, while the simulation results indicated values of 1.6 mm, 4.1 mm, and 8.7 mm. Regarding ground surface settlement, the maximum measured values during the three excavation stages were 3.3 mm, 4.4 mm, and 6.8 mm, while simulation results showed maximum values of 3.0 mm, 4.0 mm, and 6.2 mm. The measured bending moments of the supporting piles corresponded closely with the numerical simulation results. However, a noticeable discrepancy exists between the simulated and measured earth pressures. This discrepancy can be attributed to the installation effects of the supporting piles, which resulted in measured earth pressures being lower than the simulated values [51,52]. The simulations did not account for these installation effects.

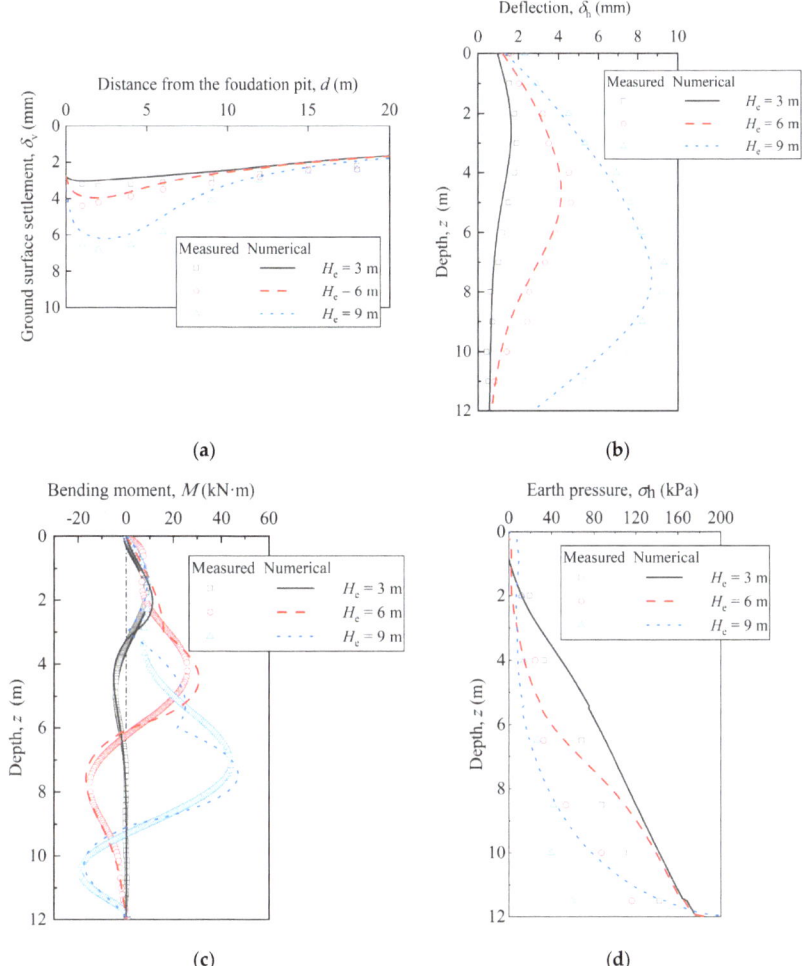

Figure 6. Comparison of measured and numerical results: (**a**) ground surface settlement; (**b**) deflection of supporting pile; (**c**) bending moment of supporting pile; (**d**) earth pressure.

Overall, the numerical simulation reasonably captured the responses of the supporting structure and surrounding soil, indicating that the finite-element model, constitutive models, and input parameters used in this study are appropriate. Based on this model and its parameters, subsequent parametric analyses can explore how varying the excavation radius affects the stress and deformation of circular foundation pits supported by PRSSs.

4.2. Influence of Excavation Radius on Deformations
4.2.1. Deflections of Supporting Piles

Figure 7 presents the influence of excavation radius on pile deflection at different excavation depths. For a foundation pit of a given radius, as the excavation depth increases, the pile deflection increases, and its profile tends to exhibit a bulging type, similar to that of multipropped rectangular foundation pits [53–55]. At the same excavation depth, the pile deflection shape is generally consistent across different excavation radii, but its magnitude increases with larger radii. When the excavation radius is less than 50 m, the pile deflection significantly increases with the expanded excavation radius, but the increase rate gradually decreases. When the excavation radius is equal to or larger than 50 m, the variation in pile deflection with an increasing excavation radius is negligible. This indicates that the spatial arching effect of circular foundation pits, which plays a role in reducing pile deflection, decreases significantly as the excavation radius increases. Consequently, the advantage of circular foundation pits over other shapes in controlling horizontal displacements is less pronounced when the excavation radius exceeds 50 m, consistent with the findings reported by Tan et al. [22].

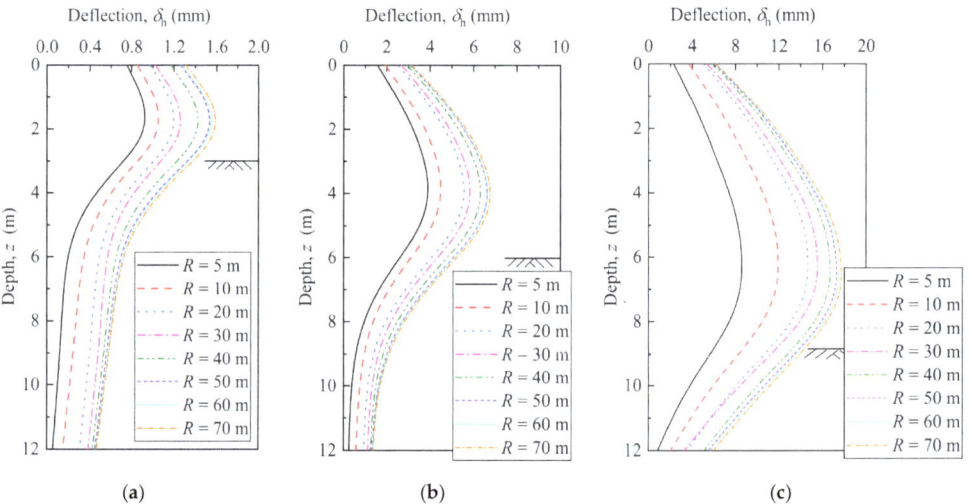

Figure 7. Variation in pile deflection with excavation radius at different excavation depths: (**a**) H_e = 3 m; (**b**) H_e = 6 m; (**c**) H_e = 9 m.

Figure 8 illustrates the variation in maximum pile deflection and its position with respect to the excavation radius during three excavation stages. At a constant excavation depth, the maximum deflection of the piles progressively increases as the excavation radius grows. However, the increase rate eventually diminishes, so when the excavation radius reaches 50 m, the maximum pile deflection tends to remain unchanged. Taking Stage 3 as an example, the maximum pile deflections at excavation radii of 10 m, 20 m, 30 m, 40 m, 50 m, 60 m, and 70 m are 1.39, 1.70, 1.81, 1.94, 2.01, 2.03, and 2.06 times those at 5 m, respectively. The rules describing pile deflection variations in Stages 1 and 2 are consistent with those observed in Stage 3. This phenomenon demonstrates that the impact of the excavation radius on pile deflection progressively attenuates as the excavation radius increases. In circular foundation pits with varying excavation depths, different retaining wall types, and disparate geologic conditions, the impact of excavation radius on retaining wall deflection is comparable. Furthermore, the maximum deflection position moves downward as the excavation depth increases. At a given excavation depth, the depth at which maximum pile deflection occurs remains relatively constant with an increased excavation radius. Under different excavation radii, the average maximum pile deflection depths at excavation depths of 3 m, 6 m, and 9 m are $0.57H_e$, $0.66H_e$, and $0.71H_e$, respectively.

The plane strain ratio (*PSR*) is calculated as the largest displacement at the center of a retaining wall from three-dimensional analysis divided by the largest displacement from plane strain analysis [56]. It is widely used to study how excavation dimensions (such as length, width, and depth) affect excavation deformations [2,4,57]. Figure 9 depicts *PSR* variation with respect to excavation radius at varying excavation depths. The *PSR* value decreases as the excavation depth increases, a trend that is more pronounced with smaller excavation radii. Moreover, for a given excavation radius, the *PSR* value increases with an increasing radius and gradually converges to 1. At Stage 3 (H_e = 9 m), the *PSR* values significantly vary from 0.51 to 0.98 for excavation radii less than 50 m; however, for larger excavation radii (greater than 50 m), the *PSR* changes moderately within a range of 0.95 to nearly 1.00. This indicates that the spatial arching effect decreases with an increasing radius, resulting in the circular foundation pit approaching a plane strain state. Consequently, for shallow excavations and radii less than 50m, designs based on plane strain conditions are likely to be conservative.

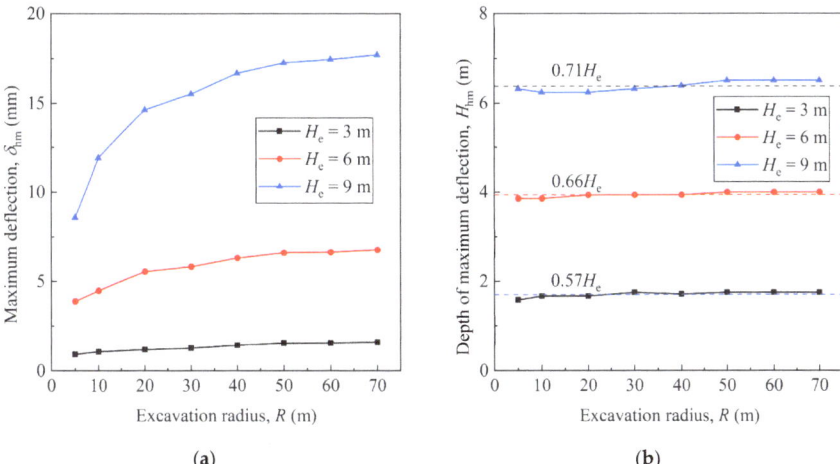

Figure 8. Variation in maximum pile deflection and its position with radius at different excavation stages: (**a**) maximum pile deflection; (**b**) depth of maximum pile deflection.

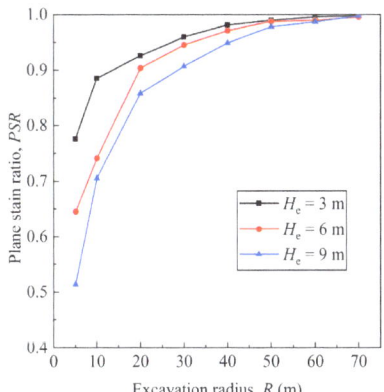

Figure 9. Variation in *PSR* with excavation radius at different excavation depths.

4.2.2. Ground Surface Settlements

The correlation between ground surface settlement and excavation radius at different excavation stages is demonstrated in Figure 10. For a foundation pit with a given radius, ground surface settlement tends to increase with the deepening excavation, displaying a concave profile corresponding to the bulging deflection of the supporting piles [53,58,59]. When the excavation depth remains constant, increasing the excavation radius below 50 m significantly increases ground surface settlement, although the increase rate gradually diminishes. However, when the excavation radius exceeds 50 m, the change in ground surface settlement with increasing radius becomes negligible. The impact of excavation radius on ground surface settlement is similar to its impact on supporting pile deflection.

Therefore, circular foundation pits demonstrate better control over horizontal and vertical deformation than rectangular pits when the excavation radius is less than 50 m. Notably, the influence of groundwater on the relationship between excavation radius and foundation pit deformation is not considered in the parametric analysis because, in the project reported in this study, the groundwater table was not progressively lowered in synchronization with the excavation process. Instead, the groundwater level in the foundation pit was intentionally lowered below the maximum excavation depth before excavation began. Therefore, unlike Figure 6a, Figure 10 shows no significant settlement in the ground surface beyond 15 m from the foundation pit when the radius is 5 m.

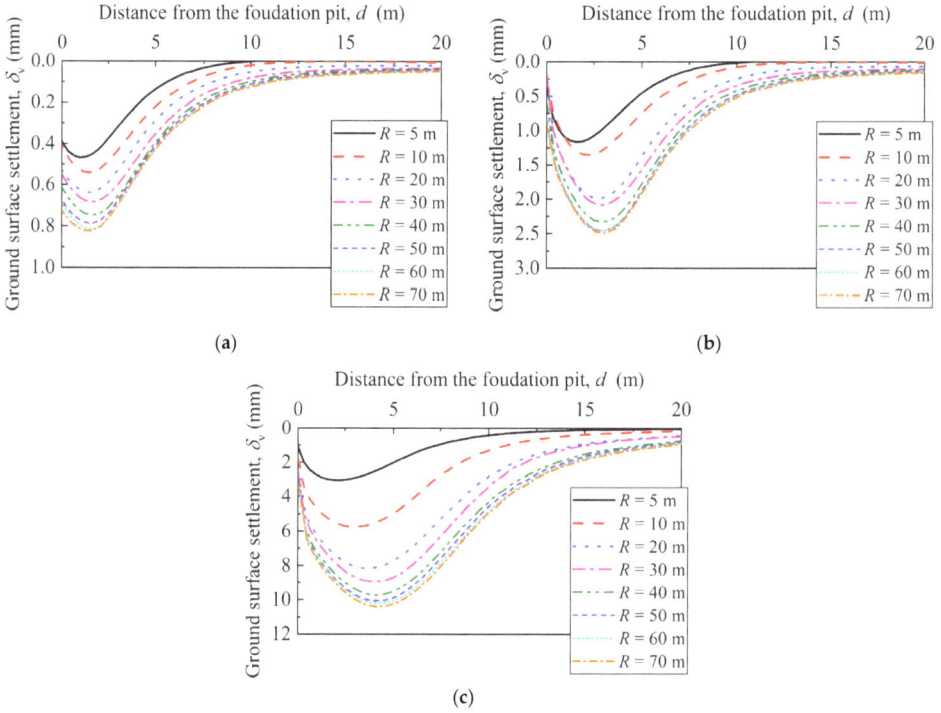

Figure 10. Variation in ground surface settlements with excavation radius: (**a**) H_e = 3 m; (**b**) H_e = 6 m; (**c**) H_e = 9 m.

Figure 11 presents the changes in the maximum ground surface settlement and its location relative to the excavation radius across various excavation stages. The maximum ground surface settlement gradually increases at a given excavation depth with an increasing excavation radius. Nevertheless, the increase rate gradually decreases until the maximum ground surface settlement reaches a point of stabilization at a 50 m excavation radius. For example, at the third excavation stage, the maximum ground surface settlement values are 1.88, 2.67, 2.92, 3.18, 3.29, 3.31, and 3.34 times those at 5 m for excavation radii of 10 m, 20 m, 30 m, 40 m, 50 m, 60 m, and 70 m, respectively. The regulations regarding changes in ground surface settlement at Stages 1 and 2 are consistent with those observed at Stage 3. It can be inferred that as the excavation radius increases, its influence on maximum ground surface settlement decreases. The impact of excavation radius on maximum ground surface settlement is more pronounced when the radius is smaller. The impact of the radius on ground surface settlement remains considerable for circular foundation pits with varying excavation depths, retaining wall types, and geological conditions. Additionally, as excavation depth increases, the distance between the maximum ground surface settlement position and the foundation pit also increases. With a constant excavation depth, this distance grows with the excavation radius, but it reaches a stable value once the radius exceeds 30m. The stable values of the distances from the pit to the maximum ground surface settlement location are $0.52H_e$, $0.50H_e$, and $0.46H_e$ for excavation depths of 3 m, 6 m, and 9 m, respectively.

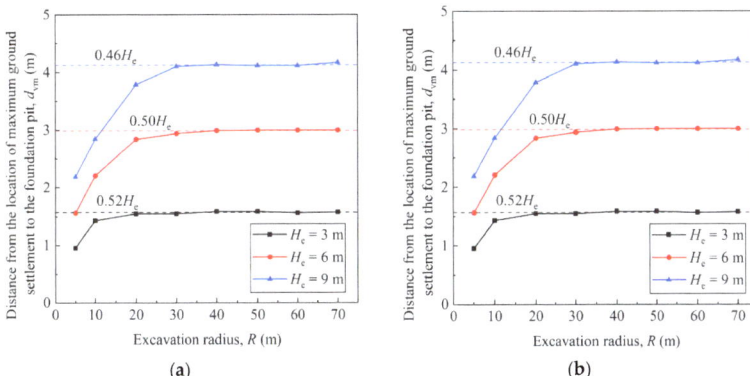

Figure 11. Variation in maximum ground surface settlement and its position with radius at different excavation stages: (**a**) maximum pile deflection; (**b**) distance from the maximum ground settlement location to the foundation pit.

Referring to the *PSR* definition above, Figure 12 illustrates how the ratio of maximum ground surface settlement from an axisymmetric model (δ_{vma}) to that of a planar strain model (δ_{vmp}) varies with excavation radius (*R*). Variations in $\delta_{vma}/\delta_{vmp}$ with excavation radius show similar trends to those of *PSR* with excavation radius. The trends imply that the excavation radii greater than 50 m result in an excavation response with a $\delta_{vma}/\delta_{vmp}$ approximately equal to 1, suggesting that axisymmetric and plane strain analysis results will yield the same maximum ground surface settlement. Once again, it is demonstrated that as the radius increases, the spatial arching effect weakens, leading the circular foundation pit to approach a plane strain state. Furthermore, $\delta_{vma}/\delta_{vmp}$ tends to decrease with increasing excavation depth, particularly for radii smaller than 50 m. Therefore, for circular deep excavations with radii greater than 50 m, the differences in results between the axisymmetric model and the plane strain model are negligible.

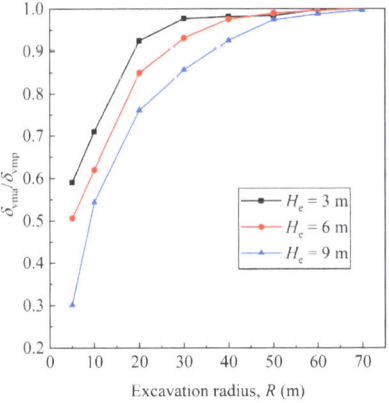

Figure 12. Variation in $\delta_{vma}/\delta_{vmp}$ with excavation radius at different excavation stages.

4.2.3. Total Ground Movements

Figure 13 illustrates contour plots of the total ground movements outside the foundation pit for different excavation radii at Stage 3 ($H_e = 9$ m). As the excavation radius increases, the total ground movements outside the pit gradually increase. Larger excavation radii lead to larger total ground movements and extend the influence areas. However, regardless of the excavation radius, the maximum total ground movement location always remains approximately 6 m below the ground surface in the vertical direction and near the wall in the horizontal direction. Once the excavation radius exceeds 50 m, the influence area, delineated by the 3 mm contour, the surface, and the supporting structure, does not change significantly, despite the continued expansion of the overall influence area with the excavation radius.

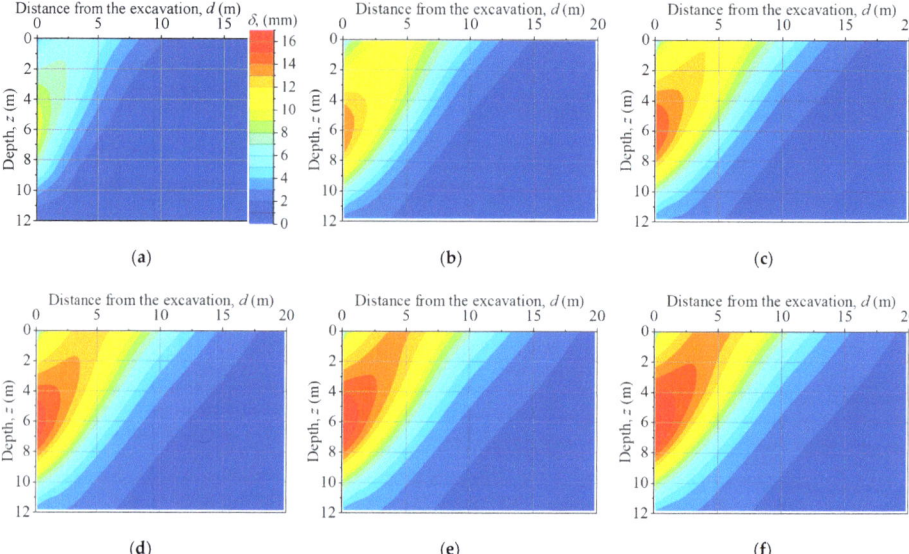

Figure 13. Contour plots of the total ground movements outside the foundation pit for different excavation radii at Stage 3: (**a**) $R = 10$ m; (**b**) $R = 20$ m; (**c**) $R = 30$ m; (**d**) $R = 40$ m; (**e**) $R = 50$ m; (**f**) $R = 60$ m.

4.3. Influence of Excavation Radius on Stresses

4.3.1. Bending Moments of Supporting Piles

Figure 14 presents the variation in supporting pile bending moments with excavation radius at different depths. The supporting pile bending moment increases with both excavation depth and radius. Similar to the effect of excavation radius on supporting pile deflection, increases in excavation radius do not significantly change the supporting pile bending moments once the radius exceeds 50 m. The bending moments of the supporting piles at the positions connected to the walings are smaller than those at other positions. This suggests that in a circular foundation pit, the walings can effectively support the retaining walls. Consequently, the bulging deflections of the supporting piles in this unpropped circular foundation pit resemble those of multipropped rectangular foundation pits.

Figure 15 displays changes in the maximum bending moments of the supporting piles and their respective locations relative to the excavation radius across various excavation stages. At the same excavation depth, the maximum bending moment gradually increases with the excavation radius. Nevertheless, the increase rate diminishes as the excavation radius increases, and the maximum bending moment remains constant when the excavation radius exceeds 50 m. For instance, at Stage 3 ($H_e = 9$ m), the maximum bending moments increase to 1.22, 1.36, 1.46, 1.47, 1.48, 1.49, and 1.49 times those at a 5 m radius, corresponding to excavation radii of 10 m, 20 m, 30 m, 40 m, 50 m, 60 m, and 70 m, respectively. Similar trends in the variation in maximum bending moments with excavation radius can be observed at Stages 1 (H_e = 3 m) and 2 (H_e = 6 m). With deeper excavation, the maximum bending moment location moves downward. However, the depth at which the maximum bending moment occurs remains relatively unchanged with an increasing excavation radius at a given excavation depth. At Stages 1, 2, and 3, the average maximum bending moment depths vary as $0.67H_e$, $0.74H_e$, and $0.83H_e$, respectively, for different excavation radii. Owing to the ring walings, the maximum bending moment occurs roughly midway between the two walings.

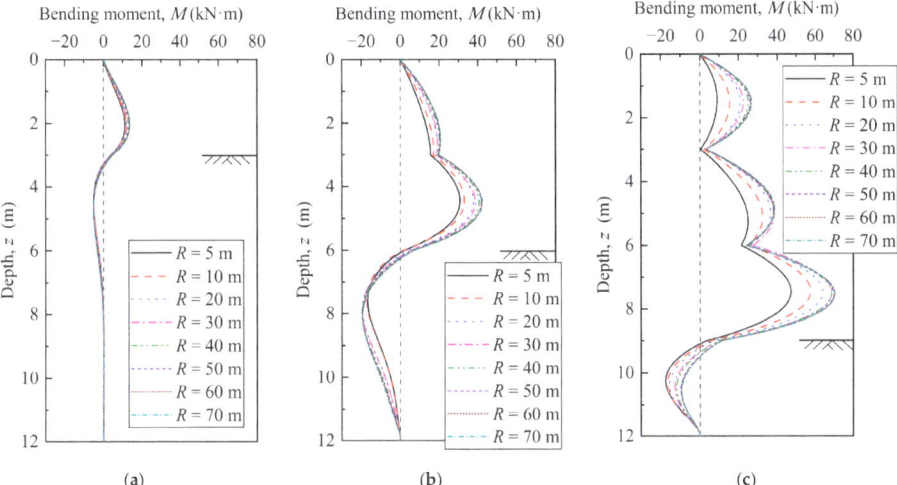

Figure 14. Variation in bending moments with excavation radius at different depths: (**a**) H_e = 3 m; (**b**) H_e = 6 m; (**c**) H_e = 9 m.

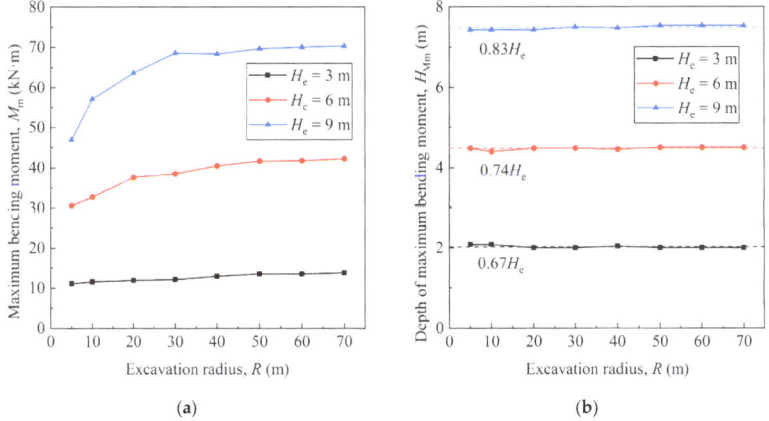

Figure 15. Variation in maximum bending moments and their locations with radii at different excavation stages: (**a**) maximum bending moments; (**b**) depths of maximum bending moments.

4.3.2. Earth Pressure

Figure 16 shows the variation in earth pressure distribution on the non-excavated side of the supporting pile with different excavation radii. The solid and dashed lines in the figure represent the axisymmetric and plane strain model results, respectively. As excavation progresses, the distribution of earth pressure along the depth changes from linear to nonlinear. Moreover, as the excavation deepens, the earth pressure borne by most parts of the supporting piles also decreases. The influence areas extend downward. However, for the supporting pile sections at depths not exceeding 4 m, the earth pressure decreases and then increases. This occurs because the supporting pile deformation gradually develops into a bulging shape (Figure 7), forming a vertical soil arching effect behind the supporting piles. The upper part of the retaining piles acts as the foot of the soil arch and is subject to greater earth pressure [60]. In the plane strain models, the earth pressure does not significantly vary with increasing excavation radius. However, in the axisymmetric models, the earth pressure increases with an increasing excavation radius, and this increase becomes more pronounced as the excavation depth increases. Overall, under identical conditions, the lateral earth pressure in axisymmetric models is lower than in plane strain models owing to the soil arching effect resulting from the circular foundation pit. This difference tends to increase with greater excavation depths and diminishes as the excavation radius increases. When the excavation radius exceeds 50 m, the difference in earth pressure between the axisymmetric models and the plane strain models is negligible.

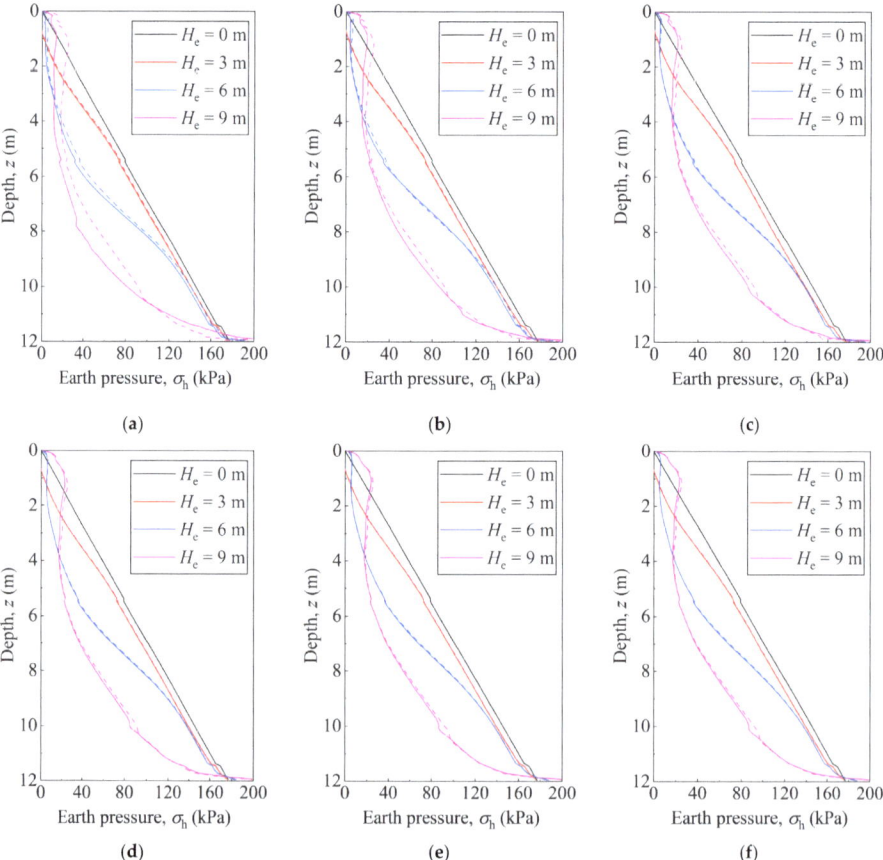

Figure 16. Variation in earth pressure distribution on the non-excavated side of the supporting pile with excavation radius: (**a**) R = 10 m; (**b**) R = 20 m; (**c**) R = 30 m; (**d**) R = 40 m; (**e**) R = 50 m; (**f**) R = 60 m.

4.3.3. Circumferential Stress

Figure 17 presents the variation in circumferential stress with excavation radius at the final excavation stage. The circular foundation pit deformations are closely related to the circumferential stress distribution since the circumferential stress affects the soil strength and the plastic zone size [17,19,61,62]. The circumferential stresses in the majority of the area affected by the excavation decrease with increasing radius. When the excavation radius exceeds 50 m, its effect on circumferential stress becomes insignificant. This suggests that the circular foundation pit spatial arching effect tends to diminish as the excavation radius increases. Furthermore, this change in circumferential stresses provides an alternative explanation for the observation that, when the radius exceeds 50 m, the foundation pit deformations tend to stabilize. The axisymmetric model results are roughly equal to those from the plane strain models.

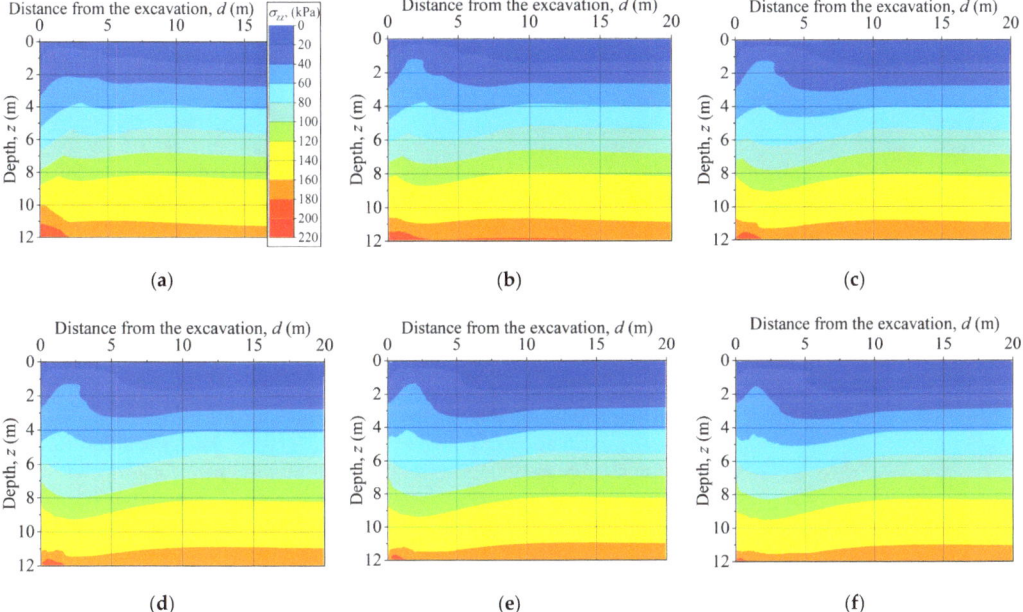

Figure 17. Contour plots of circumferential stress: (**a**) $R = 10$ m; (**b**) $R = 20$ m; (**c**) $R = 30$ m; (**d**) $R = 40$ m; (**e**) $R = 50$ m; (**f**) $R = 60$ m.

4.4. Influence of Excavation Radius on Stability

Figure 18 illustrates the safety factor (S) for varying excavation radii at the final excavation stage in both axisymmetric and plane strain conditions. The safety factor calculated from the axisymmetric models nonlinearly decreases as the excavation radius increases. As the excavation radius increases, the decrease rate in the safety factor slows down. By contrast, the safety factor obtained from the plane strain models remains relatively constant with increasing excavation radii. Furthermore, as the excavation radius increases, the safety factor under the symmetric condition tends to approach that under the plane strain condition because, as the excavation radius increases, the spatial arching effect produced by the circular excavation gradually ceases to be significant. Once the excavation radius surpasses 50 m, the safety factor derived from both the axisymmetric and plane strain models becomes largely comparable. It is important to note that various regions may have specific codes dictating minimum factors of safety based on structural type and environmental conditions. The relationship between the factor of safety and excavation radius in Figure 18 is relevant to foundation pits supported by PRSSs in silty clay. Current design methods typically calculate the factor of safety for circular foundation pits based on the plane strain assumption. Engineers can derive the factors of safety under axisymmetric conditions from plane strain results, facilitating a more economical design.

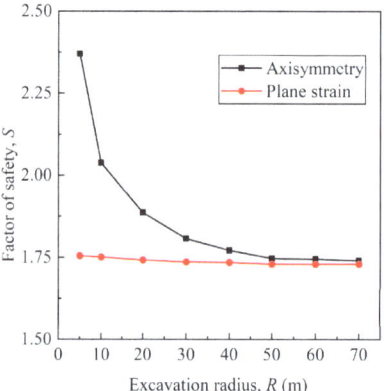

Figure 18. Correlation between the safety factor and the excavation radius under axisymmetric and plane strain conditions.

5. Conclusions

This paper presents a comprehensive study of the influence of excavation radius on the behavior of circular foundation pits supported by PRSSs. A full-scale experiment and a series of numerical simulations were performed to analyze the stress, deformation, and stability of a circular foundation pit. According to the analysis results, the following conclusions can be drawn:

1. The deflection and bending moment of the supporting pile increase significantly with an increasing excavation radius; however, the increase rate gradually slows down, making the change in deflection and the bending moment insignificant when the excavation radius exceeds 50 m. Nevertheless, the excavation radius has little effect on the depth at which the maximum pile deflection and bending moment occur. In addition, the *PSR* value increases with an increasing excavation radius and gradually converges to 1.
2. As with its influence on pile deflection, increasing the excavation radius results in greater ground surface settlement. Nevertheless, once the excavation radius is beyond 50 m, this influence becomes less pronounced, and the differences in ground surface settlement predictions using axisymmetric and planar strain models are minimal. Moreover, the distance from the maximum settlement point to the foundation pit increases with radius but stabilizes once the radius exceeds 30 m.
3. In axisymmetric models, the lateral earth pressure on the non-excavation side of the supporting pile increases as the excavation radius increases. In excavation radii exceeding 50 m, the discrepancy between the earth pressures calculated using the axisymmetric and plane strain models is negligible.
4. Circumferential stresses in the majority of the area affected by the excavation decrease with an increasing excavation radius. Once the excavation radius surpasses 50 m, its impact on circumferential stress becomes insignificant.
5. When the radius of a circular foundation pit is less than 50 m, a larger excavation radius correlates with a smaller safety factor. However, when the excavation radius is more than 50 m, the safety factor under axisymmetric conditions remains constant and approaches that under plane strain conditions.

Due to site condition limitations, the full-scale experiments and related numerical simulations in this study were conducted in silty clay. Further efforts are required to investigate the influence of excavation radius on the behavior of circular foundation pits under various geological conditions.

Author Contributions: Conceptualization, C.G. and Y.P.; software, L.C.; methodology, L.C. and Y.P.; validation, L.C.; formal analysis, L.C.; investigation, L.C., Y.P., and M.T.; resources, C.G.; data curation, L.C.; writing—original draft preparation, L.C.; writing—review and editing, C.G., Y.P. and K.Z.; visualization, L.C.; supervision, C.G., H.L., and Y.P.; project administration, H.L., Y.P., and M.T.; funding acquisition, C.G., M.T., and H.L. All authors have read and agreed to the published version of the manuscript.

Funding: This research was funded by the Science and Technology Program of Guangzhou Municipal Construction Group Co., Ltd., China, grant number 2022-KJ004. The funder had the following involvement with the study: the construction and monitoring of the PRSS.

Institutional Review Board Statement: Not applicable.

Informed Consent Statement: Not applicable.

Data Availability Statement: The data presented in this study are available on request from the corresponding author due to restrictions on privacy.

Conflicts of Interest: Authors Huqing Liang and Mengxiong Tang were employed by the company Guangzhou Municipal Construction Group Co., Ltd. The remaining authors declare that the research was conducted in the absence of any commercial or financial relationships that could be construed as a potential conflict of interest.

References

1. Tan, Y.; Fan, D.; Lu, Y. Statistical Analyses on a Database of Deep Excavations in Shanghai Soft Clays in China from 1995–2018. *Pract. Period. Struct. Des. Constr.* **2022**, *27*, 4021067. [CrossRef]
2. Hsiung, B.B.; Likitlersuang, S.; Phan, K.H.; Pisitsopon, P. Impacts of the plane strain ratio on excavations in soft alluvium deposits. *Acta Geotech.* **2021**, *16*, 1923–1938. [CrossRef]
3. JGJ 120-2012; Technical Specification for Retaining and Protection of Building Foundation Excavations. China Architecture & Building Press: Beijing, China, 2012.
4. Finno, R.J.; Blackburn, J.T.; Roboski, J.F. Three-Dimensional Effects for Supported Excavations in Clay. *J. Geotech. Geoenviron. Eng.* **2007**, *133*, 30–36. [CrossRef]
5. Cheng, K.; Xu, R.; Ying, H.; Gan, X.; Zhang, L.; Liu, S. Observed performance of a 30.2 m deep-large basement excavation in Hangzhou soft clay. *Tunn. Undergr. Space Technol.* **2021**, *111*, 103872. [CrossRef]
6. Galliková, Z.; Rehman, Z.U. Appraisal of the hypoplastic model for the numerical prediction of high-rise building settlement in Neogene clay based on real-scale monitoring data. *J. Build. Eng.* **2022**, *50*, 104152. [CrossRef]
7. Liu, Y.; Huang, F.; Wang, G.; Cao, Y.; Li, B. Study on Long-Span and Variable-Section Foundation Pit Excavation in Muddy Silty Clay. *Int. J. Civ. Eng.* **2024**, *22*, 739–755. [CrossRef]
8. Sun, Y.; Gu, Z.; Xu, Z.; Wang, C.; Song, D. Performance of a long, irregular top-down excavation in the centre of Nanjing, China. *Proc. Inst. Civ. Eng. -Geotech. Eng.* **2022**, *177*, 50–65. [CrossRef]
9. Mana, A.I.; Clough, G.W. Prediction of Movements for Braced Cuts in Clay. *J. Geotech. Eng. Div.* **1981**, *107*, 759–777. [CrossRef]
10. Wang, H. Influence of excavation width on enclosure structure stability of foundation pits. *China Civ. Eng. J.* **2011**, *44*, 120–126. [CrossRef]
11. Xiao, H.; Zhou, S.; Sun, Y. Wall Deflection and Ground Surface Settlement due to Excavation Width and Foundation Pit Classification. *KSCE J. Civ. Eng.* **2019**, *23*, 1537–1547. [CrossRef]
12. Park, C.; Joung, S. Numerical investigations on the excavation width and property of deformation of earth retaining wall. *J. Korean Geotech. Soc.* **2020**, *36*, 57–68. [CrossRef]
13. Tan, Y.; Wang, D. Characteristics of A Large-Scale Deep Foundation Pit Excavated by Central-Island Technique in Shanghai Soft Clay. Part II: Top-Down Construction of the Peripheral Rectangular Pit. *J. Geotech. Geoenviron. Eng.* **2013**, *139*, 1894–1910. [CrossRef]
14. Zeng, C.; Zheng, G.; Zhou, X.; Xue, X.; Zhou, H. Behaviours of wall and soil during pre-excavation dewatering under different foundation pit widths. *Comput. Geotech.* **2019**, *115*, 103169. [CrossRef]
15. Huang, P.; Dang, K.; Shi, H.; Yang, K.; Wu, J. Influence and Mechanism of the Excavation Width on Excavation Deformations in Shanghai Soft Clay. *Buildings* **2024**, *14*, 1450. [CrossRef]
16. Kim, K.; Lee, D.; Cho, J.; Jeong, S.; Lee, S. The effect of arching pressure on a vertical circular shaft. *Tunn. Undergr. Space Technol.* **2013**, *37*, 10–21. [CrossRef]
17. Schwamb, T.; Soga, K. Numerical modelling of a deep circular excavation at Abbey Mills in London. *Géotechnique* **2015**, *65*, 604–619. [CrossRef]

18. Qiao, Y.; Xie, F.; Bai, Z.; Lu, J.; Ding, W. Deformation characteristics of ultra-deep circular shaft in soft soil: A case study. *Undergr. Space* **2024**, *16*, 239–260. [CrossRef]
19. Tangjarusritaratorn, T.; Miyazaki, Y.; Sawamura, Y.; Kishida, K.; Kimura, M. Numerical investigation on arching effect surrounding deep cylindrical shaft during excavation process. *Undergr. Space* **2022**, *7*, 944–965. [CrossRef]
20. Tobar, T.; Meguid, M.A. Experimental Study of the Earth Pressure Distribution on Cylindrical Shafts. *J. Geotech. Geoenviron. Eng.* **2011**, *137*, 1121–1125. [CrossRef]
21. Herten, M.; Pulsfort, M. Determination of spatial earth pressure on circular shaft constructions. *Granul. Matter* **1999**, *2*, 1–7. [CrossRef]
22. Tan, Y.; Wang, D. Characteristics of a Large-Scale Deep Foundation Pit Excavated by the Central-Island Technique in Shanghai Soft Clay. I: Bottom-Up Construction of the Central Cylindrical Shaft. *J. Geotech. Geoenviron. Eng.* **2013**, *139*, 1875–1893. [CrossRef]
23. Cheng, Y.M.; Hu, Y.Y.; Wei, W.B. General Axisymmetric Active Earth Pressure by Method of Characteristics—Theory and Numerical Formulation. *Int. J. Geomech.* **2007**, *7*, 1–15. [CrossRef]
24. Cho, J.; Lim, H.; Jeong, S.; Kim, K. Analysis of lateral earth pressure on a vertical circular shaft considering the 3D arching effect. *Tunn. Undergr. Space Technol.* **2015**, *48*, 11–19. [CrossRef]
25. Meftah, A.; Benmebarek, N.; Benmebarek, S. Numerical study of the active earth pressure distribution on cylindrical shafts using 2D finite difference code. *J. Appl. Eng. Sci. Technol.* **2018**, *4*, 123–128.
26. Liu, G.; Meng, H.; Song, G.; Bo, W.; Zhao, P.; Ning, B.; Xu, X. Numerical simulation of wedge failure of rock slopes using three-dimensional discontinuous deformation analysis. *Environ. Earth Sci.* **2024**, *83*, 310. [CrossRef]
27. Zhang, J.; Li, Y.; Zhang, C. Pounding induced overturning resistance of FPB-isolated structures considering soil-structure-interactions. *Soil Dyn. Earthq. Eng.* **2024**, *177*, 108416. [CrossRef]
28. Keshavarz, A.; Ebrahimi, M. Axisymmetric passive lateral earth pressure of retaining walls. *KSCE J. Civ. Eng.* **2017**, *21*, 1706–1716. [CrossRef]
29. Guo, C.; Ye, J.; Zhao, C.; Wang, F. Mechanical and deformation characteristics of composite assembled supporting structure. *Geotech. Res.* **2020**, *7*, 230–243. [CrossRef]
30. Hu, D.; Guo, C.; Chu, X. Case Study of Flexible Prefabricated Impermeable Underground Support Structure. *Iran. J. Sci. Technol. Trans. Civ. Eng.* **2021**, *45*, 2489–2501. [CrossRef]
31. Huang, H.; Yuan, Y.; Zhang, W.; Li, M. Seismic behavior of a replaceable artificial controllable plastic hinge for precast concrete beam-column joint. *Eng. Struct.* **2021**, *245*, 112848. [CrossRef]
32. Cao, J.; Du, J.; Fan, Q.; Yang, J.; Bao, C.; Liu, Y. Reinforcement for earthquake-damaged glued-laminated timber knee-braced frames with self-tapping screws and CFRP fabric. *Eng. Struct.* **2024**, *306*, 117787. [CrossRef]
33. Pan, Y.; Fang, H.; Li, B.; Wang, F. Stability analysis and full-scale test of a new recyclable supporting structure for underground ecological granaries. *Eng. Struct.* **2019**, *192*, 205–219. [CrossRef]
34. Chen, L.; Guo, C.; Cao, D. Numerical Investigation of Earth Berm Effects on Prefabricated Recyclable Supporting Structure in Circular Excavations. *Appl. Sci.* **2024**, *14*, 4703. [CrossRef]
35. Huang, H.; Li, M.; Zhang, W.; Yuan, Y. Seismic behavior of a friction-type artificial plastic hinge for the precast beam–column connection. *Arch. Civ. Mech. Eng.* **2022**, *22*, 201. [CrossRef]
36. Huang, H.; Li, M.; Yuan, Y.; Bai, H. Experimental Research on the Seismic Performance of Precast Concrete Frame with Replaceable Artificial Controllable Plastic Hinges. *J. Struct. Eng.* **2023**, *149*, 4022222. [CrossRef]
37. *GB 50497-2019*; Technical standard for monitoring of building excavation engineering. Ministry Of Housing And Urban-Rural Development of the People's Republic of China, China Architecture & Building Press: Beijing, China, 2019.
38. Wang, F.; Chen, L.; Pan, Y.; Guo, C.; Guo, C.; Yue, L.; Chu, X. Deformation characteristics of excavation supported by prefabricated recyclable structures. *Proc. Inst. Civ. Eng. -Geotech. Eng.* **2024**, ahead of print, 1–43. [CrossRef]
39. Zhou, H.; Zheng, G.; He, X.; Wang, E.; Guo, Z.; Nie, D.; Ma, S. Numerical modelling of retaining structure displacements in multi-bench retained excavations. *Acta Geotech.* **2020**, *15*, 2691–2703. [CrossRef]
40. Brinkgreve, R.; Kumarswamy, S.; Swolfs, W.M.; Waterman, D.; Chesaru, A.; Bonnier, P.G. *PLAXIS 2016*; PLAXIS bv: Delft, The Netherlands, 2016.
41. Benz, T. *Small-Strain Stiffness of Soils and Its Numerical Consequences*; University of Sturrgart: Stuttgart, Germany, 2007.
42. Zhang, W.; Goh, A.T.C.; Xuan, F. A simple prediction model for wall deflection caused by braced excavation in clays. *Comput. Geotech.* **2015**, *63*, 67–72. [CrossRef]
43. Nejjar, K.; Dias, D.; Cuira, F.; Chapron, G.; Le Bissonnais, H. Numerical modelling of a 32 m deep excavation in the suburbs of Paris. *Eng. Struct.* **2022**, *268*, 114727. [CrossRef]
44. Hardin, B.O.; Drnevich, V.P. Shear Modulus and Damping in Soils: Design Equations and Curves. *J. Soil Mech. Found. Div.* **1972**, *98*, 667–692. [CrossRef]
45. Di Mariano, A.; Amoroso, S.; Arroyo, M.; Monaco, P.; Gens, A. SDMT-Based Numerical Analyses of Deep Excavation in Soft Soil. *J. Geotech. Geoenviron. Eng.* **2019**, *145*, 04018102. [CrossRef]
46. Brinkgreve, R.B. Selection of soil models and parameters for geotechnical engineering application. In *Soil Constitutive Models: Evaluation, Selection, and Calibration*; American Society of Civil Engineers: Austin, TX, USA, 2005; pp. 69–98.
47. Rehman, Z.U.; Zhang, G. Shear coupling effect of monotonic and cyclic behavior of the interface between steel and gravel. *Can. Geotech. J.* **2018**, *56*, 876–884. [CrossRef]

48. Potyondy, J.G. Skin friction between various soils and construction materials. *Géotechnique* **1961**, *11*, 339–353. [CrossRef]
49. *GB/T 11263-2017*; Hot-Rolled H Sections and Cut T Sections. S.A.O. of the People's Republic Of China, China Architecture & Building Press: Beijing, China, 2017.
50. Mishra, A.; Sawant, V.A. A Detailed Investigation on Contiguous Pile Wall with Homogeneous Backfill. *Geotech. Geol. Eng.* **2023**, *41*, 2065–2089. [CrossRef]
51. Richards, D.J.; Clark, J.; Powrie, W. Installation effects of a bored pile wall in overconsolidated clay. *Géotechnique* **2006**, *56*, 411–425. [CrossRef]
52. Duan, N.; Cheng, Y.P.; Liu, J.W. DEM analysis of pile installation effect: Comparing a bored and a driven pile. *Granul. Matter* **2018**, *20*, 1–16. [CrossRef]
53. Ou, C.; Hsieh, P.; Chiou, D. Characteristics of ground surface settlement during excavation. *Can. Geotech. J.* **1993**, *30*, 758–767. [CrossRef]
54. Ni, X.; Lu, J.; Wang, Y.; Shi, J.; Chen, W.; Tang, L. Field investigation of the influence of basement excavation and dewatering on ground and structure responses. *Tunn. Undergr. Space Technol.* **2021**, *117*, 104121. [CrossRef]
55. Feng, Z.; Xu, Q.; Xu, X.; Tang, Q.; Li, X.; Liao, X. Deformation Characteristics of Soil Layers and Diaphragm Walls during Deep Foundation Pit Excavation: Simulation Verification and Parameter Analysis. *Symmetry* **2022**, *14*, 254. [CrossRef]
56. Ou, C.; Chiou, D.; Wu, T. Three-Dimensional Finite Element Analysis of Deep Excavations. *J. Geotech. Eng.* **1996**, *122*, 337–345. [CrossRef]
57. Lu, T.; Wu, K.; Liu, S.; Cai, G. Method for estimating three-dimensional effects on braced excavation in clay. *Tunn. Undergr. Space Technol.* **2023**, *141*, 105355. [CrossRef]
58. Zhao, J.; Tan, Z.; Yu, R.; Li, Z.; Zhang, X.; Zhu, P. Deformation responses of the foundation pit construction of the urban metro station: A case study in Xiamen. *Tunn. Undergr. Space Technol.* **2022**, *128*, 104662. [CrossRef]
59. Maher, T.; Basha, A.M.; Abo-Raya, M.M.; Zakaria, M.H. General deformation behavior of deep excavation support systems: A review. *Glob. J. Eng. Technol. Adv.* **2022**, *10*, 39–57. [CrossRef]
60. Yang, K.; Li, Z.; Chen, Y.; Yang, X.; Lin, W. Soil Arching–Induced Lateral Earth Pressure Redistribution on the Retaining Wall in a Multistrutted Excavation in Soft Soil. *J. Geotech. Geoenviron. Eng.* **2023**, *149*, 5023004. [CrossRef]
61. Schanz, T.; Vermeer, P.A.; Bonnier, P.G. Formulation and verification of the Hardening-Soil Model. In *Beyond 2000 in Computational Geotechnics*; Routledge: Rotterdam, The Netherlands, 1999.
62. Xiong, G.; Wang, J. A rigorous characteristic line theory for axisymmetric problems and its application in circular excavations. *Acta Geotech.* **2020**, *15*, 439–453. [CrossRef]

Disclaimer/Publisher's Note: The statements, opinions and data contained in all publications are solely those of the individual author(s) and contributor(s) and not of MDPI and/or the editor(s). MDPI and/or the editor(s) disclaim responsibility for any injury to people or property resulting from any ideas, methods, instructions or products referred to in the content.

Article

Prediction of the Unconfined Compressive Strength of a One-Part Geopolymer-Stabilized Soil Using Deep Learning Methods with Combined Real and Synthetic Data

Qinyi Chen [1], Guo Hu [1,*] and Jun Wu [2]

[1] School of Urban Rail Transportation, Shanghai University of Engineering Science, Shanghai 201620, China; m405122214@sues.edu.cn
[2] School of Civil Engineering, Shanghai Normal University, Shanghai 201418, China; cvewujun@shnu.edu.cn
* Correspondence: huguo@sues.edu.cn

Abstract: This study focused on exploring the utilization of a one-part geopolymer (OPG) as a sustainable alternative binder to ordinary Portland cement (OPC) in soil stabilization, offering significant environmental advantages. The unconfined compressive strength (UCS) was the key index for evaluating the efficacy of OPG in soil stabilization, traditionally demanding substantial resources in terms of cost and time. In this research, four distinct deep learning (DL) models (Artificial Neural Network [ANN], Backpropagation Neural Network [BPNN], Convolutional Neural Network [CNN], and Long Short-Term Memory [LSTM]) were employed to predict the UCS of OPG-stabilized soft clay, providing a more efficient and precise methodology. Among these models, CNN exhibited the highest performance (MAE = 0.022, R^2 = 0.9938), followed by LSTM (MAE = 0.0274, R^2 = 0.9924) and BPNN (MAE = 0.0272, R^2 = 0.9921). The Wasserstein Generative Adversarial Network (WGAN) was further utilized to generate additional synthetic samples for expanding the training dataset. The incorporation of the synthetic samples generated by WGAN models into the training set for the DL models led to improved performance. When the number of synthetic samples achieved 200, the WGAN-CNN model provided the most accurate results, with an R^2 value of 0.9978 and MAE value of 0.9978. Furthermore, to assess the reliability of the DL models and gain insights into the influence of input variables on the predicted outcomes, interpretable Machine Learning techniques, including a sensitivity analysis, Shapley Additive Explanation (SHAP), and 1D Partial Dependence Plot (PDP) were employed for analyzing and interpreting the CNN and WGAN-CNN models. This research illuminates new aspects of the application of DL models with training on real and synthetic data in evaluating the strength properties of the OPG-stabilized soil, contributing to saving time and cost.

Keywords: unconfined compressive strength; one-part geopolymer; deep learning method; Generative Adversarial Networks; interpretable machine learning method

Citation: Chen, Q.; Hu, G.; Wu, J. Prediction of the Unconfined Compressive Strength of a One-Part Geopolymer-Stabilized Soil Using Deep Learning Methods with Combined Real and Synthetic Data. *Buildings* **2024**, *14*, 2894. https://doi.org/10.3390/buildings14092894

Academic Editor: Jan Fořt

Received: 9 August 2024
Revised: 8 September 2024
Accepted: 11 September 2024
Published: 13 September 2024

Copyright: © 2024 by the authors. Licensee MDPI, Basel, Switzerland. This article is an open access article distributed under the terms and conditions of the Creative Commons Attribution (CC BY) license (https://creativecommons.org/licenses/by/4.0/).

1. Introduction

Ordinary Portland cement (OPC) is one of the most common materials in construction engineering. Nonetheless, the production of OPC is accompanied by the generation and emission of significant quantities of carbon dioxide, which imposes substantial damage on the environment [1–3]. Therefore, in the context of the global emphasis on sustainable development, many researchers have begun to search for alternative materials and options to replace OPC. Geopolymer is a novel type of cementitious material synthesized from industrial by-products. It represents a promising alternative to conventional cement. These by-products include fly ash (FA), ground granulated blast furnace slag (GGBFS), rice husk ash, steel slag, and waste glass powder, among others [4–7]. The application of geopolymer in structural and geotechnical engineering has attracted significant attention in recent years [8,9]. Geopolymer is found to improve the strength of stabilized soil by developing a three-dimensional microstructure with calcium silicate hydrate (C-S-H) and sodium aluminosilicate hydrate (N-A-S-H) gels.

Normally, the preparation of the geopolymer involves two methods: one-part and two-part methods [7,10]. The distinguishing feature of the one-part geopolymer (OPG) lies in its unique composition, which entails a mixture of solid aluminosilicate materials (known as precursors), solid alkaline activators, and water, setting it apart from the two-part geopolymer formulations. It can be seen that OPG stands out for in situ construction projects due to its potential to reduce environmental damage and low storage and transportation costs compared to the two-part geopolymer.

As for ground improvement, the unconfined compressive strength (UCS) is commonly used to evaluate the mechanical performance of cement-stabilized soil. Time-consuming and costly laboratory experiments are often required for determining the UCS of OPG-stabilized soil. Moreover, the existing findings regarding the application of OPG in soil stabilization remain relatively limited [10–15]. It has been observed that the adoption of OPG can substantially improve the mechanical properties of soil. Notably, it has been identified that the OPG prepared by combining solid binary precursors (FA and GGBFS) and a solid activator (sodium hydroxide or sodium silicate) with water can markedly improve the UCS and shear strength of the soft soil [12,13,16–18]. Nevertheless, the mechanical behavior of geopolymer-stabilized soil is affected by various influences, including the formulation of precursors, blending processes, surrounding curing environment, etc. Especially, gaining a comprehensive understanding of how precursors and activators impact on the strength performance of OPG-stabilized soil needs a comprehensive experimental examination and study, presenting difficulties regarding time, costs, and labor [13,19–21]. Hence, accurately predicting the UCS of geopolymer-stabilized soil represents a challenging task.

In recent years, with the rapid development of Machine Learning (ML) technology, its application in the field of materials science has attracted more and more attention. The contribution of ML techniques to concrete-like materials brings a great change in the computation of physical and mechanical properties [22–28], such as the modulus, strength, durability [29,30], and impermeability [31–33]. The basic principle of ML is data driven using the logic created by computation coding, allowing the computer to independently explore implicit relationships between the data and complete specified tasks, such as predicting target values. ML is widely employed in predicting the compressive strength of concrete and demonstrates that there is significant potential for utilizing ML in evaluating the mechanical performance of geopolymer. Among them, the ensemble learning and Boosting algorithms are the most widely adopted because of their intuitive and easy-to-understand principles, ease of construction, and fast speeds of fitting and prediction. Some cutting-edge ML models, such as Random Forest (RF) [34–41], Boosted Tree (BT) [42], Extra Trees [43], Gradient Boosting Regression Tree (GBRT) [44], Adaptive Boosting (AdaBoost) [6,40,45,46], and Extreme Gradient Boosting (XGB) [34,36,47–50], have been already used to predict the materials' performance in civil and mechanical engineering. However, overfitting tends to occur for ensemble learning models when the training dataset is not ideal. For example, ensemble learning models improve predictive performance by constructing multiple base learners, particularly in cases where the training set has high dimensions and a sparse distribution. Under such circumstances, the base learners of the ensemble learning models may struggle to capture the overall features. This is because each subsequent base learner is trained based on the results of the previous one, which induces the ensemble learning model to be less effective than models such as neural networks and support vector machines.

As a subset of ML, deep learning (DL) has the ability to handle more complex data and predict the output more accurately. DL has now achieved convincing results in predicting the compressive strength of concrete and geopolymer-based concrete (GPC). Contemporary mainstream deep learning networks can be categorized into several types: fully connected networks, Convolutional Neural Networks, recurrent neural networks, attention mechanism networks, and graph convolutional networks. Notably, attention mechanism networks and graph convolutional networks are more suited for text and image data, which do not align with the data types utilized in this paper. Artificial Neural Network (ANN), a simple and effective network model that mimics the thinking behavior of the human brain [51], has been applied to predict the compressive strength of materials by many scholars [35,42,46,48,52–63]. Subsequently, advancements in computer technology and computational power have led to the development of more complex networks based on ANN. This progression gives rise to the Deep Neural Network (DNN) [37,48,56,57,64] and deep Residual Networks (ResNet) [56,57,65] which further increases the number of hidden layers and neurons. For example, the Backpropagation Neural Network (BPNN) incorporates a feedforward algorithm to adjust neuron parameters [66]. The Convolutional Neural Network (CNN) utilizes convolutional calculations for feature extraction [67], and the Long Short-Term Memory (LSTM) network incorporates the attention mechanism for extracting time series features [68,69]. Table 1 summaries the applications of the ML and DL models in predicting the compressive strength of GPC.

Table 1. Summary of the ML and DL models used to predict the compressive strength of GPC.

Reference	Type of GPC	Algorithms	Best Model (R^2)
Zhou et al. [70]	Slag- and CCA-modified GPC	GEP	GEP (0.96)
Parhi and Patro [39]	FA-based GPC	RF, NN, MARS, HEML	HEML (0.97)
Nazar et al. [55]	FA-based GPC	ANFIS, ANN, GEP	GEP (0.94)
Ngo et al. [63]	Coal ash-based GPC	RF, ANN, XGB, GB, PSO	ANN (0.9808)
Oyebisi et al. [64]	GGBFS-CCA-based GPC	DNN	DNN (0.986)
Huo et al. [48]	Calcium-based GPC	KNN, SVM, RF, GBDT, BA, ET, XGB, DNN	XGB (0.91)
Kumar Dash et al. [71]	GGBS-based GPC	ELM, ELM-CSO, ELM-ECSO	ELM-ECSO (0.94)
Shahmansouri et al. [58]	GGBS-based GPC	ANN	ANN (0.924)
Huynh et al. [65]	FA-based GPC	ANN, DNN, ResNet	ResNet (0.937)
Dong et al. [62]	FA-based GPC	ANFIS, ANN	ANFIS (0.879)

Note: CCA is corn cob ash; GGBS is ground granulated blast slag; HEML is hybrid ensemble machine learning; ECSO is enhanced cat swarm; GEP is gene expression programming; ANFIS is adaptive neuro-fuzzy inference system; MARS is multivariate adaptive regression spline.

Despite their prevalence, numerous DL models pose ongoing challenges in terms of deciphering their internal processes [72]. In the last few years, interpretable approaches have been developed to elevate the explanation of ML models [73–75]. Explainable ML techniques, such as Shapley Additive Explanation (SHAP) [47,48,76–81] and Partial Dependence Plot (PDP) [80–83], make it clear how the models predict through inputs and provide a thorough comprehension of the link between inputs and outputs.

The aforementioned findings showed that ML and DL models can be adeptly applied to assess the physical and mechanical properties of geopolymer materials. For the focuses of the current study, only relying on the limited samples obtained from laboratory and field tests may fall short of meeting the data volume requirements for typical data-driven DL models. Therefore, there is a need to introduce data augmentation techniques to expand the training dataset and consequently enhance the performance of DL models. After the data augmentation methods based on Generative Adversarial Networks (GANs) were proposed in 2014 [84], there have been significant applications and research in the field of image restoration [85–87], paving the way for one of the trending directions in DL [88]. GANs achieve the objective of dataset augmentation by learning the distribution characteristics of the original training dataset to imitate and generate convincingly realistic synthetic data. By utilizing GANs to generate convincingly synthetic samples, data augmentation serves to address the shortfall in small sample sizes for DL models, thereby improving the models' performance. In light of the data types considered in this study, the ANN, BPNN, CNN, and LSTM models were selected for predictions. This choice is justified by their distinct computational and predictive mechanisms, making them all exemplary and representative options from the perspective of predictive value. Therefore, in this study, four different DL models were first employed to predict the UCS of OPG-stabilized soil by training the experimental data. Furthermore, to enhance the performance of DL models, the Wasserstein Generative Adversarial Network (WGAN) was utilized to generate additional synthetic samples by learning the features of the experimental data. The developed DL models with and without data augmentation were then compared to achieve better performance on predicting the UCS of the OPG-stabilized soil. Finally, a sensitivity analysis and SHAP and PDP methods were applied to the DL model with data augmentation for elucidating the inherent mechanism between the input features and output. The findings of this study may stimulate the employment of DL models in assessing the strength performance of the OPG-stabilized soil by incorporating both real and synthetic data into the training process, thereby attaining a balance between resource allocation and exactitude.

2. Deep Learning Models

2.1. ANN

Neural networks are a class of ML models that simulate the functioning of neurons in the human brain. With the continuous advancement of neural networks, particularly in conjunction with the increasing scale of data, these networks have progressively transitioned from shallow architectures to deeper structures, ultimately evolving into DL models.

The most fundamental neural network is the Artificial Neural Network (ANN), which can approximate any nonlinear function by increasing the number of neurons and hidden layers. The input layer, hidden layers, and output layer make up the three primary components of the ANN's structure, as shown in Figure 1. In the ANN, the neurons are the fundamental blocks of neural networks, which are responsible for receiving input from other neurons, applying weighted sums of these inputs using activation functions, and then transmitting the results to the next layer of neurons or the output layer. This process imitates the response mechanism of biological neurons. The hidden layers, located between the input and output layers in a neural network, consist of one or multiple neurons that facilitate information transmission and processing. The output of neurons can be expressed in the computational form illustrated in Equation (1). Many neural networks derived based on the ANN are suitable for processing complex data.

$$z = f\left(\sum_{i=1}^{p} \omega_i x_i + b\right), i = 1, 2, \ldots, p, \tag{1}$$

where z is the output of a neuron, x_i represents the inputs received by the neuron. ω denotes the weights of each input node and b denotes the bias of the neuron. f is defined as the activation function.

Before training, the types of functions associated with the network in the study must be defined, primarily encompassing the activation functions, loss functions, and optimization functions. The activation function determines the information output by the neurons and is a crucial component enabling the neural network to fit nonlinear relationships. Commonly used activation functions include Rectified Linear Unit (ReLU), Sigmoid, and tanh. In this study, apart from the output layer, all other layers utilize the ReLU activation function, as expressed in Equation (2). A notable feature of the ReLU is that its derivative is 0 on the negative half-axis. Therefore, the connected neuron will output 0 via the ReLU activation function when the activation value is negative. The structure of networks can be relatively sparse under this mechanism, thereby enhancing the training efficiency and improving the model's generalization capability [89]. The selection of the loss function primarily depends on the type of data. Given that the problem addressed in this study involves regression, the Mean Squared Error (MSE) function, which is commonly used for regression problems, is employed for the loss function, as shown in Equation (3). The optimization function, also referred to as the optimizer, serves the purpose of updating the model parameters, specifically the weights and biases of the neurons, according to the gradient of the loss function. In this study, the Adam optimizer is utilized, characterized by its high computational efficiency and its suitability for non-convex optimization problems.

It is particularly effective for handling sparse gradients and noise, and does not require additional adjustments for hyperparameters such as the learning rate [90].

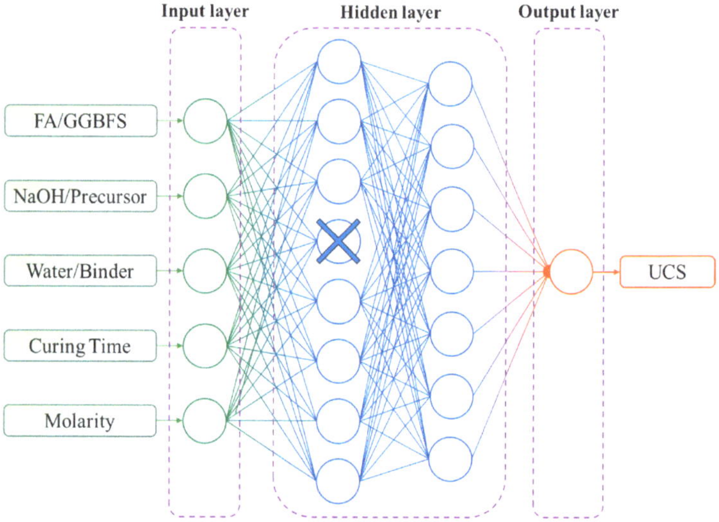

Figure 1. Framework of the ANN model for the prediction of the UCS in this study.

Furthermore, to address the issue of overfitting that may arise during training, a Dropout layer is introduced into the neural network. In the training progress, a certain proportion of neurons will randomly output 0 due to this layer. This configuration reduces the network's complexity while enhancing the model's capacity [91]. Since the current study aimed to predict the UCS value, the output layer was typically set to a single neuron.

$$f_{Relu}(x) = max(0, x), \quad (2)$$

$$MSE = \frac{\sum_{i=1}^{N} |UCS_{predict} - UCS_{true}|}{N}. \quad (3)$$

2.2. BPNN

The Back Propagation Neural Network (BPNN), first proposed by Rumelhart et al. [92], involves updating the parameters of the neural network through the backpropagation algorithm. Compared to the ANN, the BPNN exhibits a better generalization ability, enabling it to handle more complex data [93]. In the ANN, forward propagation is used solely to compute and obtain the neural network's output without adjusting the network's parameters.

Error backpropagation refers to the process of adjusting the weights and biases of the preceding layers based on the error generated by comparing the actual output values with the expected values, with the aim of minimizing this error as much as possible. This process can be encapsulated in two stages. The first stage is forward propagation, which begins at the input layer and progresses through the calculations of the hidden layers, ultimately reaching the output layer. This stage involves computing the output results at each layer and evaluating the associated errors. The second stage is backward propagation, which starts at the output layer; when the output results do not align with the actual results, the error is calculated using a loss function and subsequently, each neuron's weights are updated through an optimization function. These two steps are alternated, optimizing the parameters of each neuron and thereby reducing the discrepancy between the predicted values and the actual values [94,95].

2.3. CNN

The Convolutional Neural Network (CNN) is a type of feed-forward neural network that is similar to the ANN. The CNN model adopts Convolutional layers, Pooling layers, and fully connected layers (referred to the Dense layers) for feature extraction and classification [96,97]. Using Convolutional layers, the CNN model can identify features from input sequences, which leverages local correlations and weight sharing to reduce the model's parameter count, thereby enhancing the training speed and generalization capabilities.

A conventional CNN model is composed of the five layers: Convolutional layers, Pooling layers, Activation layers, Normalization layers, and Dense layers. The key of the CNN structure is the Convolutional layers. Adjusting the filter and kernel_size parameters in the 1D Convolutional layer can yield different effects on the feature extraction. The filter parameter determines the number of Convolutional kernels used to operate on the input data, while the kernel_size parameter plays a significant role in CNN performance. A larger kernel_size can capture broader features, while a smaller one can capture finer details. The purpose of the Pooling layer is to reduce dimensionality and accelerate the computation of the results from the Convolutional layer. Average pooling retains the overall feature information, while max pooling preserves local detailed features. As illustrated in Figure 2, for a tensor with input shape $[b, 3, 1]$ and setting f filters, a three-dimensional tensor of shape $[b, 3, f]$ is obtained, which is then dimensionally reduced by the Pooling layer to output a two-dimensional tensor of shape $[b, f]$.

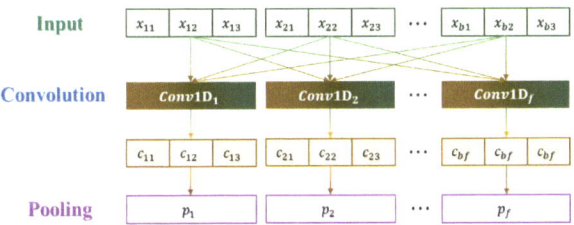

Figure 2. Calculations of the Convolutional and Pooling layers of the CNN.

2.4. LSTM

The recurrent neural network (RNN) has a greater advantage in handling time series data compared to the neural networks by using Dense layers and Convolutional layers [98,99]. The RNN is derived from the BPNN by adding a recurrent core to enhance short-term memory. In its recurrent structure, each neuron is determined not only by the parameters of the current input but also includes the output of the hidden layer from the previous time step. However, the traditional RNNs may encounter the vanishing or exploding gradient problem when dealing with long sequences, causing unstable training, an inability to increase network depth, and difficulty in effectively capturing long-range dependencies.

As one of the improved RNN models, the Long Short-Term Memory (LSTM) network has the characteristics of three gate designs, that is, the forget gate, input gate, and output gate [100,101]. These three gates manage units, which are used for the management of information forgetting and updating. The LSTM structure, as depicted in Figure 3, has x as the input feature at the current time step h_{t-1} that captures the preserved state details from the preceding time step, and h_t that stores the output for the present state. The forget gate regulates the influence of the memory from the previous time step on the current time step. The input gate controls the acceptance level of the input by the LSTM network, obtained through a non-linear transformation of x and h_{t-1}. The output gate, which is determined by the input gate and the tanh activation function, decides the output h_t at the current time step.

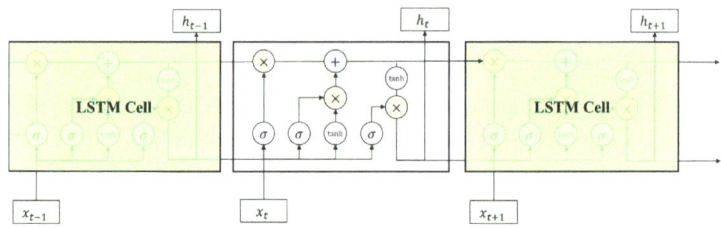

Figure 3. Structure of the LSTM network.

2.5. WGAN

Generative Adversarial Network (GAN), formally introduced in 2014 [84], consists of two neural network structures, the Generator and the Discriminator, as depicted in Figure 4. Through the adversarial interplay between these two networks, GAN can generate synthetic data. The Generator learns the distribution of real samples and then produces a series of synthetic samples, while the Discriminator distinguishes between synthetic samples generated by the Generator and real samples. The basic GAN model is prone to the issue of mode collapse, in which the Generator tends to generate a small number of high-quality synthetic samples in a narrow range. As these synthetic samples approach the real distribution, they can receive high scores from the Discriminator, inducing poor diversity and the concentration of generated synthetic samples within a small range [102,103]. Thus, various improved networks have been derived from GAN to address the mode collapse, such as the Wasserstein Generative Adversarial Network (WGAN) [103], Deep Convolutional Generative Adversarial Network (DCGAN) [104], and Cycle-Consistent Adversarial Network (CycleGAN) [105].

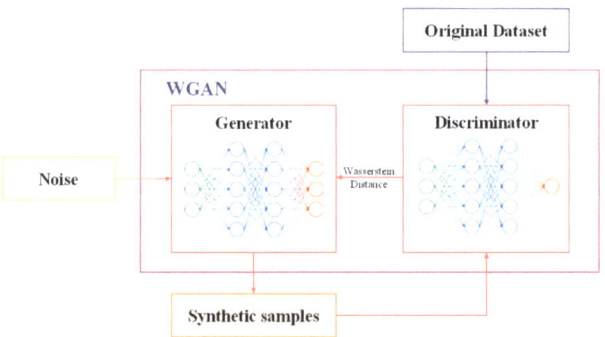

Figure 4. Structure of the WGAN.

The WGAN identifies Jensen–Shannon Divergence (JSD) as the cause of unstable GAN training. JSD is a method for measuring the similarity between two probability distributions. For non-overlapping distributions, the gradient surface is constantly zero, meaning that the distribution probability of generated samples does not overlap with that of real samples, resulting in a JSD value of log2. This leads to a situation where the gradient at the generated sample location is always zero, making it impossible to update the Generator's parameters effectively and thereby affecting training performance. In GAN, real samples are labelled as 1 and synthetic samples are set to 0, and the Discriminator's objective function is used to minimize the error between real samples (label 1) and synthetic samples (label 0).

The WGAN introduces the Wasserstein distance, also known as the Earth-Mover (EM) Distance, which calculates the minimum cost of transforming one distribution into another. The calculation of the Wasserstein distance can be expressed in Equation (4), which can effectively address the lack of gradient information due to the JSD [103,106]. Generating low-quality synthetic samples induces a greater Wasserstein distance, and thus forces the Generator's parameters to be updated. In the WGAN, the Discriminator also serves as the unit for calculating the Wasserstein distance. The more accurate the Discriminator's distance calculation, the more beneficial it is for the Generator. Therefore, in each iteration, the Generator is trained once while the Discriminator is trained five times to obtain a more accurate calculation of the Wasserstein distance. In terms of Generator design, based on the structure of the BPNN, a smaller Convolutional kernel size is used for 1D convolutions to capture the distribution and precise features of the original samples.

$$W(p,q) = \inf_{\gamma \prod(p,q)} E_{(x,y) \sim \gamma}[\|x - y\|], \quad (4)$$

where $\prod(x-y)$ represents the collection of all possible joint distributions formed by the combination of distributions p and q. For each of these potential joint distributions $y \sim \prod(x-y)$, the expected distance $E_{(x,y)\sim\gamma}[\|x-y\|]$ is computed, with (x,y) being sampled from the joint distribution γ. The term $\inf\{\cdot\}$ signifies the infimum of the set.

2.6. K-Fold Cross-Validation

K-Fold cross-validation is a common method to validate and evaluate the performance of models [107]. The basic idea is to divide a dataset into k groups, in which $k-1$ groups are used as the training set for model training and the remaining group is taken as the test set for model testing and validation, as illustrated in Figure 5. This process results in k models, in which the average results are taken as the final performance of the model. K-Fold cross-validation can extract as much valuable information as possible from limited data, thereby avoiding poor model performance due to the uneven distribution of the training set, and can further reduce the likelihood of overfitting and increase the stability of the model. Most studies recommend using 5-fold or 10-fold cross-validation to obtain the final model results [108,109]. In this study, 5-fold cross-validation was chosen, with the average values of each metric taken as the final conclusion.

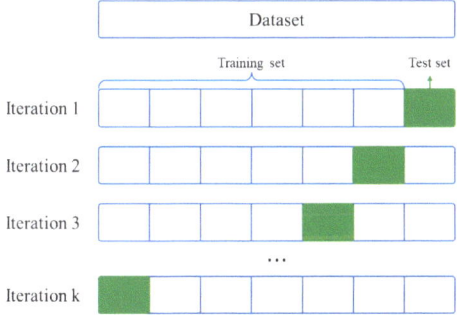

Figure 5. The diagram of K-Fold cross-validation.

2.7. Interpretable Methods

2.7.1. Sensitivity Analysis

Most ML models exhibit considerable structural complexity, particularly DL models, making it challenging to comprehend the predictive principles underlying these models. To ascertain the feasibility of such models—specifically, whether the contributions of various input features to the output values align with existing research or whether they can provide clear decision-making justifications—it is essential to implement post hoc interpretability methods [23,110].

Sensitivity analysis reveals how independent variables affect the output [111]. The specific calculation process involves randomly sampling the independent variables within a specified range and using a pre-trained model to predict the output. By employing the one-at-a-time (OAT) method to control variables, the sensitivity analysis perturbs only one independent variable at a time while keeping other variables at their nominal values, and thus the relationship between the output and that variable can be determined [112,113]. Sensitivity analysis can be divided into a global sensitivity analysis and local sensitivity analysis. In contrast to the local sensitivity analysis, the global sensitivity analysis focuses on the impacts of all input variables on the output and can consider interactions between variables. Notably, this study adopted a global sensitivity analysis method based on Sobol coefficients, which include first- and second-order sensitivity analyses. The first-order sensitivity analysis primarily focuses on the impacts of individual input parameters on the model output. The second-order sensitivity analysis reflects the degree to which interactions between two input parameters affect the model output, providing a more comprehensive understanding of how interactions between parameters influence the model output. The calculation of the first-order sensitivity Sobol index is shown in Equation (5), while the calculation of the second-order sensitivity Sobol index is shown in Equation (6).

$$S_i = \frac{V_i}{V} = \frac{Var\left(E\left(Y|X^{(i)}\right)\right)}{Var(Y)}, \tag{5}$$

$$S_{ij} = \frac{V_{ij}}{V} = \frac{Var\left(E\left(Y|X^{(i)}, X^{(j)}\right)\right) - V_i - V_j}{Var(Y)}, \tag{6}$$

where E describes the mathematical expectation. V_i is determined by the ANOVA variance decomposition formula $V_i = Var\left(E\left(Y|X^{(i)}\right)\right)$.

2.7.2. SHAP

SHAP, which is short for Shapley Additive Explanation, is an interpretive method that is deeply influenced by game theory. As indicated by its nomenclature, the SHAP method primarily facilitates post hoc explanations through the computation of Shapley values. In the context of cooperative game theory, the Shapley value (hereinafter referred to as the SHAP value) serves to quantify the contribution of each participant to the value generated by the collaboration. When applied to machine learning models, it evaluates the contribution of each input feature to the resulting output label. In SHAP methods, the model's prediction progress is interpreted as a linear function of binary variables [114], as shown in Equation (7). Additionally, the computation of SHAP value is shown in Equations (8) and (9).

$$g(z) = \phi_0 + \sum_{k=1}^{N} \phi_k z'_i, \tag{7}$$

where g is explainable DL model; z denotes the input feature; and N is the number of inputs. ϕ_k is the SHAP value of feature k. ϕ_0 is a constant.

$$\phi_k = \sum_{K \subseteq M\{i\}} \frac{|K|!(N-|K|-1)!}{N!}[g_X(K \cup \{i\}) - g_X(K)], \tag{8}$$

$$g_X(K) = E[g(x)|x_K], \tag{9}$$

where $M = \{x_1, x_2, \ldots, x_N\}$ is the set of input features. $E[g(x)|x_K]$ represents the expected value of the subset K.

2.7.3. PDP

The Partial Dependence Plot (PDP) is a visualization technique that illustrates the marginal effects of features on the predictions of the trained ML model [115]. Its advantage is to generate plots to display the relationship between the target and input variables. This makes it easier to comprehend how each input specifically affects the model's predictions, which improves the interpretability of the DL models. The PDP method elucidates the relationship between inputs and outputs by utilizing all available data points within the dataset [116,117]. The partial dependence function $f_{x_s}(x_s)$ can be estimated by calculating the mean values within the training data, as illustrated in Equation (10):

$$f_{x_s}(x_s) = \frac{1}{n}\sum_{k=1}^{n} DL\left(x_s, x_c^{(k)}\right), \tag{10}$$

where x_s is the feature of partial dependence in the set S; $x_c^{(k)}$ denotes the actual values within the dataset corresponding to the features in the feature space, excluding the specified set S; n is the total number of instances in the dataset; and DL is the trained DL model.

2.8. Performance Index

In the present study, the three metrics, including MAE, RMSE, and R^2, were employed to evaluate the performance of DL models. These metrics play crucial roles in evaluating the accuracy and explanatory power of predictive models. Specifically, MAE and RMSE quantify the disparities between the forecasted and real values, shedding light on the model's precision and consistency. On the other hand, R^2 serves as a pivotal indicator of how well the independent variable elucidates the variations in the dependent variable. Equations (11)–(13) delineate the precise methodologies for computing MAE, RMSE, and R^2, respectively.

$$MAE = \frac{1}{N}\sum_{i=1}^{N}\left|UCS_{predict} - UCS_{true}\right|, \tag{11}$$

$$RMSE = \sqrt{\frac{\sum_{i=1}^{N}\left(UCS_{predict} - UCS_{true}\right)^2}{N}}, \tag{12}$$

$$R^2 = 1 - \frac{\sum_{i=1}^{N}\left(UCS_{true} - UCS_{predict}\right)^2}{\sum_{i=1}^{N}\left(UCS_{true} - \overline{UCS_{true}}\right)^2}, \tag{13}$$

3. Methodology

3.1. Workflow of the Current Research

The framework of the current study was divided into four parts, data processing, model development, model assessment, and interpretable analysis, as illustrated in Figure 6.

In the data processing section, to mitigate the effect of different scales, the collected dataset was first standardized using Z-score normalization, as shown in Equation (14). The original real data were then divided into a training set and validation set at the ratio of 9:1. In addition, the mean UCS for the parallel samples with the same mixing proportion in the original real data was defined as the refined set. In the model development part, five different DL models were constructed: ANN, BPNN, CNN, LSTM, and WGAN-CNN. Notably, the WGAN-CNN model involved the synthetic samples generated by WGAN, which were added into the training set for the CNN model. For model assessment, three evaluation metrics (MAE, RMSE, and R^2) and the K-Fold cross-validation method were employed. In the interpretable analysis section, the best-performing DL models were further analyzed by the three types of interpretable methods (sensitivity analysis, SHAP, and PDP) to further validate the feasibility of the DL models in the prediction of the mechanical properties of the OPG-stabilized soil.

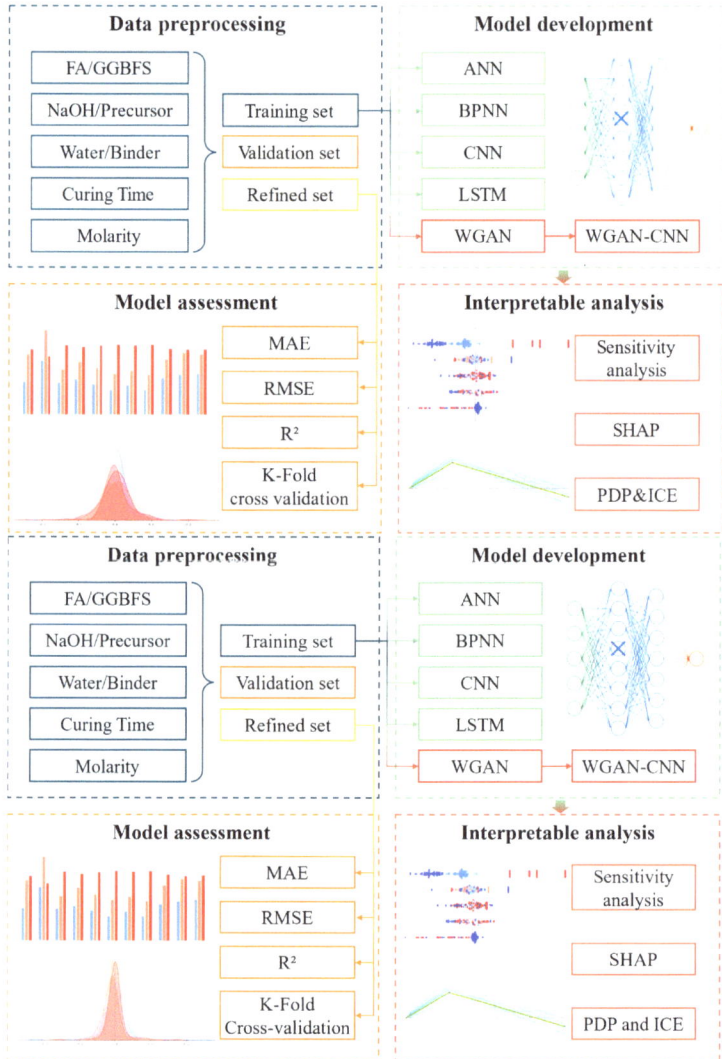

Figure 6. Workflow of the study.

$$X_i = \frac{(x_i - \mu)}{\sigma}, \tag{14}$$

where X_i is the ith input after normalization, x_i is the ith input, μ represents the sample mean, and σ represents the sample standard deviation. Standardizing the data allows them to be mapped to a range centered around zero for easier processing alongside other data.

3.2. Data Collection

The data utilized in this study originated from the laboratory experiments conducted by our study team. Initially, a solid alkali activator (NaOH), water, and binary precursors (GGBFS and FA) were blended to create the one-part geopolymer (OPG) paste. Subsequently, the OPG paste was cast into the remolded soil. The strength development of the OPG-stabilized soil was primarily influenced by the quantities of FA, GGBFS, NaOH, and water, since the one-part method was adopted in present study. Thus, the input variables for DL models were defined as the mass ratios for FA/GGBFS, NaOH/precursor, and water/binder. To investigate the impact of the alkaline concentration on the stabilized soil's strength, the molarity was also selected as an input variable in this study. Equation (15) illustrates the calculation of the molarity for the one-part geopolymer. After the casting process, the OPG-stabilized soil samples were subjected to standard curing conditions for durations of 3, 7, 14, and 28 days prior to conducting the UCS tests. Consequently, the curing time was included as an input parameter, and the UCS of OPG-stabilized soil served as the output. In current study, at least three samples for each design mixture were conducted. Therefore, a total of 390 data points were obtained from the experiment.

$$Molarity = \frac{n_{NaOH}}{V_{NaOH}} = \frac{m_{NaOH}/M_{NaOH}}{m_{NaOH}/\rho_{NaOH}}, \quad (15)$$

where m_{NaOH} represents the mass of solid NaOH. M_{NaOH} represents molar mass of NaOH. n_{NaOH} represents the molar concentration of NaOH. V_{NaOH} represents the amount of NaOH. ρ_{NaOH} represents the density of the NaOH solution.

The statistical description of the dataset is presented in Table 2, with corresponding visual representations in Figure 7 (histogram and box diagram). Figure 7a displays the distribution of UCS in a histogram. Figure 7b illustrates the distributions of the five input variables after standardization. The box diagram in Figure 7b shows that the distributions of NaOH/precursor and molarity are relatively discrete. The linear correlation coefficient was computed to clarify the relationships among the variables, as presented in Equation (16) and illustrated in Figure 8.

$$Corr(X,Y) = \frac{cov(X,Y)}{SD_X SD_Y} = \frac{\left[\sum_{i=1}^{n}(X_i - \overline{X})(Y_i - \overline{Y})\right]/(n-1)}{\sqrt{Var[X]Var[Y]}}, \quad (16)$$

where $cov(X,Y)$ is the covariance of X and Y. Var is the variance. SD denotes the standard deviation.

Table 2. Statistical description of inputs and output.

Type	Variable	Standard Deviation	Mean	Min	Max
Independent	FA/GGBFS	0.120	0.134	0	0.43
	NaOH/Precursor	0.034	0.151	0.1	0.2
	Water/Binder	0.084	0.620	0.5	0.7
	Curing time (days)	8.103	11.318	3	28
	Molarity (mol/L)	0.663	4.754	3.27	8.33
Dependent	UCS (MPa)	0.638	1.229	0.1	3.282

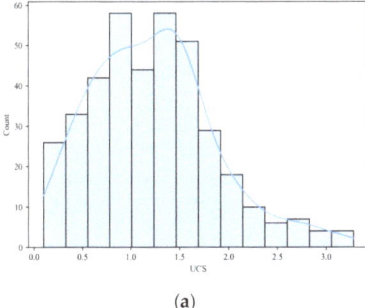
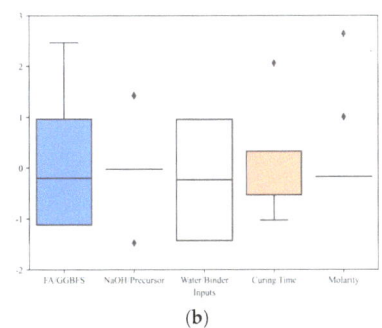

(a) (b)

Figure 7. Description of the data distribution. (a) Histogram of the UCS. (b) Box diagram of the inputs.

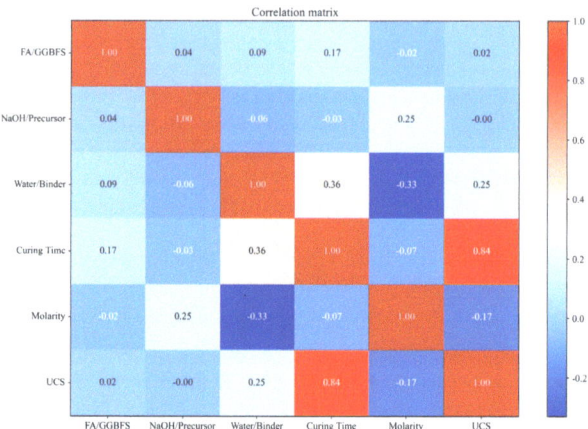

Figure 8. Correlation matrix.

4. Results and Discussion

4.1. Performance of the DL Models

The study was executed on a Windows operating system, employing Python programming within the Visual Studio Code platform. In terms of training time, the WGAN model required the most extensive training duration, while the CNN and LSTM took slightly longer than the BPNN and ANN.

The performance results and error analyses of the four DL models are shown in Figures 9–14. From the loss figures in Figures 9–12, it can be observed that the loss functions of all four DL models converged. In comparison to the other models, the loss figure of the ANN in Figure 9 shows that the loss for the validation set did not completely approach 0, but exhibited some fluctuations. This is likely due to the absence of a backpropagation algorithm in the ANN to adjust the parameters of the preceding neural network units, which caused the model's predictions for the refined set to not be completely concentrated on the best fit line.

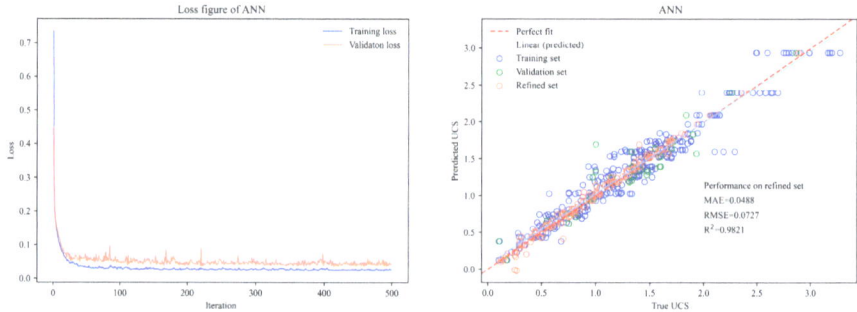

Figure 9. The performance index of the ANN model.

Among all four DL models, the CNN exhibited the best performance (as shown in Figure 11, MAE = 0.022, RMSE = 0.0409, R^2 = 0.9938), followed by LSTM (as shown in Figure 12, MAE = 0.0274, RMSE = 0.0451, R^2 = 0.9924) and BPNN (as shown in Figure 10, MAE = 0.0272, RMSE = 0.0462, R^2 = 0.9921). The linear (prediction) lines in Figures 9–12 represent the linear regression of the predicted and actual UCS of original dataset. For the BPNN, CNN, and LSTM models, these lines exhibited some deviation from the best fit line, primarily due to the limited training data for the UCS beyond 2.5 MPa and the presence of experimental errors in the samples. However, when adopting the mean UCS for the same mixing group as the refined set for DL models, the predictions from the DL models aligned with the best fit line (red dot line in the figures), indicating that the models did not exhibit overfitting and performed well in predicting the mean UCS for each group. Furthermore, the CNN, BPNN, and LSTM developed in the current study were capable of mitigating sample errors. The LSTM outperformed the BPNN in terms of R^2 and RMSE, but the BPNN had a lower MAE value than that of the LSTM, implying that the recurrent computation in the LSTM leaded to fewer outlier values during the prediction process and was less susceptible to the influence of input outliers.

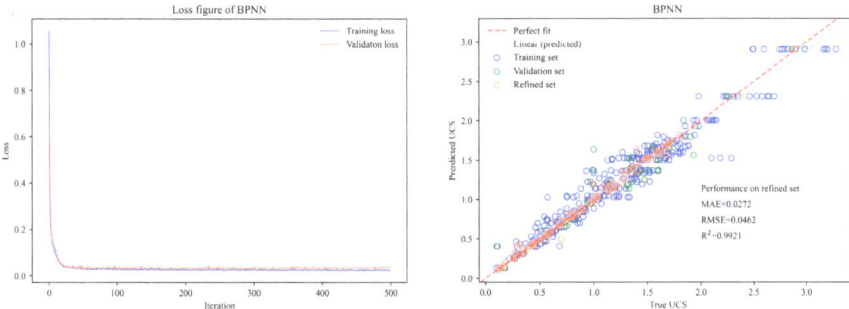

Figure 10. The performance index of the BPNN model.

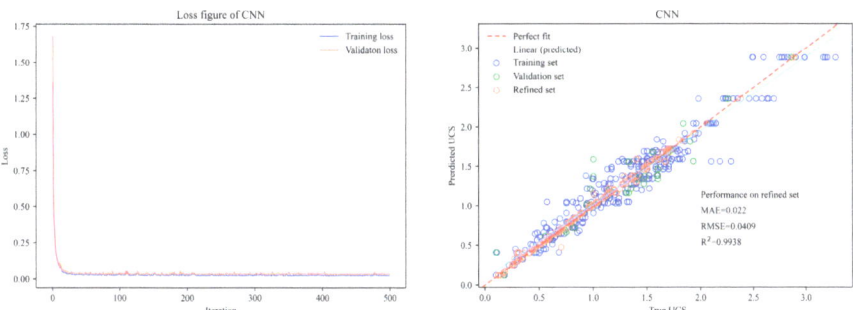

Figure 11. The performance index of the CNN model.

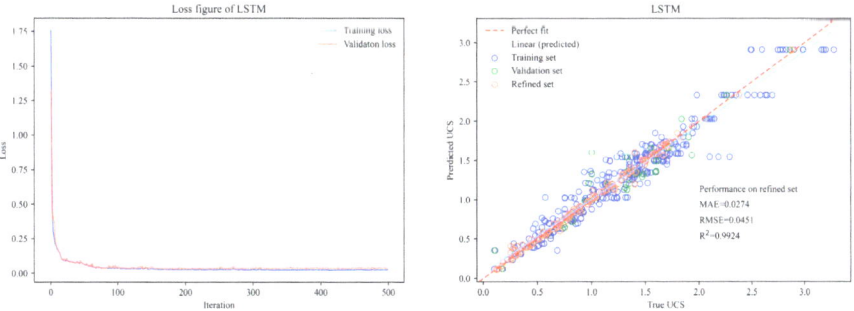

Figure 12. The performance index of the LSTM model.

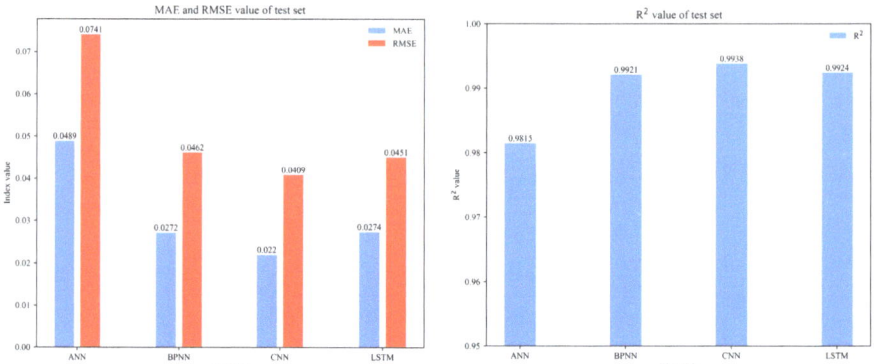

Figure 13. Performance comparison of the DL models on the refined set.

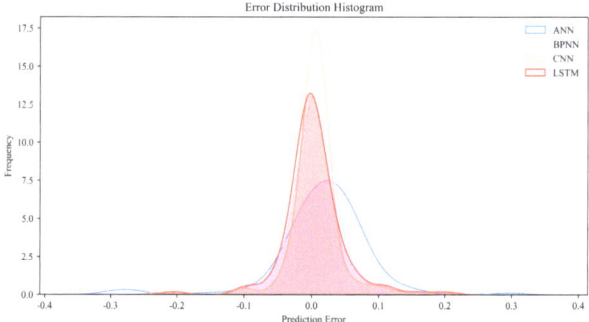

Figure 14. KDE plot of the prediction errors of DL models.

The Kernel Density Estimation (KDE) plots of the four models, which are presented in Figure 14, can be used to analyze the distribution of errors for each model. It is evident that the errors for the CNN model were most concentrated around 0, followed by the LSTM, which had smaller errors compared to the BPNN, and the ANN gave the largest errors among the four models. Based on the above analysis, the CNN model had better performance than the other DL models in the present study.

4.2. Performance of WGAN-CNN

Firstly, standardized preprocessing was applied to the source data, and then violin plots were generated using synthetic samples distributed by GAN and WGAN (Dense layers [118] and Convolutional layers [85]), as shown in Figure 15. The distribution of input variables in the original dataset is shown in Figure 15a. Based on Figure 15b, it can be observed that using GAN alone induced model collapse, in which the generated synthetic samples were concentrated within a small range and failed to effectively capture the distribution of the original data samples. At the same time, the WGAN generator with Dense layers, as shown in Figure 15c, can extract more diverse features, and the WGAN generator with Convolutional layers, as shown in Figure 15d, can capture a complementary distribution. Obviously, the combination of the generator with dense and Convolutional layers can have more comprehensive, synthetic data, compensating for the lack of distribution in some ranges. Taking the input variable of curing time as an example, the original data only included the UCS at 3, 7, 14, and 28 curing days. Through the combination of the synthetic data from the WGAN generators with Dense and Convolutional layers, the data for the UCS within a month can be obtained, further expanding the distribution for the training set.

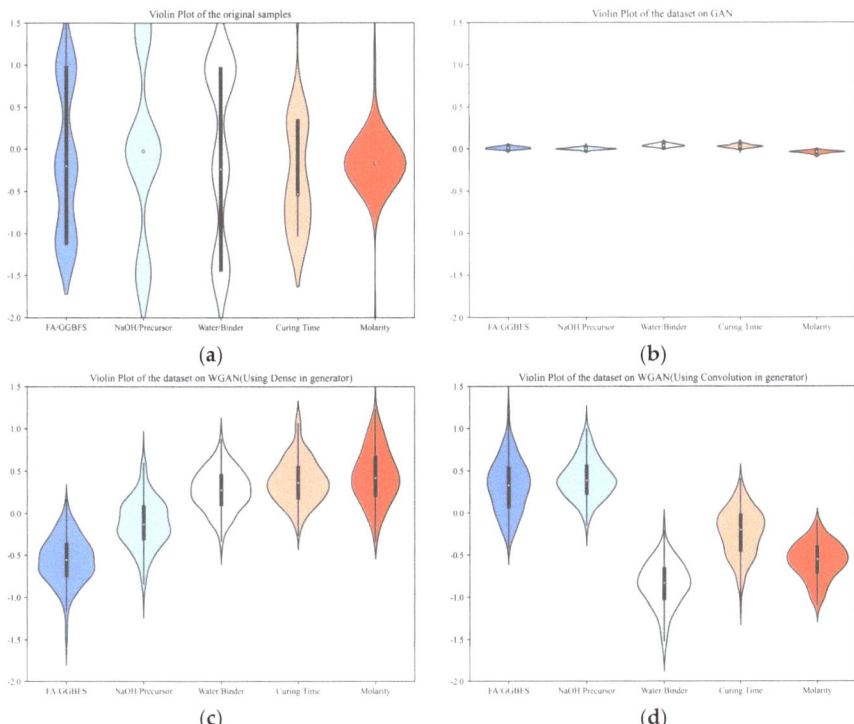

Figure 15. Violin plots of different samples. (**a**) The original dataset. (**b**) The synthetic samples generated by GAN. (**c**) The synthetic samples generated by WGAN (adopting Dense layers in the generator). (**d**) The synthetic samples generated by WGAN (adopting Convolutional layers in the generator).

Hence, in present study, the synthetic samples used to augment the training set were composed of samples generated by two different WGAN generators (Dense layers and Convolutional layers). By assigning a fixed random seed, the synthetic data were randomly sampled for each group of CNN training. Different synthetic samples were added to the original training set while keeping the refined set unchanged, resulting in the outcomes shown in Figures 16 and 17. It can be observed that the performance of the WGAN-CNN models was obviously improved when 100 to 200 synthetic samples were added in the training set. Particularly, the WGAN-CNN models with 150 and 200 groups of synthetic samples provided excellent results, in which the R^2 values approached 0.9979 and 0.9978, respectively. Additionally, the corresponding MAE values were 0.0154 and 0.0119, and the RMSE values were 0.0238 and 0.0243, respectively. According to the KDE plot illustrated in Figure 17, the WGAN-CNN model trained with 200 synthetic samples exhibited the optimum performance, with the errors being concentrated at zero. The scatter plots with linear fit lines are shown in Figure 18, which compared the predicted UCS values from these two WGAN-CNN models with the actual UCS values. It can be observed that the scatter points of the WGAN-CNN model with 200 synthetic samples were closer to the perfect fit line. Thus, it can be concluded that the performance of the WGAN-CNN model with 200 synthetic samples was slightly better than that of the model with 150 synthetic samples. In the subsequent sections, the term "WGAN-CNN" refers to the WGAN-CNN model with the incorporation of 200 WGAN-generated synthetic samples.

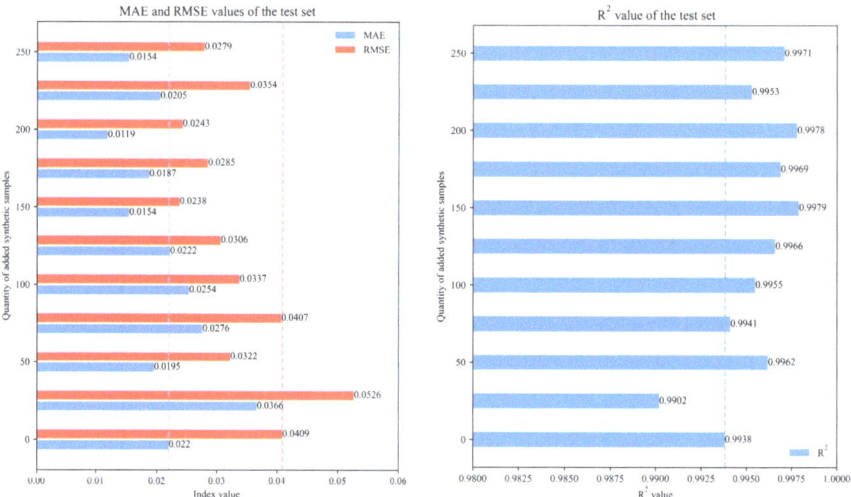

Figure 16. The comparison of the performance of the WGAN-CNN models.

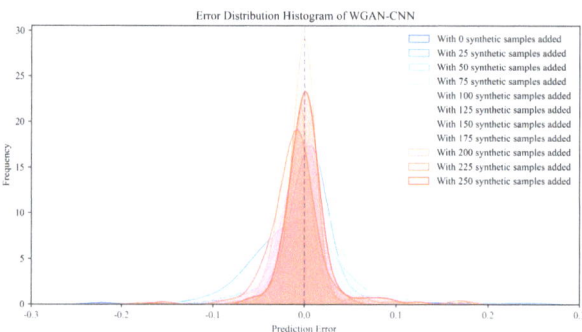

Figure 17. The KDE plot of the prediction errors of the WGAN-CNN models.

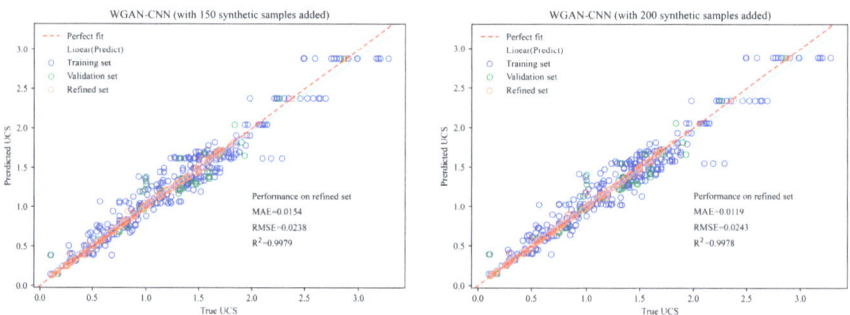

Figure 18. The performance of WGAN-CNN (with 150 and 200 synthetic samples).

4.3. Interpretable Analysis

4.3.1. Results of Sensitivity Analysis

First-order and second-order sensitivity analyses were conducted on the five DL models, and the corresponding results are shown in Figures 19 and 20, respectively. Based on the first-order sensitivity analysis, as given in Figure 19, all models indicted that the most important feature of the UCS prediction was the curing time. The top-performing CNN and WGAN-CNN models showed a consistent ranking of influencing factors, with only slight differences in the rankings of water/binder and molarity, which were placed third and fifth, respectively.

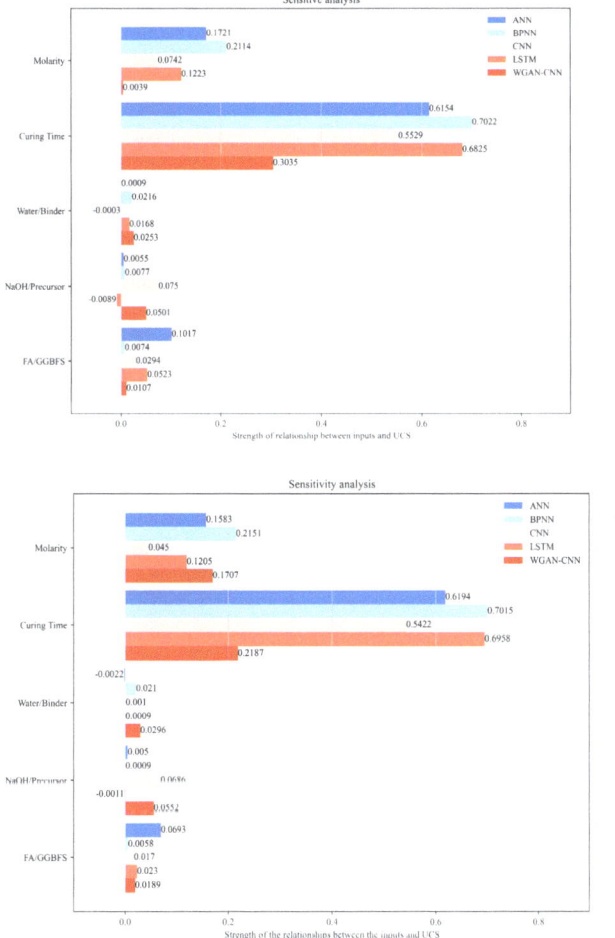

Figure 19. First order sensitive analysis of DL models.

The second-order sensitivity analysis revealed the interactions between inputs and their impacts on the UCS. The sensitivity analyses in Figure 20a,b,d did not exhibit significant interaction relationships. From Figure 20c,e, it can be observed that both the CNN and WGAN-CNN models demonstrated that the interaction between water/binder and molarity had a significant impact on the UCS. However, the sensitivity analysis only identified the degree of influence by varying the input parameters and could not reveal the nonlinear relationship between the input variable and the output. Therefore, more robust interpretability methods such as SHAP and PDP were adopted in the following analyses.

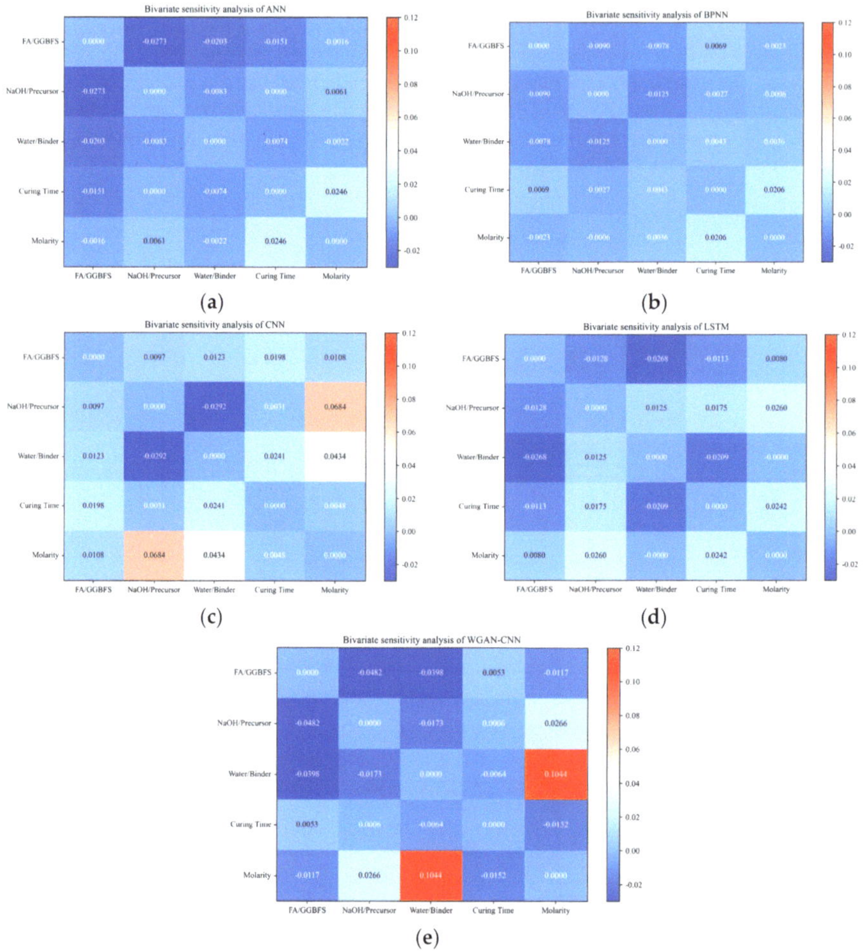

Figure 20. Second-order sensitivity analyses of DL models. (**a**) ANN. (**b**) BPNN. (**c**) CNN. (**d**) LSTM. (**e**) WGAN-CNN.

4.3.2. SHAP Results

In the interpretability analysis, the focus was on examining the CNN and WGAN-CNN models with superior performance. The SHAP values were calculated and visualized in Figures 21 and 22.

As depicted in Figure 21, the SHAP global analysis revealed that the two DL models yielded essentially identical SHAP values and global interpretations. The difference occurred in the sequence of the second-to-third and third-to-fourth rankings. This finding resonated with previous research indicating that the SHAP value increased when the curing time increased, signifying the improvement of the UCS. Furthermore, Figure 8 indicated a strong linear correlation coefficient between the UCS and curing time, further implying that the curing time could be a crucial factor in the development of UCS of the samples. As shown in Figure 21, the trend between the SHAP value and FA/GGBFS did not demonstrate a complete negative correlation. This suggested that FA/GGBFS within a lower range could improve the UCS. Similarly, lower values of molarity, as depicted by the SHAP values concentrating around 0.1, were found to have a positive impact on UCS as well. Conversely, the water/binder variable generally displayed a negative correlation with the UCS. The NaOH/precursor ratio exhibited relatively low SHAP values, making it difficult to establish a direct relationship with the UCS.

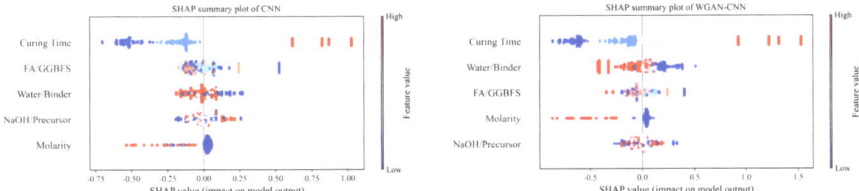

Figure 21. SHAP global explanations of the CNN and WGAN-CNN.

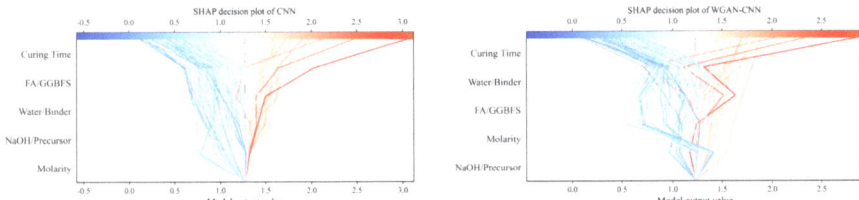

Figure 22. SHAP decision plots for the CNN and WGAN-CNN.

The decision plots for the two models, presented in Figure 22, illustrate the influence of the inputs on the models' outputs for all samples. The x-axis depicts the direction and trend of the effect of each feature on the output, and the plot can also detect outlier samples.

Through the SHAP interaction analysis, the changes in SHAP values for one input feature interacting with another can be obtained. As shown in Figures 23–25, the trends of the CNN and WGAN-CNN models in the SHAP analysis were generally consistent. By examining the interaction plot of the curing time with other factors in Figure 23, it is evident that due to the overall increase in scatter distribution with the increase in curing time, the input of curing time was found to be the dominant factor. From Figure 23a, c, it can be inferred that at lower values of the curing time (below 10 days), higher FA/GGBFS and water/binder ratios induced a decrease in the SHAP value for the curing time. Figure 23b indicates that when the curing time exceeds 15 days, a NaOH/precursor ratio greater than 0.15 increased the SHAP value of the curing time. As illustrated in Figure 23d, it is noticeable that beyond 20 days of curing time, higher molarity caused a reduction in the SHAP value for the curing time, and vice versa. This observation suggested that a certain NaOH/precursor ratio accelerated the hydration in the sample at an early curing age, implying that the UCS trend of the soil increased fast at the early curing time.

In Figure 24a, with the increase in NaOH/precursor, the SHAP value of FA/GGBFS below 0.2 increased, indicating an improvement of the UCS. Conversely, the SHAP value of FA/GGBFS above 0.2 decreased as the NaOH/precursor increased. This phenomenon was primarily attributed to the higher NaOH content in the OPG that activated more Ca and Si components in the precursor, leading to the formation of numerous hydrated areas in the soil.

Figure 24b revealed that when FA/GGBFS was less than 0.3, a higher water/binder ratio resulted in an increase in the SHAP value of FA/GGBFS. This is due to the fact that a lower water content made it more difficult for the OPG binder and soil to mix evenly, which decreased the UCS.

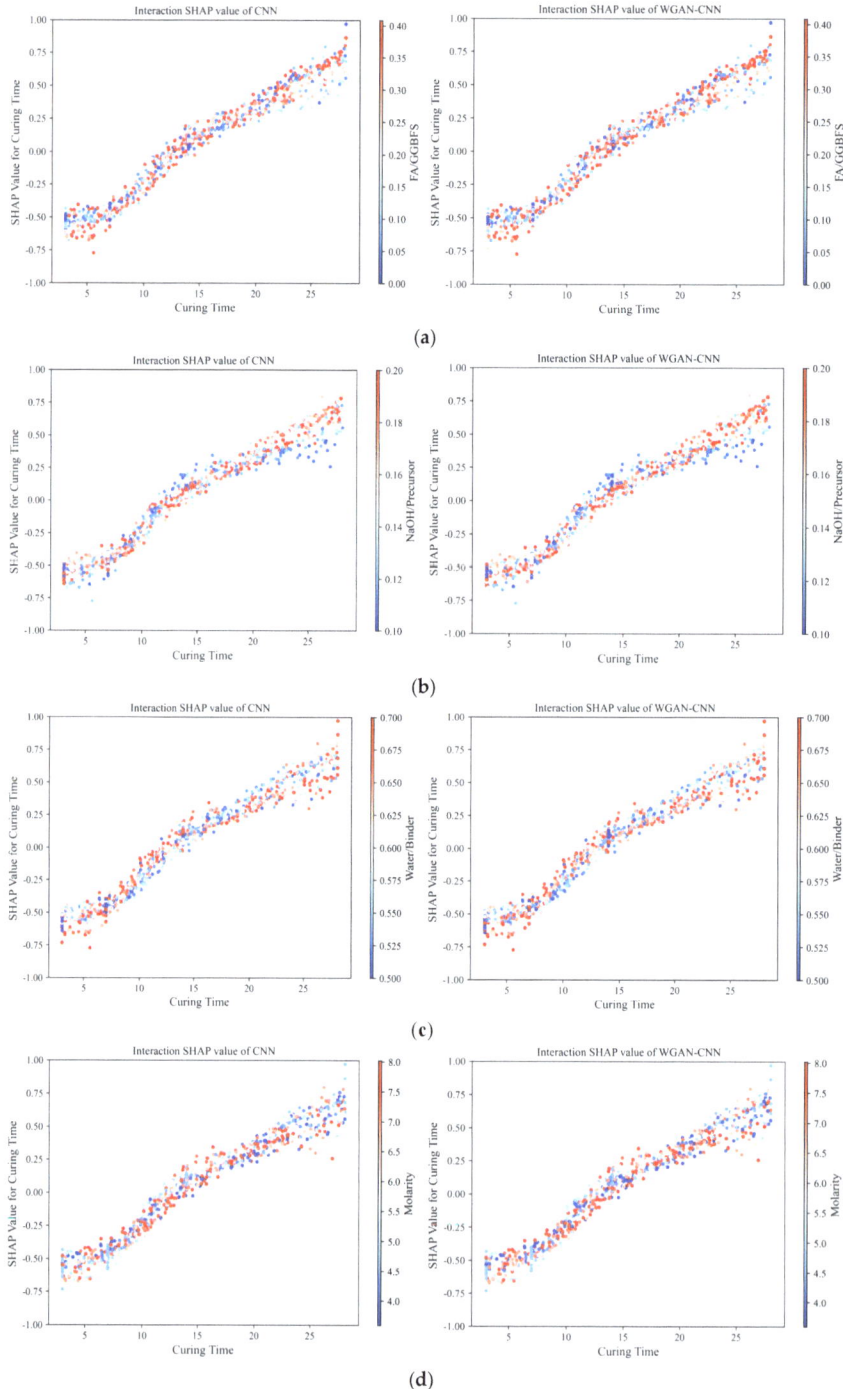

Figure 23. SHAP interaction analysis of the curing time. (**a**) Curing time versus FA/GGBFS. (**b**) Curing time versus NaOH/precursor. (**c**) Curing time versus water/binder. (**d**) Curing time versus molarity.

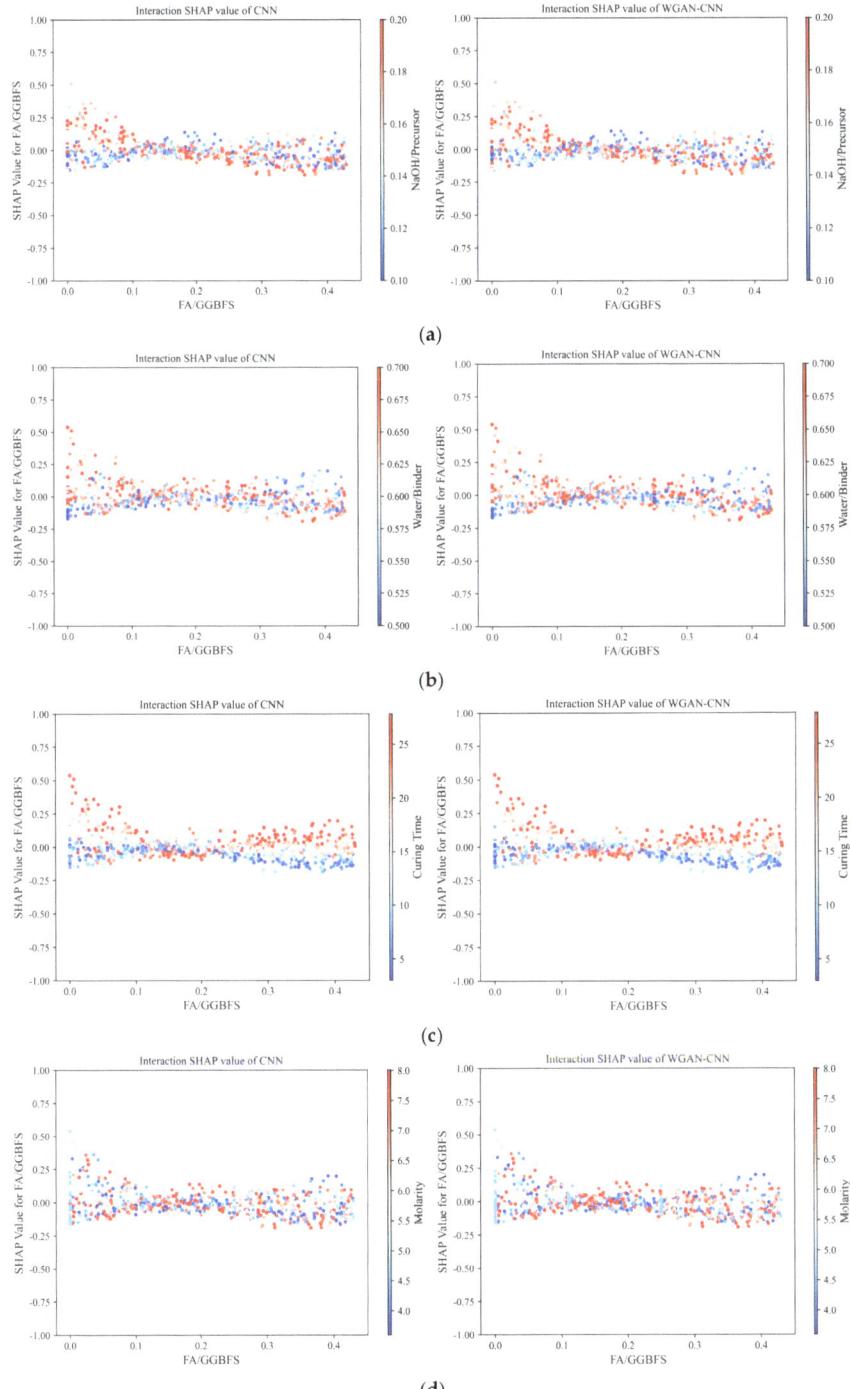

Figure 24. SHAP interaction analysis of FA/GGBFS. (**a**) FA/GGBFS versus NaOH/precursor. (**b**) FA/GGBFS versus water/binder. (**c**) FA/GGBFS versus the curing time. (**d**) FA/GGBFS versus molarity.

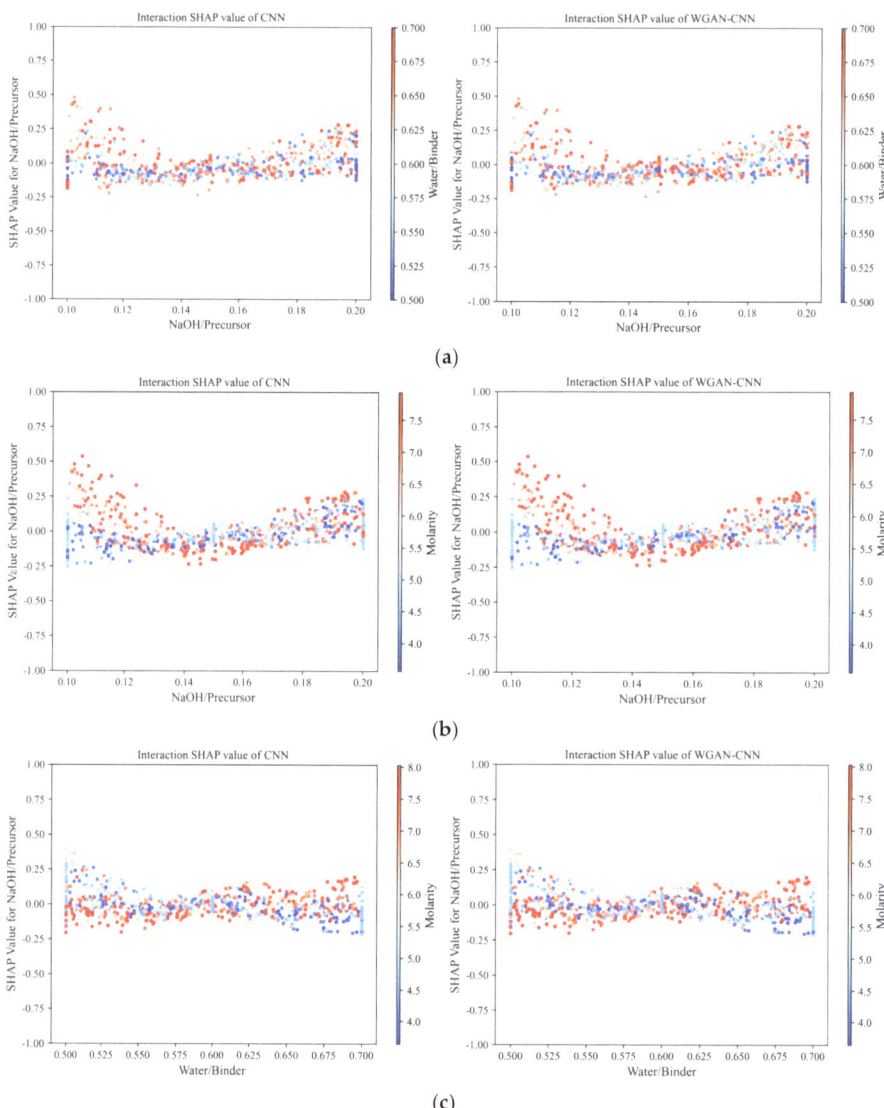

Figure 25. SHAP interaction analysis of other factors. (**a**) NaOH/precursor versus water/binder. (**b**) NaOH/precursor versus molarity. (**c**) NaOH/precursor versus water/binder.

Figure 24c illustrates the impact of curing time variations on FA/GGBFS. It is observed that FA/GGBFS in the range of 0.12 to 0.25 might reduce the model's dependence on the curing time to some extent, in which an increase in the curing time led to a reduction in the SHAP value of FA/GGBFS. However, when the FA/GGBFS was beyond 0.25, an increase in the curing time induced an increase in the SHAP value of FA/GGBFS. This might be possible because the optimal addition of FA enhanced the workability of the OPG binder, ensuring the more uniform spread of the binder in the soil. Additionally, the existence of FA participated in secondary pozzolanic reaction during later curing times, thereby enhancing the UCS of the stabilized soil.

Figure 24d demonstrates the effect of molarity variations on the SHAP value for FA/GGBFS. When FA/GGBFS ranged between 0.12 and 0.25, higher molarity could increase the SHAP value for FA/GGBFS. The findings aligned with the understanding that a lower molarity may not effectively catalyze the aluminosilicate components in FA and GGBFS to produce hydration gels, inducing a limited contribution to the improvement of the UCS of the stabilized soil. Conversely, a higher molarity could lead to a rapid release of Ca and Si ions from FA and GGBFS, thereby decreasing the OPG binder's setting time. In this case, the soil particles may not be efficiently connected by the hydration gels from the binder [12,80].

In Figure 25a, it is shown that when the NaOH/Precursor exceeded 0.14, a decrease in the water/binder led to an increase in the SHAP value for NaOH/precursor. This is because, for a specific amount of NaOH, a lower water content led to a higher concentration of the NaOH solution, which enhanced geopolymerization in OPG binder. Figure 25b,c reveals that with an increase in molarity, both the SHAP values for NaOH/precursor and water/binder exhibited a concave curve. This trend suggested that an excessively high or low molarity of the NaOH solution did not significantly enhance the properties of the soil. The OPG binder has an ideal molarity for fixed precursor or binder contents.

4.3.3. PDP Results

The analysis of 1D Partial Dependence Plots (PDPs) for the CNN and WGAN-CNN models is depicted in Figure 26. It is evident that the 1D PDP tendency for both DL models demonstrated consistency. It should be noted that the 1D PDP analysis only displayed the average responses (indicated by red line in figures). In order to visualize how the output depends on each input, the Individual Conditional Expectation (ICE) is introduced in the study (indicated by blue lines in the figures) in Figure 26. ICE provided a way to observe the influence of individual features by keeping other variables constant and analyzing how the prediction changed with variations in a single feature. For the current study, 390 samples were used, leading to the creation of 390 ICE lines. ICE, like 1D-PDP, assumed independence among variables, limiting its ability to showcase the effects of interconnected variables on the ultimate prediction of the model.

The effect of FA/GGBFS on the partial dependence is reported in Figure 26a. Overall, a slight decrease in partial dependence was observed as FA/GGBFS increased. Particularly, there was a significant decrease in partial dependence as FA/GGBFS increased from 0.25 to 0.43. This phenomenon aligned with previous findings indicating that excess FA increased the soil's porosity, thereby exerting a detrimental effect on the UCS [12,13,80,81].

In Figure 26b, it is noted that the partial dependence increased when the NaOH/precursor increased within range of 0.1 to 0.15. However, for NaOH/precursor values greater than 0.15, the partial dependence did not change. Notably, the ICE results from both DL models exhibited larger variations for NaOH/precursor at 0.2. This implied that the UCS was responsive to a NaOH/precursor ratio of 0.2.

Figure 26c shows a decreasing trend in partial dependence when the water/binder increased. It was true that for a fixed amount of the precursors, with the increase in water, the concentration of the alkaline solution became lower, which could not effectively activate the Al and Si ions from FA and GGBFS. Under such circumstances, the amount of hydrated gels was less, thereby affecting the strength development of the UCS of the sample.

In Figure 26d, a significant increase in partial dependence was observed as the curing time progressed. The ICE lines displayed more significant variations during curing durations of 14 to 28 days relative to 0 to 14 days, indicating that the strength enhancement of soil mainly took place in the later curing period [19].

Figure 26e illustrates a two-stage linear correlation between molarity and the partial dependence. A rise in molarity from 3.27 to 4.64 positively influenced the partial dependence. However, once the molarity surpassed 4.64, further increases led to a reduction in the partial dependence. This could be attributed to the dissolution of Si and Al ions from FA and GGBFS subjected to a highly concentrated NH solution, resulting in the formation of stable N-A-S-H gels. These hydrated gels were stable and could not effectively connect the soil particles, thereby weakening the strength development of the soil.

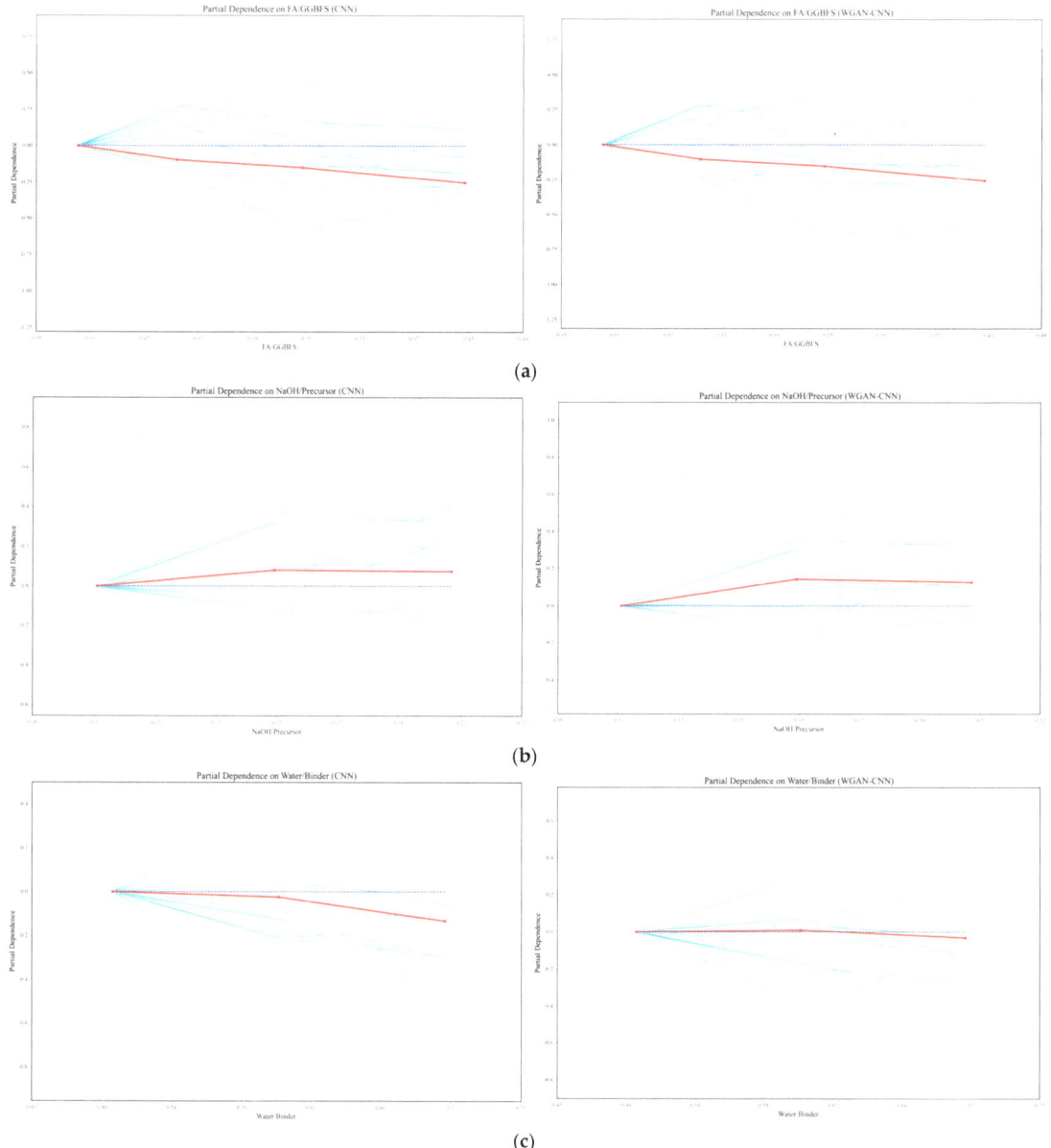

Figure 26. Cont.

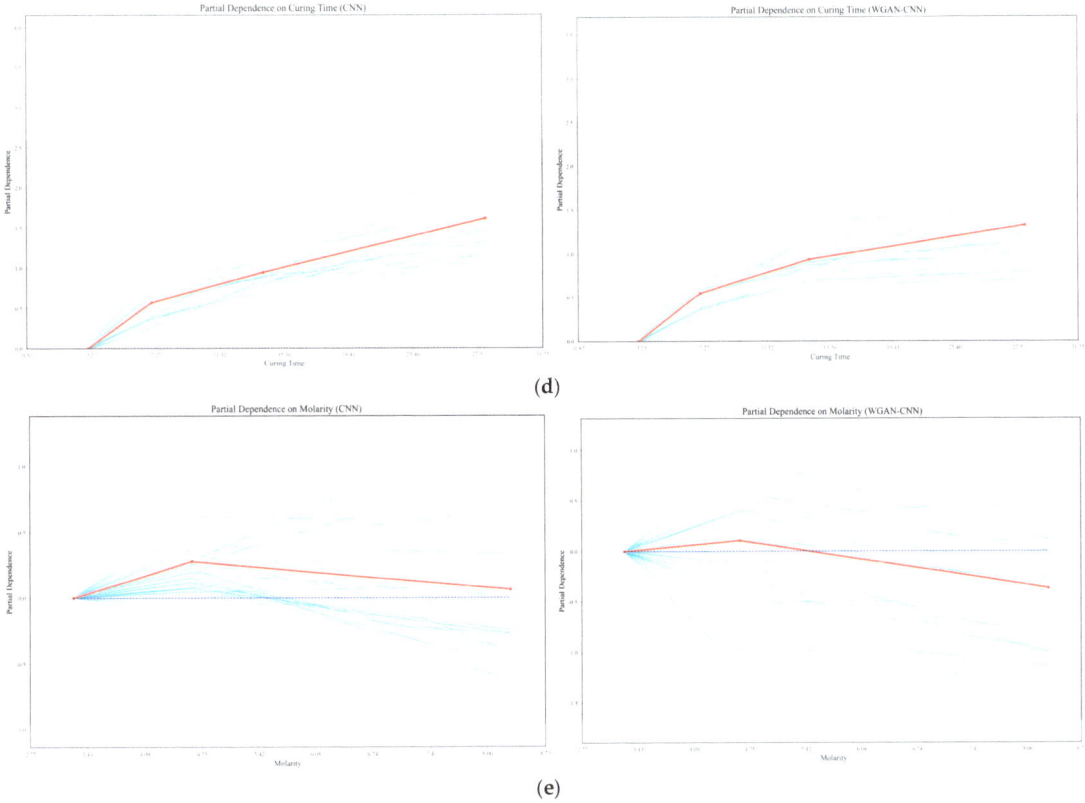

Figure 26. PDP analysis of CNN and WGAN-CNN models. (**a**) Partial dependence on FA/GGBFS. (**b**) Partial dependence on NaOH/precursor. (**c**) Partial dependence on water/binder. (**d**) Partial dependence on curing time. (**e**) Partial dependence on molarity.

5. Conclusions

This study first utilized four DL models with different principles to predict the OPG-stabilized soil's UCS. Then, the WGAN model was employed to learn the distribution of the original dataset and generate additional synthetic data for the training dataset, thereby innovatively enhancing the model's performance and robustness. Additionally, sensitivity analyses and SHAP and PDP methods were applied to elucidate the inherent mechanisms of the two DL models with higher prediction accuracy. The main conclusions were as follows:

(1) Four DL models with different principles, constructed based on original data, performed well in predicting the UCS of OPG-stabilized soil. After K-Fold cross-validation, all models achieved an R^2 above 0.98, with the MAE controlled below 0.0489. Among them, the CNN showed the best performance (MAE = 0.022, RMSE = 0.0409, R^2 = 0.9938), followed by the LSTM (MAE = 0.0274, RMSE = 0.0451, R^2 = 0.9924) and BPNN (MAE = 0.0272, RMSE = 0.0462, R^2 = 0.9921).

(2) By adding synthetic samples generated by the WGAN models with Dense and Convolutional layers to the training set, the performance of the CNN model improved. The best performance was achieved by the WGAN-CNN model trained with 200 added synthetic samples, in which the R^2 values reached 0.9978. Therefore, it can be found that in present study, the addition of synthetic data in the training set can significantly improve the accuracy of the DL model. The synthetic data generated by the WGAN

models with the combination of the Dense and Convolutional layers can have more comprehensive distributions with high quality.

(3) Three interpretability analyses (sensitivity analysis, SHAP, and PDP) were conducted on the best-performing CNN and WGAN-CNN models. The results showed that the analyses of both models were essentially the same, identifying the curing time as the most significant factor influencing the UCS. In particular, it was revealed that the UCS of OPG-stabilized soil primarily occurred at later curing times. The moderate addition of FA/GGBFS is beneficial for increasing UCS and holds practical value. The similar observation from the CNN and WGAN-CNN models implied that the DL model with the combined of the real and synthetic data can predict the mechanical properties of OPG-stabilized soil well. The conclusion is that the developed WGAN-CNN model achieved the balance between the resource and accuracy. Moreover, the observation that the WGAN-CNN exhibited the same predictive trend as the CNN based on interpretable methods further validated the effectiveness and rationality of the synthetic data generated by the WGAN model developed in this study.

The limitations of this study lie in the fact that we have only compared various DL models based on differing principles, without employing any optimization algorithms aimed at enhancing the performance of specific models. Furthermore, there remains room for broader considerations regarding the factors influencing UCS, and as the experiments are expanded, the model's capabilities can be further enhanced.

Author Contributions: Conceptualization, J.W. and G.H.; methodology, J.W. and G.H.; software, Q.C.; formal analysis, Q.C.; investigation, Q.C.; resources, J.W.; data curation, Q.C.; writing—original draft preparation, Q.C.; writing—review and editing, J.W.; supervision, J.W. and G.H.; project administration, J.W.; funding acquisition, J.W. All authors have read and agreed to the published version of the manuscript.

Funding: This research was funded by the National Natural Science Foundation of China, grant number 42377201.

Informed Consent Statement: Not applicable.

Data Availability Statement: Data will be made available on request.

Acknowledgments: Grateful acknowledgments are made to National Natural Science Foundation of China (No. 42377201) for the support of this project.

Conflicts of Interest: The authors declare no conflicts of interest.

References

1. Yang, H.; Liu, L.; Yang, W.; Liu, H.; Ahmad, W.; Ahmad, A.; Aslam, F.; Joyklad, P. A comprehensive overview of geopolymer composites: A bibliometric analysis and literature review. *Case. Stud. Constr. Mat.* **2022**, *16*, e00830. [CrossRef]
2. Cook, R.; Han, T.; Childers, A.; Ryckman, C.; Khayat, K.; Ma, H.; Huang, J.; Kumar, A. Machine learning for high-fidelity prediction of cement hydration kinetics in blended systems. *Mater. Des.* **2021**, *208*, 109920. [CrossRef]
3. Longarini, N.; Crespi, P.; Zucca, M.; Giordano, N.; Silvestro, G.D. The Advantages of Fly Ash Use in Concrete Structures. *Inżynieria Miner.* **2014**, *15*, 141–145.
4. Borçato, A.G.; Thiesen, M.; Medeiros-Junior, R.A. Incorporation of clay brick wastes and calcium hydroxide into geopolymers: Compressive strength, microstructure, and efflorescence. *J. Build. Eng.* **2024**, *88*, 109259. [CrossRef]
5. Rathnayaka, M.; Karunasinghe, D.; Gunasekara, C.; Wijesundara, K.; Lokuge, W.; David, W.L. Machine learning approaches to predict compressive strength of fly ash-based geopolymer concrete: A comprehensive review. *Constr. Build. Mater.* **2024**, *419*, 135519. [CrossRef]
6. Shamim Ansari, S.; Muhammad Ibrahim, S.; Danish Hasan, S. Conventional and Ensemble Machine Learning Models to Predict the Compressive Strength of Fly Ash Based Geopolymer Concrete. *Mater. Today Proc.* **2023**, *in press*. [CrossRef]
7. Cong, P.; Cheng, Y. Advances in geopolymer materials: A comprehensive review. *J. Traffic Transp. Eng. (Engl. Ed.)* **2021**, *8*, 283–314. [CrossRef]
8. Zhang, M.; Guo, H.; El-Korchi, T.; Zhang, G.; Tao, M. Experimental feasibility study of geopolymer as the next-generation soil stabilizer. *Constr. Build. Mater.* **2013**, *47*, 1468–1478. [CrossRef]
9. Cristelo, N.; Glendinning, S.; Teixeira Pinto, A. Deep soft soil improvement by alkaline activation. *Proc. Inst. Civ. Eng.-Ground Improv.* **2011**, *164*, 73–82. [CrossRef]

10. Lei, Z.; Pavia, S.; Wang, X. Biomass ash waste from agricultural residues: Characterisation, reactivity and potential to develop one-part geopolymer cement. *Constr. Build. Mater.* **2024**, *431*, 136544. [CrossRef]
11. Hang, Y.-J.; Heah, C.-Y.; Liew, Y.-M.; Mohd, M.A.B.A.; Lee, Y.-S.; Lee, W.-H.; Phakkhananan, P.; Ong, S.-W.; Tee, H.-W.; Hsu, C.-H. Microwave absorption function on a novel one-part binary geopolymer: Influence of frequency, ageing and mix design. *Constr. Build. Mater.* **2024**, *427*, 136264.
12. Zheng, X.; Wu, J. Early Strength Development of Soft Clay Stabilized by One-Part Ground Granulated Blast Furnace Slag and Fly Ash-Based Geopolymer. *Front. Mater.* **2021**, *8*, 616430. [CrossRef]
13. Min, Y.; Wu, J.; Li, B.; Zhang, J. Effects of Fly Ash Content on the Strength Development of Soft Clay Stabilized by One-Part Geopolymer under Curing Stress. *J. Mater. Civ. Eng.* **2021**, *33*, 04021274. [CrossRef]
14. Jaditager, M.; Sivakugan, N. Consolidation Behavior of Fly Ash-Based Geopolymer-Stabilized Dredged Mud. *J. Waterw. Port Coast. Ocean Eng.* **2018**, *144*, 4. [CrossRef]
15. Phetchuay, C.; Horpibulsuk, S.; Arulrajah, A.; Suksiripattanapong, C.; Udomchai, A. Strength development in soft marine clay stabilized by fly ash and calcium carbide residue based geopolymer. *Appl. Clay. Sci.* **2016**, *127–128*, 134–142. [CrossRef]
16. Wang, B.; Cui, C.; Xu, C.; Meng, K.; Li, J.; Xu, L. A novel analytical solution for horizontal vibration of partially embedded offshore piles considering the distribution effect of wave loads. *Ocean. Eng.* **2024**, *307*, 118179. [CrossRef]
17. Cui, C.; Liang, Z.; Xu, C.; Xin, Y.; Wang, B. Analytical solution for horizontal vibration of end-bearing single pile in radially heterogeneous saturated soil. *Appl. Math. Model.* **2023**, *116*, 65–83. [CrossRef]
18. Cui, C.; Meng, K.; Xu, C.; Liang, Z.; Li, H.; Pei, H. Analytical solution for longitudinal vibration of a floating pile in saturated porous media based on a fictitious saturated soil pile model. *Comput. Geotech.* **2021**, *131*, 103942. [CrossRef]
19. Min, Y.; Gao, M.; Yao, C.; Wu, J.; Wei, X. On the use of one-part geopolymer activated by solid sodium silicate in soft clay stabilization. *Constr. Build. Mater.* **2023**, *402*, 132957. [CrossRef]
20. Cui, C.; Xu, M.; Xu, C.; Zhang, P.; Zhao, J. An ontology-based probabilistic framework for comprehensive seismic risk evaluation of subway stations by combining Monte Carlo simulation. *Tunn. Undergr. Space Technol.* **2023**, *135*, 105055. [CrossRef]
21. Cui, C.; Meng, K.; Xu, C.; Wang, B.; Xin, Y. Vertical vibration of a floating pile considering the incomplete bonding effect of the pile-soil interface. *Comput. Geotech.* **2022**, *150*, 104894. [CrossRef]
22. Dinesh, A.; Anitha Selvasofia, S.D.; Datcheen, K.S.; Rakhesh Varshan, D. Machine learning for strength evaluation of concrete structures—Critical review. *Mater. Today Proc.* **2023**, *in press*. [CrossRef]
23. Li, Z.; Yoon, J.; Zhang, R.; Rajabipour, F.; Srubar, W.V., III; Dabo, I.; Radlińska, A. Machine learning in concrete science: Applications, challenges, and best practices. *NPJ Comput. Mater.* **2022**, *8*, 1.
24. Zhang, J.; Huang, Y.; Wang, Y.; Ma, G. Multi-objective optimization of concrete mixture proportions using machine learning and metaheuristic algorithms. *Constr. Build. Mater.* **2020**, *253*, 119208. [CrossRef]
25. Ben Chaabene, W.; Flah, M.; Nehdi, M.L. Machine learning prediction of mechanical properties of concrete: Critical review. *Constr. Build. Mater.* **2020**, *260*, 119889. [CrossRef]
26. Oey, T.; Jones, S.; Bullard, J.W.; Sant, G. Machine learning can predict setting behavior and strength evolution of hydrating cement systems. *J. Am. Ceram. Soc.* **2019**, *103*, 480–490. [CrossRef]
27. Derousseau, M.A.; Laftchiev, E.; Kasprzyk, J.R.; Rajagopalan, B.; Srubar, W.V. A comparison of machine learning methods for predicting the compressive strength of field-placed concrete. *Constr. Build. Mater.* **2019**, *228*, 116661. [CrossRef]
28. Rafiei, M.H.; Khushefati, W.H.; Demirboga, R.; Adeli, H. Neural Network, Machine Learning, and Evolutionary Approaches for Concrete Material Characterization. *ACI. Mater. J.* **2016**, *113*, 781–789. [CrossRef]
29. Felix, E.F.; Possan, E.; Carrazedo, R. Artificial Intelligence Applied in the Concrete Durability Study. In *Hygrothermal Behaviour and Building Pathologies*; Springer: Berlin/Heidelberg, Germany, 2021; pp. 99–121.
30. Taffese, W.Z.; Sistonen, E. Machine learning for durability and service-life assessment of reinforced concrete structures: Recent advances and future directions. *Automat. Constr.* **2017**, *77*, 1–14. [CrossRef]
31. Wang, L.; Wu, X.G.; Chen, H.Y.; Zeng, T.M. Iop, Prediction of impermeability of the concrete structure based on random forest and support vector machine. In Proceedings of the International Conference on Sustainable Development and Environmental Science (ICSDES), Zhengzhou, China, 19–21 June 2020.
32. Huang, J.; Duan, T.; Zhang, Y.; Liu, J.; Zhang, J.; Lei, Y.; Zhang, J. Predicting the Permeability of Pervious Concrete Based on the Beetle Antennae Search Algorithm and Random Forest Model. *Adv. Civ. Eng.* **2020**, *2020*, 8863181. [CrossRef]
33. Najigivi, A.; Khaloo, A.; Iraji Zad, A.; Abdul Rashid, S. An Artificial Neural Networks Model for Predicting Permeability Properties of Nano Silica–Rice Husk Ash Ternary Blended Concrete. *Int. J. Concr. Struct. Mater.* **2013**, *7*, 225–238. [CrossRef]
34. Hu, T.; Zhang, H.; Cheng, C.; Li, H.; Zhou, J. Explainable machine learning: Compressive strength prediction of FRP-confined concrete column. *Mater. Today Commun.* **2024**, *39*, 108883. [CrossRef]
35. Yang, S.; Sun, J.; Zhifeng, X. Prediction on compressive strength of recycled aggregate self-compacting concrete by machine learning method. *J. Build. Eng.* **2024**, *88*, 109055. [CrossRef]
36. Miao, X.; Chen, B.; Zhao, Y. Prediction of compressive strength of glass powder concrete based on artificial intelligence. *J. Build. Eng.* **2024**, *91*, 109377. [CrossRef]
37. Kurt, Z.; Yilmaz, Y.; Cakmak, T.; Ustabaş, I. A novel framework for strength prediction of geopolymer mortar: Renovative precursor effect. *J. Build. Eng.* **2023**, *76*, 107041. [CrossRef]

38. Da Silveira Maranhão, F.; De Souza Junior, F.G.; Soares, P.; Alcan, H.G.; Çelebi, O.; Bayrak, B.; Kaplan, G.; Aydın, A.C. Physico-mechanical and microstructural properties of waste geopolymer powder and lime-added semi-lightweight geopolymer concrete: Efficient machine learning models. *J. Build. Eng.* **2023**, *72*, 106629. [CrossRef]
39. Parhi, S.K.; Patro, S.K. Prediction of compressive strength of geopolymer concrete using a hybrid ensemble of grey wolf optimized machine learning estimators. *J. Build. Eng.* **2023**, *71*, 106521. [CrossRef]
40. Wang, Q.; Ahmad, W.; Ahmad, A.; Aslam, F.; Mohamed, A.; Vatin, N.I. Application of Soft Computing Techniques to Predict the Strength of Geopolymer Composites. *Polymers* **2022**, *14*, 6. [CrossRef]
41. Han, Q.; Gui, C.; Xu, J.; Lacidogna, G. A generalized method to predict the compressive strength of high-performance concrete by improved random forest algorithm. *Constr. Build. Mater.* **2019**, *226*, 734–742. [CrossRef]
42. Ouyang, B.; Song, Y.; Li, Y.; Wu, F.; Yu, H.; Wang, Y.; Sant, G.; Bauchy, M. Predicting Concrete's Strength by Machine Learning: Balance between Accuracy and Complexity of Algorithms. *ACI. Mater. J.* **2020**, *117*, 125–133.
43. Zhang, L.V.; Marani, A.; Nehdi, M.L. Chemistry-informed machine learning prediction of compressive strength for alkali-activated materials. *Constr. Build. Mater.* **2022**, *316*, 106521. [CrossRef]
44. Zhang, J.F.; Li, D.; Wang, Y.H. Toward intelligent construction: Prediction of mechanical properties of manufactured-sand concrete using tree-based models. *J. Clean Prod.* **2020**, *258*, 120665. [CrossRef]
45. Abdullah, G.M.S.; Ahmad, M.; Babur, M.; Badshah, M.U.; Al-Mansob, R.A.; Gamil, Y.; Fawad, M. Boosting-based ensemble machine learning models for predicting unconfined compressive strength of geopolymer stabilized clayey soil. *Sci. Rep.* **2024**, *14*, 2323. [CrossRef] [PubMed]
46. Ahmad, A.; Ahmad, W.; Chaiyasarn, K.; Ostrowski, K.A.; Aslam, F.; Zajdel, P.; Joyklad, P. Prediction of Geopolymer Concrete Compressive Strength Using Novel Machine Learning Algorithms. *Polymers* **2021**, *13*, 3389. [CrossRef] [PubMed]
47. Das, P.; Kashem, A. Hybrid machine learning approach to prediction of the compressive and flexural strengths of UHPC and parametric analysis with shapley additive explanations. *Case. Stud. Constr. Mat.* **2024**, *20*, e02723. [CrossRef]
48. Huo, W.; Zhu, Z.; Sun, H.; Ma, B.; Yang, L. Development of machine learning models for the prediction of the compressive strength of calcium-based geopolymers. *J. Clean Prod.* **2022**, *380*, 135159. [CrossRef]
49. Ma, G.; Cui, A.; Huang, Y.; Dong, W. A Data-Driven Influential Factor Analysis Method for Fly Ash–Based Geopolymer Using Optimized Machine-Learning Algorithms. *J. Mater. Civ. Eng.* **2022**, *34*, 7. [CrossRef]
50. Nguyen, H.; Vu, T.; Vo, T.P.; Thai, H.-T. Efficient machine learning models for prediction of concrete strengths. *Constr. Build. Mater.* **2021**, *266*, 120950. [CrossRef]
51. Mcculloch, W.S.; Pitts, W. A logical calculus of the ideas immanent in nervous activity. *Bull. Math. Biophys.* **1943**, *5*, 115–133. [CrossRef]
52. Wang, Y.; Iqtidar, A.; Amin, M.N.; Nazar, S.; Hassan, A.M.; Ali, M. Predictive modelling of compressive strength of fly ash and ground granulated blast furnace slag based geopolymer concrete using machine learning techniques. *Case Stud. Constr. Mat.* **2024**, *20*, e03130. [CrossRef]
53. Kioumarsi, M.; Dabiri, H.; Kandiri, A.; Farhangi, V. Compressive strength of concrete containing furnace blast slag; optimized machine learning-based models. *Clean. Eng. Technol.* **2023**, *13*, 100604. [CrossRef]
54. Maheepala, M.M.A.L.N.; Nasvi, M.C.M.; Robert, D.J.; Gunasekara, C.; Kurukulasuriya, L.C. Mix design development for geopolymer treated expansive subgrades using artificial neural network. *Comput. Geotech.* **2023**, *161*, 105534. [CrossRef]
55. Nazar, S.; Yang, J.; Amin, M.N.; Khan, K.; Ashraf, M.; Aslam, F.; Javed, M.F.; Eldin, S.M. Machine learning interpretable-prediction models to evaluate the slump and strength of fly ash-based geopolymer. *J. Mater. Res. Technol.* **2023**, *24*, 100–124. [CrossRef]
56. Emarah, D.A. Compressive strength analysis of fly ash-based geopolymer concrete using machine learning approaches. *Results Mater.* **2022**, *16*, 100347. [CrossRef]
57. Paruthi, S.; Husain, A.; Alam, P.; Husain Khan, A.; Abul Hasan, M.; Magbool, H.M. A review on material mix proportion and strength influence parameters of geopolymer concrete: Application of ANN model for GPC strength prediction. *Constr. Build. Mater.* **2022**, *356*, 129253. [CrossRef]
58. Shahmansouri, A.A.; Yazdani, M.; Ghanbari, S.; Akbarzadeh Bengar, H.; Jafari, A.; Farrokh Ghatte, H. Artificial neural network model to predict the compressive strength of eco-friendly geopolymer concrete incorporating silica fume and natural zeolite. *J. Clean. Prod.* **2021**, *279*, 123697. [CrossRef]
59. Aalimahmoody, N.; Bedon, C.; Hasanzadeh-Inanlou, N.; Hasanzade-Inallu, A.; Nikoo, M. BAT Algorithm-Based ANN to Predict the Compressive Strength of Concrete—A Comparative Study. *Infrastructures* **2021**, *6*, 6. [CrossRef]
60. Ahmad, W.; Farooq, S.H.; Usman, M.; Khan, M.; Ahmad, A.; Aslam, F.; Yousef, R.A.; Abduljabbar, H.A.; Sufian, M. Effect of Coconut Fiber Length and Content on Properties of High Strength Concrete. *Materials* **2020**, *13*, 1075. [CrossRef]
61. Nguyen, T.T.; Pham Duy, H.; Pham Thanh, T.; Vu, H.H. Compressive Strength Evaluation of Fiber-Reinforced High-Strength Self-Compacting Concrete with Artificial Intelligence. *Adv. Civ. Eng.* **2020**, *2020*, 3012139. [CrossRef]
62. Dao, D.; Ly, H.-B.; Trinh, S.; Le, T.-T.; Pham, B. Artificial Intelligence Approaches for Prediction of Compressive Strength of Geopolymer Concrete. *Materials* **2019**, *12*, 6. [CrossRef]
63. Ngo, A.Q.; Nguyen, L.Q.; Tran, V.Q. Developing interpretable machine learning-Shapley additive explanations model for unconfined compressive strength of cohesive soils stabilized with geopolymer. *PLoS ONE* **2023**, *18*, e0286950. [CrossRef] [PubMed]

64. Oyebisi, S.; Alomayri, T. Artificial intelligence-based prediction of strengths of slag-ash-based geopolymer concrete using deep neural networks. *Constr. Build. Mater.* **2023**, *400*, 132606. [CrossRef]
65. Huynh, A.T.; Nguyen, Q.D.; Xuan, Q.L.; Magee, B.; Chung, T.; Tran, K.T.; Nguyen, K.T. A Machine Learning-Assisted Numerical Predictor for Compressive Strength of Geopolymer Concrete Based on Experimental Data and Sensitivity Analysis. *Appl. Sci.* **2020**, *10*, 7726. [CrossRef]
66. Peng, Y.; Unluer, C. Analyzing the mechanical performance of fly ash-based geopolymer concrete with different machine learning techniques. *Constr. Build. Mater.* **2022**, *316*, 125785. [CrossRef]
67. Deng, F.; He, Y.; Zhou, S.; Yu, Y.; Cheng, H.; Wu, X. Compressive strength prediction of recycled concrete based on deep learning. *Constr. Build. Mater.* **2018**, *175*, 562–569. [CrossRef]
68. Chen, H.; Li, X.; Wu, Y.; Zuo, L.; Lu, M.; Zhou, Y. Compressive Strength Prediction of High-Strength Concrete Using Long Short-Term Memory and Machine Learning Algorithms. *Buildings* **2022**, *12*, 3. [CrossRef]
69. Latif, S.D. Concrete compressive strength prediction modeling utilizing deep learning long short-term memory algorithm for a sustainable environment. *Environ. Sci. Pollut. Res.* **2021**, *28*, 30294–30302. [CrossRef]
70. Zhou, J.; Tian, Q.; Nazar, S.; Huang, J. Hyper-tuning gene expression programming to develop interpretable prediction models for the strength of corncob ash-modified geopolymer concrete. *Mater. Today Commun.* **2024**, *38*, 107885. [CrossRef]
71. Kumar Dash, P.; Kumar Parhi, S.; Kumar Patro, S.; Panigrahi, R. Efficient machine learning algorithm with enhanced cat swarm optimization for prediction of compressive strength of GGBS-based geopolymer concrete at elevated temperature. *Constr. Build. Mater.* **2023**, *400*, 132814. [CrossRef]
72. Rudin, C. Stop explaining black box machine learning models for high stakes decisions and use interpretable models instead. *Nat. Mach. Intell.* **2019**, *1*, 206–215. [CrossRef]
73. Naser, M.Z. An engineer's guide to eXplainable Artificial Intelligence and Interpretable Machine Learning: Navigating causality, forced goodness, and the false perception of inference. *Automat. Constr.* **2021**, *129*, 103821. [CrossRef]
74. Nithurshan, M.; Elakneswaran, Y. A systematic review and assessment of concrete strength prediction models. *Case Stud. Constr. Mat.* **2023**, *18*, e01830. [CrossRef]
75. Ke, X.; Duan, Y. Coupling machine learning with thermodynamic modelling to develop a composition-property model for alkali-activated materials. *Compos. Part B Eng.* **2021**, *216*, 108801. [CrossRef]
76. Feng, J.; Zhang, H.; Gao, K.; Liao, Y.; Yang, J.; Wu, G. A machine learning and game theory-based approach for predicting creep behavior of recycled aggregate concrete. *Case Stud. Constr. Mat.* **2022**, *17*, e01653. [CrossRef]
77. Han, B.; Wu, Y.; Liu, L. Prediction and uncertainty quantification of compressive strength of high-strength concrete using optimized machine learning algorithms. *Struct. Concr.* **2022**, *23*, 3772–3785. [CrossRef]
78. Haque, M.A.; Chen, B.; Kashem, A.; Qureshi, T.; Ahmed, A.A.M. Hybrid intelligence models for compressive strength prediction of MPC composites and parametric analysis with SHAP algorithm. *Mater. Today Commun.* **2023**, *35*, 105547. [CrossRef]
79. Peng, Y.; Unluer, C. Modeling the mechanical properties of recycled aggregate concrete using hybrid machine learning algorithms. *Resour. Conserv. Recycl.* **2023**, *190*, 106812. [CrossRef]
80. Chen, Q.; Hu, G.; Wu, J. Comparative study on the prediction of the unconfined compressive strength of the one-part geopolymer stabilized soil by using different hybrid machine learning models. *Case Stud. Constr. Mat.* **2024**, *21*, e03439. [CrossRef]
81. Yao, C.; Hu, G.; Chen, Q.; Wu, J. Prediction on the freeze-thaw resistance of a one-part geopolymer stabilized soil by using deep learning method. *Case Stud. Constr. Mat.* **2024**, *21*, e03530. [CrossRef]
82. Shen, J.; Li, Y.; Lin, H.; Li, H.; Lv, J.; Feng, S.; Ci, J. Prediction of compressive strength of alkali-activated construction demolition waste geopolymers using ensemble machine learning. *Constr. Build. Mater.* **2022**, *360*, 129600. [CrossRef]
83. Li, Y.; Shen, J.; Lin, H.; Li, Y. Optimization design for alkali-activated slag-fly ash geopolymer concrete based on artificial intelligence considering compressive strength, cost, and carbon emission. *J. Build. Eng.* **2023**, *75*, 106929. [CrossRef]
84. Goodfellow, I.J.; Pouget-Abadie, J.; Mirza, M.; Xu, B.; Warde-Farley, D.; Ozair, S.; Courville, A.; Bengio, Y. Generative adversarial nets. In Proceedings of the 27th International Conference on Neural Information Processing Systems—Volume 2, Cambridge, MA, USA, 8–13 December 2014; MIT Press: Montreal, QC, Canada, 2014; pp. 2672–2680.
85. Shao, S.; Wang, P.; Yan, R. Generative adversarial networks for data augmentation in machine fault diagnosis. *Comput. Ind.* **2019**, *106*, 85–93. [CrossRef]
86. He, J.; Xu, Y.; Pan, Y.; Wang, Y. Adaptive weighted generative adversarial network with attention mechanism: A transfer data augmentation method for tool wear prediction. *Mech. Syst. Signal Proc.* **2024**, *212*, 111288. [CrossRef]
87. Du, W.Z.; Tian, S.H. Transformer and GAN-Based Super-Resolution Reconstruction Network for Medical Images. *Tsinghua Sci. Technol.* **2024**, *29*, 197–206. [CrossRef]
88. Gui, J.; Sun, Z.A.; Wen, Y.G.; Tao, D.C.; Ye, J.P. A Review on Generative Adversarial Networks: Algorithms, Theory, and Applications. *IEEE Trans. Knowl. Data Eng.* **2023**, *35*, 3313–3332. [CrossRef]
89. Hahnloser, R.H.R.; Sarpeshkar, R.; Mahowald, M.A.; Douglas, R.J.; Seung, H.S. Digital selection and analogue amplification coexist in a cortex-inspired silicon circuit. *Nature* **2000**, *405*, 947–951. [CrossRef]
90. Kingma, D.; Ba, J. Adam: A Method for Stochastic Optimization. *arXiv* **2014**, arXiv:1412.6980.
91. Hinton, G.E.; Srivastava, N.; Krizhevsky, A.; Sutskever, I.; Salakhutdinov, R. Improving neural networks by preventing co-adaptation of feature detectors. *arXiv* **2012**, arXiv:1207.0580.

92. Rumelhart, D.E.; Hinton, G.E.; Williams, R.J. Learning representations by back-propagating errors. *Nature* **1986**, *323*, 533–536. [CrossRef]
93. Li, D.; Huang, F.; Yan, L.; Cao, Z.; Chen, J.; Ye, Z. Landslide Susceptibility Prediction Using Particle-Swarm-Optimized Multilayer Perceptron: Comparisons with Multilayer-Perceptron-Only, BP Neural Network, and Information Value Models. *Appl. Sci.* **2019**, *9*, 18. [CrossRef]
94. Wan, T.; Bai, Y.; Wang, T.; Wei, Z. BPNN-based optimal strategy for dynamic energy optimization with providing proper thermal comfort under the different outdoor air temperatures. *Appl. Energy* **2022**, *313*, 118899. [CrossRef]
95. Song, H. Using Multifactor Inputs BP Neural Network to Make Power Consumption Prediction. Master's Thesis, State University of New York at Binghamton, Binghamton, NY, USA, 2018; p. 77.
96. Lecun, Y.; Bottou, L.; Bengio, Y.; Haffner, P. Gradient-based learning applied to document recognition. *Proc. IEEE* **1998**, *86*, 2278–2324. [CrossRef]
97. Waibel, A.; Hanazawa, T.; Hinton, G.; Shikano, K.; Lang, K.J. Phoneme recognition using time-delay neural networks. *IEEE Trans. Acoust. Speech Signal Process.* **1989**, *37*, 328–339. [CrossRef]
98. Lecun, Y.; Bengio, Y.; Hinton, G. Deep learning. *Nature* **2015**, *521*, 436–444. [CrossRef] [PubMed]
99. Goodfellow, I.; Bengio, Y.; Courville, A. *Deep Learning*; MIT Press: Cambridge, MA, USA, 2016.
100. Greff, K.; Srivastava, R.K.; Koutnik, J.; Steunebrink, B.R.; Schmidhuber, J. LSTM: A Search Space Odyssey. *IEEE Trans. Neural Netw. Learn. Syst.* **2017**, *28*, 2222–2232. [CrossRef]
101. Hochreiter, S.; Schmidhuber, J. Long short-term memory. *Neural. Comput.* **1997**, *9*, 1735–1780. [CrossRef]
102. Allahyani, M.; Alsulami, R.; Alwafi, T.; Alafif, T.; Ammar, H.; Sabban, S.; Chen, X. DivGAN: A diversity enforcing generative adversarial network for mode collapse reduction. *Artif. Intell.* **2023**, *317*, 103863. [CrossRef]
103. Arjovsky, M.; Chintala, S.; Bottou, L. Wasserstein Generative Adversarial Networks. In Proceedings of the 34th International Conference on Machine Learning, PMLR, Sydney, NSW, Australia, 6–11 August 2017.
104. Radford, A.; Metz, L.; Chintala, S. Unsupervised Representation Learning with Deep Convolutional Generative Adversarial Networks. *arXiv* **2015**, arXiv:1511.06434.
105. Zhu, J.Y.; Park, T.; Isola, P.; Efros, A.A. Unpaired Image-to-Image Translation Using Cycle-Consistent Adversarial Networks. In Proceedings of the 2017 IEEE International Conference on Computer Vision (ICCV), Venice, Italy, 22–29 October 2017; pp. 2242–2251.
106. Chai, P.; Hou, L.; Zhang, G.; Tushar, Q.; Zou, Y. Generative adversarial networks in construction applications. *Automat. Constr.* **2024**, *159*, 105265. [CrossRef]
107. Wong, T.T.; Yeh, P.Y. Reliable Accuracy Estimates from k-Fold Cross Validation. *IEEE Trans. Knowl. Data Eng.* **2020**, *32*, 1586–1594. [CrossRef]
108. Fushiki, T. Estimation of prediction error by using K-fold cross-validation. *Stat. Comput.* **2011**, *21*, 137–146. [CrossRef]
109. Rodríguez, J.D.; Pérez, A.; Lozano, J.A. A general framework for the statistical analysis of the sources of variance for classification error estimators. *Pattern Recognit.* **2013**, *46*, 855–864. [CrossRef]
110. Molnar, C.; Casalicchio, G.; Bischl, B. Interpretable Machine Learning—A Brief History, State-of-the-Art and Challenges. In *ECML PKDD 2020 Workshops, Communications in Computer and Information Science*; Springer: Cham, Switzerland, 2020; pp. 417–431.
111. Saltelli, A.; Andres, T.H.; Homma, T. Sensitivity analysis of model output: An investigation of new techniques. *Comput. Stat. Data Anal.* **1993**, *15*, 211–238. [CrossRef]
112. Owais, M.; Alshehri, A.; Gyani, J.; Aljarbou, M.H.; Alsulamy, S. Prioritizing rear-end crash explanatory factors for injury severity level using deep learning and global sensitivity analysis. *Expert Syst. Appl.* **2024**, *245*, 123114. [CrossRef]
113. Morio, J. Global and local sensitivity analysis methods for a physical system. *Eur. J. Phys.* **2011**, *32*, 1577. [CrossRef]
114. Ekanayake, I.U.; Meddage, D.P.P.; Rathnayake, U. A novel approach to explain the black-box nature of machine learning in compressive strength predictions of concrete using Shapley additive explanations (SHAP). *Case Stud. Constr. Mat.* **2022**, *16*, e01059. [CrossRef]
115. Molnar, C. *Interpretable Machine Learning: A Guide for Making Black Box Models Explainable*, 2nd ed.; Independently Published: Munich, Germany, 2022.
116. Kriegler, B. *Cost-Sensitive Stochastic Gradient Boosting within a Quantitative Regression Framework*; University of California: Los Angeles, CA, USA, 2007; p. 144.
117. Braun, W.J.; Murdoch, D.J.; Hlynka, M.; Iacus, S.; Atkinson, A.C.; Donev, A.; Tobias, R.D.; Arnold, B.C.; Balakrishnan, N.; Schilling, E.G.; et al. The Elements of Statistical Learning: Data Mining, Inference, and Prediction. *J. R. Stat. Soc. Ser. A Stat. Soc.* **2010**, *173*, 693–694.
118. Yang, J.; Liu, J.; Xie, J.; Wang, C.; Ding, T. Conditional GAN and 2-D CNN for Bearing Fault Diagnosis with Small Samples. *IEEE Trans. Instrum. Meas.* **2021**, *70*, 1–12. [CrossRef]

Disclaimer/Publisher's Note: The statements, opinions and data contained in all publications are solely those of the individual author(s) and contributor(s) and not of MDPI and/or the editor(s). MDPI and/or the editor(s) disclaim responsibility for any injury to people or property resulting from any ideas, methods, instructions or products referred to in the content.

Article

Influence of Fine Content and Mean Diameter Ratio on the Minimum and Maximum Void Ratios of Sand–Fine Mixtures: A Discrete Element Method Study

Huaqiao Zhong, Zhehao Zhu *, Jiajin Zhao, Lanyi Wei, Yanyan Zhang, Jiayu Li, Jiajun Wang and Wenguo Yao

School of Civil Engineering, Shanghai Normal University, Shanghai 201418, China; 1000525982@smail.shnu.edu.cn (H.Z.); 1000510775@smail.shnu.edu.cn (J.Z.); 1000531474@smail.shnu.edu.cn (L.W.); 1000531480@smail.shnu.edu.cn (Y.Z.); 1000531475@smail.shnu.edu.cn (J.L.); 1000554887@smail.shnu.edu.cn (J.W.); 1000554889@smail.shnu.edu.cn (W.Y.)
* Correspondence: zhuzhehao@shnu.edu.cn

Abstract: As urbanization accelerates and surface space becomes increasingly scarce, the development and utilization of urban underground space have become more critical. The sand–fine mixture soils commonly found in river-adjacent and coastal areas pose significant challenges to the design and construction of underground structures due to their unique mechanical properties. In soil mechanics, the minimum and maximum void ratios are crucial indicators for assessing soil compressibility, permeability, and shear strength. This study employed the discrete element method (DEM) to simulate the minimum and maximum void ratios of sand–fine mixtures under various conditions by setting six fine contents and three mean diameter ratios. The results indicate that as the fine content increases, these void ratios exhibit a trend of initially decreasing and then increasing, which can be effectively modelled using a single-parameter quadratic function. Additionally, the initial shear modulus was closely related to the uniformity of contact distribution at the microscopic level within the specimens. This study also introduced a dimensionless parameter that simultaneously described changes in contact distribution and initial shear modulus.

Keywords: sand–fine mixture; minimum void ratio; maximum void ratio; initial shear modulus; discrete element method; fine content; mean diameter ratio

1. Introduction

With the rapid pace of urbanization and the growing shortage of surface space, the development and utilization of urban underground space have become increasingly important. As an effective solution to address surface space limitations, underground space development offers new opportunities for sustainable urban growth. In river-adjacent or coastal areas, the prevalent sand–fine mixture soils present challenges to the design and construction of underground structures due to their unique mechanical properties [1]. In soil mechanics, the minimum and maximum void ratios, which define the densest and loosest states of the soil, are crucial indicators of compressibility, permeability, and shear strength. Therefore, understanding the influence of fine content and mean diameter ratio on these void ratios is essential for the future utilization of urban underground space.

Previous studies have identified several factors influencing the minimum and maximum void ratios [2], such as grain-size distribution [3,4], particle shape [5,6], and fine content [5,7–11]. Among these, the fine content (F_C) and the mean diameter ratio (D/d) are considered the most important. To describe the evolution of these void ratios, Chang et al. [12,13] proposed a bilinear model and provided empirical formulas for calibrating the model's fitting parameters. Polito [14] later improved this approach by incorporating the influence of the mean diameter ratio into the empirical formulas. Larrard [15] proposed the "loosening function" and "wall function" for computing the packing density of mixtures and subsequently determined the void ratio of the mixture. Similarly, Shen et al. [16] used random close packing theory to estimate the void ratios for both the densest and loosest packings. The minimum and maximum void ratios are also essential for predicting soil mechanical behaviour. Cubrinovski and Ishihara [2] highlighted the importance of the void ratio range ($e_{max} - e_{min}$) in normalizing Standard Penetration Test (SPT) blow counts and determining the position of the critical state line. Belkhatir et al. [17] conducted undrained shear tests on sand–fine mixtures with varying fine contents, revealing that a strong correlation exists between the void ratios and peak undrained shear strength. Chaney et al. [7] examined the impact of varying fine contents on the minimum and maximum void ratios of sand–fine mixtures, indicating a correlation between the void ratio and the static liquefaction potential of sand. Hang et al. [11] analysed the initial shear modulus of sand–fine mixtures through bender element tests and found that the normalized initial shear modulus exhibited a negative power-law correlation with both e_{min} and e_{max}.

Although the aforementioned studies have produced successful outcomes, they primarily relied on experimental methods. In experimental research, different researchers often test their own materials, leading to inconsistencies in particle shape and material properties. Moreover, the use of various testing standards [18–20] also contributes to increased data variability, complicating related research efforts. Additionally, it is challenging for soil specimens to truly reach the minimum and maximum void ratios in triaxial conditions. As a result, the relationship between the minimum and maximum void ratios and the mechanical strength of sand containing varying fine content remains underexplored in the literature. To overcome these limitations, the discrete element method (DEM) was adopted in this study. In recent years, the DEM has been widely used in geotechnical engineering, especially due to its ability to preserve geometrical characteristics and control experimental conditions [4,21–24]. More importantly, the DEM can serve as a bridge, coupling microscopic fabric parameters with corresponding mechanical properties. Several successful applications highlight the potential of this method. For instance, Zhou et al. [25] used the DEM to optimize the grading of cement-stabilized laterite granules in West Africa, reducing the need for extensive laboratory testing. Tan et al. [26] adopted the DEM to establish the relationship between grain morphology and mechanical properties in artificially crushed stones with varying shapes and gradations, revealing that the internal friction angle and cohesion increased with the enhancement of angularities and the curvature coefficient. Zhao et al. [24] acquired the fabric of sand during liquefaction via the DEM and expounded the liquefaction mechanism of sand from the viewpoints of fabric and microstructure. Barnett et al. [27] conducted undrained triaxial shear tests on sand–fine mixtures using the DEM to determine the critical state line of the mixture and explored the relationship between the parameter "b" and the critical state of the mixture. Zhang et al. [28] employed the DEM to study the failure process of a shallow shield cross-river tunnel face in saturated silty fine sand, analysed the failure mechanism of the cross-river tunnel face, and developed a new failure model for shallow shield cross-river tunnels in saturated silty fine sand. Gu et al. [29,30] employed the DEM to study the mechanical behaviour of soil under both static and dynamic loading, linking it to the contact model and describing the soil's behaviour from a microscopic perspective. They found that the coordination number (*CN*) and the mechanical coordination number (*MCN*) can serve as evaluation indicators for soil liquefaction and critical states, respectively.

This study employed the discrete element method (DEM) to create models of sand–fine mixtures with varying fine contents, simulating their minimum and maximum void ratios according to Chinese standards. Based on the simulation results, a physically meaningful model was proposed to effectively estimate the evolution of these void ratios. To further investigate the relationship between void ratios and mechanical strength, this study developed numerical sand–fines specimens under triaxial conditions to analyse the corresponding initial shear modulus. Finally, the relationship between soil fabric characteristics and the evolution of the initial shear modulus was established.

2. DEM Simulation

The PFC6.0 3D developed by Itasca was employed to conduct numerical simulations on the minimum and maximum void ratios using spherical particles and the rolling resistance linear model. Compared to other shapes of particles, spherical particles can greatly reduce the needed computing power, especially when there is a large difference in particle size between coarse grains and fine particles. By setting the correct parameters with the rolling resistance model, previous studies have already demonstrated that the utilization of spherical particles and the rolling resistance linear model can effectively simulate and replicate the mechanical behaviour of different soils [22,24].

To ensure the consistency and reliability of all DEM simulation results, the numerical simulations of the minimum and maximum void ratios were performed using the same set of contact model parameters, as listed in Table 1. In this study, three sand–fine mixtures were simulated by fixing the diameter of large grains (D = 3 mm) and gradually decreasing the diameter of small particles (d = 1.5 mm, 1 mm, and 0.5 mm). The grain-size distribution curves for the studied specimens with different fine contents and mean diameter ratios are depicted in Figure 1.

Table 1. DEM model parameters with rolling resistance model.

Linear Group		Particle–Particle	Particle–Facet	Unity
Effective Modulus	E^*	1.0×10^8	1.0×10^8	Pa
Normal-to-Shear Stiffness Ratio	κ^*	2.0	2.0	-
Friction Coefficient	μ	0.55	0	-
Dashpot Group				
Normal Critical Damping Ratio	β_n	0.2	0.2	-
Shear Critical Damping Ratio	β_s	0.2	0.2	-
Dashpot Mode	M_d	3	3	-
Rolling Resistance Group				
Rolling Friction Coefficient	μ_r	0.20	0	-

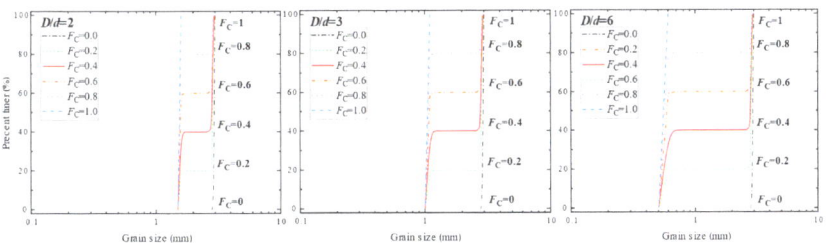

Figure 1. Grain-size distribution curve of the mixture with varying mean diameter ratios and fine contents.

For these sand–fine mixtures, we also performed DEM triaxial drained tests to establish the relationship between the initial shear modulus and the evolution of the minimum and maximum void ratios.

2.1. Minimum Void Ratio Test Simulation

The numerical simulation for the minimum void ratio was designed based on the main principles outlined in the Chinese national standard GB/T 2015 50123 [20]. Particles with the specified fine content F_C were initially generated with overlaps inside a cylindrical container measuring 437 mm in height and 100 mm in radius. The dimensions of this container significantly exceed ten times the maximum particle size (D = 3 mm), thereby avoiding the consideration of any boundary effects. Due to the initial overlaps, the particles were uniformly dispersed throughout the container and subsequently settled to the bottom under a low gravity of g = 3 m/s². Once the particles reached an initial equilibrium at the bottom, a top cover was placed to apply an axial stress of 950 kPa. Under the maintenance of this load, the container with the whole particles was subjected to cyclic vibration (as shown in Figure 2). This forced the particles to continuously consolidate until the densest state was reached. At this state, the total volume and the particles' volume were measured, allowing the value of the minimum void ratio to be calculated.

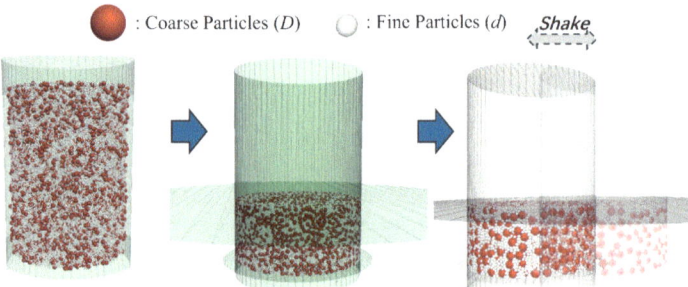

Figure 2. Determination of the minimum void ratio in DEM.

2.2. Maximum Void Ratio Test Simulation

As for the maximum void ratio, the sand–fine mixtures were first prepared inside a bottom-sealed container. Once the initial equilibrium was achieved, the container's bottom was substituted with a cylindrical diffuser (see Figure 3). This change allowed the particles to commence free fall with a real gravity of $g = 9.81$ m/s^2. In this step, the purpose of the diffuser was to minimize the kinetic energy during free fall for the achievement of the loosest state. After the free fall ended, the particles in the upper layer that formed a cone owing to friction were removed. The remaining portion was thus used to determine the corresponding maximum void ratio.

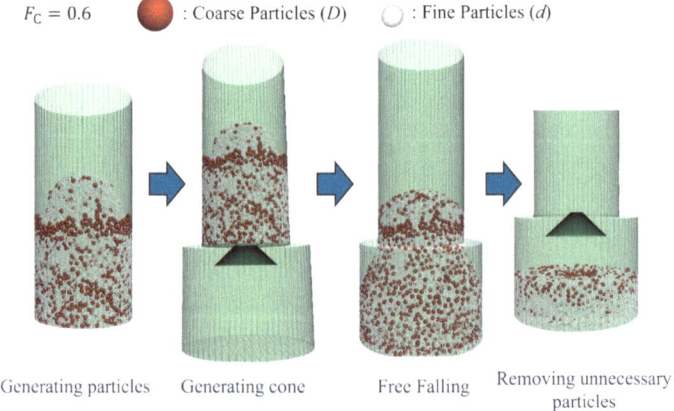

Figure 3. Determination of the maximum void ratio in DEM.

2.3. Initial Shear Modulus DEM Test

In this study, the initial shear modulus G_0 was determined by simulating small-strain triaxial shear tests. As shown in Figure 4, the sand–fine mixture was generated with overlaps and later uniformly distributed inside a square container equipped with six servo-controlled walls. This configuration permitted precise control over the boundary conditions. The velocities of the upper and lower side walls were precisely adjusted to continuously apply the shear strain (10^{-6}/s). At the same time, the two pairs of lateral walls exerted a constant confining pressure of 200.5 kPa on the mixture to establish a triaxial loading condition. During the shearing process, the axial strain was limited to a very small range ($\varepsilon_a \leq 10^{-5}$), ensuring that the specimen remained within its elastic deformation regime to accurately determine its initial shear modulus G_0 [21,31–36]. The following equations were used to measure the initial shear modulus G_0:

$$G = \frac{1}{3} \times \frac{dq}{d\varepsilon_q} \tag{1}$$

$$d\varepsilon_q = \frac{2}{3}(d\varepsilon_1 - d\varepsilon_3) \tag{2}$$

$$q = d\sigma_1 - d\sigma_3 \tag{3}$$

where q is the deviator stress; σ_1 is the axial stress; σ_3 is the horizontal stress; ε_q is the shear strain; and ε_1, ε_3 are the axial and horizontal strains, respectively.

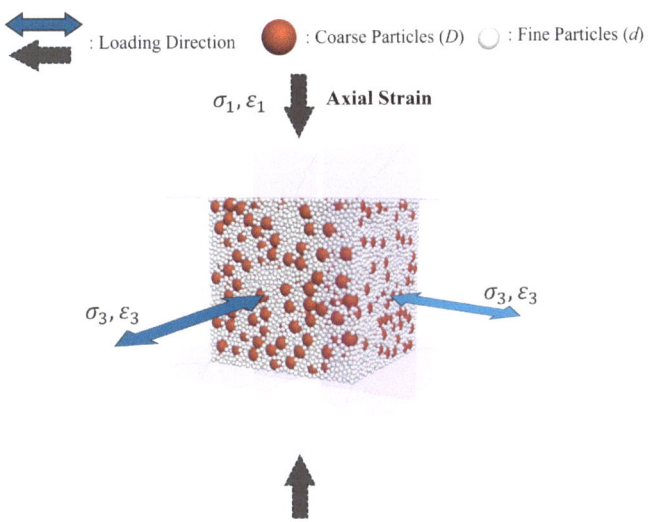

Figure 4. The triaxial shear test in DEM.

2.4. Validation of Contact Model Parameters

The contact model governs the mechanical interactions between particles, so any changes to the contact model parameters can result in significantly different mechanical behaviours of the entire specimen. Therefore, setting and validating the parameters within the contact model is essential. To ensure the reliability of the simulation data and that the results accurately reflect real-world conditions, we implemented a rigorous validation programme for the contact model parameters. Using the rolling resistance model and spherical particles specified in Table 1, we simulated the mechanical behaviour of a reference silica sand Hostun 31 (HN31) under cyclic triaxial shear conditions [37].

The whole validation process can be decomposed into three steps [24]:

(i) Spherical particles were generated within a cubic domain measuring 0.2 m × 0.2 m × 0.2 m, maintaining a uniform void ratio. The generated particle size distribution strictly followed the actual grain-size distribution curve of the HN31 sand. At the same time, the contact model was established between particle–particle and particle–facet interactions, and the unbalanced forces between particles were eliminated.

(ii) When the particle generation was completed, confining pressure was applied to the specimen by controlling the velocity of the walls, which was calculated by measuring the stress on all walls at each time step. Based on the difference between the measured value and the target value, the velocity and direction of each wall were adjusted to ensure precise servo control. Once the consolidation stress reached 200.5 kPa, it was maintained for a period until the void ratio stabilized.

(iii) After consolidation, a stress-controlled constant-volume cyclic triaxial shear test was performed on the specimen using a sine wave consistent with that used in the laboratory tests. The sine wave had a frequency of 0.1 Hz with a cyclic stress ratio (CSR) of 0.22 (the amplitude of shear stress divided by the consolidation stress). During the application of shear stress, both the shear stress and the effective mean stress were recorded. After the sample failed, the effective stress path was plotted and compared with the results obtained from laboratory tests on the HN31 sand.

As seen in Figure 5, with the application of cyclic shear stress, the mechanical behaviour exhibited by the DEM simulation aligns well with the indoor test: both started from the point (200,0) and gradually moved towards (0,0), eventually forming a butterfly orbit near (0,0). Additionally, the amplitude of the shear stress was precisely controlled at 105 kPa, with the curve remaining smooth and exhibiting minimal fluctuation, indicating the precision and reliability of the servo system. Based on these validation results, it can be concluded that the contact model and parameters used in this study can accurately reflect the mechanical properties of sandy soil.

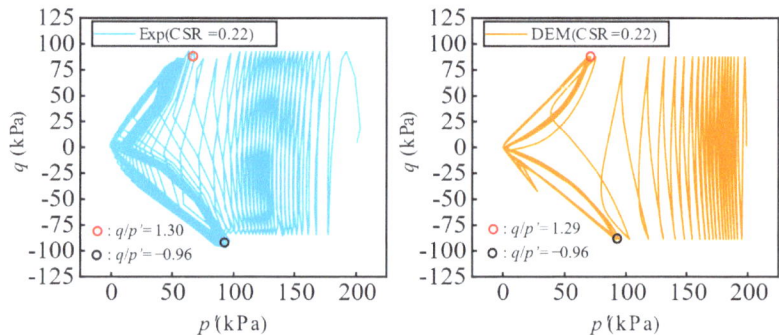

Figure 5. Comparison of effective stress paths obtained from the laboratory test and the DEM simulation [38].

3. Results and Discussion

3.1. Minimum and Maximum Void Ratio

The variation in the minimum void ratio with different fine contents and mean diameter ratios is illustrated in Figure 6. This figure demonstrates that the minimum void ratio initially decreases as the fine content increases until reaching a transitional fine content. After passing this transitional point, the minimum void ratio begins to rise in conjunction with the fine content reaching 1.0. This inflexion trend reflects the transformation in the predominance of the main skeleton within sand–fine mixtures. Prior to the transition point e_{min}^T, as shown in Figure 6, coarse grains build the main soil matrix, and the fine particles primarily fill the voids between coarse particles [2,8,9]. This phenomenon causes the sand–fine mixture to become denser and thus results in a decrease in the minimum void ratio. On the contrary, beyond the transition point, as the fine content increases, fine particles gradually replace the coarse grains and construct their own skeleton. In general, fine particles have a larger surface area as compared to coarse grains, which increases the number of contact points between them. This hinders the particles from arranging closely with one another, thereby increasing the void ratio.

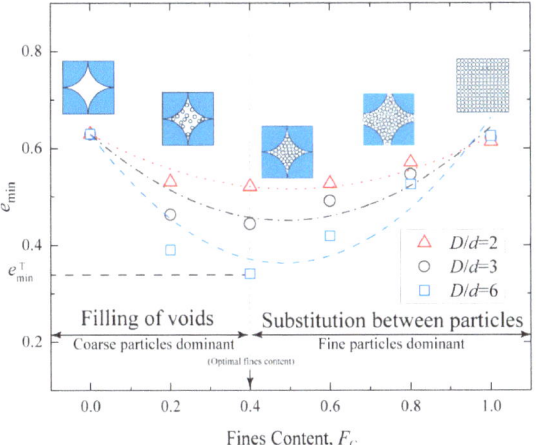

Figure 6. The impact of mean diameter ratio and fine content on minimum void ratio.

The relationship of the transitional minimum void ratio (e_{min}^T) with the mean diameter ratio D/d is displayed in Figure 7. It can be observed that the transition fine content and e_{min}^T steadily decreases as the mean diameter ratio increases and gradually converges to a constant. When the size difference between coarse grains and fine particles becomes more pronounced, fine particles are more likely to be accommodated within the voids created by the coarse grains. This enhances the filling effect of fine particles, thereby decreasing the value of the transitional minimum void ratio [2,7,39].

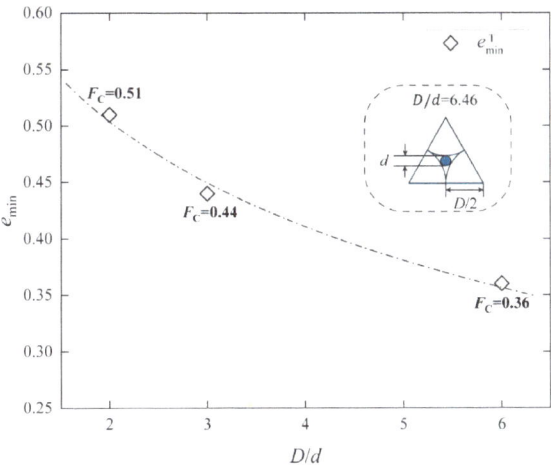

Figure 7. The correlation between the transitional minimum void ratio and mean diameter ratio.

To establish the functional relationship between e_{min} and F_C, a quadratic function ($y = ax^2 + bx + c$) was employed to fit the numerical results at various mean diameter ratios. As shown in Figure 6 and Table 2, the clear benefit of choosing such a function is that it is smooth in form without any cusps, and it can be easily controlled with only three fitting parameters. First, in the quadratic function, the fitting parameter "c" represents the intercept on the y-axis, which refers to the clean sand composed of only coarse grains without fine particles ($F_C = 0$). This value was directly set as the minimum void ratio of the provided coarse grains with $D = 3$ mm, regardless of the mean diameter ratio. Second, since the quadratic function attains its minimum point at $x = -b/2a$ (the $e_{\min}^T$ mentioned earlier), the fitting parameter "a" and "b" must satisfy a specific relationship with $e_{\min}^T$. By combining the above two arguments, the fitting parameters "b" and "c" are expressed in the following form:

$$e_{\min} = a \times (F_C)^2 + (-2a \times e_{\min}^T) \times F_C + e_{\min(F_C=0)} \quad (4)$$

Table 2. The fitting function and parameters for the minimum void ratio.

D/d	Fitting Function ($F_C \in [0,1]$)	a	b	c	R^2
2	$e_{\min} = 0.44 \times (F_C)^2 - 0.45 \times F_C + 0.63$	0.44	−0.45	0.63	0.91
3	$e_{\min} = 0.74 \times (F_C)^2 - 0.73 \times F_C + 0.63$	0.74	−0.73	0.63	0.86
6	$e_{\min} = 1.13 \times (F_C)^2 - 1.10 \times F_C + 0.63$	1.13	−1.10	0.63	0.87

Regarding the functional relationship between the fitting parameter "a" and the mean diameter ratio D/d, two special cases can be hereinafter discussed. In scenarios where the mean diameter ratio equals one, the two materials in a binary sand–fine mixture are exactly the same size, and the mixture can be considered uniform soil. In this case, the fitting parameter "a" should equal zero to maintain a constant minimum void ratio, regardless of the variation in fine content. On the other hand, when the mean diameter ratio approaches infinity, fine particles are notably smaller than coarse grains. The addition of fine particles with very small volume in the soil theoretically leads to limited changes in the minimum void ratio. Combining the above arguments, the function curve between the fitting parameter "a" and the mean diameter ratio should satisfy the following two conditions: (i) the curve passes through the point (1,0); (ii) the curve converges to a fixed value as the mean diameter ratio approaches infinity.

For this purpose, a modified inverse proportional function $y = 1.198 * (x-1)/x$ was used to fit the scatter points displayed in Figure 8. The function theoretically passes through the point (1,0) and exhibits a horizontal asymptote as the x-coordinate tends to infinity. Both the aforementioned requirements can be satisfied with this function. In conclusion, this study proposes a methodology that uses only a single intermediate fitting parameter "a" to establish the relationship between the minimum void ratio and the mean diameter ratio. As a dimensionless indicator, the mean diameter ratio measures the size disparity between coarse grains and fine particles, which is the key physical characteristic to understanding the evolution of binary soil–fine mixtures. Hence, the consideration of the mean diameter ratio (Equations (5) and (6)) offers explicit physical meaning for the selection of the fitting parameters and avoids the constraints associated with a reliance on any specific empirical equation.

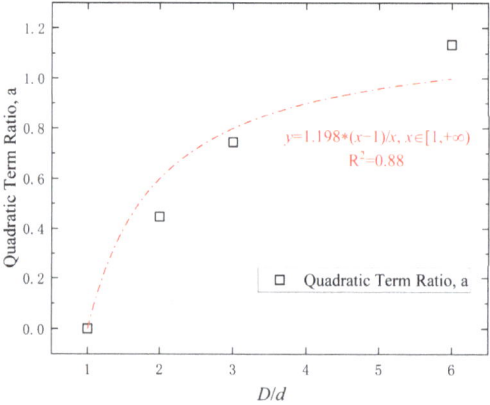

Figure 8. The functional relationship between the quadratic team ratio and mean diameter ratio.

Combined with Equation (4), the following can be obtained:

$$e_{min} = a \times (F_C)^2 + \left(-2a \times e_{min}^T\right) \times F_C + e_{min(F_C=0)} \tag{5}$$

$$a = 1.198 \times \frac{\left(\frac{D}{d} - 1\right)}{\frac{D}{d}} \tag{6}$$

Figure 9 displays the maximum void ratio (e_{max}) with varying mean diameter ratios and fine contents. Similar to the minimum void ratio, the maximum void ratio exhibits the same trend. As the fine content increases, the maximum void ratio initially decreases and then increases after a transitional point of about 0.4. Consequently, the quadratic function can continue to be used here to describe the evolution of the maximum void ratio. Following the same logic, the fitting parameter "c" was set the same (see Table 3) for different mean diameter ratios, corresponding to the maximum void ratio of pure coarse grains. The fitting parameter "b" was coupled with the fitting parameter "a" through the transitional fine content. Finally, the fitting parameter "a" was determined in relation to the mean diameter ratio, providing a clear physical interpretation for the description of the maximum void ratio.

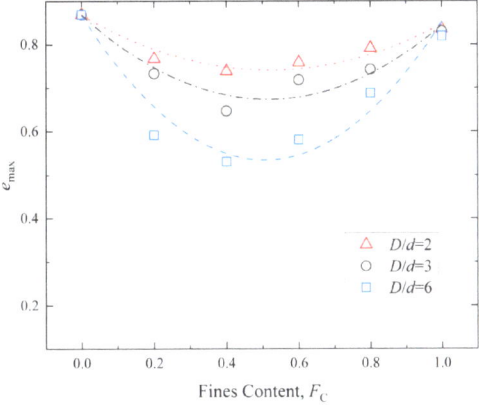

Figure 9. The impact of mean diameter ratio and fine content on maximum void ratio.

Table 3. The fitting function and parameters for the maximum void ratio.

D/d	Fitting Function ($F_C \subset [0,1]$)	a	b	c	R^2
2	$e_{max} = 0.46 \times (F_C)^2 - 0.49 \times F_C + 0.86$	0.46	−0.49	0.86	0.91
3	$e_{max} = 0.73 \times (F_C)^2 - 0.49 \times F_C + 0.86$	0.73	−0.75	0.86	0.89
6	$e_{max} = 1.30 \times (F_C)^2 - 1.31 \times F_C + 0.86$	1.30	−1.31	0.86	0.91

Figure 10 shows the correlation between the minimum and maximum void ratio of the investigated sand–fine mixtures. For the provided mean diameter ratio, a strong linear correlation exists between the minimum and maximum void ratio. In particular, despite changes in fine content, both the minimum and maximum void ratios exhibit a consistent trend. The phenomena indicate that the introduction of particles of different sizes into a uniform soil effectively creates a new mixture. Consequently, both the minimum and maximum void ratios automatically adjust in response to changes in fine content. Furthermore, in any specific type of sand–fine mixtures, the minimum and maximum void ratios are highly correlated. This strong correlation reinforces the notion that these ratios should be considered the intrinsic properties of the new material.

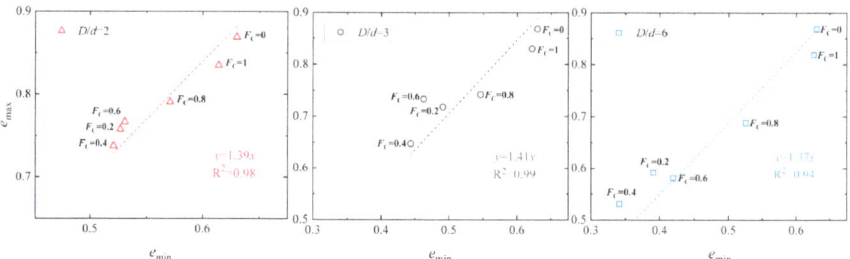

Figure 10. Correlation between the maximum void ratio and minimum void ratio.

3.2. Initial Shear Modulus

As the fine content increases, the primary load-bearing structure within a sand–fine mixture gradually shifts from a matrix of coarse grains to one dominated by fine particles. This transition leads to a significant change in its mechanical properties. For granular material, the initial shear modulus G_0 is one of the most important indicators for characterizing the shear strength. Figure 11 displays the initial shear modulus G_0 of different sand–fine mixtures subjected to a confining pressure of 200 kPa, using small-strain DEM triaxial shear tests. It is evident from the figure that G_0 likewise exhibits an initial decreasing trend followed by an increasing trend. This is in line with the variations in the minimum and maximum void ratios. However, no obvious correlation is observed between the G_0 and fine content as the mean diameter ratio increases. Interestingly, the initial shear modulus for the specimens, with mean diameter ratios of three and six, exhibits a striking similarity when the fine content is below 0.8; however, both curves exceed that curve with a mean diameter ratio of two.

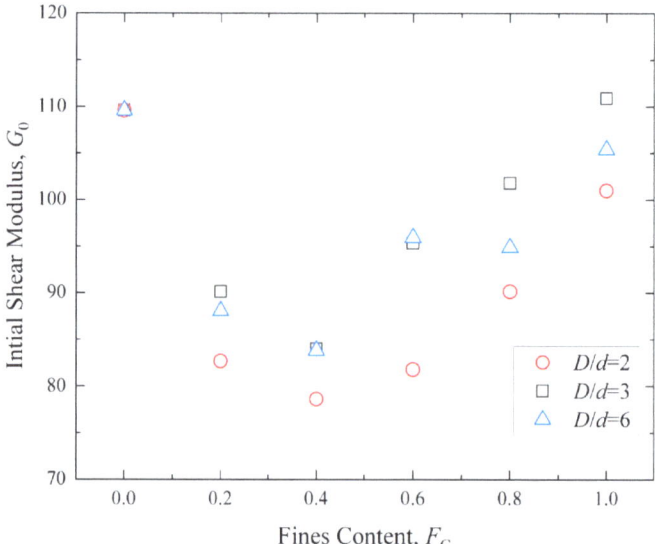

Figure 11. The impact of mean diameter ratio and fine content on initial shear modulus.

In general, the mobility of fine particles is much greater than that of coarse grains. Therefore, as fine particles are introduced, the number of coarse grains that can form the global load-bearing structure against external load decreases. This results in a reduction in the initial shear modulus. On the contrary, once the transitional fine content is exceeded, fine particles begin to form their own structure while coarse particles become loosely distributed. Consequently, the overall load-bearing structure is enhanced with the addition of fine particles, leading to a gradual increase in the initial shear modulus.

The DEM triaxial shear tests were equally used to capture the force chain structures with varying fine contents, as depicted in Figures 12 and 13. Each force chain is represented as a "bar" connecting the centre of each particle, where the thickness and colour indicate the magnitude of the force. A thicker bar signifies a greater transmitted force, while a thinner bar denotes a lower force. Additionally, the magnitudes of all the contact forces were collected to compute the coefficient of variation (CV) for the entire specimen. As a dimensionless indicator, the CV is derived from the standard deviation (S) and the mean value (AVG), serving as an indicator of force chain dispersion. In this study, the CV reflects the homogeneity of the force chain system. A higher CV suggests that contact forces are more concentrated on a limited number of contacts, resulting in less uniformity across the entire force chain. The CV, S, and AVG can be calculated using Equations (7)–(9), respectively.

$$CV = \frac{S}{AVG} \tag{7}$$

$$S = \sqrt{\frac{1}{n}\sum_{i=1}^{n}(x_i - AVG)^2} \tag{8}$$

$$AVG = \frac{1}{n}\sum_{i=1}^{n} x_i \tag{9}$$

where n is the number of contacts in the specimen and x_i is the magnitude of the contact force. The coefficient of variation of contact force with varying fine contents is illustrated in Figure 12.

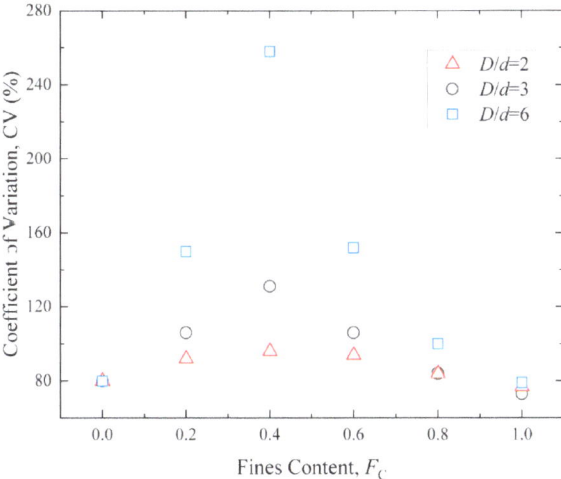

Figure 12. The coefficient of variation in contact force with varying fine contents.

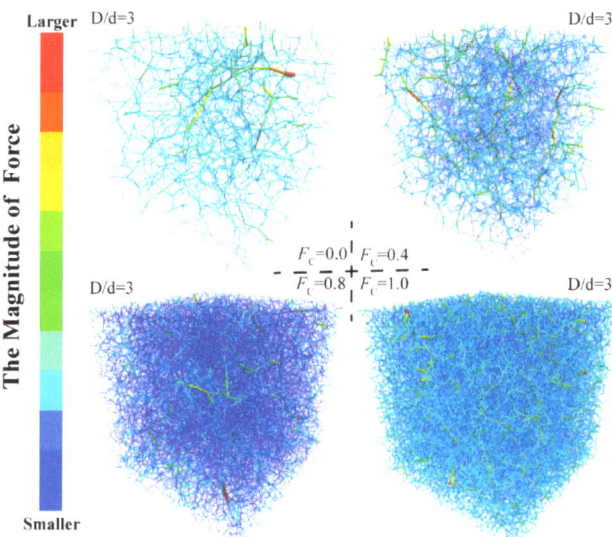

Figure 13. The variation in force chain structure with fine content.

In the case of a clean specimen with a uniform particle size ($F_C = 0$) in Figure 12, the entire force chain is evenly distributed, and the small CV indicates less stress concentration in the main soil skeleton. With the initial addition of fines (i.e., $0 < F_C < 0.4$), the original structure, primarily supported by coarse grains, the stress concentration becomes prevailing, as evidenced by the increase in CV in Figure 12. This indicates a pronounced stress concentration with only a few contact points responsible for the transmission of external load. Meanwhile, many other contact points remain inactivated, contributing minimally to the structural integrity. This likely accounts for the observed reduction in the initial shear modulus up to e_{min}^T in Figure 11. Beyond this point (i.e., $F_C > 0.4$), the force chain formed by fine particles becomes prevailing. According to Figure 13, the stress concentration within this structure gradually decreases, leading to a more uniformly distributed load across the specimen. Consequently, a larger number of contact points are engaged, enhancing the structure's ability to withstand external loads. This shift is responsible for the increase in the initial shear modulus observed after reaching e_{min}^T.

The influence of the mean diameter ratio on the force chain is illustrated in both Figures 12 and 14. In the overall trend, the increase in the mean diameter ratio amplifies the concentration of the contact force, further accentuating the disparity between the main and branch force chains. Meanwhile, this impact becomes increasingly pronounced as the fine content approaches the transitional state. When reaching the transitional fine content, the main soil skeleton is in a critical transitional state, dominated by both coarse grains and fine particles. Therefore, for the particle skeleton formed by the sand–fine mixture, an increase in the mean diameter ratio leads to a more pronounced force concentration at limited contacts.

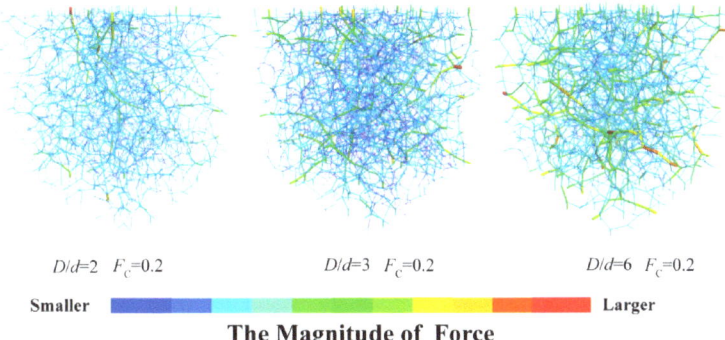

Figure 14. The variation in force chain structure with mean diameter ratio.

To correlate the physical characteristics of sand–fine mixtures with their mechanical properties, it is necessary to establish a connection between the initial shear modulus and a physical parameter that can aptly reflect the strength of either the force chains or the main soil skeleton. The minimum void ratio, indicative of the densest state, serves as a direct measurement of the potential compactness under external stresses. As long as the introduction of fine particles alters the value of the minimum void ratio, the overall force chain certainly undergoes a remarkable change. Consequently, the minimum void ratio measured when $F_C = 0$ can be used as a reference baseline, and the deviation from this baseline $\Delta e_{\min}$ can be recorded at various F_C values. This leads to the establishment of a functional relationship between them, as displayed in Figure 15. It is evident from the graph that there exists an obvious linear relation between G_0 and $\Delta e_{\min}$. The three functions all originate from the point $F_C = 0$, and the magnitude of the slope increases as the mean diameter ratio becomes greater. The $\Delta e_{\min}$ signifies the transformation of dominant particles within the skeleton. From the microscopic perspective, the increase in mean diameter ratio enhances the stress concentration with fewer activated contact points, amplifying its impact on G_0. Combining Formula 5 and 6, the $e_{\min}$ can be obtained by determining its mean diameter ratio, fine content, and minimum void ratio when $F_C = 0$. Thus, it is feasible to determine the initial shear modulus through limited minimum void ratio tests and a grading curve.

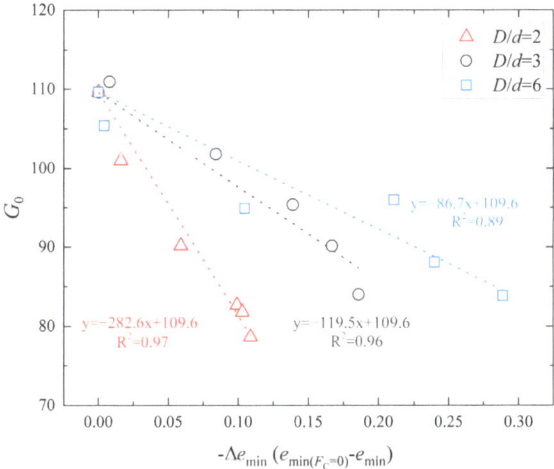

Figure 15. Correlation between the initial shear modulus and the deviation of minimum void ratio.

4. Summary and Conclusions

This paper employed the DEM to investigate the influence of the fine content and mean diameter ratio on the minimum and maximum void ratios by using the rolling resistance linear model. The quadratic function was employed to describe the relationship between the minimum/maximum void ratios and fine content. By conducting small-strain triaxial shear DEM tests, the initial shear modulus of the sand–fine mixtures was analysed with the evolution of the minimum void ratio to establish the relationship between the mechanical and physical characteristics. The main findings are summarized as follows:

1. Both the minimum and maximum void ratios initially decrease as the fine content increases until they reach a transitional fine content. The relationship between maximum and minimum void ratios exhibits an obvious linear pattern regardless of the fine content and mean diameter ratio.
2. An increase in the mean diameter ratio corresponds to a decrease in both the minimum and maximum ratios. This trend loses its effect as the ratio approaches a critical value of 6.5. This suggests a bounded impact for the influence of the mean diameter ratio.
3. The evolution of the minimum void ratio follows a quadratic function characterized by a single fitting parameter. Due to the strong linear correlation between the minimum and maximum void ratios being independent of the fine content and the mean diameter ratio, the latter can be effectively predicted using this linear function.
4. In parallel with the evolution of the maximum and minimum void ratios, the initial shear modulus equally demonstrates a trend that begins with an increase and subsequently declines. This trend is punctuated by a transitional fine content, delineating the above two distinct regimes.
5. From the microscopic perspective, an increase in fine content leads to a transformation of the global force chain. While approaching the transitional fine content, the stress concentrates at limited contact points and the force chain thus becomes much more localized. This explains the initial decrease with the addition of fines ($F_C < 0.4$). With the further addition of fines ($F_C > 0.4$), fine particles prevail in the global force chain. At this stage, the addition of fine particles significantly enhances the homogeneity of the global chain. Because most particles contribute to these force chains, the initial shear modulus is consequently increased.

It is important to note that the contact model used in this study is uniform, meaning that the material properties of coarse and fine particles are identical. However, in real-world conditions, the materials of the two particle types in a mixture often differ, necessitating additional research. Additionally, the fitted quadratic equation obtained in this study applies to cohesionless mixtures, and additional research is required to verify its applicability in other scenarios.

Author Contributions: Conceptualization, H.Z. and Z.Z.; methodology, J.Z.; software, J.W.; validation, H.Z., Z.Z. and J.Z.; formal analysis, L.W.; investigation, Y.Z.; resources, J.L.; data curation, H.Z.; writing—original draft preparation, H.Z.; writing—review and editing, H.Z.; visualization, W.Y.; supervision, Z.Z.; project administration, Z.Z.; funding acquisition, Z.Z. All authors have read and agreed to the published version of the manuscript.

Funding: The financial support provided by the National Natural Science Foundation of China (Grant Nos. 42307190 and 41931286) is deeply acknowledged.

Data Availability Statement: The raw data supporting the conclusions of this article will be made available by the authors upon request.

Conflicts of Interest: The authors declare no conflicts of interest.

References

1. Jebelli, J.; Meguid, M.A.; Sedghinejad, M.K. Excavation Failure during Micro-Tunneling in Fine Sands: A Case Study. *Tunn. Undergr. Space Technol.* **2010**, *25*, 811–818. [CrossRef]
2. Cubrinovski, M.; Ishihara, K. Maximum and Minimum Void Ratio Characteristics of Sands. *Soils Found.* **2002**, *42*, 65–78. [CrossRef] [PubMed]
3. Iwasaki, T.; Tatsuoka, F. Effects of Grain Size and Grading on Dynamic Shear Moduli of Sands. *Soils Found.* **1977**, *17*, 19–35. [CrossRef]
4. Liu, X.; Yang, J.; Zou, D.; Li, Z.; Chen, Y.; Cao, X. Utilizing DEM and Interpretable ML Algorithms to Examine Particle Size Distribution's Role in Small-Strain Shear Modulus of Gap-Graded Granular Mixtures. *Constr. Build. Mater.* **2024**, *428*, 136232. [CrossRef]
5. Sarkar, D.; Goudarzy, M.; König, D.; Wichtmann, T. Influence of Particle Shape and Size on the Threshold Fines Content and the Limit Index Void Ratios of Sands Containing Non-Plastic Fines. *Soils Found.* **2020**, *60*, 621–633. [CrossRef]
6. Cho, G.-C.; Dodds, J.; Santamarina, J.C. Particle Shape Effects on Packing Density, Stiffness, and Strength: Natural and Crushed Sands. *J. Geotech. Geoenviron. Eng.* **2006**, *132*, 591–602. [CrossRef]
7. Chaney, R.; Demars, K.; Lade, P.; Liggio, C.; Yamamuro, J. Effects of Non-Plastic Fines on Minimum and Maximum Void Ratios of Sand. *Geotech. Test. J.* **1998**, *21*, 336. [CrossRef]
8. Rahman, M.M.; Lo, S.R.; Gnanendran, C.T. On Equivalent Granular Void Ratio and Steady State Behaviour of Loose Sand with Fines. *Can. Geotech. J.* **2008**, *45*, 1439–1456. [CrossRef]
9. Cabalar, A.F. The Effects of Fines on the Behaviour of a Sand Mixture. *Geotech. Geol. Eng.* **2011**, *29*, 91–100. [CrossRef]
10. Zhu, Z.; Zhang, F.; Dupla, J.-C.; Canou, J.; Foerster, E. Investigation on the Undrained Shear Strength of Loose Sand with Added Materials at Various Mean Diameter Ratios. *Soil Dyn. Earthq. Eng.* **2020**, *137*, 106276. [CrossRef]
11. Hang, T.; Fan, H.; Xiao, X.; Zhang, L.; Liang, K.; Wu, Q.; Chen, G. Prediction Model for Small-Strain Shear Modulus of Non-Plastic Fine–Coarse-Grained Soil Mixtures Based on Extreme Void Ratios. *Soil Dyn. Earthq. Eng.* **2024**, *176*, 108279. [CrossRef]
12. Chang, C.S.; Wang, J.-Y.; Ge, L. Modeling of Minimum Void Ratio for Sand–Silt Mixtures. *Eng. Geol.* **2015**, *196*, 293–304. [CrossRef]
13. Chang, C.S.; Wang, J.Y.; Ge, L. Maximum and Minimum Void Ratios for Sand-Silt Mixtures. *Eng. Geol.* **2016**, *211*, 7–18. [CrossRef]
14. Polito, C.P. Correlations for Estimating Coefficients for the Prediction of Maximum and Minimum Index Void Ratios for Mixtures of Sand and Non-Plastic Silt. *Geotechnics* **2023**, *3*, 1033–1046. [CrossRef]
15. De Larrard, F. *Concrete Mixture Proportioning*; CRC Press: Boca Raton, FL, USA, 1999; ISBN 978-1-4822-7205-5.
16. Shen, C.; Liu, S.; Xu, S.; Wang, L. Rapid Estimation of Maximum and Minimum Void Ratios of Granular Soils. *Acta Geotech.* **2019**, *14*, 991–1001. [CrossRef]
17. Belkhatir, M.; Schanz, T.; Arab, A. Effect of Fines Content and Void Ratio on the Saturated Hydraulic Conductivity and Undrained Shear Strength of Sand–Silt Mixtures. *Environ. Earth Sci.* **2013**, *70*, 2469–2479. [CrossRef]
18. Selig, E.; Ladd, R. (Eds.) Evaluation of Relative Density Measurements and Applications. In *Evaluation of Relative Density and Its Role in Geotechnical Projects Involving Cohesionless Soils*; ASTM International: West Conshohocken, PA, USA, 1973; ISBN 978-0-8031-0081-7.
19. Lo Presti, D.; Pedroni, S.; Crippa, V. Maximum Dry Density of Cohesionless Soils by Pluviation and by ASTM D 4253-83: A Comparative Study. *Geotech. Test. J.* **1992**, *15*, 180–189. [CrossRef]
20. *GB/T 50123*; Standard for Soil Test Method. China Planning Press: Beijing, China, 2015.
21. Reddy, N.S.C.; He, H.; Senetakis, K. DEM Analysis of Small and Small-to-Medium Strain Shear Modulus of Sands. *Comput. Geotech.* **2022**, *141*, 104518. [CrossRef]
22. Cundall, P.A.; Strack, O.D.L. A Discrete Numerical Model for Granular Assemblies. *Géotechnique* **1979**, *29*, 47–65. [CrossRef]
23. Zhao, J.; Zhu, Z.; Liu, J.; Zhong, H. Damping Ratio of Sand Containing Fine Particles in Cyclic Triaxial Liquefaction Tests. *Appl. Sci.* **2023**, *13*, 4833. [CrossRef]
24. Zhao, J.; Zhu, Z.; Zhang, D.; Wang, H.; Li, X. Assessment of Fabric Characteristics with the Development of Sand Liquefaction in Cyclic Triaxial Tests: A DEM Study. *Soil Dyn. Earthq. Eng.* **2024**, *176*, 108343. [CrossRef]
25. Zou, G.; Yang, B.; Yu, J.; Yang, S.; Chen, Q. Strength Formation and Failure Mechanism Analysis of Cement-Stabilized Laterite Granules Based on Numerical Simulation. *Buildings* **2023**, *13*, 3093. [CrossRef]
26. Tan, X.; Qiu, Z.; Yin, X.; Hu, Y.; Liu, X.; Zeng, L. Effects of Particle Shape and Packing Density on the Mechanical Performance of Recycled Aggregates for Construction Purposes. *Buildings* **2023**, *13*, 2153. [CrossRef]
27. Barnett, N.; Rahman, M.M.; Karim, M.R.; Nguyen, H.B.K.; Carraro, J.A.H. Equivalent State Theory for Mixtures of Sand with Non-Plastic Fines: A DEM Investigation. *Géotechnique* **2021**, *71*, 423–440. [CrossRef]
28. Zhang, Z.; Xu, W.; Nie, W.; Deng, L. DEM and Theoretical Analyses of the Face Stability of Shallow Shield Cross-River Tunnels in Silty Fine Sand. *Comput. Geotech.* **2021**, *130*, 103905. [CrossRef]
29. Gu, X.; Zhang, J.; Huang, X. DEM Analysis of Monotonic and Cyclic Behaviors of Sand Based on Critical State Soil Mechanics Framework. *Comput. Geotech.* **2020**, *128*, 103787. [CrossRef]
30. Gu, X.; Huang, M.; Qian, J. DEM Investigation on the Evolution of Microstructure in Granular Soils under Shearing. *Granul. Matter* **2014**, *16*, 91–106. [CrossRef]
31. Hardin, B.O.; Black, W.L. Sand Stiffness Under Various Triaxial Stresses. *J. Soil Mech. Found. Div.* **1966**, *92*, 27–42. [CrossRef]
32. Viggiani, G.; Atkinson, J.H. Stiffness of Fine-Grained Soil at Very Small Strains. *Géotechnique* **1995**, *45*, 249–265. [CrossRef]

33. Atkinson, J.H. Non-Linear Soil Stiffness in Routine Design. *Géotechnique* **2000**, *50*, 487–508. [CrossRef]
34. Miwa, S.; Ikeda, T. Shear Modulus and Strain of Liquefied Ground and Their Application to Evaluation of The Response of Foundation Structures. *Struct. Eng. Earthq. Eng.* **2006**, *23*, 167s–179s. [CrossRef]
35. Clayton, C.R.I. Stiffness at Small Strain: Research and Practice. *Géotechnique* **2011**, *61*, 5–37. [CrossRef]
36. Chiaro, G.; Koseki, J.; Sato, T. Effects of Initial Static Shear on Liquefaction and Large Deformation Properties of Loose Saturated Toyoura Sand in Undrained Cyclic Torsional Shear Tests. *Soils Found.* **2012**, *52*, 498–510. [CrossRef]
37. Yao, C.; Zhong, H.; Zhu, Z. Development of a Large Shaking Table Test for Sand Liquefaction Analysis. 2024. Available online: https://pubs.geoscienceworld.org/gsw/lithosphere/article/2024/2/lithosphere_2024_137/645133/Development-of-a-Large-Shaking-Table-Test-for-Sand (accessed on 9 September 2024).
38. Benahmed, N. Comportement Mécanique d'un Sable Sous Cisaillement Monotone et Cyclique: Application Aux Phénomènes de Liquéfaction et Mobilité Cyclique. Ph.D. Theis, ENPC, Champs-sur-Marne, France, 2001.
39. McGEARY, R.K. Mechanical Packing of Spherical Particles. *J. Am. Ceram. Soc.* **1961**, *44*, 513–522. [CrossRef]

Disclaimer/Publisher's Note: The statements, opinions and data contained in all publications are solely those of the individual author(s) and contributor(s) and not of MDPI and/or the editor(s). MDPI and/or the editor(s) disclaim responsibility for any injury to people or property resulting from any ideas, methods, instructions or products referred to in the content.

Article

Upper Bound Analysis of Two-Layered Slopes Subjected to Seismic Excitations Using the Layer-Wise Summation Method

Lili Jin [1,*] and Youfang Liao [2]

[1] School of Municipal Construction and Transportation, Guangxi Polytechnic of Construction, Nanning 530007, China
[2] Guangxi Ruiyu Construction Technology Co., Ltd., Nanning 530012, China
* Correspondence: litiemei666@163.com

Abstract: Due to natural sedimentation and artificial filling, slopes exhibit heterogeneity in the form of multi-layer soils, namely, layered slopes. Compared with homogenous slopes, the failure mechanism of layered slopes is more complex owing to the different shear strengths of each soil layer. Therefore, it is of great importance to gain insight into the stability of layered slopes. In this study, the upper bound theorem of limit analysis incorporated with a pseudo-static approach is utilized to investigate the seismic stability of two kinds of two-layered slopes: one with a stiff lower soil layer and the other with a weak lower soil layer. Three failure patterns, namely face failure, toe failure and base failure, are taken into account. A depth coefficient (Δ) is introduced to describe the distribution of two soil layers. The layer-wise summation method is adopted to calculate the safety factor and yield acceleration coefficient more conveniently. Based on Newmark's method, the earthquake-induced horizontal displacement is estimated. The calculated results are validated by comparisons with published literature and the numerical method in terms of safety factor, critical failure surface and yield acceleration coefficient. The results show that the depth coefficient has a significant influence on the failure mechanism of two-layered slopes by determining whether the stability of upper-layered soil is dominant in the overall slope stability or not. Inaccurately identifying the failure patterns will overestimate the seismic performance of two-layered slopes in the aspects of safety factor and yield acceleration coefficient, leading to an underestimation of earthquake-induced horizontal displacement.

Keywords: slope stability; seismic displacement; limit analysis; layered slope; safety factor

Citation: Jin, L.; Liao, Y. Upper Bound Analysis of Two-Layered Slopes Subjected to Seismic Excitations Using the Layer-Wise Summation Method. *Buildings* **2024**, *14*, 1990. https://doi.org/10.3390/buildings14071990

Academic Editors: Bartolomeo Pantò, Harry Far and Antonio Formisano

Received: 27 March 2024
Revised: 28 May 2024
Accepted: 25 June 2024
Published: 1 July 2024

Copyright: © 2024 by the authors. Licensee MDPI, Basel, Switzerland. This article is an open access article distributed under the terms and conditions of the Creative Commons Attribution (CC BY) license (https://creativecommons.org/licenses/by/4.0/).

1. Introduction

The upper bound theorem of limit analysis is widely applied to the problems of stability analysis, i.e., slope stability [1], retaining wall stability [2], tunnel face stability [3] and embankment stability [4]. Generally, the Mohr–Coulomb failure criterion, represented by cohesion and internal friction angle of soils, is employed in the stability analysis of earth slopes [5–7]. The log-spiral rotational failure mechanism is proved to be the critical failure mechanism in slope stability [8]. Based on this failure mechanism, extensive research has recently been conducted on slope stability problems under different conditions and useful conclusions are drawn, providing guidance to the practical design of slopes. For instance, two- and three-dimensional stability charts and displacement charts of uniform slopes with the presence of seismic excitation and pore water pressure are established in order to quickly evaluate the stability of slopes for engineering interests [9–13]. Meanwhile, much attention has been paid to the failure pattern of slopes to further investigate the scale of landslides. Three primary failure patterns include face failure, toe failure and base failure in two- and three-dimensional slope stability analysis [14]. Toe failure commonly occurs in most cases. Base failure is triggered in mild slopes with low internal friction angle. Strong seismic excitation and large pore water pressure increase the likelihood of base failure. Face failure takes place when the slope is subjected to a large surcharge or when the three-dimensional effect is considered. Moreover, a rotational–translational combined failure is established when slopes involve a weak interlayer with lower shear strengths because landslides could occur along this interlayer [15]. In addition, the geometry of slopes has a significant influence on failure patterns. For instance, Rao et al. [16] and Zhang and Yang [17] explored the different failure patterns of two-staged slopes subjected to seismic excitations in two and three dimensions, respectively.

The aforementioned slope stability analyses are all aimed at homogenous slopes. However, owing to the natural geological action and artificial filling, slopes often exhibit heterogeneity and anisotropy [18], such as linear distributions of shear strengths along the depth or layered slopes composed of multi-layer soils. Therefore, it is of great importance to investigate the stability of slopes with heterogeneous and anisotropic soil. Within the framework of limit analysis, the same conclusion was drawn that heterogeneity and anisotropy of cohesion has a significant influence on slope stability and that a decrease in the heterogeneity coefficient and an increase in the anisotropy coefficient make slopes unstable [19,20]. In contrast, the anisotropy of the internal friction angle affects slope stability little [21,22]. For slopes composed of multi-layer soils, owing to the different shear strengths of each soil layer, the failure surface of each soil layer should be different. Therefore, the failure mechanism is composed of a series of failure surfaces instead of a single failure surface. Currently, numerous works have been conducted on the stability of layered slopes [23–27]. Li and Jiang [28] proposed three failure mechanisms to evaluate the stability of two-layered slopes. They found that face failure (failure mechanism A in their study) could occur for steeply two-layered slopes subjected to the large surcharger near the slope crest, and the rotational–translational failure mechanism (failure mechanism C in their study) is more critical than the rotational mechanism for gently two-layered slopes. Based on the combined failure mechanism, Deng et al. [29] adopted the limit equilibrium stress method to establish the stability charts for two-layered slopes for facilitating the design of slopes. Yao and Wang [30] established a horizontal layer slope failure mechanism for multi-layered slopes by combining a discrete algorithm with the upper bound theorem of limit analysis. Recently, a kinematic approach incorporated with the discretization technique has been developed to address this issue more conveniently than the traditional kinematic approach does. For instance, Chen et al. [31] calculated the earthquake-induced horizontal displacement of two-layered slopes with tension cutoff using the discretized failure mechanism. On the other side, a numerical method is an alternative way to conduct the stability analysis of multi-layered slopes. Based on the finite element method, Chatterjee and Krishna [32] found that translational failure occurred in the coarse-grained soil layer, while rotational failure took place in the fine-grained soil layer. However, few studies focus on the influence of the distribution of soil layers on the stability of the multi-layered slope, i.e., safety factor, failure mechanism and earthquake-induced horizontal displacement.

The objective of this study is to investigate the influence of the distribution of soil layers on the seismic stability of two-layered slopes in the application of the upper bound theorem of limit analysis. Two kinds of two-layered slopes are considered: one with a stiff lower soil layer and the other with a weak lower soil layer. To better describe the distribution of two soil layers, a depth coefficient (Δ) is introduced and defined as the ratio of the height of upper-layered soil to the height of the slope. Next, the pseudo-static approach is utilized to characterize the seismic forces acting on the slope. Both horizontal and vertical seismic forces are taken into consideration. A layer-wise summation method [33] is adopted to calculate external work rates and internal energy dissipation more efficiently. Subsequently, the safety factor (FS) and yield acceleration coefficient (k_y) are obtained by establishing an energy balance equation. Once the yield acceleration coefficient is determined, the earthquake-induced horizontal displacement (U_x) is calculated based on Newmark's method [34]. Afterward, the calculated results are compared and verified with the published literature and upper bound solutions of the finite element limit analysis method, including k_y, FS and critical failure surfaces. Parametric studies including slope geometry and seismic excitation on the FS and failure pattern of selected slopes are conducted with different values of Δ. Finally, the influence of Δ on the seismic performance (i.e., k_y and U_x) of selected slopes is investigated, and some interesting conclusions are drawn.

2. Methodology

2.1. Upper Bound Solutions of FS for Two-Layered Slopes

Within the framework of limit analysis, the upper bound theorem is commonly applied to the stability analysis of slopes for finding rigorous upper bound values to the limit forces or loads causing failure or collapse of slopes. The application of the upper bound theorem requires that the soil mass should be perfectly plastic and obey the Mohr–Coulomb yield criterion. The deformation is governed by the associated flow rule that the angle between the tangent line at each point on the failure surface and the velocity vector is the internal friction angle. In other words, the internal friction angle controls the shape of the failure surface. The log-spiral rotational failure mechanism is proved to be a more critical failure mechanism than the translational failure mechanism. But for layered slopes, due to the different internal frictional angles of each soil layer, the failure mechanism is composed of a series of log-spiral failure surfaces instead of a single log-spiral failure surface. To comprehensively investigate the failure mechanism of two-layered slopes, three failure patterns, namely face failure, toe failure and base failure, are taken into consideration in this study, as illustrated in Figure 1. Herein, face failure is assumed to occur within the upper soil layer, which is verified by the finite element limit analysis method in Section 3.

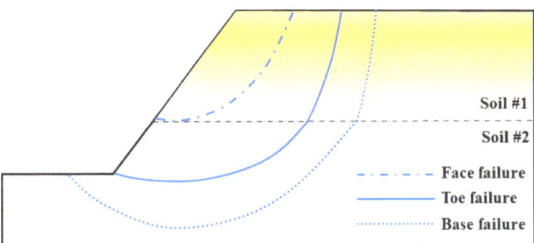

Figure 1. Failure pattern of a two-layered slope.

2.1.1. Base Failure and Toe Failure

Since base failure can degenerate into toe failure, the calculation of upper bound solutions for base failure is presented in detail. Figure 2 shows how base failure is made up of two log-spiral rotational failure surfaces due to different internal friction angles in two soil layers. To describe the distribution of two soil layers, a depth coefficient (Δ) is introduced, which is defined as the ratio of the height of the upper soil layer (h) to the total height of the slope (H). In this study, the external work rates are represented by soil weight and seismic forces. Both horizontal and vertical seismic forces are considered. The internal energy dissipation is represented by soil cohesion along the failure surface. Then, the energy balance equation is established by equating the external work rates to the internal energy dissipation, which can be expressed as

$$W_\gamma + W_{kv} + W_{kh} = D \tag{1}$$

where W_γ is the work rate of the soil weight; W_{kh} and W_{kv} are the work rates of the horizontal and vertical seismic forces, respectively; and D is the internal dissipation of the soil cohesion. To account for the calculation of seismic forces, the pseudo-static approach is employed to treat seismic forces as a uniformly distributed inertial force, acting on the center of gravity of sliding soil mass [35]. This approximate but user-friendly approach is favored by engineers and is commonly applied in the assessment of seismic stability. Next, the calculation of the external work rates and the internal energy dissipation is elaborated by using the layer-wise summation method (LSM) [33] as follows.

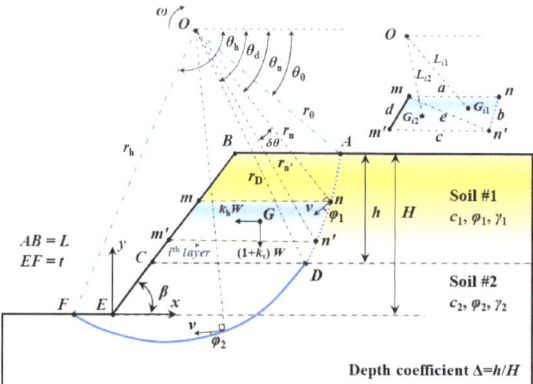

Figure 2. Computation diagram of base failure.

Compared with the classical limit analysis, the LSM can better address the problems of highly nonlinear features of soil property, especially for layered soil. The core of the LSM is, firstly, to horizontally divide the sliding soil mass into several layers and, secondly, to calculate the external work rates and internal energy dissipation of each soil layer and sum them up. As shown in Figure 2, the sliding soil mass as one rigid body rotates around point O with angular velocity ω in the polar coordinate system. For the convenience of calculation, a cartesian coordinate system is established by setting the toe of the slope (point E) as the origin ($E(0,0)$). Point F is the intersection of the failure surface and the bottom of the slope ($F(t,0)$). When $EF = 0$, base failure degenerates into toe failure. Hence, t is set as an independent variable to distinguish two different failure patterns, and the value of t is negative. CD is the interface of the upper and lower soil layer. According to the LSM, the failure mechanism composed of two log-spiral failure surfaces is discretized by dividing the polar angles at the interval of $\delta\theta$ (0.1°). Then, the rigid sliding soil mass is divided into horizontal soil layers. The location of the ith soil layer (block $mnn'm'$) can be expressed in the polar coordinate system as

$$\theta = \begin{cases} \theta_0 + (i-1)\delta\theta, & \theta_0 \leq \theta < \theta_D \\ \theta_D + (i-1)\delta\theta, & \theta_D \leq \theta \leq \theta_h \end{cases} \quad (2)$$

$$r = \begin{cases} r_0 e^{(\theta-\theta_0)\tan\varphi_1}, & \theta_0 \leq \theta < \theta_D \\ r_D e^{(\theta-\theta_D)\tan\varphi_2}, & \theta_D \leq \theta \leq \theta_h \end{cases} \quad (3)$$

$$r_D = r_0 e^{(\theta_D-\theta_0)\tan\varphi_1} \quad (4)$$

where θ_0, θ_D and θ_h are the angles of points A, D and F on the failure surface with the horizontal direction, respectively. r_0 and r_D are the length of OA and OD, respectively; φ_1 and φ_2 are the internal friction angles of upper and lower soil layers, respectively. According to the geometrical features, θ_D can be deduced by a given Δ as

$$\Delta = \frac{h}{H} = \frac{e^{(\theta_D-\theta_0)\tan\varphi_1} \cdot \sin\theta_D - \sin\theta_0}{e^{(\theta_D-\theta_0)\tan\varphi_1} \cdot e^{(\theta_h-\theta_D)\tan\varphi_2} \cdot \sin\theta_h - \sin\theta_0} \quad (5)$$

For the convenience of calculation, the discrete horizontal soil layer is further divided into two triangle blocks (block mnn' and block $mm'n'$). The gravity centers of two triangle blocks should first be determined due to the fact that the soil weight and seismic forces act on the gravity center. According to the geometrical features, the coordinates of gravity centers of block mnn' and block $mm'n'$ can be obtained by coordinate transformation as, respectively,

$$\begin{cases} x_{G_{i1}} = \frac{2r_h\cos(\pi-\theta_h)+r_n\cos\theta_n+r_{n'}\cos\theta_{n'}+[r_h\sin(\pi-\theta_h)-r_n\sin\theta_n]\cot\beta}{3}+t \\ y_{G_{i1}} = \frac{3r_h\sin(\pi-\theta_h)-2r_n\sin\theta_n-r_{n'}\sin\theta_{n'}}{3} \end{cases} \quad (6)$$

$$\begin{cases} x_{G_{i2}} = \frac{r_h\cos(\pi-\theta_h)+r_{n'}\cos\theta_{n'}+[2r_h\sin(\pi-\theta_h)-r_n\sin\theta_n-r_{n'}\sin\theta_{n'}]\cot\beta}{3}+t \\ y_{G_{i2}} = \frac{3r_h\sin(\pi-\theta_h)-r_n\sin\theta_n-2r_{n'}\sin\theta_{n'}}{3} \end{cases} \quad (7)$$

where (x_{Gi1}, y_{Gi1}) and (x_{Gi2}, y_{Gi2}) are the coordinates of gravity center of block mnn' and block $mm'n'$ in cartesian coordinate system, respectively; r_h, r_n and $r_{n'}$ are the length of OF, On and On', respectively; and θ_n and $\theta_{n'}$ are the angles of point n and point n' of the ith soil layer with the horizontal direction, respectively ($\theta_{n'} = \theta_n + \delta\theta$).

Secondly, the total work rates of sliding soil mass duo to soil weight and seismic forces can be expressed by the sum of work rates of the ith soil layer, which are calculated by the dot product of soil gravity, seismic forces and velocity at the gravity center, respectively.

$$W_\gamma = \sum \gamma_i A_{i1} \cdot \omega \cdot (x_{G_{i1}} - x_O) + \sum \gamma_i A_{i2} \cdot \omega \cdot (x_{G_{i2}} - x_O) \quad (8)$$

$$W_{kh} = k_h \left[\sum \gamma_i A_{i1} \cdot \omega \cdot (y_O - y_{G_{i1}}) + \sum \gamma_i A_{i2} \cdot \omega \cdot (y_O - y_{G_{i2}}) \right] \quad (9)$$

$$W_{kv} = k_v W_\gamma \quad (10)$$

$$\begin{cases} x_O = r_h \cos(\pi - \theta_h) + t \\ y_O = r_h \sin(\pi - \theta_h) \end{cases} \quad (11)$$

where γ_i is the soil unit weight of the ith soil layer; A_{i1} and A_{i2} are the areas of block mnn' and block $mm'n'$, respectively; (x_O, y_O) is the coordinates of point O in the cartesian coordinate system; and k_h and k_v are the horizontal and vertical acceleration coefficient, respectively. Herein, $k_v = \lambda k_h$. λ is the vertical-to-horizontal acceleration coefficient ratio, generally ranging from −0.5 to 0.5.

Owing to the sliding soil mass as one rigid block, the internal energy dissipation only occurs along the failure surface, which can be derived as

$$\begin{aligned} D = \sum \Big[&c_i \omega \sqrt{(r_n\cos\theta_n)^2 + (r_n\sin\theta_n)^2} \\ &\times \sqrt{(r_n\cos\theta_n - r_{n'}\cos\theta_{n'})^2 + (r_n\sin\theta_n - r_{n'}\sin\theta_{n'})^2} \cos\varphi_i \Big] \end{aligned} \quad (12)$$

where c_i and φ_i are the cohesion and internal friction angle of the ith soil layer, respectively.

2.1.2. Face Failure

In this study, face failure is assumed to only occur within the upper soil layer, as depicted in Figure 3. Hence, the two-layered slope can be treated as a homogenous slope with upper-layered soil. The total height of the slope (H) is replaced by the height of the upper soil layer (h) in the calculation. The classical upper bound theorem of limit analysis is utilized to establish the energy balance equation. The work rates of the soil weight and seismic forces can be expressed in the polar coordinate system as [11,36]

$$W_\gamma = \gamma_1 \omega r_0^3 (f_1 - f_2 - f_3) \quad (13)$$

$$W_{kh} = k_h \gamma_1 \omega r_0^3 (f_4 - f_5 - f_6) \quad (14)$$

$$W_{kv} = k_v W_\gamma \quad (15)$$

where γ_1 is the soil unit weight of the upper soil layer, and $f_1 \sim f_6$ are non-dimensional functions, which can be found in Appendix A in detail. The internal energy dissipation along the failure surface D can be calculated as

$$D = \frac{c_1 \omega r_0^2}{2 \tan \varphi_1} \left[e^{2(\theta_h - \theta_0) \tan \varphi_1} - 1 \right] \quad (16)$$

where c_1 and φ_1 are the cohesion and internal friction angle of upper soil layer, respectively.

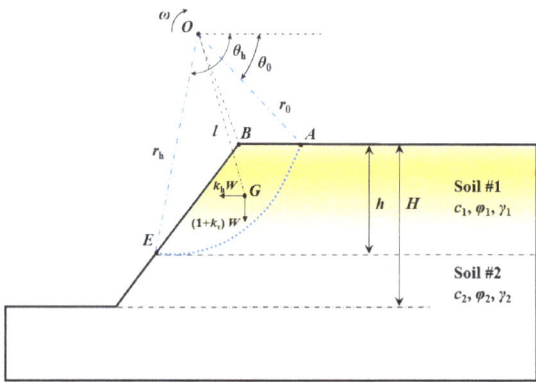

Figure 3. Computation diagram of face failure.

2.1.3. Safety Factor

As an indicator of the state of the slope, the safety factor (FS) is favored by engineers and commonly used in practice. FS can be calculated by the strength reduction method.

$$\begin{cases} c' = c/\text{FS} \\ \varphi' = \arctan(\tan \varphi / \text{FS}) \end{cases} \quad (17)$$

where c and φ are the actual cohesion and internal friction angle of soil mass, respectively; c' and φ' are the cohesion and internal friction angle of soil mass in the limit equilibrium state, respectively. Substituting Equation (17) into Equation (1) and rearranging, a variable η, as a function of three independent variables, θ_0, θ_h and t (t for base failure only), is introduced to describe the stability of the slope as

$$\eta = \frac{D}{W_\gamma + W_{kv} + W_{kh}} = f(\theta_0, \theta_h, t, \text{FS}) \quad (18)$$

When the minimum of η is equal to 1.0, the slope is considered to be in the state of limit equilibrium, and the value of FS represents the safety factor of slopes. Owing to the implicit relationship between FS and η, an iteration method is adopted to determine the value of FS and the detailed procedure is described as follows.

Step 1. Input the information of a two-layered slope, including slope geometry (β and H), soil properties (c_i and φ_i of each soil layer), the distribution of two soil layers (Δ) and earthquake intensity (k_h and λ).

Step 2. Set FS = 1.0 and search the minimum of $\eta = f(\theta_0, \theta_h, t, \text{FS})$. The search domain of independent variables θ_0 and θ_h range from $\pi/6$ to ($\pi - \beta$) and t ranges from $-H$ to 0. The constraint condition is $\theta_0 < \theta_h$. In the process of minimizing η, θ_0 and θ_h are varied with an increment of 0.01° and t is varied with a minimum of 0.001. The minimization procedure does not terminate until the difference between adjacent calculated results is less than 10^{-6} [14].

Step 3. If $|\eta - 1| \leq 10^{-3}$, which means the value of FS is an upper bound of the safety factor of the slope, stop the iteration. If not, set FS = $\sqrt{\text{FS}}$ and take the updated FS back to **Step 2** for the next iteration.

2.2. Yield Acceleration Coefficient and Seismic Permanent Displacements

Apart from FS, Newmark first proposed the basic elements of a procedure, namely Newmark's method, to estimate the earthquake-induced displacement of an embankment in the evaluation of seismic stability [34], which is widely adopted by scholars [37–41]. To calculate the earthquake-induced displacement, the yield acceleration ($k_y g$) or yield acceleration coefficient (k_y) of a specific slope should be first determined. By equating the sum of external work rates of the soil weight and seismic forces to the internal energy dissipation, k_y can be deduced by rewriting Equation (1) as

$$k_y = \frac{\left\{\begin{array}{c}\sum\left[c_i\omega\cos\varphi_i\sqrt{(r_n\cos\theta_n)^2+(r_n\sin\theta_n)^2}\right.\\ \left.\times\sqrt{(r_n\cos\theta_n-r_{n'}\cos\theta_{n'})^2+(r_n\sin\theta_n-r_{n'}\sin\theta_{n'})^2}\right]\\ -\left[\sum\gamma_i A_{i1}\cdot\omega\cdot(x_{G_{i1}}-x_O)+\sum\gamma_i A_{i2}\cdot\omega\cdot(x_{G_{i2}}-x_O)\right]\end{array}\right\}}{\left\{\begin{array}{c}\sum\gamma_i A_{i1}\cdot\omega\cdot(y_O-y_{G_{i1}})+\sum\gamma_i A_{i2}\cdot\omega\cdot(y_O-y_{G_{i2}})\\ +\lambda\left[\sum\gamma_i A_{i1}\cdot\omega\cdot(x_{G_{i1}}-x_O)+\sum\gamma_i A_{i2}\cdot\omega\cdot(x_{G_{i2}}-x_O)\right]\end{array}\right\}} \quad (19)$$

for base failure and toe failure and

$$k_y = \frac{\frac{c_1 \omega r_0^2}{2\tan\varphi_1}\left[e^{2(\theta_h-\theta_0)\tan\varphi_1}-1\right]-\gamma_1\omega r_0^3(f_1-f_2-f_3)}{\lambda\gamma_1\omega r_0^3(f_1-f_2-f_3)+\gamma_1\omega r_0^3(f_4-f_5-f_6)} \quad (20)$$

for face failure. Therefore, k_y can be obtained by minimizing Equation (19) or Equation (20) with three independent variables: θ_0, θ_h and t (t for base failure only). The minimization procedure is the same as that of searching the minimum of η, while the value of FS is always set to 1.0, indicating the limit equilibrium state of the slope.

Once the external acceleration exceeds the yield acceleration, the soil mass starts to slide, causing its angular acceleration around point O to be not zero. Due to the inertial force, an additional moment should be considered in the energy balance equation. Equation (1) can be rewritten as

$$W_\gamma + W_{kv} + W_{kh} = D + W_M \quad (21)$$

where W_M is the work rate induced by the inertial forces. For base failure and toe failure, the formula of W_M can be expressed as [31]

$$W_M = \omega I_M \ddot{\theta} \quad (22)$$

$$I_M = \sum\left\{\left[\frac{1}{36}\gamma_i A_{i1}(a^2+b^2+e^2)+\gamma_i A_{i1}L_{i1}\right]+\left[\frac{1}{36}\gamma_i A_{i2}(c^2+d^2+e^2)+\gamma_i A_{i1}L_{i2}\right]\right\} \quad (23)$$

where I_M is the inertia moment of the sliding soil mass rotating around point O; $\ddot{\theta}$ is the angular acceleration of the sliding soil mass; L_{i1} and L_{i2} are the length of OG_{i1} and OG_{i2}, respectively; a, b, c, d and e represent the length of each side of triangle block mnn' and triangle block mnn', respectively, as shown in Figure 2.

For face failure [11], it can be expressed as

$$W_M = \frac{G}{g}l^2\ddot{\theta} \quad (24)$$

$$l = \frac{\gamma_1 r_0^3}{G}\sqrt{(f_1 - f_2 - f_3) + (f_4 - f_5 - f_6)} \qquad (25)$$

$$G = \frac{1}{2}\gamma_1 r_0^2 \left[\frac{e^{2(\theta_h - \theta_0)\tan\varphi_1} - 1}{2\tan\varphi_1} - \frac{L}{r_0}\sin\theta_0 - \frac{h}{r_0}\frac{\sin(\beta + \theta_h)e^{(\theta_h - \theta_0)\tan\varphi_1}}{\sin\beta}\right] \qquad (26)$$

where G is the weight of sliding soil mass; g is gravity acceleration; l is the length of OG, as shown in Figure 3. The expressions of h/r_0 and L/r_0 are provided in Appendix A. Based on Newmark's method, the horizontal displacement is accumulated when the external acceleration coefficient exceeds k_y. By substituting Equations (8)–(18) and Equations (22)–(26) into Equation (21), the expression of $\ddot{\theta}$ can be obtained after rearrangement.

For base failure and toe failure, we obtain the following:

$$\ddot{\theta} = \frac{k - k_y}{I_M}\left\{\left[\sum\gamma_i A_{i1}\cdot\omega\cdot(y_O - y_{G_{i1}}) + \sum\gamma_i A_{i2}\cdot\omega\cdot(y_O - y_{G_{i2}})\right] + \lambda\left[\sum\gamma_i A_{i1}\cdot\omega\cdot(x_{G_{i1}} - x_O) + \sum\gamma_i A_{i2}\cdot\omega\cdot(x_{G_{i2}} - x_O)\right]\right\} \qquad (27)$$

For face failure, we obtain the following:

$$\ddot{\theta} = (k - k_y)\frac{\gamma_1 r_0^3}{\frac{G}{g}l^2}(f_4 - f_5 - f_6) \qquad (28)$$

where k is the actual horizontal acceleration coefficient of an earthquake which varies with time, while k_y is presumed to keep constant for a specific slope. The earthquake-induced horizontal displacement (U_x) can be calculated by double integrating $\ddot{\theta}$ over time interval dt, and displacement coefficient (C) is determined simultaneously.

$$u_x = r_h\sin\theta_h\int_t\int_t\ddot{\theta}\,\mathrm{d}t\mathrm{d}t = C\int_t\int_t(k - k_y)\mathrm{d}t\mathrm{d}t \qquad (29)$$

For base failure and toe failure, we obtain the following [31]:

$$C = \frac{r_h\sin\theta_h}{I_M}\left\{\left[\sum\gamma_i A_{i1}\cdot\omega\cdot(y_O - y_{G_{i1}}) + \sum\gamma_i A_{i2}\cdot\omega\cdot(y_O - y_{G_{i2}})\right] + \lambda\left[\sum\gamma_i A_{i1}\cdot\omega\cdot(x_{G_{i1}} - x_O) + \sum\gamma_i A_{i2}\cdot\omega\cdot(x_{G_{i2}} - x_O)\right]\right\} \qquad (30)$$

For face failure, we obtain the following [11]:

$$C = r_h\sin\theta_h\frac{\gamma_1 r_0^3}{\frac{G}{g}l^2}(f_4 - f_5 - f_6) \qquad (31)$$

3. Results

3.1. Verification

As previously mentioned, the formulas of safety factor (FS) and the yield acceleration coefficient (k_y) are derived to evaluate the seismic performance of a two-layered slope. Herein, the results of published literature and the upper bound solutions calculated by the finite element limit analysis method (FELAM) are utilized to verify the correctness and effectiveness of the proposed method. Firstly, Figure 4 presents the comparisons of k_y for a homogenous slope and a two-layered slope. Different from the classical limit analysis, Chen et al. [31] employed the discretization technique to calculate the work rates and internal energy dissipation more conveniently, especially for heterogeneous slopes. Despite the different calculated methods, k_y of the proposed method matches well with the results of Chen et al. [31] with little difference. To exhibit the flexibility of the seismic stability analysis of two-layered slopes, the failure mechanism and FS of a 26.6° two-layered slope with a stiff lower soil layer (Slope 1) are calculated by using the proposed method and FELAM, respectively. The soil property is shown in Table 1. As illustrated in Figure 5, both the failure mechanism and FS in this paper are in line with the solutions of FELAM under different values of the depth coefficient (Δ). Moreover, Δ does have an influence on the failure mechanism of the two-layered slope with a stiff soil layer, indicating that the occurrence of face failure is controlled by Δ. Overall, it can be inferred from the comparisons that the proposed method is fully validated for seismic stability analysis of two-layered slopes.

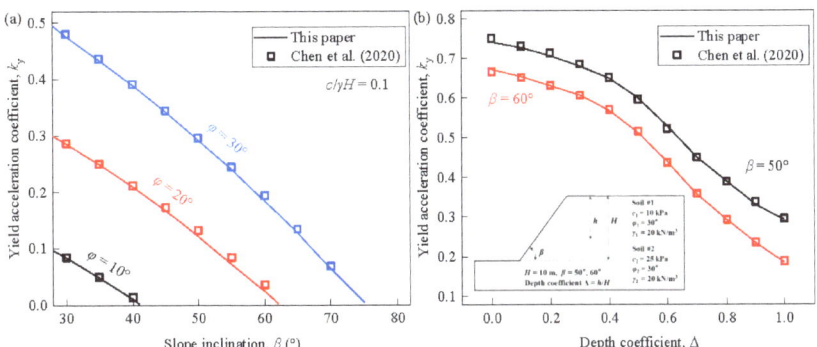

Figure 4. Comparison of yield acceleration coefficient [31]: (**a**) a homogenous slope; (**b**) a two-layered slope.

Table 1. The soil property of a two-layered slope (Adapted from Li and Jiang [28]).

Case	Layer	γ (kN/m³)	c (kPa)	φ (°)
Slope 1 with a stiff lower soil layer	#1	17.50	18.0	12.0
	#2	19.85	25.0	21.5
Slope 2 with a weak lower soil layer	#1	19.85	25.0	21.5
	#2	17.50	18.0	12.0

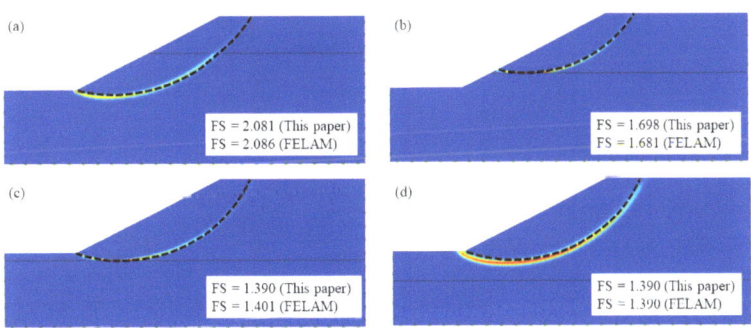

Figure 5. Comparison of FS and critical failure surface of a 26.1° two-layered slope calculated by the proposed method and FELAM: (**a**) Δ = 0.5; (**b**) Δ = 0.8; (**c**) Δ = 1.1; (**d**) Δ = 1.4.

3.2. Safety Factor and Failure Pattern

To investigate the depth coefficient (Δ) on the seismic stability of the two-layered slope, both the safety factor (FS) and the failure pattern of the two-layered slopes possessing different slope inclination (β) and soil strength (i.e., cohesion (c) and internal friction angle (φ)) are calculated subjected to different Δ ranging from 0 to 1.4. The soil property of the two kinds of two-layered slopes is shown in Table 1: Slope 1 with a stiff lower soil layer and

Slope 2 with a weak lower soil layer. Figure 6a,b show the negative correlation between β and FS for both Slope 1 and Slope 2, which is acknowledged by scholars [14,17]. Note that the range of Δ triggering face failure or base failure becomes narrow as β increases, indicating that gently layered slopes are more susceptible to the distribution of soil layers than steeply layered slopes are. The reason may be that Δ controls whether the stability of upper-layered soil is dominant in the overall slope stability or not. In addition, Figure 6c,d depict the different failure patterns with the same value of Δ for Slope 1 and Slope 2. It can be observed that FS will be overestimated if face failure or base failure are mistaken for toe failure, which demonstrates that the stability of two-layered slopes could be overestimated if the failure pattern is not accurately recognized, especially for the gently layered slopes ($\beta \leq 26.6°$) (Figure 6a,b). Interestingly, the failure patterns with different methods exhibit distinct differences. Figure 7 compares the failure patterns obtained from the proposed method and FELAM. For Slope 1, the result of FELAM shows that toe failure along with face failure occurs when the two-layered slope becomes unstable, while only face failure takes place in the proposed method. For Slope 2, despite the base failure occurring in both methods, the results of FELAM show that rotational failure (base failure) and translational failure (near the toe of the slope) simultaneously take place. In addition, the difference in failure patterns leads to the difference in FS. This can be attributed to the deficiency in considering only one failure pattern in the stability analysis of the proposed method.

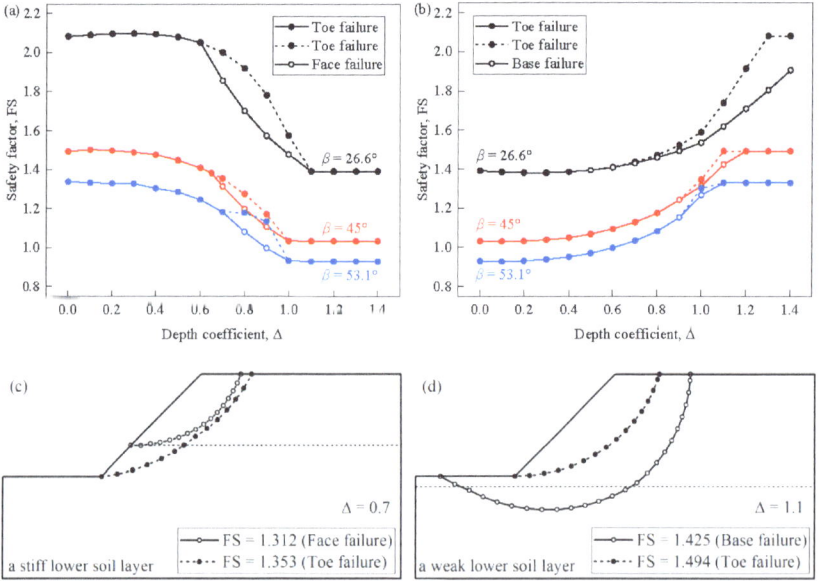

Figure 6. The effect of slope inclination on safety factor: (**a**) Slope 1; (**b**) Slope 2; (**c**) different failure patterns of Slope 1 with $\beta = 45°$ and $\Delta = 0.7$; (**d**) different failure patterns of Slope 2 with $\beta = 45°$ and $\Delta = 1.1$.

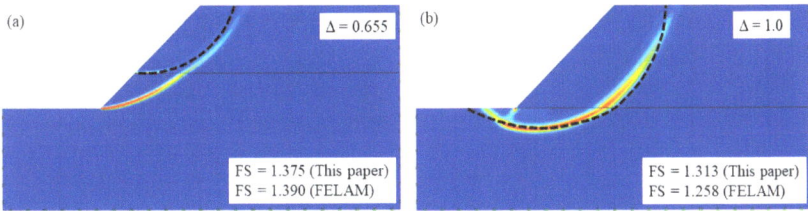

Figure 7. Failure mechanism of a 45° two-layered slope: (**a**) Slope 1; (**b**) Slope 2.

As expected, the presence of an earthquake weakens the slope stability in Figures 8 and 9. However, the failure pattern is hardly affected by the horizontal acceleration coefficient (k_h) and the vertical-to-horizontal acceleration coefficient ratio (λ). The occurrence of face failure for Slope 1 and base failure for Slope 2 only depends on the value of Δ. For example, as shown in Figures 8a and 9a, face failure occurs when Δ ranges from 0.6 to 1.0, and toe failure takes place when $\Delta \leq 0.6$ and $\Delta \geq 1.0$ regardless of the value of k_h and λ. In addition, Figure 9 also indicates that the downward vertical seismic excitation ($\lambda = 0.5$) has the greatest weakening effect on slope stability.

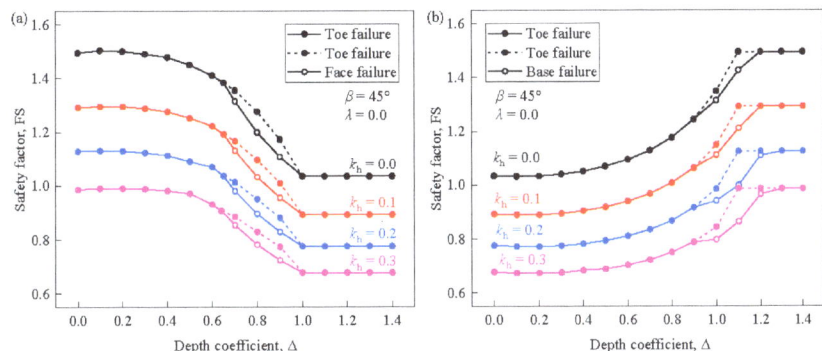

Figure 8. The effect of horizontal acceleration coefficient on safety factor: (**a**) Slope 1; (**b**) Slope 2.

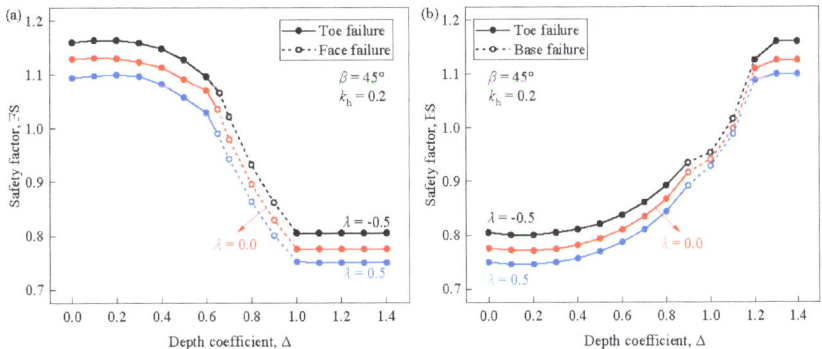

Figure 9. The effect of acceleration coefficient ratio on safety factor: (**a**) Slope 1; (**b**) Slope 2.

3.3. Earthquake-Induced Horizontal Displacement

To explore the depth coefficient (Δ) on yield acceleration coefficient (k_y) and earthquake-induced horizontal displacement (U_x) of the two-layered slope, the slope subjected to a specific earthquake is studied. Figure 10 depicts the acceleration–time records of the San

Fernando earthquake, and its peak gravity acceleration (PGA) is 1.22 g. The slope inclination of two kinds of two-layered slopes is 45°, and the soil property is shown in Table 1. Based on Equations (19), (20) and (29)–(31), k_y, C (displacement coefficient) and U_x of Slope 1 and Slope 2 are presented in Figures 11 and 12, respectively. Herein, the vertical acceleration is not included. For Slope 1, an increase in Δ leads to a decrease in k_y and C (Figure 11a,b), indicating the weakened seismic performance; consequently, U_x becomes larger. However, k_y, C and U_x remain constant when Δ exceeds 1.0 owing to the fact that the dominant role of the stability of the upper soil layer in the overall slope stability treats the two-layered slope as a homogenous slope composed of upper-layered soil, with the lower soil layer regarded as a firm stratum. In addition, U_x increases rapidly when face failure occurs, meaning that the seismic performance will be overestimated if face failure is treated as toe failure. For Slope 2, the opposite variations of k_y, C and U_x can be observed owing to the increasing soil strength of the overall slope when Δ ranges from 0.0 to 1.4. Similarly, mistaking base failure for toe failure will overestimate the seismic stability of the slope. Figures 11d and 12d describe the detailed displacement–time curves under the cases of two different failure patterns with the same value of Δ. The displacement difference of different failure patterns is presented in Tables 2 and 3. For Slope 1, compared with U_x under face failure, U_x under toe failure is reduced by 24.12%, 35.16% and 33.11% for $\Delta = 0.7 \sim 0.9$, respectively. For Slope 2, the reductions in U_x under toe failure are, respectively, 11.74% and 46.66% for $\Delta = 1.0$ and $\Delta = 1.1$ if base failure is replaced by toe failure. Therefore, accurately identifying the failure patterns of two-layered slopes under a specific value of Δ is of great importance to evaluate slope stability.

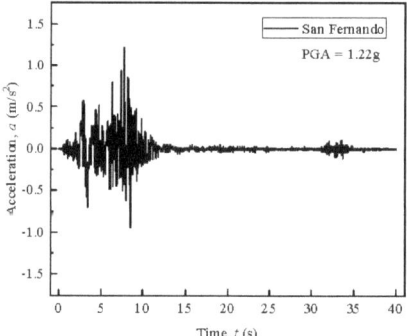

Figure 10. Acceleration–time history of San Fernando earthquake in 1971 (Pacoima Dam Station).

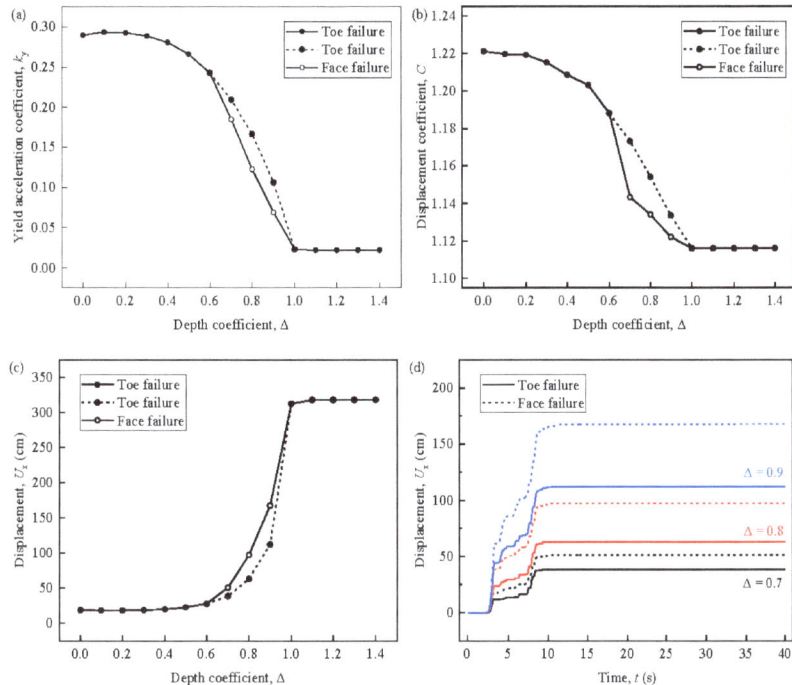

Figure 11. Seismic parameters of Slope 1: (**a**) yield acceleration coefficient; (**b**) displacement coefficient; (**c**) displacement; (**d**) detailed variation of displacement.

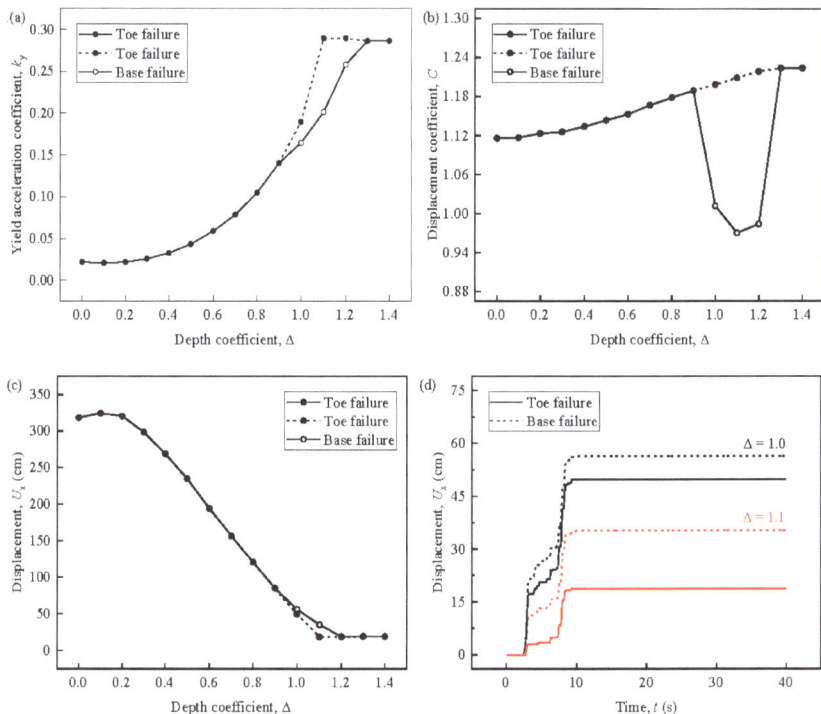

Figure 12. Seismic parameters of Slope 2: (**a**) yield acceleration coefficient; (**b**) displacement coefficient; (**c**) displacement; (**d**) detailed variation of displacement.

Table 2. Earthquake-induced horizontal displacements of different failure patterns for Slope 1.

Depth Coefficient, Δ	Horizontal Displacement, U_x (cm)		Difference $(U_{xF} - U_{xT})/U_{xF} \times 100\%$
	Face Failure	Toe Failure	
0.7	50.74	38.50	24.12%
0.8	97.18	63.01	35.16%
0.9	167.93	112.33	33.11%

Note: U_{xF} and U_{xT} are the horizontal displacements of face failure and toe failure, respectively.

Table 3. Earthquake-induced horizontal displacements of different failure patterns for Slope 2.

Depth Coefficient, Δ	Horizontal Displacement, U_x (cm)		Difference $(U_{xB} - U_{xT})/U_{xB} \times 100\%$
	Base Failure	Toe Failure	
1.0	56.42	49.79	11.74%
1.1	35.26	18.81	46.66%

Note: U_{xT} and U_{xB} are the horizontal displacements of toe failure and base failure, respectively.

4. Conclusions

Based on the upper bound theorem of limit analysis, this study mainly investigates the influence of the distribution of two soil layers on the seismic stability of two-layered slopes in the aspects of failure pattern, safety factor (FS), yield acceleration coefficient (k_y) and earthquake-induced horizontal displacement (U_x). Two kinds of two-layered slopes are considered: one with a stiff lower soil layer (Slope 1) and the other with a weak lower soil layer (Slope 2). A pseudo-static approach is employed to describe the presence of seismic forces. The upper bound theorem of limit analysis incorporated with a layer-wise summation method is employed to calculate the external work rates and internal energy dissipation. The calculated results are in line with the solutions of the published literature and finite element limit analysis. Emphasis is placed on the influence of the depth coefficient (Δ) on FS, k_y, U_x and critical failure surfaces of two-layered slopes. Some major conclusions are drawn as follows:

(1) The distribution of two soil layers significantly affects the stability of two-layered slopes, especially for the failure pattern. The failure pattern of gently two-layered slopes is more susceptible to the variation of Δ than that of steeply two-layered slopes is. The range of Δ triggering face failure for Slope 1 and base failure for Slope 2 narrows with an increase in slope inclination. It can be attributed to the fact that Δ determines whether the stability of the upper soil layer dominates the overall slope stability.

(2) The presence of an earthquake induces the reduction in FS of two-layered slopes. The horizontal acceleration coefficient (k_h) and the vertical-to-horizontal acceleration coefficient ratio (λ) have little influence on the failure patterns, which are only controlled by Δ.

(3) Inaccurate recognition of failure pattern will overestimate the seismic performance (i.e., FS, k_y and U_x) of two-layered slopes with some range of Δ. For example, the earthquake-induced horizontal displacement will be underestimated by 24%~35% for Slope 1 and 11%~46% for Slope 2, respectively, if face failure or base failure are mistaken for toe failure. In practical engineering, much attention should be paid to the distribution of two soil layers to accurately identify the failure pattern of two-layered slopes.

Author Contributions: Conceptualization, L.J.; methodology, L.J.; software, Y.L.; validation, Y.L.; formal analysis, L.J.; writing—original draft preparation, L.J.; writing—review and editing, L.J. and Y.L.; visualization, L.J. All authors have read and agreed to the published version of the manuscript.

Funding: This research was funded by the Project of Promoting the Basic Ability of Scientific Research of Young and Middle-aged Teacher in Universities of Guangxi (No. 2023KY1193).

Data Availability Statement: Dataset available on request from the authors.

Conflicts of Interest: Author Youfang Liao was employed by Guangxi Ruiyu Construction Technology Co., Ltd. The remaining author declares that the research was conducted in the absence of any commercial or financial relationships that could be construed as a potential conflict of interest.

Appendix A

$$f_1 = \frac{\left[(3\tan\varphi_1 \cos\theta_h + \sin\theta_h)e^{3(\theta_h-\theta_0)\tan\varphi_1} - (3\tan\varphi_1 \cos\theta_0 + \sin\theta_0)\right]}{3(1+9\tan^2\varphi_1)}$$

$$f_2 = \frac{1}{6}\frac{L}{r_0}\left(2\cos\theta_0 - \frac{L}{r_0}\right)\sin\theta_0$$

$$f_3 = \frac{1}{6}\frac{h}{r_0}\frac{\sin(\beta+\theta_h)}{\sin\beta}\left[2\cos\theta_h e^{(\theta_h-\theta_0)\tan\varphi_1} + \frac{h}{r_0}\cot\beta\right]e^{(\theta_h-\theta_0)\tan\varphi_1}$$

$$f_4 = \frac{\left[(3\tan\varphi_1 \sin\theta_h - \cos\theta_h)e^{3(\theta_h-\theta_0)\tan\varphi_1} - (3\tan\varphi_1 \sin\theta_0 + \cos\theta_0)\right]}{3(1+9\tan^2\varphi_1)}$$

$$f_5 = \frac{1}{3}\frac{L}{r_0}\sin^2\theta_0$$

$$f_6 = \frac{1}{6}\frac{h}{r_0}\frac{\sin(\beta+\theta_h)}{\sin\beta}\left[2\sin\theta_h e^{(\theta_h-\theta_0)\tan\varphi_1} - \frac{h}{r_0}\right]e^{(\theta_h-\theta_0)\tan\varphi_1}$$

$$\frac{h}{r_0} = \sin\theta_h e^{(\theta_h-\theta_0)\tan\varphi_1} - \sin\theta_0$$

$$\frac{L}{r_0} = \frac{1}{\sin\theta_h}\left[\sin(\theta_h-\theta_0) - \frac{h}{r_0}\frac{\sin(\beta+\theta_h)}{\sin\beta}\right]$$

References

1. Bacharz, K.; Bacharz, M.; Trąmpczyński, W. Estimating the Slope Safety Factor Using Simple Kinematically Admissible Solutions. *Materials* **2023**, *16*, 7074. [CrossRef] [PubMed]
2. Chehade, H.A.; Dias, D.; Sadek, M.; Jenck, O.; Chehade, F.H. Seismic internal stability of saturated reinforced soil retaining walls using the upper bound theorem of limit analysis. *Soil Dyn. Earthq. Eng.* **2022**, *155*, 107180. [CrossRef]
3. Khezri, N.; Mohamad, H.; Fatahi, B. Stability assessment of tunnel face in a layered soil using upper bound theorem of limit analysis. *Geomech. Eng.* **2016**, *11*, 471–492. [CrossRef]
4. Yingchaloenkitkhajorn, K. Analysis of embankment slope stability: The comparison of finite element limit analysis with limit equilibrium methods. In Proceedings of the MATEC Web of Conferences, Shanghai, China, 13–14 October 2018; Volume 270, p. 02004.
5. Chwała, M. Upper-bound approach based on failure mechanisms in slope stability analysis of spatially variable c-φ soils. *Comput. Geotech.* **2021**, *135*, 104170. [CrossRef]
6. Yang, T.; Zou, J.F.; Pan, Q.J. Three-dimensional seismic stability of slopes reinforced by soil nails. *Comput. Geotech.* **2020**, *127*, 103768. [CrossRef]
7. Wang, Y.; Chai, J.; Cao, J.; Qin, Y.; Xu, Z.; Zhang, X. Effects of seepage on a three-layered slope and its stability analysis under rainfall conditions. *Nat. Hazards* **2020**, *102*, 1269–1278. [CrossRef]
8. Chen, W.F. *Limit Analysis and Soil Plasticity*; Elsevier Science: Amsterdam, The Netherlands, 1975; pp. 399–445.
9. Cui, H.; Ji, J.; Song, J.; Huang, W. Limit state line-based seismic stability charts for homogeneous earth slopes. *Comput. Geotech.* **2022**, *146*, 104749. [CrossRef]
10. Michalowski, R.L. Limit analysis and stability charts for 3D slope failures. *J. Geotech. Geoenviron. Eng.* **2010**, *136*, 583–593. [CrossRef]
11. You, L.; Michalowski, R.L. Displacement charts for slopes subjected to seismic loads. *Comput. Geotech.* **1999**, *25*, 45–55. [CrossRef]
12. Michalowski, R.L.; Nadukuru, S.S. Three-dimensional limit analysis of slopes with pore pressure. *J. Geotech. Geoenviron. Eng.* **2013**, *139*, 1604–1610. [CrossRef]
13. Rao, P.P.; Wu, J.; Chen, Q.S.; Nimbalkar, S. Three-dimensional assessment of cracked slopes with pore water pressure using limit analysis. *Environ. Earth Sci.* **2021**, *80*, 1–13. [CrossRef]
14. Park, D.; Michalowski, R.L. Intricacies in three-dimensional limit analysis of earth slopes. *Int. J. Numer. Anal. Methods Geomech.* **2018**, *42*, 2109–2129. [CrossRef]
15. Huang, M.; Fan, X.; Wang, H. Three-dimensional upper bound stability analysis of slopes with weak interlayer based on rotational-translational mechanisms. *Eng. Geol.* **2017**, *223*, 82–91. [CrossRef]
16. Rao, P.P.; Wu, J.; Jiang, G.Y.; Shi, Y.W.; Chen, Q.S.; Nimbalkar, S. Seismic stability analysis for a two-stage slope. *Geomech. Eng.* **2021**, *27*, 189–196.
17. Zhang, Z.L.; Yang, X.L. Unified solution of safety factors for three-dimensional compound slopes considering local and global instability. *Comput. Geotech.* **2023**, *155*, 105227. [CrossRef]
18. Cui, J.; Jin, Y.; Jing, Y.; Lu, Y. Elastoplastic solution of cylindrical cavity expansion in unsaturated offshore island soil considering anisotropy. *J. Mar. Sci. Eng.* **2024**, *12*, 308. [CrossRef]
19. Nian, T.K.; Chen, G.Q.; Luan, M.T.; Yang, Q.; Zheng, D.F. Limit analysis of the stability of slopes reinforced with piles against landslide in nonhomogeneous and anisotropic soils. *Can. Geotech. J.* **2008**, *45*, 1092–1103. [CrossRef]
20. Chen, G.H.; Zou, J.F.; Sheng, Y.M.; Chen, J.Y.; Yang, T. Three-dimensional seismic bearing capacity assessment of heterogeneous and anisotropic slopes. *Int. J. Geomech.* **2022**, *22*, 04022148. [CrossRef]
21. Duncan, J.M.; Seed, H.B. Anisotropy and stress reorientation in clay. *J. Soil Mechan. Found. Div.* **1996**, *92*, 21–50. [CrossRef]
22. Al-Karni, A.A.; Al-Shamrani, M.A. Study of the effect of soil anisotropy on slope stability using method of slices. *Comput. Geotech.* **2000**, *26*, 83–103. [CrossRef]
23. Kumar, J.; Samui, P. Stability determination for layered soil slopes using the upper bound limit analysis. *Geotech. Geol. Eng.* **2006**, *24*, 1803–1819. [CrossRef]
24. Sazzad, M.M.; Mazumder, S.; Moni, M.M. Seismic stability analysis of homogeneous and layered soil slopes by LEM. *Int. J. Comput. Appl.* **2015**, *117*, 12–17.

25. Sarkar, S.; Chakraborty, M. Stability analysis for two-layered slopes by using the strength reduction method. *Int. J. Geo-Eng.* **2021**, *12*, 24. [CrossRef]
26. Qian, Z.G.; Li, A.J.; Merifield, R.S.; Lyamin, A.V. Slope stability charts for two-layered purely cohesive soils based on finite-element limit analysis methods. *Int. J. Geomech.* **2015**, *15*, 06014022. [CrossRef]
27. Qin, C.; Chen Chian, S. Kinematic stability of a two-stage slope in layered soils. *Int. J. Geomech.* **2017**, *17*, 06017006. [CrossRef]
28. Li, C.; Jiang, P. Failure mechanism of two-layered slopes subjected to the surcharge load. *Int. J. Geomech.* **2020**, *20*, 06019024. [CrossRef]
29. Deng, D.P.; Li, L.; Zhao, L.H. Stability analysis of a layered slope with failure mechanism of a composite slip surface. *Int. J. Geomech.* **2019**, *19*, 04019050. [CrossRef]
30. Yao, Y.; Wang, Z. Study on upper bound limit analysis of horizontal layers slope stability based on optimization method. *Sci. Rep.* **2023**, *13*, 6106. [CrossRef] [PubMed]
31. Chen, G.H.; Zou, J.F.; Pan, Q.J.; Qian, Z.H.; Shi, H.Y. Earthquake-induced slope displacements in heterogeneous soils with tensile strength cut-off. *Comput. Geotech.* **2020**, *124*, 103637. [CrossRef]
32. Chatterjee, D.; Murali Krishna, A. Stability analysis of two-layered non-homogeneous slopes. *Int. J. Geotech. Eng.* **2021**, *15*, 617–623. [CrossRef]
33. Wang, L.; Yao, Y.; Wu, L.; Xu, Y. Kinematic limit analysis of three-dimensional unsaturated soil slopes reinforced with a row of piles. *Comput. Geotech.* **2020**, *120*, 103428. [CrossRef]
34. Newmark, N.M. Effects of earthquakes on dams and embankments. *Géotechnique* **1965**, *15*, 139–160. [CrossRef]
35. Zhang, F.; Gao, Y.F.; Wu, Y.X.; Zhang, N.; Qiu, Y. Effects of vertical seismic acceleration on 3D slope stability. *Earthq. Eng. Eng. Vib.* **2016**, *15*, 487–494. [CrossRef]
36. Qin, C.B.; Chian, S.C. Kinematic analysis of seismic slope stability with a discretisation technique and pseudo-dynamic approach: A new perspective. *Géotechnique* **2018**, *68*, 492–503. [CrossRef]
37. Yiğit, A. Prediction of amount of earthquake-induced slope displacement by using Newmark method. *Eng. Geol.* **2020**, *264*, 105385. [CrossRef]
38. Lu, L.; Lin, Y.L.; Guo, D.D.; Xing, H.; Zhang, Z.; Duan, J.Y. A modified Newmark block method for determining the seismic displacement of a slope reinforced by prestressed anchors. *Comput. Geotech.* **2023**, *162*, 105697. [CrossRef]
39. Chang, C.J.; Chen, W.F.; Yao, J.T. Seismic displacements in slopes by limit analysis. *J. Geotech. Eng.* **1984**, *110*, 860–874. [CrossRef]
40. Li, X.; He, S.; Wu, Y. Seismic displacement of slopes reinforced with piles. *J. Geotech. Geoenviron. Eng.* **2010**, *136*, 880–884. [CrossRef]
41. Loukidis, D.; Bandini, P.; Salgado, R. Stability of seismically loaded slopes using limit analysis. *Géotechnique* **2003**, *53*, 463–479. [CrossRef]

Disclaimer/Publisher's Note: The statements, opinions and data contained in all publications are solely those of the individual author(s) and contributor(s) and not of MDPI and/or the editor(s). MDPI and/or the editor(s) disclaim responsibility for any injury to people or property resulting from any ideas, methods, instructions or products referred to in the content.

Article

Structural Stability and Mechanical Analysis of PVC Pipe Jacking under Axial Force

Rudong Wu, Kaixin Liu, Peng Zhang *, Cong Zeng, Yong Xu and Jiahao Mei

Faculty of Engineering, China University of Geosciences, Wuhan 430074, China; rudongwu@cug.edu.cn (R.W.); lkx@cug.edu.cn (K.L.); zengcong@126.com (C.Z.); xyong@cug.edu.cn (Y.X.); meijiahao@cug.edu.cn (J.M.)
* Correspondence: cugpengzhang@cug.edu.cn

Abstract: PVC pipe jacking is prone to cause yielding or buckling under the jacking force and may lead to engineering failure. The relationship between the buckling modes, ultimate bearing capacity, different diameter–thickness ratios, and length–diameter ratios of PVC pipe jacking under different load forms was analyzed. The calculation methods for allowable jacking force and the single allowable jacking distance are obtained through theoretical analysis and three-dimensional finite elements. The buckling mode of the pipe under uniform load changes from symmetric buckling to asymmetric buckling and then to the overall Euler buckling form as the length–diameter ratio increases. The ultimate bearing capacity of the pipe approaches the theoretical value of yield failure when L/D ≤ 6. For L/D > 6, the pipe undergoes buckling, and the ultimate bearing capacity determined by the axial buckling value and the buckling load can be calculated according to the long pipe theory formula when L/D > 8.5. Under eccentric loads, the failure mode transitions from local failure to Euler buckling with increasing pipe length. The ultimate bearing capacity of pipe is obviously lower than that of uniform load, but as the length–diameter ratio increases, this difference decreases until it becomes consistent.

Keywords: pipe jacking; structural stability; buckling load; ultimate bearing capacity

1. Introduction

Pipe jacking is an advanced underground pipe-laying technology with less environmental impact [1–4]. Only high-load-bearing pipe materials could be used in the early stages of micro tunnels, such as concrete pipes, fiberglass-reinforced plastic pipes, and steel pipes [5–7]. Although PVC is a high-quality material for water supply and drainage pipes, it is often used for buried pipelines rather than trenchless methods. A low-load-bearing pipe jacking system was developed, allowing PVC to be used in pipe jacking as technology progressed [8,9].

An important factor that limited the use of PVC pipes in micro tunnels was its axial bearing capacity [10,11]. An experimental setup was developed by Jemii et al. [12] to study the circumferential mechanical characteristics of PVC pipes. Furthermore, a finite element model was created to predict the mechanical response of the pipes under radial loads. The stress characteristics of arch-shaped axial hollow wall PVC pipes, as well as the impact of the pipe wall layout form on pipe stiffness and strength performance, were analyzed by Tang et al. [13] based on buried model tests and simulation analysis. The conclusion that the axial hollow wall is structurally preferable with a circular hole configuration was attained. When considering the stability of PVC pipe jacking under axial load during construction, studies on the stability of steel pipe jacking can serve as a reference. The relationship between critical axial pressure for steel pipe jacking and various parameters has been extensively researched by many scholars [14–16]. The theoretical derivation for axially loaded cylindrical shells was conducted by scholars in the early 20th century. Fok [17] used the energy method combined with the Rayleigh–Ritz trial function to analyze the

buckling of long cylindrical shells under far-field hydrostatic pressure. The compressive strain capacity of a pressurized pipeline under eccentric axial compression was numerically studied by Tu [18]. At the same time, the effects of internal pressure and the ratio of pipe diameter to wall thickness on the compressive strain capacity were studied.

Thus far, the current literature has seldom focused on the mechanical characteristics and axial bearing capacity of PVC pipe jacking. Most of the research literature is mainly focused on the circumferential bearing performance of buried pipes and the buckling stability of steel pipe jacking [19–22]. Compared to steel pipes, the strength of PVC pipes is lower, and yield failure or buckling in PVC might be observed when subjected to significant axial pressure. Therefore, a study on the mechanical characteristics of PVC pipe jacking under axial pressure is essential. The relationship between the ultimate bearing capacity and PVC pipes with different lengths and diameters is also important to study, to prevent the failure of the PVC pipe caused by jacking force.

This paper investigates the failure modes and mechanical properties of PVC pipe jacking under axial uniform force and two eccentric loads through theoretical research and numerical simulation. The influence of the diameter–thickness ratio and the length–diameter ratio on the ultimate bearing capacity of PVC pipes are analyzed and compared with theoretical formulas. Furthermore, the elastic buckling load and ultimate bearing capacity of PVC pipes are obtained and, when combined with the study of the bearing capacity of a single PVC pipe, the calculation method for the allowable jacking force and the single allowable jacking distance are derived.

2. Methodology
2.1. Failure Modes under Axial Loads

A low-load one-time construction method is to use PVC pipe for jacking. In this method, the frontal resistance required by the cutter head jacking acts on the spiral rod inside the pipe. The PVC pipe only bears the friction resistance between the surrounding soil and the outer surface of the pipe and is not affected by the head-on resistance. The axial force of the PVC pipe is greatly reduced, and the risk of buckling of the PVC pipe during jacking is also reduced. The force transfer mechanism enables PVC pipe to be applied in pipe jacking engineering. The principle of PVC micro pipe jacking is shown in Figure 1.

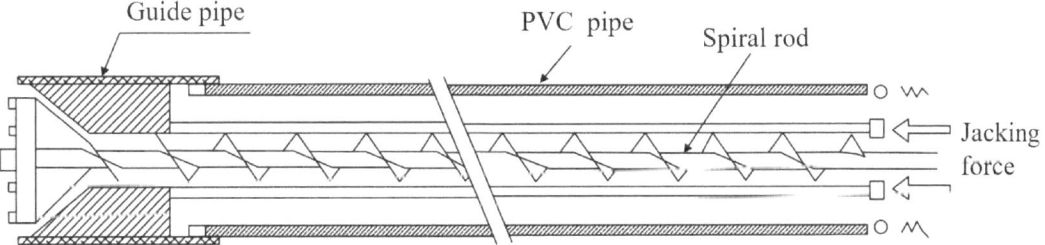

Figure 1. Schematic diagram of PVC pipe jacking principle.

However, although this method can be used to apply PVC pipe to the pipe jacking, it still has the risk of buckling or yield failure under the action of axial force. It is of great significance to clarify the ultimate bearing capacity and buckling modes of PVC pipe under different conditions for pipe jacking construction to determine which type of failure is more likely to occur in PVC pipes under different axial loads. The finite element model of PVC pipe was established by ABAQUS 6.14 software. The shape change energy density theory and cylindrical shell analysis theory were analyzed. The corresponding flow chart of this paper is shown in Figure 2.

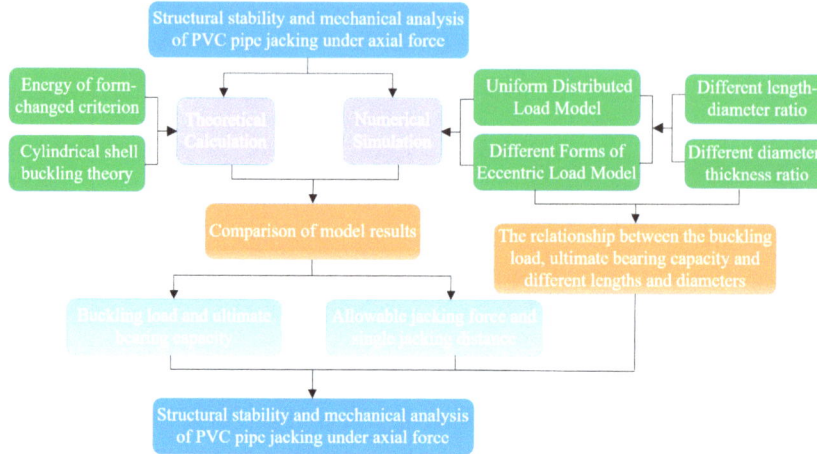

Figure 2. The main research content flow chart of this paper.

(1) Energy of form-changed criterion

The energy of form-changed criterion refers to a strength theory used to determine if a material undergoes yield failure, also known as the fourth yield criterion [23,24]. Yield failure will occur when the shape changes specific energy at a point that reaches the level at which the material yields under the complex state of stress. The formula for strength conditions is shown in Equation (1):

$$\sqrt{\frac{1}{2}\left[(\sigma_1 - \sigma_2)^2 + (\sigma_2 - \sigma_3)^2 + (\sigma_1 - \sigma_3)^2\right]} \leq [\sigma] \qquad (1)$$

where σ_1, σ_2, and σ_3 represent the three principal stresses at the critical point of the component in the formula.

For PVC pipes under axial uniform force, yield failure is determined according to Equation (2).

$$P_d = A_p * \sigma_u \qquad (2)$$

where A_p is the cross-sectional area of the pipe, m^2, and σ_u is the yield strength of the pipe material, Pa.

(2) Cylindrical shell buckling theory

The failure form of PVC pipe jacking under axial loads can be similar to the buckling of cylindrical shells. The buckling load of axially compressed cylindrical shells is influenced by the length. They are classified into short cylindrical shells [25,26] and long cylindrical shells [27] based on different buckling modes. The buckling load for short cylindrical shells is calculated using Equation (3), while the buckling load for long cylindrical shells is calculated using Equation (4).

$$P_{cr} = \frac{2\pi E t^2}{\sqrt{3(1-\nu^2)}} \qquad (3)$$

$$P_{cr} = \frac{\pi^3 E D^3 t}{8(\mu_0 l)^2} \qquad (4)$$

In the formula, E is the elastic modulus (N/m^2), D is the diameter of the cylindrical shell (m), t is the thickness of the cylindrical shell (m), ν is the Poisson ratio, l indicates the length of the cylindrical shell (m), and μ_0 is the effective length factor, which varies depending on boundary conditions.

2.2. Finite Element Model

The finite element models of the PVC pipe were developed using the ABAQUS 6.14 finite element software. To obtain more accurate results of PVC pipe jacking failure modes and bearing capacity, the model was set as follows.

(1) Element and material: The PVC pipe was simulated by a three-dimensional shell element and the elastic-plastic constitutive model was adopted for PVC pipe. According to the experimental research and numerical simulation of previous scholars [12,28,29], the elastic modulus can be taken as 3000 MPa and the compressive yield strength and tensile yield strength are 86.71 MPa and 51.58 MPa, respectively. The finite element model of the PVC pipe is shown in Figure 3, and the pipe parameters are listed in Table 1.

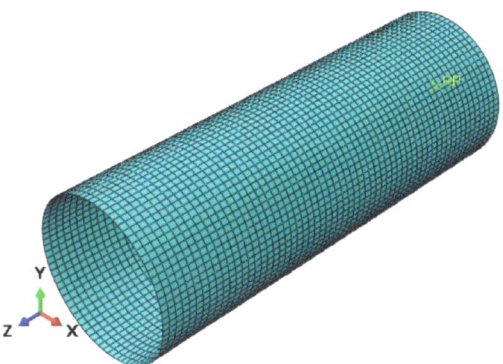

Figure 3. Numerical calculation model for PVC pipes.

Table 1. Pipe parameters of finite element model.

Material	Density (kg/m³)	Diameter (mm)	Wall Thickness (mm)	Pipe Length (m)	Elastic Modulus [28] (MPa)	Compressive Yield Strength [12,28] (MPa)	Tensile Yield Strength [29] (MPa)	Poisson Ratio
PVC Pipe	1360	223.6	11.8	0.6	3000	86.71	51.58	0.319

(2) Element selection and mesh division: The simulation employed three-dimensional shell elements referred to as S4R (four-node reduced integral shell element). S4R has good applicability and can be automatically adjusted between thin and thick shell elements, which can be used for large deformation calculations. The accuracy of the calculation results is greatly affected by the number of elements [30]. To determine the selection of element type and density, many simulations were carried out in this paper. The elastic buckling results of S4R (four node reduced integral shell element) and S8R (eight-node reduced integral shell element) at the mesh density of 0.01 and 0.005 were compared under method B, as shown in Table 2. The calculation results of the S4R type were closer to the theoretical values, and the mesh density did not change much after 0.01. Therefore, the three-dimensional S4R (four-node reduced integral shell element) was employed and the number of pipe meshes for a 0.6 m length was 4186.

Table 2. The influence of mesh type and density on the results.

Mesh Type	Mesh Density	Simulated Values (kN)	Theoretical Value (kN)
S4R	0.01	1421	
	0.005	1414	1617
S8R	0.01	1337	
	0.005	1389	

(3) Boundary condition and compression load: For the boundary condition setting of the model, one end of the PVC pipe was fixed while the other end was hinged and the two were coupled by the coupling command. The reference points were set at the center of both ends of the shell and the two were coupled by the coupling command, and the boundary conditions were set at these two reference points. The compressive load selects the force load and the displacement load. The force load was applied by applying a concentrated force at the force action or applying a shell edge load at the pressurized end section. The displacement load controls its motion or deformation by applying a vector displacement to the target force.

(4) Simulation methods: The static general analysis step is usually used to calculate the structure with constant or increased structural stiffness in ABAQUS 6.14. If the structure buckles or collapses, it is easy to have non-convergence problems which may prevent it from calculating the post-buckling state. To compare the results of the Buckle–Riks analysis step, two methods were used. The soil layers were not established and the interaction between the pipe and the soil was not considered in the model. Method A: the static general analysis step is selected, the axial pressure is simulated by applying the displacement load to the reference point of the pressure end, and the load-displacement curve is output to determine its bearing capacity. Method B: Buckle–Riks is used to calculate the buckling eigenvalue, and then the defect is introduced to calculate the post-buckling result through the Riks analysis step.

3. Results under Uniform Load

The buckling modes of PVC pipes under uniform axial load obtained using Method A and Method B are shown in Figures 4 and 5, respectively. As shown in Figure 4, the model was compressed in a corrugated manner under the static general analysis step, and the compressive stress on the model was symmetrically distributed. Additionally, the load-analysis step curve in Method A first increased and then decreased. It can be seen from Figure 5 that in Method B, where the Buckle analysis step was used, the five buckling modes of the short pipe exhibited varying deformation patterns.

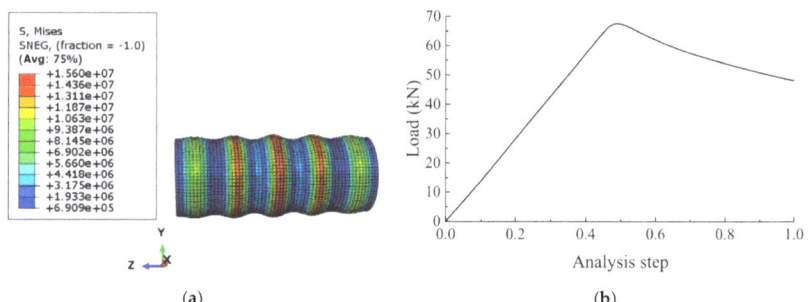

Figure 4. Numerical results of Method A: (**a**) model failure mode; (**b**) load-step curve.

The first two buckling modes showed anti-symmetric buckling for two symmetric points on the pipe; one is convex while the other is concave. The last three buckling modes exhibited symmetric buckling, the number of circumferential waves generated on the pipe gradually decreased, and the peak position appeared in the middle of the pipe. The deformation of the pipeline under axial compression was mainly composed of circumferential deformation and vertical deformation on the cross-section. The buckling mode of the pipeline was greatly affected by the eigenvalue. In the fifth mode, only the middle of the pipe produced a depression. From the first to the fifth mode, the length of the deformed pipe gradually decreased, and the number of deformation waves also decreased. The characteristic values were consistent with the buckling modes.

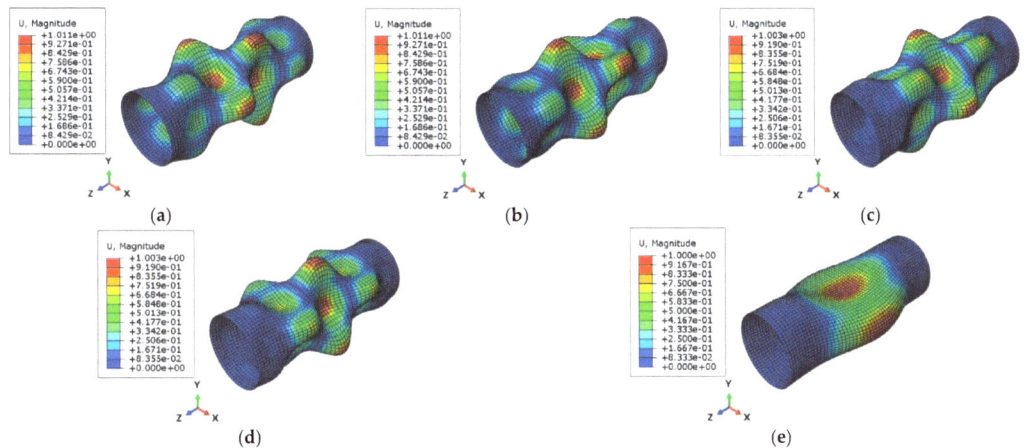

Figure 5. Buckling mode under the Buckle analysis step: (**a**–**e**) eigenvalue of mode 1~eigenvalue of mode 5.

The comparison of results from different theories and two simulation methods is shown in Table 3. The results of simulation Method A were more aligned with the fourth yield criterion, while the results from Method B were closer to the classical critical buckling solution for short pipes. This size of PVC pipe was more likely to experience yield failure first based on the results.

Table 3. Comparison between numerical results and theoretical results.

	Fourth Yield Criterion	Method A	Short Pipe Theory	Method B
Critical buckling load/kN	683.1	676.4	1617	1421

3.1. Method A Results

The comparison and error between the simulated and theoretical values under different lengths, wall thicknesses, and diameters are shown in Table 4. The error in Table 4 is obtained by 1 minus the simulated value divided by the theoretical value and the error between the two is small, which can correctly reflect the accuracy of the simulation. The changes in the simulated values and theoretical values of the axial bearing capacity of the pipe with length, diameter, and wall thickness are shown in Figure 6. Only the length of the pipe changed; the theoretical value for the PVC pipe's bearing capacity remained constant. This is because the axial bearing capacity of the pipe was not influenced by the pipe length in the fourth yield criterion. The simulation values showed minor variations with changes in pipe length but were generally stable. The curve fluctuations when the pipe was shorter were affected by the boundary conditions.

When the wall thickness and diameter of a PVC pipe increased, its axial bearing capacity also increased, and the two were approximately linearly related. When the wall thickness of the PVC pipe increased from 4.4 mm to 22.3 mm, its bearing capacity rose from 244.93 kN to 1264.49 kN. For every 100 mm increase in the pipe diameter, the bearing capacity increased by about 300 kN. The bearing capacity of pipes under axial uniform force showed strong consistency with the results from yield theory under Method A. Combined with the observed deformation patterns under axial pressure, it mainly reflected the nonlinearity of the material. The simulation results for all three scenarios aligned well with the theoretical values, which also showed the accuracy of the simulation in this paper.

Table 4. Effects of pipe length, diameter, and wall thickness on simulated and theoretical values.

		Simulation Value (kN)	Theoretical Value (kN)	Deviation (%)
Length (m)	0.6	676.4	683.1	0.98
	0.9	685.9	683.1	0.41
	1.2	675.6	683.1	1.09
	2.0	676.2	683.1	1.01
	3.0	674.3	683.1	1.30
Diameter (mm)	223.6	676.4	683.09	0.98
	300	892.26	929.49	4.00
	400	1172.87	1252.01	6.32
	500	1527.97	1547.52	1.26
	600	1787.63	1897.04	5.77
Wall thickness (mm)	4.48	244.93	267.84	8.55
	5.59	320.36	333.09	3.82
	7.45	404	440.13	8.21
	8.94	514	524.51	2.00
	11.95	676.4	683.09	0.98
	14.91	866.96	850.45	1.90
	22.36	1264.49	1229.86	2.74

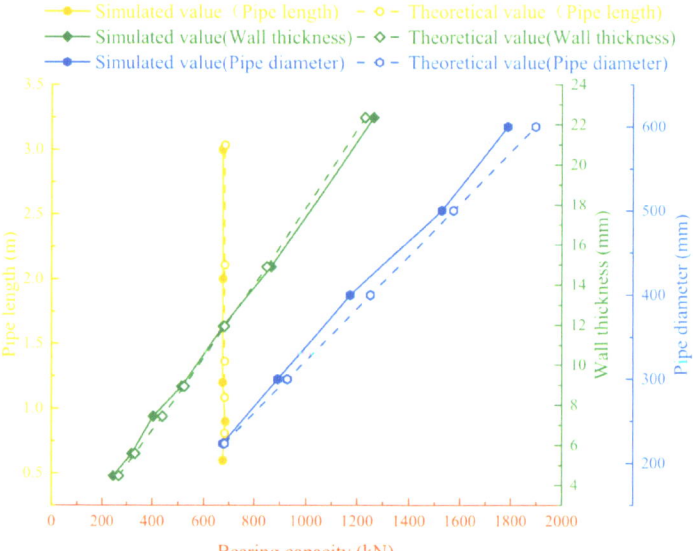

Figure 6. Comparison of theoretical and simulated values for different lengths, wall thicknesses, and diameters.

3.2. Method B Analysis

Elastic theory analysis was conducted on the buckling model. A force was applied to the reference point of the hinged end, and the concentrated force along the axial direction of the pipe was used as the axial uniform force. The length and wall thickness of the pipe were varied. The buckling modes for pipes with $L/D \leq 6$, $6 < L/D \leq 8.5$, and $L/D > 8.5$ are shown in Figure 7. The first mode buckling values under uniform axial load for different sizes of PVC pipes are presented in Table 5. As shown in Figure 7, as the length–diameter ratio increased, the buckling mode of the pipe transitioned from symmetric buckling to anti-symmetric buckling and ultimately to the overall Euler buckling pattern. The number of radial and circumferential waves on the pipe also decreased with an increasing length–diameter ratio.

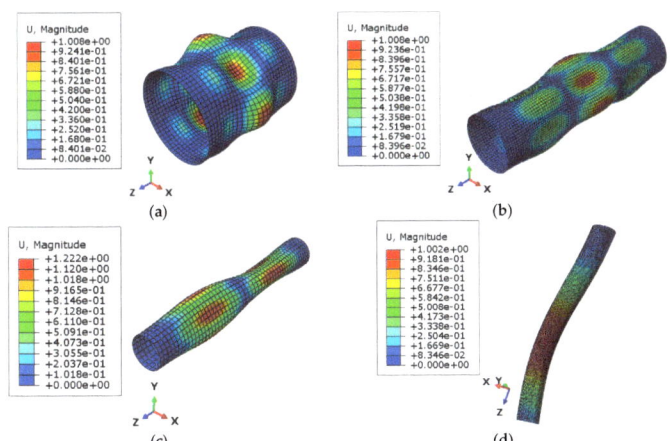

Figure 7. Buckling modes of different lengths: (**a**) 0.3 m; (**b**) 0.9 m; (**c**) 1.6 m; (**d**) 2 m.

Table 5. Elastic buckling values under axial uniform force (kN).

t (mm) \ L (m)	0.3	0.6	1.2	2.0	3.0	7.0
5.59	351.62	341.96	312.41	265.46	148.28	26.89
7.45	612.51	573.59	523.37	409.68	194.41	31
8.94	855.42	804.56	700.95	485.33	230.21	36.65
11.8	1485.95	1421	1138.59	624.64	296.12	47.02
14.91	2274.79	2004.92	1716.59	767.41	363.65	57.60
22.36	4575.95	3892.12	3486.38	1073.37	508.47	80.08

The curve of the elastic buckling load for PVC pipes with different lengths as a function of the diameter–thickness (D/t) ratio is shown in Figure 8a. The curve showing the elastic buckling load for PVC pipes with different wall thicknesses as a function of the length–diameter ratio is plotted in Figure 8b. The buckling load for PVC pipes of various lengths decreased as the D/t ratio increased, and when the D/t ratio was low, the buckling load for shorter PVC pipes was significantly higher than that of longer pipes. When the D/t ratio was 10, the buckling load for a 0.3 m long PVC pipe was about 4575 kN, which is approximately 57 times the buckling load of a 7 m long PVC pipe. As the D/t ratio increased, the effect of length on the buckling load of PVC pipes gradually diminished, eventually tending to be consistent.

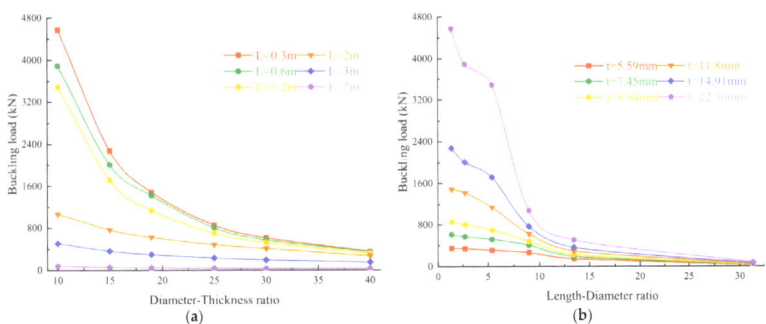

Figure 8. The curve of elastic buckling load as a function of diameter–thickness ratio and length–diameter ratio: (**a**) diameter–thickness ratio; (**b**) length–diameter ratio.

As seen in Figure 8b, the elastic buckling load of the pipe is inversely correlated with the length–diameter (L/D) ratio. At an L/D ratio of 1.34, the wall thickness had the greatest impact on the buckling load. At this ratio, the buckling load for a wall thickness of 22.36 mm was approximately 14.6 times that for a wall thickness of 5.59 mm. However, as the L/D ratio increased, the buckling loads for PVC pipes with different wall thicknesses gradually decreased and converged. The variations in buckling load across different L/D ratios demonstrated a more staged behavior, influenced by the buckling modes.

The comparison of elastic buckling values for PVC pipes under axial uniform force with the short pipe theory is presented in Figure 9a. When the L/D ratio was low, the buckling load of the pipe was close to the results calculated using the short pipe theory. However, this consistency gradually diminished as the L/D ratio increased. When the L/D ratio exceeded 6, a significant deviation occurred, indicating that the short pipe theory was no longer suitable for calculating the buckling load of PVC pipes.

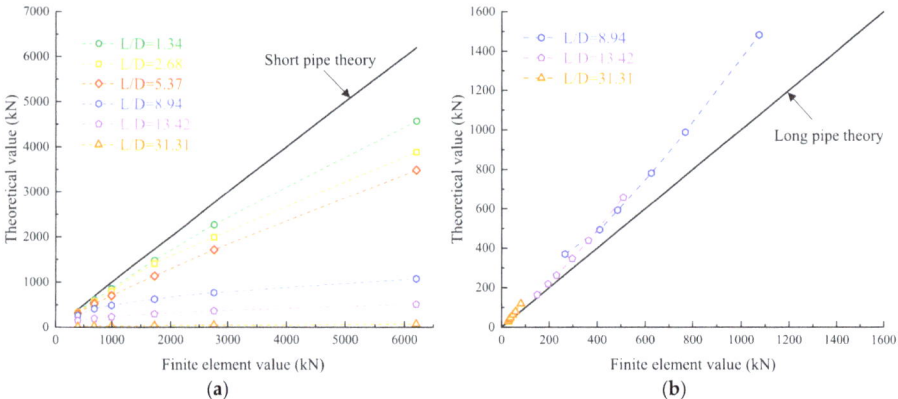

Figure 9. Comparison of finite element results with theoretical values: (**a**) short pipe theory; (**b**) long pipe theory.

Figure 9b plots a comparison between the elastic buckling loads for PVC pipes with an L/D ratio greater than 8.5 and the long pipe theoretical formula. As shown in Figure 9b, when L/D > 8.5, the results for elastic buckling load aligned well with the long pipe theoretical formula. Consequently, under axial uniform force, buckling loads were close to the short pipe theoretical formula when L/D was approximately 6 and converged toward the long pipe theoretical formula when L/D was around 8.5.

The results reflect elastic bearing capacity; the post-buckling stage was not considered. The first buckling mode was introduced into the pipe model as an initial imperfection to analyze post-buckling. The first-order axial buckling mode was scaled by a certain factor and then applied to the structure as an initial defect, with the defect size not exceeding 1% of the pipe's diameter. The ultimate axial bearing capacity for PVC pipe of different lengths and wall thicknesses under uniform axial loading is listed in Table 6.

Table 6. Ultimate bearing capacity of PVC pipe under axial uniform load.

t (mm) \ L (m)	0.3	0.6	1.2	2.0	3.0	7.0
5.59	173.46	150.02	173.49	209.23	144.40	23.60
7.45	297.17	309.7	383.92	366.42	191.98	30.89
8.94	410.43	420.54	489.19	444.15	228.78	35.63
11.8	633.33	635.78	681.99	590.37	296.35	46.12
14.91	856.82	889.27	887.28	726.01	365.77	56.93
22.36	1364.97	1367.53	1378.56	1044.29	511.73	80

Figure 10a,b display the variation in the ultimate bearing capacity of PVC pipes under axial uniform force as a function of the L/D ratio and D/t ratio. The ultimate bearing capacity showed a stepped pattern of variation as the L/D ratio increased. The ultimate bearing capacity remained relatively constant with only slight fluctuations at L/D = 6. This is because deformations in the model are more likely to be influenced by boundary conditions at lower L/D ratios. However, when the L/D ratio was greater than 6, the ultimate bearing capacity gradually decreased as the L/D ratio increased. When the L/D ratio became sufficiently large, the ultimate bearing capacity of PVC pipes was no longer affected by wall thickness. The ultimate bearing capacity for PVC pipes with different wall thicknesses tended to decrease and eventually converge to similar values.

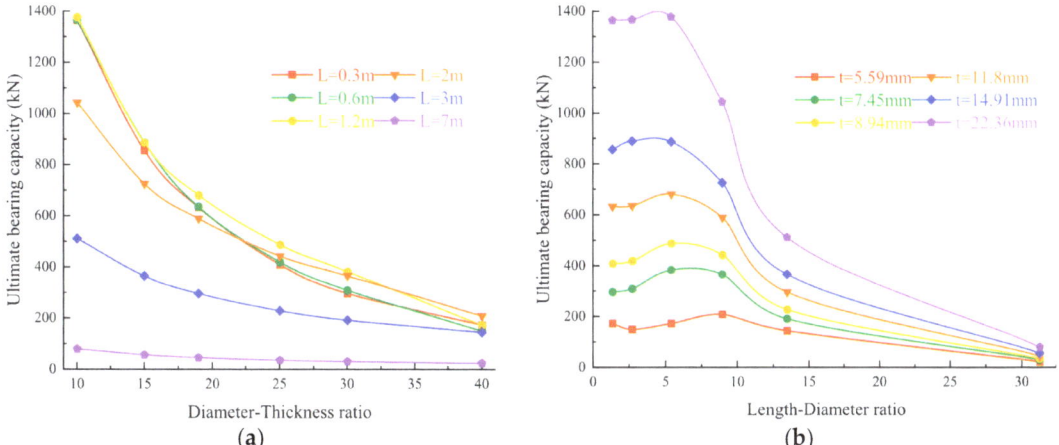

Figure 10. The curve of the ultimate bearing capacity of the pipe changing with the diameter–thickness ratio and the length–diameter ratio: (**a**) diameter–thickness ratio; (**b**) length–diameter ratio.

As can be seen from Figure 10b, the ultimate bearing capacity of PVC pipes gradually decreased as D/t increased. The ultimate bearing capacity curves of the PVC pipes with lengths of 0.3 m and 0.6 m were almost identical, and shorter pipes are more easily affected by the wall thickness ratio. For pipes with lengths of 0.3 m and 0.6 m, as the D/t ratio increased from 10 to 40, the ultimate bearing capacity decreased from 1364 kN to 173 kN—a reduction of about 1191 kN. In contrast, for a 7 m-long PVC pipe, the ultimate bearing capacity decreased from 80 kN to 23.6 kN as the D/t ratio increased from 10 to 40. This indicates that shorter pipes are significantly more affected by changes in the D/t ratio, whereas longer pipes are less influenced by these variations.

The results from Method A and Method B were compared, as shown in Figure 11. The ultimate bearing capacity of PVC pipes under axial uniform force was close to the results from Method A when the L/D ratio was less than 6. However, the difference between the ultimate bearing capacity and Method A's results increased as the L/D ratio exceeded 6. When the L/D ratio was less than 6, the ultimate bearing capacity of the pipe was primarily determined by the material's yield strength. When the L/D ratio was greater than 6, the buckling failure of the pipe was mainly governed by its axial buckling load. Zhen [14] studied the influence of the slenderness ratio of the steel pipe jacking on the critical buckling load and found that there is a critical slenderness ratio, which causes local buckling and global buckling of the steel pipe jacking. When the slenderness ratio was less than 37, local buckling occurred in the steel pipe jacking, and the critical bearing capacity was determined by the buckling load. The length of PVC pipe used in pipe jacking is shorter than that of steel pipe jacking, and the critical slenderness ratio of PVC pipe jacking is 6.

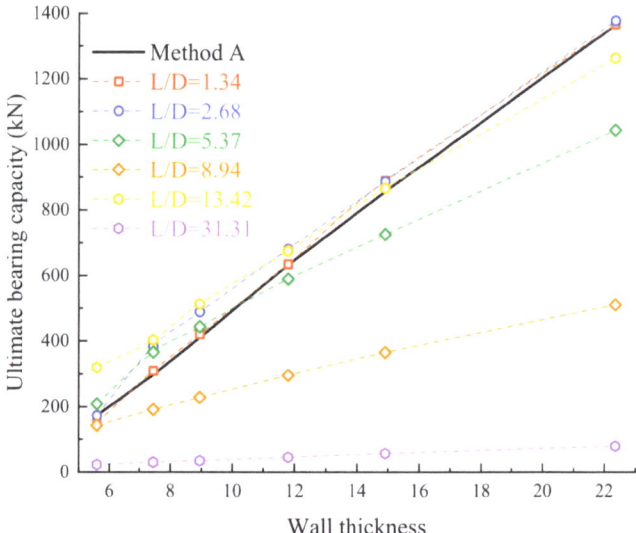

Figure 11. Comparison of results between Method A and Method B.

To compare the critical values of elastic instability with those of elastoplastic instability, the elastic buckling values from Table 5 were divided by the corresponding ultimate bearing capacity values from Table 6 to derive Table 7. As can be seen in Table 7, as the length of the pipe increased, the elastic buckling load for PVC pipe jacking gradually approached the ultimate bearing capacity under axial uniform force. When the length reached 2 m, the elastic buckling load and the ultimate bearing capacity were nearly identical. Considering the comparison between the elastic buckling results and the long pipe theory formula, it can be found that the buckling load at this time should also approach the result of the Euler compression rod theory formula.

Table 7. The ratio of elastic buckling load to ultimate bearing capacity.

t (mm) \ L (m)	0.3	0.6	1.2	2.0	3.0	7.0
5.59	0.49	0.44	0.56	0.79	0.97	0.88
7.45	0.49	0.54	0.73	0.89	0.99	1.00
8.94	0.48	0.52	0.70	0.92	0.99	0.97
11.8	0.43	0.45	0.60	0.95	1.00	0.98
14.91	0.38	0.44	0.52	0.95	1.01	0.98
22.36	0.30	0.35	0.40	0.97	1.01	1.00

4. Results under Eccentric Load

The axis deviation caused by uneven softness and improper correction of the stratum will cause the pipe to be pressed by the eccentric axis during the pipe-jacking construction. Currently, the pipe is unevenly stressed, the stability of the pipe is often reduced accordingly, and the safety of the pipe jacking structure is greatly affected. To investigate the stability of PVC pipes under eccentric axial pressure, two scenarios were analyzed in this paper:

a. Full-section radial triangular load with an eccentricity of $r/2$, as shown in Figure 12a, hereinafter referred to as L1;

b. Half-section uniformly distributed load with an eccentricity of $2r/\pi$, as shown in Figure 12b, hereinafter referred to as L2.

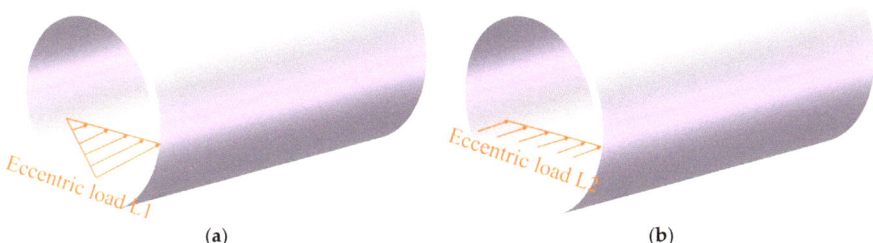

Figure 12. Schematic diagram of two types of eccentric loads: (**a**) L1 load; (**b**) L2 load.

4.1. Buckling Load of PVC Pipe

The PVC pipes were subjected to boundary conditions with one end fixed and the other hinged in the eccentric axial pressure model. Two pressurization methods were adopted: full-section radial triangular load (L1) and half-section uniformly distributed load (L2). The buckling modes for these two eccentric loading conditions of different lengths and different wall thicknesses are shown in Figures 13 and 14, respectively. The buckling modes for 3 m-long PVC pipes under the two different loading conditions are shown in Figure 15a and 15b, respectively.

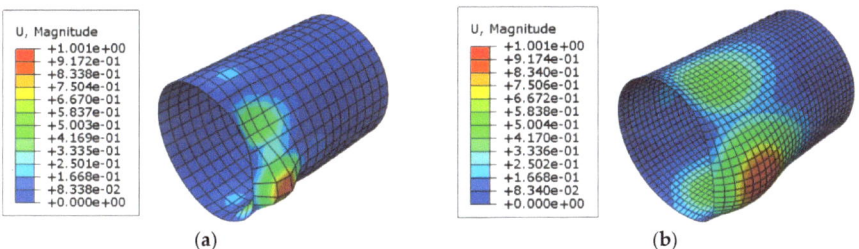

Figure 13. Buckling mode of 0.3 m pipe under L1 load: (**a**) t = 5.59 mm; (**b**) t = 22.36 mm.

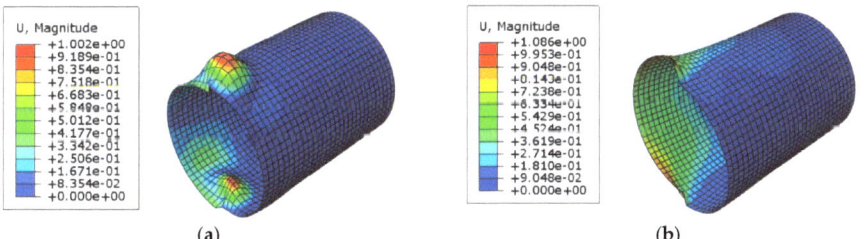

Figure 14. Buckling mode of 0.3 m pipe under L2 load: (**a**) t = 5.59 mm; (**b**) t = 22.36 mm.

Under the two eccentric loading conditions, the buckling modes of the pipes transitioned from localized failure in short pipes to an Euler buckling pattern in longer pipes as the L/D ratio increased. The number of circumferential waves also decreased in shorter pipes, and the wave peaks shifted toward the top and bottom ends of the pipe. For longer pipes, the buckling modes under both eccentric loading conditions were nearly identical to those under axial uniform force. It indicates that in this failure pattern, the impact of wall thickness on the critical buckling load can be amplified, while the impact of the length–diameter ratio may be reduced.

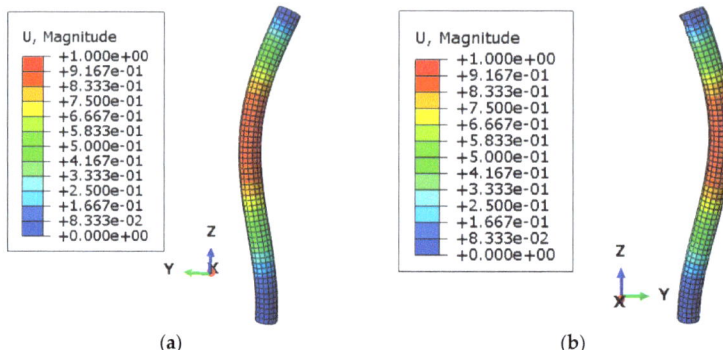

Figure 15. Buckling mode of 3 m pipe: (**a**) L1 load (**b**) L2 load.

The pipe length and thickness were changed, and the curves showing how the buckling values of PVC pipes changed with the D/t ratio and L/D ratio under two different loading conditions are depicted in Figure 16a and 16b, respectively. As seen in Figure 16a, the elastic buckling values gradually decreased with increasing D/t and L/D ratios. Additionally, the decrease in elastic buckling as the L/D ratio increased appears to be more staged. For the same diameter–thickness ratio, shorter pipes often have higher yield loads, but this trend diminished as the D/t ratio increased. At a D/t ratio of 10, the buckling load of a 0.3 m PVC pipe was 3059 kN, while the buckling load of a 7 m PVC pipe was only 80 kN, making the shorter pipe's buckling load 38 times greater. When the D/t ratio increased to 40, the difference was reduced to just 9 times. It indicates that as the pipe wall thickness decreases beyond a certain point, the influence of the length on the pipe buckling load will be gradually weakened.

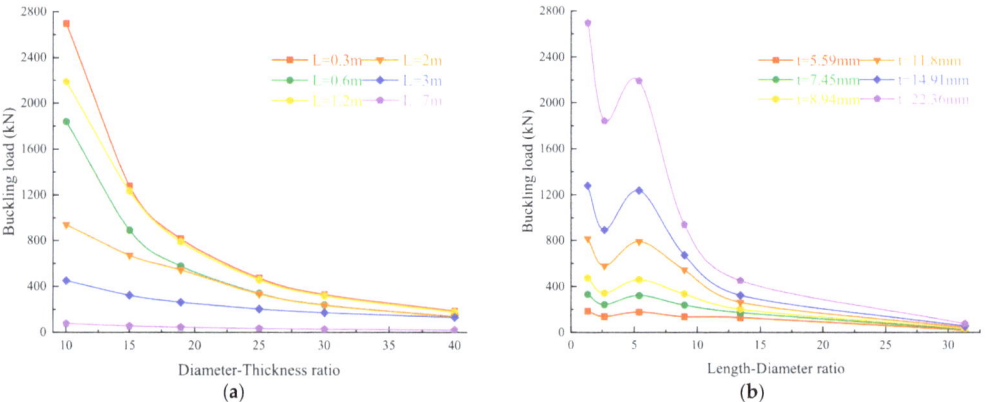

Figure 16. Variation curve of elastic buckling load with diameter–thickness ratio and length–diameter ratio under L1 load: (**a**) diameter–thickness ratio; (**b**) length–diameter ratio.

It can be observed from Figure 16b that under the action of eccentric load L1, the buckling load exhibits fluctuating variations when the L/D ratio is less than 6, with more significant fluctuations for PVC pipes with greater wall thickness. When the L/D ratio was greater than 6, the buckling load gradually decreased as the L/D ratio increased, eventually approaching zero. The main reason for this phenomenon is that the buckling modes of PVC pipes vary significantly with changes in the L/D ratio, and the critical buckling load will be affected.

Figure 17a,b exhibit the buckling load changing curves with the D/t ratio and L/D ratio under L2 load, respectively. The overall pattern was similar to that observed under the L1 load: the buckling load decreased with an increase in the D/t ratio, and the changes concerning the L/D ratio exhibited a phased pattern, with the buckling load gradually decreasing as the L/D ratio increased, particularly when L/D exceeded 6.

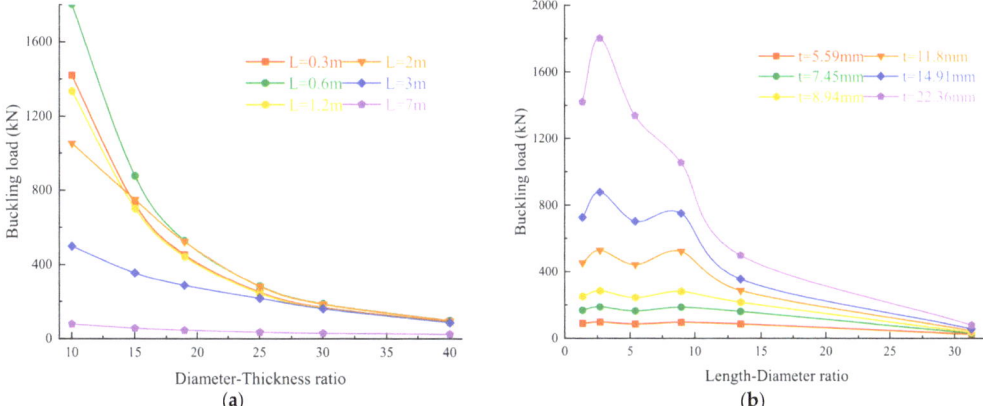

Figure 17. Variation curve of elastic buckling load with diameter–thickness ratio and length–diameter ratio under L2 load: (**a**) diameter–thickness ratio; (**b**) length–diameter ratio.

However, a notable difference is that the buckling loads obtained with the L2 loading form were significantly lower than those from the L1 loading form, with the maximum buckling loads differing by up to 900 kN. Furthermore, when the L/D ratio was 6, the buckling load under the L2 load first increased and then decreased, whereas under the L1 load, it first decreased and then increased. This indicates that under eccentric axial force when the pipe is shorter, the mode and magnitude of failure are strongly influenced by the type of loading and the point of load application.

4.2. Ultimate Bearing Capacity Analysis

The ultimate bearing capacity was obtained by introducing the previously calculated elastic buckling load results into the elastoplastic buckling analysis in the same manner. The computed results are shown in Table 8. The curves depicting the ultimate bearing capacity of PVC pipe jacking under the two eccentric loadings as the length–diameter ratio and diameter–thickness ratio are shown in Figures 18 and 19, respectively.

Table 8. Ultimate bearing capacity of PVC pipe under two eccentric loads.

Eccentric Load Form	L (m) t (mm)	0.3	0.6	1.2	2.0	3.0	7.0
L1	5.59	96.68	75.56	85.44	74.82	75.00	22.05
	7.45	171.81	121.50	140.74	118.97	112.90	30.49
	8.94	232.34	158.79	205.29	155.01	141.40	35.31
	11.8	334.60	253.97	317.27	233.80	208.95	46.91
	14.91	459.54	392.48	436.82	342.94	278.25	57.27
	22.36	789.55	804.28	717.45	640.23	392.23	79.13
L2	5.59	40.61	41.43	39.75	40.53	38.54	23.38
	7.45	65.64	67.33	64.57	66.40	68.64	30.82
	8.94	89.14	91.63	86.64	90.54	88.18	36.59
	11.8	135.84	140.69	137.45	134.11	127.10	47.13
	14.91	187.95	183.76	163.29	174.34	167.92	57.86
	22.36	272.44	292.72	228.76	275.72	275.33	81.32

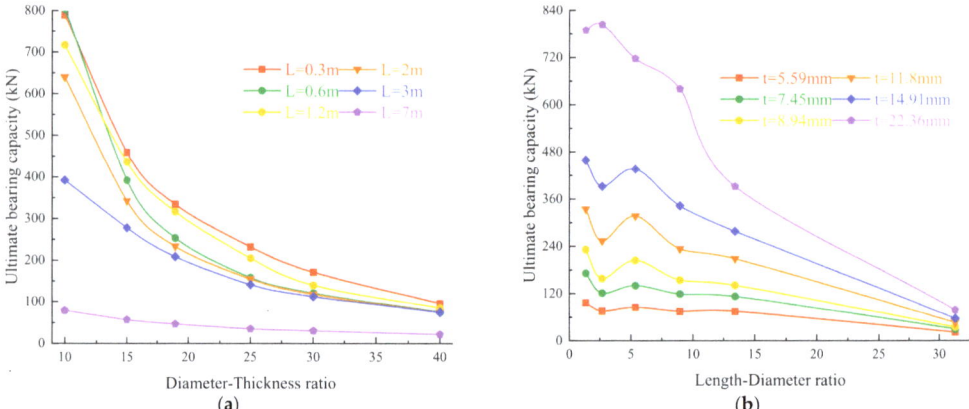

Figure 18. Change curve of ultimate bearing capacity under L1 load: (**a**) diameter–thickness ratio; (**b**) length–diameter ratio.

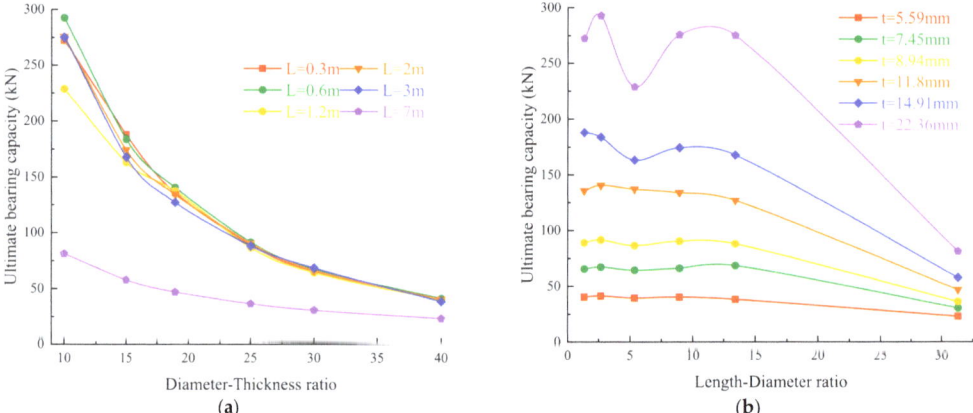

Figure 19. Change curve of ultimate bearing capacity under L2 load: (**a**) diameter–thickness ratio; (**b**) length–diameter ratio.

As plotted in Figure 18a, the ultimate bearing capacity of PVC pipes gradually decreased as the D/t ratio increased, with shorter pipes being more significantly affected by changes in D/t. As D/t increased from 10 to 40, the ultimate bearing capacity of a 0.3 m-long pipe decreased by about 700 kN. It gradually decreased, and finally the ultimate bearing capacity tended to be equal. When the pipe length was between 0.3 m and 2 m, the ultimate bearing capacity of PVC pipes was not much different.

As can be seen from Figure 18b, under the L1 loading condition, the ultimate bearing capacity exhibited a staged relationship with wall thickness when the L/D ratio was less than 6. When the wall thickness was less than or equal to 14.91 mm, the numerical results first decreased and then increased with increasing L/D ratio. However, when the wall thickness was greater than 22 mm, the trend was reversed: the ultimate bearing capacity first increased and then decreased with the increasing L/D ratio. When the L/D ratio exceeded 6, the ultimate bearing capacity generally decreased as the L/D ratio increased.

Figure 19 displays the variation of the ultimate bearing capacity with the diameter–thickness ratio and length–diameter ratio under L2 eccentric load. The overall trend of the curves was consistent with that under the L1 loading condition—both decreased as

D/t and L/D increased. The ultimate bearing capacity under L2 remained at roughly the same level when L/D was greater than 14, but when L/D = 6 the ultimate bearing capacity decreased significantly, which was also mainly controlled by the change in buckling mode. The maximum ultimate bearing capacity for the pipe was only about 300 kN under the L2 loading condition, significantly lower than that under L1. Therefore, with the L2 type of eccentric loading, failure of the pipe may occur more readily, which should be noted.

To study the impact of eccentricity on the ultimate load capacity of pipes, 0.3 m-, 3 m-, and 7 m-long pipes were selected, and the ultimate bearing capacities under L1 and L2 loads were compared with those under axial uniform force. As depicted in the figure, when the pipe length was 0.3 m and 3 m, with increasing wall thickness, the ratio of the ultimate bearing capacity under L1 and L2 loads to that under axial uniform force tended to stabilize. It can be seen from Figure 20 that with an eccentricity of 0.5, corresponding to the L1 load, the ultimate bearing capacity was about 55% of that under axial uniform force. With an eccentricity of 0.6366, representing the L2 load, the ultimate bearing capacity was approximately 22% of the capacity under axial uniform force.

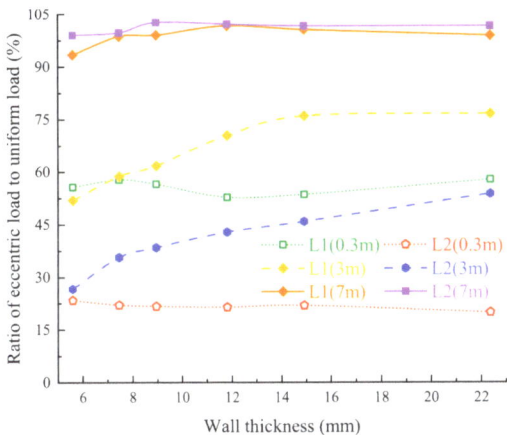

Figure 20. The ratio of ultimate bearing capacity under eccentric load and uniform load for different pipe lengths.

When the length of the pipe increased to 3 m, the proportion of L1 and L2 to the uniform load increased from 55% to about 80% and 22% to about 50%, respectively, both of which are significantly improved. It was found that with the increase of the L/D ratio, the influence of the load distribution form on the ultimate bearing capacity gradually decreased, and the ultimate bearing capacity under the two eccentric loads continued to rise. Moreover, at lower L/D ratios, loads with higher eccentricity led to a greater reduction in the ultimate bearing capacity of the pipes. However, when the pipe length increased to 7 m, the ratio of the ultimate bearing capacity of the two eccentric loads to the uniform axial compression was almost the same, both of which were about 100%, indicating that the ultimate bearing capacity under L1 and L2 loads was almost the same as that under uniform axial compression.

The relationship between the bearing capacity under two types of eccentric loading and the length–diameter ratio was compared. The greater impact of initial defects when the wall thickness was smaller was considered, and a thickness of t = 22.36 mm was chosen. The comparison results are shown in Figure 21. For L/D ratios $\leq$ 6, the buckling mode exhibited localized failure, and the bearing capacity should primarily be influenced by the failure mode and material strength. The ratios of L1 and L2 to the uniform load were maximized at around 22% and 60%, respectively.

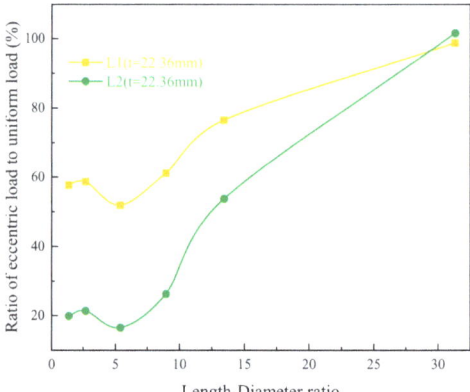

Figure 21. Ratio of ultimate bearing capacity under two eccentric loads and uniform load.

At L/D greater than 6, the buckling mode of the pipe gradually transitioned to Euler buckling with increasing length–diameter ratio. However, the development of the buckling mode under uniform loading and different eccentric loadings varied during the process of increasing the length–diameter ratio. Overall, the ratio of the ultimate bearing capacity under both types of eccentric loading to the ultimate bearing capacity under uniform loading increased continuously with an increasing L/D ratio. When L/D reached 30, it tended to be consistent with the ultimate bearing capacity under uniform loading.

5. Discussion

When PVC pipe jacking is subjected to axial pressure, material failure may occur first or buckling may occur first according to the numerical analysis above. Under axial uniform force when L/D ≤ 6, PVC pipes are prone to experience yield failure first, the magnitude of which is determined by the yield strength of the pipe material. When L/D is greater than 6, the pipe is likely to experience buckling instability first, the magnitude of which is determined by the axial buckling value of the structure.

When L/D is less than or equal to 6, the ultimate bearing capacity is $\bar{F}_d = A_p \sigma_u$

$$F_p - F_0 \leq F_d = A_p \sigma_u \tag{5}$$

The allowable jacking distance L is calculated according to Equation (6).

$$L \leq \frac{A_p \sigma_u}{\mu(N+W)} \tag{6}$$

In the formula, F_p is the allowed thrust force; F_0 is the resistance faced; A_p is the pipe cross-sectional area, m^2; σ_u is the yield strength of the pipe material, Pa; μ is the friction coefficient; N is the pipe pressure; and W is the pipe gravity.

In the range of 6 < L/D ≤ 8.5, the ultimate bearing capacity of the pipe is less than the theoretical value of full-section yielding. The finite element analysis method can be used to analyze its buckling type and determine its critical buckling load to accurately calculate its ultimate bearing capacity.

When L/D is greater than 8.5, the ultimate bearing capacity depends on its axial buckling value. At this point, the ultimate bearing capacity of the pipe is close to the elastic buckling value, thus exhibiting good consistency with the Euler formula for long pipes.

$$F_p - F_0 \leq F_d = \frac{\pi^3 E D^3 t}{8(\mu_0 l)^2} \tag{7}$$

$$L \leq \frac{\pi^3 E D^3 t}{8\mu(N+W)(\mu_0 l)^2} \tag{8}$$

According to the CECS-2020 [31], the maximum allowable jacking force of the dowel surface for pipe jacking is calculated according to the following Formula (9). In the design process of pipe jacking engineering, it is slightly conservative to select the value of pipe–soil friction resistance according to the current standard specification. The relationship between the change of the length–diameter ratio and the buckling of the pipeline is considered in this paper. The allowable jacking force and jacking distance derived from different length–diameter ratios are more applicable.

$$F_d = K_d \frac{f_p A_p}{\gamma_d \times 10^3} \tag{9}$$

$$f_p = \frac{f_{p,k}}{\gamma_c} \tag{10}$$

In the formula, K_d is the eccentric compression allowing the jacking force reduction factor. γ_d is the allowable jacking force comprehensive coefficient, and the value of the PVC pipe is 1.11. $f_{p,k}$ is the standard value of axial compressive strength of the pipe, and the value of the PVC pipe is 66 MPa. γ_c is the partial coefficient of axial compressive strength, and the value of the PVC pipe is 1.2.

Under the eccentric axial pressure L1, the short pipe exhibits asymmetric local buckling along the axial direction. Based on the comparative analysis with axial uniform force, the ratio of the ultimate bearing capacity of L1 to that of axial uniform force fluctuates around a certain value at $L/D \leq 6$, with this ratio varying with the wall thickness, generally around 50%. For $6 < L/D < 30$, the ultimate bearing capacity of L1 gradually approaches that of axial uniform force with the increase of L/D. For accurate calculation, finite element analysis methods can be employed. When $30 \leq L/D$, the ultimate bearing capacity of L1 approaches that of axial uniform force, calculated according to Equation (7).

Under the eccentric axial pressure L2, when $L/D \leq 14$, the ultimate bearing capacity of the pipe fluctuates around a certain value as a whole; when $14 < L/D < 30$, the ultimate bearing capacity under L2 increases with the length–diameter ratio. The increase gradually approaches the ultimate bearing capacity under axial uniform force. If you want to calculate accurately, you can use the finite element analysis method; when $30 \leq L/D$, the ultimate bearing capacity is calculated using Equation (7).

PVC pipes typically have outer diameters ranging from 200 to 600 mm and lengths of around 1 m in micro tunneling. When only the axial uniform force is considered, when the pipe diameter is greater than 333 mm, the yield strength of the pipe is mainly considered. However, for pipe diameters ranging from 200 to 333 mm, a specific analysis needs to be conducted in conjunction with the pipe length.

6. Conclusions

The failure forms and buckling modes of PVC pipes under uniform and eccentric loads were investigated, and the buckling load and ultimate bearing capacity at different length–diameter ratios and diameter-thickness ratios were obtained through theoretical research and numerical simulation. The key conclusions were drawn as follows:

(a) The elastic buckling load of PVC pipes decreases continuously with an increasing length–diameter ratio and diameter–thickness ratio under axial uniform force. It closely approximates the short pipe theory formula when L/D is less than or equal to 6 and tends to approach the long pipe theory formula when L/D exceeds 8.5. The elastic-plastic buckling is calculated by introducing an initial defect, and the ultimate bearing capacity of the pipe is obtained. When the L/D ratio is less than or equal to 6, the ultimate bearing capacity of the pipe tends to approach the theoretical yield failure value. When L/D is greater than 6, the pipe buckles and becomes unstable, and its magnitude is determined by the axial buckling value of the structure.

(b) The mode of failure and the magnitude of the buckling load of the pipe are significantly influenced by the manner and location of the loading under eccentric axial loading. Short pipes exhibit asymmetric local failures under eccentric loading, gradually transitioning to Euler buckling modes as the length–diameter ratio increases. The buckling load of the pipe under eccentric axial loading is notably lower than that under axial uniform force. However, as the length–diameter ratio increases, the difference between the two decreases, indicating that the influence of the loading mode and distribution diminishes with an increasing length–diameter ratio.

(c) Based on the consideration of the load capacity of a single pipe and the relationship between the ultimate bearing capacity of the pipe under different L/D ratios and the fourth yield criterion and Euler's formula, the calculation methods of allowable jacking force and single allowable jacking distance is derived.

(d) To prevent PVC pipes from buckling during jacking, when the length–diameter ratio is less than 6, priority should be given to the yield failure of the pipe. When the length–diameter ratio is greater than 6, priority should be given to the axial buckling value of the pipe under a certain length–diameter ratio of the pipe. The increase in wall thickness can increase the strength failure value and the axial buckling failure value of the pipe. However, it also increases the production cost of the pipe. Therefore, the wall thickness of the pipe should be determined based on the permissible jacking force.

However, there are still limitations in the FEM and results that can be further investigated. In the simulation, the soil–structure interaction (SSI) is not considered. The frictional resistance is derived from soil pressure acting on the pipe and the shear behavior of the SSI. The uncertainty of soil parameters has a significant effect on the structure [32]. The frictional resistance is also affected by soil properties and tends to be higher in dense or cohesive soils. The excessive frictional resistance induced by soil pressure increases the total jacking force and decreases the allowable jacking distance in a practical jacking drive since the critical buckling load decreases with the increase in pipe length, and the pipe is more prone to buckle under the action of jacking force. Meanwhile, the pipe jacking project is also affected by soil deformation [33,34]. The settlement of the pipe induced by the soil movement in long-distance pipe jacking will cause a deviation of the pipe axis, resulting in additional eccentricity and reduced critical buckling load and ultimate bearing capacity. Furthermore, the earth pressure generated by the SSI causes extrusion and contact with the pipes and may lead to the deformation of the pipe, resulting in a decrease in the buckling confining pressure, and the buckling of the pipe will occur under a relatively small jacking force [16].

Author Contributions: Conceptualization, R.W., K.L. and P.Z.; methodology, R.W. and K.L., P.Z.; software, R.W., K.L. and Y.X.; validation, R.W., P.Z. and J.M.; formal analysis, R.W., P.Z. and C.Z.; investigation, C.Z., J.M. and Y.X.; resources, R.W., K.L. and C.Z.; data curation, P.Z. and C.Z.; writing—original draft preparation, R.W., K.L. and P.Z.; writing—review and editing, R.W. and J.M.; visualization, K.L. and P.Z.; supervision, P.Z. and C.Z.; project administration, P.Z.; funding acquisition, P.Z. All authors have read and agreed to the published version of the manuscript.

Funding: This work is supported by the National Natural Science Foundation of China (No. 52008383) and the China Scholarship Council (No. 202306410063).

Data Availability Statement: All data that support the findings of this study are available from the corresponding author upon reasonable request.

Conflicts of Interest: The authors declare no conflicts of interest.

References

1. Ma, B.; Najafi, M. Development and applications of trenchless technology in China. *Tunn. Undergr. Space Technol.* **2008**, *23*, 476–480. [CrossRef]
2. Zhang, P.; Behbahani, S.S.; Ma, B.; Iseley, T.; Tan, L. A jacking force study of curved steel pipe roof in Gongbei tunnel: Calculation review and monitoring data analysis. *Tunn. Undergr. Space Technol.* **2018**, *72*, 305–322. [CrossRef]

3. Liu, K.; Ariaratnam, S.T.; Zhang, P.; Chen, X.; Wang, J.; Ma, B.; Zhang, Y.; Feng, X.; Xu, T. Mechanical response of diaphragm wall supporting deep launch shaft induced by braced excavation and pipe jacking operation. *Tunn. Undergr. Space Technol.* **2023**, *134*, 104998. [CrossRef]
4. Liu, K.; Xiao, A.; Zhang, P.; Zhou, H.; Chen, Z.; Xu, T.; Ma, B.; Ai, H.; Wang, Q. Study on mechanical response of steel pipe jacking considering the effect of pipe sticking. *Tunn. Undergr. Space Technol.* **2022**, *127*, 104617. [CrossRef]
5. Ji, X.; Ni, P.; Barla, M. Analysis of jacking forces during pipe jacking in granular materials using particle methods. *Undergr. Space* **2019**, *4*, 277–288. [CrossRef]
6. Li, C.; Zhong, Z.; Bie, C.; Liu, X. Field performance of large section concrete pipes cracking during jacking in Chongqing—A case study. *Tunn. Undergr. Space Technol.* **2018**, *82*, 568–583. [CrossRef]
7. Zhang, P.; Feng, X.; Zeng, C.; Ariaratnam, S.T. Field performance of steel pipes during curve jacking in Gongbei tunnel. *Tunn. Undergr. Space Technol.* **2022**, *128*, 104585. [CrossRef]
8. Najafi, M.; Iseley, D.T. Evaluation of PVC Pipe for Microtunneling. In *Buried Plastic Pipe Technology: 2nd Volume*; ASTM Special Technical Publication; ASTM: West Conshohocken, PA, USA, 1994; Volume 1222, p. 220.
9. Chapman, D.N.; Rogers, C.D.F.; Burd, H.J.; Norris, P.M.; Milligan, G.W.E. Research needs for new construction using trenchless technologies. *Tunn. Undergr. Space Technol.* **2007**, *22*, 491–502. [CrossRef]
10. Ryan, P.K.; Finney, A.J. Pipe materials and joint selection for trenchless construction. In Proceedings of the Pipelines 2012: Innovations in Design, Construction, Operations, and Maintenance, Doing More with Less 2012, Miami Beach, FL, USA, 19–22 August 2012; pp. 928–939.
11. Kramer, S.R.; McDonald, W.J.; Thomson, J.C.; Kramer, S.R.; McDonald, W.J.; Thomson, J.C. Pipe jacking and microtunnelling. In *An Introduction to Trenchless Technology*; Springer: Berlin/Heidelberg, Germany, 1992; pp. 86–120.
12. Jemii, H.; Bahri, A.; Boubakri, A.; Hammiche, D.; Elleuch, K.; Guermazi, N. On the mechanical behaviour of industrial PVC pipes under pressure loading: Experimental and numerical studies. *J. Polym. Res.* **2020**, *27*, 240. [CrossRef]
13. Tang, P.; Hu, S.; Liu, G.; Ye, Y.; Pan, F.; Hou, Z. Mechanical Properties and Structural Optimization Analysis of PVC Axial Hollow-wall Pipe for Drainage. *Adv. Eng. Sci.* **2023**, 1–11. (In Chinese) [CrossRef]
14. Zhen, L.; Qiao, P.; Zhong, J.; Chen, Q.; Chen, J.J.; Wang, J. Design of steel pipe-jacking based on buckling analysis by finite strip method. *Eng. Struct.* **2017**, *132*, 139–151. [CrossRef]
15. Wang, Y.; Qiao, P.; Lu, L. Buckling analysis of steel jacking pipes embedded in elastic tensionless foundation based on spline finite strip method. *Thin-Walled Struct.* **2018**, *130*, 449–457. [CrossRef]
16. Zhen, L.; Chen, J.-J.; Qiao, P.; Wang, J.-H. Analysis and remedial treatment of a steel pipe-jacking accident in complex underground environment. *Eng. Struct.* **2014**, *59*, 210–219. [CrossRef]
17. Fok, S.L. Analysis of the buckling of long cylindrical shells embedded in an elastic medium using the energy method. *J. Strain Anal. Eng. Des.* **2002**, *37*, 375–383. [CrossRef]
18. Tu, S.; Shuai, J. Numerical study on the buckling of pressurized pipe under eccentric axial compression. *Thin-Walled Struct.* **2020**, *147*, 106542. [CrossRef]
19. Huang, C.; Chen, J.; Sun, Y. Mechanical simulation and calculation methodology of buried steel pipes under multiple loads. *Case Stud. Constr. Mater.* **2022**, *17*, e01662. [CrossRef]
20. Alotaibi, E.; Omar, M.; Shanableh, A.; Zeiada, W.; Fattah, M.Y.; Tahmaz, A.; Arab, M.G. Geogrid bridging over existing shallow flexible PVC buried pipe–Experimental study. *Tunn. Undergr. Space Technol.* **2021**, *113*, 103945. [CrossRef]
21. Costa, Y.D.; Zornberg, J.G.; Costa, C.M. Physical modeling of buried PVC pipes overlying localized ground sub-sidence. *Acta Geotech.* **2021**, *16*, 807–825. [CrossRef]
22. Mei, Z.; Xiao, A.; Mei, J.; Hu, J.; Zhang, P. Experimental Study on Interface Frictional Characteristics between Sand and Steel Pipe Jacking. *Appl. Sci.* **2023**, *13*, 2016. [CrossRef]
23. Hu, Q.; Li, X.; Han, X.; Li, H.; Chen, J. A normalized stress invariant-based yield criterion: Modeling and validation. *Int. J. Plast.* **2017**, *99*, 248–273. [CrossRef]
24. Małachowski, E.; L'vov, G.; Daryazadeh, S. Numerical prediction of the parameters of a yield criterion for fibrous composites. *Mech. Compos. Mater.* **2017**, *53*, 589–600. [CrossRef]
25. Fajuyitan, O.K.; Sadowski, A.J.; Wadee, M.A.; Rotter, J.M. Nonlinear behaviour of short elastic cylindrical shells under global bending. *Thin-Walled Struct.* **2018**, *124*, 574–587. [CrossRef]
26. Luo, Z.; Zhu, Y.P.; Zhao, X.Y.; Wang, D.Y. Hi28gh-order vibrations' dynamic scaling laws of distorted scaled models of thin-walled short cylindrical shells. *Mech. Based Des. Struct. Mach.* **2015**, *43*, 514–534. [CrossRef]
27. Farshidianfar, A.; Farshidianfar, M.H.; Crocker, M.J.; Smith, W.O. Vibration analysis of long cylindrical shells using acoustical excitation. *J. Sound Vib.* **2011**, *330*, 3381–3399. [CrossRef]
28. Saad, N.A.; Al-Maamory, M.H.; Mohammed, M.R.; Hashim, A.A. The effect of several service and weathering parameters on tensile properties of PVC pipe materials. *Mater. Sci. Appl.* **2012**, *3*, 784–792. [CrossRef]
29. Burn, S.; Davis, P.; Schiller, T.L. *Long-Term Performance Prediction for PVC Pipes*; AWWA Research Foundation: Denver, CO, USA, 2006.
30. Baysal, E.; Koçar, O.; Anaç, N.; Darıcı, F. Eşit Kanallı Açısal Presleme Yönteminde Kanal Açılarının ve İç Köşe Ka-visinin Deformasyona Etkisinin Sonlu Elemanlar Metodu ile İncelenmesi. *Çukurova Üniv. Mühendis. Fak. Derg.* **2023**, *38*, 859–873. [CrossRef]

31. *CECS246-2020*; Technical Specification for Pipe Jacking of Water Supply and Sewerage Engineering. China Engineering Construction Association, CECS: Beijing, China, 2020. (In Chinese)
32. Mina, D.; Forcellini, D. Soil–structure interaction assessment of the 23 November 1980 Irpinia-Basilicata earthquake. *Geosciences* **2020**, *10*, 152. [CrossRef]
33. Rajeev, P.; Tesfamariam, S. Seismic fragilities of non-ductile reinforced concrete frames with consideration of soil structure interaction. *Soil Dyn. Earthq. Eng.* **2012**, *40*, 78–86. [CrossRef]
34. Rathje, E.; Pehlivan, M.; Gilbert, R.; Rodriguez-Marek, A. Incorporating site response into seismic hazard assessments for critical facilities: A probabilistic approach. In *Perspectives on Earthquake Geotechnical Engineering: In Honour of Prof. Kenji Ishihara*; Springer: Berlin/Heidelberg, Germany, 2015; pp. 93–111.

Disclaimer/Publisher's Note: The statements, opinions and data contained in all publications are solely those of the individual author(s) and contributor(s) and not of MDPI and/or the editor(s). MDPI and/or the editor(s) disclaim responsibility for any injury to people or property resulting from any ideas, methods, instructions or products referred to in the content.

Article

Multifractal Characteristics and Displacement Prediction of Deformation on Tunnel Portal Slope of Shallow Buried Tunnel Adjacent to Important Structures

Xiannian Zhou [1], Yurui He [1], Wanmao Zhang [2,*] and Dunwen Liu [2]

1. Road & Bridge International Co., Ltd., Beijing 101100, China; 235501005@csu.edu.cn (X.Z.); yrhe.s9@cccecrl.com (Y.H.)
2. School of Resources and Safety Engineering, Central South University, Changsha 410083, China; dunwen@csu.edu.cn
* Correspondence: zhangwm@csu.edu.cn

Abstract: The tunnel portal section is often in extremely weak and fragmented strata, and the deformation of the portal side and slope will affect the stability of the surrounding rock and the tunnel-supporting structure. However, the deformation characteristics and displacement development patterns of slopes in the tunnel portal section are not clear. In this paper, the multifractal characteristics and displacement prediction of the deformation sequence of the tunnel portal slope at of a weak and water-rich shallow buried tunnel adjacent to an important structure are studied in depth. Combined with the deformation characteristics of the tunnel portal slope, a suitable slope monitoring and measurement scheme is designed to analyze the deformation pattern of the tunnel portal slope. Based on the multifractal detrended fluctuation analysis (MF-DFA) method, the multifractal characteristics of the deformation monitoring sequences at each monitoring point of the tunnel portal slope are analyzed. The multifractal characteristics of displacement sequences at different monitoring points of the tunnel portal slope are consistent with the actual monitoring results. Furthermore, the Long Short-Term Memory (LSTM) model is optimized using the Particle Swarm Optimization (PSO) algorithm to predict the deformation of the tunnel portal slope. The results show that the maximum mean square error (MSE) of the horizontal displacement test set prediction results is 0.142, and the coefficient of determination (R^2) is higher than 91%. The maximum value of MSE for vertical displacement test set prediction is 0.069, and the R^2 are higher than 91%. The study shows that the performance of the PSO-LSTM prediction model can meet the requirements for predicting the displacement of the tunnel portal slope. Based on the MF-DFA method and PSO-LSTM prediction model, the fluctuation characteristics of the displacement value of the tunnel portal section can be accurately identified and the displacement development pattern can be effectively predicted. The conclusions of the study are of great practical significance for the safe construction of the tunnel portal section.

Keywords: tunnel portal slope; displacement; prediction; multifractal detrended fluctuation analysis method; long short-term memory

Citation: Zhou, X.; He, Y.; Zhang, W.; Liu, D. Multifractal Characteristics and Displacement Prediction of Deformation on Tunnel Portal Slope of Shallow Buried Tunnel Adjacent to Important Structures. *Buildings* **2024**, *14*, 1662. https://doi.org/10.3390/buildings14061662

Academic Editors: Binsheng (Ben) Zhang and Eugeniusz Koda

Received: 12 April 2024
Revised: 29 May 2024
Accepted: 3 June 2024
Published: 4 June 2024

Copyright: © 2024 by the authors. Licensee MDPI, Basel, Switzerland. This article is an open access article distributed under the terms and conditions of the Creative Commons Attribution (CC BY) license (https:// creativecommons.org/licenses/by/ 4.0/).

1. Introduction

With the implementation of China's "The Belt and Road Initiative" strategy, more and more Chinese engineering construction enterprises have gone abroad. They have undertaken a large number of overseas highways, railroads, and other infrastructure projects, contributing to the infrastructure construction of many countries in Asia and Europe. Influenced by the terrain, most of the highway and railroad projects needed to cross a large number of mountainous areas. Therefore, tunneling occupies a very important position in the construction of high-speed infrastructure in mountainous areas [1–3]. Numerous influencing factors need to be considered in the design and alignment of railroads. Although the engineering community has now recognized the importance of geological conditions at the tunnel portal for construction safety, tunnel construction is still unavoidable in the case of unfavorable geological conditions such as high slope, large deflections, and shallow burials [4–6]. In this case, if the excavation method and auxiliary construction measures chosen for tunnel construction are unreasonable, the construction process is very prone to accidents such as roofing, collapse, lining cracking, slope instability, and landslides [7,8]. It will not only cause schedule delays and economic loss but also easily lead to casualties of construction personnel on site. Therefore, how to ensure the stability of the surrounding rock and the tunnel portal slope, and understand the safety of entering and exiting the tunnel, has become one of the important researches of many experts and scholars in the field of tunnel engineering.

Existing research shows that the main factor restricting the safe entry and exit of tunnels is the stability of the surrounding rock at the tunnel entrance [9,10]. The stability of the surrounding rock of the tunnel portal section can be divided into the stability of the side slope of the tunnel portal and the stability of the surrounding rock and lining of the excavation surface of the tunnel body. At the same time, the research shows that the two are also interacting with each other. The deformation of the uphill side of the tunnel entrance will affect the stability of the surrounding rock and supporting structure of the tunnel body, and the rock and soil disturbance caused by tunnel excavation will also affect the stability of the uphill side of the tunnel entrance [11–14]. In the theoretical study of the stability of tunnel portal rock, Aygar et al. [11] analyzed the relationship between highway tunnel stability and portal slope in Turkey using numerical simulation. Wang et al. [15,16] performed a large-scale shaking table test on a tunnel portal and developed a method for detecting dynamic damage based on the Hilbert–Huang transform. This method accurately identifies macroscopic damage in tunnel linings and portal slopes. Genis et al. [17] utilized a dynamic analysis program based on the three-dimensional finite-difference method and determined that peak accelerations exceeding 0.5 g may lead to severe damage in tunnel portal slopes and the area 20–50 m from the tunnel entrance. In addition, many researchers [18–22] have also emphasized the significance of tunnel portal stability in tunnel construction through various studies. In applying the theory of perimeter rock stability in tunnel portal sections, Li et al. [23,24] established a three-dimensional numerical model and proposed the use of the center diaphragm and circular reserved core soil methods to excavate shallow buried tunnels. This method effectively controls peripheral rock deformation, surface settlement, and slope stability in conditions of loose and fragmented rock. Aygar and Gokceoglu [25] highlighted the impact of opening excavation on tunnels lacking cohesive foundations. Ayoublou et al. [12] emphasized the importance of slope displacement measurements and monitoring at tunnel portals. Taromi et al. [26] investigated the collapse mechanism of water conveyance tunnel portals and presented potential solutions.

In addition, in the process of tunnel construction, it is necessary to continuously monitor the slope at the entrance [27]. Analyzing and predicting the deformation pattern of the slope during tunnel portal construction can provide technical support and theoretical guidance for the early warning of tunnel portal construction safety, which is of great significance for improving the safety of tunnel portal construction. After obtaining the original tunnel portal slope monitoring data, to further prevent the occurrence of tunnel disasters, it is necessary to analyze the deformation trend and predict the displacement development in advance [28–30]. The deformation monitoring data of the side and elevation slopes are usually shown as complex nonlinear and non-stationary time series. The deformation sequence is characterized by discontinuous multi-scale. Compared with the simple fractal dimension, the multifractal method describes the fractal structure through the spectral function, which can more finely characterize the volatility of the deformation sequence at different levels [31,32]. In recent years, some researchers have applied multifractals to the field of geotechnical engineering [33–36]. Therefore, the multifractal theory can be used to analyze the fluctuation characteristics of the deformation sequence of the tunnel portal slope.

Tunnel slope engineering is a complex nonlinear dynamical system, and the stability and deformation of the slope are affected by many uncertain factors [37,38]. Due to the complexity, ambiguity, and randomness of the deformation of the slope during the construction of the tunnel portal. Therefore, simple statistical methods do not apply to the complex nonlinear time series slope deformation problem [39,40]. Machine learning methods can effectively replace traditional statistical methods due to their nonlinear learning ability. Support Vector Regression and Extreme Gradient Boost are the most commonly used machine learning methods in time series prediction [41]. Compared with statistical methods, machine learning methods are more likely to capture the complexity, dynamics, and nonlinear characteristics of nonlinear time series data on slope. At present, machine learning methods have achieved certain results in the research of slope deformation prediction [42,43]. In recent years, deep learning has developed rapidly [43]. Many studies have shown that its performance is better than traditional machine learning models. Commonly used deep learning methods for time series prediction include deep neural network [44,45], convolutional neural network [46], recurrent neural network (RNN) [47], and so on. Among them, RNN models have a strong fitting ability to sequence data. Long Short-Term Memory (LSTM) solves the defects of the gradient explosion problem in traditional RNN and is the most widely used RNN model [48]. The LSTM is better than traditional RNN in fitting long sequence data and has achieved better prediction results in a large number of engineering applications [49–52]. However, when the input sequence is long, the performance of the LSTM model is still poor. Optimization algorithms of group intelligence such as particle swarm algorithm (PSO) can effectively improve the performance of the LSTM, and in recent years, some related studies have applied the PSO-LSTM model to slope deformation prediction [53].

The tunnel portal section is often in extremely weak and broken strata, and the construction of the portal and the excavation of the slope uplift will disturb the slope and the internal surrounding rock [54,55]. The self-stabilizing surrounding rock will make it difficult to form an effective bearing arch, and it is very easy to have engineering accidents such as collapses, toppling, and landslides seriously affect the construction progress and the economic benefits of the project. In Malaysia, a railroad tunnel portal section can easily form a soil slope due to shallow depth. Construction disturbance during the excavation of the tunnel portal can easily induce landslides and sidewall instability, and the safety coefficient of the slope will be greatly reduced. Therefore, during the construction of the tunnel portal section, analyzing and predicting the monitoring data of the portal side and slope can provide a basis for the dynamic design and information construction of the tunnel. It is of great practical significance to improve the stability of the tunnel side slope and ensure the safe construction of the tunnel portal section.

Therefore, this study takes the construction of a soft, water-rich, and shallow buried tunnel portal section near a high-voltage power tower in Malaysia as the engineering background. Combined with on-site monitoring and measurement, multifractal analysis, and deep learning methods, an in-depth study is carried out on the multifractal characteristics of deformation and deformation prediction of the tunnel portal slope. The main research includes the following aspects. (1) Combining the deformation characteristics of the tunnel portal slope, designing a suitable monitoring and measurement scheme, and analyzing the deformation pattern of the tunnel portal slope. Evaluate the stability of the tunnel portal slope. (2) Based on the multifractal detrended fluctuation analysis method (MF-DFA), analyze the multifractal characteristics of the deformation monitoring sequences at each monitoring point of the tunnel portal slope. Analyze the change characteristics of the displacement sequence of the slope at the tunnel entrance and compare it with the actual situation. (3) Optimize the LSTM model using the PSO algorithm to predict the deformation of the tunnel portal slope. Combined with the MF-DFA multifractal features, the PSO-LSTM model is applied to predict the displacement development of the deformation monitoring points of the slope at the entrance of the tunnel.

2. Materials and Methods

2.1. Overview of the Tunnel Project

A railroad project on the east coast of Malaysia is located in Selangor State in the coastal belt of western Malaysia. The study relies on the No. 3 tunnel mileage pile number CH48 + 511~CH49 + 168, north-south direction, the total length of the tunnel is 657 m. The tunnel crosses the first peak of Cheraka Mountain, with a maximum depth of 104 m. The shallow section is 137 m long, with a maximum depth of 109 m and a minimum depth of 1.3 m. The surrounding rock is fully weathered, strongly weathered sandstone, with high mud content, and the rock body is broken. The peripheral rock of the tunnel is fully weathered and strongly weathered sandstone, with high mud content, broken rock, and local extremely broken rock. The inlet is prone to form soil slope, and the construction disturbance is prone to landslides and sidewall instability. In addition, there are two fracture zones in the tunnel, including CH48 + 537~CH48 + 580 and CH48 + 800~CH49 + 080, with a total length of about 323 m. The rock is fractured, and the fissure water is abundant, which makes the tunnel construction risk high, and there is a potential danger of landslides. Meanwhile, there are high voltage towers on the east side of the tunnel area about 140 m–200 m, and the vibration requirement for high voltage towers from the local power company in Malaysia is 3 mm/s. An aerial photo of the tunnel project route is shown in Figure 1.

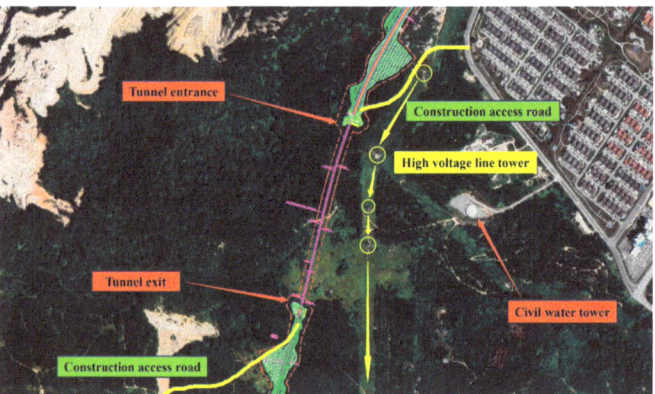

Figure 1. The tunnel project roadmap and layout plan.

2.2. Deformation Monitoring Program for Tunnel Portal Slope

According to the ground investigation drawings, the surrounding rock at the tunnel entrance is mainly composed of fully weathered to moderately weathered residual flooding clay, fine sand, and granite, and the rock body is broken to extremely broken. Before excavation of the tunnel entrance and exit and the shallow buried section of the tunnel body, overrun pipe shed grouting support is done in strict accordance with the design. The excavation adopts the method of reserving core soil, weak blasting, or non-blasting excavation method. Into the hole, Φ108 large pipe shed combined with Φ42 small conduit for pre-protection to strengthen the initial support. At the same time, strengthen the ground surface pre-injection grouting reinforcement treatment measures, and do a good job of holes outside the anti-drainage measures. Strengthen the surface subsidence measurement during construction. The inlet section of the tunnel is a high-slope tunnel, with a large excavation volume and complicated slope protection measures. After excavation, monitoring and measuring are carried out in time, support is strengthened according to the design requirements, and the construction of back arch closure is completed in time. Before construction, the horizontal displacement and vertical settlement values of the slope at the entrance were continuously monitored. Firstly, determine the monitoring area and choose the suitable location of monitoring points. A total of 7 monitoring points are arranged on the surface of the slope at the entrance, forming 3 monitoring lines. The detailed arrangement of deformation monitoring points on the up slope of the tunnel portal side is shown in Figure 2.

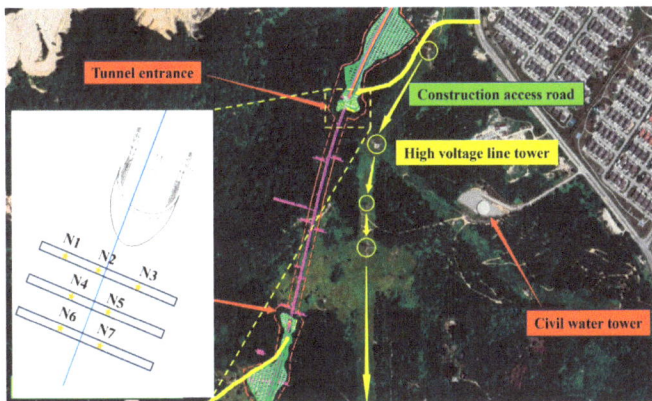

Figure 2. Arrangement of deformation monitoring points of tunnel portal slope.

Combined with the deformation monitoring results of the tunnel portal slope, the deformation pattern of the tunnel portal slope is analyzed. Further, based on the MF-DFA method, the multifractal characteristics of the deformation sequences at each monitoring point of the slope are analyzed. The PSO-LSTM model is utilized to predict the displacement development of the deformation monitoring points. The specific flow chart of the study is shown in Figure 3.

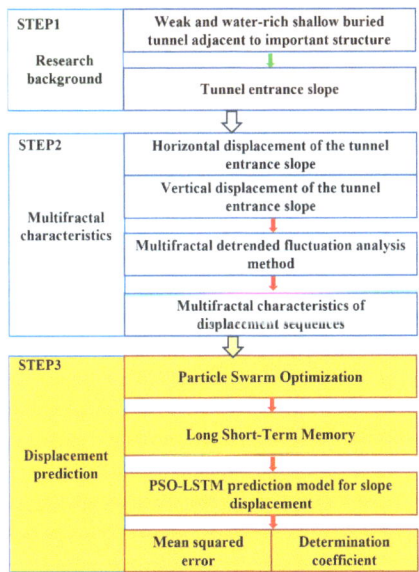

Figure 3. Flow chart of the study.

2.3. Multifractal Detrended Fluctuation Analysis Method

MF-DFA is a method for analyzing non-stationary finite time series. MF-DFA can effectively reveal the fractal structure and nonlinear dynamic properties in the data [56–58].

The method combines multifractal theory and the detrended technique to reveal the complex structure and dynamic patterns of the data by analyzing the multifractal properties of the data and removing the trending components in the data. In MF-DFA, the Hurst index of the original time series is first calculated, and then the time series is divided into different sub-series according to different Hurst indices. Then, each subsequence is de-trended, i.e., the long-term trend in the subsequence is removed, and then the respective Hurst index is calculated again. By comparing the Hurst indices of the sub-series after the detrended process, the fractal characteristics in the data series can be analyzed more accurately. Specifically, the calculation of MF-DFA contains the following five steps.

Step 1: Given a time series $x(t)$. The length of the sequence is N and the mean value is $\bar{x}$, find the cumulative deviation sequence $y(t)$:

$$y(t) = \sum_{i=1}^{t}(x(i) - \bar{x}) \tag{1}$$

Step 2: The sequence will be $y(t)$ equalized in terms of the time scale s.

$$m = int(N/s) \tag{2}$$

Since N may not be an exact multiple of s, there will be leftover values in the division process $y(t)$. The $2m$ equal-length subintervals are obtained by using the reverse-order processing method.

Step 3: The corresponding residual series are obtained $z_v(t)$.

$$z_v(t) = y_v(t) - p_v^k(t) \tag{3}$$

Equation: $y_v(t)$ is the subinterval. $p_v^k(t)$ denotes a kth order fitting polynomial to the vth subinterval. The variable v ranges from 1 to $2m$, and t ranges from 1 to s.

Step 4: Calculate the residual sequence $z_v(t)$ of the residual series $F^2(s,v)$.

$$F^2(s,v) = \frac{1}{s}\sum_{t=1}^{s}(z_v(t))^2 \tag{4}$$

Step 5: For the $F^2(s,v)$ dataset, take the mean value and calculate the q-order volatility function of the series $F_q(s)$.

$$F_q(s) = \left\{\frac{1}{2m}\sum_{v=1}^{2m}\left[F^2(s,v)\right]^{q/2}\right\}^{1/q} \tag{5}$$

where q can theoretically assume any non-zero real value, and the value of q is related to the $F_q(s)$ the degree of exposure to fluctuations. In particular, the MF-DFA degenerates to the standard DFA when q = 2. In particular, a limiting form of Equation (5) emerges when q = 0:

$$F_0(s) = exp\left\{\frac{1}{4m}\sum_{v=1}^{2m}\ln\left[F^2(s,v)\right]\right\} \tag{6}$$

A sliding window is used to optimize the traditional MF-DFA for dividing subintervals. Let the window length be s, the sequence length be N, and the sliding step be 1.

$$F_q(s) = \begin{cases} \left\{\dfrac{1}{N-s+1}\sum_{v=1}^{N-s+1}\left[F^2(s,v)\right]^{q/2}\right\}^{1/q}, q \neq 0 \\ exp\left\{\dfrac{1}{2(N-s+1)}\sum_{v=1}^{N-s+1}\ln\left[F^2(s,v)\right]\right\}, q = 0 \end{cases} \tag{7}$$

The q-order fluctuation function for a specific scale s is derived through the aforementioned steps $F_q(s)$. Adjusting the values of s and iterating through the steps yields a series of $s - F_q(s)$ point values. When a long-range correlation is present in this time series, a power law connection between $F_q(s)$ and s is evident, as depicted in Equation (8):

$$F_q(s) \propto s^{h(q)} \tag{8}$$

Taking logarithms of the above equation yields the following form:

$$\lg F_q(s) = h(q) \lg s + \lg b \tag{9}$$

$F_q(s)$ is the q-order volatility function of the series. The $h(q)$ is the corresponding generalized Hurst exponent. b is the constant coefficient.

Make $\lg F_q(s) - \lg s$ double logarithmic scatterplot and fit it. Its slope is the generalized Hurst exponent $h(q)$. If $h(q)$ is a nonlinear subtractive function of q, then the sequence is characterized by multifractal.

The multifractal spectrum $f(\alpha)$ characterizing the fractal intensity and fractal singularity of a time series can typically be determined in Equations (10)–(12) as follows:

$$\tau(q) = qh(q) - 1 \tag{10}$$

$$\alpha = \tau'(q) \tag{11}$$

$$f(\alpha) = q\alpha - \tau(q) \tag{12}$$

$\tau(q)$ is the Renyi index, also known as the scalar function. If it is a nonlinear up-convex function of q, the sequence is characterized by multifractal. Here, α represents the singular intensity, while $f(\alpha)$ represents the multifractal spectrum. When $\alpha - f(\alpha)$ is a single-peak up-convex shaped like a quadratic function, it means that the sequence has multifractal characteristics.

2.4. PSO-LSTM Algorithm

2.4.1. Principles of the LSTM Algorithm

LSTM Network is a special type of Recurrent Neural Network mainly used for the task of processing and predicting sequential data. LSTM was proposed by Hochreiter and Schmidhuber in 1997 and was initially designed to solve the problem of disappearing or exploding gradients faced by conventional RNN when processing long sequential data [59]. LSTM can capture long-term dependencies through the introduction of gating mechanisms and cell states, it can maintain information over a longer period, thus capturing long-term dependencies. The main advantage of LSTM is that it can effectively handle long sequence data. The specific computational steps of LSTM are as follows:

Step 1: Data normalization. $x(i, j)$ is the original data and $x'(i, j)$ is the normalized data.

Step 2: The LSTM model comprises multiple cells, each with specific formulas for the forgetting gate, input gate, and output gate.

$$\begin{cases} f_t = \sigma\left(W_f h_{t-1} + W_f x_t + b_f\right) \\ i_t = \sigma(W_i h_{t-1} + W_i x_t + b_i) \\ O_t = \sigma(W_o h_{t-1} + W_o x_t + b_o) \end{cases} \tag{13}$$

where f_t, i_t, and O_t are the results of the oblivion gate, input gate, and output gate state settlements, respectively. The h_{t-1} is the hidden state of the moment before the time, the σ is the sigmoid function. W_f, W_i, and W_o are the weight matrices of the forgetting gate, input gate, and output gate, respectively. b_f, b_i, and b_o are the forgetting gate, input gate, and output gate bias terms, respectively.

Step 3: For the candidate value vector, the product of the input value and the candidate value vector is used to update the cell state, calculated as:

$$\begin{cases} C_t = \tan h(W_c h_{t-1} + W_c x_t + b_c) \\ C_t = f_t C_{t-1} + iC_t \\ h_t = o_t \tan h(C_i) \\ f(x) = \frac{1}{1+e^{-x}} \\ f(x) = \tan h(x) \end{cases} \quad (14)$$

where W_c is the input unit state weight matrix. b_c is the input unit state bias term. $\tan h$ is the activation function. o_t is the neuron output value. h_t is the current moment hidden state.

2.4.2. Principles of the PSO Algorithm

PSO is a particle swarm algorithm that simulates the foraging behavior of a flock of birds [60]. The algorithm uses the information-sharing mechanism in the biota to produce the behavior of synchronizing information between individuals and groups with each other. It is a stochastic search algorithm based on group collaboration. In the PSO algorithm, "particle" is used as an intermediate choice. Individual particles exchange information with each other, and many particles form a group to form a particle population. The objective of PSO is to facilitate numerous particles in discovering the optimal solution within a multidimensional space. This multidimensional space, often referred to as the multi-dimensional solution space, serves as the search domain for the particle swarm to locate the optimal solution. Each optimization problem corresponds to a particle within this search space. These particles are expanded into a D-dimensional space and possess a function that evaluates the quality of the particle's current position, along with a velocity vector that dictates its movement and direction. Each iteration is a continuous search of the particles in the solution space in the direction of the current optimal particle.

The algorithm of PSO is implemented as follows: in a D-dimensional solution space, there exist N particles. Each particle possesses a velocity vector that varies in real time due to many factors. The particle velocity of the ith evolution is V_{id}^k, with the previous velocity WV_{id}^{k-1}, the individual optimal position $C_1 r_1 \left(pbest_{id} - x_{id}^{k-1}\right)$, and the population optimal position $C_2 r_2 \left(gbest_{id} - x_{id}^{k-1}\right)$. The velocity update in the dth dimension of particle i is calculated as follows.

$$V_{id}^k = WV_{id}^{k-1} + C_1 r_1 \left(pbest_{id} - x_{id}^{k-1}\right) + C_2 r_2 \left(gbest_{id} - x_{id}^{k-1}\right) \quad (15)$$

In addition, each iteration updates the position information of each particle. The position of the particle for the ith evolution x_{id}^k is changed by the position information of the previous x_{id}^{k-1}, and the velocity information of the previous iteration V_{id}^{k-1} are linearly summed up. The dth dimensional position update of particle i is computed as follows.

$$x_{id}^k = x_{id}^{k-1} + V_{id}^{k-1} \quad (16)$$

In the optimization process, the position vector in the dth dimension of the search space fluctuates within the range of $[x_{min}, x_{max}]$, while the velocity vector ranges within $[-V_{min}, V_{max}]$. During iterations, if the values of V_{id} and x_{id} exceed the boundaries, the velocity or position in that particular d-dimension is set to the maximum boundary velocity or position. Here, V_{id}^k represents the dth dimensional component of the flight velocity searched by particle i at the kth iteration, and x_{id}^k denotes the dth dimensional component of the position searched by particle i at the kth iteration. The parameters w, C_1, and C_2 stand for the inertia weight (non-negative), acceleration constants, and r_1, r_2 are random numbers within the range [0,1].

2.4.3. PSO Optimized LSTM Model

LSTM has excellent feature extraction ability for data with spatio-temporal correlation. In this study, the LSTM model is used to predict the displacement data of the tunnel portal slope. To obtain better training effects and prediction accuracy, the hyperparameters of the LSTM model need to be optimized. Since the monitoring system and monitoring data are changing in real-time, the data may have different volatility in different periods. To select the most suitable hyperparameters for the predicted data, the PSO algorithm is used to optimize the three hyperparameters of the LSTM model, namely, learning rate, iteration rounds, and the number of hidden layer units.

The PSO-LSTM model was developed to evaluate the error between the prediction results and the measured values. The Mean Square Error (MSE) and the Coefficient of Determination (R^2) of the test dataset were documented. The MSE value falls within the range of $[0, +\infty)$, with a lower value signifying a reduced prediction model error. On the other hand, R^2 elucidates the portion of variance in the dependent variable elucidated by the independent variable through the regression relationship. A higher R^2 value indicates superior model performance. The formulas for calculating the MSE and the R^2 are presented below:

$$MSE = \frac{1}{n}\sum_{i=1}^{n}(\hat{y}_i - y_i)^2 \tag{17}$$

$$R^2 = 1 - \frac{\sum_{i=1}^{n}[\hat{y}_i - y_i]^2}{\sum_{i=1}^{n}[y_i - \overline{y_i}]^2} \tag{18}$$

where n represents the number of predicted outcomes, y_i represents the true results, $\hat{y}_i$ represents the predicted results, and y_i represents the mean of the true values.

3. Results

3.1. Deformation Monitoring Results of Tunnel Portal Slope

To accurately assess the stability of the tunnel portal slope, the horizontal displacement and vertical settlement values of the slope at the portal are continuously monitored. Firstly, the monitoring area and the location of suitable monitoring points are determined, and the overall safety of the tunnel portal slope is determined from point to point by obtaining the monitoring data of multiple monitoring points. The results of deformation monitoring at each monitoring point are shown in Figures 4–6.

As can be seen from Figure 4, the trends of horizontal displacement at the three monitoring points in the first section of the tunnel portal slope are basically the same. The horizontal displacements peaked at about the 25th day, which were 15.4 mm, 12.4 mm, and 11.2 mm, respectively, and the horizontal displacements at the monitoring points stabilized after the 85th day. The horizontal displacements after deformation stabilization were about 4.5 mm, 7.0 mm, and 7.5 mm. The vertical displacements at monitoring points N1 and N3 of the tunnel portal slope had similar trends. The vertical displacement at monitoring point N1 was characterized by settlement. However, the displacement at monitoring point N3 shows upward bulging. The vertical displacements peaked at about day 75 at 2.5 mm and 4.2 mm, respectively. The settlement value of monitoring point N3 stabilized after 90 days, and the stabilized vertical displacement was about 2.0 mm. The settlement value of monitoring point N2 peaked at about 25 days at 5.1 mm. The settlement value of monitoring point N2 stabilized after 60 days, and the stabilized vertical displacement was about 3.0 mm. The vertical displacements of monitoring points N1 and N3 are similar in trend.

As can be seen from Figure 5, the horizontal displacement at monitoring point N4 in the second section of the tunnel portal slope peaked at 9.4 mm on the 90th day, while the horizontal displacement at monitoring point N5 peaked at 13.6 mm on the 25th day, and the horizontal displacement stabilized after the 80th day. The horizontal displacement after stabilization is about 5.5 mm. The vertical displacement value of the N4 monitoring point on the slope of the tunnel entrance reached its peak on the 70th day, which was −6.2 mm. The vertical displacement value tends to stabilize after the 95th day, and the settlement after stabilization is about −2.0 mm. The vertical displacement value of the N5 monitoring point has not yet stabilized after the 100th point, with a vertical displacement value greater than 4.0 mm. However, the vertical displacement of the N5 monitoring point shows an upward uplift.

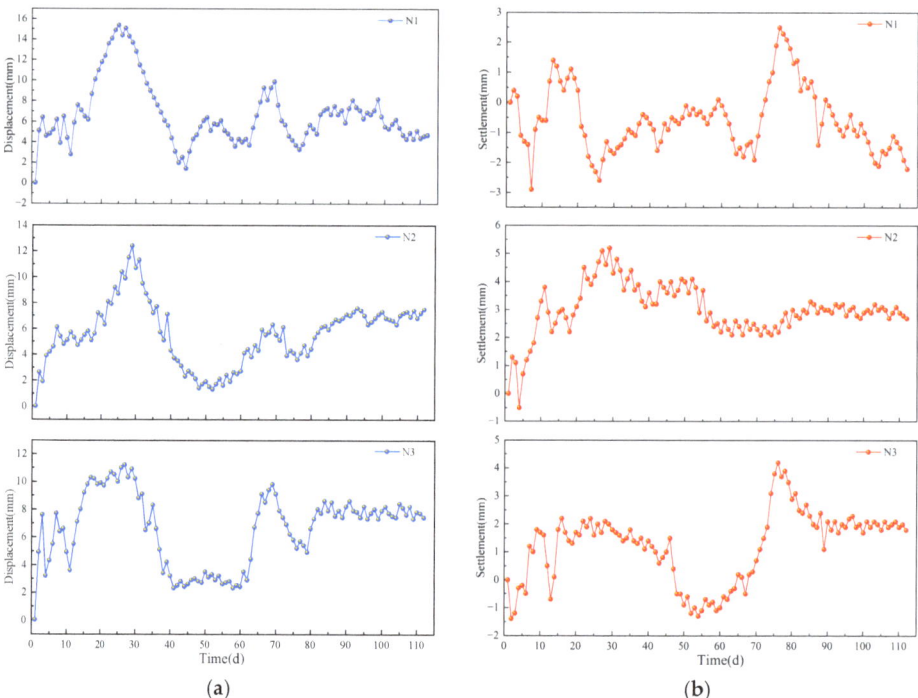

Figure 4. Deformation monitoring results of the first section of the portal slope: (**a**) horizontal displacement value, (**b**) vertical displacement value.

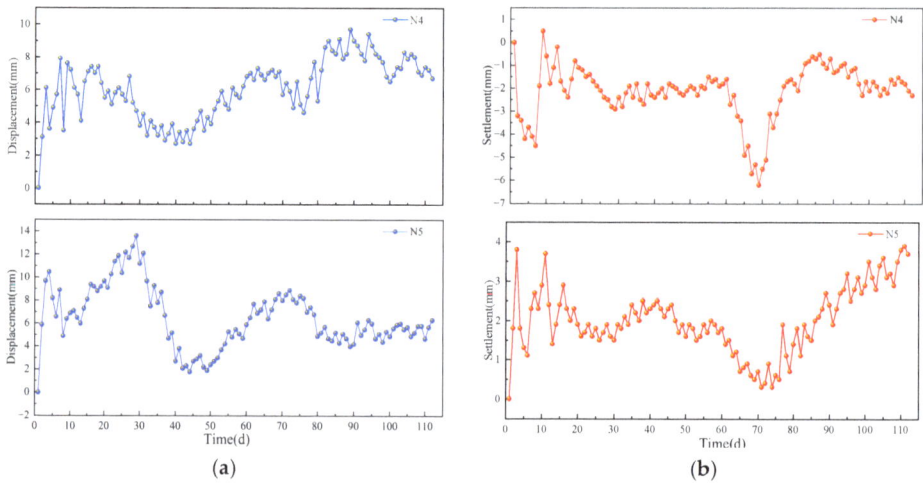

Figure 5. Deformation monitoring results of the second section of the portal slope: (**a**) horizontal displacement value, (**b**) vertical displacement value.

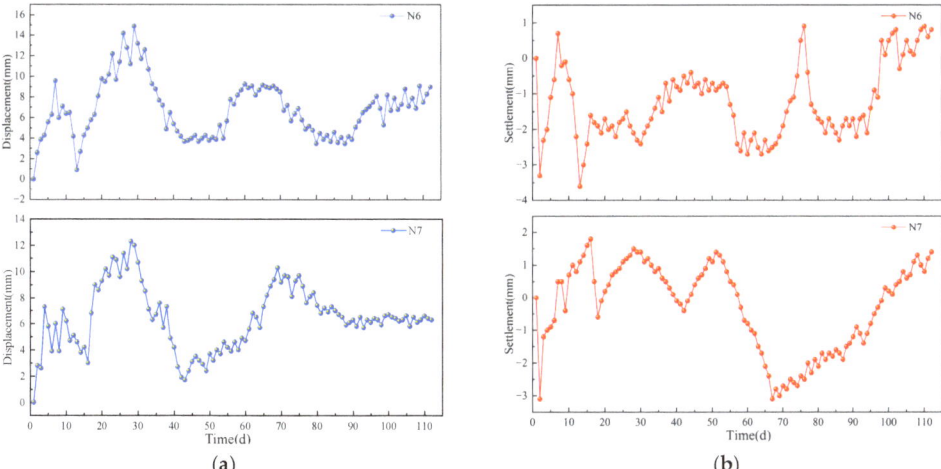

Figure 6. Deformation monitoring results of the third section of the portal slope: (**a**) horizontal displacement value, (**b**) vertical displacement value.

As can be seen from Figure 6, the trend of horizontal displacement at the monitoring points of the third section of the tunnel portal slope is basically the same. The horizontal displacements peaked at about the 28th day, at 14.9 mm and 12.3 mm, respectively, and the horizontal displacements at N7 tended to stabilize after the 90th day. The horizontal displacement after stabilization is about 6.3 mm. The vertical displacement values of the three sections of the tunnel portal side slope monitoring points show multiple peaks of about −3 mm. The vertical displacement value of the N7 monitoring point still does not stabilize after the 100th day, and the performance of the vertical displacement changes from settlement to upward bulging.

From the above analysis, it can be seen that during the monitoring period, the maximum value of horizontal displacement of the slope at the entrance is 15.4 mm, and the maximum value of vertical settlement is −6.2 mm, and after the deformation and stabilization of the slope at the entrance, the horizontal displacement is about 6–8 mm, and the value of vertical settlement is not more than −2 mm. Therefore, the horizontal displacement and vertical settlement of the slope at the entrance are small, and the stability of the slope at the entrance of the tunnel is relatively high.

3.2. MultiFractal Characteristics of Deformation of Elevation Slope at Tunnel Portals

3.2.1. Horizontal Displacement Multifractal Characterization

The sliding time window optimization MF-DFA is used to perform multifractal analysis on the deformation monitoring sequences of each monitoring point of the side slope of the tunnel portal, respectively. The generalized Hurst exponent and Renyi exponent are computed for the horizontal displacement sequences at each monitoring point. The variation of the indices corresponding to the sequence of monitoring points is shown in Figure 7. Further, the multifractal spectrum of the horizontal displacement sequence is shown in Figure 8.

As can be seen from Figure 7, when q varies between [−10,10], the generalized Hurst indices of the horizontal displacement sequences of different monitoring sections of the tunnel portal slope sides are all nonlinearly decreasing with q. The generalized Hurst indices of the horizontal displacement sequences of different monitoring sections of the elevation slope of the tunnel portal are all nonlinearly decreasing with q. This indicates that the horizontal displacement sequences at each monitoring point are characterized by multifractal. Under different fluctuation orders q, the generalized Hurst exponent curves of the horizontal displacement series at N1, N2, N4, and N6 are concentrated in the lower fluctuation of N3, N5, and N7, which show a weaker multifractal characteristic. However, the values of the horizontal displacement series at each monitoring point are significantly larger than 0.5. $h(q)$ values are significantly larger than 0.5, indicating that all the monitoring point sequences have better memory and long-range correlation from the whole to the local components. In addition, from Figure 7, it can be seen that the scale function $\tau(q)$ of the horizontal displacement series at each monitoring point is in good agreement. The middle part of the scale function curve is upconvex, satisfies $\tau(0) = -1$, as well as the overall nonlinear relationship. It indicates that the horizontal displacement sequence of each monitoring point has multifractal characteristics.

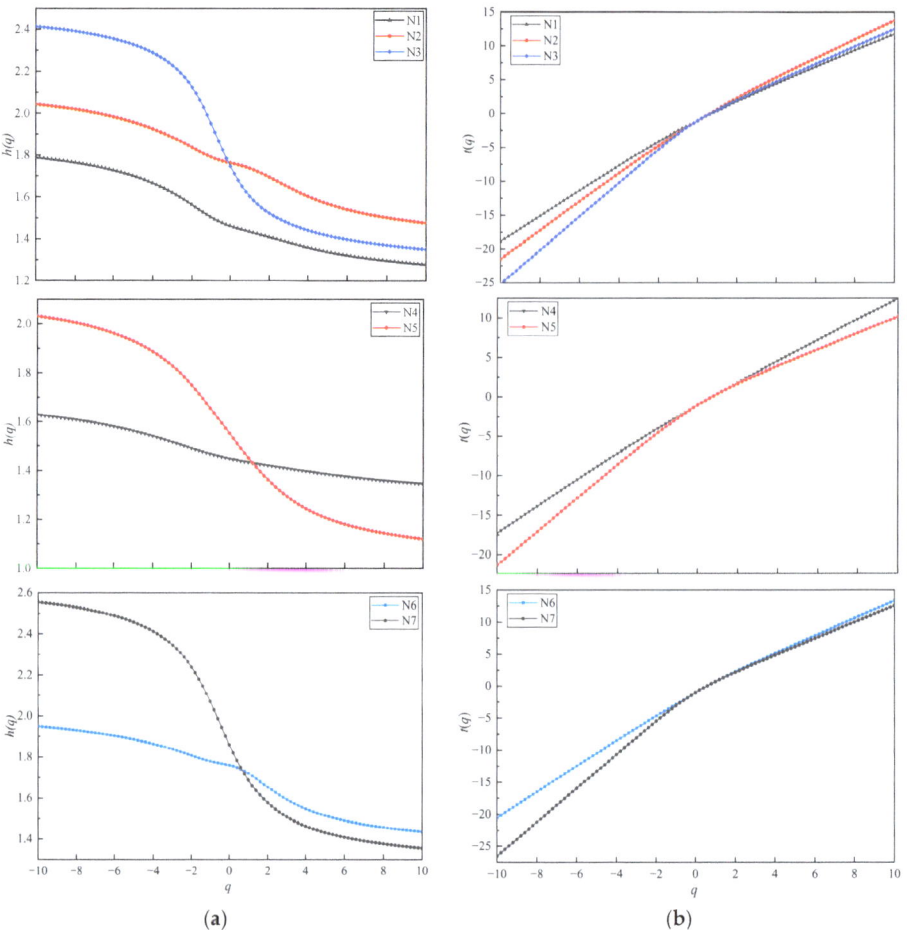

Figure 7. Variation of each index of the horizontal displacement series: (**a**) generalized Hurst index, (**b**) scaling function $\tau(q)$.

As can be seen in Figure 8, for the multifractal spectra of the horizontal displacement sequences of the monitoring points at different monitoring sections, the images of the multifractal spectra show a typical single-peak convex distribution, which resembles a quadratic function curve. The local scales of the multifractals of the horizontal displacement series are not constant, indicating the diversity of local changes at different moments. The singular intensities of most of the horizontal displacement sequences are distributed on both sides of the image, reflecting the diversity of local variations at different moments. α are distributed on both sides of the image, reflecting the uneven distribution of the fractal structure of the monitoring point sequences. This further illustrates the multifractal nature of the horizontal displacement sequence. The multifractal spectral curves of the horizontal displacement sequences are basically symmetrical, and the overall development state is stable.

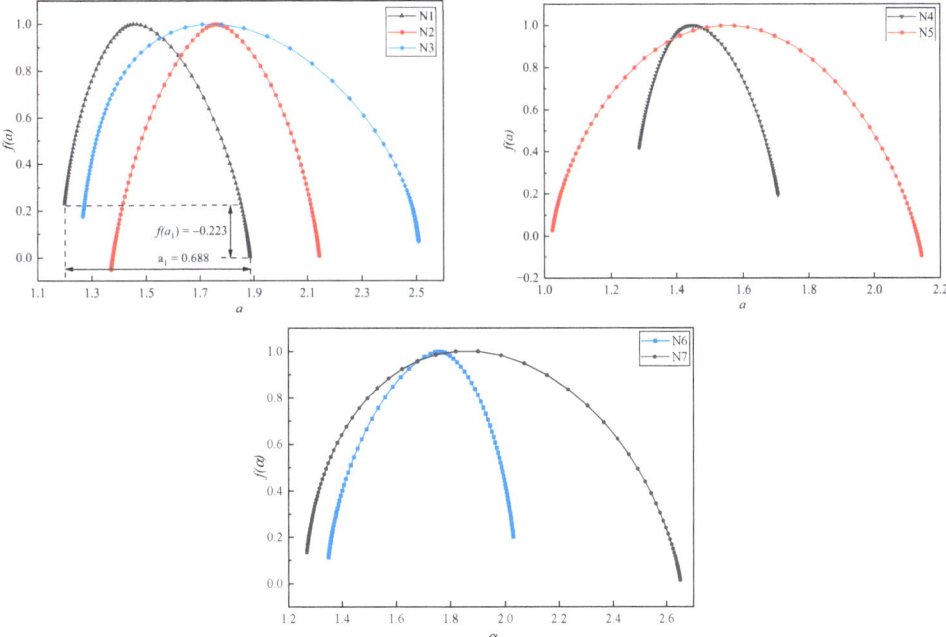

Figure 8. Multifractal spectrum of the horizontal displacement sequence.

In Figure 8, $\Delta\alpha$ represents the multifractal spectral width, which signifies the multifractal strength and complexity of the fluctuations at the monitoring point. A larger $\Delta\alpha$ indicates stronger multifractal strength and more intense, complex fluctuations in the sequence. Meanwhile, $\Delta f(\alpha)$ denotes the proportion of large and small fluctuations in the sequence. A higher $\Delta f(\alpha)$ signifies a greater proportion of small and medium fluctuations in the sequence. The calculations for $\Delta\alpha$ and $\Delta f(\alpha)$ are as follows:

$$\Delta\alpha = \alpha_{max} - \alpha_{min} \tag{19}$$

$$\Delta f(\alpha) = \Delta f(\alpha_{max}) - \Delta f(\alpha_{min}) \tag{20}$$

Calculate the multifractal characteristic statistics of the horizontal displacement series of the monitoring points of different monitoring sections; the calculation results are shown in Table 1.

Table 1. Multifractal characteristic statistics for horizontal displacement.

Monitoring Points	Cross-Section 1			Cross-Section 2		Cross-Section 3	
Eigenvalue	N1	N2	N3	N4	N5	N6	N7
$\Delta\alpha$	0.688	0.773	1.241	0.421	1.118	0.681	1.383
$\Delta f(\alpha)$	−0.223	0.060	−0.108	−0.225	−0.123	0.087	−0.121

As can be seen from Table 1, comparing the width of the multifractal spectrum of the horizontal displacement sequence at each monitoring point $\Delta\alpha$. For Section 1, the multifractal spectral widths of the horizontal displacement sequences at monitoring points N1 and N2 are smaller than those at monitoring point N3. $\Delta\alpha$ is smaller than that of N3. It means that the multifractal intensity of the horizontal displacement sequence at N3 is larger, and the horizontal displacement fluctuation is more complicated. Similarly, for Sections 2 and 3, the multifractal intensity of the horizontal displacement series at points N5 and N7 is larger, and the displacement fluctuations are more complicated. Comparison of the proportion of large and small fluctuations in the horizontal displacement series at each monitoring point. The proportion of large and small fluctuations in the horizontal displacement sequence of each monitoring point is compared. For Section 1, the horizontal displacement sequence of N2 is slightly larger than that of N1 and N3. $\Delta f(\alpha)$ is slightly larger than that of N1 and N3. This indicates that the proportion of small fluctuations in the horizontal displacement sequence at N2 is larger. Similarly, for Sections 2 and 3, the proportion of small fluctuations in the horizontal displacement sequences of monitoring points N5 and N6 is larger than that of monitoring points N1 and N3.

It can be seen that the results of the multifractal eigenvalues of the horizontal displacement sequences of different monitoring sections at the tunnel portal are more in line with the actual monitoring results, and the multifractal intensity of the horizontal displacement sequences at monitoring points N3, N5, and N7 is more intense, and the fluctuation of the displacement sequences at the monitoring points is slightly more complicated. When evaluating the stability of the tunnel portal slope, more attention should be paid to the horizontal displacement changes at monitoring points N3, N5, and N7.

3.2.2. Vertical Displacement Multifractal Characterization

The multifractal analysis is performed on the vertical displacement sequences of each monitoring point of the upward slope of the tunnel portal respectively. The generalized Hurst index, Renyi index, and multifractal spectrum of the vertical displacement sequence at each monitoring point are obtained, and the index changes of the corresponding monitoring point sequence are shown in Figures 9 and 10.

As can be seen from Figure 9, when q varies between $[-10,10]$, the generalized Hurst indices of the vertical displacement sequences of different monitoring sections of the tunnel portal slope are all nonlinearly decreasing with q. The generalized Hurst indices of the vertical displacement sequences of different monitoring sections of the tunnel portal slope are all nonlinearly decreasing with q. This indicates that the vertical displacement sequences at each monitoring point are characterized by multifractal. At different fluctuation orders q, the $h(q)$ values of the vertical displacement series at each monitoring point are significantly larger than 0.5, indicating that all the sequences have good memory and long-range correlation from the whole to the local components. In addition, from Figure. 9, it can be seen that the scale function $\tau(q)$ of the vertical displacement series at each monitoring point is in good agreement. The middle part of the scalar function curve is upconvex and satisfies $\tau(0) = -1$ The scale function curve has an upward convex shape in the center, which indicates that the vertical displacement sequence of each monitoring point has multifractal characteristics.

In Figure 10, the multifractal spectra of the vertical displacement sequences at various monitoring points across different sections exhibit a distinctive single-peak convex distribution, resembling a quadratic function curve. The local scales of these multifractals display variability, highlighting the diverse local changes occurring at different instances. The singular intensities of the vertical displacement sequences are dispersed on both sides of the image, showcasing the heterogeneous local variations over time. The distribution of α values on either side of the image further underscores the uneven fractal structure distribution within the monitoring point sequence, emphasizing its multifractal nature. Notably, the multifractal spectral curves of the vertical displacement sequences exhibit a symmetrical pattern, indicating a stable overall development state.

Calculate the multifractal characteristic statistics of the vertical displacement sequences of monitoring points in different monitoring sections; the calculation results are shown in Table 2.

Table 2. Vertical displacement multifractal characterization statistics.

Monitoring Points Eigenvalue	Cross-Section 1			Cross-Section 2		Cross-Section 3	
	N1	N2	N3	N4	N5	N6	N7
$\Delta \alpha$	1.018	0.998	1.599	1.247	1.004	1.194	0.955
$\Delta f(\alpha)$	0.014	0.203	−0.019	0.108	0.153	−0.142	0.083

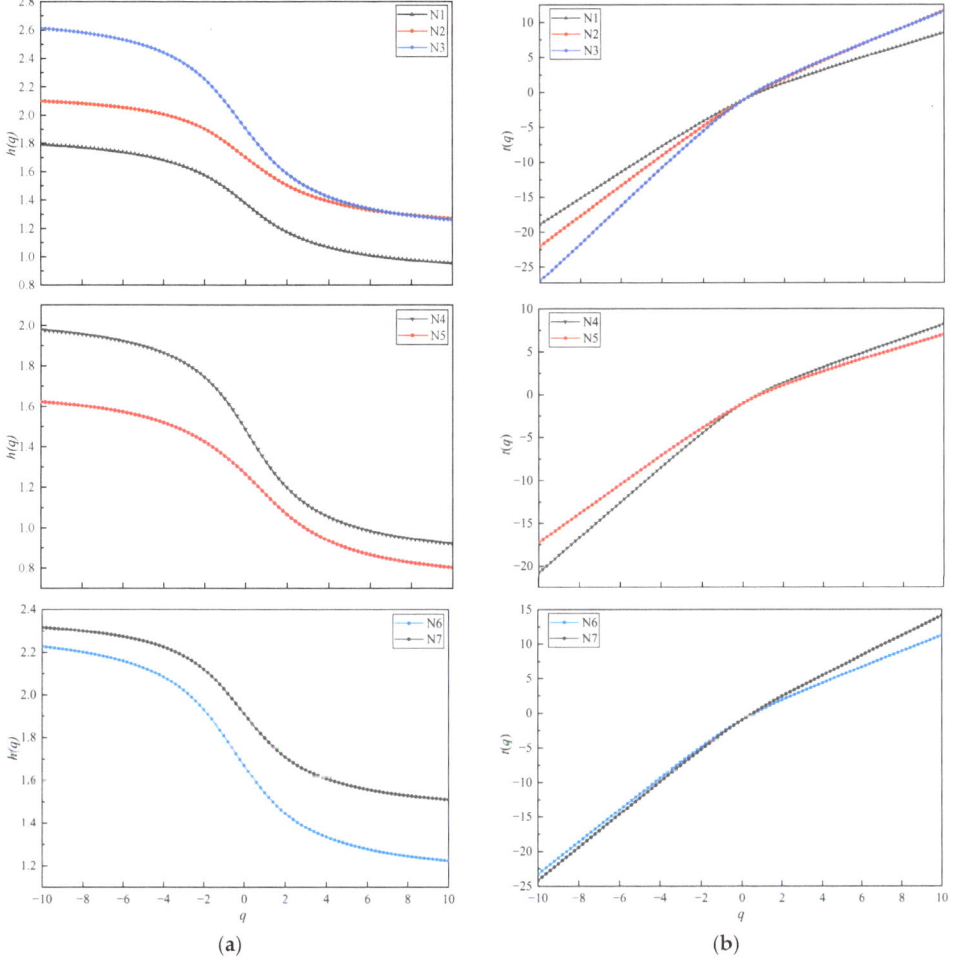

Figure 9. Variation of each index of the vertical displacement sequence: (**a**) generalized Hurst index, (**b**) scaling function $\tau(q)$.

As can be seen from Table 2, we compare the widths of the multifractal spectra of the vertical displacement series at each monitoring point $\Delta \alpha$. For Section 1, the multifractal spectral widths of the vertical displacement sequences at monitoring points N1 and N2 are smaller than those at monitoring point N3. $\Delta \alpha$ is smaller than that of N3. This means that the vertical displacement sequence at N3 has a larger intensity of multifractals, and the vertical displacement fluctuation is more complicated. Similarly, for Sections 2 and 3, the multifractal strengths of the vertical displacement series at N4 and N6 are larger, and the displacement fluctuations are more complicated. Comparing the proportion of large and small fluctuations in the vertical displacement series at each monitoring point, the proportion of large and small fluctuations in the vertical displacement series at N4 and N6 is larger. The proportion of large and small fluctuations in the vertical displacement sequences at each monitoring point is compared. For Section 1, the vertical displacement sequence $\Delta f(\alpha)$ at monitoring point N2 is slightly larger than that at monitoring points N1 and N3. This indicates that the proportion of small fluctuations in the vertical displacement sequence at N2 is larger. Similarly, for Sections 2 and 3, the proportion of small fluctuations in the vertical displacement sequences of monitoring points N5 and N7 is larger.

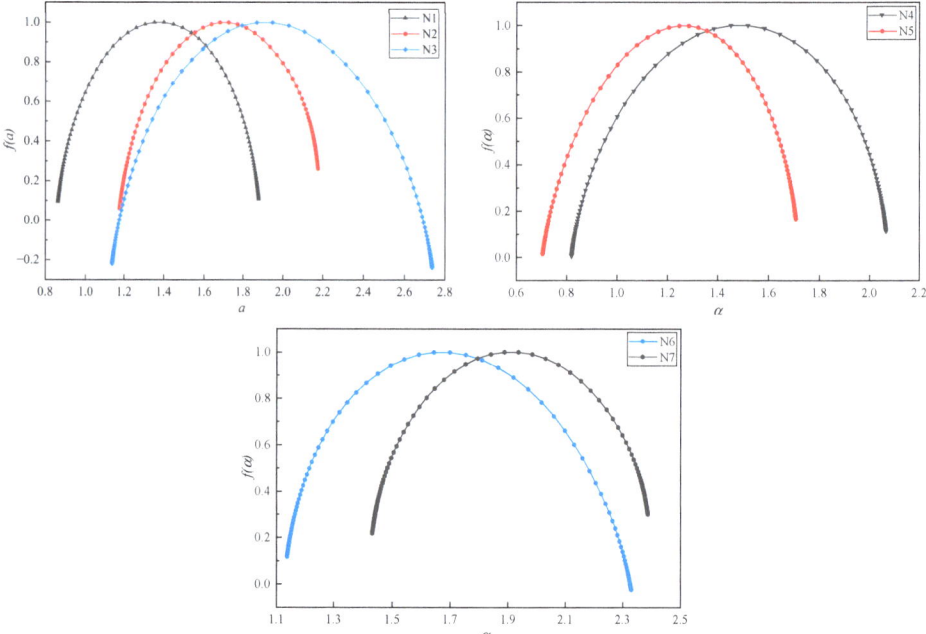

Figure 10. Multifractal spectrum of vertical displacement sequence.

It can be seen that the results of the multifractal eigenvalues of the vertical displacement sequences of different monitoring sections at the tunnel portal side slope are more in line with the actual monitoring results, and the multifractal strengths of the vertical displacement sequences at monitoring points N3, N4, and N6 are more intense, and the fluctuations of the displacement sequences of the monitoring points are slightly more complicated. More attention should be paid to the vertical displacement changes at monitoring points N3, N4, and N6 when evaluating the stability of the tunnel portal slope.

3.3. PSO-LSTM Prediction of Slope Deformation at Tunnel Portal Sides

The results of the previous study show that the results of the multifractal eigenvalues of the displacement sequences of the different monitoring sections of the tunnel portal slope are more in line with the actual monitoring results. Among them, the horizontal displacements at N3, N5, and N7 are more intense, and the vertical displacements at N3, N4, and N6 are more intense. Therefore, the PSO-LSTM method is used to predict the horizontal displacements at N3, N5, and N7 and the vertical displacements at N3, N4, and N6 when evaluating the stability of the tunnel portal slope.

3.3.1. Horizontal Displacement Prediction Results

The hyperparameters obtained after PSO optimization are used to input the LSTM model. Model training is performed on the input data. Based on several iterations and training, the accuracy of the model prediction was made to reach a reasonable range. The daily data of monitoring data from different monitoring sections of the tunnel portal slope were selected for prediction, totaling about 100 sets of data. Furthermore, 70% of the data is used as the training set and the remaining 30% of the data is the test set. The PSO-LSTM model was trained and tested, and the predicted horizontal displacements of the N3, N5, and N7 monitoring points of the tunnel portal slope are shown in Figure 11.

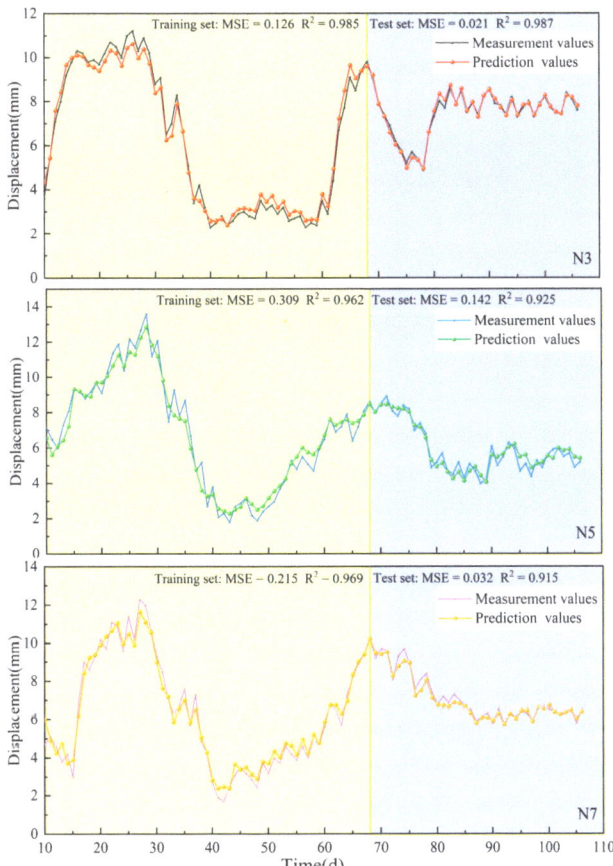

Figure 11. Predicted horizontal displacement of the tunnel portal slope.

As can be seen from Figure 11, the PSO-LSTM model predicts the horizontal displacements of the tunnel portal slope at monitoring points N3, N5, and N7, which are closer to the actual monitoring results. The maximum MSE value of the horizontal displacement training set fitting results for each measurement point is 0.309, and the R^2 is higher than 96%. The maximum MSE value of the prediction results of the test set is 0.142, and the R^2 is higher than 91%. From the prediction curves, it can be seen that the predicted horizontal displacements of measuring points N3 and N7 after the 85th day almost coincide with the actual monitoring results. It can be seen that the PSO-LSTM model is more effective in predicting the horizontal displacement in the middle and late stages of the monitoring sequence.

To further evaluate the error between the PSO-LSTM model's prediction of horizontal displacement sequences at monitoring points N3, N5, and N7 and the measured values, the results of the PSO-LSTM model's horizontal displacement prediction error calculations are shown in Figure 12.

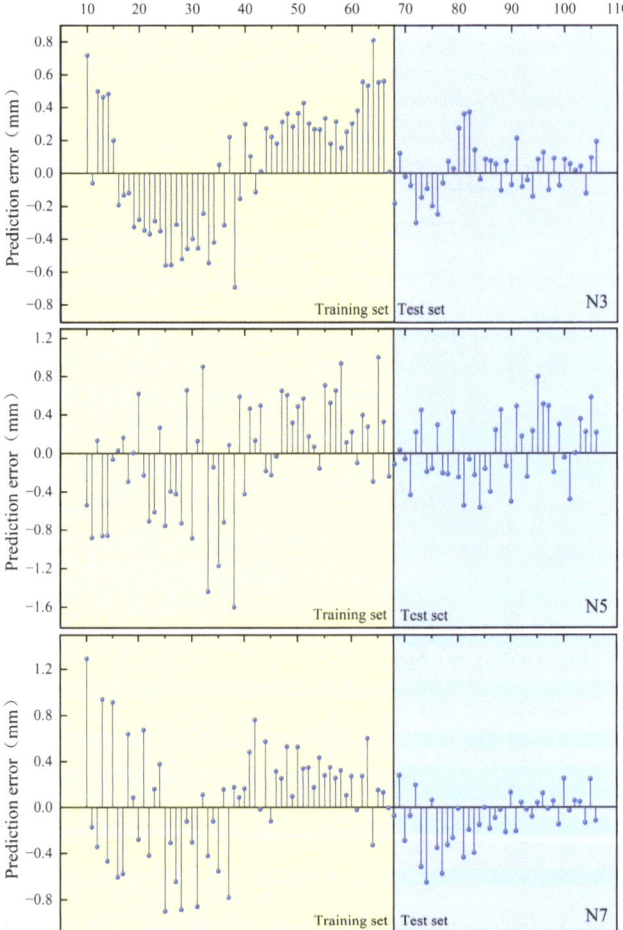

Figure 12. Calculation results of horizontal displacement prediction error.

As can be seen from Figure 12, by comparing the sample error calculation results of the PSO-LSTM model for the prediction of the horizontal displacement sequences of the N3, N5, and N7 monitoring points, it is found that the maximum value of the horizontal displacement prediction error of the N3 monitoring point is 0.81 mm. It is found that the maximum value of the horizontal displacement prediction error of the N3 monitoring point is 0.81 mm, and about 90% of the sample prediction errors can be controlled within ±0.5 mm, the maximum value of the horizontal displacement prediction error of the N5 monitoring point is −1.6 mm, about 90% of the sample prediction errors can be controlled within ±0.8 mm, the maximum value of the horizontal displacement prediction error of the N7 monitoring point is 1.29 mm, and about 90% of the sample prediction errors can be controlled within ±0.6 mm can be controlled within ±0.6 mm. It can be seen from the figure that the maximum prediction error of the model test set is significantly smaller than the training set prediction error. It shows that the PSO-LSTM model can predict the horizontal displacement sequences of N3, N5, and N7 with small sample errors. This indicates that the PSO-LSTM prediction model has better performance.

3.3.2. Vertical Displacement Prediction Results

The PSO-LSTM model was trained and tested to predict the vertical displacements at the N3, N4, and N6 monitoring points on the portal slope of the tunnel portal. The corresponding prediction results are shown in Figure 13.

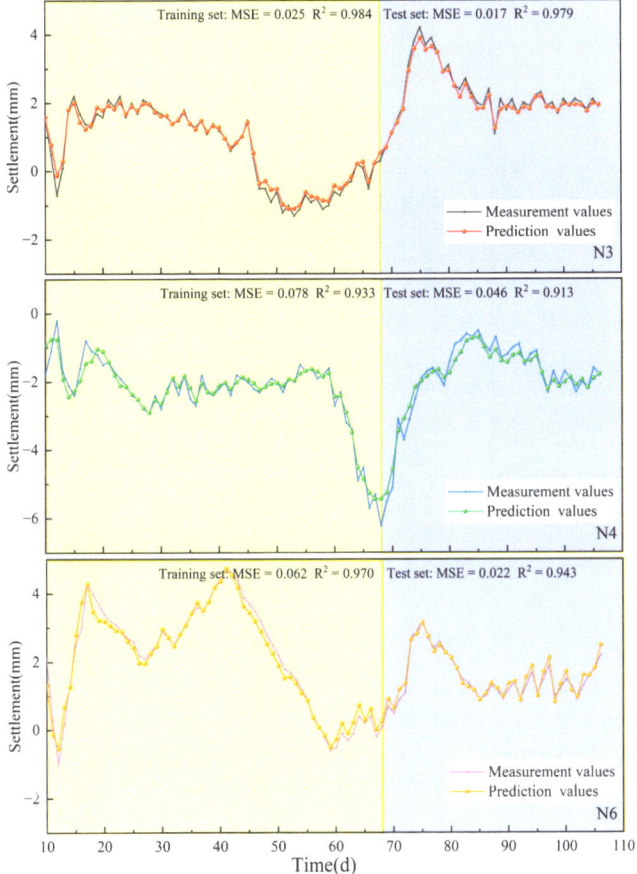

Figure 13. Vertical displacement prediction results of tunnel portal slope.

As can be seen from Figure 13, the PSO-LSTM model predicts the vertical displacements of the tunnel portal slope at monitoring points N3, N4, and N6, which are closer to the actual monitoring results. The maximum MSE value of the vertical displacement training set fitting results for each measurement point is 0.078, and the R^2 is higher than 93%. The maximum MSE value of the prediction results of the test set is 0.069, and the R^2 is higher than 91%. From the prediction curves, it can be seen that the predicted vertical displacements of monitoring points N3 and N6 after the 75th day almost coincide with the actual monitoring results. It can be seen that the PSO-LSTM model is more effective in predicting the vertical displacement monitoring sequence in the middle and late stages.

To further evaluate the error between the PSO-LSTM model's prediction of vertical displacement sequences at monitoring points N3, N4, and N6 and the measured values, the results of the PSO-LSTM model's vertical displacement prediction error calculations are shown in Figure 14.

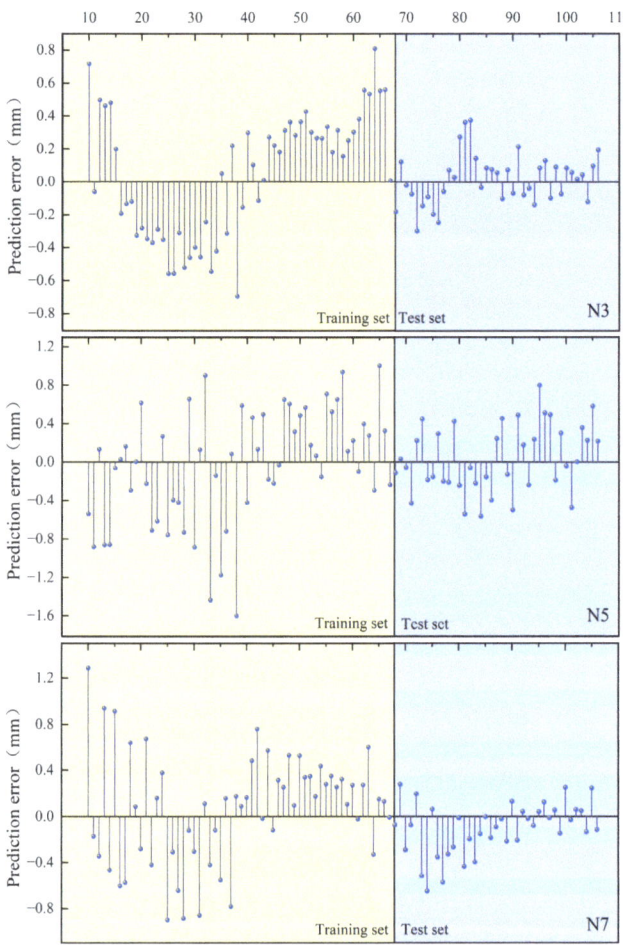

Figure 14. Calculation results of vertical displacement prediction error.

As can be seen in Figure 14, by comparing the sample error calculation results of the PSO-LSTM model for the prediction of vertical displacement sequences at the N3, N4, and N6 monitoring points, it is found that the maximum value of the prediction error of vertical displacement at N3 is 0.58 mm, and about 90% of the sample prediction errors can be controlled within ±0.2 mm, the maximum value of the prediction error of vertical displacement at N4 is 0.85 mm, and about 90% of the sample prediction errors can be controlled within ±0.35 mm. The maximum value of the prediction error of vertical displacement at N6 is −0.77 mm and about 90% of the sample prediction errors can be controlled within ±0.30 mm. The maximum prediction error of vertical displacement at N6 is −0.77 mm, and the prediction error of about 90% of the samples can be controlled within ±0.30 mm. From the figure, it can be seen that the maximum prediction error of the model test set is slightly smaller than the training set error. It shows that the PSO-LSTM model predicts the vertical displacement sequences of the N3, N4, and N6 monitoring points with small sample errors. It shows that the PSO-LSTM model has good performance and can meet the requirements of vertical displacement prediction for the tunnel portal slope.

4. Discussion

Tunnel construction is often challenging due to the presence of difficult geological conditions such as high slopes, bias pressure, and shallow burial. These conditions can lead to engineering accidents like collapse, slope instability, and landslides during the tunnel portal construction. As a result, ensuring the stability of the surrounding rock and side slopes at the tunnel portal has become a crucial focus of research in tunnel engineering. In the theoretical study of the stability of the surrounding rock at the tunnel portal, numerical simulation is commonly used to analyze the tunnel and its entrance slope [19,22,24]. Some scholars have also carried out large-scale shaking table tests to determine the macro damage of tunnel lining and entrance slopes. Additionally, monitoring slope displacement in the tunnel portal section is deemed essential for field application. Various excavation methods for shallow tunnels have been adopted to control deformation and stabilize slopes at the entrance. However, the complexity of tunnel portal slope engineering as a nonlinear dynamic system means that stability and deformation are influenced by numerous uncertain factors. Theoretical methods like numerical simulation may not fully guarantee stability during tunnel excavation, especially in unfavorable geological conditions. Continuous monitoring of entrance side slope elevation is necessary to analyze deformation trends, predict displacement development, and prevent tunnel disasters.

To address challenges in constructing a weak, water-rich, and shallow buried tunnel portal next to an important structure, this study focuses on designing a monitoring and measurement scheme to analyze tunnel portal side slope deformation. Monitoring results indicate high stability after stabilization, with minimal horizontal and vertical displacement. By using the MF-DFA method, the study analyzes multifractal characteristics of monitoring sequences at each measurement point of the tunnel portal slope. Results show good consistency with actual monitoring data, revealing higher multifractal intensity in horizontal and vertical displacement sequences at certain measurement points. Furthermore, the PSO-LSTM model is utilized to predict displacement developments at measurement points on the tunnel portal slope. Prediction accuracy is notably high, indicating the model's effectiveness in forecasting displacement sequences.

In conclusion, tunnel portal sections face challenges in unfavorable geological environments, making it crucial to mitigate engineering risks and ensure stability. Analyzing and predicting slope monitoring data can inform dynamic design, optimize tunnel excavation and support programs, and enhance the safety and stability of adjacent structures like high-voltage towers.

5. Conclusions

Analyzing and predicting the deformation pattern of the portal slope during tunnel portal construction can provide technical support and theoretical guidance for the early warning of tunnel portal section construction safety. Therefore, this paper takes the construction of a soft, water-rich, and shallow buried tunnel portal section near a high-voltage power tower in Malaysia as the background. Combined with on-site monitoring, multifractal analysis, and deep learning methods, it carries out an in-depth study of the multifractal characteristics and displacement prediction of the deformation of the tunnel portal slope. The main research conclusions are as follows.

1. Combined with the deformation characteristics of the tunnel portal slope, design a suitable monitoring and measuring program to analyze the deformation pattern of the tunnel portal slope. After the deformation of the tunnel portal slope is stabilized, the horizontal displacement is about 6–8 mm, the vertical settlement value is not more than 2 mm, and the stability of the tunnel portal slope is high.
2. Based on the MF-DFA method, analyze the multifractal characteristics of the deformation monitoring sequences at each monitoring point of the tunnel portal slope. The

MF eigenvalues of the displacement sequences at different monitoring sections of the tunnel portal slope are more in line with the actual monitoring results. For the horizontal displacement sequences, the multifractal strengths of monitoring points N3, N5, and N7 are larger. For the vertical displacement sequence, the multifractal intensities of monitoring points N3, N4, and N6 are larger.

3. The PSO-LSTM prediction model was utilized to predict the deformation development of the side slope of the tunnel portal. The maximum MSE value of the horizontal displacement test set prediction result is 0.142, and R^2 is higher than 91%. The maximum MSE value of the vertical displacement test set prediction result is 0.069, and R^2 is higher than 91%. The PSO-LSTM model has a small error in predicting the displacement sequence of each monitoring point, and the performance of the prediction model can meet the requirements for predicting the displacement of the portal slope of the tunnel portal.

The tunnel portal section under study has a single nature of surrounding rock, and the values of side and elevation slope deformation are generally small. In future studies, multifractal characterization can be carried out to analyze the slope displacement sequences of tunnels with different surrounding rock properties. In addition, more factors affecting the slope deformation can be considered to further improve the prediction accuracy of the PSO-LSTM model.

Author Contributions: Methodology, X.Z. and Y.H.; software, W.Z.; validation, X.Z. and Y.H.; formal analysis, W.Z. and D.L.; data curation, X.Z. and W.Z.; writing—original draft preparation, W.Z.; writing—review and editing, X.Z. and D.L.; project administration, Y.H. and D.L.; funding acquisition, X.Z. and Y.H. All authors have read and agreed to the published version of the manuscript.

Funding: This research received no external funding.

Data Availability Statement: The data that support the findings of this study are available upon request from the authors.

Acknowledgments: The authors would like to thank Road & Bridge International Co., Ltd. for their assistance with conducting the field experiments.

Conflicts of Interest: Authors Xiannian Zhou and Yurui He were employed by the company Road & Bridge International Co., Ltd. The remaining authors declare that the research was conducted in the absence of any commercial or financial relationships that could be construed as a potential conflict of interest.

References

1. Gong, C.; Ding, W.; Mosalam, K.M.; Gunay, S.; Soga, K. Comparison of the structural behavior of reinforced concrete and steel fiber reinforced concrete tunnel segmental joints. *Tunn. Undergr. Space Technol.* **2017**, *68*, 38–57. [CrossRef]
2. Lei, M.; Liu, L.; Shi, C.; Tan, Y.; Lin, Y.; Wang, W. A novel tunnel-lining crack recognition system based on digital image technology. *Tunn. Undergr. Space Technol.* **2021**, *108*, 103724. [CrossRef]
3. Zhou, Z.; Zhang, J.; Gong, C. Automatic detection method of tunnel lining multi-defects via an enhanced You Only Look Once network. *Comput.-Aided Civ. Infrastruct. Eng.* **2022**, *37*, 762–780. [CrossRef]
4. Bandini, A.; Berry, P.; Boldini, D. Tunnelling-induced landslides: The Val di Sambro tunnel case study. *Eng. Geol.* **2015**, *196*, 71–87. [CrossRef]
5. Zhao, C.; Lei, M.; Shi, C.; Cao, H.; Yang, W.; Deng, E. Function mechanism and analytical method of a double layer pre-support system for tunnel underneath passing a large-scale underground pipe gallery in water-rich sandy strata: A case study. *Tunn. Undergr. Space Technol.* **2021**, *115*, 104041. [CrossRef]
6. Jia, C.; Zhang, Q.; Lei, M.; Zheng, Y.; Huang, J.; Wang, L. Anisotropic properties of shale and its impact on underground structures: An experimental and numerical simulation. *Bull. Eng. Geol. Environ.* **2021**, *80*, 7731–7745. [CrossRef]
7. Huang, L.; Ma, J.; Lei, M.; Liu, L.; Lin, Y.; Zhang, Z. Soil-water inrush induced shield tunnel lining damage and its stabilization: A case study. *Tunn. Undergr. Space Technol.* **2020**, *97*, 103290. [CrossRef]
8. Lei, M.; Lin, D.; Huang, Q.; Shi, C.; Huang, L. Research on the construction risk control technology of shield tunnel underneath an operational railway in sand pebble formation: A case study. *Eur. J. Environ. Civ. Eng.* **2020**, *24*, 1558–1572. [CrossRef]
9. Zhang, Y.; Yang, J.; Yang, F. Field investigation and numerical analysis of landslide induced by tunneling. *Eng. Fail. Anal.* **2015**, *47*, 25–33. [CrossRef]

10. Zhou, Z.; Ding, H.; Miao, L.; Gong, C. Predictive model for the surface settlement caused by the excavation of twin tunnels. *Tunn. Undergr. Space Technol.* **2021**, *114*, 104014. [CrossRef]
11. Aygar, E.B.; Gokceoglu, C. Effects of Portal Failure on Tunnel Support Systems in a Highway Tunnel. *Geotech. Geol. Eng.* **2021**, *39*, 5707–5726. [CrossRef]
12. Ayoublou, F.F.; Taromi, M.; Eftekhari, A. Tunnel portal instability in landslide area and remedial solution: A case study. *Acta Polytech.* **2019**, *59*, 435–447. [CrossRef]
13. Kaya, A.; Karaman, K.; Bulut, F. Geotechnical investigations and remediation design for failure of tunnel portal section: A case study in northern Turkey. *J. Mt. Sci.* **2017**, *14*, 1140–1160. [CrossRef]
14. Lei, M.; Li, J.; Zhao, C.; Shi, C.; Yang, W.; Deng, E. Pseudo-dynamic analysis of three-dimensional active earth pressures in cohesive backfills with cracks. *Soil Dyn. Earthq. Eng.* **2021**, *150*, 106917. [CrossRef]
15. Wang, Q.; Geng, P.; Li, P.; Chen, J.; He, C. Dynamic damage identification of tunnel portal and verification via shaking table test. *Tunn. Undergr. Space Technol.* **2023**, *132*, 104923. [CrossRef]
16. Wang, Q.; Geng, P.; Chen, J.; He, C. Dynamic discrimination method of seismic damage in tunnel portal based on improved wavelet packet transform coupled with Hilbert-Huang transform. *Mech. Syst. Signal Process.* **2023**, *188*, 110023. [CrossRef]
17. Genis, M. Assessment of the dynamic stability of the portals of the Dorukhan tunnel using numerical analysis. *Int. J. Rock Mech. Min. Sci.* **2010**, *47*, 1231–1241. [CrossRef]
18. Tuncay, E. Assessments on slope instabilities triggered by engineering excavations near a small settlement (Turkey). *J. Mt. Sci.* **2018**, *15*, 114–129. [CrossRef]
19. Wang, X.; Chen, J.; Zhang, Y.; Xiao, M. Seismic responses and damage mechanisms of the structure in the portal section of a hydraulic tunnel in rock. *Soil Dyn. Earthq. Eng.* **2019**, *123*, 205–216. [CrossRef]
20. Jia, J. Application of PS-INSAR Technique on Health Diagnosis of the Deformable Body on Front Slope beside Mountain Tunnel Portal. *Math. Probl. Eng.* **2020**, *2020*, 8823382. [CrossRef]
21. Feng, H.; Jiang, G.; He, Z.; Guo, Y.; Hu, J.; Li, J.; Yuan, S. Dynamic response characteristics of tunnel portal slope reinforced by prestressed anchor sheet-pile wall. *Rock Soil Mech.* **2023**, *44S*, 50–62.
22. Zhang, Q.; Wang, J.; Zhang, H. Attribute recognition model and its application of risk assessment for slope stability at tunnel portal. *J. Vibroeng.* **2017**, *19*, 2726–2738. [CrossRef]
23. Li, X.; Li, X.; Yang, C. A comparison study of face stability between the entering and exiting a shallow-buried tunnel with a front slope. *Front. Earth Sci.* **2022**, *10*, 987294. [CrossRef]
24. Li, C.; Zheng, H.; Hu, Z.; Liu, X.; Huang, Z. Analysis of Loose Surrounding Rock Deformation and Slope Stability at Shallow Double-Track Tunnel Portal: A Case Study. *Appl. Sci.* **2023**, *13*, 50248. [CrossRef]
25. Aygar, E.B.; Gokceoglu, C. Problems Encountered during a Railway Tunnel Excavation in Squeezing and Swelling Materials and Possible Engineering Measures: A Case Study from Turkey. *Sustainability* **2020**, *12*, 11663. [CrossRef]
26. Taromi, M.; Eftekhari, A.; Hamidi, J.K.; Aalianvari, A. A discrepancy between observed and predicted NATM tunnel behaviors and updating: A case study of the Sabzkuh tunnel. *Bull. Eng. Geol. Environ.* **2017**, *76*, 713–729. [CrossRef]
27. Zhu, B.; Lei, M.; Gong, C.; Zhao, C.; Zhang, Y.; Huang, J.; Jia, C.; Shi, C. Tunnelling-induced landslides: Trigging mechanism, field observations and mitigation measures. *Eng. Fail. Anal.* **2022**, *138*, 106387. [CrossRef]
28. Xi, N.; Yang, Q.; Sun, Y.; Mei, G. Machine Learning Approaches for Slope Deformation Prediction Based on Monitored Time-Series Displacement Data: A Comparative Investigation. *Appl. Sci.* **2023**, *13*, 46778. [CrossRef]
29. Intrieri, E.; Gigli, G.; Mugnai, F.; Fanti, R.; Casagli, N. Design and implementation of a landslide early warning system. *Eng. Geol.* **2012**, *147*, 124–136. [CrossRef]
30. Dai, F.C.; Lee, C.F.; Ngai, Y.Y. Landslide risk assessment and management: An overview. *Eng. Geol.* **2002**, *64*, 65–87. [CrossRef]
31. Lopes, R.; Betrouni, N. Fractal and multifractal analysis: A review. *Med. Image Anal.* **2009**, *13*, 634–649. [CrossRef]
32. Liu, J.; Li, Q.; Wang, X.; Wang, Z.; Lu, S.; Sa, Z.; Wang, H. Dynamic multifractal characteristics of acoustic emission about composite coal-rock samples with different strength rock. *Chaos Soliton Fract.* **2022**, *164*, 112725. [CrossRef]
33. Ehlen, J. Fractal analysis of joint patterns in granite. *Int. J. Rock Mech. Min. Sci.* **2000**, *37*, 909–922. [CrossRef]
34. Li, W.; Zhao, H.; Wu, H.; Wang, L.; Sun, W.; Ling, X. A novel approach of two-dimensional representation of rock fracture network characterization and connectivity analysis. *J. Petrol. Sci. Eng.* **2020**, *184*, 106507. [CrossRef]
35. Zhang, W.; Liu, D.; Tang, Y.; Qiu, W.; Zhang, R. Multifractal Characteristics of Smooth Blasting Overbreak in Extra-Long Hard Rock Tunnel. *Fractal Fract.* **2023**, *7*, 84212. [CrossRef]
36. Liu, D.; Zhang, W.; Jian, Y.; Tang, Y.; Cao, K. Damage precursors of sulfate erosion concrete based on acoustic emission multifractal characteristics and b-value. *Constr. Build. Mater.* **2024**, *419*, 135380. [CrossRef]
37. Wasowski, J.; Bovenga, F. Investigating landslides and unstable slopes with satellite Multi Temporal Interferometry: Current issues and future perspectives. *Eng. Geol.* **2014**, *174*, 103–138. [CrossRef]
38. Gariano, S.L.; Guzzetti, F. Landslides in a changing climate. *Earth-Sci. Rev.* **2016**, *162*, 227–252. [CrossRef]
39. Li, Z.; Cheng, P.; Zheng, J. Prediction of time to slope failure based on a new model. *Bull. Eng. Geol. Environ.* **2021**, *80*, 5279–5291. [CrossRef]
40. Feng, X.T.; Zhao, H.B.; Li, S.J. Modeling non-linear displacement time series of geo-materials using evolutionary support vector machines. *Int. J. Rock Mech. Min. Sci.* **2004**, *41*, 1087–1107. [CrossRef]

41. Huang, Y.; Zhao, L. Review on landslide susceptibility mapping using support vector machines. *Catena* **2018**, *165*, 520–529. [CrossRef]
42. Ma, Z.; Mei, G.; Prezioso, E.; Zhang, Z.; Xu, N. A deep learning approach using graph convolutional networks for slope deformation prediction based on time-series displacement data. *Neural Comput. Appl.* **2021**, *33*, 14441–14457. [CrossRef]
43. Ma, Z.; Mei, G.; Piccialli, F. Machine learning for landslides prevention: A survey. *Neural Comput. Appl.* **2021**, *33*, 10881–10907. [CrossRef]
44. Xiao, L.; Zhang, Y.; Peng, G. Landslide Susceptibility Assessment Using Integrated Deep Learning Algorithm along the China-Nepal Highway. *Sensors* **2018**, *18*, 443612. [CrossRef]
45. Lian, C.; Zeng, Z.; Yao, W.; Tang, H. Multiple neural networks switched prediction for landslide displacement. *Eng. Geol.* **2015**, *186*, 91–99. [CrossRef]
46. Pei, H.; Meng, F.; Zhu, H. Landslide displacement prediction based on a novel hybrid model and convolutional neural network considering time-varying factors. *Bull. Eng. Geol. Environ.* **2021**, *80*, 7403–7422. [CrossRef]
47. Wang, H.; Zhang, L.; Luo, H.; He, J.; Cheung, R.W.M. AI-powered landslide susceptibility assessment in Hong Kong. *Eng. Geol.* **2021**, *288*, 106103. [CrossRef]
48. Yang, B.; Yin, K.; Lacasse, S.; Liu, Z. Time series analysis and long short-term memory neural network to predict landslide displacement. *Landslides* **2019**, *16*, 677–694. [CrossRef]
49. Liu, Z.; Gilbert, G.; Cepeda, J.M.; Lysdahl, A.O.K.; Piciullo, L.; Hefre, H.; Lacasse, S. Modelling of shallow landslides with machine learning algorithms. *Geosci. Front.* **2021**, *12*, 385–393. [CrossRef]
50. Yan, L.; Chen, C.; Hang, T.; Hu, Y. A stream prediction model based on attention-LSTM. *Earth Sci. Inform.* **2021**, *14*, 723–733. [CrossRef]
51. Li, C.; Li, J.; Shi, Z.; Li, L.; Li, M.; Jin, D.; Dong, G. Prediction of Surface Settlement Induced by Large-Diameter Shield Tunneling Based on Machine-Learning Algorithms. *Geofluids* **2022**, *2022*, 4174768. [CrossRef]
52. Cao, Y.; Zhou, X.; Yan, K. Deep Learning Neural Network Model for Tunnel Ground Surface Settlement Prediction Based on Sensor Data. *Math. Probl. Eng.* **2021**, *2021*, 9488892. [CrossRef]
53. Yang, C.; Huang, R.; Liu, D.; Qiu, W.; Zhang, R.; Tang, Y. Analysis and Warning Prediction of Tunnel Deformation Based on Multifractal Theory. *Fractal Fract.* **2024**, *8*, 1082. [CrossRef]
54. Tian, X.; Song, Z.; Zhang, Y. Monitoring and reinforcement of landslide induced by tunnel excavation: A case study from Xiamaixi tunnel. *Tunn. Undergr. Space Technol.* **2021**, *110*, 103796. [CrossRef]
55. Ouyang, C.; Zhou, K.; Xu, Q.; Yin, J.; Peng, D.; Wang, D.; Li, W. Dynamic analysis and numerical modeling of the 2015 catastrophic landslide of the construction waste landfill at Guangming, Shenzhen, China. *Landslides* **2017**, *14*, 705–718. [CrossRef]
56. Kong, X.; Wang, E.; Hu, S.; Shen, R.; Li, X.; Zhan, T. Fractal characteristics and acoustic emission of coal containing methane in triaxial compression failure. *J. Appl. Geophys.* **2016**, *124*, 139–147. [CrossRef]
57. Kong, X.; Wang, E.; He, X.; Li, Z.; Li, D.; Liu, Q. Multifractal characteristics and acoustic emission of coal with joints under uniaxial loading. *Fractals* **2017**, *25*, 17500455. [CrossRef]
58. Kong, B.; Wang, E.; Li, Z.; Lu, W. Study on the feature of electromagnetic radiation under coal oxidation and temperature rise based on multifractal theory. *Fractals* **2019**, *27*, 19500383. [CrossRef]
59. Hochreiter, S.T.U.M.; Schmidhuber, J. Long short-term memory. *Neural Comput.* **1997**, *9*, 1735–1780. [CrossRef]
60. Eberhart, R.; Kennedy, J. New optimizer using particle swarm theory. In Proceedings of the 1995 6th International Symposium on Micro Machine and Human Science, Nagoya, Japan, 4–6 October 1995.

Disclaimer/Publisher's Note: The statements, opinions and data contained in all publications are solely those of the individual author(s) and contributor(s) and not of MDPI and/or the editor(s). MDPI and/or the editor(s) disclaim responsibility for any injury to people or property resulting from any ideas, methods, instructions or products referred to in the content.

Article

Dynamic Response Analysis Method of a High-Strength RC Beam Subjected to Long-Duration Blast Loading

Haochuan Zhao [1], Fan Zeng [2,3,*], Xiaowei Feng [1,*], Shouqian Wang [1], Chao Huang [2,3], Na Liu [2,3] and Jian Zhang [4]

1. Institute of Systems Engineering, China Academy of Engineering Physics, Mianyang 621999, China; 15520478354@163.com (H.Z.); w1188759202@163.com (S.W.)
2. CAEP Software Center for High Performance Numerical Simulation, Beijing 100088, China; huang_chao@iapcm.ac.cn (C.H.); liu_na@iapcm.ac.cn (N.L.)
3. Institute of Applied Physics and Computational Mathematics, Beijing 100088, China
4. North Hua'an Industrial Group Co., Ltd., Qiqihaer 161000, China; z113014492@126.com
* Correspondence: zeng_fan@iapcm.ac.cn (F.Z.); xiaowei_feng@126.com (X.F.)

Abstract: An analysis method of normalized pressure–impulse (*P-I*) diagrams related to the ductility ratio of structural components is proposed, to quickly estimate the dynamic response of high-strength reinforcement concrete (RC) beams subjected to long-duration blast loading. Firstly, the overall bending deformation mode of RC beams is uncovered via explosion tests in a closed chamber, where the durations of the near-planar blast loadings are varied within 80–105 ms. Then, a single-degree-of-freedom (SDOF) model is established based on the bending deformation mode. The resistance function for the uniform pressure loading is developed using a novel approach, consisting of (1) developing and benchmarking a three-dimensional (3D) improved steel–concrete separated finite-element (FE) model; (2) using the benchmarked FE model to conduct numerical simulations for uniform pressure loading; and (3) idealizing the resistance function for uniform pressure using a bilinear relationship. Finally, the SDOF model is used to conduct parametric analyses and develop a normalized *P-I* diagram that can be used to analyze or design RC beams for far-field blast effects. This *P-I* diagram is verified using results from blast load tests that are primarily in the dynamic region. A total of 188 additional 3D nonlinear FE analyses of RC beams are conducted to expand the database in the impulse and quasi-static regions. Considering the limitations of the proposed method in predicting the shear-dominated deformation and the fracture behavior of members, the *P-I* diagram is applicable to the dynamic response of the bending deformation of members under far-field explosion, which can provide an important reference for the blast-resistant design and analysis of high-strength RC beams.

Keywords: long duration blast loading; bilinear resistance model; *P-I* diagram

Citation: Zhao, H.; Zeng, F.; Feng, X.; Wang, S.; Huang, C.; Liu, N.; Zhang, J. Dynamic Response Analysis Method of a High-Strength RC Beam Subjected to Long-Duration Blast Loading. *Buildings* **2024**, *14*, 1612. https://doi.org/10.3390/buildings14061612

Academic Editor: Duc-Kien Thai

Received: 20 April 2024
Revised: 23 May 2024
Accepted: 28 May 2024
Published: 1 June 2024

Copyright: © 2024 by the authors. Licensee MDPI, Basel, Switzerland. This article is an open access article distributed under the terms and conditions of the Creative Commons Attribution (CC BY) license (https://creativecommons.org/licenses/by/4.0/).

1. Introduction

In recent years, the number of underground explosion accidents is increasing. For example, in March 2010, the "Lubyanka" subway station and "Cultural Park" subway station in the center of Moscow exploded one after another, resulting in 40 deaths and nearly 100 injuries. In September 2017, five people were killed and more than 30 injured in a bombing at Parsons Green Underground station in west London, as well as a subway station bombing in Belarus. The positive pressure region of the shock wave generated by these explosion events can be as high as $10^2 \sim 10^3$ ms, belonging to the long-pulse-width explosion load [1–3]. Long-duration blast waves are typically defined by positive pressure durations over 100 ms, which develop in later stages of shock wave propagation, i.e., in the 'far field' from the source of detonation.

As one of the load-bearing structures of underground buildings, high-strength reinforced concrete (RC) beams are also important components under the action of long-pulse-width shock waves. Studying their dynamic response and blast-resistant performance under the action of a long-pulse-width shock wave has important theoretical significance and engineering value for improving the blast-resistant safety of RC structures.

As a common component of major blast-resistant structures, high-strength beams are generally improved from the aspects of materials and section properties, etc., and the influences of concrete strength, steel fiber content, steel strength, and reinforcement ratio on the blast resistance and deformation degree of beams are mainly studied [4–14].

In terms of experiments, several explosive experimental research studies were carried out based on special experimental equipment. For example, LIAL Z et al. [9] used the explosion pressure simulator to study the blast-resistant behavior of high-reinforcement-ratio and high-strength steel bars against beams, respectively, and the results showed that both high-reinforcement-ratio and high-strength steel bars could effectively reduce the peak displacement of members and reduce the length and width of cracks. Zhou Xiwu et al. [10] adopted the domestic advanced ultra-high weight hammer impact testing machine system and found that the overall stiffness of the beam was effectively improved with the reinforcement ratio increasing. Magnusson et al. [11] used a shock tube device to study the effects of high-strength concrete and steel fiber content on the deformation degree and failure mode of beams. Wang, Y.D et al. [15] investigated the reinforcing effect of an expanded section on the ductility and ultimate shear strength of concrete beams. Li, C.J et al. [16] investigated the effects of ultra-high-performance fiber-reinforced concrete jacketing on the static and blast behavior of reinforced beams. Though the displacement response of the beam was derived from the explosion experiment accurately, several limitations were still reserved. For instance, concerning the loading condition of planar wave, it is difficult to realize. For example, the loading condition of plane shock wave is difficult to achieve; for the newly designed high-strength beams, it is necessary to carry out blast-resistant performance experiments in batches, and the experiment cost is too high. Due to the limitations of explosion experiments, the research on the dynamic response of high-strength beams under a long pulse width explosion load is insufficient.

In terms of numerical calculation, the single-degree-of-freedom (SDOF) model has been widely used in dynamic analysis in the explosion resistance of structure [17,18] due to its high computational efficiency [19]. When the SDOF model is used to analyze the displacement of high-strength beams, a corresponding resistance model [20] should be established to determine the parameters such as equivalent stiffness and yield resistance. For the far-field explosion effect, the blast wave acts uniformly on the target surface, so the resistance model must be applicable to the uniformly distributed load environment [21]. At present, the resistance model used to analyze the response and displacement of beam members under an explosion load is relatively simple. For example, Xu Juechun et al. [22] used elastic and plastic resistance models to obtain the dynamic response equation of the direct shear failure of components under an explosion load, and Nassr et al. [23] used the rigid–plastic resistance model to study the influence of the axial force effect on the strength and stability of an H-shaped steel beam. The ideal elastic–plastic or rigid–plastic models ignore the effect of resistance on the SDOF system and have not studied the hardening effect of resistance deeply.

In this paper, based on the dynamic response analysis of a high-strength beam subjected to long-pulse blast loading, the normalization P-I diagram related to the ductility ratio of high-strength beam is constructed by the fusion of numerical values and a few experiments, so as to realize the rapid calculation of its dynamic response. First of all, we select a typical ordinary strength beam; based on this, by improving the strength of concrete and steel bars and increasing the ratio of reinforcement, we design a different bearing capacity of the beam. And then, the deformation mode of the reference beam is studied through the underground closed reinforced concrete explosion chamber [24]. Combined with the deformation pattern, the SDOF model based on bilinear resistance model is established, and the calculation accuracy of the SDOF model is verified by a small number of explosion experiments. Among them, the results of resistance and mid-span displacement simulated by the finite-element model [25] of uniformly loaded beams are summarized, and a bilinear resistance model is formed by reasonable simplification. Finally, the verified SDOF model is used to obtain the normalized *P-I* diagram related to the ductility ratio of the high-strength beam. The validity of the *P-I* diagram is verified by the explosion experiment results of a few reference beams and a large number of finite-element simulation results.

2. Design of High-Strength Beams

In this paper, the commonly used RC beam of ordinary strength is selected as a reference. Four kinds of high-strength beams are established, improving their bearing capacity by increasing the concrete strength, number of rebars, and reinforcement ratio based on the reference beam (see Figure 1). The reference beam is numbered B1-C40-HRB400-D14, with a geometric size of 200 mm × 200 mm × 2500 mm, made of C40 concrete, reinforced with HRB400 steel bars with a diameter of 14 mm at the top and bottom, and HRB400 steel bars with a diameter of 8 mm at the hoop. The spacing is 150 mm (see Table 1). The geometry of the beam section, the area, and the reinforcement ratio of the tensile reinforcement, as well as the reinforcement ratio and the spacing of the hoop reinforcement, have been taken into account in the design code [26]. The longitudinal reinforcement consisted of diameters of 14 mm or 20 mm (steel areas equal to 307 mm^2 and 626 mm^2), resulting in reinforcement ratios of 0.85% and 1.74%, not exceeding the 2.5% required in the design code [26].

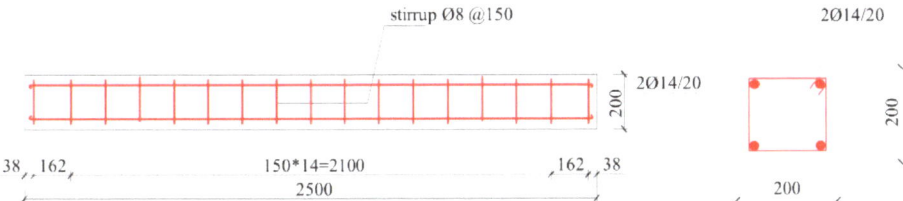

Figure 1. Dimensions and reinforcement of a reference beam (unit: mm).

Table 1. Design parameters of high-strength RC beams.

Beam Sample	Grand of Concrete	Longitudinal Bar Grade	Diameter of Longitudinal bar/mm	Reinforcement Ratio
B1-C40-HRB400-D14	C40	HRB400	14	0.85%
B2-C110-HRB400-D14	C110	HRB400	14	0.85%
B3-C40-HRB400-D20	C40	HRB400	20	1.74%
B4-C40-HRB700-D14	C40	HRB700	14	0.85%
B5-C110-HRB700-D20	C110	HRB700	20	1.74%

3. Reference Beam Explosion Test

In order to generate the long-duration explosion loadings, an underground confined RC shot cavity was designed and excavated [24], as shown in Figure 2. The internal dimensions of the cavity were 3800 mm × 3500 mm × 3000 mm. An equipment mounting well with pre-drilled holes was prefabricated on the side of the blast pit to connect the sensor wires inside the cavity to the data acquisition room (Figure 2a). During experiments, the specimen and related supporting facilities were first placed in the cavity, and steel cover plates were placed on both sides of the specimen and the steel plates of the upper steel cover plate. The specimen and concrete support at the bottom were combined and connected by bolts to realize the simply supported constrained boundary conditions (Figure 2b). The flexural stiffness of the support was calculated to be about 2.5×10^9 N/m^2, which is much larger than that of RC beams. Hence, it is reasonable that the end supports of the beam have been assumed to be rigid and simple during experiments. In order to attenuate the rigid reflection of the blast wave, a layer of rubber was attached to the inner wall of the crater.

In experiments, the multi-point charge initiation technology was used to realize the plane explosion wave acting on the specimen by adjusting the blast height, mass, and plane position of the charge. Five charges C1 to C5, adopting high explosive 8701, were tied on the suspended iron wires in the shot cavity, and the detonating cords converged to ensure simultaneous detonation, as shown in Figure 2c.

In order to evaluate the failure pattern and explosion wave distribution of the specimen, three pressure sensors (with a measuring range of 0~1 MPa), P1~P3, were placed flush with the upper surface of the specimen under each working condition, as shown in Figure 2d. Meanwhile, displacement sensors with a measuring range of 100 mm and an accuracy of 2‰ were installed on the bottom surface of the specimen at the positions of 1/4, 1/2, and 3/4 of the net span of the beams.

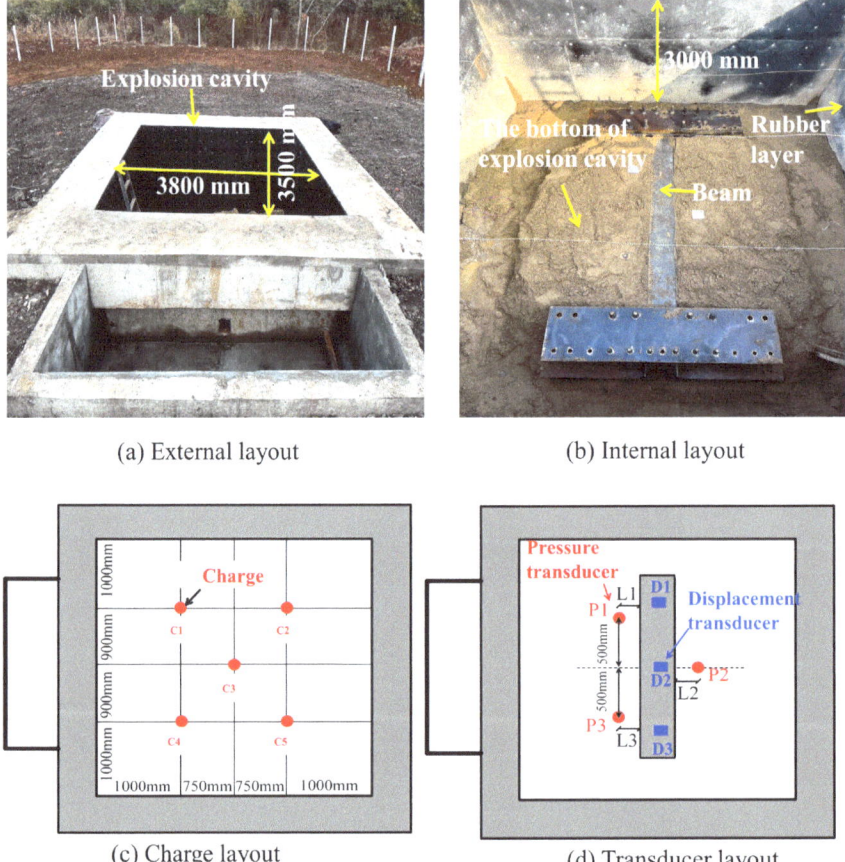

(a) External layout (b) Internal layout

(c) Charge layout (d) Transducer layout

Figure 2. Various main views and parts of the experimental setup: (**a**) External layout; (**b**) Internal layout; (**c**) Charge layout; (**d**) Transducer layout.

The reference beam numbered B1-C40-HRB400-D14 was selected as the experimental object. The vertical distance between the 5-point distributed explosive center and the test piece was about 1 m, and a total of three explosion experiments were carried out. The explosive yield and experimental conditions are shown in Table 2.

Table 2. Experimental conditions.

Experimental Conditions	P1 Explosion Height (mm)	P2 Explosion Height (mm)	P3 Explosion Height (mm)	P4 Explosion Height (mm)	P5 Explosion Height (mm)	Charge Mass (kg)
Exp 1	990	990	990	980	980	0.5
Exp 2	950	930	945	900	910	0.9
Exp 3	950	940	920	900	900	1.15

Figures 3 and 4 show the measured results and corresponding impulse time-history curves of the P1~P3 pressure sensors under different explosion conditions. The variation tendencies of pressure time-history curves at different points match well with each other, which indicates that the blast shock wave load acting on the beam surface can be approximated as a uniform distribution load. At the same time, the positive pressure region time of the shock wave is about 80~105 ms. In addition, with the increase in charge, the overpressure and impulse of blast loading acting on beam members increase significantly.

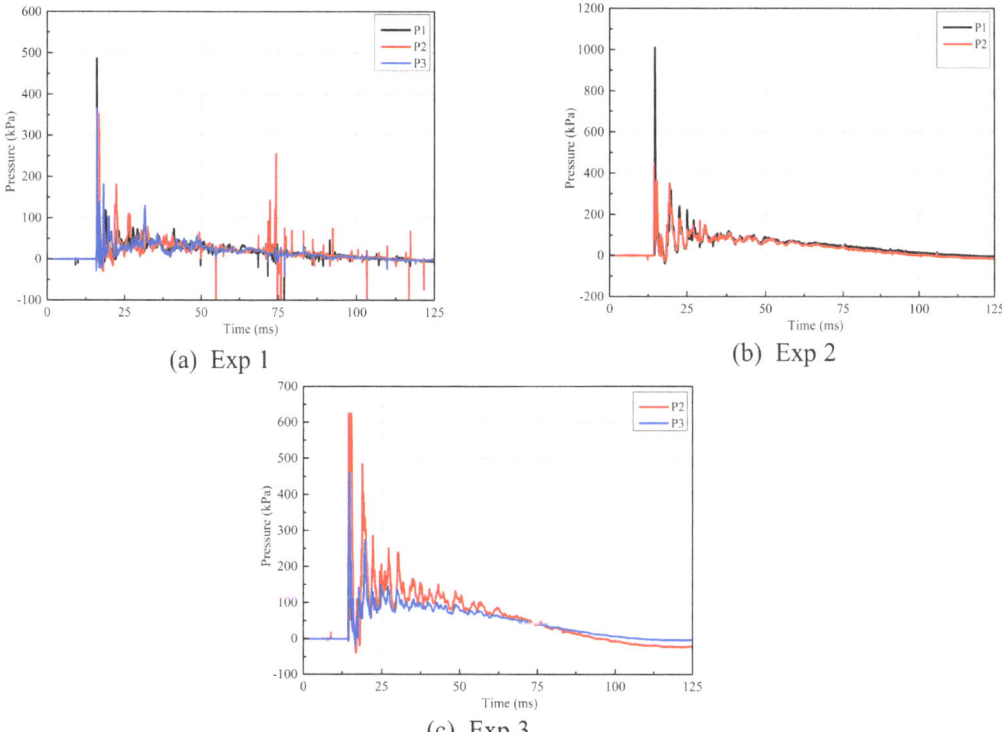

Figure 3. Time-history plots of the pressure for three experiments: (a) Exp 1, (b) Exp 2, and (c) Exp 3.

Figure 5 shows the damage morphology of the beam. As for Exp 1, the whole specimen is in elastic deformation except for a small number of transverse cracks in the middle span of the back of the specimen. With the increase in charge, such as in Exp 2 and Exp 3, crack initiation positions gradually develop from the middle span to the two ends, and the number, width, and length of cracks increase significantly. The deformation degree of the specimen was gradually intensified, and obvious residual deformation appeared.

The damage mode of the overall bending of members was obtained, which was basically consistent with the other results [4,5,9].

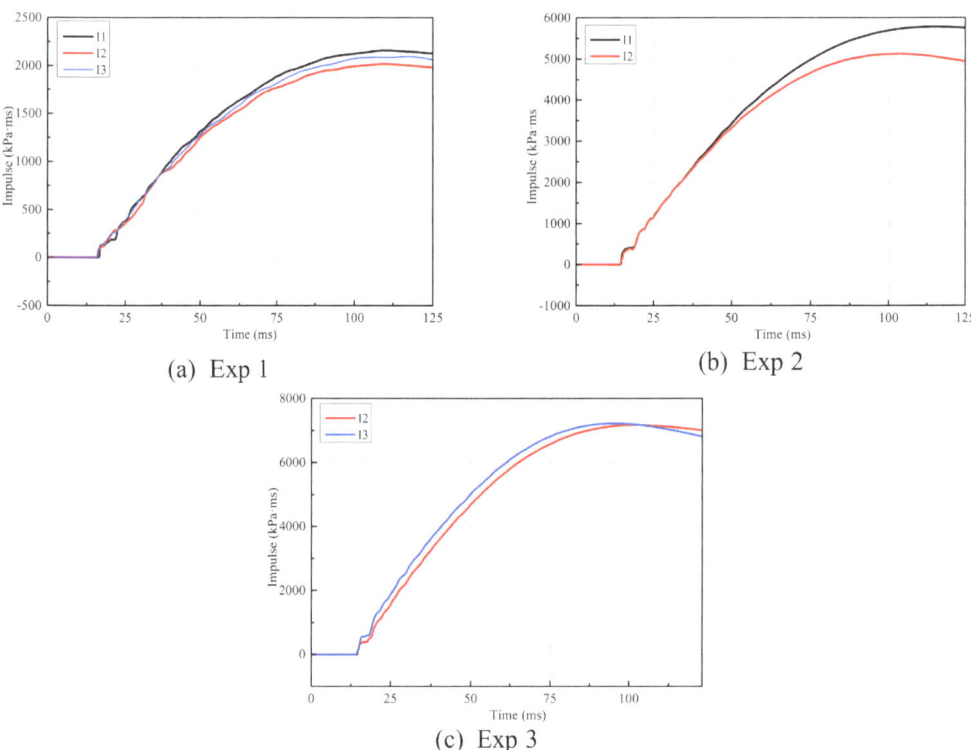

Figure 4. Time-history plots of the impulse for three experiments: (**a**) Exp 1, (**b**) Exp 2, and (**c**) Exp 3.

Figure 5. Failure morphology of various beam specimens.

Figure 6 shows the measurement results of the D1~D3 displacement time-history of the displacement sensor located at the measurement point on the back of the beam. As for Exp 1, the maximum deflection of D1, D2, and D3 of the three displacement meters of the specimen was 4.08 mm, 6.10 mm, and 4.30 mm, respectively. And the residual deflection was 1.02 mm, 1.61 mm, and 0.59 mm, respectively. As for Exp 2, the maximum deflection of the three displacement meters D1, D2, and D3 of the specimen was 9.91 mm, 13.60 mm, and 10.93 mm, respectively. And the residual deflection was 3.30 mm, 2.37 mm, and 2.30 mm, respectively. As for Exp 3, the maximum deflection of D1, D2, and D3 of the three displacement meters of the specimen was 16.28 mm, 24.94 mm, and 16.07 mm, respectively. And the residual deflection was 2.66 mm, 7.82 mm, and 5.31 mm, respectively. According to measurable damage and displacement of beams, it can be found that the beam presents an overall bending deformation mode subjected the planar blast wave at a magnitude of 100 milliseconds.

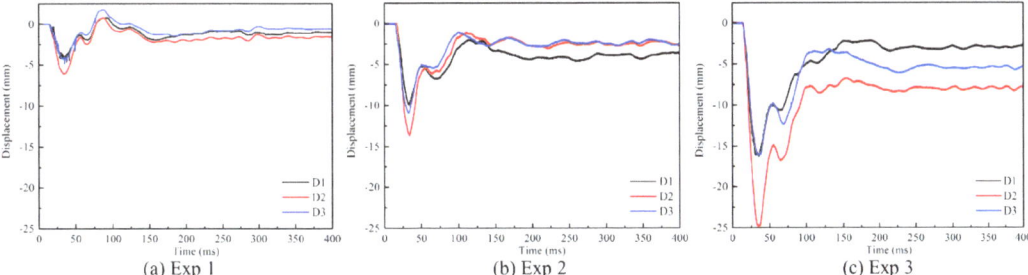

Figure 6. Time-history plots of the maximum deflection of three specimens: (a) Exp 1, (b) Exp 2, and (c) Exp 3.

4. Numerical Modeling

Since the beam presents an overall bending failure subjected the planar blast wave at a magnitude of 100 milliseconds, the single-degree-of-freedom model of the equivalent bending system can be used for simplified calculation, as shown in Figure 7, and its motion equation is as follows:

$$K_{LM} m \ddot{x}(t) + C \dot{x}(t) + R(x) = F(t) \tag{1}$$

where m is the system mass, x is the mid-span vertical displacement of the beam member, C is the damping coefficient, $R(x)$ is the resistance function of the bending deformation mode of the beam member, $F(t)$ is the equivalent external force of the uniform load, and K_{LM} is the load mass transformation coefficient.

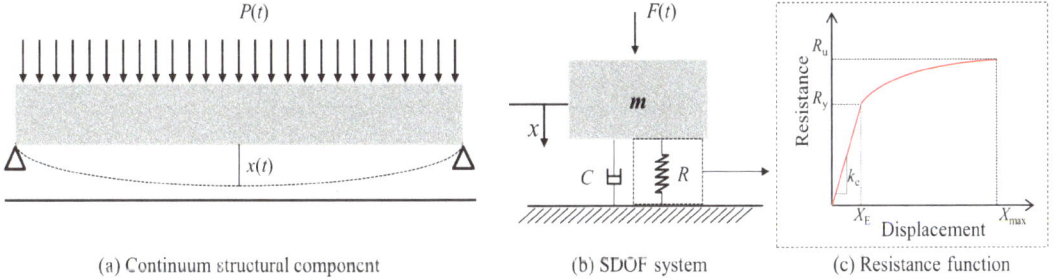

Figure 7. Constructing the SDOF system for the loaded beam.

Selecting the yield resistance R_y, mid-span elastic limit displacement X_E, and mass m to be the basic physical quantities, the dimensionless form of the single-degree-of-freedom motion equation can be written as follows:

$$\ddot{x}^* + 2\xi \dot{x}^* + R^*(x^*) = F^*(t^*) \tag{2}$$

In this formula, the dimensionless quantity $x^* = x/X_E$, $R^* = R(x)/R_y$, $F^* = F(t)/R_y$, $t^* = tw$, elastic stiffness $k_e = R_y/X_E$, frequency $w = \sqrt{k_e/mK_{LM}}$, damping rate satisfies $C = 2\xi k_e/w$. ξ is the flexural damping ratio and the value is 0.1. m is the mass of the beam member. The values of the load–mass equivalence factor K_{LM} are 0.78 in the elastic stage of the beam and 0.66 in the elastic–plastic stages of the beam, respectively.

The resistance of the beam is the internal force tending to restore the element to its unloaded static position. There are several functional forms of resistance, and for the bilinear resistance function, the following relation is satisfied:

$$R(x) = \begin{cases} k_e x & x \leq X_E \\ R_y + k_p(x - X_E) & X_E \leq x \leq X_{\max} \end{cases} \quad (3)$$

where k_e is the effective stiffness of the elastic stage of the beam member, and k_p is the effective stiffness of the plastic stage of the beam member.

According to the dimensionless motion equation, under the condition of a uniform distribution load, the main controlling factor of the displacement response is the resistance model of the member. There are several resistance models frequently used, including the ideal elastic–plastic model, rigid–plastic model, elastic–plastic-hardening model, and elastic–plastic-softening model. In order to obtain the resistance model of high-strength beams under a uniform load, the improved separated finite-element model of reinforced concrete proposed by our research group [25] was applied, using it on the above five kinds of beams. And then, we analyzed the displacement response using evaluation software of the damage grade of the strong shock wave structure [27]. Next, we carried out analysis of the key physical parameters such as yield resistance, elastic limit displacement, and stiffness from the beam resistance model to establish an idealized bilinear resistance model.

Figure 8 shows the improved separated finite-element model of the RC beam with a uniform load. The model consists of two types of grids: one is the grid containing the steel skeleton lines, which is defined as the reinforced concrete grid; the other type is the grid that does not contain the reinforcement skeleton line, which is defined as plain concrete grid. The classical Holmquist–Johnson–Cook (HJC) model is adopted for a plain concrete mesh, and the reinforced concrete composite constitutive model based on modified mixture theory is adopted for a reinforced concrete mesh.

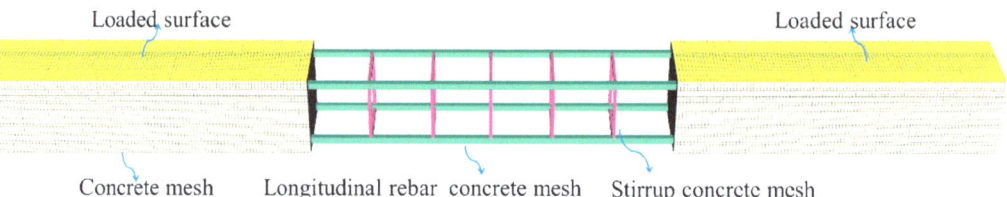

Figure 8. Improved discrete numerical model for RC beams.

The plain concrete grid adopts the HJC constitutive model, and its stress–strain relationship is as follows:

$$\sigma_m = f_m \left[A_m(1-D) + B_m(P/f_m)^{N_m} \right] \left[1 + C_m \ln(\dot{\varepsilon}/\dot{\varepsilon}_0) \right] \quad (4)$$

where the subscript m represents the physical quantity related to the concrete matrix; σ_m represents the stress of concrete; f_m represents the concrete compressive strength; A_m represents the cohesion parameter; B_m represents the pressure hardening coefficient; N_m represents the pressure hardening index; C_m represents the strain rate parameter; and $\dot{\varepsilon}_0$ represents the reference strain rate.

The reinforced concrete grid adopts the composite material constitutive model, and its stress–strain relationship is as follows:

$$\sigma = V_m \sigma_m + V_f \sigma_f^{eq} \quad (5)$$

where σ_m is established by the nondestructive concrete matrix constitutive Equation (3) which does not consider the pressure sensitivity. And σ_f^{eq} is the equivalent stress of the steel bar considering the interface bond slip effect, and its expression is as follows:

$$\sigma_f^{eq} = \left(f_y^{eq} + H_f^{eq}\varepsilon_p\right)\left[1 + C_f\ln(\dot{\varepsilon}_p/\dot{\varepsilon}_0)\right] \quad (6)$$

where f_y^{eq} represents the actual yield strength of steel bars embedded in concrete, which satisfies $f_y^{eq} = f_y\left[0.93 - 2(f_{mr}/f_y)^{1.5}/\rho\right]$; ρ represents the effective reinforcement ratio; f_{mr} represents the tensile fracture stress of concrete; H_f^{eq} represents the equivalent plastic modulus, which satisfies $H_f^{eq} = \int_{\delta_y}^{\delta_c}(\sigma_f - f_y)/(\varepsilon_p + \delta/l)d\delta/(\delta_c - \delta_y)$; δ represents the interface slip displacement of reinforced concrete; δ_y and δ_c represent the displacements at different stages of interface slip; l represents the length of the interfacial bonding zone; ε_p represents the plastic strain; and C_f represents the strain ratio coefficient.

Taking B3-C40-HRB400-D20 as an example, the material parameters in numerical simulation are briefly given. The mesh size was 10 mm. The concrete mesh adopted the HJC concrete constitutive model, and the parameters were as follows: the initial density was 2.4 g/cm³, the shear modulus was 14.4 GPa, Poisson's ratio was 0.20, f_m was 50.16 MPa, A_m was 0.28, B_m was 1.84, N_m was 0.84, and C_m was 0.007.

The parameters of the longitudinal reinforcement were as follows: the tensile yield strength was 466.7 MPa; the ultimate strength was 601.3 MPa; the elastic modulus was 200 GPa; and the plastic hardening modulus was 1.12 GPa. And the parameters of the stirrup were as follows: the tensile yield strength was 483.5 MPa; the ultimate strength was 582.4 MPa; the elastic modulus was 200 GPa; and the plastic hardening modulus was 0.94 GPa.

For reinforced concrete mesh, in the numerical model considering interface bond slip, the length of the interface bond zone was 300 mm, and the equivalent material parameters of longitudinal reinforcement and stirrup were calculated as follows: The longitudinal bar's equivalent strength f_y^{eq}, equivalent elastic modulus E_f^{eq}, and equivalent hardening modulus H_f^{eq}H were 425.0 MPa, 162.2 GPa, and 788.8 MPa, respectively, and the stirrup's equivalent strength f_y^{eq}, equivalent elastic modulus E_f^{eq}, and equivalent hardening modulus H_f^{eq}H were 368.1 MPa, 150.2 GPa, and 656.5 MPa, respectively. Then, according to the concrete's parameters, combined with Formula (4), the composite material model parameters in the reinforced concrete grid were obtained.

The influence of finite-element mesh size on numerical simulation results was studied. Taking the B3-C40-HRB400-D20 beam as an example, the pressure time history measured by Exp 3 was used as the pressure load on the surface of the beam. Three mesh sizes, 20 mm, 10 mm, and 5 mm, were selected and the corresponding grid scales were 12,500, 100,000, and 800,000, respectively. Figure 9 shows the time history of the mid-span displacement of the RC beam with different element sizes. The numerical simulation results of the three mesh sizes could be summarized as follows. The numerical simulation results are related to the mesh size; for example, the simulation results of 20 mm and 10 mm are slightly different. As the mesh size decreases gradually, the difference in the time history of the mid-span displacement curve decreases and converges gradually (10 mm and 5 mm). Further refinement of the mesh size can improve the calculation accuracy, but the calculation cost is doubled, so the mesh size of 10 mm is used to balance the computational accuracy and cost.

Figure 10a shows the bending moment–angle curve results of five kinds of beams, respectively. According to the conversion relationship between bending moment and resistance, the resistance–displacement curve of the beam is further given, as shown in Figure 10b. By increasing the strength of concrete, the strength of rebar, and the diameter of rebar, the bending mechanical properties of the member are significantly improved. Under a uniform load, the beam presents two stages of elastic and plastic hardening. Further, the yield resistance R_y and elastic limit displacement X_E of five beam samples were extracted, and the dimensionless resistance–displacement curves were obtained, as shown in Figure 11. It is found that the resistance model has a good normalization property and can be further simplified into a bilinear model. Table 3 shows the yield resistance R_y, stiffness k_e in the elastic stage, stiffness k_p in the plastic stage, and the ratio of the two-stage stiffness of the five kinds of beams. By comparison, it is found that the stiffness ratio of k_p/k_e in the plastic stage and elastic stage of the five beam samples is small, and its average value is 0.017. A more conservative ideal elastoplastic resistance model, $k_p = 0$, can be used in the design and blast-resistant analysis of high-strength RC beams. The key physical parameters in the bilinear resistance model, such as yield resistance, elastic stiffness, and plastic stiffness, can quantify the resistance model of beam members and, as important input parameters of the SDOF model, effectively analyze the dynamic response of RC beams under a uniform load of support.

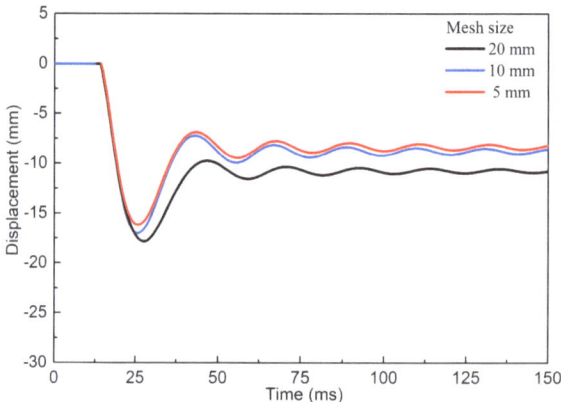

Figure 9. Mid-span displacement–time histories of RC beams with different mesh sizes.

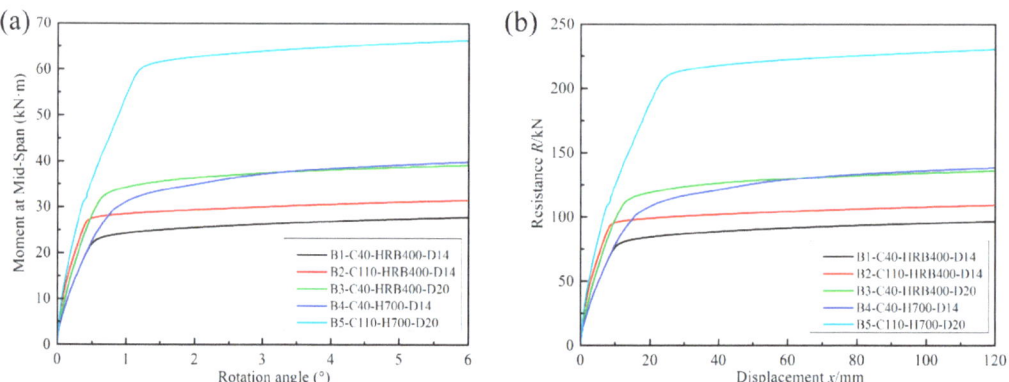

Figure 10. Results from uniform pressure loaded FE models: (**a**) moment–angle; and (**b**) resistance–displacement.

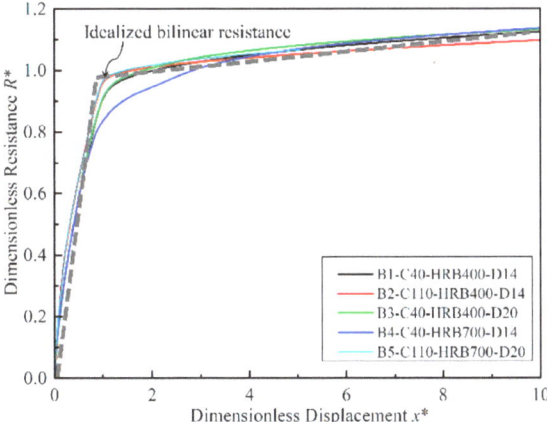

Figure 11. Results of nondimensional resistance–displacement curves.

Table 3. Bilinear resistance model.

Beam Sample	Yield Strength R_y (kN)	Elastic Stiffness k_e (kN/m)	Plastic Stiffness k_p (kN/m)	k_p/k_e
B1-C40-HRB400-D14	77.3	8.63×10^3	123.5	0.015
B2-C110-HRB400-D14	88.9	11.33×10^3	154.7	0.014
B3-C40-HRB400-D20	109.8	9.79×10^3	203.1	0.021
B4-C40-HRB700-D14	112.2	8.58×10^3	167.1	0.019
B5-C110-HRB700-D20	197.5	13.23×10^3	242.1	0.018

5. Numerical Model Validation

The accuracy of the SDOF model and the finite-element model is verified by the measured results of the displacement time history of the midpoint D1 of the beam member. In the process of numerical calculation, the pressure time history curve measured by experiment is taken as the input of explosion load. In the SDOF analysis, the Newmark–Beta method is used to solve the differential equation of the single-degree-of-freedom model, and the time step is 0.1% of the natural vibration period. The finite-element model integrated into the evaluation software of the damage grade of the strong shock wave structure [27,28] is used to analyze the dynamic response of an RC beam subjected to blast loading, and the data of the mid-span displacement are outputted.

Figure 12 shows the comparison of the SDOF calculation results with the finite-element calculation results and experimental results. For the working condition of Exp 1, the maximum displacement of D1 calculated by the SDOF is 6.13 mm, and the maximum displacement of D1 calculated by the finite-element model is 6.25 mm. The deviation between the SDOF and finite-element model is 0.5% and 2.4% compared with the experimental results. For the working condition of Exp 2, the maximum displacement of D1 calculated by the SDOF model is 14.6 mm, and that by the finite-element model is 14.9 mm. Compared with the experimental results, the deviations of D1 and the SDOF are 7.3% and 9.5%, respectively. For the working condition of Exp 3, the maximum displacement of D1 calculated by the SDOF model is 23.7 mm, and that by the finite-element model is 27.6 mm. Compared with the experimental results, the deviations between the two are −4.9% and 10.8%. These results verified the simulation accuracy of the SDOF model and finite-element model by the comparison of the results of three working conditions. Additionally, in the plastic rebound stage, the simulation results of the SDOF model and finite-element model differ greatly from the experimental results, leading to the discrepancy between the simulated residual displacement and the experimental results. The numerical model used can simulate the dynamic response of beams under long-duration blast loading. However, there are still some differences between the numerical model and experiments, as follows: (1) the numerical model lacks an elaborate method to simulate the interaction process between the reinforcement layer and the concrete; (2) the propagation, refraction, and reflection of the stress wave in structures lead to a complex state of stress due to the non-uniform medium characteristics of reinforced concrete, which is difficult to be reasonably described by mathematical means; (3) the load-blast-enhanced strategy to simulate the shock wave loading did not take into account the diffraction effect of the explosion wave and wave-structure interaction, and it also ignored the thermal effect of high-temperature gas acting on the structure.

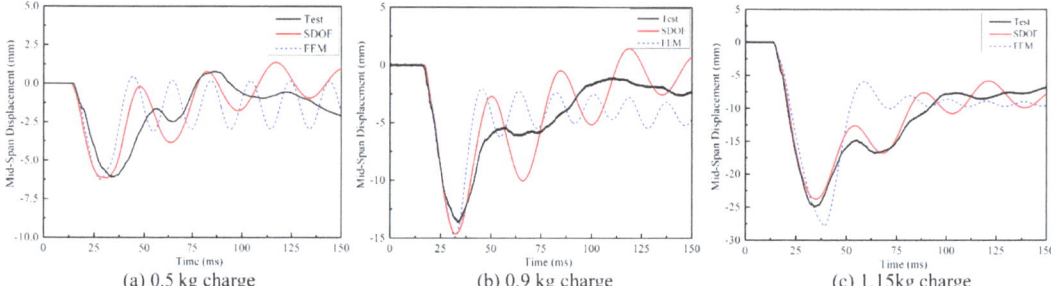

Figure 12. Comparison of mid-span displacement of beam specimens.

In the P-I curve analysis in the following section, the maximum displacement at the mid-span position is used as a physical quantity to evaluate the dynamic response degree of the component.

6. Pressure–Impulse Curve

6.1. Reference Beam P-I Curve

The pressure–impulse curve is an important analysis method for dynamic response analysis and the blast-resistant design of components. At the same time, the displacement ductility ratio μ (the ratio of the maximum displacement x max to the elastic limit displacement X_E during deformation) can quantify the degree of deformation or damage of the component. Therefore, P-I curves based on the ductility ratio can provide an effective means for the blast-resistant design and dynamic response analysis of high-strength beams.

The displacement analysis of reference beams numbered B1-C40-HRB400-D14 was carried out using the SDOF model verified by experiments, and P-I curves related to ductility ratio were drawn. According to the classification of explosion load, the pressure–impulse space can be divided into three load regions: impulse load, quasi-static load, and dynamic load. The validity of P-I curves based on the SDOF model in three load zones is evaluated by combining the experimental results of shock wave explosion and finite-element simulation. Figure 13 shows the P-I curves corresponding to the ductility ratio of the reference beam when $\mu = 1, 2$, and 4, and the comparison with the experiment. The displacement ductility ratios of the components corresponding to the three explosion experiments are 0.62, 1.34, and 2.46, respectively, which correspond to the numbers close to the red mark symbol. The experimental explosion load belongs to the dynamic load, and the corresponding ductility ratio points of the three experimental load spaces all fall within the corresponding interval, which verifies the validity of the P-I curve in the dynamic load interval. Furthermore, 44 finite-element calculation examples are carried out in the quasi-static load and pulse load regions combined with finite-element model. Figure 14 shows the comparison between the ductility ratio results obtained based on the finite-element model and the ductility ratio contour lines obtained based on the SDOF model. The finite-element simulation results basically fall within the corresponding ductility ratio interval, which further verifies the validity of the curve obtained based on the SDOF model.

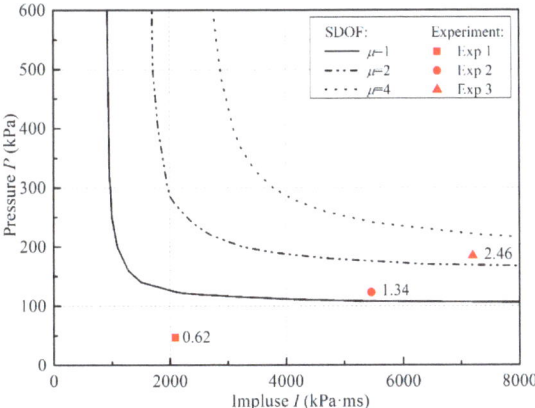

Figure 13. *P-I* diagram for the reference beam with experimental results.

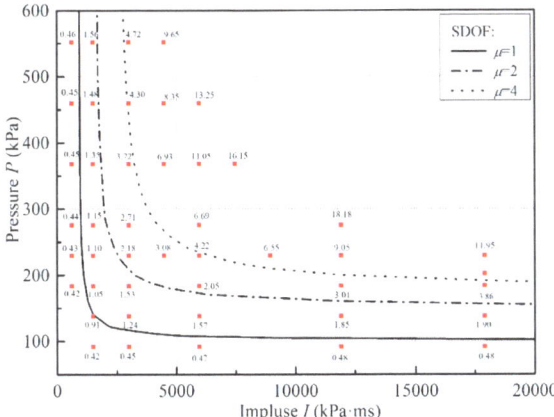

Figure 14. *P-I* diagram for the reference beam based on the finite-element method.

6.2. P-I Curve of the High-Strength Beam

The SDOF model was used to analyze the dynamic response of four kinds of high-strength beam samples and then draw P-I curves. Figure 15 shows the P-I curve corresponding to the ductility ratio $\mu = 1$ of a high-strength beam. It is found that compared with the reference beam, the pressure asymptote and impulse asymptote of the high-strength beam can be improved by increasing the strength of concrete, the strength of reinforcement, and the diameter of reinforcement. Further, the normalized P-I curve is obtained by the yield resistance R_y and frequency w. Figure 16 shows the dimensionless pressure–impulse curves (P^*-I^*) corresponding to the ductility ratio $\mu = 1, 4,$ and 10, where the dimensionless pressure $P^* = PA/R_y$ and dimensionless impulse $I^* = IAw/R_y$, and A is the stress area of the member. As can be seen from the figure, although the yield resistance and stiffness of beams with different strengths vary greatly (see Table 3 for details), the P^*-I^* based on the ductility ratio has a normalized property; that is, through the dimensionless pressure–impulse curve of the reference beam, combined with the yield resistance and circular frequency parameters of the high-strength beam sample, the results show that the pressure–impulse curve of a high-strength beam under a plane shock wave load can be obtained quickly and accurately, which is convenient for the explosion response analysis and blast-resistant design of beam members. According to the damage criterion for ductility ratios exceeding 10, given by the UFC 3-340-02 design code [29], when the peak overpressure of blast loading is 202 kPa, an ordinary RC beam such as B1 is close to yield failure, while a high-strength RC beam, such as B5, begins to yield failure when the peak overpressure value is 500 kPa. These results are basically consistent with the other results [9].

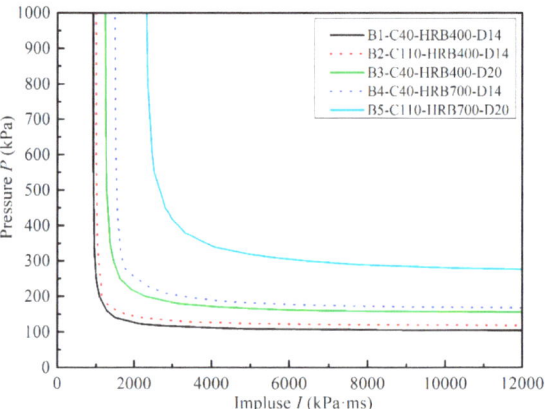

Figure 15. *P-I* diagram for high-strength beams with a ductility ratio of 1.

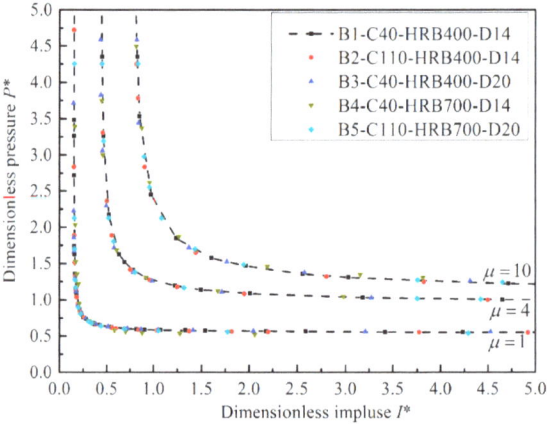

Figure 16. P^*-I^* diagram for five types of beams with ductility ratios of 1, 4, and 10.

In order to further verify the normalized properties of dimensionless pressure–impulse curves, the finite-element model was used to analyze the ductility of three kinds of high-strength beams, including B3-C40-HRB400-D20, B4-C40-HRB700-D14, and B5-C110-HRB700-D204, under a uniform explosive load, and the results were compared with the dimensionless pressure–impulse diagram. Figure 17 shows the comparison between the P^*-I^* diagrams and 144 finite-element simulation results corresponding to ductility ratios μ = 1, 2, and 4. The following trends are shown in Figure 17: (1) Most of the finite-element simulation results fall within the ductility ratio interval of the corresponding P^*-I^* graph. (2) In the three load areas of pulse load, quasi-static load, and dynamic load, the ductility ratio of the beam under the same (P^*, I^*) load is consistent. For example, the pulse load (P^*, I^*) = (5, 0.75), and the ductility ratios of the three beams are 7.70, 7.94, and 7.71, respectively. The dynamic load (P^*, I^*) = (5, 0.75), and the ductility ratios of the three beams are

6.61, 6.51, and 6.68, respectively. The quasi-static loads $(P^*, I^*) = (0.75, 5)$, and the ductility ratios of the three beams are 1.24, 1.19, and 1.22, respectively. (3) In some areas, there are certain differences in beam ductility ratios; for example, when $(P^*, I^*) = (1.1, 5)$, the ductility ratios of the three beam samples are 8.79, 7.84, and 9.47, respectively. (4) In the quasi-static load area, the finite-element results are more conservative than the SDOF results. For example, if the load point $(P^*, I^*) = (1, 5)$, the ductility ratios of the B3-C40-HRB400-D20 and B5-C110-HRB700-D204 beams are 4.42 and 4.44, which are higher than the isoline of the SDOF ductility ratio.

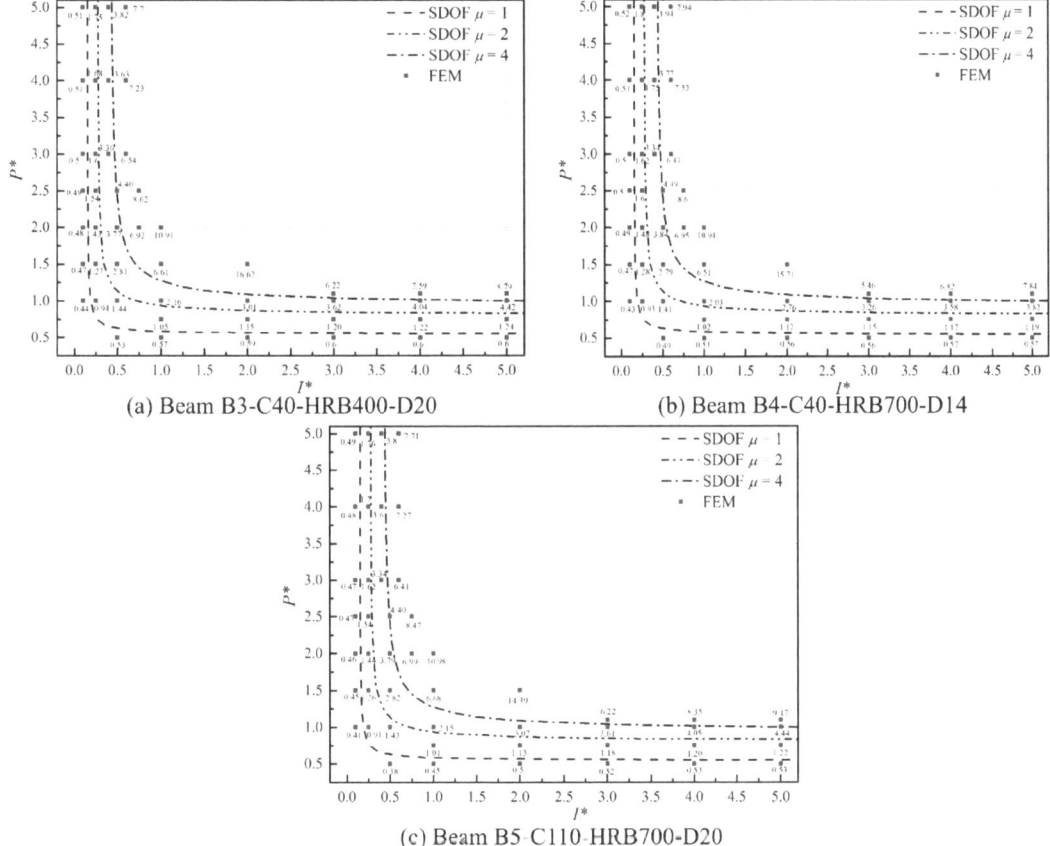

Figure 17. P^*-I^* diagram with finite-element results.

By correlating the P-I diagram with industry design standards, Figure 17 shows the P-I damage contours for the damage levels for the high-strength RC beams defined in UFC 3-340-02 [29] and ASCE 2010 [30], which can be used to analyze the far-field explosion in specified explosion scenarios such as long-range large equivalent chemical explosions and industrial gas explosions. For example, for high-strength RC beams (B5-C110-HRB700-D20 sample), a critical overpressure peak of 500 kPa is obtained, agreeing with experimental results [9].

P-I diagrams for high-strength beams have been partially verified via some experimental results (see Figure 18). However, they also have certain limitations. First of all, the experimental verification is limited to three test points, which mainly belong to the dynamic load region in the figure. For the pulse load and quasi-static load region, the calibrated finite-element model is used to study the effectiveness of the two load regions. Then, the second limitation is that the pressure–impulse diagram is valid only for far-field explosions, assuming that the explosion pressure is evenly distributed on the surface of the member and that the pressure time history curve is reasonably approximated as a triangular pulse. This figure is not suitable for analyzing the near-field explosion effect on high-strength beams. The third limitation is derived from the deformation mode of the beam, which means the SDOF model used to generate the pressure–impulse diagram assumes the deformation mode of the beam. For pulsed loads, this assumed deformation shape may not be accurate because of the risk of shear failure near the beam end support.

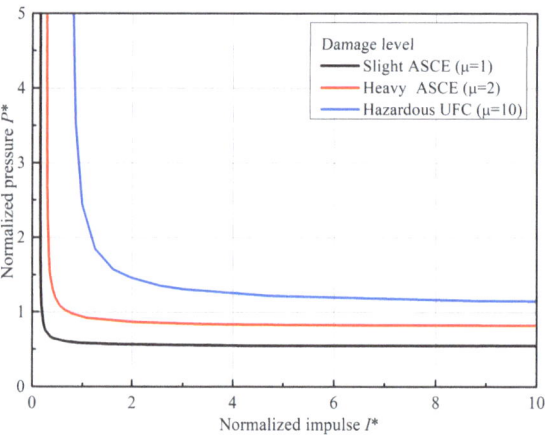

Figure 18. P^*-I^* diagram for design of high-strength RC beams.

7. Conclusions

An experimentally validated P-I diagram for reinforced concrete beams for far-field blast effects was developed and proposed. The ductility contours for P-I diagrams were developed using an experimentally validated SDOF model that used, as input, an idealized bilinear resistance function for reinforced concrete beams subjected to uniform load. P-I diagrams can quickly predict the critical overpressure peak corresponding to the hazardous level of reinforced concrete beams in specified explosion scenarios such as large equivalent chemical explosions and industrial gas explosions.

(1) The overall bending of reinforced concrete beams is obtained via explosive chamber experiments with a long-duration pulse of 80–105 ms.

(2) A single-degree-of-freedom model with an idealized bilinear resistance function is proposed based on the overall bending mode. The resistance function is developed using a novel approach combined with a three-dimensional improved steel–concrete separated finite-element model.

(3) Through the normalized P-I analysis method with the ductility criterion given by the UFC 3-340-02 design code, the peak overpressure 202 kPa, corresponding to the hazardous state of the ordinary beams, is obtained, while the peak overpressure thresholds for high-strength beams reaches 500 kPa, significantly higher than that of ordinary beams.

(4) The analytical method does not accurately predict the shear-dominated deformation and fracture behavior of each member. Meanwhile, the validation of damage overpressure thresholds for high-strength beams is insufficient.

(5) In the next work, long-duration blast loading experiments of high-strength concrete beams will be carried out to explore the damage mode, especially for the end-supported shear failure. Meanwhile, the pulse of the shock wave will be broadened

from 100 ms to the order of seconds, supporting the validation of *P-I* diagrams in the quasi-static region.

Author Contributions: Conceptualization, H.Z.; Software, F.Z., C.H. and N.L.; Writing—original draft, H.Z.; Writing—review & editing, H.Z., F.Z. and X.F.; Visualization, J.Z.; Supervision, X.F., S.W. and J.Z. All authors have read and agreed to the published version of the manuscript.

Funding: This research was supported by the National Natural Science Foundation of China (grant number 11971070).

Data Availability Statement: Data are contained within the article.

Acknowledgments: The authors would like to extend their sincere appreciation to the National Natural Science Foundation of China for support.

Conflicts of Interest: Author Jian Zhang was employed by the company North Hua'an Industrial Group Co., Ltd. The remaining authors declare that the research was conducted in the absence of any commercial or financial relationships that could be construed as a potential conflict of interest.

References

1. Clubley, S.K. Long duration blast loading of cylindrical shell structures with variable fill level. *Thin-Walled Struct.* **2014**, *85*, 234–249. [CrossRef]
2. Denny, J.W.; Clubley, S.K. Long-duration blast loading & response of steel column sections at different angles of incidence. *Eng. Struct.* **2019**, *178*, 331–342. [CrossRef]
3. Cannon, L.; Clubey, S.K. Structural response of simple partially-clad steel frames to long-duration blast loading. *Structures* **2021**, *32*, 1260–1270. [CrossRef]
4. Li, Y.; Algassem, O.; Aoude, H. Response of high-strength reinforced concrete beams under shock-tube induced blast loading. *Constr. Build. Mater.* **2018**, *189*, 420–437. [CrossRef]
5. Aoude, H.; Dagenais, F.P.; Burrell, R.P.; Saatcioglu, M. Behavior of ultra-high performance fiber reinforced concrete columns under blast loading. *Int. J. Impact Eng.* **2015**, *80*, 185–202. [CrossRef]
6. Mahmoud, A.; Ehab, E.S. Seismic Performance of GFRP-Reinforced Concrete Rectangular Columns. *J. Compos. Constr.* **2016**, *20*, 04015074. [CrossRef]
7. Yang, S.; Liu, Z.; Wang, S.; Zhong, W.; Zhang, R.; Yao, X. Dynamic response and failure analysis for urban bridges under far-field blast loads. *Eng. Struct.* **2023**, *285*, 116043. [CrossRef]
8. Wang, Y.; Chen, Q.; Zhao, Z.; Qiang, H.; Yang, K.; Wang, X. Design and performance evaluation framework for seismically isolated reinforcement concrete columns subjected to blast loads. *Structures* **2022**, *45*, 2239–2252. [CrossRef]
9. Liao, Z.; Tang, D.; Li, Z.; Xue, Y.; Shao, L. Study on explosion resistance performance experiment and damage assessment model of high-strength reinforcement concrete beams. *Int. J. Impact Eng.* **2019**, *133*, 103362. [CrossRef]
10. Zhou, X.W.; Wang, X.; Zhang, R.; Zhang, G.; Xiong, R. An Experimental Study of the Effects of Different Reinforcement Ratios on the Impact Resistance Behaviors of Reinforced Concrete Beams. *J. Texting Eval.* **2020**, *48*, 2162–2184. [CrossRef]
11. Magnusson, J.; Hallgren, M.; Ansell, A. Air-blast-loaded, high-strength concrete beams, Part I: Experimental investigation. *Mag. Concr. Res.* **2010**, *62*, 127–136. [CrossRef]
12. Guo, X.; Ding, C.X.; Wei, P.J.; Yang, R.S. Theoretical analysis of the interaction between blasting stress wave and linear interface crack under high in-situ stress in deep rock mass. *Int. J. Rock Mech. Min. Sci.* **2024**, *176*, 105723. [CrossRef]
13. Zhang, C.W. The active rotary inertia driver system for flutter vibration control of bridges and various promising applications. *Sci. China Technol. Sci.* **2023**, *66*, 390–405. [CrossRef]
14. Huang, H.; Yao, Y.F.; Liang, C.J.; Ye, Y.X. Experimental study on cyclic performance of steel-hollow core partially encased composite spliced frame beam. *Soil Dyn. Earthq. Eng.* **2022**, *163*, 107499. [CrossRef]
15. Wang, Y.D.; Yang, S.; Han, M.; Yang, X. Experimental Study of Section Enlargement with Reinforced Concrete to Increase Shear Capacity for Damaged Reinforced Concrete Beams. *Appl. Mech. Mater.* **2013**, *256*, 1148–1153. [CrossRef]
16. Li, C.J.; Hassan, A. Influence of UHPFRC jacketing on the static, blast and post-blast behaviour of doubly-reinforced concrete beams. *Int. J. Impact Eng.* **2023**, *179*, 104656. [CrossRef]
17. Krauthammer, T.; Bazeos, N.; Holmquist, T. Modified SDOF Analysis of RC Box-Type Structures. *J. Struct. Eng.-ASCE* **1986**, *112*, 726–744. [CrossRef]
18. Krauthammer, T. Shallow-Buried RC Box-Type Structures. *J. Struct. Eng.* **1984**, *110*, 3. [CrossRef]
19. Carta, G.; Stochino, F. Theoretical models to predict the flexural failure of reinforced concrete beams under blast loads. *Eng. Struct.* **2013**, *49*, 306–315. [CrossRef]
20. Al-Thairy, H. A modified single degree of freedom method for the analysis of building steel columns subjected to explosion induced blast load. *Int. J. Impact Eng.* **2016**, *94*, 120–133. [CrossRef]
21. Bruhl, J.C.; Varma, A.H. Analysis and Design of One-Way Steel-Plate Composite Walls for Far-Field Blast Effects. *J. Struct. Eng.* **2021**, *147*, 04020288. [CrossRef]

22. Xu, J.; Wu, C.; Li, Z.X. Analysis of direct shear failure mode for RC slabs under external explosive loading. *Int. J. Impact Eng.* **2014**, *69*, 136–148. [CrossRef]
23. Nassr, A.A.; Razaqpur, A.G.; Tait, M.J.; Campidelli, M.; Foo, S. Strength and stability of steel beam columns under blast load. *Int. J. Impact Eng.* **2013**, *55*, 34–48. [CrossRef]
24. Peng, Q.; Zhou, D.Y.; Wu, H.; Ma, L.L.; Fang, Q. Experimental and numerical studies on dynamic behaviors of RC slabs under long-duration near-planar explosion loadings. *Int. J. Impact Eng.* **2022**, *160*, 104085. [CrossRef]
25. Zeng, F.; Feng, X.W.; Huang, C.; Xu, Q.; Xiao, G.Z.; Tain, R. Modified discrete numerical model for reinforced concrete structures. *Explos. Shock Waves* **2022**, *42*, 065102. [CrossRef]
26. *GB 55002-2021*; Building Design Code. China Construction Industry Press: Beijing, China, 2021.
27. Zeng, F.; Liu, N. Evaluation software of damage grade of strong shock wave structure JUST-PANDA and its application. In Proceedings of the National Conference on Explosive Mechanics, Tongxiang, China, 3–5 November 2018.
28. Zeng, F.; Xiao, G.Z.; Feng, X.W.; Huang, C.; Tian, R. A damage assessment method for masonry structures subjected to long duration blast loading. *Explos. Shock Waves* **2021**, *41*, 105101. [CrossRef]
29. *UFC 3-34002-2008*; Structures to Resist the Effects of Accidental Explosions. US Department of Defense: Washington, DC, USA, 2008.
30. Task Committee on BlastResistant Design. *Design of Blast Resistant Buildings for Petrochemical Facilities*, 2nd ed.; ASCE: Reston, VA, USA, 2010.

Disclaimer/Publisher's Note: The statements, opinions and data contained in all publications are solely those of the individual author(s) and contributor(s) and not of MDPI and/or the editor(s). MDPI and/or the editor(s) disclaim responsibility for any injury to people or property resulting from any ideas, methods, instructions or products referred to in the content.

Article

Parametric Study of the Deep Excavation Performance of Underground Pumping Station Based on Numerical Method

Jiani Zhang [1,2], Zhenkun Yang [1,3,4,*] and Rafig Azzam [4]

1. Department of Civil Engineering, University of Shanghai for Science and Technology, Shanghai 200093, China; 86cjf911@usst.edu.cn
2. Shanghai Institute of Quality Inspection and Technical Research, Shanghai 200214, China
3. Department of Civil Engineering and Architecture, Linyi University, Linyi 276000, China
4. Chair of Engineering Geology and Hydrology, RWTH-Aachen University, 52064 Aachen, Germany; azzam@lih.rwth-aachen.de
* Correspondence: yangzhenkun@lyu.edu.cn

Abstract: Environmental responses to deep excavations are combined results of numerous factors. The effects of some factors are relatively straightforward and can be considered carefully during the design. On the other hand, more features impact excavation-induced performances indirectly, making their influences difficult to be clearly understood. Unfortunately, the complexity and non-repeatability of practical projects make it impossible to thoroughly understand these issues through realistic deep excavation projects. Therefore, parametric studies based on repeatable laboratory and numerical tests are desired to investigate these issues further. This work examines the influence of several key features on excavation-induced displacements through a series of 3D numerical tests. The study includes the choice of soil constitutive models, the modeling method of the soil–wall interface, and the influences of various key soil parameters. The comparison shows that the MCC model can yield a displacement field similar to the HSS model, while its soil movement is greatly improved compared to the MC model. Both the soil–wall interface properties and soil parameters impact the excavation-induced displacement to a large extent. In addition, the influence mechanisms of these parameters are analyzed, and practical suggestions are given. The findings of this paper are expected to provide practical references to the design and construction of future deep excavation projects.

Keywords: deep excavation; pipe galleries; deformation; elastic foundation; analytical solution

1. Introduction

The urbanization process has led to a depletion of internal land resources, prompting the placement of numerous municipal facilities, such as water supply pumping stations and substations, underground. Consequently, a significant number of deep excavation projects have been undertaken. The design, construction, and performance of deep excavations are closely interrelated, and it is not easy to carry out an excavation both efficiently and safely. From a design perspective, many factors (e.g., ground conditions, retaining schemes, construction methods, and construction costs) should be considered [1,2]. The existing design methods, which are generally based on observations of past case studies, are no longer capable of generating reliable predictions for new cases with increasingly complex construction conditions. Therefore, improved methods for predicting excavation-induced displacements should be developed to provide guidelines for designing the retaining systems.

Several approaches are generally used to conduct deformation analyses of deep excavations: simplified theoretical analyses (e.g., linear- and elastic-based close form approach, beam-spring approach, and limit equilibrium method), empirical/semi-empirical methods [3–7], laboratory tests [8–12], and numerical approaches [13–15]. Simplified theoretical methods are generally used to provide some basic understanding of the performance of deep excavations during the design, but they have many limitations because they are oversimplified [16]. Empirical and semi-empirical approaches are used to extrapolate the performance of deep excavations from the analyses of previously reported field data [6]. Since empirical approaches are based on numerous field measurements of different regions, they can generally provide results consistent with regional experiences [4]. Therefore, a large number of well-documented field measurements from different areas are required to improve the applicability of empirical/semi-empirical methods. Laboratory tests generally include centrifuge tests and large-scale model tests, through which the deformation law of deep excavations can be investigated. However, laboratory tests are both oversimplified and relatively prohibitive, making the approach rarely applied in practical engineering [8,10].

Numerical methods are the only available methods that can consider both geotechnical, structural, and constructional aspects of deep excavation problems [13,17]. Therefore, these approaches have the potential to be an effective tool for deep excavation analyses. With the developments in both hardware and software, numerical approaches are becoming more powerful and less consuming, which has resulted in considerable advances in deformation analyses of deep excavations. However, the complexity of numerical methods makes their results vulnerable to numerous factors, and neglecting some of these factors will reduce the accuracy of the model. On the other hand, it is unrealistic to consider all of these factors in a single model [17,18]. Therefore, it is more practical to study the impact of these factors individually in parametric studies. However, studies focusing on the influence of several key individual factors are missing, making their influence mechanisms unclear. To address these issues, the current work is undertaken.

This work presents several parametric studies to examine the influence of several key features on excavation-induced displacements. To achieve this, a series of numerical tests based on the ABAQUS (2018) software are carried out. Considering that including too many features in a single numerical model is cumbersome for practical application in the design and analysis of deep excavations, a simplified model is generated to investigate the isolated influence of these features. The examined factors include the choice of constitutive soil models, the modeling method of the soil–wall interface, and the sensitivity of the calculated results to several key parameters of the soil. The findings of the current work are expected to have practical value in the design and construction of deep excavations.

2. Development of the Idealized Model

As mentioned in the last section, the study in this work is based on an idealized hypothetical deep excavation. In fact, investigations on some general characteristics of deep excavations based on hypothetical projects were not unusual in previous studies. For example, several researchers discussed the influence of different modeling techniques (e.g., different mesh types and element types for the soil and structural components) and structural features such as the operational stiffness of the diaphragm wall, horizontal supports, and vertical piles [15,18]. Based on an idealized excavation project, [19] evaluated the efficiency of isolation walls outside an excavation in modifying the excavation-induced displacement field. In order to have a comparison, a hypothetical deep excavation model of a similar size and construction procedure in the study of [15] is developed in this work. In addition, because the parametric studies in this paper aim to capture the general influence tendencies of several specific features, many aspects irrelevant to these features are simplified significantly. Detailed descriptions and simplifications of the applied model are described subsequently in this section.

2.1. Geometry of the Model

The idealized excavation (40 × 40 m in plane and 12 m in depth) is the simplification of a typical square, three-level excavation. The enclosure structures are diaphragm walls (1 m in thickness and 30 m deep) supported by three levels of floor slabs (0.15 m in thickness) with beams (0.4 m × 0.6 m in section) and a base slab (1 m thick). The horizontal structures are supported by erect column piles with diameters of 0.8 m and lengths of 30 m. The vertical distance between adjacent horizontal structures is 4 m, and the horizontal distance between adjacent beams (adjacent erect column piles) is 8 m. Besides four erect column piles firmly connected with the columns, 25 engineering piles are also included in the quarter-model (as shown in Figure 1). These engineering piles are assumed to be uniformly distributed below the base slab and duplicate other properties from the erect column piles.

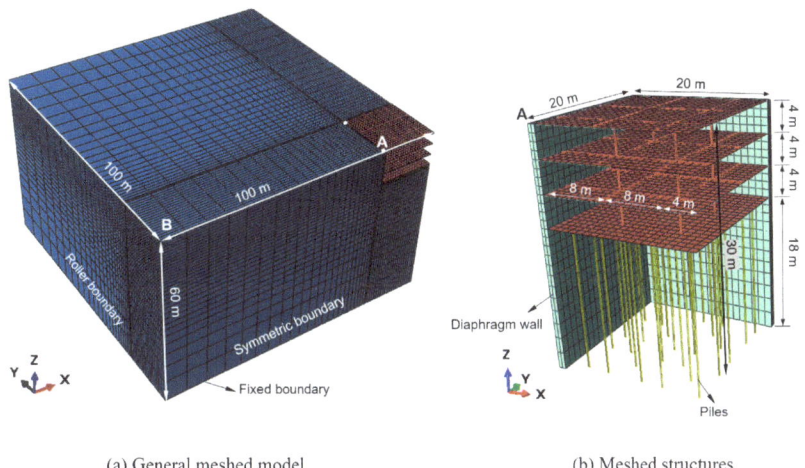

(a) General meshed model (b) Meshed structures

Figure 1. Geometric features and mesh of the model.

The model comprises 50,424 nodes and 45,397 elements, in which the soil mass is modeled with 41,070 linear hexahedral elements of type C3D8I (where the "I" refers to the incompatible modes method), the diaphragm wall is modeled with 2016 linear hexahedral elements of type C3D8R (where the "R" refers to the reduced integration method), the slabs are modeled with 1600 linear quadrilateral elements of type S4R (where the "R" also refers to the reduced integration method), and the beams and piles are modeled with 711 linear line elements of type B31. The bottom boundary of the model is fixed; two of the vertical boundaries are symmetrical, and the other two are rollers. The roller boundary makes sure that the horizontal movements of the model are restrained while the meshes are free in the vertical plane. The piles are assumed to be embedded into the soil without interface properties. The assumption is made according to the conclusion that the impact of the soil–pile interface on excavation performance is minimal [18]. Different from the soil–pile interaction, the soil–wall contact properties influence the excavation behavior more dramatically. Unfortunately, a systematic study on the influence of the soil–wall contact properties is still missing. Therefore, several parametric studies regarding this issue will also be included in the current work.

2.2. Construction Sequence

Without any doubt, construction procedures impact the excavation-induced performance significantly. Consequently, numerical models aiming at replicating the performance of realistic projects should capture the construction procedures in practice as much as possible. However, the studies conducted in this paper are based on a simplified hypothetical project, which does not aim to discuss the influence of different construction procedures or different modeling methods. Therefore, the simulation of the construction process can be simplified significantly. The main construction sequence of the excavation in this article is summarized in Table 1.

Table 1. Modeled construction sequence.

Steps	Description
1	Geostatic
2	Installation of the diaphragm wall, piles, and the beams and floor slab at the ground level;
3	(Exc-1) Excavation to 4 m below ground surface (BGS);
4	Installation of the beams and floor slab at the second level;
5	(Exc-2) Excavation to 8 m BGS;
6	Installation of the beams and floor slab at the third level;
7	(Exc-3) Excavation to 12 m BGS;
8	Installation of the base slab.

2.3. Constitutive Models and Input Parameters

Since a number of input parameters of the soil and the soil–wall interface are variables in the subsequent parametric studies, the current section only presents the input parameters applied in the basic analysis (i.e., denoted as the BA model subsequently), as described in Section 2.1.

The floor slab, beams, and piles in the model are reinforced concrete materials and are assumed to behave linearly and elastically for simplicity. The density of these reinforced concrete components is assumed to be 2500 kg/m^3, the Poisson's ratio is assumed to be 0.2, and the nominal Young's modulus is 30 GPa. To consider the effect of imperfection in the concrete as well as the workmanship, the applied Young's modulus for those reinforced concrete components in the calculations is reduced by 20% of the nominal value.

The diaphragm wall is represented by the cross-anisotropic material introduced by a previous study to consider the joints between different wall panels [19], and the input parameters are described in Table 2.

Table 2. Input parameters of the diaphragm wall.

E_1	E_2	E_2	ν_{12}	ν_{13}	ν_{23}	G_{12}	G_{13}	G_{23}
30 GPa	3 GPa	30 GPa	0	0.2	0	1.5 GPa	12.5 GPa	1.5 GPa

For the convenience of carrying out parametric studies, a single soil layer is applied to the models. The soil adopted in the basic analysis is a typical soil (i.e., silty clay) in Shanghai (specified in Table 3) reported in a substation project [19]. In the basic analysis, the MCC model is applied, and the detailed input parameters are presented in Table 3.

Table 3. Input parameters of the MCC model.

γ, (kN/m^3)	ν	K_0	e_0	Modified Cam-Clay Parameters		
				M	λ	κ
18.6	0.3	0.49	0.877	1.327	0.0704	0.01

The isotropic Coulomb friction model with a shear stress limit is applied to represent the soil–wall interface properties in the basic analysis. Its detailed parameters (i.e., μ = 0.3, τ_{max} = 25 kPa) are decided by referring to a case study in Shanghai reported by Cui [13]. More possible methods to consider the soil–wall interface, as well as the influence of μ and τ_{max}, will be further investigated through several parametric studies in the next section.

3. Parametric Investigations

3.1. Strategy of Analyses

A comparison study of different constitutive soil models (e.g., the MCC model, the MC model, and the HSS model) is first presented in Section 3.2. Additionally, three groups of parametric studies, which discuss the methods of considering soil–wall contact, the impact of the value of μ, and the influence of the value of τ_{max}, respectively, are conducted. The results and analyses of these parametric studies are presented in Section 3.3. Finally, a series of parametric studies discussing the impact of different soil features based on the MCC model are carried out, and the results are illustrated in Section 3.4. To be noted, for models without special notes in this work, the applied input parameters are the same as the basic analysis.

3.2. Comparison of Different Soil Models

The MC model (i.e., the Mohr–Coulomb model), the MCC model (i.e., the Modified Cam-Clay model), and the HSS model (i.e., the Hardening Soil–small model) are three commonly applied soil models in deep excavation analyses. However, straight comparisons of them are lacking from previous studies. Based on the hypothetical excavation project, the performances of the three models are compared in this section. To be noted, the comparison is made based on a hypothetical project, which means there is no field data to calibrate the results of these models. Therefore, the study in this section only aims to find the difference rather than provide an evaluation of different models. Despite the lack of field data, a previous study by Dong [18] has calculated a model sharing the same geometry as the current research, the results of which can be used as references. The input parameters of the MC model are shown in Table 4, and the input parameters of the HSS model are presented in Table 5.

Table 4. Input parameters of the MC model.

γ, (kN/m^3)	E, (MPa)	ν	c', (kPa)	φ' (°)
18.6	44.65	0.3	18.6	32.9

Table 5. Input parameters of the HSS model.

γ, (kN/m^3)	ν_{ur}	c', (kPa)	φ' (°)	E_{50}^{ref} (MPa)	E_{oed}^{ref} (MPa)	E_{oed}^{ref} (MPa)	G_0^{ref} (MPa)	$\gamma_{0.7}$	e_0
18.6	0.2	18.6	32.9	7.003	4.902	21.008	77.02	1×10^{-4}	0.877

The calculated diaphragm wall deflections, ground surface settlements, and ground surface horizontal movements at the middle section are presented and compared in Figure 2. In this figure, the detailed description of the legend is presented in Table 6.

Table 6. Description of curves in Figure 2.

Name	Description
MCC model	the result of the numerical model with a soil model described in Table 3;
HSS model	the result of the numerical model with a soil model described in Table 5;
MC model	the result of the numerical model with a soil model described in Table 4;
Dong's study	the result of a published work reported by Dong [18].

In general, all three models yield displacement patterns similar to Dong's results [18]. The calculated maximum wall deflections of the MCC model, MC model, and HSS model are 13.3 mm, 14.1 mm, and 11.8 mm, respectively. In general, the differences in the wall deflections calculated from different models are insignificant; all of them (i.e., the MCC model, MC model, and the HSS model) seem to be applicable if the wall deflection is the main concern of a deep excavation.

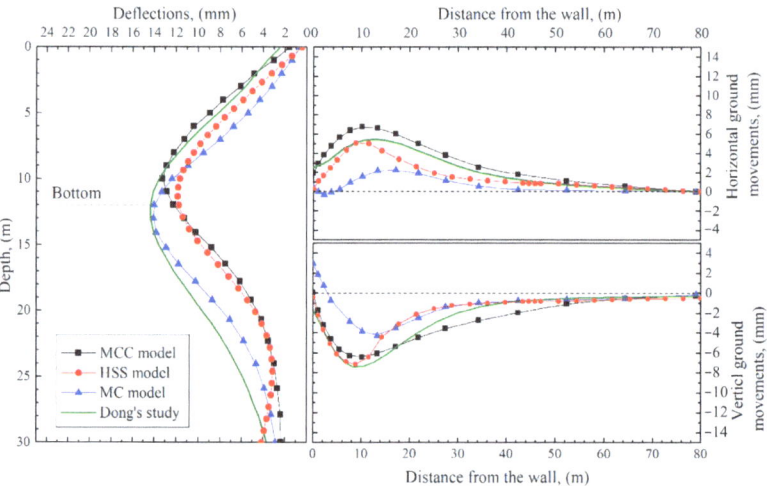

Figure 2. Calculated displacement fields of models with different soil constitutive models.

By further examination, the comparison suggests that the HSS model yields the smallest wall deflection. However, it is not safe to say the reason for the small wall deflections of the HSS model is its consideration of the small strain stiffness of soil. The reason is that the determination of the parameters of the HSS model relies very much on experience correlations and an inverse analysis, which makes its parameters more flexible and favorable. In contrast, methods for determining the MCC parameters are relatively unified, and they all can be obtained from conventional laboratory tests. This advantage makes the MCC model a more appropriate choice for design purposes.

In terms of the ground settlements behind the wall, it is apparent that the MC model underestimates the settlement significantly. This is because the MC model produces unrealistically large upward movements of deep soils [20], which has offset the settlement at the ground surface. The MCC model and the HSS model yield similar maximum ground settlements, and both of them are close to Dong's results [18]. However, considering the larger maximum wall deflection of the MCC model and the close relationship between the maximum wall deflection and the maximum ground settlement, it is safe to say that the MCC model would yield smaller maximum ground surface settlements if the wall deflection were the same as the HSS model. Meanwhile, the ground settlements far from the wall calculated from the MCC model are more evident than the HSS model and Dong's result. This tendency should arise from the MCC model's inability to account for the small strain behavior of the soil. In fact, a similar tendency was also reported from previous studies; for example, Kung [21] concluded that soil models without considering small strain stiffness tend to underestimate surface settlements near the walls while overestimating settlements far from the walls. The horizontal ground movements show the same tendency with the settlements: the MC model underestimates the deformation significantly, and the MCC model and the HSS model yield a similar displacement profile.

Because of the lack of field data, the current study can only provide a preliminary comparison between different soil models. Assuming that Dong's results [18] are reliable, it can be said that both the MCC model (also denoted as the BA model subsequently) and the HSS model yield acceptable displacement fields, while the MC model underestimates the ground movements significantly. Considering that it is more convenient to determine the input parameters of the MCC model, the subsequent parametric studies in this work will be carried out based on the BA model.

3.3. Soil–Wall Interface Properties

3.3.1. Methods to Consider Soil–Wall Interaction

Several methods for considering soil–wall interactions (e.g., tie constraints, embedded approach, and surface-to-surface contact with different tangential behaviors) have been applied in previous studies. However, most of these studies generally assumed the methods used were reliable without detailed descriptions. To improve the understanding of this issue, the first parametric study in this section investigates the difference between different methods in considering the soil–wall contact. The analysis strategy and the corresponding descriptions of different cases are described in Table 7.

Table 7. Strategy of analyses on different methods of soil–wall contact.

Case	Description
Tie	Use Tie constraints to connect the diaphragm wall and the soil
Embedded	The nominal diaphragm wall is embedded in the soil without interface properties
Embedded (modified)	The modified diaphragm wall is embedded in the soil without interface properties
BC (basic analysis)	Surface-to-surface contact with the tangential behavior represented by the basic Coulomb friction model ($\mu = 0.3$).
BA (basic analysis)	Surface-to-surface contact with the tangential behavior represented by the Coulomb friction model with a shear stress limit ($\mu = 0.3$, $\tau_{max} = 25$ kPa).
Frictionless	Surface-to-surface contact with frictionless tangential behavior
Rough	Surface-to-surface contact with rough tangential behavior

Notice that there are two "Embedded" scenarios (i.e., the "Embedded" and the "Embedded (modified)") in Table 7. This is because when applying the "Embedded region" approach, the soil at the location of the diaphragm wall cannot be removed. Therefore, both the weight and stiffness of the soil accumulate in the diaphragm wall's properties during the subsequent simulation processes, which may impact the calculated results. To quantify this impact, the "Embedded (modified)" case, in which the diaphragm wall applies a modified unit weight (i.e., by reducing the unit weight of the soil from the nominal concrete value), is further included in this study.

The calculated results of different models described in Table 7 are presented in Figure 3. According to the figure, the excavation-induced displacement field is sensitive to different modeling methods of soil–wall contact. Typically, the "Frictionless" model yields particularly large displacements from all aspects, indicating the significant impact of the friction at the soil–wall contact. On the other hand, all the models except the "Embedded" case yield the same displacement patterns, while the magnitudes vary with different modeling methods. The discrepancy of the "Embedded" model arises from the great accumulated weight of the diaphragm wall, which causes dramatic settlements. When the weight is modified (i.e., "Embedded (modified)"), the calculated ground displacement profiles become nearly identical with the "Rough" and "Tie" models. At the same time, despite the unrealistic ground movements of the "Embedded" case, the lateral wall deflection is similar to the "Rough" and "Tie" models (only with a difference of around 1 mm). This tendency suggests that the weight of the diaphragm wall has a significant impact on the surrounding soils while influencing the lateral deformations of the retaining structures negligibly.

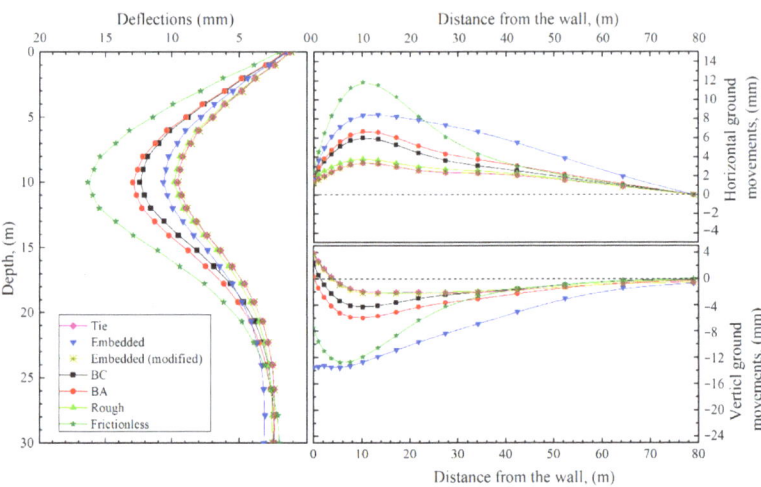

Figure 3. Deformations of models with different soil–wall contact types.

The similar vertical ground movements near the wall (i.e., where the x coordinate is 0) between the "BC" model and the "Tie", "Rough", and "Embedded (modified)" models suggest that the relative sliding between the wall and the soil outside the pit of the "BC" model is minimal. However, the lateral wall deflection of the "BC" scenario is larger than the "Tie", "Rough", and "Embedded (modified)" cases significantly. This discrepancy might be because of different normal behaviors of the contact. In the "Tie", "Rough", and "Embedded (modified)" scenarios, the separation of the surfaces once they are closed is prohibited, while the "Hard contact" applied to represent the normal behaviors in the "BA" and "BC" models allows separations after contact. However, the contact problems are so complicated that more possibilities explaining the differences are likely. Overall, even if the relative sliding between the soil and the wall does not occur, the approaches of Tie constraints, Embedded region, and Rough tangential property should be applied with caution because they generally yield conservative lateral wall deflections.

3.3.2. Influence of the Shear Stress Limit, τ_{max}

The difference between the "BC" and "BA" models, although very limited, is observed in Figure 3, illustrating the influence of the shear stress limit, τ_{max}, set in the "BA" model. In order to make clear this influence, a further parametric study concerning the soil–wall contact was conducted. According to a previous study [14], the value range of ultimate side friction of cast-in-place piles is 15 kPa~100 kPa. In the current parametric study, a domain of 5 kPa~100 kPa for the values of τ_{max} is considered. To be noted, the coefficient of friction, μ, is kept to be 0.3 for all the models in this study. The results of this study, as well as the results of the "Frictionless" and "Rough" models described in Table 7, are compared in Figure 4.

As expected, the results from models with different values of τ_{max} are bounded by the "Frictionless" model and the "Rough" model (in which no shear stress limit is defined), and the displacements (in all aspects) generally increase with a decreasing τ_{max} value. At the same time, Figure 4 shows that the "τ_{max} = 50 kPa", "τ_{max} = 100 kPa", and "BC" (i.e., τ_{max} = ∞) models produce identical results, indicating that the vertical shear stress between the diaphragm wall and the soil in this study is smaller than 50 kPa. Furthermore, the difference between the "τ_{max} = 15 kPa" and "τ_{max} = 50 kPa" (i.e., the possible range for Shanghai soft soils) models is limited (e.g., about 2 mm of the lateral wall deflections, around 3 mm of horizontal ground movements, and approximately 3 mm of ground settlements), which indicates that the excavation-induced displacements are insensitive to τ_{max} values.

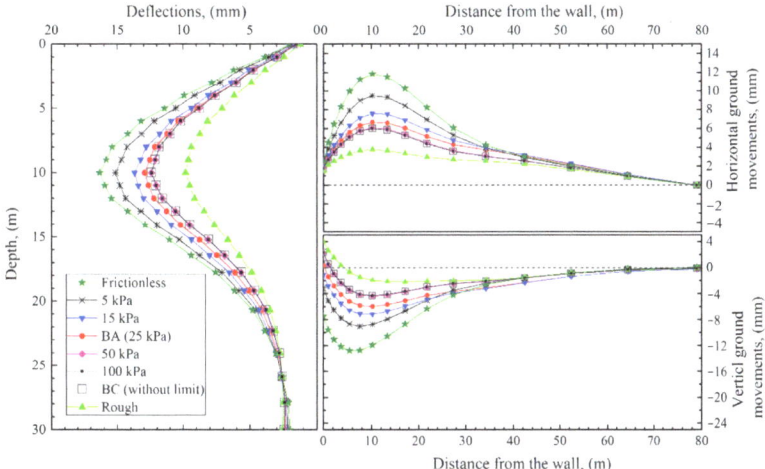

Figure 4. Deformations of models with different shear stress limit.

3.3.3. Influence of the Coefficient of Friction, μ

No specific scope of the μ values of soil–wall contact has been reported previously; practitioners in Shanghai generally apply a scope of 0.25~0.75 by referring to the friction coefficient between the cushion cap bottom and foundation soils regulated by the Technical Code for Building Pile Foundations [22]. This parametric study, fixing the shear stress limit at τ_{max} = 25 kPa, considers a μ scope of 0.005~1.0. In addition, the results from the "Frictionless" and "Rough" cases are also included for comparison. The calculated displacements are presented in Figure 5.

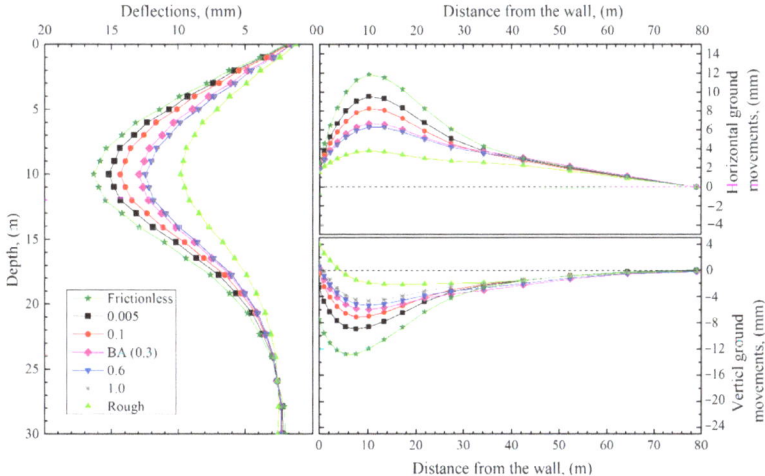

Figure 5. Deformations of models with different coefficient of friction.

In general, the displacements decrease with the increasing μ values, while all the results are bounded by the "Frictionless" and "Rough" models. The identical results between the "μ = 0.6" and "μ = 1.0" models demonstrate that when μ is larger than 0.6, the interface property will be dominated by the shear stress limit. Considering the close results between the "$\mu = 0.3$" and "$\mu = 0.6$" models, the maximum value of μ should be somewhere slightly larger than 0.3. Similar to the shear stress limit, the difference between different models is insignificant, which suggests that calculated displacements are not sensitive to the coefficient ratio of friction, either.

3.3.4. General Evaluation

In general, the parametric studies in this section suggest that the soil–wall interface properties can impact the excavation-induced displacement fields. Typically, the modeling methods to consider the contact affect the calculated results dramatically. Even under situations without relative sliding between the wall and the soils, Tie constraints, Embedded region, and Rough tangential properties are not recommended because they generally produce over-conservative lateral wall deflections. When the soil–wall contact is simulated by surface-to-surface contact with a tangential behavior represented by the Coulomb friction model with a shear stress limit, both the coefficient ratio of friction and the shear stress limit, if not values that are apparently unreliable, influence the displacements negligibly. Therefore, the μ and τ_{max} values can generally be determined according to experiences.

3.4. Soil Parameters

Studies in this work generally involve the MCC model and the HSS model. Numerous studies concerning the input parameters of the HSS model have been reported [23–25]. In contrast, the influence of the input parameters of the MCC model on the excavation-induced displacement has never been investigated. In order to fill this gap in knowledge, as well as to improve the understanding of the application of the MCC model in deep excavation problems, this section presents a series of parametric studies based on the MCC model.

The discussed items include Poisson's ratio, ν, a void ratio, e_0, the coefficient of lateral earth pressure at rest, K_0, a frictional constant, M, an isotropic logarithmic compression index, λ, and the swelling index, κ. To be noted, there will be only one variable, which is the corresponding discussed parameter, in each parametric study, while the possible correlation between the discussed parameter and other unchanged ones (e.g., λ and κ; ν, M, and K_0) is not considered. The parameter bound of each group of the input parameters can generally cover most of the possible values of Shanghai soft soils, while specific values within the bounds applied in the parametric studies are only to describe an increasing or decreasing order but do not necessarily correspond to particular soils.

3.4.1. Influence of the Poisson's Ratio, ν

Figure 6 presents the calculated results of models with different Poisson's ratios, ν, which range from 0.2 to 0.4. According to the figure, the changing Poisson's ratio impacts the excavation performance significantly. Both deformations and the influence weight of ν increase with an increasing value in ν. For example, the maximum wall deflection increased by 19%, 23%, 28%, and 37%, respectively, for each 0.5 increment of the ν value from 0.2 to 0.4. When the value of ν changed from 0.2 to 0.4, the maximum wall deflection, the maximum ground surface settlement, and the maximum horizontal movement of the ground surface increased by 98%, 98%, and 151%, respectively.

The influence of the Poisson's ratio can be explained by the expression of Young's modulus in the MCC model:

$$E = 3K(1 - 2\nu) \quad (1)$$

where K is the bulk modulus, which can be expressed by

$$K = \frac{(1 + e_0)p'}{\kappa} \quad (2)$$

where e_0 is the void ratio, p' is the mean effective stress, and κ is the unloading–reloading line slope. Substituting Equation (1) into Equation (2), we can obtain

$$E = \frac{3(1-2\nu)(1+e_0)p'}{\kappa} \qquad (3)$$

Therefore, when other variables in the expression remain unchanged, a larger Poisson's ratio reflects a weaker stiffness of the soil, and thus larger deformations occur under the excavation-induced unloading.

Unfortunately, despite the great impact of Poisson's ratio on the calculated performance of deep excavations, corresponding values for in situ soils can only be determined empirically or computed through back analyses.

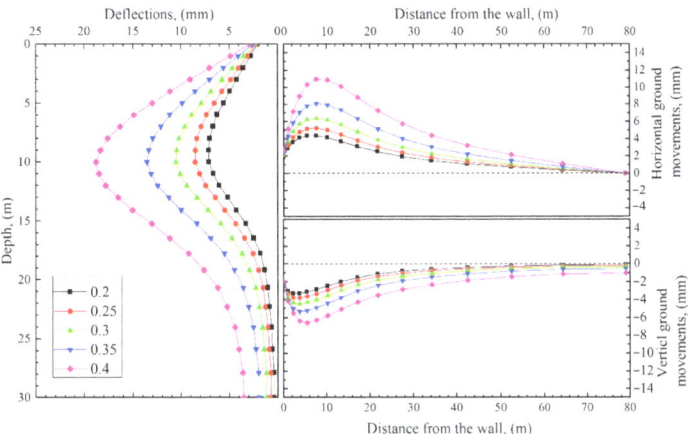

Figure 6. Deformations of models with different ν.

3.4.2. Influence of the Void Ratio, e_0

According to the Technical Code for Building File Foundations [22], the void ratio of Shanghai soft soils is generally between 0.6 and 1.6. To cover this range, five e_0 values (i.e., 0.5, 0.9, 1.2, 1.6, and 2.0) are compared in Figure 7.

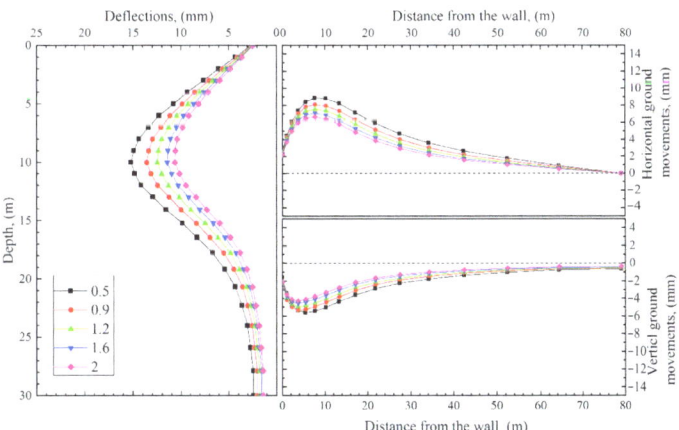

Figure 7. Deformations of models with different e_0.

In general, all aspects of deformations decreased with the increasing void ratio. When the input value of e_0 reduced from 2.0 to 0.5, the maximum wall deflections, the maximum ground surface settlements, and the maximum horizontal ground surface movements increased by 43%, 31%, and 33%, respectively. According to Equation (2), the bulk modulus, K, of soils is proportional to the void ratio, e_0. Therefore, soils with a larger void ratio accordingly have a larger bulk modulus and, thus, a smaller rebound during unloading. In addition, the results also indicate that, compared with the ground surface movements, the lateral wall deflection was more sensitive to the value of e_0.

3.4.3. Influence of the Coefficient of Lateral Earth Pressure at Rest, K_0

The impact of the coefficient of lateral earth pressure at rest on deep performance reflects the influence of the magnitude of the initial horizontal stresses in the ground. The sensitivity of the excavation-induced deformations to different values of K_0 is investigated in Figure 8.

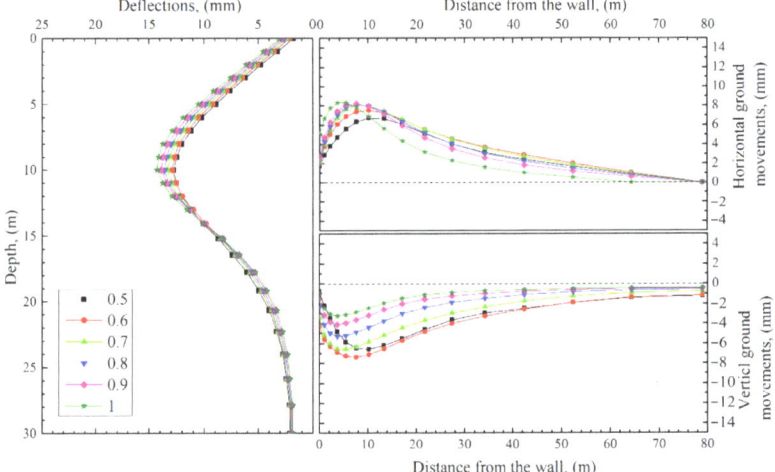

Figure 8. Deformations of models with different K_0.

The figure shows that the differences of the wall deflections, the vertical and the horizontal ground movements between the "$K_0 = 0.5$" model and the "$K_0 = 1$" model were around 12%, 50%, and 23%, respectively. The diaphragm wall deflections increased negligibly during K_0 value's increase from 0.5 to 1. Theoretically, larger values of K_0 mean larger lateral earth pressure on the back of the diaphragm wall and, thus, a larger lateral stress relief when the soil inside the excavation is removed. However, the influence of the K_0 is insignificant. Furthermore, the limited differences of the lateral wall deflections with different K_0 values are generally above the bottom of the excavation, while the lower part of the wall inserted into the soil remains stable.

However, the obtained results might only represent the current idealized excavation because the tendency is not observed universally. In fact, the general influence of the value of K_0 is much more complicated. Several researchers have previously investigated the impact of the coefficient of lateral earth pressure at rest on excavation performances, but no consistent conclusion has been drawn. For example, Potts [26] carried out a series of 2D numerical analyses and found that the wall displacements were very much dependent on the values of K_0, in which a larger value of K_0 led to much larger wall deflections. A series of 3D numerical analyses conducted by Dong [18] indicated that changes in the values of the coefficient of lateral earth pressure at rest had an insignificant influence on diaphragm wall movements. At the same time, Xu [27], through his parametric studies, summarized that the diaphragm wall deflections decrease along with the increasing K_0 values. Although the influence tendency of K_0 in this study is minimal, it is opposite to Xu's results [27]. These contradictory conclusions might arise from various factors (such as different modeling methods, excavation scales, and constitutive models), which need more targeted investigations. Unmistakably, the impact of K_0 on excavation-induced displacements is still ambiguous, and further research is desired.

Unlike the lateral wall deflections, the ground surface movements seem to be less complicated. The lateral movements generally increased, while the vertical movements generally decreased with an increasing value of K_0. Nevertheless, considering that the excavation-induced ground movements are closely related to lateral wall deflections, the influence of K_0 on ground movements should be further investigated.

3.4.4. Influence of the Slope, λ, of the Normal Consolidation Line in the $e - \ln p'$ Plane

The values of λ reported from the several realistic projects in Shanghai range from 0.07 to 0.17, reflecting a general scope of the parameter for Shanghai soft soils [13,14]. This parametric study expands this scope to 0.03~0.4, and the calculated results are compared in Figure 9.

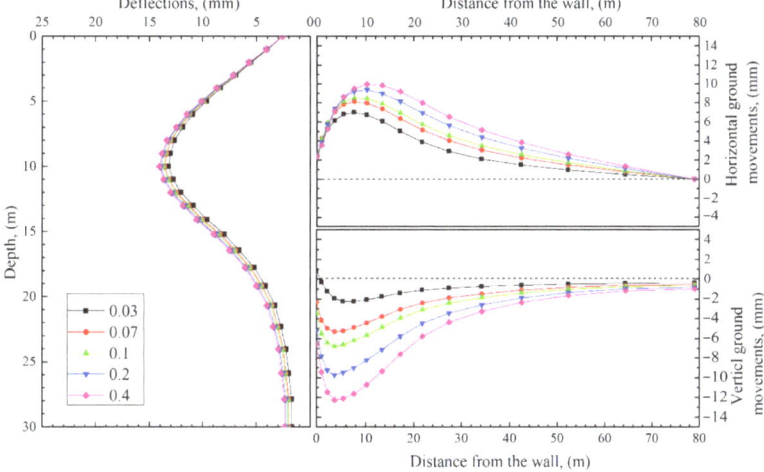

Figure 9. Deformations of models with different λ.

The figure shows that λ values have a very limited impact on the lateral wall deflections (i.e., the maximum wall deflections only increased by 6.5% when the λ value increased from 0.03 to 0.4). This is because λ mainly reflects soil characteristics under loading conditions, but deep excavations are basically unloading processes.

Different from the lateral wall deflections, the ground outside the pit is very sensitive to the variation in the value of λ; i.e., when the λ value differs from 0.03 to 0.4, the maximum settlements and the maximum horizontal movements of the ground surface increased by 445% and 42%, respectively. This tendency indicates the existence of loading conditions outside the pit during the excavation. In fact, the loading conditions arise from the upward movement of the deep soil caused by the excavation process.

3.4.5. Influence of the Slope, κ, of the Unloading–Reloading Line in the $e - \ln p'$ Plane

The influence of the values of κ is described in Figure 10. The parameter is the slope of the unloading–reloading lines in the $e - \ln p'$ plane and mainly reflects the unloading behavior of the soils. During the excavation, the soil in front of the wall was in the unloading condition. Consequently, the wall deflections were directly related to the swelling index.

Moreover, according to Equation (2), the bulk modulus is in inverse proportion to the value of κ. Therefore, as shown in the figure, the maximum wall deflections increased by as much as 115% when the κ value increased from 0.005 to 0.025.

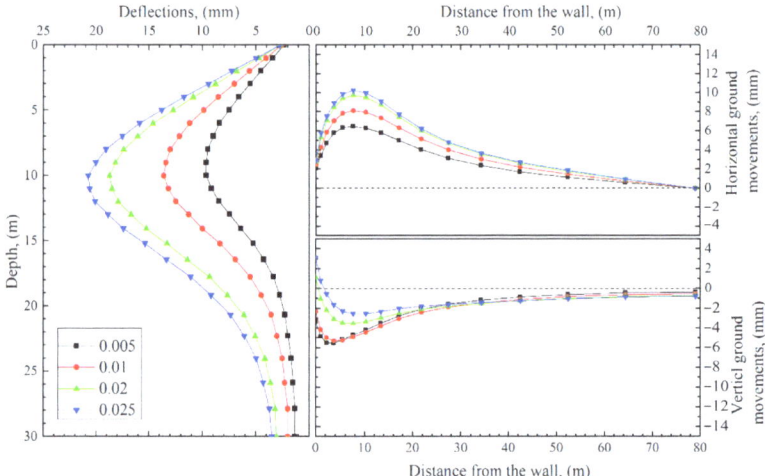

Figure 10. Deformations of models with different κ.

Theoretically, the great increase in the lateral wall deflections brings great volume loss to the ground behind the wall and hence should increase the ground settlements. Yet, as shown in Figure 10, the ground settlements decrease with the increasing value in κ. This indicates that the deep soil is more sensitive to the value of κ. The larger κ causes more significant upward movements of the deep soil, which outweighs the additional volume loss caused by the increased lateral wall deflections, and thus, decreasing settlements are produced.

3.4.6. Influence of the Slope, M, of the Critical State Line in the $p'-q$ Plane

The MCC model does not involve a cohesion parameter, and M is derived from the effective friction angle through Equation (4):

$$M = \frac{6\sin\varphi'}{3-\sin\varphi'} \tag{4}$$

In addition, M is the only parameter reflecting the shear strength of MCC soils. The results of models with different M values are presented in Figure 11. In general, the diaphragm wall deflections decrease with the increase in the M value, and the deformations are very sensitive to M with small values. This tendency is because M affects the shape of the plastic surface, and a small value of M means the soil can enter the plastic zone easily. When the value of M was larger than one, the diaphragm wall was no longer sensitive to the change of M, indicating the soil was in the elastic behavior.

The ground settlements increased slightly when the value of M differed from 0.3 to 0.5. When the value of M was larger than 0.5, however, the settlements decreased with the increasing value in M. Different from the diaphragm wall, a further increase in the value of M when it is larger than one can still reduce the ground settlements, which should arise from the additional upward movement of the deep soil. Meanwhile, the lateral ground movement seems to be insensitive to the change in the value of M.

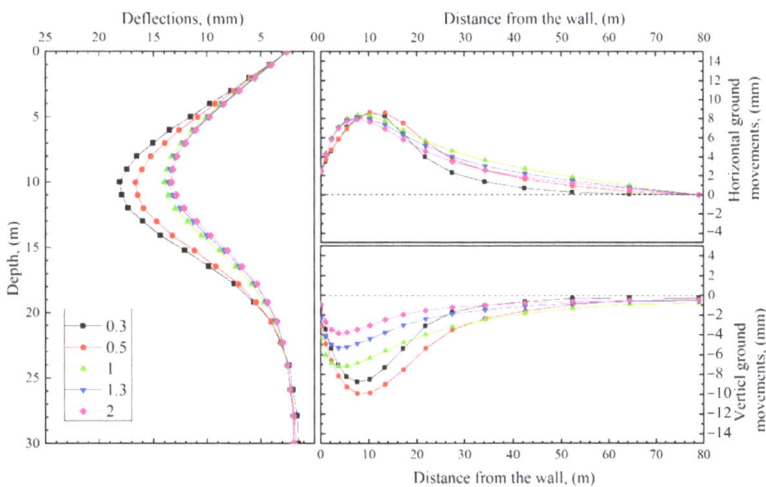

Figure 11. Deformations of models with different M.

4. Conclusions

This work first developed an idealized square basement excavation. Based on the development of the hypothetical project, the procedure of a finite element analysis of deep excavations was introduced. Thereafter, the results of several calculations with different soil models were compared. The comparison with other models proves the reliability of the MCC model in deep excavation problems. Finally, a series of parametric studies based on the idealized excavation was carried out to investigate the influence of several critical aspects (e.g., soil–wall contact properties and several soil properties based on the MCC model). On the basis of the parametric studies, the following conclusions are drawn.

1. The soil–wall interface properties can impact the excavation-induced displacements from all aspects. Typically, the modeling methods to consider the contact affect the calculated results dramatically, in which the model assuming the tangential behavior of the soil–wall contact as frictionless yields the most significant displacements. On the contrary, the "Tie", "Embedded (modified)", and "Rough" models, which generally assume no relative sliding between the wall and where the soil occurs, produce the smallest displacements. At the same time, the results of the two models using the Coulomb friction model to consider the tangential behavior of the soil–wall interface lie somewhere in between. Although it is the same without relative sliding between the wall and the soil, Tie constraints, Embedded region, and Rough tangential property yield much smaller wall deflections than the BC model because the former three generally do not allow separation between the soil and the wall. Therefore, the approaches of "Tie constraints", "Embedded region", and "Rough tangential property" to represent the soil–wall contact are not recommended because they may produce over-conservative lateral wall deflections.

2. When the soil–wall contact is simulated by surface-to-surface contact with a tangential behavior represented by the Coulomb friction model with a shear stress limit, both the coefficient ratio of friction and the shear stress limit, if not values that are apparently unreliable, influence the displacements negligibly.

3. The discussion of the soil parameters of the MCC models shows that different parameters influence the displacements to various degrees. The lateral wall deflections are sensitive to Poisson's ratio, ν, the void ratio, e_0, the frictional constant, M, and the swelling index, κ. The ground settlements behind the wall are sensitive to Poisson's ratio, ν, the coefficient of lateral earth pressure at rest, K_0, the frictional constant, M, the isotropic logarithmic compression index, λ, and the swelling index, κ. The

lateral ground movements are sensitive to Poisson's ratio, ν, the isotropic logarithmic compression index, λ, and the swelling index, κ. Typically, the parametric study on the lateral earth pressure at rest highlights the ambiguity of its impact, and further examinations are needed to make clear the issue.

This study investigated the influencing mechanisms of different factors in deep excavation analyses based on FEM and highlighted the importance of several key parameters. The findings and conclusions drawn in this study provide valuable references to the design and construction of deep excavations.

Author Contributions: Conceptualization, J.Z. and Z.Y.; methodology, J.Z.; software, Z.Y.; formal analysis, R.A.; investigation, R.A.; data curation, Z.Y.; writing—original draft preparation, J.Z. and Z.Y.; writing—review and editing, R.A. All authors have read and agreed to the published version of the manuscript.

Funding: This research was funded by the National Natural Science Foundation of China (Grant 52108328).

Data Availability Statement: The original contributions presented in the study are included in the article, further inquiries can be directed to the corresponding authors.

Conflicts of Interest: The authors declare no conflicts of interest.

References

1. Cui, J.; Jin, Y.; Jing, Y.; Lu, Y. Elastoplastic Solution of Cylindrical Cavity Expansion in Unsaturated Offshore Island Soil Considering Anisotropy. *J. Mar. Sci. Eng.* **2024**, *12*, 308. [CrossRef]
2. Chao, Z.; Shi, D.; Zheng, J. Experimental research on temperature—Dependent dynamic interface interaction between marine coral sand and polymer layer. *Ocean. Eng.* **2024**, *297*, 117100. [CrossRef]
3. Fuentes, R.; Devriendt, M. Ground Movements around Corners of Excavations: Empirical Calculation Method. *J. Geotech. Geoenviron. Eng.* **2010**, *136*, 1414–1424. [CrossRef]
4. Moormann, C. Analysis of wall and ground movements due to deep excavations in soft soil based on a new worldwide database. *Soils Found.* **2004**, *44*, 87–98. [CrossRef]
5. Bolton, M.D.; Lam, S.-Y.; Vardanega, P.J.; Ng, C.W.W.; Ma, X. Ground movements due to deep excavations in Shanghai: Design charts. *Front. Struct. Civ. Eng.* **2014**, *8*, 201–236. [CrossRef]
6. Clough, G.G.; O'Rourke, T.T. Construction Induced Movements of Insitu Walls. In *Specialty Conference on Design and Performance of Earth Retaining Structures 1990*; Geo-Institute: Reston, VA, USA, 1990; pp. 439–470. Available online: https://www.researchgate.net/profile/Wayne-Clough/publication/279565072_Construction_induced_movements_of_in_situ_wall/links/5924b776a6fdcc4443127b81/Construction-induced-movements-of-in-situ-wall.pdf (accessed on 11 April 2024).
7. Ou, C.-Y.; Hsieh, P.-G.; Chiou, D.-C. Characteristics of ground surface settlement during excavation. *Can. Geotech. J.* **1993**, *30*, 758–767. [CrossRef]
8. Wei, H.; Wang, H.; Akira, H.; Yang, J. Experimental Study on Bearing Capacity of Doubled Steel Tubular Piles. In *Foundation Analysis and Design*; American Society of Civil Engineers: Reston, VA, USA, 2006; pp. 242–248. [CrossRef]
9. Trupp, T.; Marulanda, C.; Hashash, Y.; Liu, L.; Ghaboussi, J. Novel Technologies for Tracking Construction Progress of Deep Excavations. In *Geotechnical Engineering for Transportation Projects*; American Society of Civil Engineers: Reston, VA, USA, 2004; pp. 2254–2262. [CrossRef]
10. Wang, H.-L.; Peng, F.-L.; Tan, Y. Site Monitoring and Development of Real-Time Monitoring Program for New Pneumatic Caisson Construction. In *Geo-Frontiers 2011: Advances in Geotechnical Engineering*; American Society of Civil Engineers: Reston, VA, USA, 2011; pp. 182–191. [CrossRef]
11. Pearson, J.E.; Hannen, W.R.; Soderberg, E. Development of Fatigue Monitoring System for a Hydraulic Excavator. *Pract. Period. Struct. Des. Constr.* **2004**, *9*, 221–226. [CrossRef]
12. Xie, X.Y.; Ning, Z.W.; Liu, X.R.; Liu, F.Z. Centrifuge Model Study of Impact on Existing Undercrossing Induced by Deep Excavation. In *Deep and Underground Excavations*; American Society of Civil Engineers: Reston, VA, USA, 2010; pp. 132–143. [CrossRef]
13. Cui, J.; Yang, Z.; Azzam, R. Field measurement and numerical study on the effects of under-excavation and over-excavation on ultra-deep foundation pit in coastal area. *J. Mar. Sci. Eng.* **2023**, *11*, 219. [CrossRef]
14. Yang, Z.; Chen, Y.; Azzam, R.; Yan, C. Performance of a top-down excavation in Shanghai: Case study and numerical exploration. *Eur. J. Environ. Civ. Eng.* **2021**, *26*, 7932–7957. [CrossRef]
15. Dong, Y.; Burd, H.; Houlsby, G. Finite element parametric study of the performance of a deep excavation. *Soils Found.* **2018**, *58*, 729–743. [CrossRef]

16. Xiang, B.; Liu, Y.; Cui, J.; Yang, Z. Analytical Solution for the Deformation of Pipe Galleries Adjacent to Deep Excavation. *Buildings* **2024**, *14*, 1103. [CrossRef]
17. Yang, Z.; Fuentes Gutierrez, R.; Azzam, R. *Deformation Analysis of Deep Excavations in Shanghai Soft Soils*; Lehrstuhl für Ingenieurgeologie und Hydrogeologie: Aachen, Germany, 2022.
18. Dong, Y. Advanced Finite Element Analysis of Deep Excavation Case Histories. Ph.D. Thesis, University of Oxford, Oxford, UK, 2014.
19. Yang, Z.; Chen, Y.; Yan, C.; Azzam, R. Numerical Evaluation of Isolation Walls in Modifying Excavation-Induced Displacement Field. *Arab. J. Sci. Eng.* **2022**, *48*, 12693–12708. [CrossRef]
20. Brinkgreve, R.B.J. Selection of soil models and parameters for geotechnical engineering application. In *Soil Constitutive Models: Evaluation, Selection, and Calibration*; American Society of Civil Engineers: Reston, VA, USA, 2005; pp. 69–98.
21. Kung, G.T.-C.; Ou, C.-Y.; Juang, C.H. Modeling small-strain behavior of Taipei clays for finite element analysis of braced excavations. *Comput. Geotech.* **2009**, *36*, 304–319. [CrossRef]
22. *JGJ 94-2008*; Technical Code for Building Pile Foundations. Ministry of Construction: Beijing, China, 2008.
23. Goh, A.T.; Xuan, F.; Zhang, W. Reliability Assessment of Diaphragm Wall Deflections in Soft Clays. In *Foundation Engineering in the Face of Uncertainty*; American Society of Civil Engineers: Reston, VA, USA, 2013; pp. 487–496. [CrossRef]
24. Franza, A.; Ritter, S.; Dejong, M.J. Continuum solutions for tunnel—Building interaction and a modified framework for deformation prediction. *Géotechnique* **2020**, *70*, 108–122. [CrossRef]
25. Hashash, Y.M.A.; Dashti, S.; Musgrove, M.; Gillis, K.; Walker, M.; Ellison, K.; Basarah, Y.I. Influence of Tall Buildings on Seismic Response of Shallow Underground Structures. *J. Geotech. Geoenviron. Eng.* **2018**, *144*, 04018097. [CrossRef]
26. Potts, D.M.; Fourie, A.B. The behaviour of a propped retaining wall: Results of a numerical experiment. *Géotechnique* **1984**, *34*, 383–404. [CrossRef]
27. Xu, Z.H. Deformation Behavior of Deep Excavations Supported by Permanent Structures in Shanghai Soft Deposit. Ph.D. Thesis, Shanghai Jiao Tong University, Shanghai, China, 2007.

Disclaimer/Publisher's Note: The statements, opinions and data contained in all publications are solely those of the individual author(s) and contributor(s) and not of MDPI and/or the editor(s). MDPI and/or the editor(s) disclaim responsibility for any injury to people or property resulting from any ideas, methods, instructions or products referred to in the content.

Article

Analytical Solution for the Deformation of Pipe Galleries Adjacent to Deep Excavation

Binhui Xiang [1,2], Ying Liu [1,*], Jifei Cui [3] and Zhenkun Yang [4,5]

1. Department of Civil Engineering, Nanchang Institute of Technology, Nanchang 330099, China; xiangbin@nit.edu.cn
2. Jiangxi Zhengde Engineering Testing Co., Ltd., Nanchang 330072, China
3. Department of Civil Engineering, University of Shanghai for Science and Technology, Shanghai 200093, China; cuijifei@usst.edu.cn
4. Department of Engineering Geology and Hydrogeology, RWTH Aachen University, 50264 Aachen, Germany; yangzhenkun@lyu.edu.cn
5. Department of Civil Engineering, Linyi University, Linyi 276000, China
* Correspondence: 2008994071@nit.edu.cn

Abstract: Deep excavations clearly impact adjacent existing properties and threaten their operational safety. Predicting the deformation of existing infrastructure induced by nearby underground construction is the main concern of urban underground development. This paper presents an analytical calculation method for predicting underground pipe gallery deformations induced by adjacent deep excavations. First, the authors assume the existing pipe gallery to be nonexistent in the soil and propose a solution to calculate the excavation-induced vertical movements of the soil at the position of the existing pipe gallery. Thereafter, the authors simplify the existing pipe gallery as an elastic beam on a Winkler foundation to calculate its deformation. Finally, the method is verified by the good agreement found between the calculated result and the field measurement of the construction of the Shanghai Hongqiao CBD project. The proposed analytical method of this work can provide accurate evaluation results for similar engineering projects.

Keywords: deep excavation; pipe galleries; deformation; elastic foundation; analytical solution

1. Introduction

With the development of urbanization, more and more high-rise buildings and underground structures are being constructed in cities. This process inevitably requires a large number of underground constructions. At the same time, deep excavations near existing infrastructures are unavoidable because of the limited available space in urban areas [1–7]. The presence of adjacent urban underground pipe galleries has become a necessary consideration for the construction of a deep foundation pit. The excavation of a pit can lead to displacements of its surrounding strata, potentially impacting the functionality of the nearby urban underground pipe gallery and disrupting its normal operations. Understanding the interaction mechanism between the displacement of the surrounding strata of a foundation pit and the nearby underground pipe gallery, as well as analyzing the deformation behavior of the pipe gallery during the construction of its adjacent foundation pit, is a pressing challenge and requirement in current research [8–10].

In recent years, emphasis has been placed on the study of responses of existing properties to deep excavations. Several commonly used techniques to investigate deformation behaviors and the corresponding environmental effects of braced excavations are FEM analyses based on numerical tools [11–16], empirical/semiempirical methods based on field measurements [17–22]; or a published database [23–26], analytical solutions [27–32], and model tests [33,34]. In addition, machine learning (ML), artificial intelligence (AI), and artificial neural network (ANN) algorithms are becoming increasingly accurate and reliable in predicting elastic fields of soil around retaining walls under various scenarios of wall movements [35–41]. Of these methods, numerical methods are most widely used to investigate the interaction between new excavations and existing properties because they can consider most of the factors in practice. For example, Huang et al. [42] presented a finite element parametric study to investigate tunnel behavior caused by nearby deep excavation in Shanghai. This study researched the effects of several factors (e.g., the relative position of the tunnel to the foundation pit, the diameter of the tunnel, the dimension of the pit, and several tunnel protection measures) that may affect the tunnel response. Yang et al. [15] analyzed the influence of a top-down excavation on an adjacent elevated road as well as a simultaneously constructed foundation pit based on a verified 3D FE model, in which the responses both of ground and underground properties to the top-down excavation were studied. These previous studies prove the effectiveness of FE methods. However, the establishment of a numerical model always includes many hypothetical parameters that need to be defined, and very limited constitutive models are available for different soils, making numerical simulations inconvenient [32]. Another effective technique to study the influences of deep excavations is laboratory tests [33,34]. For example, Choudhury et al. [17] performed a series of centrifuge models to investigate pile responses to deep excavations in sands with various relative densities, and valuable results were obtained. Laboratory tests have many advantages, e.g., the variables are controllable, and the results are relatively reliable. Nevertheless, equipment for these tests is so prohibitive and laboratories are so limited that only very few projects can have access to model tests.

Analytical solutions can provide quick and relatively accurate predictions if the calculation conditions are appropriately simplified [30,43–46]. In addition, analytical methods are clear and simple, making them available to most researchers and engineers. Moreover, once an analytical solution is developed and verified, it can effectively predict the performance of similar projects. At present, a widely applied analytical method is the two-step method. The method calculates the displacement of the greenfield soil or the vertical load induced by the excavation at the desired position and then applies the obtained displacement or load to the target property to determine its responses. The effectiveness of the method has been verified by various researchers. A typical example is as follows: based on the traditional two-step method, Zhang et al. (2016) [43] developed and verified a new analytical method for predicting tunnel responses caused by upside excavation. In addition, this verified method also considered the role of dewatering in the interaction between the excavation and the tunnel.

Previous studies mostly focused on the deformation of nearby buildings, underground pipelines, and tunnels caused by deep excavations. However, studies on the excavation-induced deformation of comprehensive pipe galleries are missing. In fact, pipe galleries are extremely vulnerable to the movements of the surrounding soil. In addition, resembling blood vessels in the human body, pipe galleries play crucial roles in urban functions. Therefore, it is necessary to make clear the potential impact of an underground project on its adjacent underground pipe galleries before construction to ensure the normal life of urban residents. Once the interaction mechanism between excavation-induced ground movements and the displacements of underground pipe galleries is understood, proper construction measures can be proposed. This work, based on the traditional two-stage method, develops a new method to calculate the displacements of pipe galleries caused by adjacent deep excavations. The establishment of the new method can be described as follows: (1) based on the control equation of the elastic plane strain problem, the displacement distribution of the soil outside the wall is calculated using the separation of variables method; (2) the developed two-dimensional solution is then extended to obtain a spatial distribution expression of the displacement of the soil behind the diaphragm wall; (3) the deformation of the pipe galleries under certain soil displacements is calculated using a simplified interaction model between the pipe gallery and soil. Finally, the method is checked by comparing the calculated results to the field measurements of a typical deep excavation project in Shanghai. Based on this verified method, several influencing factors are further analyzed to provide valuable references for practical engineering.

2. Basic Solution to Elastic Plane Strain Problems

The theoretical analysis method in this article has four assumptions: (1) soil is assumed to be elastic without considering the pore water pressure; (2) deep excavation problems are generally simplified as plane strain problems; (3) soil is saturated; and (4) pipe galleries are assumed as Winkler subgrade moduli.

2.1. Mechanical Model for Elastic Plane Strain Problems

When the body forces are not considered, the equilibrium equation for elastic plane strain problems can be described as

$$\left.\begin{array}{l}\frac{\partial \sigma_x}{\partial x} + \frac{\partial \tau_{zx}}{\partial z} = 0 \\ \frac{\partial \sigma_z}{\partial z} + \frac{\partial \tau_{xz}}{\partial x} = 0\end{array}\right\} \qquad (1)$$

where σ_x and σ_z are the normal stresses along the x and z directions, respectively, and τ_{zx} and τ_{xz} are the shear stresses along the x and z directions, in which, according to the Shearing Stress Theorem, $\tau_{zx} = \tau_{xz}$.

The geometric equation for elastic plane strain problems is

$$\left.\begin{array}{l}\varepsilon_x = \frac{\partial u}{\partial x} \\ \varepsilon_z = \frac{\partial w}{\partial z} \\ \gamma_{xz} = \frac{\partial u}{\partial z} + \frac{\partial w}{\partial x}\end{array}\right\} \qquad (2)$$

where u and w are the displacements along the x and z directions, respectively; ε_x and ε_z are the normal strains along the x and z directions, respectively; and γ_{xz} is the shear strain in the x-z direction.

The physical equation with Lame constants is

$$\left.\begin{array}{l}\sigma_x = (\lambda + 2G)\varepsilon_x + \lambda \varepsilon_z \\ \sigma_z = (\lambda + 2G)\varepsilon_z + \lambda \varepsilon_x \\ \tau_{xz} = G\gamma_{xz}\end{array}\right\} \qquad (3)$$

where $\lambda = \frac{E\nu}{(1+\nu)(1-2\nu)}$, $G = \frac{E}{2(1+\nu)}$.

Substituting Equations (2) and (3) into Equation (1) yields the basic equation for plane strain problems as

$$\left.\begin{array}{l}(\lambda + 2G)\frac{\partial^2 u}{\partial x^2} + G\frac{\partial^2 u}{\partial z^2} + (\lambda + G)\frac{\partial^2 w}{\partial x \partial z} = 0 \\ (\lambda + 2G)\frac{\partial^2 w}{\partial z^2} + G\frac{\partial^2 w}{\partial x^2} + (\lambda + G)\frac{\partial^2 u}{\partial x \partial z} = 0\end{array}\right\} \qquad (4)$$

2.2. Method of Separation of Variables for Plane Strain Problems

According to Equation (2), the volume strain, θ, and rigid body rotation angle, ω, can be expressed as

$$\left.\begin{array}{l}\theta = \frac{\partial u}{\partial x} + \frac{\partial w}{\partial z} \\ \omega = \frac{1}{2}\left(\frac{\partial w}{\partial x} - \frac{\partial u}{\partial z}\right)\end{array}\right\} \qquad (5)$$

Using Equations (4) and (5), we have

$$\nabla^2 \theta = 0 \qquad (6)$$

$$\nabla^2 \omega = 0 \qquad (7)$$

where $\nabla^2 = \frac{\partial^2}{\partial x^2} + \frac{\partial^2}{\partial z^2}$.

According to the boundary conditions of the model, the strain of the soil at infinity is zero, and we have $\theta|_{x=+\infty} = 0$. Using the method of separation of variables to solve Equation (6), its general solution can be obtained as

$$u = \int \frac{1}{\alpha}[K_1 \cos(\alpha z) + K_2 \sin(\alpha z)](A + \alpha x)e^{-\alpha x}d\alpha \tag{8}$$

Similarly, we can obtain the general solution of Equation (7) as

$$w = \int \frac{1}{\alpha}[-K_2 \cos(\alpha z) + K_1 \sin(\alpha z)]\left(A - \frac{\lambda + 3G}{\lambda + G} + \alpha x\right)e^{-\alpha x}d\alpha \tag{9}$$

Noting that $\tau_{xz} = G\left(\frac{\partial u}{\partial z} + \frac{\partial w}{\partial x}\right)$, $\tau_{xz}|_{z=0} = 0$; thus, $K_2 = 0$. Therefore, we can rewrite Equations (8) and (9) as

$$\left. \begin{array}{l} u = \int \frac{1}{\alpha} K_1 \cos(\alpha z)(A + \alpha x)e^{-\alpha x}d\alpha \\ w = \int \frac{1}{\alpha} K_1 \sin(\alpha z)\left(A - \frac{\lambda + 3G}{\lambda + G} + \alpha x\right)e^{-\alpha x}d\alpha \end{array} \right\} \tag{10}$$

Letting $K_3 = K_1 A$, we can obtain

$$\left. \begin{array}{l} u = \int \frac{1}{\alpha} \cos(\alpha z)(K_3 + K_1 \alpha x)e^{-\alpha x}d\alpha \\ w = \int \frac{1}{\alpha} \sin(\alpha z)\left(K_3 - K_1 \frac{\lambda + 3G}{\lambda + G} + K_1 \alpha x\right)e^{-\alpha x}d\alpha \end{array} \right\} \tag{11}$$

Assuming that the back of the diaphragm wall is smooth, i.e., $\tau_{xz}|_{x=0} = 0$, we have

$$K_3 = \frac{\lambda + 2G}{\lambda + G}K_1 \tag{12}$$

3. Analytical Solution of Excavation-Induced Ground Movement

3.1. The Translation Mode of the Wall Movement

When the retaining wall develops inward translation movement, as shown in Figure 1, the corresponding boundary condition of the model is $0 \leq z \leq H$, $u(0,z) = -d$. According to Equation (11), we have

$$u = \int \frac{1}{\alpha} K_3 \cos(\alpha z)d\alpha = -d \tag{13}$$

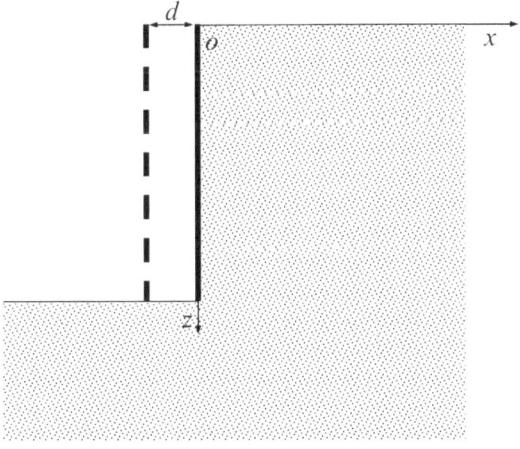

Figure 1. Inward translation of the retaining wall.

Using a Fourier transform on variable d, we can obtain

$$-d = -\frac{2d}{\pi} \int \frac{\sin(H\alpha)}{\alpha} \cos(\alpha z) d\alpha \qquad (14)$$

Comparing Equation (13) with Equation (14), it is easy to find that

$$K_3 = -\frac{2d}{\pi} \sin(H\alpha) \qquad (15)$$

Substituting Equations (12) and (15) into Equation (11), the following is obtained:

$$\left.\begin{aligned} u &= -\frac{2d}{\pi} \int_0^\infty \frac{1}{\alpha} \cos(\alpha z) \left(1 + \frac{\lambda+G}{\lambda+2G} x\alpha\right) \sin(H\alpha) e^{-\alpha x} d\alpha \\ w &= -\frac{2d}{\pi} \int_0^\infty \frac{1}{\alpha} \sin(\alpha z) \left(1 + \frac{\lambda+G}{\lambda+2G} x\alpha - \frac{\lambda+3G}{\lambda+G}\right) \sin(H\alpha) e^{-\alpha x} d\alpha \end{aligned}\right\} \qquad (16)$$

Thus, we can obtain the vertical movement and the normal stress at the ground surface as

$$w|_{z=0} = 0 \qquad (17)$$

$$\sigma_z|_{z=0} = \frac{dH(H^2 - x^2)}{\beta\pi(H^2 + x^2)^2} \qquad (18)$$

where

$$\beta = \frac{1 - \mu^2}{E} \qquad (19)$$

In other words, the ground surface settlement is zero, and there is a stress with a magnitude represented by Equation (18) distributed on the ground surface. Therefore, the wall-translation-induced settlement is equivalent to the displacement caused by the following load being applied to the ground surface:

$$F(x) = -\frac{dH(H^2 - x^2)}{\beta\pi(H^2 + x^2)^2} \qquad (20)$$

Assuming that the settlement is zero when $x = x_{ref}$, according to the Boussinesq Flamant solution, the ground surface settlement caused by F is

$$w = \frac{2\beta F}{\pi} \ln \frac{s}{\rho} \qquad (21)$$

in which F is the concentrated load, s is the distance between where we want to obtain the settlement and the reference point x_{ref}, and ρ is the distance between where we want to obtain the settlement and the concentrated load F. The three variables can be represented by

$$\left.\begin{aligned} \rho &= |\xi - x| \\ s &= |\xi - x_{ref}| \\ F(\xi) &= -\frac{dH(H^2 - \xi^2)}{\beta\pi(\xi^2 + H^2)^2} \end{aligned}\right\} \qquad (22)$$

Combining Equations (20)–(22), we have

$$w = -\frac{2dH}{\pi^2} \int_{-\infty}^{+\infty} \frac{(\xi^2 - H^2)}{(\xi^2 + H^2)^2} \ln\left|\frac{\xi - x}{\xi - x_{ref}}\right| d\xi \qquad (23)$$

The wall's inward translation can be obtained as

$$w = \frac{2dH^2}{\pi^2} \left(\frac{1}{x^2 + H^2} - \frac{1}{x_{ref}^2 + H^2}\right) \qquad (24)$$

250

3.2. The Rotating Mode of the Wall Movement

When the retaining wall rotates around the corner at the bottom of the pit, as shown in Figure 2, the boundary condition of the model is $0 \leq z \leq H$, $u(0,z) = \frac{z}{H}d - d$. According to Equation (11), it can be obtained that

$$u = \int_0^\infty \frac{1}{\alpha} K_3 \cos(\alpha z) \mathrm{d}\alpha = \frac{z}{H}d - d \qquad (25)$$

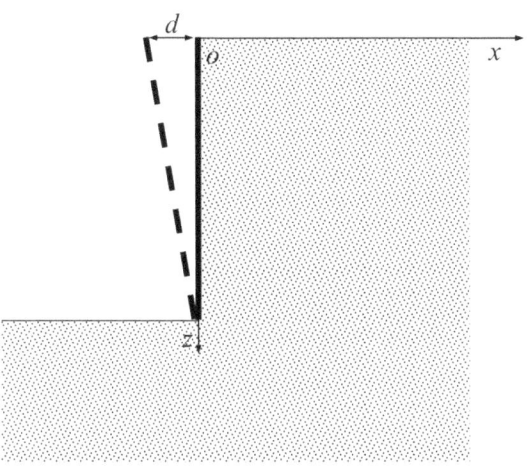

Figure 2. Retaining wall's rotation around its toe.

Performing a Fourier transform on $u(0,z) = \frac{z}{H}d - d$, we obtain

$$\frac{z}{H}d - d = \frac{2d}{\pi H}\int_0^\infty \frac{\cos(H\alpha) - 1}{\alpha^2} \cos(\alpha z)\mathrm{d}\alpha \qquad (26)$$

Comparing Equation (25) with Equation (26), we can obtain

$$K_3 = \frac{2d}{\pi H} \frac{\cos(H\alpha) - 1}{\alpha} \qquad (27)$$

Similar to the derivation of Equations (17) and (18), the boundary conditions at the ground surface of this model are

$$w|_{z=0} = 0 \qquad (28)$$

$$\sigma_z|_{z=0} = -\frac{dH}{\beta\pi}\frac{1}{x^2 + H^2} - \frac{1}{4}\frac{d}{\pi H \beta}\frac{x^4}{(x^2 + H^2)^2} \qquad (29)$$

In other words, the ground settlement caused by wall rotation is equivalent to the displacement caused by the following load acting on the ground surface:

$$F(x) = \frac{dH}{\beta\pi}\frac{1}{x^2 + H^2} + \frac{1}{4}\frac{d}{\pi H \beta}\frac{x^4}{(x^2 + H^2)^2} \qquad (30)$$

Substituting Equation (30) into Equation (21), we obtain

$$w = \frac{2d}{\pi^2}\int_{-\infty}^{+\infty}\left(\frac{H}{\xi^2 + H^2} + \frac{1}{2H}\ln\frac{\xi^2}{\xi^2 + H^2}\right)\ln\left|\frac{\xi - x}{\xi - x_{ref}}\right|\mathrm{d}\xi \qquad (31)$$

3.3. The Triangle Mode of the Wall Movement

When the retaining wall develops triangle-type movement, the boundary conditions of the model are shown in Figure 3. Assuming that the inward movement of the retaining wall at a depth of $H/2$ is $-d$, the movement can be regarded as the difference between two rotation-type movements, as described in Figure 3, which can be represented by

$$w = w_1 - w_2 \tag{32}$$

where w_1 and w_2 are the movements of the retaining wall with depths of H and $H/2$, and lateral movements of $-2d$ at the ground surface, when they develop rotation-type movements. The solution of the ground settlement behind the retaining wall caused by the wall's triangle-type displacement is

$$w = \frac{4d}{\pi^2 H} \int_{-\infty}^{+\infty} \left(\frac{1}{2} \ln \frac{\left(\xi^2 + \frac{H^2}{4}\right)^2}{\xi^2(\xi^2 + H^2)} - \frac{2H^2}{4\xi^2 + H^2} + \frac{H^2}{\xi^2 + H^2} \right) \cdot \ln \left| \frac{\xi - x}{\xi - x_{ref}} \right| d\xi \tag{33}$$

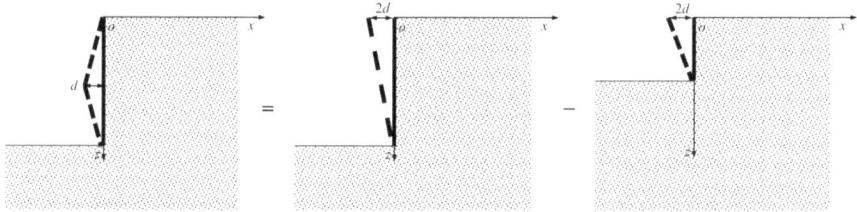

Figure 3. The triangle-pattern movement of the retaining wall.

3.4. The Parabolic Mode of the Wall Movement

The retaining wall may also develop parabolic-pattern movement, as shown in Figure 4. In such a scenario, the model's boundary condition is $0 \leq z \leq H$, $u(0,z) = \frac{4d}{H^2}z(z-H)$. According to Equation (11), we have

$$u = \int_0^\infty \frac{1}{\alpha} K_3 \cos(\alpha z) d\alpha = \frac{4d}{H^2} z(z - H) \tag{34}$$

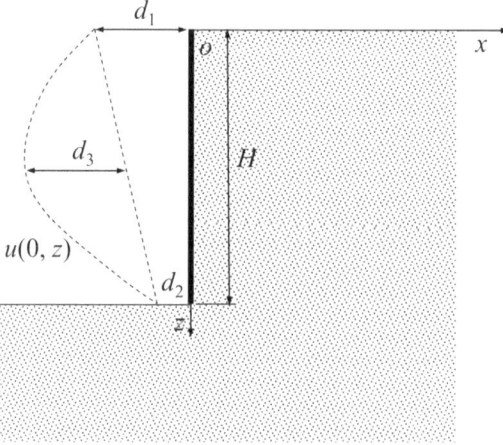

Figure 4. The parabolic mode of the wall movement.

Performing a Fourier transform on $u(0,z) = \frac{4d}{H^2}z(z-H)$, we obtain

$$\frac{4d}{H^2}z(z-H) = \frac{1}{\pi}\int_0^\infty \frac{8d(1+\cos(\alpha H))}{\alpha^2 H} - \frac{16d\sin(\alpha H)}{\alpha^3 H^2}\cos(\alpha z)d\alpha \qquad (35)$$

Comparing Equation (34) with Equation (35), we obtain

$$K_3 = \frac{8d}{\pi H^2}\left[\frac{H(1+\cos(\alpha H))}{\alpha} - \frac{2\sin(\alpha H)}{\alpha^2}\right] \qquad (36)$$

Similar to the derivation of Equation (17), and Equation (18), the boundary conditions at the ground surface of this model are

$$w|_{z=0} = 0 \qquad (37)$$

$$\sigma_z|_{z=0} = \frac{4dE}{\beta\pi H^2}\left(\frac{H}{2}\ln\left(\frac{x^2}{x^2+H^2}\right) + 3H + \frac{Hx^2}{x^2+H^2} - 4x\arctan\left(\frac{H}{x}\right)\right) \qquad (38)$$

In such conditions, the ground settlement caused by wall movement is equivalent to the displacement caused by the following load acting on the ground surface:

$$F(x) = -\frac{4dE}{\beta\pi H^2}\left(\frac{H}{2}\ln\left(\frac{x^2}{x^2+H^2}\right) + 3H + \frac{Hx^2}{x^2+H^2} - 4x\arctan\left(\frac{H}{x}\right)\right) \qquad (39)$$

Using Equations (21) and (39), it can be obtained that when the retaining wall develops parabolic-type movement, the ground settlement behind the wall is

$$w = -\frac{8d}{\pi^2 H^2}\int_{-\infty}^{+\infty}\left(\frac{H}{2}\ln\left(\frac{\zeta^2}{\zeta^2+H^2}\right) + 3H + \frac{H\zeta^2}{\zeta^2+H^2} - 4\zeta\arctan\left(\frac{H}{\zeta}\right)\right)\ln\left|\frac{\zeta-x}{\zeta-x_{ref}}\right|d\zeta \qquad (40)$$

3.5. Distribution Patterns of Ground Surface Settlement under Different Wall Movement Types

In order to analyze the distribution patterns of ground surface settlement under various wall movement types, a hypothetic model with a wall depth of $H = 10$ m is developed. Taking $x_{ref} = 10H$ and $d = 0.5\%H$, the normalized ground settlements of different wall movement cases are drawn in Figure 5. According to the figure, two settlement patterns (i.e., arc shoulder distribution and trough distribution) are generally observed. The ground surface settlements caused by the translation and rotation types of wall movement are arch shoulder types, characterized by the maximum settlements appearing immediately behind the wall, and the settlements gradually decrease to zero with increasing distance to the retaining wall. In the triangular and parabolic types of wall movement models, the grounds behind the wall develop trough settlements. Typical characteristics of trough settlements are that the maximum settlements occur at a certain distance behind the wall, and the settlements gradually decrease to zero with increasing distance to the wall. According to previous studies [14,18,21,23,47], ground settlements caused by triangle-type wall movements and parabolic-type wall movements are in accordance with realistic responses of the ground to deep excavations.

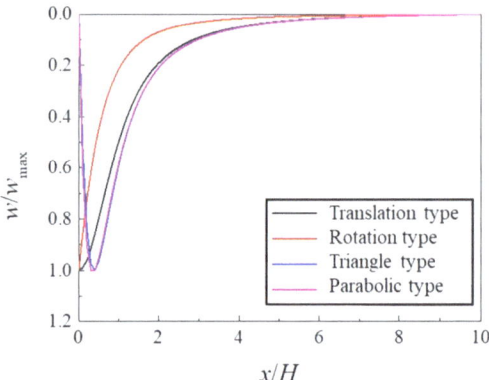

Figure 5. Normalized ground settlements behind the wall under different wall movement types.

4. The Excavation-Induced Settlement of the Pipe Gallery behind the Retaining Wall

4.1. Method Description

Existing theoretical predictions of excavation-induced performance have generally been limited to simplified two-dimensional models (i.e., plane-strain, half-sections) that are assumed to generate worst-case scenarios for wall deflections and ground deformations. However, it is readily apparent that the distribution and magnitude of excavation-induced deformations around the perimeter of the site have strong spatial effects. Accordingly, it is also necessary to consider the spatial characteristics of excavation-induced displacements when studying the responses of surrounding pipelines, subway tunnels, pipe galleries, and other facilities to excavation projects.

For rectangular excavations, as shown in Figure 6, ground movements behind the retaining wall can generally expressed as

$$w(x,y) = w_{\max} f(x) g(y) \qquad (41)$$

where $f(x)$ is the distribution function of ground settlements along the direction perpendicular to the side of the pit, and $g(y)$ is the distribution function of ground settlements along the direction parallel to the retaining wall.

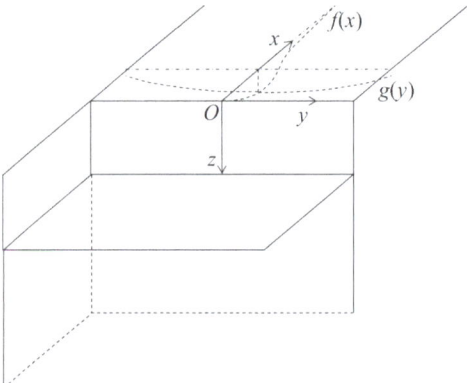

Figure 6. Spatial distribution of the excavation-induced settlement.

The analytical formula of $w_{max}f(x)$ can be derived from the theoretical solution in previous sections of this paper. In terms of the distribution function of ground settlements along the direction parallel to the retaining wall, $g(y)$, it is affected by various factors and so, unfortunately, has no accurate theoretical solution. Therefore, the calculations in this section adopt empirical expressions obtained from field measurements.

Zhang et al. (2012) [48] summarized the collected data in Shanghai and obtained a distribution function of ground settlements along the direction parallel to the retaining structures as

$$g(y) = e^{-\pi(\frac{y}{A})^2}, A = \frac{L}{2}\left[0.069 \ln\left(\frac{H_e}{L}\right) + 1.03\right] \quad (42)$$

in which A is the influence radius of the displacement, and L and H are the longitudinal length and the excavation depth of the pit, respectively.

An alternative expression was developed by Finno and Calvello (2005) [49]. Based on experimental studies on excavation projects in Chicago, they proposed that the surface settlement distribution along the direction parallel to the retaining wall can be corrected using a correction function erfc(y):

$$w(y) = w_{\max}g(y) = w_{\max}\left(1 - \frac{1}{2}\text{erfc}\left(\frac{2.8\{y + L[0.015 + 0.035\ln(H_e/L)]\}}{0.5L - L[0.015 + 0.035\ln(H_e/L)]}\right)\right) \quad (43)$$

The correction function erfc(y) in Equation (43) is expressed as

$$\text{erfc}(y) = \int_0^y e^{-u^2} du \quad (44)$$

where y is the projection length of the distance between the desired point to the corner of the pit on the y-axis, and $y < L/2$.

After obtaining the spatial distribution of ground movements using the solution presented in previous sections of this paper, the interaction between the soil and the pipe galleries can be analyzed using the two-stage method. Thereafter, excavation-induced displacements of the pipe galleries can be calculated.

The first step of the two-stage method is to deduce the ground settlement, d, at the position of the pipe gallery, in which the stiffness of the gallery should first be neglected. In this step, the current work involves two formulas to deduce the soil movement (i.e., Equations (42) and (43)). Therefore, both formulas are used, and their results are compared later in this paper.

In the second step, the obtained settlement at the position of the pipe gallery is then treated as an additional displacement exerted on the pipe gallery, while the pipe gallery is modeled as an elastic foundation beam. Then, the mechanical responses of the pipe gallery under the addition displacement can be calculated using the Winkler foundation model, which can be expressed as

$$E_t I_t \frac{\partial^4 w}{\partial y^4} + kDw = kDd \quad (45)$$

where the parameter k can be obtained using the Vesic formula [50]:

$$k = 0.65 \sqrt[12]{\frac{E_s D^4}{E_t I_t}} \frac{E_s}{(1 - v_s^2)D} \quad (46)$$

where $E_t I_t$ is the bending stiffness of the pipe gallery; E_s and v_s are Young's modulus and Poisson's ratio of the soil foundation, respectively; and D is the outer diameter of the gallery.

The boundary condition of Equation (45) is that the excavation-induced additional displacement of the gallery is zero at an infinite distance from the middle of the pit. The differential equation given by Equation (45) can be solved using the difference method to obtain the pipe gallery's deformation under a given addition displacement of the soil at the corresponding position.

4.2. Verification of the Method by Field Measurements

The Hongqiao CBD project is located in downtown Shanghai. This study focuses on the response of the energy pipe gallery on the south side of the pit to the excavation. The excavation has a depth of 18.4 m and is supported by an 800 mm thick and 36 m deep diaphragm wall. As described in Figure 7, the pipe gallery, buried 8–10 m below the ground surface, is located on the south side of the pit, with a distance of 3.6 m from the retaining wall. During the excavation process of the foundation pit, the settlements of the pipe gallery were extensively monitored. In the calculations, the soil is assumed to be homogeneous and exhibit elastic characteristics with Young's modulus of E_s = 10 MPa. The material of the pipe gallery is C30 concrete with Young's modulus of E_t = 30 GPa. The inertia moment of the pipe gallery can be obtained as I_t = 17 m^4.

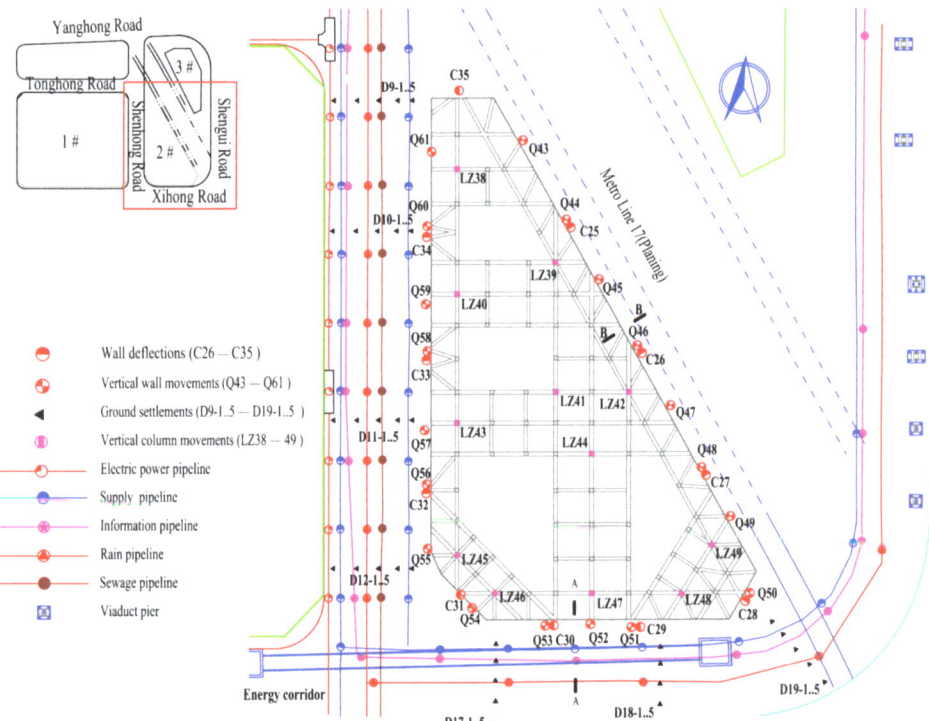

Figure 7. The plane view and instrumentation of the project.

Figure 8 presents the monitored deflections of the diaphragm wall in the middle of the pit boundary. Based on the displacement mode proposed in Section 3, the wall deflection can be fitted using a triangular-type displacement. In this perspective, the ground surface behind the retaining wall performs a settlement pattern as shown in Figure 9. Clearly, the ground surface presents a spoon-shape settlement. Specifically, as the distance from the diaphragm wall increases, the settlement first increases rapidly and then gradually decreases. In addition, soil at an infinite distance from the pit is barely influenced by the excavation.

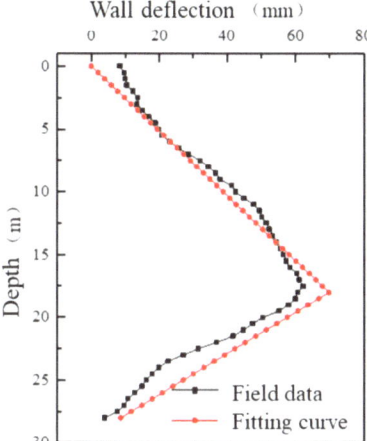

Figure 8. Wall deflection.

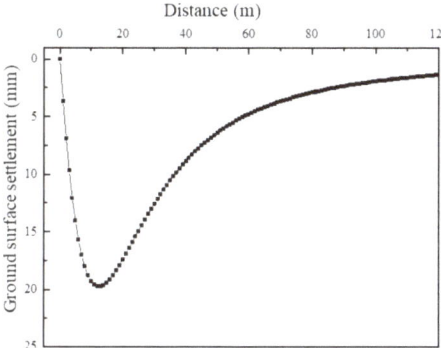

Figure 9. Ground surface settlement behind the wall.

Using the method proposed in this paper, combined with the two distribution formulas given by Zhang et al. (2012) [48] and Finno and Calvello (2005) [49], the authors deduce the ground settlement at the position of the pipe gallery and denote the results as the Z-result and F-result, respectively.

The two results are presented and compared in Figure 10. The Z-result suggests that the soil at the pipe gallery develops the most settlement at the middle point of the pit. With increasing distance from the middle, the ground settlement decreases rapidly. According to the F-result, on the other hand, the maximum ground settlement is maintained within a certain range near the middle of the pit, in which the size of the range is determined by Equation (42). Obviously, the F-result is more in accordance with realistic engineering performance.

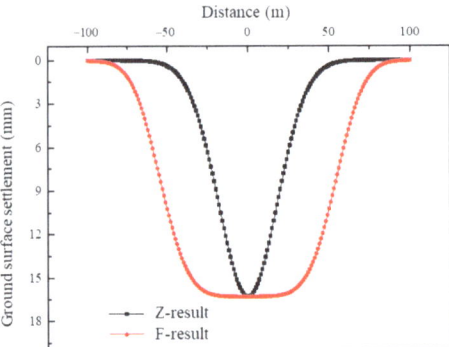

Figure 10. Ground settlements at the position of the pipe gallery.

Figure 11 compares the calculated pipe gallery deformations (i.e., Z-result and F-result) with the field data to verify the ability of the method proposed in this paper in predicting the responses of pipe galleries to excavations. The figure shows that the deformation patterns of the pipe gallery obtained using the two methods are basically consistent, with the maximum deformation occurring in the middle and then decreasing gradually towards the corners of the pit. On the other hand, the F-result undergoes a larger deformation than the Z-result because the maximum ground settlement of the F-result is maintained within a certain range near the middle of the pit. The comparison shows that the F-result is more reliable. This indicates that the solution proposed in this article combined with Finno's (Finno and Calvello 2005) [49] empirical formula, i.e., Equation (43), can provide ideal predictions for excavation-induced deformations of pipe galleries.

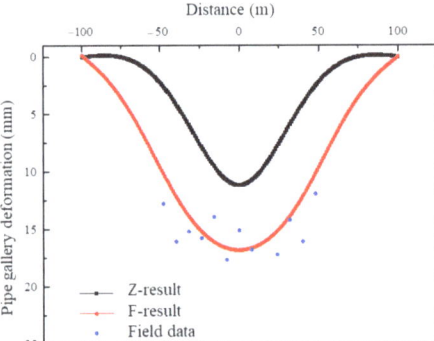

Figure 11. Pipe gallery deformations.

5. Parametric Studies on Excavation-Induced Pipe Gallery Settlements

The analyses in Section 4 proved the capability of the proposed method to reproduce the displacement of pipe galleries adjacent to deep excavations. Based on this verified solution, two additional parametric studies are carried out in this section to explore the impacts of two key factors, i.e., the distance of the pipe gallery to the pit and the stiffness of the pipe gallery. Because the combination of the proposed solution of this article and Finno's (Finno and Calvello 2005) [49] empirical formula is more reliable, it is applied to carry out the parametric studies in this section.

5.1. Distance to The Pit

When considering the effects of the distance of the pipe gallery to the excavation, four values are compared. These distances are 0.5, 1, 1.5, and 2 times the excavation depth, while other parameters are assumed to be the same as the model in Section 4. Figures 12 and 13 present the ground settlement at the position of the pipe gallery and the deformation of the pipe gallery, respectively.

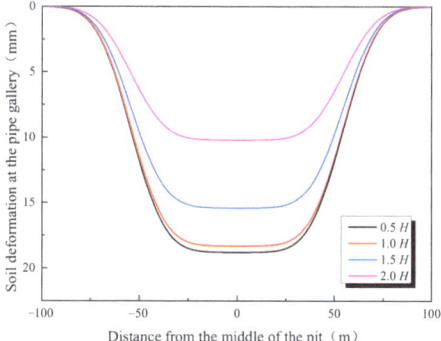

Figure 12. Ground settlements at the position of the pipe gallery.

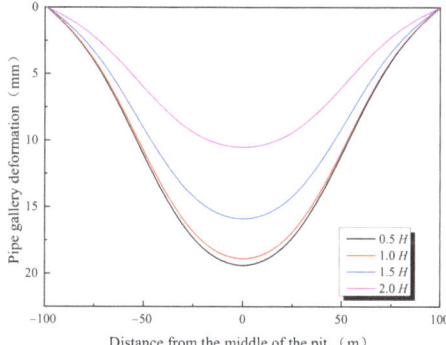

Figure 13. Pipe gallery deformations.

Figure 12 shows that the results of 0.5H and 1.0H are very close to each other, which is because, for the current case, the ground settlement reaches its maximum within a range of 0.5–1.0 times the excavation depth. At the same time, according to Figure 12, the result of 1.5H is much smaller than those of 0.5H and 1.0H (i.e., the settlement of the 1.5H scenario is 15.4 mm, decreasing by 15.8% compared with the 1.0H scenario), and the result of 2.0H is smallest among the calculated scenarios (i.e., the settlement of the 2.0H scenario is 10.2 mm, decreasing by 33.8% compared with the 1.0H scenario and 44.3% compared with the 2.0H scenario). The result indicates that the ground settlement gradually decreases with increasing distance to the wall after its maximum, which is in accordance with the summarized spoon-shape settlement pattern of the ground settlement behind retaining structures in engineering practice. In fact, the excavation-induced ground settlement will finally reach a negligible value when the distance to the diaphragm is sufficiently large.

The calculated pipe gallery deformations of different scenarios are presented and analyzed in Figure 13. In accordance with the distribution of the ground settlement, the deformation of the pipe gallery also shows an increasing-then-decreasing trend with increasing distance from the pit. The maximum pipe gallery deformation of the 1.5H scenario is 15.9 mm, decreasing by 15.8% from the 1.0H scenario (i.e., 18.9 mm), and the maximum gallery deformation of the 2.0H scenario is 10.5 mm, decreasing by 34.0% from the 1.5H scenario and 44.4% from the 1.0H scenario. Therefore, it is recommended to control the designed foundation pit to twice its excavation depth away from nearby pipe galleries. Otherwise, reinforcement measures should be taken for the surrounding soil.

5.2. The Stiffness of the Pipe Gallery

Keeping other parameters the same as the case in Section 4.2, the authors further calculate the pipe galley deformations under changing gallery stiffness. Four cases with different gallery stiffness are analyzed, in which Young's moduli of the gallery are 750, 1500, 3000, and 6000 times the soil modulus, denoted as E_t/E_s = 750, E_t/E_s = 1500, E_t/E_s = 3000, and E_t/E_s = 6000, respectively. The pipe gallery deformations of the four cases, as well as the calculated ground settlement at the position of the gallery, are presented in Figure 14.

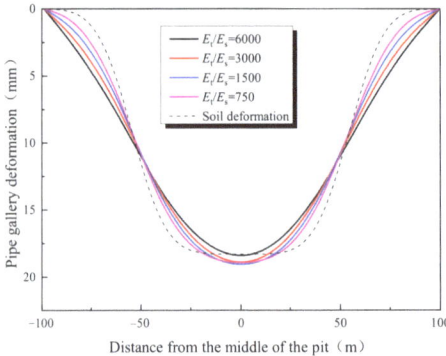

Figure 14. The influence of pipe gallery stiffness.

Clearly, the calculated pipe gallery deformations of all four cases share the same deformation pattern. In terms of the influence of the gallery stiffness, it can be seen that the maximum gallery deformation (occurs near the middle of the pit), from a magnitude close to the soil settlement, decreases with increasing gallery stiffness. On the contrary, the gallery near the corners of the pit tends to develop larger displacement when its stiffness increases. It can be seen that properly increasing the stiffness of the pipe gallery can be beneficial for resisting deformation caused by displacements of surrounding soil layers.

6. Conclusions

This work first proposes a new solution to determine the displacement distribution of the ground behind the retaining wall using the control equation of the elastic plane strain problem combined with the method of separation of variables. Then, the deduced 2D solution is extended to 3D problems to obtain the spatial distribution expression of the ground settlement. Afterward, the authors, by simplifying the soil–pipe gallery interaction to the Winkler foundation–Beam model, calculate the excavation-induced pipe gallery displacement using the two-stage method. After being verified by a realistic case in Shanghai, the proposed solution is applied to explore the potential influence of various factors on the excavation-induced displacement of pipe galleries. The following results are drawn:

1. During the extension from 2D to 3D of the proposed solution in this work, two experimental formulas of the ground settlement distribution along the longitudinal direction of retaining structures (i.e., Zhang's formula and Finno's formula) are used and evaluated. The comparison with field data shows that the proposed solution of this work combined with Finno's formula provides more desirable results, while Zhang's formula tends to provide overconservative pipe gallery deformation.
2. The ground settlement behind the retaining structure follows a spoon-shape pattern, i.e., the settlement first increases with the increase in distance from the pit until its maximum value; then, the settlement gradually decreases to a negligible value.

The deformation distribution of the pipe gallery is closely in accordance with the distribution of ground settlement at the corresponding location.
3. From a magnitude close to the ground settlement at the corresponding position, the maximum deformation of the pipe gallery decreases with increasing stiffness.

Author Contributions: Conceptualization, B.X. and Y.L.; methodology, Y.L. and J.C.; software, B.X.; formal analysis, Y.L.; investigation, J.C.; resources, Z.Y.; data curation, Y.L.; writing—original draft preparation, B.X. and Y.L.; writing—review and editing, J.C. and Z.Y. All authors have read and agreed to the published version of the manuscript.

Funding: This research was funded by the National Natural Science Foundation of China (Grant 52108328).

Data Availability Statement: The data are contained within the article.

Conflicts of Interest: Author Binhui Xiang was employed by Jiangxi Zhengde Engineering testing Co. Ltd. The remaining authors declare that the research was conducted in the absence of any commercial or financial relationships that could be construed as a potential conflict of interest.

References

1. Wang, C.; Liang, F.; Yu, X. A review of bridge scour: Mechanism, estimation, monitoring and countermeasures. *Nat. Hazards* **2017**, *87*, 1881–1906. [CrossRef]
2. Rehman, Z.; Zhang, G. Three-dimensional elasto-plastic damage model for gravelly soil-structure interface considering the shear coupling effect. *Comput. Geotech.* **2021**, *129*, 103868. [CrossRef]
3. Gallikova, Z.; ur Rehman, Z. Appraisal of the hypoplastic model for the numerical prediction of high-rise building settlement in neogene clay based on real-scale monitoring data. *J. Build. Eng.* **2022**, *50*, 104452. [CrossRef]
4. Rao, P.; Feng, W.; Ouyang, P.; Cui, J.; Nimbalkar, S.; Chen, Q. Formation of plasma channel under high-voltage electric pulse and simulation of rock-breaking process. *Phys. Scr.* **2023**, *99*, 015604. [CrossRef]
5. Shao, W.; Qin, F.; Shi, D.; Soomro, M.A. Horizontal bearing characteristic and seismic fragility analysis of CFRP composite pipe piles subject to chloride corrosion. *Comput. Geotech.* **2024**, *166*, 105977. [CrossRef]
6. Shao, W.; Li, Q.; Zhang, W.; Shi, D.; Li, H. Numerical modeling of chloride diffusion in cement-based materials considering calcium leaching and external sulfate attack. *Constr. Build. Mater.* **2023**, *401*, 132913. [CrossRef]
7. Cui, J.; Jin, Y.; Jing, Y.; Lu, Y. Elastoplastic Solution of Cylindrical Cavity Expansion in Unsaturated Offshore Island Soil Considering Anisotropy. *J. Mar. Sci. Eng.* **2024**, *12*, 308. [CrossRef]
8. Attewell, P.B.; Yeates, J.; Selby, A.R. *Soil Movements Induced by Tunnelling and Their Effects on Pipelines and Structures*; Methuen, Inc.: New York, NY, USA, 1986.
9. Fang, K.; Zhang, Z.; He, J.; Liu, X. *Pipelines Deformation Control for Double-Row Supported Excavation*; ICPTT 2011; American Society of Civil Engineers: Reston, VA, USA, 2011; pp. 440–447.
10. Jia, X.; Zhang, H.; Wang, C.; Liang, F.; Chen, X. Influence on the lateral response of offshore pile foundations of an asymmetric heart-shaped scour hole. *Appl. Ocean. Res.* **2023**, *133*, 103485. [CrossRef]
11. Liu, H.; Lv, S.; Jia, J. *Numerical Analysis of the Influence of Foundation Pit Excavation on Many Underground Pipelines Nearby*; ICPTT 2011; American Society of Civil Engineers: Reston, VA, USA, 2011; pp. 1358–1364.
12. Wang, Y.; Shi, J.; Ng, C.W.W. Numerical modeling of tunneling effect on buried pipelines. *Can. Geotech. J.* **2011**, *48*, 1125–1137. [CrossRef]
13. Wang, Z.Z.; Whittle, A.J. Effects of Movement Induced by Ground Improvement on the Performance of an Excavation Support System in Underconsolidated Clay. *J. Geotech. Geoenviron. Eng.* **2024**, *150*, 5023008. [CrossRef]
14. Yang, Z.; Chen, Y.; Azzam, R.; Yan, C. Performance of a top-down excavation in shanghai: Case study and numerical exploration. *Eur. J. Environ. Civ. Eng.* **2021**, *26*, 7932–7957. [CrossRef]
15. Yang, Z.; Chen, Y.; Yan, C.; Azzam, R. Numerical Evaluation of Isolation Walls in Modifying Excavation-Induced Displacement Field. *Arab. J. Sci. Eng.* **2022**, *48*, 12693–12708. [CrossRef]
16. Yao, A.; Xu, T.; Zeng, X.; Jiang, H. Numerical Analyses of the Stress and Limiting Load for Buried Gas Pipelines under Excavation Machine Impact. *J. Pipeline Syst. Eng. Pract.* **2013**, *6*, A4014003. [CrossRef]
17. Choudhury, D.; Shen, R.; Leung, C.; Chow, Y. *Centrifuge Model Study on Pile Responses Due to Adjacent Excavation. Foundation Analysis and Design*; American Society of Civil Engineers: Reston, VA, USA, 2006; pp. 145–151.
18. Cui, J.; Yang, Z.; Azzam, R. Field measurement and numerical study on the effects of under-excavation and over-excavation on ultra-deep foundation pit in coastal area. *J. Mar. Sci. Eng.* **2023**, *11*, 219. [CrossRef]
19. Hsieh, P.-G.; Ou, C.-Y. Shape of ground surface settlement profiles caused by excavation. *Can. Geotech. J.* **1998**, *35*, 1004–1017. [CrossRef]
20. Li, Y.; Wang, Z. *Study of Influence of Subway Station Excavation on Existing Metro Deformation*; ICCTP 2009; American Society of Civil Engineers: Reston, VA, USA, 2009; pp. 1–7.

21. Tan, Y.; Huang, R.; Kang, Z.; Bin, W. Covered semi-top-down excavation of subway station surrounded by closely spaced buildings in downtown Shanghai: Building response. *J. Perform. Constr. Facil.* **2016**, *30*, 4016040. [CrossRef]
22. Tan, Y.; Wei, B.; Diao, Y.; Zhou, X. Spatial Corner Effects of Long and Narrow Multipropped Deep Excavations in Shanghai Soft Clay. *J. Perform. Constr. Facil.* **2013**, *28*, 4014015. [CrossRef]
23. Clough, G.G.; O'Rourke, T.T. *Construction Induced Movements of Insitu Wall, Design and Performance of Earth Retaining Structure*; American Society of Civil Engineers: Reston, VA, USA, 1990; pp. 292–308.
24. Long, M. Database for retaining wall and ground movements due to deep excavations. *J. Geotech. Geoenviron. Eng.* **2001**, *127*, 203–224. [CrossRef]
25. Ou, C.-Y.; Hsieh, P.-G.; Chiou, D.-C. Characteristics of ground surface settlement during excavation. *Can. Geotech. J.* **1993**, *30*, 758–767. [CrossRef]
26. Wang, L.; Luo, Z.; Khoshnevisan, S.; Juang, C. *Robust Design of Braced Excavations Using Multiobjective Optimization-Focusing on Prevention of Damage to Adjacent Buildings*; Geo-Congress 2014 Technical Papers; American Society of Civil Engineers: Reston, VA, USA, 2014; pp. 3178–3187.
27. Xu, Y.S.; Ma, L.; Du, Y.J.; Shen, S.L. Analysis of urbanisation-induced land subsidence in Shanghai. *Nat. Hazards* **2012**, *63*, 1255–1267. [CrossRef]
28. Calvello, M.; Finno, R.J. Selecting parameters to optimize in model calibration by inverse analysis. *Comput. Geotech.* **2004**, *31*, 411–425. [CrossRef]
29. Cui, J.; Ouyang, P.; Zhang, J.; Yang, Z. Theoretical Analysis of Deformation and Internal Forces of Used Piles Due to New Static-Pressure Pile Penetration. *Appl. Sci.* **2023**, *13*, 2714. [CrossRef]
30. Kingshuk, D.; Bikas, S.R. Estimation of Ground Movement and Wall Deflection in Braced Excavation by Minimum Potential Energy Approach. *Int. J. Geomech.* **2018**, *18*, 4018068.
31. Li, D.; Xiao, M.; Zeng, Q. Impact of Deep Excavations on Adjacent Buried Pipelines. In *New Pipeline Technologies, Security, and Safety*; American Society of Civil Engineers: Reston, VA, USA, 2003; pp. 1116–1125.
32. Schuster, M.; Kung, G.; Juang, C.; Hashash, Y. Simplified Model for Evaluating Damage Potential of Buildings Adjacent to a Braced Excavation. *J. Geotech. Geoenviron. Eng.* **2009**, *135*, 1823–1835. [CrossRef]
33. Chen, R.; Yin, X.; Tang, L.; Chen, Y. Centrifugal model tests on face failure of earth pressure balance shield induced by steady state seepage in saturated sandy silt ground. *Tunn. Undergr. Space Technol.* **2018**, *81*, 315–325. [CrossRef]
34. Zheng, G.; Wei, S.W.; Peng, S.Y.; Diao, Y.; Ng, C.W.W. Centrifuge modeling of the influence of basement excavation on existing tunnels. In *Physical Modelling in Geotechnics, Two Volume Set*; Zheng, G., Wei, S.W., Peng, S.Y., Eds.; CRC Press: Boca Raton, FL, USA, 2010; pp. 549–554.
35. Geng, P.; Yang, X.; Zhang, Y.; Huang, X.M. Research on prediction method of pipe gallery environment based on lstm circular convolution neural network. *Int. Core J. Eng.* **2020**, *6*, 340–346.
36. Zhang, R.; Meng, R.; Sang, J.; Hu, Y.; Li, X.; Zheng, C. Modelling individual head-related transfer function(hrtf)based on anthropometric parameters and generic hrtf amplitudes. *CAAI Trans. Intell. Technol.* **2023**, *8*, 364–378. [CrossRef]
37. Zhang, Y.; Hu, Y.; Gao, X.; Gong, D.; Guo, Y.; Gao, K.; Zhang, W. An embedded vertical-federated feature selection algorithm based on particle swarm optimisation. *CAAI Trans. Intell. Technol.* **2023**, *8*, 734–754. [CrossRef]
38. Katkade, S.N.; Bagal, V.C.; Manza, R.R.; Yannawar, P.L. Advances in real-time object detection and information retrieval: A review. *Artif. Intell. Appl.* **2023**, *1*, 139–144. [CrossRef]
39. Yi, T.; Shi, M.; Shang, W.; Zhu, H. A privacy-preserving method for publishing data with multiple sensitive attributes. *CAAI Trans. Intell. Technol.* **2023**, *9*, 222–238. [CrossRef]
40. Groumpos, P.P. A critical historical overview of artificial intelligence: Issues, challenges, opportunities, and threats. *Artif. Intell. Appl.* **2023**, *1*, 197–213.
41. Luo, C.T.; Luo, C. A kernel-embedded local learning for data-intensive modeling. *Artif. Intell. Appl.* **2024**, *2*, 38–44. [CrossRef]
42. Huang, X.; Schweiger, H.; Huang, H. Influence of Deep Excavations on Nearby Existing Tunnels. *Int. J. Geomech.* **2011**, *13*, 170–180. [CrossRef]
43. Zhang, X.; Ou, X.; Yang, J.; Fu, J. Deformation Response of an Existing Tunnel to Upper Excavation of Foundation Pit and Associated Dewatering. *Int. J. Geomech.* **2016**, *17*, 4016112. [CrossRef]
44. Boscardin, M.; Cording, E. Building Response to Excavation-Induced Settlement. *J. Geotech. Eng.* **1989**, *115*, 1–21. [CrossRef]
45. Osman, A.; Bolton, M. Ground Movement Predictions for Braced Excavations in Undrained Clay. *J. Geotech. Geoenviron. Eng.* **2006**, *132*, 465–477. [CrossRef]
46. Zhou, H.; Kong, G.; Liu, H. A semi-analytical solution for cylindrical cavity expansion in elastic–perfectly plastic soil under biaxial in situ stress field. *Géotechnique* **2016**, *66*, 584–595. [CrossRef]
47. Hwang, R. *Performance of Deep Excavations in the Taipei Basin. Earth Retention Conference 3*; American Society of Civil Engineers: Reston, VA, USA, 2010; pp. 55–68.
48. Zhang, C.; Yu, J.; Huang, M. Deformation controlling criterion of effect on underground pipelines due to foundation pit excavation. *Rock Soil Mech.* **2012**, *33*, 8. (In Chinese)

49. Finno, R.J.; Calvello, M. Supported excavations: Observational method and inverse modeling. *J. Geotech. Geoenviron. Eng.* **2005**, *131*, 826–836. [CrossRef]
50. Kalinli, A.; Acar, M.C.; Gündüz, Z. New approaches to determine the ultimate bearing capacity of shallow foundations based on artificial neural networks and ant colony optimization. *Eng. Geol.* **2011**, *117*, 29–38. [CrossRef]

Disclaimer/Publisher's Note: The statements, opinions and data contained in all publications are solely those of the individual author(s) and contributor(s) and not of MDPI and/or the editor(s). MDPI and/or the editor(s) disclaim responsibility for any injury to people or property resulting from any ideas, methods, instructions or products referred to in the content.

MDPI AG
Grosspeteranlage 5
4052 Basel
Switzerland
Tel.: +41 61 683 77 34

Buildings Editorial Office
E-mail: buildings@mdpi.com
www.mdpi.com/journal/buildings

Disclaimer/Publisher's Note: The title and front matter of this reprint are at the discretion of the Guest Editors. The publisher is not responsible for their content or any associated concerns. The statements, opinions and data contained in all individual articles are solely those of the individual Editors and contributors and not of MDPI. MDPI disclaims responsibility for any injury to people or property resulting from any ideas, methods, instructions or products referred to in the content.

www.ingramcontent.com/pod-product-compliance
Lightning Source LLC
LaVergne TN
LVHW072323090526
838202LV00019B/2344